Public Administration and Information Technology

Volume 40

Public Administration and Information Technology publishes authored and edited books that examine the application of information systems to common issues and problems in public administration. This series examines both the successes of Information and Communication Technology (ICT) adoption and some of the most important challenges to implementation. The books published in this series will address all areas of public administration, through the use of information technology adoption in the public and nonprofit sectors, and in the private sector where important lessons can be learned for public managers and policy analysts. New and emerging technologies that will have a lasting impact on public administration will be featured in this series. Both developed and developing countries will be examined in this series. The series particularly welcomes books that cover international dimensions of public administration and information technology. The research in this series will be able to bridge both theory and practice to provide relevance to public managers. The series will cover all aspects of e-governance/e-government research, and new and emerging trends and issues in this research. The series publishes edited books, monographs, upper-level textbooks and research handbooks. For authors interested in submitting a book proposal, please email the editor.

Manuel Pedro Rodriguez Bolívar
University of Granada
manuelp@ugr.es

Hans Jochen Scholl • Eric E. Holdeman •
F. Kees Boersma
Editors

Disaster Management and Information Technology

Professional Response and Recovery Management in the Age of Disasters

Springer

Editors
Hans Jochen Scholl
Information School
University of Washington
Seattle, WA, USA

Eric E. Holdeman
Eric Holdeman Associates
Puyallup, WA, USA

F. Kees Boersma
Department of Organization Sciences
VU University Amsterdam
Amsterdam, The Netherlands

ISSN 2512-1812 ISSN 2512-1839 (electronic)
Public Administration and Information Technology
ISBN 978-3-031-20938-3 ISBN 978-3-031-20939-0 (eBook)
https://doi.org/10.1007/978-3-031-20939-0

This Springer imprint is published by the registered company Springer Nature Switzerland AG
The registered company address is: Gewerbestrasse 11, 6330 Cham, Switzerland

Foreword

We are living in a world of information overload. Whether it is from a variety of social media platforms, the growing and increasingly connected internet-of-things, expanding citizen journalists, traditional media outlets or professional and amateur pundits adding their voice to the fray, the information we receive, whether voluntary or involuntary, can be overwhelming, clouding our ability to make even the simplest of decisions.

When a disaster strikes, managing time-critical information adds to the complexity for those disaster survivors in need of accurate information and is nearly impossible for those charged with making life-saving decisions to alleviate the pain and suffering of those survivors.

I have spent the last 13 years as a professional emergency manager, at every level, local, state, and federal, using various technologies such as Crisis Information Management Systems (CIMS) to add clarity to the disaster "fog of war." As a profession, we are still hunting for the ultimate disaster management decision support system; it has been elusive.

Let me reflect on my time as the Federal Emergency Management Agency (FEMA) Administrator during the Nation's response to coronavirus disease 2019 (COVID-19) starting in February 2020. It was clear we did not have all the data we needed to make well-informed decisions. In some cases, the data we needed did not exist. In other cases, the data existed but not in a form that was useful or digestible. For the remainder data that existed, the sheer volume of data became all-consuming. Everything from the amount of personal protective equipment (PPE) in each state, to hospital visits by those with COVID-19 symptoms, to providing resources for natural disasters intertwined with COVID-19 impacts, a comprehensive common operating picture (COP) was unclear. With time the COP became clearer, but in many cases, the data remained unavailable, or the timeliness of information quickly perished.

It remains critical to have access to and understanding of real-time data, from government, private and public sectors in order to drive timely decisions. This information must be linked directly to critical infrastructure and interdependencies; the emergency manager must have access to comprehensive key data sets and how they may impact the unfolding disaster. Most importantly we must have the apparatus; the technological solutions and the human skill sets to drive decisions that we humans can only make.

Information overload is the primary enemy of timely decision-making. Too much information strains the decision-making process and can grind progress to a halt. Early in a disaster, emergency managers are seeking *any* bit of information that may point them to a solution but often those first reports are mischaracterized or plain wrong. With piles of sometimes random information, the task is now to sift through all the information with the hopes of finding that golden nugget that will change the tide of the rapidly deteriorating disaster. Instead of taking positive actions to mitigate the disaster, emergency managers are now in a race against the ticking "decision-action clock" looking for mission-critical information. If you miss the time that your "timely decision" will change the outcome in a positive way, then it is back to the starting line to start the process all over again. While you are head-down digging for critical information, the unfolding situation continues to spin out of control out of your view. If you fail to intervene, then what was once a straightforward problem now turns chaotic, creating additional challenges and information requirements. In the military planning community, there is a term used to help narrow down critical information; "latest time information is of value" or LTIOV. Our current-day CIMS are not built to meet this requirement.

To better meet this requirement, the "creators" of future CIMS should adopt another foundational element of information derived from the military called Priority Intelligence Requirements, or PIRs. A PIR is an intelligence requirement associated with a decision that will critically affect the overall success of the unit's mission. PIRs are in four buckets: (1) what we want to know; (2) why we need it (linked to operational decision-making); (3) when we need it (LTIOV); and (4) how we want it (format). Although technology theoretically makes our tasks easier, it is important that the foundation of any technology is built on a solid foundation of proven doctrine and principles.

The authors have crafted an extensively researched and logical series of chapters from the history of CIMS; technology successes and challenges; how we communicate, store, and transfer data; and what emergency manager practitioners with need in the future to meet the needs of managing disasters. They lay out a compelling argument for the need for technology that is open and interoperable and that can expand and integrate with technology innovations. Additionally, they discuss the role of technology in supporting system-level resilience and the development of system standards and governance to ensure mission performance when it counts.

Their treatise is an important exploration in a world that continues to be complex and chaotic. It is critical to have access to and understanding of real-time data, from both the private and public sectors, to drive timely decisions, all with the goal of minimizing suffering and protecting property and the environment. The emergency management profession desperately needs to understand these complicated, complex, and sometimes obscure interdependencies well before a disaster occurs. We need a system and people that allow us to be least reactive, leaving us more time to think and act. *Disaster Management and Information*

Technology is a great roadmap for both emergency managers and innovators that will shape the future of crisis decision-making.

Acting Secretary, Department of Homeland Security Peter T. Gaynor
11th Administrator, Federal Emergency Management Agency

Foreword

Crisis Information Management Systems from the Perspective of Academic Research

The linkage between academic research and field experience is vital to achieving an informed, insightful grasp of the complexity and uncertainty inherent in decision-making in crisis conditions. The collection of chapters included in this volume, *Disaster Management and Information Technology: Professional Response and Recovery Management in the Age of Disasters*, provides a major contribution to this challenging task. Over the last three decades, advances in information technology have promised to increase the capacity of crisis management organizations to collect, analyze, and transmit timely information to practicing managers in real time. In fact, substantial increases have been achieved in the volume of data that can be processed, types of analysis that can be conducted, speed of processing time, visual representation of results, and the range, extent, and rapidity at which information can be transmitted in near-real time to decision makers at multiple points in the emergence and escalation of a crisis, as well as its de-escalation and recovery. The co-authors contributing to this volume address many of these issues in four related sections: Crisis Management Information Systems (CIMS) in Emergency Management Practice; CIMS Functionalities and Features; CIMS Requirements, Development, and Testing; and CIMS Assessment, Evaluation, and Data Management.

Yet, crisis managers are constrained by human limits in cognitive capacity to absorb new information under stressful conditions in contrast to the volume of information generated in even minor crises. It becomes a major challenge to organize, analyze, comprehend, and translate into action evidence from the field, especially in novel conditions that do not fit prior planning scenarios. Technologies are essential to manage the deluge of information generated in crisis management operations, as digital information systems increasingly are embedded in mechanisms that monitor the operation of technical systems such as electrical power, communication, transportation, water, wastewater, and gasoline distribution systems. Crisis operations can benefit significantly from investment in Internet of Things (IOT) environments to generate alerts or indicate limits in technical performance. Yet, each sub-system is subject to its own vulnerabilities, failure, and error-prone performance that can lead to cascading failures in large-scale, dynamic, multi-level systems as sub-systems interact across organizations, disciplines, and jurisdictions. Such interactions likely generate feedback loops and novel dynamics not anticipated in the logical design of crisis management systems, a compelling reminder to conduct rigorous research as crisis events unfold, even as the limitations of systematic research cannot be denied. To the extent that the veil of uncertainty is pushed back in complex dynamic systems even modestly, informed action can save lives, losses, and societal disruption.

The chapters in this book address high-risk dilemmas and offer promising frameworks of discovery, integration of multi-level findings, and collaboration to inform present-day practice. Distinctively, the chapters in this book acknowledge that crisis information management is fundamentally a sociotechnical process. In today's rapidly changing world, the information management and communication processes essential to anticipate hazards and inform timely decision-making rely on a range of technologies. Yet, the reverse is also true. Technologies, from simple flip phones to supercomputers, rely on human intelligence to design, program, operate, and maintain them, interpreting the information that is transmitted through them in the context of known risk. More challenging is the next generation of sociotechnical models, tools, and programs that may signal unknown hazards for a wider society, but scale that information to decision-makers at multiple levels of operation to inform coordinated action. Taken together, the chapters in this book represent a fresh, vital approach to the role of intelligence in crisis management practice. It is the foundation of the adaptive, learning system that characterizes professional emergency management.

Professor Emerita,
University of Pittsburgh
and
Affiliated Scholar, CITRIS
University of California, Berkeley

Louise K. Comfort

Crisis Information Management Systems—in Crisis? In Winning Ways? Or, in a Blend of Both?

Introduction to the PAIT Volume on Disaster Management and Information Technology

Twenty-five years after Enrico Louis Quarantelli (1924–2017) published his cautionary article entitled "Problematic Aspects of the Information/Communication Revolution for Disaster Planning and Research: Ten Non-technical Issues and Questions" (Quarantelli, 1997), it is worthwhile revisiting some of those issues and questions, when publishing a volume on "Disaster Management and Technology," in general, and on "Crisis Information Management Systems," in particular.

Since 1997, when Quarantelli raised his concerns, a massive proliferation and a widespread use of all kinds of information and communication systems (ICTs) have been witnessed across the entire spectrum of practical disaster management, that is, in mitigation, preparedness, response, and recovery. A trained sociologist and pioneering scholar in the field of disaster sociology, and although not a technologist, Quarantelli nevertheless had a clear understanding of the massive impacts of ICTs ("revolution") in this particular context. In his words,

> [A] new major technological innovation always changes the world into which it is introduced... However, we need to make a distinction between quantitative and qualitative changes. Sometimes what is produced are only changes in degree, but at other times there are transformations of kind. In the instance of the revolution we are discussing, our view is that what is occurring is also bringing about qualitative changes and basic trans- formations over and above only quantitative modifications and alterations in degree. (p. 95)

In that, he was concerned with "possible negative consequences" and "unintended effects" (p. 96), among which he enumerated the danger of ICTs in disaster management to be viewed as fixes for all kinds of problems, and, as a consequence, turn from sheer means into ends in and by themselves (p. 97). What he also correctly foresaw, in particular, was the "information overload problem" already known from the military, where ICT advances "produce more information than can be handled during crises" (p. 97), which also might include misinformation, which "means more likelihood of greater and quicker diffusion of incorrect information, which is even a problem now..., although relatively minor compared to what could occur in the future" (p. 99). And, in summary, he admonished that the "existence of better communication facilities does not necessarily lead in itself to a better exchange of knowledge and intelligence, and/or a greater understanding of what is occurring" (p. 101). When reading through the two forewords to this volume, that is, Gaynor's practitioner perspective as well as Comfort's academic perspective along with Holdeman's account (Chapter "Emergency Management's Journey with Technology") of practical experiences with ICT-based disaster management for the last few decades, it becomes clear that Quarantelli's foresights and cautions were not only warranted but rather remain a concern that carries on.

Disaster management is first and foremost a practical endeavor, which depends on multidisciplinary managerial skills and well-rehearsed practical coordination capabilities. When it comes to the scientific side of these things, academicians shall be clear amongst themselves that disaster management-related science is an endeavor geared in great part at better understanding and improving practice, which scholars in some theory-heavy fields might readily dismiss as sort of a "craft" rather than true science. In fact, while they are neither theory-starved nor theory-thin (Johnson, 2011), applied sciences have not been known for creating groundbreaking theoretical frameworks, and along these lines, no "Grand Theory of Disaster Management" can be expected to ever emerge. Neither fancy nor lofty theoretical frameworks along with ethereal academic discourses in the highest abstract will have any chance of ever gaining any significance nor relevance, which shields disaster management research from becoming a self-referential academic enterprise, which, as an inevitable consequence, would then lack tight relationships to the real world. Conducting theory-informed research in the context of application (Carrier & Nordmann, 2010), in general, and, in particular, using scientific methods, when carried out in stewardship of informing, benefiting, and enhancing disaster management practice, represents not only a noble academic contribution, but rather can also be of highest relevance and significance to society. An in-depth understanding of actual practices as well as coherent and consistent analytical frameworks is required for serving this purpose. The main aim of scientific research in the context of application (in this case, disaster management) is the production, and not only the application, of knowledge that contributes to both a better understanding of disaster and crisis situations as well as an improved disaster management. We do not assume any unproblematic transfers of academic knowledge to practical challenges (Fuller, 2019). Instead, application-oriented research emphasizes theorizing on disaster management processes informed by various sub-disciplines through various empirical studies aiming at insights in concrete practical contexts. This volume is intended to mark an early milestone in the accumulating knowledge regarding Crisis Information Management Systems (CIMS), which have become instrumental in disaster management practice overall and central to disaster information management.

Information management (IM) is distinct from information systems research (ISR), which has been researched and taught for decades in management of information systems departments of business schools. While ISR maintains its focus on "systems" and the "IT artifact" (Benbasat & Zmud, 2003), IM encompasses a wider array of variables, which includes organizational entities such as data, systems, structures, processes, cultures, and relationships that pertain to information access, generation, dissemination, and security (to name a few) (Earl, 1996; Choo, 2002). Interestingly, over decades ISR has been vexed with finding and explaining "information systems failures" or "successes," focusing on technical aspects and has begun rather reluctantly to recognize the inescapable contextual embeddedness of information systems. As ISR found out time and again, systems that work well in one particular context did not work as well, or even at all, in a different context. As early as 1975, scholars pointed at the context dependency and proposed the study of organizational and other context variables for better understanding failures and successes of information systems in practice (Lucas, 1975).

Since then information system failures have remained an unrelenting concern for practitioners and academicians alike as the non-ebbing tide of respective reports indicate (Liebowitz, 1999; Fowler & Horan, 2007; Cecez-Kecmanovic et al., 2014; Dwivedi et al., 2015; Kim & Kishore, 2019; Baghizadeh et al., 2020). More recent ISR has attempted to correct the confining perspective on "IT artifacts" (Benbasat & Zmud, 2003) and has introduced a multi-level study orientation capable of including some context variables (Bélanger et al., 2014). When it comes to CIMS, it appears therefore intuitively clear that the specific context variables of disaster management need study and that the evaluation of technical features of any given CIMS and its functionalities alone can hardly suffice when planning for, implementing, and using such systems. As central part of disaster management, disaster information management encompasses a set of capabilities and capacities, which are specific to the four areas of mitigation, preparedness, response, and recovery. Moreover, these are also specific when it comes to the magnitude of the crisis, that is, the scale, scope, and duration of an emergency (Fischer, 2003). CIMS used in such wide ranges of contexts appear in need of not only versatility with regard to purpose but rather also regarding their resilience, which requires "reduced failure probabilities," "reduced consequences from failures," and "reduced time to recovery" (Bruneau et al., 2003, p. 736), all of which translate into the four classic resilience dimensions of (1) robustness, (2) redundancy, (3) resourcefulness, and (4) rapidity (Bruneau et al., 2003, pp. 737–738) applied to CIMS.

We owe it to Turoff and friends that not only the context sensitivity of CIMS was identified but rather also the special needs and requirements for so-called DERMIS (Dynamic Emergency Response Management Information Systems) were spelled out, an earlier synonymous term for CIMS (Turoff et al., 2004; Van De Walle et al., 2010). Among the context-specific observations presented as "nine premises" were, for example, the need for unobtrusiveness and inconspicuousness of CIMS during disaster management operations along with extreme ease of use. Also, exception-handling capabilities were seen as essential along with role transferability and the actionability and validity of information provided along with other specifics (Turoff et al., 2004). Among the requirements for CIMS, the authors emphasized (a) "easy to learn" and use; (b) usability by trained emergency responders; (c) minimal learning requirements; (d) versatility in terms of "tailoring" and "filtering";

(e) support of "planning, evaluation, training, exercises, and system updating and maintenance between crisis events"; (f) functioning "without the need for a single operational physical center"; and (g) support of "structured communication processes" irrespective of crisis particulars (Turoff et al., 2004, p. 12).

As Quarantelli had already noticed, the introduction of technology also introduces new points for potential failure and likely increases the overall vulnerability in disaster management. However, while this is undoubtedly the case with respect to CIMS, it also presents a tradeoff situation between the probability of CIMS failure and the benefits derived from CIMS usage. In this particular regard, it is again helpful to invoke Fisher's emergency and disaster categorization scheme for analysis (Fischer, 2003). While the probability of total and non-recoverable system loss is highly unlikely for lower disaster categories, when it comes to the highest, that is, DC-9 (catastrophe) or DC-10 (annihilation), then total system loss is not unlikely at all. In these most severe cases of extreme events, the incident's scale, scope, and duration are major, thus affecting several populated areas, or even society at large, for an extended period of time. Examples include catastrophes such as the 2004 Indonesian earthquake and tsunami, the 2011 Eastern Japan earthquake and tsunami, and nuclear or geographically widespread advanced conventional warfare. During extreme events of this magnitude (Quarantelli, 2006), critical infrastructures such as the power plants, power grids, and power substations can become inoperable and even permanently dysfunctional for extended periods of time. With the loss of power, however, also major CIMS-based capabilities can disappear with catastrophic consequences for disaster management. In the case of the looming Cascadia Subduction Zone mega thrust in the Pacific Northwest of the United States, it is estimated that widespread power outages might last for 12–18 months. Despite some currently built-in redundancy with fuel-driven power generators and cell tower infrastructures, the loss of information-sharing and communication capabilities will be dramatic under this scenario, and consequently, the coordinated effectiveness of the response will be greatly hampered. Studies and exercises involving CIMS need to address this extreme scenario.

In an analytical report published elsewhere, when taking author-provided "keywords" as indicators one co-editor found that current disaster information management research has veered away in large numbers from studying CIMS along with "decision support" and "situational awareness" as prerequisite for a "common operating picture" and redirecting its attention and focus toward inquiring the uses of social media, in particular, Twitter, around the occurrence of emergencies and disasters. Most recently, a large portion of this social-media and Twitter-related research in disaster information management has revolved around the COVID-19 pandemic. "Sentiment analysis" has been found a popular theme in this research. Social sciences have been known for producing a certain "faddishness" in topics and methods for some time (Abrahamson, 2009; Aguirre & Best, 2014). However, just having a plethora of ready-made, inexpensive, and easily available data does not mean that these data have any relevance to disaster information management. They might be more related to sentiments uttered inside certain strata of net and smartphone savvy persons within certain age groups in the overall context or in the geographical vicinity of emergencies or disasters. Nothing is wrong with that. But is this selection of easily collected data relevant to the phenomenon of disaster information management? What do these data really represent? What is the relationship to overall disaster management? Why are these studies becoming so numerous in our relatively small domain of study? When it comes to CIMS, with all due respect to our colleagues engaged in this area, it is hoped that the social media/Twitter/Covid fad is coming to a "well-deserved" end at some time soon.

The chapters in this edited volume are organized within four topical sections: (1) CIMS in Emergency Management Practice; (2) CIMS Functionalities and Features; (3) CIMS Requirements, Development, and Testing; and (4) CIMS Assessment, Evaluation, and Data Management. Please note that in the following we will use the terms "emergency management" and "disaster management" interchangeably. We may refer to them under the acronyms of EM/DM.

In the first section, *CIMS in Emergency Practice*, three chapters provide accounts of and insights into the evolution of CIMS usage and deployment in disaster management practice.

In the chapter entitled "Emergency Management's Journey with Technology," drawing from his own multi-decade practitioner experience, during which he left a mark as a strong proponent of and an outspoken advocate for the implementation and use of modern ICTs, Eric Holdeman presents what he calls the technology journey of emergency management. One of the enduring dilemmas already encountered early in ICT uses during emergencies is that CIMS, which are helpful and effective in regular emergency management might not scale well, if at all. As Holdeman observes, this is owed to the nature and rapidly growing complexity of larger disasters. He provides a historical account of the origin of modern disaster management in the United States, which finds its roots in the Civil Defense Era of the 1950s and 1960s. Founded in that era, "Emergency Operations Centers" (EOCs) were military-inspired command centers, around which the civil defense was organized. The EOCs were to become the nuclei of emergency management as we know it today. Technology adoption was rather slow and relied for decades on traditional means such as landlines and later fax machines. The advent of computers did not occur until the late 1990s, at least not at the local and county levels according to Holdeman's account. However, since the early 2000s, both the Internet and Internet-based mobile technologies finally have had a major impact on daily routines and responses. Part of the slow technology adoption appears to have been technology aversion on part of the "first generation" of responders and emergency professionals. With a more technology-affine generation surely taking over the reins in emergency management this aversion may fade. However, what will remain in Holdeman's view is the relative exposure and potential over-reliance when using leading-edge technologies, which may introduce unwanted additional risks.

In the chapter entitled "Deploying Modern Technology for Disaster Management Practitioners," Johnson, McIntosh, and Tropasso cast a light on shortfalls of technology implementation in EM/DM, and how such shortfalls might be avoided. The authors present and discuss "common mistakes" when implementing and managing CIMS. They emphasize that in order to stay on top of the technological and organizational challenges, EM/DM like other organizational entities require a sound technology governance framework, which also includes data access, storage, and dissemination plans. Effective CIMS they point out need to support and incorporate standard operating procedures (SOPs), which make their use consistent throughout emergencies. Planning, implementation, and operation of CIMS have "human-factor" and "social" sides, which need attention to unleash the full potential of these supporting tools.

In the final chapter of this section entitled "Technology and Information Management Supporting Resilience in Healthcare and Rescue Systems," Väyrynen, Vainikainen, Paunu, Helander, and Tenhovuori study how CIMS add to resilience in healthcare-related EM/DM. The authors take the COVID-19 pandemic as a case to investigate how respective response systems have been adjusted, modified, and connected so that information could be shared. Although the healthcare sector is governed by fairly stringent data management and privacy protection laws, the pandemic response enabled an environment for innovation and related policies, which fostered research opportunities in consultation, research grants, collaboration platforms, and research support infrastructure, which added to the overall resilience of the pandemic response. Sharing technology-based innovations quickly throughout the multi-national research and practice network during the unfolding crisis made the response more robust and sophisticated. Through the urgent need imposed by the pandemic, it appears new avenues of technology use and application were quickly found and incorporated in the response.

The second section of the volume is dedicated to *CIMS Functionalities and Features*. This section contains some more technical chapters.

The chapter by Barth, Kabbinahithilu, de Cola, Barters, and Pantazis provides the description of a specific EM/DM system, the HEIMDALL system. Under the title "A System for Collaboration and Information Sharing in Disaster Management," the authors describe the architecture and components of the HEIMDALL system, which allows for scenario building, response planning, information sharing, collaboration, and incident cataloging. Integrated with external geographic information system (GIS) functionality as well as with other inputs including mobile field units, the system has been conceived to support responders in incidents of wildfires, landslides, and floods. The system is designed for satellite-based networking and data exchange. In its federated architecture, local units can connect to a backbone (a so-called catalog architecture) for data sharing and access. The system underwent several practice trials ranging from fire fighters, police, and medical services to civil protection and command-and-control centers.

In the chapter entitled "A Decade of Netcentric Crisis Management: Challenges and Future Development," Wolbers, Treurniet, and Boersma describe the adaptation of the concept of net-centric information management developed by the military into the realm of civil disaster management. The authors distinguish the tenets held in either domain, which favor distributed sense making, transparency, and connectivity in the civil domain, whereas self-synchronization, information superiority, and also connectivity dominate the military domain. However, as the authors demonstrate while the two domains are distinct they may have important practice elements and insights to share. For example, information transparency and information superiority may be balanced in a way that they result in a unity-of-command approach across jurisdictions in a civil disaster response scenario.

In the chapter entitled "Common Operational Picture and Interconnected Tools for Disaster Response: The FASTER Toolkit," Konstantinos Konstantoudakis and colleagues give a detailed account of the architecture and the components of the comprehensive and integrated toolkit for emergency management called FASTER, which integrates a range of mobile and stationary devices along with sensory and surveillance equipment into a communication and services hub, which is capable of providing incident commanders with a detailed real-time common operating picture (COP). The FASTER COP toolkit has undergone several field trials to test its real-world operational readiness and viability.

In the chapter entitled "Intelligent Building Evacuation: From Modeling Systems to Behaviors," Moghaddam, Muccini, and Dugdale report on how an algorithm-based evacuation system, which utilizes a smart Internet-of-Things (IoT) infrastructure, can be used for optimizing rapid and flexible evacuations from buildings of various architectural layouts in case of emergencies. The design of the algorithm was informed via an agent-based model that simulated human behavior in emergency evacuation situations. Like the system described in the previous chapter, the IoT-based evacuation algorithm is still in a pre-production experimental phase.

In the final chapter in this section entitled "Challenges of Integrating Advanced Information Technologies with 5G in Disaster Risk Management," Velev and Zlateva explore and discuss the potential quantitative and qualitative expansion and increased integration of services once a fully fledged 5G cellular infrastructure has become available and serves as a backbone. The authors predict that integrating in new ways on the basis of this backbone, social media, IoT, big data, cloud computing, artificial intelligence, and virtual reality will lead to novel opportunities and applications hugely relevant to disaster management, in general, and to disaster information management, in particular. As an example, 5G-backed drone technology could serve as an important additional capability in disaster-related surveillance, search and rescue, and transportation.

The third section of the volume focuses on *CIMS Requirements, Development, and Testing*. The six chapters in this section demonstrate the wide range of challenges and areas to be addressed in designing, building, and testing CIMS.

In the chapter entitled "An Integrated Framework to Evaluate Information Systems Performance in High-Risk Settings: Experiences from the iTRACK Project," Abdelgawad and Comes discuss the importance of software system testing, and they describe as the three pillars of system evaluation the dimensions of quality, usability, and usefulness, which system testing needs to consider. The authors take the European iTRACK system as a case in point. iTrack integrates and controls personnel deployment and action, equipment allocation and use, and provides services for mission steering and control, which includes secure communication, data access and storage, threat detection, logistics support, along with information collection and decision support. The framework-based, comprehensive test of the iTRACK system was performed for all three dimensions, which integrated objective and subjective, that is, user perception-informed measures.

In the chapter entitled "Rural First Responders and Communication Technology: A Mixed Methods Approach to Assessing Their Challenges and Needs," Buchanan, Choong, Dawkins, and Spickard Prettyman present and discuss the specific barriers to using modern ICTs in rural settings in disaster management. In their mixed-method study, the authors identify as ICT usage barriers in rural areas (a) lack of cell coverage, (b) lack of system interoperability, (c) high cost of ICTs, (d) inappropriate physical ergonomics of devices, and (e) lack of device and network reliability. These barriers lead to inaccurate information, lack of tracking capabilities, and inaccurate geographic information. While the needs for responders in rural areas are not much different from their urban colleagues, the rural setting adds a number of additional barriers to the effectiveness of responses, when using modern ICTs.

The chapter by Elmasllari and Kirk is entitled "Designing Well-Accepted IT Solutions for Emergency Response: Methods and Approaches." Significant mismatches between user needs and actual system implementations have been known and documented for decades. Disaster ICTs, which can be characterized as complex and complicated, appear to be no exception. The authors therefore propose an approach to system design, which narrows the gap between needs and actual implementations, and which focuses on the four need categories (Rasmussen), explicit, observable, tacit, and latent. Elmasllari and Kirk also used a mixed method approach for identifying design issues and propose remedies. Deep domain knowledge of and practical experience with disaster response situations along with participatory development approaches appear to be indispensable prerequisites for successful CIMS development.

In the chapter entitled "Mobile Device-to-Device Communication for Crisis Scenarios Using Low-Cost LoRa Modems," Höchst and colleagues present a technical solution for long-range peer-to-peer (i.e., smartphone-to-smartphone) communication in crisis situations. The chapter specifies hardware and firmware prerequisites. Based on such extensions, smartphones can incorporate a direct device-to-device messaging application, which makes them independent from carrier availability. The authors developed a so-called Bundle Broadcasting Connector, which lets smartphones transmit and receive messages. Device-to-device communications were tested to work in rural settings for distances under 2 km and in urban settings under 3 km. The authors analyzed the robustness and throughputs under various payloads and found the approach technically feasible while scalable at low equipment-related cost and low energy consumption.

The chapter co-authored by Pilemalm and Mojir is entitled "Digitalized Cross-Sector Collaboration for an Effective Emergency Response: Emerging Forms of Network Governance." In a cross-case comparative study, the authors investigate and analyze three cases in the Swedish public sector, in which CIMS are used for collaboration and coordination. The research project studies challenges and issues of organizational collaboration and coordination and the governance thereof, and it connects these with the enabling capabilities and uses of ICTs, in general, and CIMS, in particular. The researchers find as one missing link for improved cross-jurisdictional collaboration the lack of ICT and CIMS use, whose enabling capacities were underutilized. The study acknowledges and emphasizes the hybrid character of CIMS. The design of these systems has to reflect the dual nature of the hierarchical (government) form of governance and the network form of governance in cross-jurisdictional collaboration.

In the final chapter of this section entitled "Defining Common Information Requirements for Supporting Multiagency Emergency Operations," co-authors Steen-Tveit and Munkvold study responder information requirements and information sharing practices in a disaster management context of Norway. The research identifies eight categories (location, critical infrastructure, victims, evacuation routes and means, resources, weather conditions, critical buildings, and situational development), for all of which integrated CIMS support would be required. Such CIMS then would be effective in capturing a dynamic situation leading to enhanced situational awareness (SA) for incident management and enable the emergence of a common operating picture (COP).

In the fourth and final section of the volume, *CIMS Assessment, Evaluation, and Data Management*, five chapters give accounts and evaluations of existing CIMS that are currently used in disaster information management practice.

In the chapter entitled "A Commercial Cloud-Based Crisis Information Management System: How Fit and Robust Is It in Response to a Catastrophe?", Nolan and Scholl focus on one of the most widely used CIMS in the United States known under its product name, WebEOC. As the name suggests, this CIMS is Web-based, which makes it accessible almost anywhere as long as the communication infrastructure is mainly intact. The authors uncover that the widespread proliferation of this commercial-off-the-shelf CIMS in disaster information management was coincidental and in perceived absence of better alternatives rather than based on systemic evaluation and informed choice, in particular, at the Federal Emergency Management Agency (FEMA). Among other severe problems, the authors report on serious scalability, interoperability, security, and performance problems found with the practical use of WebEOC as soon as a given emergency situation requires multi-jurisdictional coordination and collaboration.

The chapter entitled "Practitioners' Perceptions of Fitness to Task of a Leading Disaster Response Management Tool," by Scholl and Holdeman, also focuses on WebEOC, the commercial-of-the-shelf CIMS. The authors conducted an investigation via survey among first responders and emergency managers regarding their experiences when using WebEOC in a range of practical emergency and disaster responses. Despite its widespread use, the CIMS was found lacking robustness, ease of use, scalability, and interoperability. The study empirically, more widely, and squarely confirmed previous study results, which called into question the readiness and fitness of this particular CIMS.

In the chapter entitled "From Digital Public Warning Systems to Emergency Warning Ecosystems," the focus is given on public alert and warning systems. In the chapter, Bonaretti and Fischer-Preßler describe and analyze the component parts of current public warning systems (PWS). Emergency management agencies still use traditional means such as FM or AM radio alerts, TV alerts, sirens, warning lights, electronic reader boards, and even old-style billboards among others to warn the public of threats and hazards. However, these agencies increasingly also incorporate and rely on smartphone notifications in the blend of instantly alerting the public. As the authors describe in detail, these PWS are advancing through four sequential steps, activation and representation (by the emergency management agency), dispatch (through various channels), and counteraction (when the alert has been received by the population and is acted upon). Based on their analysis, the authors propose an even tighter integration of warning methods, systems, and sectors that connects the digital data ecosystems of various sectors including the private sector and the healthcare sector.

The chapter by Correia, Água, and Simões-Marques entitled "The Role of Ontologies and Linked Open Data in Support of Disaster Management" focuses on data management within disaster management by means of various hierarchical ontologies. The authors point out that data used in disaster management are extremely heterogeneous as are the systems that produce and use these data as are the agencies involved in disaster management. An unfolding disaster itself adds to these complexities. For addressing these complexities at the data end, the authors investigate how ontologies at various levels might help mitigate the problem. Linked open data, the authors argue, provide a wealth of information to responders, if they can be readily accessed and interpreted by responders in real time. Such ontology-based system would be a major step toward intelligent decision support in emergency management the authors argue.

In the last, but not least, contribution to the volume, "Toward a Taxonomy for Classifying Crisis Information Management Systems," Borges, Canós, Penadés, Labaka, Bañuls, and Hernantes propose a classification approach to CIMS. In this chapter, following Nickerson et al.'s guidance the authors first define the dimensions of a useful taxonomy as to be "concise," "robust," "comprehensive," "extendible," and "explanatory." On this basis in an iterative process, the authors developed what they call the "Tax-CIM" taxonomy, which resulted in seven dimensions (coordination, information management and retrieval, presentation/visualization, communication, collaboration, intelligence, and general support). In another iterative process, the authors validated the emerging taxonomy against 12 real-world CIMS and refined Tax-CIM in the process. The taxonomy helps classify existing CIMS and those under development. It also informs about what might be missing in a CIMS under consideration.

By this point, it is in order to highlight important comments from the two foreword contributors to this volume, former FEMA administrator, Peter T. Gaynor and Prof. emerita Dr. Louise K. Comfort, of the University of Pittsburgh. While both contributors approach the area of Crisis Information Management Systems, or CIMS, from different angles, broadly speaking from practice as opposed to research, they converge in important ways. Gaynor views CIMS as indispensable tools, but rather not as panaceas to all decision support problems that incident command have in the disaster information management context. He helps sharpen the academic perspective on CIMS toward priority information requirements (PIR), which rest on a set of principles and a doctrine, which is inspired by the military. Comfort also asserts that the focus on the relevant pieces of information are what matters most to responders, since human cognitive capacities deteriorate under duress and in the face of simultaneous information overload. Both foreword contributors are also highly aware of the additional vulnerabilities that even sophisticated CIMS introduce. Throughout this volume and in their comments, in their own contributions, their topical selections, and directions, the co-editors have emphasized the need for the closest possible relationship between disaster management in practice and the study of disaster management in academia. We strongly hope that the publication of this volume provides another stepping stone in this direction.

Seattle, WA, USA — Hans Jochen Scholl
Puyallup, WA, USA — Eric E. Holdeman
Amsterdam, The Netherlands — F. Kees Boersma
June 2022

References

Abrahamson, E. (2009). Necessary conditions for the study of fads and fashions in science. *Scandinavian Journal of Management, 25*(2), 235–239.

Aguirre, B. A., & Best, E. (2014). How not to learn: Resilience in the study of disaster. In *Learning and calamities* (pp. 236–252). Routledge.

Baghizadeh, Z., Cecez-Kecmanovic, D., & Schlagwein, D. (2020). Review and critique of the information systems development project failure literature: An argument for exploring information systems development project distress. *Journal of Information Technology, 35*(2), 123–142.

Bélanger, F., Cefaratti, M., Carte, T., & Markham, S. E. (2014). Multilevel research in information systems: Concepts, strategies, problems, and pitfalls. *Journal of the Association for Information Systems, 15*(9), 1.

Benbasat, I., & Zmud, R. W. (2003). The identity crisis within the IS discipline: Defining and communicating the discipline's core properties1. *MIS Quarterly, 27*(2), 183–194.

Bruneau, M., Chang, S. E., Eguchi, R. T., Lee, G. C., O'Rourke, T. D., Reinhorn, A. M., Shinozuka, M., Tierney, K., Wallace, W. A., & von Winterfeldt, D. (2003). A framework to quantitatively assess and enhance the seismic resilience of communities. *Earthquake Spectra, 19*(4), 733–752.

Carrier, M., & Nordmann, A. (2010). *Science in the context of application*. Springer Science & Business Media.

Cecez-Kecmanovic, D., Kautz, K., & Abrahall, R. (2014). Reframing success and failure of information systems. *MIS Quarterly, 38*(2), 561–588.

Choo, C. W. (2002). *Information management for the intelligent organization: The art of scanning the environment* (3rd ed.). Information Today.

Dwivedi, Y. K., Wastell, D., Laumer, S., Henriksen, H. Z., Myers, M. D., Bunker, D., Elbanna, A., Ravishankar, M., & Srivastava, S. C. (2015). Research on information systems failures and successes: Status update and future directions. *Information Systems Frontiers, 17*(1), 143–157.

Earl, M. J., Oxford Institute of Information Management, & PA Consulting Group. (1996). *Information management: The organizational dimension.* Oxford University Press.

Fischer, H. W. (2003). The sociology of disaster: Definitions, research questions, & measurements continuation of the discussion in a post-September 11 environment. *International Journal of Mass Emergencies and Disasters, 21*(1), 91–107.

Fowler, J. J., & Horan, P. (2007). Are information systems' success and failure factors related? An exploratory study. *Journal of Organizational and End User Computing (JOEUC), 19*(2), 1–22.

Fuller, S. (2019). *Philosophy of science and its discontents*. Routledge.

Johnson, A. (2011). Everything new is old again: What place should applied science have in the history of science? In M. Carrier & A. Nordmann (Eds.), *Science in the context of application* (pp. 455–466). Springer.

Kim, J. U., & Kishore, R. (2019). Do we fully understand information systems failure? An exploratory study of the cognitive schema of IS professionals. *Information Systems Frontiers, 21*(6), 1385–1419.

Liebowitz, J. (1999). A look at why information systems fail. *Kybernetes, 28*(1), 61–67.

Lucas, H. C. (1975). *Why information systems fail.* Columbia University Press.

Quarantelli, E. L. (1997). Problematical aspects of the information/communication revolution for disaster planning and research: Ten non-technical issues and questions. *Disaster Prevention and Management: An International Journal, 6*(2), 94–106.

Quarantelli, E. L. (2006). Catastrophes are different from disasters: Some implications for crisis planning and managing drawn from Katrina. In *Understanding Katrina: Perspectives from the social sciences.*

Turoff, M., Chumer, M., van de Walle, B. A., & Yao, X. (2004). The design of a dynamic emergency response management information system (DERMIS). *JITTA: Journal of Information Technology Theory and Application, 5*(4), 1.

Van De Walle, B., Turoff, M., & Hiltz, S. R. (2010). *Information systems for emergency management.* Routledge.

Contents

Part I
CIMS in Emergency Management Practice

Emergency Management's Journey with Technology

Eric E. Holdeman

Abstract There is no one single journey when it comes to technology. For those who did not grow up as "digital natives" each has taken their own path in accepting, developing technological skills and expanding them by integrating them into their everyday work environment. Indeed, the journey continues with no hard-set destination before us. We only know that technological development and use of technology continue to expand exponentially with each passing day. What follows is therefore just one American perspective on how the profession of emergency management has adopted technologies over the decades in which the profession has existed. All the while, working daily to plan for, train, and practice for future emergency and disaster response events that are sure to come.

Keywords Emergencies · Disasters · Catastrophes · History of emergency management · Emergency Operations Center · EOC · Mobile technologies · Alert and warning systems · Modern information technologies · Situational awareness · Common operating picture · COP · Rapid damage assessment · Technology aversion · Data management · Disaster information management

There is no one single journey when it comes to technology. For those who did not grow up as "digital natives," each has taken their own path in accepting and developing technological skills and expanding them by integrating them into their everyday work environment. Indeed, the journey continues with no hard-set destination before us. We only know that technological development and the use of technology continue to expand exponentially with each passing day.

E. E. Holdeman (✉)
Eric Holdeman Associates, Puyallup, WA, USA
e-mail: ericholdeman@ericholdeman.com

H. J. Scholl et al. (eds.), *Disaster Management and Information Technology*, Public Administration and Information Technology 40,
https://doi.org/10.1007/978-3-031-20939-0_1

What follows is therefore just one American perspective on how the profession of emergency management has adopted technologies over the decades in which the profession has existed, all the while, working daily to plan, train, and practice for future emergency and disaster response events that are sure to come.

Emergencies, Disasters, and Catastrophes

Before going further with a review of technology and how it has been incorporated into the emergency management profession, it must first be explained what the differences are between emergencies, disasters, and catastrophes.

Emergencies are the most typical, day-to-day type of events that involve fire and police agencies. These are the daily traffic accidents, house fires, heart attacks, and lost or missing person's type of low-level events. First responder agencies are sized and equipped to handle these events. Should there be a larger-scale emergency that exceeds the capabilities of a single department, e.g., a mass shooting of five people or a large apartment fire, agencies can call upon other like agencies from neighboring jurisdictions to come and assist them. It is these events that usually do not include the use of emergency management resources. Emergencies are considered routine.

Disasters are those types of events that exceed the normal capabilities of first responder agencies and require a more coordinated response to the situation either due to the large scale of a disaster or the number of people or properties that are being impacted. Flooding is the most common disaster. Other natural disasters caused by severe weather include tornadoes, winter storms, and hurricanes. Human-caused events can also tip the scale of an event. These can include terrorism, hazardous material incidents, cybersecurity attacks, and the like. In the above cases, a more coordinated response is needed. Typically, a jurisdiction will activate what is called an emergency operations center (EOC) where representatives from a wide range of agencies and even the private sector can come together physically to coordinate a response to the events impacting the community. Each level of government, from a city to a county, to the state and even the federal government will operate an EOC in a disaster situation.

Catastrophes are disasters on a much bigger scale. The impacts to people and property are the same as you see in disasters, only with either a larger footprint or more devastating impact to, for example, a high population density geographic area. A catastrophe will automatically require the injection of federal resources and other states outside of the impacted area due to the overwhelming impact of the disaster. An example for what will be categorized as a catastrophe will be a full-rip Cascadia subduction fault earthquake that impacts the coasts of the states of Washington, Oregon, and parts of Northern California. Local and immediately available regional resources will be overwhelmed.

The challenge of technology is that it is likely to be used daily for emergencies and then also be needed for disasters and even catastrophes. The ability of technology to "scale up" is one of the challenges people and agencies must plan for. Additionally, with the larger-scale events, electrical power may not be available, so an overdependence on technology can hinder a community's response at the worst possible moment. Communities must look at mitigating all the possible impacts that could take their technology "offline" when the solutions provided by the technological system are at their highest need.

Another challenge with any technology being used in a larger event is the interoperability of the technology across the first responder and federal assets coming to assist in responding to the disaster. Much money has been invested in communications interoperability, following the events of the terrorist attacks of 9/11, which in itself remains a challenge. As we continue to adopt more sophisticated technological systems, not all of them will be interoperable across the responding agencies that flow into a disaster zone to assist with the response and recovery operations.

History of Emergency Management

The Civil Defense Era

It is important to put the history of emergency management into context. Before there was an emergency management profession, there was civil defense. Civil defense sprung from the beginnings of the Cold War and the threat of nuclear attack by the Soviet Union. Once intercontinental ballistic missiles with nuclear warheads were developed, the need for an organized function of civil defense was promulgated.

The primary activities of the civil defense era focused on trying, to the best of the nation's capability, to have the maximum number of people survive a nuclear attack. The planning function was oriented on two major areas. The first area was identifying publicly available civil defense shelters. These were primarily commercial buildings made out of concrete, steel, and stone. The basements of these buildings were identified as places where people could congregate and achieve some modicum of protection from an initial nuclear blast and the subsequent nuclear fallout that would follow.

The second planning function included planning for the evacuation of major population centers that were believed to be targets in a nuclear war. The principal function of the planning was purely evacuating people out of cities with little thought to where they would go or how they would be cared for following the evacuation.

The preparedness phase of this era focused on distributing federally supplied civil defense supplies to the previously identified civil defense shelter. This included food and water stored in 55-gallon fiber drums. Medical kits were also provided that had the very basics and included morphine.

The preparedness aspect of civil defense also included the distribution of radiation detection equipment. Radiac meters and personal dosimeters were part of the equipment stockpile maintained by states and distributed to local civil defense agencies associated with cities and counties. These instruments were further distributed out to individual civil defense shelters and to local first responders, who were primarily fire and police, with perhaps hospitals also having these in their inventory of supplies and equipment.

City and county local civil defense agencies were often located in the basements of courthouses and other public buildings. Staffing for these agencies primarily initially came from the US military, with personnel completing their military service and continuing to serve in a civilian capacity in these civil defense agencies.

The concept of the emergency operations center (EOC) which came out of the military was adopted as the location where government officials would gather to garner information on the status of their community and plan the response to disaster events. The EOC would at best have had physical blackboards and then eventually white boards to record the status of an incident. Data such as the number of shelters operational with the number of people located at each shelter would be recorded on these boards. A map displaying the individual jurisdiction would display the location of shelters and also annotate other information like the radiological readings that would be passed to the EOC by first responders.

The technology and communication's tools available back then were very limited. Landline phones were the most reliable form of communications. Radio frequencies were dedicated to use by state-wide civil defense organizations. The EOC might have a dedicated radio room for this equipment, with the addition of amateur radio systems and operators augmenting the governmental professionals.

The national to state warning system that was developed and indeed continues to this day is the National Warning System (NAWAS). This is a ringdown system where all parties on a line can hear the caller when they pick up the phone. The principle function of NAWAS was to distribute a nation-wide warning that inbound missiles or bombers had been detected, and there was an imminent threat of a nuclear strike in the United States. Each state maintains a second ringdown system as part of NAWAS where they can pass this warning down to individual counties. Major cities might be included in this communications loop, but not necessarily.

The only immediate warning system available to cities and counties was air raid warning sirens. These were tone only, with no technology available to warn of other hazards. However, in areas of the nation susceptible to tornadoes, these were dual purposed to provide a tornado warning.

All of the above was the general extent of the technology available for communications and warning.

The Beginnings of Emergency Management

Fast forward to 1979, the federal government established what we now know as the Federal Emergency Management Agency (FEMA). The impetus for the formation of FEMA had not to do with nuclear attack but how the federal government had underperformed when responding to large-scale natural disasters which included hurricane Carla in 1962, the San Fernando earthquake in 1971, and hurricane Agnes in 1972 and led to more agitation for a better agency coordination. Centralizing the coordination function under one agency was done to foster a more cohesive disaster response by multiple federal agencies with different disaster missions, like debris cleanup and disaster housing as examples.

The national defense/civil defense aspect of emergency management continues until this day. It peaked in the 1980s as the United States continued to respond to the potential for a Russian nuclear attack. Even with the fall of the Berlin Wall in 1989 and then the dissolution of the Soviet Union in 1991, two-thirds of FEMA's efforts were directed toward surviving a nuclear attack on the homeland and the continuity of the US government following such an attack.

The focus on civil defense, the civil defense shelters, supplies, and radiological equipment, ceased having federal funding around 1993. This ended these programs at the state and local levels. In truth, the disaster supplies were likely never renewed and replaced once they were distributed in the early era of civil defense.

Moving forward from 1992 onward, much more of the focus of emergency management has been on natural disasters. There have been significant events that have swung the pendulum of focus back and forth. The terrorist attacks of September 11, 2001, created a total focus on funding and activities of the federal, state, and local levels on terrorism.

That event also led to the creation of the Department of Homeland Security (DHS) and the inclusion of FEMA into that larger department. Immediately preceding the 9/11 attacks, it had been a cabinet level agency in President Clinton's administration.

The advent of the focus on terrorism led to much more federal funding being distributed to state and local agencies, up to $3.2 billion for approximately 10 years. Those funds have continued to decrease over the years. More details on the use of those funds for technological purposes will be discussed later in this chapter. This influx of federal funding was way beyond any level of funding that had been seen previously.

The last major disaster event that shaped emergency management in any significant manner was Hurricane Katrina. Once again, the performance of FEMA and the other federal agencies was called into question. The Post-Katrina Emergency Reform Act on October 4, 2006, once again reoriented FEMA to provide optimized performance in natural disasters. Katrina was also the event that swung FEMA back from its "terrorism-centric" focus following 9/11 that came from their inclusion into the Department of Homeland Security (DHS) to a more balanced approach to hazards and what the focus of the agency should be. The term typically used is an "all-hazards approach."

The Technology Odyssey of Emergency Management

From the civil defense era of the 1950s–1960s onward, landline phones and radio communications dominated what technology was available to emergency management agencies.

The first real technological advance was the adoption of numeric pagers. These were number-only pagers that select management personnel could carry for the purposes of recalling them for an emergency. As funding became available, then more pagers could be distributed to line staff to facilitate notifications of events.

Later innovation of pager technology included text messaging and then also the addition of a keyboard to the pager, allowing the recipient of a pager text message to reply. By the end of the 1980s, these devices were seeing wide adoption and use.

It was also in the 1980s that brought the wide use of the FAX machine that allowed the transmission of documents over telephone lines. This was the first true data transmission of information between agencies and levels of government. Subsequent innovations of FAX machine technology allowed for multiple document scanning and the sending of group faxes to multiple addressees in one single "FAX and send." This technology remained the key multi-jurisdictional communications tool until the development and adoption of computers and email. The transmission of daily situation reports during an incident would be an example for the use of a FAX machine in a disaster.

Still in this era, information was collected usually by phone and then displayed on white boards or chart paper that was arrayed on the walls of an EOC. These "boards" might include topical areas such as road closures, shelters open and occupancy numbers, significant events occurring during the event, and paper maps. These were sometimes covered with clear acetate that allowed individuals to write information using markers or grease pencils on multiple overlays of data, displaying spatially the status of the disaster by highlighting damaged areas, supply points, etc.

Copy machines were also fielded during this period, and they replaced the old mimeograph machines that required the production of stencils for each individual page of a document. Documents were then run off and typically hand collated for assembly and stapling.

The next development that actually moved emergency management into the digital age was the fielding of desktop personal computers. These were not ubiquitous in organizations. It was not unusual for state and local emergency offices to have computers that were shared by multiple people. The assignment of individual computers to people most likely did not occur until the late 1990s.

Laptops, while in existence, were much more expensive than desktop computers and therefore in short supply. Perhaps one or two laptops might be available to be "checked out" for people on field deployments in a travel status or for instructional purposes.

Even in this era of new computers, the preferred method of group presentations and presenting information was with an overhead projector and what were called "overhead slides." These dominated presentations up until and into the 2000s.

Email began to have widespread application in the late 1990s. Its evolution has changed much about how emergency management shares information between individuals, agencies, and levels of government.

One simple example is illustrative of how email has functioned. Prior to email, a DRAFT plan had to be printed and physically mailed using the US Post Office to individual recipients for review. Agencies had a printing budget. Enough time had to be allowed for the time for mail to be sent and received, along with a period for the actual physical review. Annotated copies of the plan, with pen and ink changes, would be sent back by the recipients for review, page by page from the agency which sent the plan out. There might be physical cover letters and also summaries of comments from each reviewer. The final plans had to be physically printed again and sent via email to a distribution list of agencies and organizations.

As email capabilities have increased overtime, these plans could be distributed at the push of a button and reviewees commented digitally right in the document and sent those comments back to the originator. The development of the World Wide Web and the Internet has also enhanced this review process and will be discussed more below.

Mobile Technologies

Field disaster response and communications connectively has been totally realized by cellular communications. Again, progress to where we are today was slow. The first cell phones known as "bricks" were fielded in emergency management in the early 1990s. These were far and few between, often reserved for directors and maybe upper management.

Once consumer cell phones became more commonplace, it became more the rule than the exception for essential emergency management staff, not everyone, to have some form of cell phone. By the late 1990s, it was not uncommon for emergency management staff at all levels to have a government-issued cell phone.

Blackberries were the first system that allowed for email to be used in a cellular environment. With the subsequent fielding of the iPhone and touch technology, access to the Internet was the final realization of a mobile platform for managing technology while away from the office.

The 2010 release of the Apple iPad sped up the transition to mobile technology. Because of its size and the addition of a keyboard, the less technological emergency oriented managers now had more familiarity with technology, and it sped up the adoption of mobile solutions within the discipline. The use of these mobile technologies will be discussed later in this chapter.

The Advent of the Internet

As with most of our modern twenty-first century, it is the widespread adoption of the Internet in all its forms that has advanced the discipline of emergency management. In the late 1990s and early 2000s, the use of the Internet for emergency management purposes exploded—in a good way. The first permutation was the development of individual agency webpages. Initially, these were very static affairs with very basic information posted to them providing information on the agency, contact information, and perhaps copies of plans.

Early in the adoption of the Internet by government agencies, the use of this new tool was restricted to a select few. Usually public information officers (PIO) would be the type of position authorized access to the Internet. Its use by everyday emergency management staff was considered frivolous, and staff were not generally trusted to use the tool. Note that this was before the widespread use of social media by individuals.

As the use of the Internet expanded within the mainstream of popular culture, the Internet and agency websites became collection places for the posting of all types of documents and information. Instead of being static, they became the go-to location to find out current information about events, such as conferences and trainings. With new mobile payment options, it became common for the registration process for trainings and conferences to all be handled over the Internet.

Websites became the repository of all forms of information. Another trend that developed was individual governments began to establish agency templates for websites to achieve a common look and theme. As websites became the repository of information, it was not uncommon for people logging into the agency website to find it difficult to access the information they were seeking. It was there but hidden in plain sight.

Previously, agencies had printing budgets. They were used to publish paper copies of plans for distribution to other agencies. They were also used for the printing of public education materials. Today, printing budgets are almost nonexistent. Publications are converted to PDFs and distributed via email or available and searchable on individual agency websites. The previously time-intensive nature of physically mailing of plans via the United States Postal Service for comment and review and then final formal promulgation of documents has been relegated to emailing a link to the PDF documents. Individuals and agencies may then print a copy themselves if they want a paper copy.

While some printed materials still do exist in the form of public education documents, the primary method for the distribution of information is now done via the Internet. The federal government remains the largest single producer of printed public education materials.

Document sharing as previously described has become widespread. What has made the availability of documents much easier has been the use of "the Cloud" for the storage of information which has also aided the retention of documents for continuity of government purposes.

Alert and Warning

One of the first duties of emergency management agencies is to provide alert and warning messages to the public when there is a threat to persons or property. As noted earlier, siren systems tied originally to warning the public of a nuclear attack were the first warning systems. These became dual use in some communities that have tornado hazards.

There are also some "fixed site" industrial areas that might have dedicated siren systems that warn of a hazardous materials spill or in the case of a nuclear power plant, a radiation emergency. Modern siren systems now may have voice capabilities that allow them to function as multi-hazard warning systems.

National Warning System (NAWAS)

There are 2200 locations in the United States connected to NAWAS, as described earlier. It is basically a party line where a call from one person is heard throughout the system. While originally envisioned as a warning system for nuclear attack, today it primarily serves as an all-hazard warning system providing a physical telephone link between national command authorities, the National Weather Service, and state and local warning points. The reliability of the system is one reason for continuing to maintain its function and service.

Emergency Alert System (EAS)

The Emergency Alert System (EAS) is a national public warning system that works in cooperation with radio and TV broadcasters, cable TV, satellite, and wireline providers to transmit warning messages from the government to the general public. Only Presidential EAS messages must be transmitted by broadcasters. It was not until January of 2010 that the first test of this national warning system was conducted by FEMA.

Participating agencies that are authorized to transmit EAS warnings must have specialized equipment installed at their locations. Likewise, media stations must purchase and maintain similar equipment that allows for the transmission of these warning messages on their broadcast channels, which includes radio, television, and cable channels.

EAS was formerly known as the Emergency Broadcast System (EBS). EAS replaced EBS in 1997 which is when the signals used became digital. Thirty years ago, the EBS was the only technological tool available to emergency managers, which allowed a federal, local, or state agency to send an electronic alert to the entire population within their jurisdiction. The last EAS-related innovation added was the addition of Amber Alerts for missing children.

Telephone Notification Systems

Commercially there are now a number of mass alerting systems available. Many, but not all counties and cities have opted to have one of these commercial systems. They became popular after the 2007 mass shooting incident at Virginia Tech led to an explosion of commercial mass notification systems. At one time, there were over 100 of these commercial offerings available. Over time, these have been consolidated to be many fewer.

These commercial services have become a preferred option for many emergency management organizations. The limitation is that residents must "opt in" to receive these notifications. Thus, there might be thousands of subscribers to the system, but in reality, it equates in most cases, to a very small percentage of actual residents who have taken the step to subscribe and receive notifications.

Wireless Notification Systems

One significant technological challenge that occurred was the switch by people from wireline telephones to the use of wireless phones in their homes. Today, 80% of all calls to 911 now come from wireless phones. The use of wired phone systems meant that each terminal had a geolocation for that phone, a physical US Postal System address. Mobile communications created another challenge in identifying the location of the caller. This has been addressed by telephone system providers using either satellite data or triangulation, determining the caller's location by means of cell towers.

IPAWS and WEA

The Integrated Public Alert & Warning System (IPAWS) is FEMA's national system for local alerting that provides authenticated emergency and life-saving information to the public through mobile phones using Wireless Emergency Alerts (WEA), to radio and television via the Emergency Alert System, and on the National Oceanic and Atmospheric Administration's Weather Radio.

The Wireless Emergency Alerting (WEA) system was rolled out in 2012. It allows for the issuing agency to specify a geographic area to receive the alert. An initial significant limitation was that originally only a maximum of 90 characters were available for formatting a message. In 2019 that was increased to 360 characters. The advantage of this system is that people do not have to "opt in" to get these alerts, meaning that visitors who do not live in the area where an alert is being issued will also be notified. Each wireless carrier may use different technologies to make the system work on their devices. Again, only selected government entities can issue these warnings and these agencies must have applied to do so.

The Human Part of Warning

For a warning to be successful it requires three separate actions. First, the threat or hazard has to be detected. Second, a timely warning must be issued that provides information about the hazard people may face, and then directs them to take protective measures. Lastly, and most importantly, people who receive the warning must act on that warning to protect themselves from danger. This last step is sometimes the hardest. Part of the human psychic is that people appear to want confirmation that they are doing the right thing. The behavior is called "milling" which is when people seek to know what others are doing in response to the warning. For instance, when the fire alarm goes off, people look around to see what others are doing. Better more complete warning messages are believed to shorten the time needed for people to take the right action.

Social Media

The adoption and use of social media were perhaps one of the slowest timelines for emergency management agencies. The initial perception of social media was that it was for personal use only and that it had no function in government. The use of social media in the workplace was actually banned in some organizations. It was restricted, as described above, as was the case with the Internet. Only certain categories of people, e.g., public information officers, were allowed to access social media sites. The potential for using social media for emergency management purposes was not recognized by most emergency managers. Some of this reluctance to use social media internal to emergency management could have been the age of senior leadership within emergency management at the time. They feared going out on a limb using a new technology that there was no expectation they should use. Doing so might only get them in trouble with elected officials, if mistakes were made by line staff in its implementation.

The first social media tool created in 2006 that showed immense promise was Twitter. Here you now had a mobile social media platform operated by a smartphone that allowed people to see what was happening at a specific time and place and document that by either a simple 140 character narrative or even the addition of a photograph.

One of the challenges made by emergency managers and others was that citizen reports of an event using social media were the "unverified" nature of the report. There was and still continues to today, some reluctance by emergency managers who do not trust the ability of the general public to "crowd source" what is happening in the field during an event. This has been hotly debated by some, in that the public are not trained observers and may erroneously report event—accidently. Now with the coming of active disinformation and misinformation campaigns, there is even less trust in what is coming in from the public.

The two advantages of using social media in general and Twitter in particular are the ability to formulate a better situational assessment of the impacts of a disaster by monitoring social media and ensuring that only original observations are used and that the retweets that can become very common are disregarded.

Secondly, there is a function called "rumor control." Before social media, it was normal that public information officers (PIO) would be assigned to listen to commercial radio and watch local television stations to find out what was being reported about an incident. If a news report was incorrect in its reporting, then that station would be contacted, and the correct information is given to them. Agency news releases might call attention to the incorrect information and correct the record in writing.

Still today, in most emergency management agencies, the typical use of social media remains the pushing out of information rather than using it to garner situational awareness and assist in rumor control. The progression from sending information out via a fax machine, and then via email by the Internet and now by social media, remains much more of a "push vs. a pull" of information. Social media use by emergency management, in general, is just another information distribution tool.

Blogs and Podcasts

Many people think of blogs and podcasts as a form of social media. They have developed overtime as a means to share information on a broader scale with people and organizations inside and outside of emergency management. Generally, they are a tool for information sharing and commentary about a wide variety of topics.

Still, because of the many people in emergency management who are not technically oriented, there are those who refer to a blog as a newsletter, reflecting their more traditional expectations of the profession. In recent years, more and more podcasts have emerged providing a broad spectrum of information and commentary on the emergency management topics and the profession.

It has been the continued emergence of new forms of technology in the civilian sector that has motivated the expansion of these tools within government and, more particularly, in emergency management.

Video Teleconferencing

Video teleconferencing has been around in emergency management circles as far back as the early to the mid-1990s. Early videoconferencing solutions required staff to go to a physical site where the technology was offered and then meet remotely with another person or persons, also operating from another dedicated video teleconferencing center. These were expensive to operate due to the cost of the facility, staff, and equipment. Thus, the fees were also expensive to schedule for use.

Other more personalized video teleconferencing solutions were developed and fielded. These were more personalized devices that were dedicated videoconferencing tools. They provided much more of a personal interaction between senior executives in government. The downside was that they required a fiber-optic connection to have the video quality. In one instance, these were used to connect a major metropolitan area city's mayor, its corresponding county executive, and their state's governor.

The last giant leap forward in videoconferencing was made as the result of the COVID-19 pandemic. Multiple systems existed before the pandemic, but they gained wide acceptance and use because of the pandemic. These software solutions operated over the Internet and personal computers, be they laptop or desktop.

Because of the requirements for social distancing brought about by the pandemic, home videoconferencing became the norm for conducting business from routine staff meetings to more formal webinars, training classes, and individual one-on-one sessions.

Each organization has adopted a platform for its internal use. While there is a wide variety of systems, not every system is allowed to be used by their staffs, so that interoperability can still be an issue for some. Typically, it was a concern over the security of a system that limited staff from using it or being a guest on such a system.

Of any technology used by emergency management, it is video teleconferencing that has rapidly integrated itself into everyday and disaster use. Now, it is hard to imagine a scenario where videoconferencing is not used to assist in the coordination of a disaster response and recovery.

It is believed that one outcome of video teleconferencing is that it may be difficult moving forward to have individuals report to a physical EOC. People have become accustomed to operating remotely, and the thought of braving severe weather such as snow or ice storms will make people reluctant to physically report to an EOC or Emergency Coordination Center (ECC). While the videoconference capability has been a force multiplier for the pandemic, it could hinder future disaster coordination efforts since videoconferencing is still not as effective as having in-person coordination and collaboration between individuals and organizations that may not have ever worked together in the past.

Information Management Systems

One of the greatest technological challenges that the emergency management discipline has experienced is the much sought-after information management system for use in responding to disasters. It has been the equivalent of the quest for the Holy Grail.

The efforts to find an information management system extend back to the MS-DOS Prompt era. The goal was to have a system that could take the manual methods for collecting, displaying, and sharing information and have it become digitized to speed and collection and sharing of information within an EOC and between EOCs. The ultimate goal was to have a system that was interoperable between the levels of governments, local, state, and federal.

The personal efforts this author was involved failed miserably. A single-state license was purchased so that state and local jurisdictions could be on the same system. That effort began in around 1993. One of the significant challenges was that smaller emergency management agencies in rural areas did not even own a computer. While a good faith effort was made to provide computers and training, the system was just too complex and difficult to manage for digital neophytes who were involved with trying to implement the system.

Other software solutions were coming forward. It was not unusual for a technology startup to work with a local emergency management agency to develop and fine-tune an information management software solution. Then, that software provider would look to expand the reach of their marketing to other states in the nation. One such solution looked to be more appealing and easier to use than the above described MS-DOS Prompt software. However, their pricing for the solution was to pay an annual fee of $500.00 a seat. This pricing puts the solution out of reach of all but the largest and best funded emergency management agencies.

A breakthrough solution was developed and became widely adopted over a number of years throughout the nation and at all levels of emergency management. That solution was WebEOC. There is another chapter in this book on that particular software that covers it in much more detail.

The initial fielding of WebEOC provided a web-based solution at a relatively low price point, which made it very appealing to the emergency management profession as a whole. You could tailor the individual "boards" to have the information you desired on them and digitally display the information. The promise of this software was that cities could submit logistics requests up the chain through their parent counties. From there, the request could be resourced at the county level or forwarded up to a state EOC, to be resourced there and, if not there, forwarded onto FEMA, all the while providing situational awareness of the status of the request to the requesting organization.

One cannot state categorically that it did not work everywhere, but it can be said that over time emergency agencies may have retained the software but not used it effectively or extensively. Many have continued to pay the license fee but have shelved the use of the system.

With all the above systems, the other common denominator is the lack of a digitized situation map that displays a visual picture of an incident, where damages are located and perhaps the location of responding resources. The integration of computer maps into these systems has, in general, failed miserably. The speed with which data can be entered and manipulated has been difficult to achieve to have a real-time map that can be used to manage the disaster.

Because of the COVID-19 pandemic, most emergency management agencies struggled to have a digital solution that provided a means for remote workers to maintain situational awareness while attempting to coordinate their actions with others. This was particularly true for the development of a digital map that could provide a visual display of the status of the pandemic response.

What has emerged out of the pandemic is that many communities that were already paying for and using Microsoft Teams to manage projects adopted MS Teams and modified it for use to manage their emergency operations centers information coordination needs. The only needed addition to MS Teams is a digital map that provides the common operating picture spatially for all to see and to share with other levels of government.

At this writing, there is not one digital information system that is commonly used across state boundaries and used to transmit disaster information to FEMA. While WebEOC still enjoys some national use, more and more agencies are seeking alternative solutions.

Cybersecurity

With the coming of technological solutions into emergency management, the profession has also exposed itself to the risks and dangers that come from cybersecurity intrusions into their operational systems.

Unfortunately, many early systems were designed for functionality and not for security. Security in many cases was a total afterthought. Thus, with many technology systems, security has had to be reengineered back into the system rather than integrating security from the outset during the design phase.

The sophistication of criminals, foreign and domestic, along with foreign national sponsored cyber threats has created an additional human-caused disaster. Besides being a community threat, it is an internal threat to emergency management operational systems to be mitigated and perhaps responded to. The current types of cyber threats include:

- Phishing/social engineering attacks
- Internet of Things (IoT)-based attacks
- Denial of service
- Ransomware

- Internal attacks
- Asynchronous Procedure Calls in System Kernels
- Uneven Cybersecurity Protections (i.e., Security Gaps)
- Unpatched Security Vulnerabilities and Bugs

The United States has slowly awakened to the dangers of cyberattacks in America's homeland. The critical infrastructure of the nation is primarily owned and operated by the private sector with an estimated 86% of all infrastructures being private. While much work has been done, high-profile successful attacks on critical infrastructure operating systems have shown the vulnerability and the risks to even presumably well-protected and sophisticated companies operating large segments of the nation's infrastructure.

As noted, emergency management is also not immune from these attacks, and as more and more technology solutions are adopted, those risks can compound. Continued diligence is needed to protect these twenty-first-century systems and also to develop and maintain backup policies and procedures that can be used when those systems are not available due to natural causes or human intervention in the operating systems.

Artificial Intelligence and Predictive Systems

The next step in the progression of disaster information systems is to achieve predictive modeling for what will happen when disasters strike, further perfecting the modeling using artificial intelligence to take those models and have them be in play during an actual event "in real time." Doing so will enhance the capability for first responders and emergency managers to have at their fingertips an immediate geospatial snapshot of where they can expect the most damages to be occurring. These will of course need to be confirmed by direct observation, but it will allow faster decision-making on which geographic areas of a city or county to examine for damages. This technology could be the first step in conducting a rapid damage assessment.

In reality, we are only at the beginning of the development of these technologies. Besides the use in crisis situations, the same predictive modeling can be applied to longer-term threats like climate change impacts as built environment, for instance, being predictive for when heat emergencies will impact the most vulnerable populations.

To have these predictive systems to work will require the integration of the "as built environment" along with hazard information. Earthquake risks are a great example for how this might work, taking and identifying areas with older building stock that can include unreinforced masonry (URM) buildings that are very susceptible to collapse in an earthquake and then taking and overlaying data on the geological formations and soil conditions for these same areas, in order to identify the scope and scale of possible damages. Using census data, low-income populations and traditionally more impacted minority areas of a community can also be integrated into the predictions.

Rapid Damage Assessment

Rapid damage assessments following a disaster have traditionally been ascribed to what is called "Windshield Surveys." Via preplanning, fire departments have established routes that are to be driven by fire trucks to survey specific segments of the community. These might be schools, places of congregate care, hospitals, and other significant structures or infrastructure that exists in the community. While driving these preassigned routes, they are not to respond to emergency situations but to aggregate the information they collect and transfer that data to the community's EOC, either by radio, written reports, or in-person. This is the first effort to establish a situational assessment from first responder personnel. Police departments might also be tasked to do the same with their officer resources.

A second rapid damage assessment occurs when citizens are requested to call into a citizen hotline or enter damage information at a predetermined website where they report damages to their personal properties. Due to FEMA disaster recovery procedures, only uninsured losses can potentially obtain federal reimbursement.

Jurisdictions will of necessity have government representatives go out and inspect areas of the community that have been reported as having more significant damages. This latter process is used to compile information for forwarding to FEMA to support a community's request for a presidential declaration.

Before a presidential declaration will be approved, joint damage assessment teams with representatives from local jurisdictions, the state, and FEMA will selectively tour damaged areas to jointly assess the extent of the damages.

All of the above has traditionally been very much a manual process with damages being collected and recorded and documented via paper forms. It is now possible via multiple software solutions to automate this process by having a digital record of the damages, supported by photographs that are geolocated to the damage site. These can be transmitted wirelessly as the assessment occurs or downloaded upon a return to a location that still has operational communications.

These solutions are available now, but not in widespread use. The technology is proven and relatively simple to integrate. The advantage of a technology solution is the rapid collection and display of the damages that can then be transmitted digitally to the state and federal authorities. However, it is likely that the final joint physical inspection will still be required since processes and procedures will have to be adopted at the state and federal levels that allow for the digital transmission of the damage information.

Professionalization of the Workforce

Emergency management began with a workforce that was many times entering a second career after a career in the military or as a first responder. It was a male-dominated workforce in the civil defense era. With the attacks of 9/11, we now have colleges and universities in every state in the nation offering degree programs in emergency management and homeland security. These programs are producing young professionals eager to use their education in government or the civilian sector. Additionally, today these people coming into the workforce are digital natives. They grew up with technology and that familiarity with it allows them to quickly adapt to and seek to adopt new technological solutions.

This younger and more technologically capable workforce can only advance the adoption of new technologies, finding better ways to use the systems and ensuring that the tools provide the promised improvements in performance that we all seek. They are also replacing the technology adverse and nontechnical older professionals who have managed emergency management programs previously.

Technology Adverse

At this writing, we are only entering the second generation of emergency managers to be in the workforce following the low-tech civil defense era. As discussed earlier, the first generation of emergency managers was often not technology savvy and indeed resistant to incorporating early versions of technology to use in emergency management administration and operations.

Adopting New Technologies Can Be Risky Business

Every agency and jurisdiction has purchased technology solutions that have not fulfilled the promises that were expected from the purchase and the use of the technology. Some of these failures can be placed on the software or device solutions themselves, but more often the problems encountered come from within an organization.

Organizations purchase technology solutions, be they equipment/device related or software, that are never or perhaps poorly integrated into the operations of the agency. Every new technology solution must be incorporated into an organization. Policies and procedures need to be written that define the uses of the technology along with training for the users. There are plenty of examples of new technologies that have been purchased that have had political ramifications. These include the use of small aerial drones or license plate readers to name only two. The technology can be of tremendous value for day-to-day uses, but the purchase of the new technology was never socialized with elected officials or the general population of a community. The end result can be that political pressures are brought to bear and agencies have to discontinue use of the new technology solution.

While not directly related to emergency management and disasters, the use of body cameras by law enforcement shows the many pitfalls of acquiring and then implementing new technology. The users of the technology must have training on its use. Before training, there must be written policies on when and what situations the cameras are turned on. Where will the video content be stored? How long will recordings be maintained, and by who? Can just anyone edit the video content? When will such video content be released to the media or the general public? What about the right to privacy of people also caught in the camera frame not engaged specifically in what was the rationale for recording an incident or interaction?

The easiest phase of technology acquisition is the purchase of equipment or software. Following that, the implementation and maintenance of these systems are where the hardest work will occur.

There is the concept of "fail fast" in the technology world. Private sector companies are often cited as examples for how to acquire technology, implement it quickly, and then evaluate it for performance. If the solution is not up to snuff, then quickly abandon the technology and seek another solution.

This concept does not work in government. There are inherent risks to trying a new technology. If that technology is not what it was envisioned to be, the decision-maker or organization that promoted the purchase of the technology cannot just abandon the technology and say, "I made a mistake!" Their reputation is on the line, and the wasting of taxpayer dollars is considered an unforgivable sin. The media and others are more than happy to exploit these errors to garner subscribers for media or score political points for those who wish to make political hay from the mistake that was made.

For this reason, a person or agency will stay with a failed system or solution long after it is no longer being used, if only to avoid the embarrassment of having to acknowledge they made a mistake. This then generates a reluctance on the part of many to embrace new technologies in the future due to the fear and experience of their previous embrace of a technology solution.

Data: The Final Frontier

Data will define the future. It is like the gold or other valuable mineral that is buried in the earth. The organizations that are successful will find ways to mine the data to improve their daily operations, develop ways to achieve disaster reduction solutions, and enhance their disaster responses. This will accelerate their disaster recovery by using existing data that they have already collected over myriad of systems and processes.

The problem with data collection and storage today is that it is all in silos within individual departments and jurisdictions. There it sits, perhaps untapped except for specific tasks and individual programs that collected the data. While it seems simple to say that all data collected will be made available to other agencies and purposes, there is a whole host of issues associated with data sharing. In today's world, privacy and security is one of the biggest concerns facing organizations that collect and store data.

Like with mapping, there is also a reluctance on the part of agencies to share the information they have collected. This hesitancy can come from numerous motivations, ranging from pure selfishness to a lack of trust in other agencies and to concerns about how they might be associated with an inappropriate application of the data that they have shared. While the technical aspect of data sharing can be complex, the human aspect may prove to be the thorniest of issues to overcome.

To overcome all of the above obstacles will require executive leadership that has authority over an entire enterprise. With authorities and directives in place, there is a chance that progress can be made on data sharing. However, it is not unheard for individuals to drag their feet on implementation. They do this knowing that executive level personnel who are either elected officials or senior appointed ones may have relatively short tenures in their positions and implementation of directives can be delayed until those people have rotated out of their positions.

Finally, with policies and procedures in place, there will need to be information management systems developed that can access the data being made available and present it in a manner that is understandable to those trying to make sense of a disaster situation. Information that can be geolocated and displayed on a map will always help in digesting the impact of what is being displayed. Unfortunately, today most information management systems are designed to service a single agency or jurisdiction. Expanding the capability to collect a broad array of data from across a discipline or geographic region will require a tailoring of the software to make it more interoperable with multiple users accessing data for different purposes.

Seeking Technological Solutions That Work

The emergency management profession has turned a corner on the use of technology. Rather than being totally wary of technology, there is a younger breed of emergency managers who have not had negative experiences in adopting technologies of the past and are more open to what technology can do.

One of the ongoing challenges is that technology companies want to provide their software as a service with the requirement for an annual renewal of the software license. These annual costs continue to weigh on basically limited operational budgets since the increasing use of technology has not been a traditional expense for the profession.

Typical questions that will be asked about new technological innovation are:

- Is a technology-based solution actually needed?
- What does it cost to purchase?

- What are the ongoing direct costs for software and indirect costs of personnel to maintain the system and continue to input and keep data updated?
- What added benefit will it provide?
- How often will the technology be used?
- What is the alternative for using this technology?
- What have you been using up until now that isn't working today?

Conclusions

After a very slow start in the adoption of technological solutions, there are now new innovations being developed that will benefit the broader emergency management and first responder community.

The emergency management workforce is now younger and more technology savvy than their predecessors. They are not averse to trying new technological solutions; however, the implementation of those new systems needs to be well thought-out in advance of adoption and purchase so as to have a successful outcome. See Chapter "Deploying Modern Technology for Disaster Management Practitioners", for a more thorough examination for how technology can be strategically integrated into any organization.

Deploying Modern Technology for Disaster Management Practitioners

Russ Johnson, Chris McIntosh, and Carrie Tropasso

Abstract The rapid evolution of modern technology with access to enormous amounts of data has created a new set of problems and challenges for emergency management practitioners and mission managers. "Keeping up" with the continuous development of new technologies (drones, sensors, location intelligence, artificial intelligence, IOT, GIS, etc.) emphasizes the importance of technology that is open, interoperable, and can expand and integrate with new technology innovations. Adding to the challenge is assuring an organization has the capacity to manage, use, and provide the required information products for decision-makers when, where, and how they need them.

Implementing technology without a comprehensive analysis of key mission requirements, personnel capability, and standard operating procedures (exactly how technology will be used) can create disruption and frustration. Newer technology capabilities may be interesting but not necessary to support the organization's primary mission. If new technology is appropriate, it should be deployed with updated policy and procedures to be effective.

This chapter will examine common technology deployment shortfalls and what's required to overcome them to implement technology that supports emergency management practitioners and decision-makers.

Keywords Situational awareness · Technology for disaster management · Disaster management technology implementation · Virtual technology disaster management · Modern technology governance · Standard Operating Procedures (SOP's) · Cyber security · Disaster management technology workflows · Data for disaster management · Training and exercise technology · Managing disruptive technology · Selecting new disaster management technology

R. Johnson (✉) · C. McIntosh · C. Tropasso
Bent Ear Solutions, Alexandria, VA, USA
e-mail: Rjohnson@Bentearsolutions.com; CMcIntosh@Bentearsolutions.com; Ctrpasso@Bentearsolutions.com

H. J. Scholl et al. (eds.), *Disaster Management and Information Technology*, Public Administration and Information Technology 40,
https://doi.org/10.1007/978-3-031-20939-0_2

Introduction

Disaster management organizations rely upon and have benefited from the rapid advancement and increasing capabilities of technology. From modeling events to developing mitigation strategies and to maintaining real-time situational awareness, technology can enable more accurate and timely decision support during disasters and emergencies. However, many organizations have not effectively adapted to the capabilities modern technology can deliver. It was not long ago that technology solutions were very "application centric," designed to solve specific problems with fixed functionality and workflows. These tools were typically designed for a single user or a limited group of users. As the internet and network availability expanded, technology moved toward "platform designs" that integrate data from other disparate systems and scale to accommodate large numbers of continuously connected users and stakeholders. Platforms enable flexibility in configuring various applications supporting a broader range of mission requirements. These solutions can be delivered as software as a service (SAS) or on-premise or a combination of both often referred to as hybrid. Cloud computing, access to external systems, open-source, and streaming real-time data (often referred to as the Internet of Things or IoT) are all now possible. These expanded capabilities can connect everyone in the organization to improve communications, rapidly share information, and dramatically change how and for what technology can be used. They also present challenges that require a programmatic approach to implement, deploy, and maintain. With more practitioners and stakeholders connected, what are the right technologies for an organization to support its mission? How will these technologies be used? Who will be using them, and how will they be managed and maintained? There are many choices and interesting capabilities, but are they really necessary to meet mission requirements? These challenges and requirements have often not been fully understood by organizational leadership. Technologies are frequently implemented without a comprehensive vision, strategic plan, or defined end state.

The important questions and information required for critical disaster management decisions should be clearly identified long before technology is acquired or deployed. Failure to recognize the importance of doing the essential preparatory work before modern technology is acquired and deployed is often an ineffective use of valuable resources and may put the program's operational effectiveness at risk.

The remainder of this chapter will focus on the issues and the requirements for deploying, managing, and sustaining modern technology to support the disaster management mission.

Common Mistakes in Implementing and Managing Modern Technology

Implementing technology without a comprehensive analysis of critical mission requirements, personnel buy-in, training, and standard operating procedures (exactly how it will be used) is the most common mistake organizations make. With multiple users and wide-ranging capabilities, the deployment of modern platform technology can be daunting. The organization's leadership must stay actively involved and "champion" the implementation process that directs and balances the synchronization of personnel, procedures, and technology. This includes the following:

- Establishing and executing a technology governance framework
- Evaluating and choosing technology
- Developing a data plan
- Managing technology deployment
- Developing new and updated standard operating procedures
- Implementing a training and exercise regimen
- Monitoring and measuring performance

Establishing and Executing a Technology Governance Framework

Establishing a governance framework to manage and navigate the changes modern technology requires is essential. Generally, governance refers to the mechanisms, relations, and processes by which an organization is controlled and directed. It involves balancing the many interests of the practitioners, stakeholders, the organization, its priorities, and how it completes its mission. Governance sets direction for the major decisions required to deploy modern technology to fulfill the organization's mission responsibilities. The overall goal of establishing a governance process is to improve organization's performance, consistency, and accountability supported by the appropriate tools and technology within the constraints of resources and budget.

The governance process is set in motion by reviewing and evaluating the organization's current mission, performance, and technology effectiveness. Interviews with staff and stakeholders are an effective way to identify required changes, understand different perspectives, and begin to develop support for new or updated technology. Interviews also shed light on potential resistance, gaps in understanding mission priorities, and current technology performance. Some of the interview questions and points of discussion should include the following:

- Is the current organization's vision/mission statement still accurate?
- Are the organization's goals/objectives current and effectively supporting the mission?
- Is there an increase in the volume, complexity, or the nature of incidents or responsibilities the organization is expected to support?
- What are critical questions the organization must respond to on a daily basis and during a crisis?
- How effective is the current technology in providing information to answer required questions?
- Does the organization have access to the data required to provide actionable information?
- What does the staff find frustrating in working with their current technology?
- Are staff roles and responsibilities effectively aligned to meet mission requirements?
- Are the stakeholder's, who depend upon the organization, expectations being met?

After staff interviews have been conducted and reviewed, the organization's current technology limitations should be determined:

- Where does existing technology fall short?
- Is it optimized to its full potential or underutilized?
- Can it be upgraded to meet desired requirements?
- Will it or will components interoperate with newer modern technologies?
- Is it able to consume required data from existing legacy systems?

Many organizations own technology that is not properly configured, fully deployed, or used to its full potential. This often leads to the current solution(s) being labeled as problematic or insufficient when the real problem could be how it is deployed or being used. It is important to obtain the required assistance and expertise to evaluate existing technology before making investments in new capabilities.

Evaluating and Choosing Technology

Selecting the most appropriate technology to support the organizations mission can be difficult. There are many different products, vendors, and solutions to choose from when working toward technology decisions. First and foremost, the technology should demonstrate the functional support required to meet the organization's priority mission requirements. It should overcome the issues and shortfalls of current technology and provide ease of use for practitioners. These capabilities should be demonstrated, tested, and thoroughly evaluated before any procurement consideration is made. In addition to supporting priority functional requirements, other important technical capabilities include:

- Interoperability – Is the technology interoperable with existing systems?
- Configurability – Can the technology be configured to address new problems or changes in mission requirements?
- Ease of use – Will the technology be intuitive and suitable for practitioners and operations personnel?
- Scalability – Will the technology scale and expand when required for complex events and operations?
- Cloud capabilities – Can the technology deploy across both on-premise and cloud environments in an easy and seamless manner or in a hybrid configuration?
- Security – Does the technology provide the required security, access controls, and credentialing?
- Sustainability – Is the technology supported by a stable and reputable vendor?
- Installation – Will the initial installation, development, and deployment be done by in-house personnel or a vendor, or a combination?

These considerations are often not sufficiently addressed or well understood when functionality requirements become the primary decision criteria. Assuring the technology can be configured, is scalable, interoperates with existing systems, is supported by a reliable vendor, and is intuitive for those who use it is as important as functional requirements.

Developing a Data Plan

Technology, no matter how powerful, without access to the required underlying data, is ineffective and results in underutilization of expensive resources. In concert with researching technology, data needs and requirements should be determined:

- Does the organization have permission and access to the specific data necessary to provide the required information products?
- Is data "locked" in proprietary systems that require programming costs to unlock and access?
- Are data sharing agreements in place or required with other departments or mutual mission partners in neighboring jurisdictions?
- Do any new data sources or data services need to be acquired or subscribed to?
- Will additional streaming "real-time" data (sensor data, tracking data, traffic, weather, etc.) be required and will the new technology effectively consume, analyze, and display it?

With the vast amounts of data availability, having a data management plan is necessary to maximize technology investments. Data from sensors, field devices, open-source portals, social media, and subscription data services and data from other internal systems can be overwhelming and confusing if not effectively managed and planned for.

Managing Technology Deployment

After new technology has been thoroughly researched and selected, the process of implementation is the next challenge. If a vendor will be contracted for installation and implementation or to assist the organization's in-house technical personnel, the following due diligence should be performed:

- Request references, past performance, and referrals from potential vendors.
- Seek vendors that have experience and understand the disaster management industry.
- Document and provide potential vendors a detailed description of the requirements, timelines, benchmarks, communication frequency, training, and reporting expectations.
- Meet and interview potential vendors to determine:
  - How well does the vendor understand the organization's requirements from the project description provided?
  - Is the vendor's experience relevant to the size and requirements of the organization's needs?
  - Does the vendor have experience in implementing technology using an agile methodology?
- The vendor is flexible and follows up on questions provided by the organization.
- The vendor provides modern security provisions in the design and implementation of the system.
- The vendor provides adequate post implementation training and support.

As implementation begins, leadership must reiterate and articulate the purpose and benefits with staff and stakeholders. They must also be attentive and responsive to unintended consequences, disruptions, or other sources of resistance to reduce frustrations that delay implementation. To expedite the implementation process and maintain continuity, a timeline with benchmarks, checkpoints, and functional performance goals must be maintained and adhered to.

For disaster management organizations, when critical life and property decisions can arise without notice, a parallel deployment strategy is standard. New technology is deployed and tested, while the legacy system is operational and serves as primary mission support. This enables the newer technology to be tested and exercised to evaluate performance and develop staff familiarity and confidence. This is often accomplished by employing an agile implementation methodology introducing new capabilities in segments.

Agile implementation follows a pattern of breaking the overall project into smaller pieces. These project segments are delivered and tested in work sessions with the organizations staff called sprints. Sprints enable staff and practitioners to test sections of the technology for desired performance and make adjustments as necessary. This helps reduce confusion and shortens the learning curve and anxiety of dealing with a new system. It also increases the likelihood of staff acceptance, speeds up familiarity with capabilities, and reduces the overall time from initial implementation to operational readiness. The agile approach emphasizes the following:

- Smaller deployment cycles – The implementation of technology is done in smaller manageable sections.
- Flexibility and feedback – Technology can be modified or reconfigured as sprint deliveries are tested and evaluated.
- Value of teamwork – The team members work closely together to develop an understanding of their roles and responsibilities with new technology.
- Staff Interaction – Interaction, communication, and feedback are valued equally to the implementation of technology and tools.

Organizations that rely upon technology for critical decision support must include robust cybersecurity provisions in their implementation plan. Cybersecurity can generally be defined as activities that are undertaken to minimize threats and vulnerabilities and enforcing the required policies for prevention, data assurance, recovery, and other cybersecurity-related impacts.

Historically the most common form and least secure method of authentication is single factor which relies upon a username and password to gain system access and prevent unauthorized use. This approach is susceptible to many attacks such as "brute force, key logging, credential stuffing, dictionary attack, and password spraying," which can put the organization at high risk from legitimate credentials being used by threat actors with malicious intent. This holds especially true for organizations that use a traditional security architecture in which the inside network is trusted and outside the network is not.

Today's workforce, with distributed people connected and interacting remotely, accessing data from multiple sources, cloud computing, etc., increases vulnerability to cybersecurity-related threats. More secure practices recommend verifying anything and everything trying to connect before granting access. This approach requires additional, technical design requirements, planning, and processes which can include multifactor authentication, encryption of sensitive data, robust inspection and logging of traffic, and continuously verifying the integrity of assets and connection points.

From a practitioner's perspective, what does this mean? Practitioners need to be aware of the consequences of not following security best practices and planning with security first in mind. Reducing these potentially devastating events is a responsibility for everyone who is credentialed to access any of the organization's system. Leadership must emphasize the need for everyone to understand and safeguard the organization's valuable data and report concerns. These practices include assuring all assets and devices are continuously updated with latest software patches and updates, multifactor authentication, complex passwords, and following other best practice security recommendations. Leadership must create a security conscious culture to assure everyone in the organization is well informed and supportive. This includes identifying how the technology will be maintained, monitored, and who to contact when issues or concerns are discovered.

Implementing new modern technology requires the organization's leadership to initiate actions that require a careful balance between the needs of the staff, the process of installation, deployment, and maintaining a new system. Creating an organizational culture that emphasizes and continuously reinforces system security and operational continuity is essential for organizations that depend upon technology for critical decision support.

Developing Standard Operating Procedures

The next step in the process is developing clear and concise standard operating procedures (SOPs). SOPs identify how the technology will be used and who will use it to provide the priority information products to meet mission requirements. They are step-by-step instructions compiled and documented to help carry out routine and complex operations. They are developed to achieve efficiency, quality, accountability, and uniformity of performance while reducing miscommunication and complying with the organizations policies. Well-written SOPs are essential to meet user and stakeholder expectations. Organizations without a robust procedure system will struggle in today's complex environments. Disaster management units that perfect day-to-day activities have more time to focus on being agile and responsive to the events and uncertainties of everyday business. The ability to increase agility is partially realized through efficient and effective standard operating procedures. The purpose of SOPs is to enable the organization to optimize its ability to use technology consistently with higher quality, increased customer service, and accountability.

Effective SOPs codify how things are done and memorialize what's been done in the past to serve as potential tools and reference for future events. They bring together technology and operations and develop a synergy between the two. This helps to ensure communication and alignment so technical staff know what stakeholders and practitioners need and leadership understands what functions can be automated. Important tasks in developing SOPs include the following:

- Identify tasks and workflows that technology can support to solve priority problems necessary to support the mission.
- Determine the information products required, how they will be produced, who should receive them, and when they are needed.
- Identify the roles and responsibilities of the staff and practitioners who will be using the technology to provide information products.
- Document identified tasks into step-by-step SOPs that everyone has access to and understands.

Standard operating procedures should be reviewed and updated frequently. As new technology is acquired or new circumstances arise, updated standard operating procedures are necessary.

For example, many of the newer disaster management platforms are built on or integrate with modern Geospatial Information Systems (GIS). These systems can produce various views of map-based geographic areas with dynamic data streams to produce real-time situational awareness. These may include current operations status, logistical supply and resource locations, damage assessment, shelter locations/status, public information, weather, and more. In order to develop consistency, a display plan may be required. Standard operating procedures will direct what information products (map views, situation reports, etc.) will be produced, who is responsible, and when and where they will reside on a large display panel or panels on a daily basis and throughout the life cycle of an emergency.

Another example is the global COVID-19 pandemic that caused organizations to work differently and deal with new unexpected challenges such as remote working, social distancing, virtual EOC operations, hospital capacity issues, new requirements for shelter management, etc. and establish new procedures.

Standard operating procedures describe how work is performed and who is responsible. They become the "playbook" for the organization and enable new personnel to become operational and understand their roles in a standardized, repeatable way, in less time.

Implementing a Training and Exercise Regiment

Public safety organizations of all types purchase a variety of tools and equipment to respond to and recover from emergencies and disasters. This includes fire apparatus, heavy rescue equipment, emergency medical units, hazardous material units, etc. The personnel that operate this equipment train and exercise regularly to remain proficient. But for many organizations, crisis management systems and applications fall into a pattern of being deployed and extended to meet complex requirements only when a major event occurs. The same level of training and exercise emphasis does not exist for these important technology decision support tools. This can lead to the possibility of mission failure, poor performance, or misinterpretation of critical information when it matters most.

To overcome this "blind spot," leadership must make ongoing training and exercises a priority. Before having to extend or scale technology during a major event, under the stress of a crisis, practitioners should have the familiarity and proficiency to scale during complex disaster or emergency without difficulty. Exercises can also test if standard operating procedures work under simulated crisis conditions or if adjustments are required. The ability to have technology readiness and preparedness can only be achieved when a programmatic training and exercising program drive frequent system usage and practice.

Training and exercises can take many forms. Contrary to traditional trends, training can be a daily routine with short exercises that take 20 minutes or less to solve specific problems. Short, quick-hitting exercises simulating various scenarios keep staff and practitioners sharp and confident in the use of their modern crisis management systems. These can supplement more formal or extensive exercises that occur less frequently. As personnel within organizations change, and technology advances, frequent and ongoing training is essential to maintain efficiency and preparedness.

Monitoring and Measuring Performance

As new technology is deployed, monitoring performance and making timely adjustments are essential for ongoing adoption and operational efficiency. Modern technology expands upon disaster management organization's ability to provide timely and accurate decision support. These capabilities depend upon external networks, internal networks, the software and devices on which they operate, and the staff and practitioners who use technology to sustain operational readiness. With these expanded capabilities, more users, and stakeholders continuously connected, both the value and complexity of new technology become apparent. Monitoring and maintaining these system components, maintaining appropriate security measures, and transitioning personnel to new roles must be incorporated into the implementation plan for both the initial and long-term success of modern technology deployment.

Conclusion

Modern technology provides powerful tools and capabilities to support the disaster management mission. However, implementing new technology is challenging and disruptive. The presence of new tools, with more people continuously connected, *will* change how organizations do business, and managing that change is what separates successful programs from the ones that fall short. When modern technology is deployed without a comprehensive plan guided by a comprehensive governance framework, the desired outcomes will not be achieved. Organizations are typically resistant to change, and modern technology modifies how the organization achieves its mission. Working with staff and stakeholders to gain support, acceptance, and the use of new technology and the changes it brings is a substantial challenge.

To successfully implement change, an organization's leadership must be prepared to develop and implement a comprehensive technology plan. Establishing a governance framework is an effective way to develop, socialize, implement, operationalize, and monitor the impacts and benefits of modern technology. The potential power of modern technology cannot be realized without an implementation strategy that embodies an inclusive approach emphasizing the "human factor" that supports, trains, and empowers practitioners to confidently and securely perform their roles when it matters most.

Technology and Information Management Supporting Resilience in Healthcare and Rescue Systems

Hannele Väyrynen, Jasmin Vainikainen, Annamaija Paunu, Nina Helander, and Sini Tenhovuori

Abstract Health care and rescue system resilience is the multifactoral sum of technology, humans, information, processes, and management. The coronavirus (COVID-19) pandemic has been a catalyst for transformation globally and tested the resilience of health care and rescue systems in many ways. The relevant use of technology has been acknowledged as one important element in developing resilience, but there are still very few empirical studies that have studied the role of technology in supporting system-level resilience. This chapter examines how information system solutions have advanced system resilience during the COVID-19 crisis through a literature review and empirical case study of the Finnish health care and rescue sector. According to the results of this study, the use of different technology solutions and digital services in health care and rescue has increased during the pandemic, as the crisis has accelerated the development of an information system (IS) for data sharing as well as experiments on AI and robotics. However, in developing IS solutions, several challenges arise that are specific to the health care and rescue sector that need to be taken into account: strict legislation, the privacy of health data, and the fact that implementation of a digital service cannot compromise patient care.

Keywords Healthcare system · Rescue system · Resilience · Technology · Information management · COVID-19

H. Väyrynen (✉) · J. Vainikainen · A. Paunu · N. Helander
Tampere University, Information and Knowledge Management, Tampere, Finland
e-mail: hannele.vayrynen@tuni.fi; jasmin.vainikainen@tuni.fi; annamaija.paunu@tuni.fi; nina.helander@tuni.fi

S. Tenhovuori
Wellbeing Services County of Pirkanmaa, Pirkanmaa, Finland
e-mail: sini.tenhovuori@pirha.fi

H. J. Scholl et al. (eds.), *Disaster Management and Information Technology*, Public Administration and Information Technology 40,
https://doi.org/10.1007/978-3-031-20939-0_3

Introduction

Healthcare systems are one of the most critical systems in societies (European Observatory on Health Systems and Policies, 2020) constituting a solid foundation for daily life. In a crisis, situations are solved with ad hoc solutions causing complex networks of a human- technology mixture (Bakos, 2020). There may be signals of a sudden crisis, but the preparedness and resilience to shocks of health systems vary (European Observatory on Health Systems and Policies, 2020; Thomas & Rutter, 2008). Resilience can be seen as the ability of an individual, system, or organization to survive crises or shocks (Huey & Palaganas, 2020; Tariverdi et al., 2019) and actions to prepare for, adapt and respond to, and recover from stressful conditions or disruptive events, e.g., a natural disaster, pandemic, cyberattacks, economic crisis, conflicts, mass migration, or terrorist attacks (Linkov et al., 2013; Crowe et al., 2014; Ceferino et al., 2018; Landeg et al., 2019; Lo Sardo et al., 2019; Zhao et al., 2019; Hundal et al., 2020). A resilient organization needs the ability to prioritize and identify problems and respond proactively to crises, resilience concerns systems/leadership, organization culture, training and simulation, cross-domain communication, and a cooperative approach. The focus of this chapter is organization-level resilience. Health care and resilience are considered from diverse approaches, e.g., systems that support health infrastructure resilience (Atallah et al., 2018). Healthcare resilience is affected by both the interdependencies of hospital departments and services and by critical lifelines and infrastructure, such as transportation, supply chains, power and water networks, and internal and external communications systems (Cimellaro et al., 2018; Tariverdi et al., 2019; Zhao et al., 2019). However, in the context of health care, the resilience debate has been focusing more on the individual level and human factors, leaving room for studies that focus on system and organization level resilience, especially from the aspect of technology in supporting resilience.

The chapter construes a more comprehensive picture of resilience, and the crucial triangle of technology, adoption, and information management (IM). In the best-case scenario, technology solutions and information communication technology can support healthcare and rescue personnel in their daily work, enable supply chain management, ensure healthcare financing with efficient processes, and produce transparent processes for governance and service delivery (Otto et al., 2015) to advance healthcare system resilience.

The theoretical framework of the chapter leans on Ristvej and Zagorecki's classification of an information system (IS) in crisis management (CM), namely, early warning systems, geographical information systems, *training applications*, *decision support systems*, and *document and data sharing tools*. An IS has four specific functions: data collection, data storage, data processing and analysis, or data transfer and distribution (Ristvej & Zagorecki, 2011). While the focus here is on crisis management and technology, crisis management is considered through the lens of

IM, and ISs are considered to support certain functions in the organization (e.g., human resources compared with patient flows, patient appointment systems) or technology applications in the healthcare/hospital and rescue context (pilot projects, e.g., patient monitoring or pandemic infection tracking). This chapter examines this subject through a literature review and a qualitative empirical study focused on the Finnish healthcare (hospital context) and rescue services during the COVID-19 crisis; we seek answers to the questions of how IS solutions have advanced system resilience during the COVID-19 crisis and how these solutions have affected the operations of the healthcare and rescue agencies. The three following classification elements are considered in the empirical part of this chapter: training applications for personnel, decision support systems in pandemic operations, and document and data sharing tools between the actors.

Information systems and different applications in health care and rescue are not only a technical development but also a mindset, a way of thinking, an attitude, and a commitment for networked, global thinking, to improve health care locally, regionally, and worldwide by using information and communication technology (Eysenbach, 2001). Thus, we are especially interested in identifying the role of IS in applications and tools in healthcare system resilience during the COVID-19 crisis, and we are also interested in taking a broader view of the phenomenon as a complex mixture of human operators, hardware, and software, where information management plays a crucial role, as stated by Bakos (2020).

The chapter continues with a brief introduction to resilience, technology, and information technology (IT). After reviewing the literature, the chapter describes data as a resource potential, the challenges of data utilization, and barriers to data and information exchange between institutions. After the theoretical approach, examples of digital technology solutions and innovations are introduced, and empirical insights are provided of technology support in a healthcare and rescue system case from Finland during the COVID-19 crisis. The chapter ends with a discussion and conclusion section that calls for interaction and cooperation between human technology and regional, national, and global data sources and practice models.

Resilience, Technology, and Information Management in a Healthcare and Rescue System

Resilience can be seen as the ability of an individual, system, or organization to survive crises or shocks (Huey & Palaganas, 2020; Tariverdi et al., 2019). The resilient organization also needs the ability to prioritize and identify problems and respond proactively to crises (Cimellaro et al., 2018; Falegnami et al., 2018). The resilience of systems can be influenced by leadership (Mansour et al., 2012; Deutsch et al., 2016), organization culture (Huey & Palaganas, 2020), training and simulation (Cimellaro et al., 2018; Huey & Palaganas, 2020; Hundal et al., 2020), procedures, and cross-domain communication and cooperation (Linkov et al., 2013; Cimellaro et al., 2018).

Health and resilience are considered from diverse approaches, e.g., systems that support health infrastructure resilience (Atallah et al., 2018). The resilience of the healthcare system can be seen, in other words how quickly and at what capacity health care can produce and provide healthcare services to the entire community in the event of a shock. Disruptive events in healthcare systems often lead to an unexpected increase in the number of patients or reduction in the number of healthcare providers (Lo Sardo et al., 2019). Both the interdependencies of hospital departments and services and critical lifelines and infrastructures affect healthcare resilience (such as transportation, supply chains, power and water networks, and internal and external communications systems) (Cimellaro et al., 2018; Tariverdi et al., 2019; Zhao et al., 2019). The resilience of healthcare systems can be measured and defined by economic losses during the crisis, casualties, recovery time, patient waiting time, bed capacity, and quality of service and care (Cimellaro et al., 2018; Crowe et al., 2014; Low et al., 2017; Tariverdi et al., 2019; Hundal et al., 2020).

Considering the practical infrastructure level, transportation, power and water networks, internal and external communication systems in organizations, and crucial supplies like oxygen, blood, medical equipment, and medication supplies are subject to technological reliability (Cimellaro et al., 2018; Tariverdi et al., 2019; Zhao et al., 2019). All these functions produce fragmented data. Technology platforms are one way to unify outspread data and information. At best, platforms can integrate and offer real-time data, enabling operational flexibility and response, and supporting decision-making in changing situations (Vecchi et al., 2002; Cimellaro et al., 2018).

Data per se is not valuable but has to be transformed into understandable information that brings some value to the recipient. It is said that "healthcare is undergoing a data revolution" (Panesar, 2019) and data is a crucial resource, as highlighted by the COVID-19 pandemic in the healthcare sector, for example. Increasingly, real-time data analysis to create predictive modeling during the crisis supports the mitigation of risks (Mensah et al., 2015; Lo Sardo et al., 2019; Hundal et al., 2020). Despite data being a potential resource, the challenges of data utilization culminate in unintegrated information systems or non-syncretized data, formulating barriers for data and information exchange between institutions (Liapis et al., 2015). Challenges in healthcare informatics were identified (e.g., Guah, 2004) nearly 20 years ago, yet the same stumbling blocks still exist. Besides technology solutions, technology absorptive capacity and the management of information and knowledge are needed as well (Bose, 2003; Raymond et al., 2017). Table 1 describes some operational guidelines for crisis management in healthcare and rescue organizations and the role of information management.

Table 1 Operational guidelines for CM in healthcare and rescue organizations (Wang & Wu, 2021)

Precrisis phase	Crisis phase	Postcrisis phase
Keep alert to detect potential threats Prepare CM plans Plan pandemic prevention routes Check inventory of reserve medical supplies Launch awareness campaigns	Identify competency/knowledge requirements Assemble CM team Define specific responsibilities Convene response consensus meetings Reduce the risk of exposure to contagion Contain nosocomial infections Protect the safety of healthcare workers Strict separation among zones of risk Patient risk stratification	Review and correct action planning Gradually resume activities Institutionalize and internalize lessons learned from the crisis

Deploying Digital Technology and Innovations in Practice in a Crisis

National and global collaboration and communication as well as open innovation (OI) practices between different organizations are needed to succeed in a crisis situation (e.g., government, education, and research institutions) (Patrucco et al., 2022). Innovations need *a place* to happen, and cooperative innovation processing with several actors can produce quick solutions in a shock or disaster situation. Digital innovations are almost never made in isolation but need a cooperation group or innovation ecosystem around them (e.g., Iyawa et al., 2016). Different innovation clusters like FabLabs (fabrication laboratory, often digital) have played a crucial role in problem-solving COVID-19 initiatives, e.g., using 3D printing for equipment production (Abbassi et al., 2021). However, in the public sector, innovation management is not an easy task, although many innovations are designed for the public sector, mostly by private sector actors. The structures of public organizations are still very bureaucratic and hierarchical. The information flows between organization levels may be slow, and understanding of the innovation and the knowledge problem behind it is lacking. In other words, the value of the innovation is not identified or recognized (Jalonen, 2013).

Regarding innovation and technology solutions, an evaluation process is needed to optimize the utilization of new technology in the organization. One example for evaluation is the activity checklist made by Kaptellin et al. back in 1990 that considers human and technology in addition to environment issues: *means and ends*, i.e., what the technology is for and how it helps humans to operate; *social and physical aspects of the environment* which integrates technology with them; *learning, cognition, and articulation*, i.e., internal or external activities that support technology utilization; and *development*, which frames the comprehensive development and transformation view (Kaptellin et al., 1999).

New research and analyzing methods for the healthcare and rescue research have been developed to understand epidemiology, for example, or to produce different scenarios such as environmental risks. To mention a few, next-generation sequencing technology (NGS) is not only intended for the analysis of samples or monitoring diseases, but it also affects the personnel's operational practices by creating easy-to-use automated workflows (Iyawa et al., 2016). Stratuscent (2021) has helped to build resilience during COVID-19 with its technical solution for scent detection, NOZE, a digitized sense of smell that can be integrated with several products. Another solution for air sensoring is Konikore (Koniku, 2021). These solutions can be used for monitoring the risk level of the airborne virus or for identifying some diseases or some safety-threatening issues (e.g., in travel or logistics) (Koniku, 2021; Stratuscent, 2021). High technology is fabulous, but let's keep our feet on the ground at the health and rescue operational level.

Operating clinical services in remote mode made a rapid leap at the beginning of the COVID-19 pandemic, globally enabling new health IT, on the one hand with organized trials and pilots, and on the other hand with new established practices with new IT in operations as well as knowledge sharing. Regardless of the name of the digital source (e.g., e-health, health apps, health platforms, or telemedicine), the functions around the solution are more relevant: individual level monitoring and data collection for healthcare or rescue staff, provision of health services to customers, remote communication and evaluation or monitoring the situation between customer and personnel, or wider data and information documentation platforms for information sharing at local, national, or global level (e.g., Iyawa et al., 2016).

At the very beginning of the COVID-19 situation, the Sheba Medical Center in Israel used InTouch Telepresence robots and the Hospital District of Helsinki, and Uusimaa (HUS) in Finland used the Murffi robot to communicate with and monitor patients remotely, allowing better communication between staff and patient to provide care with minimal physical contact and minimized virus infection. The robots were controlled from another room by doctors, nurses, and pharmacists (Wetzler, 2020; Kahri, 2021; Oborn et al., 2021). Cardmedic digital flashcards have been used in the UK for patient communication by phone, tablet, or computer, allowing the sharing of vital information and questions with the patient (Orlikowski & Scott, 2021). Remote monitoring and examination tools for COVID-19 include TytoCare to listen to the patient's heart and lungs as well as examining the throat and ears, and EarlySense to measure continuous heart rate and respiration rate through a sensor placed under the mattress of the bed. Both TytoCare and EarlySense sensors can be taken home by the patient, which saves hospital bed capacity (Wetzler, 2020).

During the COVID-19 pandemic, digital innovations have created new ways to support care work around the world. For example, the challenges of communicating with patients while using personal protective equipment (PPE) and staff's fear of contamination have contributed to the use of digital technologies in hospitals.

In Finland alone, there are over 50 Finnish start-ups or growth companies with innovative health and health technology solutions to tackle among other things the pandemic in healthcare and other healthcare service challenges, e.g., diagnostics and test manufacturing, remote operations, or platforms (HealthCapitalHelsinki, 2021). There are multiple ISs and huge amounts of different data that could be used and analyzed by healthcare and rescue actors. The challenge is how interoperable the ISs are and how to deliver real-time knowledge, for example, to support decision-making in crisis situations.

Support and Benefits of IT When Operating During a Crisis: Empirical Insights from Finland

In an acute crisis situation, the role of information management has been critical. At the beginning of the COVID-19 pandemic, several challenges occurred related to information management, not only at national and local levels but also at international level. The biggest city area (Greater Helsinki) as well as other smaller regions in Finland had challenges to see the comprehensive operational picture; however, after half a year, the structure of knowledge acquisition for the operational picture had improved, becoming more systematic, faster, and established in daily practices. The challenging issue is the huge amount of data, how to identify the relevant data in a crisis situation (e.g., KPMG, 2021).

Massive improvements were made very soon in gathering the data and in sharing timely status data at national level. Thus, the pandemic crisis has improved data acquisition and sharing practices tremendously in a short time window. The pandemic shock forced information management teams to develop operational picture systems rapidly, e.g., to control the inventory situation, treatment equipment, number of hospital beds, and human resources. Even though the analysis and reports have advanced during the pandemic, the information systems do not currently eliminate the manual work of analysis and reporting in Finnish institutions. Although the pandemic was an unknown, data was at the core of all decisions and public recommendations that led to actions. Only the future will show what kind of disaster information management model will be formulated from the current and functional operation models in Finland.

In Finland, the COVID-19 e-system for national symptom testing was organized by the biggest university hospital, HUS, to ensure clear and sufficient capacity for the testing system. In the first phase, a symptomatic individual made an electronic symptom assessment so as to avoid physical contact, and the application guided the person to the next steps, e.g., testing. However, at municipality level, the information systems occasionally crashed when reserving a test, inflicting congestion in the service. Citizens had a big role in utilizing digital services, simultaneously reducing the workload of the healthcare professionals at the beginning of the pandemic. In the Finnish online service, *Omaolo*, nearly 330,000 symptom checks were made during 60 days by citizens, which can be considered a great figure considering that Finland only has 5.53 million habitants. Similarly, the UK healthcare system has put into operation a digital online symptom checker (NHS 111 online) (Chambers et al., 2019); Singapore has the COVID-19 Symptom Checker (Singapore, 2021), and Japan the Stop COVID-19 Symptom Checker (Tokyo Government, 2021). However, symptom checkers have received criticism on both the reliability of the identification of the patients' symptoms and forwarding to medical care (Mansab et al., 2021), since in a crisis situation the reliability of the digital solution must be at the highest level.

In order to achieve a deeper understanding of the role of IS in crisis management in Finland during the COVID-19 pandemic, we carried out an empirical case study in one of the healthcare and rescue system districts in Finland. The Pirkanmaa Hospital District is a joint municipal authority owned by 23 municipalities. Tampere University Hospital (TAYS) is the hospital that provides services to hospital districts serving nearly 1 million inhabitants in the catchment area (TAYS, 2021a). We gathered the data through a series of facilitated workshops in which over 100 healthcare and rescue professionals participated during autumn 2021. The empirical data gathering focused on the themes of IS solutions and practices, as well as IS development targets in organizations. Questions were addressed as to what kind of IS works in a crisis, which practices are functional in coordination and cooperation, what kind of data and information production supports decision-making, and how geographical information can be integrated into regional information. All workshop participants were encouraged to have open dialogue instead of being guided by the selected theoretical framework. Some of the identified results are described below.

The use of different e-health services in health care has increased during the pandemic. The other example from TAYS is *OmaTays*, established in 2017, a digital service between customers or patients and TAYS. OmaTays is a service to manage functions from patient booking of an appointment or doctor's appointments to laboratory requests, offering an easy way to reschedule, ask questions, or attend a remote consultation. In May 2020, there were 45,000 application users, while by spring 2021, this number had grown to 100,000 users. The exhilarating speed of adoption can partly be explained by the COVID-19 pandemic. A new service in the OmaTays application was released in spring 2020, i.e., a COVID-19 tracking enquiry for those that were exposed to the COVID-19 virus and for people who tested positive for COVID-19. Over 50,000 coronavirus enquiries were filled in by citizens during the first year after the pandemic became active in the Tampere restriction area (Pasanen, 2021).

TAYS has also developed the TAYS TABU application to assist, for example, COVID-19 situation analysis at TAYS. TABU is a reporting visualization tool that allows staff, through one user interface, to read and analyze multiple data from various data collection databases. Further, it offers various user groups different reports to help them in their daily routines, supporting decision-making and developing operations (TAYS, 2021b).

TAYS aims to be the most digital university hospital in Finland in the future. They have been actively developing and implementing digitalization widely in their organization. In a case study where the participants represented the municipalities of Pirkanmaa Hospital District, especially healthcare personnel involved with human resources, it became evident that the comprehensive knowledge and information management process, i.e., data collection, data storage, data processing and data analysis, or data transfer and distribution needed restructuring from strategic goal setting to implementation. The process should be shared with common understanding by the personnel, described in detail, and process and operating models should be adopted and be accepted by all the users. In the case organizations, the present data is gathered and to some extent analyzed. However, the purpose of data collection is unclear to the personnel and thus can lead to neglect or unintended mistakes, for example, in data collection.

However, information technology is only a tool. In the case study, technology challenges often appeared because of the personnel's lack of competence to utilize the information systems. On the other hand, the remote services were implemented quickly; technological interaction between health professionals and customers became the new normal and was learnt through practice. For example, the shift to remote working and social distancing during COVID-19 improved and helped the adoption of different kinds of digital services by both the professionals and customers, such as remote doctor's appointments or the tracking enquiry system. By the middle of the pandemic, the responsiveness to rapidly changing situations and, for instance, action proposals, had improved, and learning by doing had consolidated routines in healthcare operations (KPMG, 2021).

Overall, ICT applications enable improvements in healthcare availability and in the quality and efficiency of services. Such tools and solutions include electronic patient databases, health network pages, personal wearable and portable communication systems, and various e-health services. These tools and solutions can be used as an aid in the prevention, diagnosis, and treatment of diseases and to support the delivery of high-quality, cost-effective, and customer-oriented services. In a crisis, a comprehensive operation picture of the crisis is valuable, and technology applications can support the decision-making processes and priorities of the operation chain. The other benefit is benchmarking and utilizing data sources from other regions nationally and globally.

Conclusions

The COVID-19 pandemic is a public health crisis where decision-makers are under pressure to respond quickly and to prove their capability to meet public health needs (El-Jardali et al., 2020). Various preparedness plans and models for crisis management have been made and anticipated by Finnish municipalities, hospital districts, and individual hospitals, as well as other authorities. As Dwight D. Eisenhower once said, "In preparing for battle I have always found that plans are useless, but planning is indispensable" (Eisenhower, 2021). As Maritsa and Kalemis point out, "many of the current healthcare systems and organizations are ruled over hierarchical conceptualizations governed by order and rules, thereby agonize to achieve immediate respond [sic] to the complex system pressures" (Maritsa & Kalemis, 2020). However, the crisis management and decision-making processes of healthcare systems and organizations have to respond to these pressures and have now been dynamically developed in the midst of a pandemic in terms of these processes, models, and new services.

The aim of the chapter was to analyze how IS solutions have advanced system resilience during the COVID-19 crisis and how these solutions have affected the operations of the agencies involved. The literature revealed that resilience can be defined as the ability of a system or organization to absorb and recover from shocks such as natural disasters, conflicts, or pandemics (Cimellaro et al., 2018; Hundal et al., 2020). Critical infrastructure, cooperation, cross-domain communication, organizational culture, and training affect healthcare resilience (Linkov et al., 2013; Cimellaro et al., 2018; Tariverdi et al., 2019; Huey & Palaganas, 2020). Information management involves knowledge sharing, data validation, and dissemination whose efficiency affects the outcome of the crisis. The efficiency of knowledge sharing and management is influenced by communication templates and models, situation awareness, and organizational culture (Bakos, 2020; Maritsa & Kalemis, 2020). It is important to notice the impact and importance of digital technologies during a crisis, in addition to resilience and knowledge management. Digital technologies, such as telemedicine and e-health, enable organizations to respond to the crisis (Gkeredakis et al., 2021), and during COVID-19, a number of digital innovations have been made in health care to promote remote communication, monitoring, and examination. Innovation, collaboration, and e-health solutions are the key components of recovery in times of crisis (Wetzler, 2020). During a crisis like COVID-19, organizations cooperate with stakeholders and across boundaries to produce new ways of creating knowledge, data sharing, and innovation (Gkeredakis et al., 2021).

It seems that complicated and interdisciplinary cooperation is needed when reforming an information system. Pioneers that have boldly developed technological solutions are already ahead of others in adapting their operations in the crisis. The cases of the robots presented here have reduced the demand for patient rooms, minimizing the risk of infection and consumption of protective equipment. The functions of the operation are guided by the analysis of the infection situation regionally, nationally, and globally. The health professionals have learned to identify the most relevant data from the huge amount of data and information they receive (KPMG, 2021), and, as practice has shown in the COVID-19 situation, learning has taken place "by doing," using technology solutions rather than training applications. Multidisciplinary cooperation is essential to create a real-time and comprehensive operation picture and to optimize the available human and economic resources. For instance, when robots are accepted as a partner and personnel have learned to utilize them in crisis operations, based on these results, robots provoke positive emotions among both personnel and patients.

However, sometimes a coincidence affects how to work in a crisis. One example comes from the case where a surgical hospital was modified into a COVID-19 hospital and the existing robot solution on the market, the Elisa Telecommunications and HUS Murffi robot, was piloted in the medical nursing of COVID-19 patients. A wider standpoint in technology utilization is needed. Now, new concepts of existing technology solutions and application utilization in other sectors are needed. For example, several robotic solutions exist in manufacturing operations that could be converted for health care and rescue operations. A coincidence may also happen via contact networks. Knowledge sharing between network contacts is an efficient way of learning, both for technology utilization and best operation practices. It is important to obtain integrated geo-information and regional information as well as integrated ISs to design an operational crisis information management system.

Resilience and the capability to react to shocks in health care or rescue and in the wider national context are worth ensuring and organizing. For example, not an easy thought, foreign investments in innovations or companies may consider how resilient operations in a certain region or country are (e.g., Le, 2021). In addition to lockdowns in society because of pandemics, a low level of investment, employability, or, on the other hand, a lack of employees (e.g., in health care) due to the crisis will affect the economy, leading to economic shock (Buchetti et al., 2021; Thomson et al., 2021).

According to the systematic literature review specified in the case of COVID-19, the use of different technology solutions and digital services in health care and rescue has increased during the pandemic. The crisis has accelerated the development of digital applications and data sharing as well as experiments on artificial intelligence (AI) and robotics in health care and rescue. IS applications, for instance, enable improvements in the availability of health care and in the quality and efficiency of services. However, in developing IS solutions, several challenges specific to the healthcare sector and rescue need to be taken into account: strict legislation, the privacy of health data, and the implementation of a digital service cannot compromise patient care. Patrucco et al. (2022) confirm that, even though there is an increased use of innovation policies promoting open innovation during the crisis, there is little evidence of consistency between the policy strategy used pre-COVID and during the crisis for each country. However, there is an increased use of four types of innovation policy instruments, i.e., those entailing formal consultation with stakeholders and experts, fellowships and postgraduate loans and scholarships, networking and collaborative platforms, and dedicated support for research infrastructure.

Although this chapter describes some experiences of healthcare resilience, the examples are only taken from a narrow group of countries, and there are many more excellent examples of technical solutions on the market and in the operational environment. Healthcare resilience and e-health solutions or robotics in health care merit deeper examination. Multi-professional cooperation is needed in research and innovation for preparing for the future and to solve challenges (Oborn et al., 2021); for example, the established virtual labs and Innovation Centers for Social and Health Care are brilliant spaces for developing new innovations and healthcare practices in preparation for a crisis. The purpose of these innovation cooperation platforms is to promote collaboration and innovations between start-ups, the healthcare industry and research partners, clinicians, and academia (Wetzler, 2020;

Oborn et al., 2021; Sote Virtual Lab, 2021). Further, besides technology solutions, the softer side, namely, human-technology interaction, the capability to utilize technology, and engagement of the personnel, is worthy of consideration.

Management models are not the only areas that have to prove their capability, logistics, material arrangements, and other infrastructure also matter, including how these elements and processes need to function in crisis events (Gkeredakis et al., 2021). Usually, disaster protocols are planned based on readiness, response, and recovery (Farazmand, 2009; Maritsa & Kalemis, 2020). When making an aftermath analysis of this pandemic crisis, these models will require thorough iterations.

References

Abbassi, W., Harmel, A., Belkahla, W., & Rejeb, H. B. (2021). Maker movement contribution to fighting COVID- 19 pandemic. *R & D Management*, 13. https://doi.org/10.1111/radm.12503

Atallah, D. G., Djalali, A., Fredricks, K., Arlington, L., Bussio, M., & Nelson, B. D. (2018). Developing equitable primary health care in conflict-affected settings: Expert perspectives from the frontlines. *Qualitative Health Research, 28*(1), 98–111.

Bakos, L. (2020). Knowledge management issues during organizational crisis: How human-machine communication helps. In A. Wensley & M. Evans (Eds.), *Proceedings of the 17th international conference on intellectual capital, knowledge management & organisational learning ICICKM*.

Bose, R. (2003). Knowledge management-enabled health care management systems: Capabilities, infrastructure, and decision-support. *Expert Systems with Applications, 24*(1), 59–71.

Buchetti, B., Parbonetti, A., & Pugliese, A. (2021). Covid-19, corporate survival and public policy: The role of accounting information and regulation in the wake of a systemic crisis. *Journal of Accounting and Public Policy*.https://doi.org/10.1016/j.jaccpubpol.2021.106919

Ceferino, L., Kiremidjian, A., & Deierlein, G. (2018). Probabilistic model for regional multiseverity casualty estimation due to building damage following an earthquake. *Asce-Asme Journal of Risk and Uncertainty in Engineering Systems Part A-Civil Engineering, 4*(3), 16.

Chambers, D., Cantrell, A., Johnson, M., Preston, L., Baxter, S. K., Booth, A., & Turner, J. (2019). Digital and online symptom checkers and health assessment/triage services for urgent health problems: Systematic review. *BMJ Open, 9*, e027743. https://doi.org/10.1136/bmjopen-2018-027743

Cimellaro, G. P., Malavisi, M., & Mahin, S. (2018). Factor analysis to evaluate hospital resilience. *Asce-Asme Journal of Risk and Uncertainty in Engineering Systems Part A-Civil Engineering, 4*(1), 7.

Crowe, S., Vasilakis, C., Skeen, A., Storr, P., Grove, P., Gallivan, S., & Utley, M. (2014). Examining the feasibility of using a modelling tool to assess resilience across a health-care system and assist with decisions concerning service reconfiguration. *Journal of the Operational Research Society, 65*, 1522–1532.

Deutsch, E. S., Dong, Y., Halamek, L. P., Rosen, M. A., Taekman, J. M., & Rice, J. (2016). Leveraging health care simulation technology for human factors research: Closing the gap between lab and bedside. *Human Factors, 58*(7), 1082–1095.

Eisenhower, D. D. Quotes. (n.d.). Available at BrainyQuote.com. Retrieved 10.6.2021.

El-Jardali, F., Bou-Karroum, L., & Fadlallah, R. (2020). Amplifying the role of knowledge translation platforms in the COVID-19 pandemic response. *Health Research Policy and Systems, 18*(1), 58. https://doi.org/10.1186/s12961-020-00576-y

European Observatory on Health Systems and Policies, Thomas, S., Sagan, A., Larkin, J., Cylus, J., et al. (2020). *Strengthening health systems resilience: Key concepts and strategies*. World Health Organization. Regional Office for Europe.
Eysenbach, G. (2001). What is e-health? *Journal of Medical Internet Research, 3*(2), E20.
Falegnami, A., Bilotta, F., Pugliese, F., Costantino, F., Di Gravio, G., Tronci, M., & Patriarca, R. A. (2018). A multicountry comparative survey about organizational resilience in anaesthesia. *Journal of Evaluation in Clinical Practice, 24*(6), 1347–1357.
Farazmand, A. (2009). Hurricane, Katrina, the crisis of leadership, and Chaos management: Time for trying the surprise. *Public Organization Review, 9*, 399–412.
Gkeredakis, M., Lifshitz-Assaf, H., & Barrett, M. (2021). Crisis as opportunity, disruption and exposure: Exploring emergent responses to crisis through digital technology. *Information and Organization, 31*(1), 12.
Guah, M. (2004). *Today's health care demands knowledge management strategy*. 26th international conference on information technology interfaces, 1, pp. 461–467.
HealthCapitalHelsinki. (2021). *Finnish companies with innovative health tech solutions to COVID-19 – Health Capital Helsinki*. Available Finnish companies with innovative health tech solutions to COVID-19 – Health Capital Helsinki. Retrieved 12.1.2022.
Huey, C., & Palaganas, J. (2020). What are the factors affecting resilience in health professionals? *A synthesis of systematic reviews, Medical Teacher, 42*(5), 550–560. https://doi.org/10.1080/0142159X.2020.1714020
Hundal, G. S., Thiyagarajan, S., Alduraibi, M., Laux, C. M., Furterer, S. L., Cudney, E. A., & Antony, J. (2020). Lean Six Sigma as an organizational resilience mechanism in health care during the era of COVID-19. *International Journal of Lean Six Sigma, 12*(4), 762–783.
Iyawa, G. E., Herselman, M., & Botha, A. (2016). Digital health innovation ecosystems: From systematic literature review to conceptual framework. *Procedia Computer Science, 100*, 244–252.
Jalonen, H. (2013). The knowledge-innovation nexus in the welfare service ecosystem. *International Journal of Knowledge-Based Development, 4*(1), 34–49.
Kahri, P. (2021). Case: murffi-videorobotticovid-19 hoitotyössä. HUS. presentation.
Kaptellin, V., Nardi, B., & Macaulay, D. (1999). The activity checklist: A tool for representing the "space" of context. *Interactions, 6*(4), 27–39. https://doi.org/10.1145/306412.306431
Koniku. (2021). Konikore. Available at https://koniku.com/. Retrieved 10.12.2021.
KPMG. (2021). *Jatkoselvitys koronakriisiin liittyvien toimenpiteiden toteutuksesta.*. Available at https://www.hel.fi/static/helsinki/korona/jatkoselvitys-koronakriisin-toteutuksesta-raportti-08062021.pdf. Retrieved 8.12.2021.
Landeg, O., Whitman, G., Walker-Springett, K., Butler, C., Bone, A., & Kovats, S. (2019). Coastal flooding and frontline health care services: Challenges for flood risk resilience in the English health care system. *Journal of Health Services Research & Policy, 24*(4), 219–228.
Le, N. P. (2021). *The impacts of COVID-19 pandemic on Foreign Direct Investment: The case of Southeast Asian Nations*. Academia letters. Available at Academia.edu | Search | The impacts of COVID-19 pandemic on Foreign Direct Investment: The case of Southeast Asian Nations. Retrieved 16.12.2021.
Liapis, A., Kostaridis, A. I., Ramfos, A., Hall, I., Gaetano, A. D., Koutras, N., Dobrinkova, N., Leventakis, G., Olunczek, A., Seynaeve, G., & Boustras, G. (2015). A position paper on improving preparedness and response of health services in major crises. *ISCRAM-med*.
Linkov, I., Eisenberg, D. A., Plourde, K., Seager, T. P., Allen, J., & Kott, A. (2013). Resilience metrics for cyber systems. *Environments Systems and Decisions, 33*, 471–476.
Lo Sardo, D. R., Thurner, S., Sorger, J., Duftschmid, G., Endel, G., & Klimek, P. (2019). Quantification of the resilience of primary care networks by stress testing the health care system. *Proceedings of the National Academy of Sciences of the United States of America, 116*, 201904826.
Low, S. P., Gao, S., & Wong, G. Q. E. (2017). Resilience of hospital facilities in Singapore's healthcare industry: A pilot study. *International Journal of Disaster Resilience in the Built Environment, 8*(5), 537–554.

Mansab, F., Bhatti, S., & Goyal, D. (2021). Performance of national COVID-19 'symptom checkers': A comparative case simulation study. *BMJ Health Care Inform, 28*, e100187. https://doi.org/10.1136/bmjhci-2020-100187

Mansour, M., James, V., & Edgley, A. (2012). Investigating the safety of medication administration in adult critical care settings. *Nursing in Critical Care, 17*(4), 189–197.

Maritsa, E. & Kalemis, K. (2020). *Leadership readiness in crisis context: Health preservation through shared knowledge.* 17th international conference on intellectual capital, knowledge management & organisational learning ICICKM 2020.

Mensah, P., Merkuryev, Y., & Longo, F. (2015). Using ICT in developing a resilient supply chain strategy. *Procedia Computer Science, 43*, 101–108.

Oborn, E., Pilosof, N., Hinings, B., & Zimlichman, E. (2021). Institutional logics and innovation in times of crisis: Telemedicine as digital 'PPE'. *Information and Organization, 31*(1), 8.

Orlikowski, W., & Scott, S. (2021). Liminal innovation in practice: Understanding the reconfiguration of digital work in crisis. *Information and Organization, 31*(1), 6.

Otto, K., Shekar, M., Herbst, C. & Mohammed, R. (2015). *Information and communication technologies for health systems strengthening: Opportunities, criteria for success, and innovation for Africa and beyond.* Health, Nutrition, and Population Discussion Paper; World Bank, Washington, DC. © World Bank.

Panesar, A. (2019). *Machine learning and AI for healthcare: Big Data for improved health outcomes.* Apress L. P, Print.

Pasanen, P. (2021). *Sähköinen asiointi kasvanut vauhdilla - OmaTaysilla jo 100 000 käyttäjää.* Available at https://www.tays.fi/fi-I/Sairaanhoitopiiri/Digitalisaatio/Sahkoinen_asiointi_kasvanut_vauhdilla__O(122999). Retrieved 13.12.2021.

Patrucco, A. S., Trabucchi, D., Frattini, F. & Lynch, J. (2022). The impact of Covid-19 on innovation policies promoting Open Innovation. *R & D Management, 52*(2), 273–293. https://doi.org/10.1111/radm.12495

Raymond, L., Pare, G., & Maillet, E. (2017). IT-based clinical knowledge management in primary health care: A conceptual framework. *Knowledge and Process Management, 24*(4), 247–256.

Ristvej, J., & Zagorecki, A. (2011). Information systems for crisis management – Current applications and future directions. *Communications, 2*, 59–63.

Singapore COVID-19 Symptom Checker (2021). Available at https://sgcovidcheck.gov.sg. Retrieved 13.12.2021.

Sote Virtual Lab. (2021). *Virtual lab for social and health care – about.* Available at About | Virtual Lab for Social and Health Care | Tampere Universities (tuni.fi). Retrieved 10.12.2021.

Stratuscent. (2021). *Bringing the sense of smell to devices everywhere.* Available at https://www.stratuscent.com/. Retrieved 10.12.2021.

Tariverdi, M., Fotouhi, H., Moryadee, S., & Miller-Hooks, E. (2019). Health care system disaster-resilience optimization given its reliance on interdependent critical lifelines. *Journal of Infrastructure Systems, 25*(1), 16.

TAYS. (2021a): *Pirkanmaa Hospital District.* Available at https://www.tays.fi/en-US/Hospital_District. Retrieved 11.12.2021.

TAYS. (2021b). *TABU.* Available at Digitalisaatio uudistaa toimintaa ja joustavoittaa asiointia | Tampereen yliopistollinen sairaala (tays.fi). Retrieved 11.12.2021.

Thomas, P., & Rutter, P. M. (2008). A computer literacy skills profile of pharmacists residing in two counties of England. *Health Information & Libraries Journal, 25*(4), 288–294.

Thomson, S., Garcia-Ramirez, J., Akkazieva, B., Habicht, T., Cylus, J., & Evetovits, T. (2021). How resilient is health financing policy in Europe to economic shocks? Evidence from the first year of the COVID-19 pandemic and the 2008 global financial crisis. *Health Policy.* https://doi.org/10.1016/j.healthpol.2021.11.002

Tokyo Government COVID-19 task force website. (2021). *How to get help if you suspect having COVID-19.* Available at https://stopcovid19.metro.tokyo.lg.jp/en/flow/. Retrieved 13.12.2021.

Vecchi, V., Cusumano, N., & Boyer, E. J. (2002). Medical supply acquisition in Italy and the United States in the era of COVID-19: The case for strategic procurement and public-private partnerships. *American Review of Public Administration, 50*(6–7), 642–649.

Wang, W.-T., & Wu, S.-Y. (2021). Knowledge management based on information technology in response to COVID-19 crisis. *Knowledge Management Research & Practice, 19*(4), 468–474. https://doi.org/10.1080/14778238.2020.1860665

Wetzler, D. (2020). *ARC battles Covid-19 with technology, The Sheba Medical Center at Tel Hashomer*. Available at Webinar #4: ARC Battles COVID-19 With Technology - Canadian Friends of Sheba Medical Center (shebacanada.org) Retrieved 13.4.2020.

Zhao, X. L., Miers, I., Green, M., & Mitrani-Reiser, J. (2019). Modeling the cybersecurity of hospitals in natural and man-made hazards. *Sustainable and Resilient Infrastructure, 4*(1), 36–49.

Part II
CIMS Functionalities and Features

A System for Collaboration and Information Sharing in Disaster Management

Benjamin Barth, Govinda Chaithanya Kabbinahithilu, Tomaso de Cola, Alexandros Bartzas, and Spyros Pantazis

Abstract Natural and man-made hazards are complex situations involving multiple organizations that need to collaborate. Communication and information exchange are critical for responding to these situations, while at the same time organizations can locally and internationally benefit from expertise, knowledge, and information exchange also outside of an ongoing response for preparation. In order to improve the capabilities of these involved organizations, a communication system is designed based on a content-oriented federated architecture tailored to disaster management. It includes a catalogue that is offering web services for publishing, subscribing, and discovery of disaster information and further services for collaboration of agencies and first responders. The main requirement is access control as responders deal with sensitive data. The system has been designed and successfully evaluated together with end users from several disciplines involved in disaster management.

Keywords Information sharing · Preparedness · Response · Disaster management · Content-oriented architectures

Introduction

Natural and man-made hazards are highly complex situations involving a lot of actors and organizations such as command and control centers, civil protection and medical services, and police and fire fighting units. Communication means are critical for a successful response; a coordinated response is not possible without sharing information, knowledge, actions, and plans. The scale of the hazard thereby

B. Barth (✉) · G. C. Kabbinahithilu · T. de Cola
German Aerospace Center (DLR), Cologne, Germany
e-mail: Benjamin.Barth@dlr.de; Govinda.Kabbinahithilu@dlr.de; Tomaso.deCola@dlr.de

A. Bartzas · S. Pantazis
Space Hellas S.A., Athina, Greece
e-mail: abartzas@space.gr; span@space.gr

H. J. Scholl et al. (eds.), *Disaster Management and Information Technology*, Public Administration and Information Technology 40,
https://doi.org/10.1007/978-3-031-20939-0_4

influences the complexity, the bigger the event, the more actors are involved. In cross-border case, it becomes an international event requiring bilateral agreements and interoperability which is a major gap as identified by the International Forum to Advance First Responder Innovation (IFAFRI). Ten common capability gaps have been defined out of which Gap 5 is the lag of maintaining interoperable communications with first responders (The International Forum to Advance First Responders Innovation, 2018).

On the other hand, the climate change leads to more extreme weather situations in regions that were known to be moderate. This leads, for instance, to heat waves, droughts in all over Europe, or to forest fires like in Sweden in 2018, where the authorities and first responders are not so used to respond to these hazards as, for example, in the South of Europe where during the fire season forest fires are frequent events. The experience of Southern European countries can help the first responders in the north in this case. Similar conditions and requirements for knowledge exchange can be found in other regions in the world as well.

Our goal is to foster data and information sharing among multidisciplinary stakeholders of multiple organizations also in an international context in order to improve the cooperation capabilities. The work presented in this chapter has been supported by end users from European firefighters, civil protection, medical services, police, and command-and-control organizations and is tailored for the needs of those. We consider the preparedness and response phase of the disaster management cycle in which there are three potential use cases for collaboration and data sharing:

1. During the response of an ongoing incident. Multiple organizations are usually involved either in national or international context. Information exchange and communication among the involved organizations is critical, for example, firefighters are in charge to respond to forest fire situations, but also the police might be involved to for blocking roads and other tasks. Information exchange is the basis for building and maintaining a common operational picture (COP) in this use case. It includes also the communication to the political level and the decision-makers. A good picture about the situation, plans, conditions, and possibilities has to be communicated to them in order to find or justify a good decision and decide for a way forward. Also, the public needs to be considered.
2. Preparedness and training for such an incident. Responsible organizations can prepare by building appropriate scenarios that are used as basis for drills and trainings. Partner organizations, for example, of neighboring countries, could share their information about past incidents and prepare in cooperation scenarios and common response plans.
3. To build a network of end users to exchange expert knowledge, experiences and general information for instance about hazards, scenarios and response plans. Organizations are not necessarily affected by the same incident in this case but are benefitting from the knowledge that other organization have about hazards with similar conditions, for example, by exchanging scenarios and lessons learnt.

In order to improve the interoperability of disaster management organizations, a cloud-based approach is investigated by (Flachberger & Gringinger, 2016; Pottebaum et al., 2016). However, not all organizations have the legal framework for this, or they even have legal constraints that can block end users from uploading data into a cloud drive and share data this way. Response plans and scenarios can include sensitive data such as critical infrastructure which must be handled with care, especially in an international context. The end users need at any point in time information and control about who can access the data.

To address these issues, we propose a content-oriented federated architecture consisting of multiple local units (LU) and a catalogue that provides multiple services for communication and collaboration via RESTful web services, for example, for publications and subscriptions. Thereby, the catalogue is a web server where the LUs connect to for information discovery and other services. As LU, in general, the system for disaster management of an organization can be seen where we take LU as an instance of a HEIMDALL system (Barth et al., 2019). The HEIMDALL project developed a system for scenario building, response planning, and collaboration including the catalogue which was integrated into the system to connect several instances. In principle, the idea is that an LU is owned and managed by an organization having access to its own data sources and other external systems (e.g., weather services). The LU generates and collects data belonging to this organization which can include, for instance, information about the current situation that could also be beneficial for other involved stakeholders.

The content-oriented architecture increases the efficiency of data sharing and allows for access control. The catalogue organizes the communication and data sharing but has no access to the data itself. Data is transmitted from LU to LU in a peer-to-peer-like mode using direct links but with the overall organization of the catalogue, that is, the catalogue stores a description of the data and the LU where it is located and forwards only this information. In this way, the first responders have full control about who can access the data which might be necessary given the sensitivity of some data they deal with or legal constraints they have.

Content-oriented approaches describe a new paradigm of networking that has drawn quite big attention in the research community. The goal is to overcome problems of the host-centric approach of today's internet with high request for digital content of the modern society by using a content-centric approach. Users looking for content request it directly from the network and not from a specific host. Multiple copies of the content can be available in the network which is identified by its name or content descriptor (CD). The nearest copy to the requester is usually delivered which increases the efficiency of the network. In principle, the new paradigm needs a dedicated network consisting of nodes that are able to perform content-oriented routing and provide caching, but it is also possible to run such a network on top of TCP/IP.

Seedorf et al. (2020) presented the use of information-centric networks (ICN) during disaster situations with the focus on damaged communication infrastructures. ICN is a dedicated implementation of a content-oriented architecture. Open research topics are pointed out, and benefits are highlighted. The scenario considered in the study deals with data sharing to users in the field and among the users in the field, while we are considering the data is shared among different organizations at command and control (C&C) level that are usually placed outside the disaster area. Nevertheless, some of the benefits are still interesting for this scenario. By using a content-based approach, we see the following advantages for the communication system:

1. Authentication of named data objects
2. Decentralized content-based access control
3. Publish/subscribe mechanism
4. Sessionless
5. Discovery by name

The approach provides flexibility since it can be adapted to other systems and can provide additional services via the catalogue in future implementations and at the same time due to access control and direct exchange of the data among users ensure security of the data. The remainder of the chapter is organized as follows: the design of the system architecture is detailed including the content-oriented approach, the services and implementation details of the catalogue are presented, and finally, we conclude the chapter.

System Architecture

The content-oriented sharing and collaboration system are integrated in the HEIMDALL system for scenario building and response planning, but its design can be generalized also to use cases outside of disaster management and independently from the integrated system. The integrated system architecture can be seen in Fig. 1. The system has been codesigned with end users during the EU-H2020 HEIMDALL project. It is a modular design based on RESTful web services which allows for an open and flexible access to data products, scalability, and facilitated updates (Barth et al., 2019). It includes various data sources and modules in a single platform offering the services via a web-based graphical user interface (GUI) to the user. The primary users considered are the command and control centers, but the web-based approach allows remote access if connectivity is available, for example, at incident command posts. A service platform connects the modules and provides general integration services such as a geographic information system (GIS) database. User and role management provide security by authentication and access control on a local basis.

The system makes use of different inputs that are shown directly to the user or used as basis to provide further services. During the project, a terrain movement monitoring system and satellite-based earth observation systems have been integrated; other external services can be any web-based services or sensor network and include, for example, weather services which are also used as basis for simulation tools, or the European Forest Fire Information System (EFFIS).

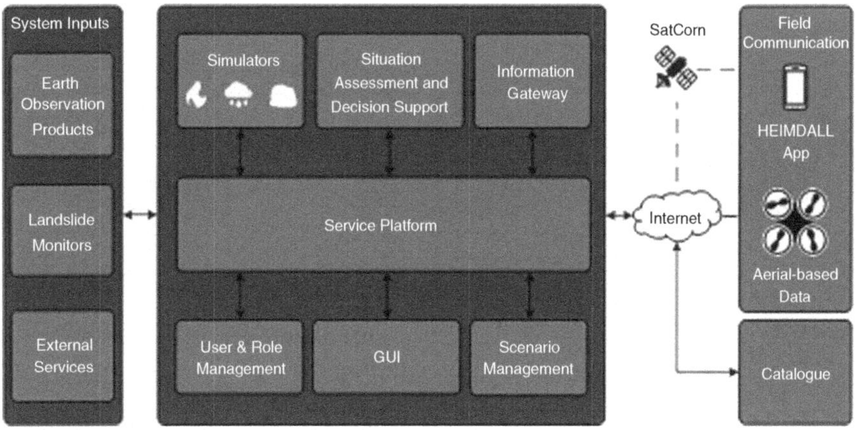

Fig. 1 HEIMDALL system architecture

The system inputs together with the core functionality form the LU, a system instance that is meant to be managed by an organization. The scenario management module is the heart of the system fusing all information flows and feeding a scenario data structure. The scenario data structure has been designed during the project with the end users and allows to store information in a standardized way. It includes, among others, hazard characteristics, decisions and plans, collected data from sensors, and lessons learnt. It is used during the response to record data or to create hypothetical or historical scenarios for preparedness. For interoperability, the scenario data structure can fully be mapped to the EDXL-SitRep format (OASIS, 2016) allowing to share the data with standard compliant receivers.

Furthermore, the HEIMDALL system includes simulation tools to determine the evolution of the hazards; weather conditions for this can be loaded from web services or set manually. The system integration focused on forest fires, floods, and landslides. Therefore, a simulator module for each hazard is provided, but due to the modular design, it can be extended to other types of hazards. Situation/impact assessment and decision support services are provided based on the simulation results.

The HEIMDALL system considers two use cases for information sharing. The first is field communication and information sharing within an organization and the second is communication and collaboration with other organizations. For the first, the HEIMDALL system, including all available information, can be accessed by web browser from anywhere after authentication, for example, from the field. However, for specific situations, it is not helpful to have all information available, especially first responders in the field can be overloaded by the amount of information. For them, an app has been designed that connects via the information gateway to the HEIMDALL platform. Using EDXL-SitRep, a light version of the scenario data is transmitted via the information gateway to the app which includes only the necessary data for first responders in the field. The other way around, the

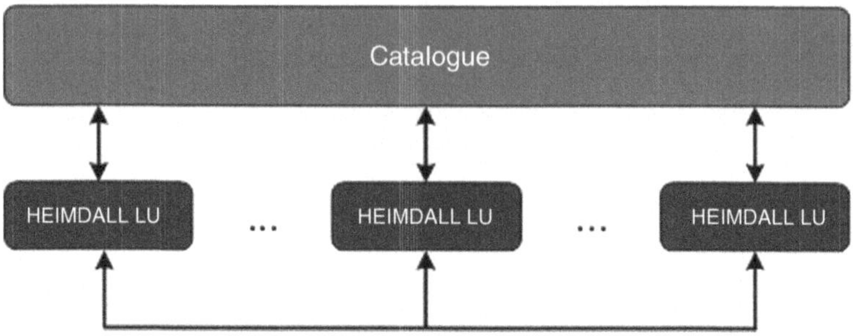

Fig. 2 Federated architecture

app can be used to transmit messages, pictures, locations, and waypoints to get information from the field. Furthermore, the information gateway provides alerting features based on the common alerting protocol (CAP) that can be used for field communication, activation of responders, or warning of the general public.

For field connectivity, a satellite channel or general internet access by mobile networks is considered. The satellite is the backup if terrestrial infrastructure is damaged. A satellite terminal provides a Wi-Fi access point to be able to connect commercial smartphones and equipment.

For the second case, the collaboration with other organizations, the catalogue module connects multiple LUs. The selected approach is based on the Content Oriented Pub/Sub System (COPSS) (Chen et al., 2011). The network structure can be seen in Fig. 2. A global catalogue serves as a so-called rendezvous point that deals in our case with data related to hazards and disaster management, but in principle, it is not limited to this. For scalability, a setup with multiple catalogue modules which exchange information among each other is also possible. In contrast to COPSS, data is not transmitted over the rendezvous point because of data security issues. The data is transmitted using a direct link among LUs. The catalogue helps with the information discovery and the connection to other authorities and offers additional services, which is also a diversion from the underlying COPSS approach. The catalogue is a webserver offering RESTful web services by an application programmable interface (API) that connects to the LUs' components. The basic function is the provision of publish and subscribe features (pub/sub). The LUs are connected to the catalogue on the one hand, and on the other, they can use dedicated interfaces to establish data exchange among themselves via a direct link.

The LUs are the source of the data shared and are owned by the according first responder organization; in content-oriented view, they are also called content owner. They might have access to their own data source, like sensors, etc., or access other external systems like weather providers. The basic idea is that if a content owner wants to share data, it publishes the data using the catalogue by sending a content descriptor (CD). The CD can, for instance, be the name of the data or a meta-data file describing the content. Important is that the CD is unique for each content in the network so that it can be explicitly identified. Subscribers also use a CD to subscribe to topics; here no limitations are given, the more detailed a subscriber defines its CD for subscription, the narrower will be the results. For instance, if there is an interest in lessons learnt for forest fires with wind speeds above 200 km/h, users can subscribe to this or only to forest fires. In the latter case, the results are still fitting, but it might lead to an overhead with data the user is not interested in. Consequently, a defined format for the CDs tailored to the specific needs of first responders supports the approach and improves the user experience.

Our setup is built on top of a TCP/IP network: the catalogue maps between the content-oriented world of the first responder data and the IP world by maintaining tables with CDs and the corresponding LU addresses or identifiers (IDs). If a user wants to subscribe to content, it sends a subscription message (containing a CD to which the user wants to subscribe) to the catalogue which initiates the next steps. In contrast to COPSS, as mentioned, the data is not transmitted via the RP, and the LUs directly exchange the data which on the other hand means that the publisher and subscriber are not decoupled. As communication system, the catalogue is agnostic to the CD format and values, but as mentioned, a well-defined format of the CD is beneficial and more efficient. Our design is based on a JSON meta-data file which can simply be mapped to a URL-based naming scheme as it is common for content-oriented approaches. We defined for each data type in the system a dedicated JSON structure that is completed by the data source and identifies the data uniquely. The meta-data consists of a root element, common for all data types available in the system, and a dedicated part which is specific for each type. Since our approach is JSON based, the format of the CD follows a key value principle; an example in URL form would be:

```
Response Plan/Discipline/Fire Fighters/Hazard/Forest Fire/Area/
Spain/Catalonia/La Jonquera/Key/Value ...
```

Some of the included fields are mandatory from development side; others are tailored directly for the need of first responders. The following fields are specified in the root element:

1. An ID of the organization (LU ID)
2. Role of the user publishing the data, for example, incident commander
3. The discipline of the content owner, for example, emergency medical service, police
4. The area the data applies, subdivided into country, state, and municipality
5. The country the content owner is based
6. The language

This root element structure can be in general be used to describe data for first responders as it holds the main parameters for sharing; it could also be applied to other architecture concepts and can be extended with further fields in the future.

Access Control

As mentioned, security and access control are major requirements, and it is emphasized to be based on role, discipline, and area. With this, data can, for example, be shared only with firefighters, firefighters of a dedicated country, incident commanders of a dedicated country, or any combination. Also, it shall be possible to set it to public so that all participants in the network will be able to access it. As technical solution for the access control, three options have been identified.

In the first option, access control rights are included in the root element of the CD when data is published. In this case, access rights are a mandatory field. The catalogue checks at subscription requests for the necessary access rights before informing the publishers. If access rights are updated at the LU, the updated rights must be forwarded to the catalogue.

The second considers the design presented in (Fotiou et al., 2012) where access control provider (ACP) is a dedicated user and role management module of the LU, that is, a distributed ACP approach. The catalogue does not receive any information about access rights. Received subscriptions are forwarded to the publishers which check on their side if they grant access to this request or not. The check is consequently moved to the LU and allows for a maximum of control.

Last option for access control is attribute-based encryption (Ion et al., 2013). In this approach, the data is authenticated and encrypted at the same time. A key authority (which could be the catalogue) distributes keys based on the access roles set by the data owner. The access roles depend on so-called attributes. Only subscribers fulfilling the attributes can decrypt the data. Attributes, for example, can be the role, discipline, area, or any logical combination.

Catalogue Design

The catalogue itself is based on RESTful web services and offers an API as access point. The architecture of the catalogue is presented in Fig. 3. It includes database tables, for publications and for subscriptions, to offer the basic pub/sub services. Additionally, other services for collaboration and information sharing are provided that have been designed with end users and are presented in the following. Inherently, the web-based architecture offers sustainability by being flexible for possible future services and enhancements.

- Publish (Pub): This is used if a data owner wants to share data with other entities or stop sharing data. For publication, the CD including the root element is sent to the catalogue. The catalogue updates the table of publications and matches it with the subscription table. Subscribers are informed about the update. The CD needs to be completed in order to have a unique name and enabling discovery by name. Given the three options for access control, eventually the first one was implemented: access rights included in the CD. This was an implementation

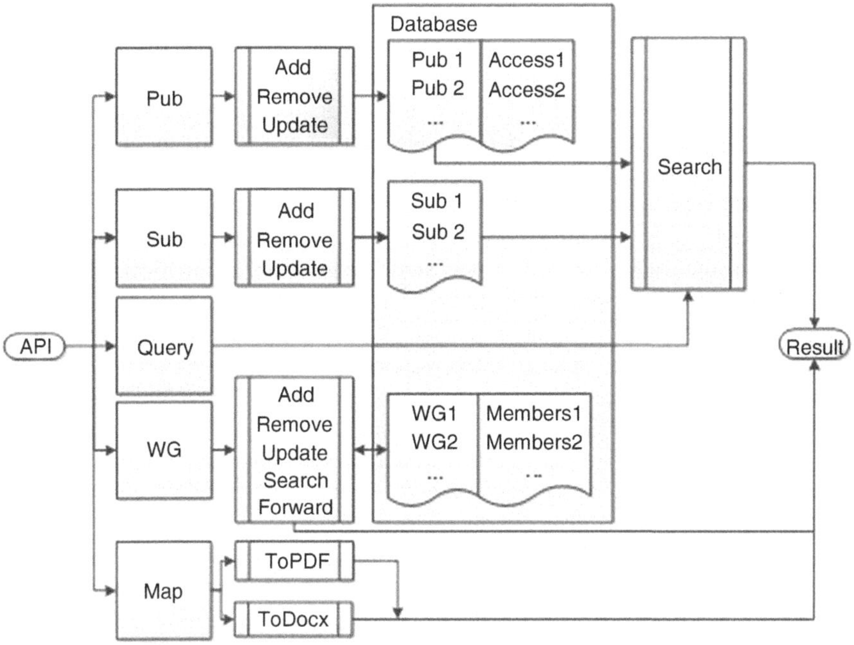

Fig. 3 Catalogue architecture

choice; the other options are valid, have their benefits as discussed, and could replace the selected choice without negative effects. The current implementation foresees that the access rights are transmitted included in the root CD structure. Access rights can be set by combination of LU ID, roles, discipline, and area where area is further divided into country, state, and region as introduced in the section system architecture. It follows the logical equation:

$$(\text{LU ID} \wedge \text{role}) \vee (\text{role} \wedge \text{discipline} \wedge \text{area})$$

This allows sharing it with a specific organization and specific roles of this organization or with certain types of organizations, roles, and areas. It is possible, for instance, to share data with all firefighters of one country, or all incident commanders of a dedicated region. The catalogue applies the access control while matching subscriptions and queries with publications. Access rules are optional; if no rules are set, data is accessible by any entity, and user connected to the catalogue, that is, it is within the network publicly accessible. This enables a network of users and knowledge exchange.

- Subscription (Sub): This is called if a user wants to un-/subscribe to a dedicated topic. A CD including the root element needs to be sent to the catalogue which stores the request in the table of subscriptions and informs publishers that provided suitable content. If subscribed and access rights match, the user will receive a notification for new content once available in the system and can access the data via direct link. In difference to publications, a subscribe request does not include access rights. Subscribing CDs can include only parts of a full descriptor. The more detailed a subscriber defines its CD for subscription, the narrower the results will be. A fully defined CD for subscription will lead to only one result as it defines a unique CD. If the CD contains less fields, for example, only data type and hazard type, more results will be delivered. This very much depends on the user's needs and grants all freedom to define search parameters.

- Query: In contrast to subscription with stored request and automatic notifications, a query is a single request of matching data available in the network. It can be basically understood as a search for data. Queries are performed by CD where search parameters are attached to corresponding part of the CD. The catalogue does not store the data. Consequently, it cannot perform a complete match itself, but it uses the publications table to determine a list of possible matches. If the content fits and access control allows, data is transmitted using the direct user link.
- Map: The map method allows for mapping the EDXL-SitRep files of the scenario data structure to predefined user-friendly reports in PDF or docx format. This enables sharing event information to involved actors that do not have access to EDXL standard receivers or the HEIMDALL system such as, for example, politicians. It creates a formatted printout of the scenario data providing a report of the situation. The data is transmitted to the catalogue with the selected format, and the catalogue returns the converted data. Optionally, a list of addresses can be added. In this case, the catalogue automatically shares the converted data with the addresses.
- Working group (WG): WG enables live collaboration on a scenario structure synchronized among all members. A responsible agency invites other partners to the work group where any scenario can be used as a starting point. During response, members are able to update the scenario structure based on certain access rules to stay compliant with legal formalities; however, after consultation with the end user, all partners of the group shall able to read the information. This means, a fast way of sharing all information among the involved actors as they all get the same information fosters the cooperation capabilities and improves the COP of all involved organizations. Nevertheless, read and write rights are a matter of configuration and could be adapted case by case. After closing the WG, a local copy of the scenario can be distributed for documentation, and it can be used as recorded historical event for training, analyses, and lessons learnt process. Any entity can create a new group and add or remove members by sending a scenario ID, a group name, and the LU IDs of the members. Confirmation requests are sent out in this case. The creator owns the scenario and can decide to close the group. The idea is that it will be the legally responsible organization triggering the group. Creating a new work group returns a unique work group ID (WID). Access to the scenario is locally granted to the members of the group, that is, the data is not shared with the catalogue. An update of data structure triggers a notification to every member of the group informing them

about new entries. Using the WID, any member of a group is allowed to push a message to all others in the group.

Conclusion and Future Work

The design of the catalogue module for data sharing and collaboration of actors in disaster management was presented. The catalogue is the connecting unit and enabler of a decentralized federated content-oriented architecture of multiple local units (LUs) offering services for data publication, subscription, discovery, and other services for collaboration and networking. Data security and access control are major requirements considered. Data is neither forwarded nor stored at the catalogue. Content descriptors (CDs) are tailored for first responders for improved user experience. Furthermore, it offers options to map data to standardized formats generating reports in a predefined structure.

With the federated architecture based on content-oriented design, a flexible solution is provided that at the same time ensures security and holds extension opportunities for future implementations. This includes services available at the local units and at the catalogue. An example could be a translation service: especially, in cross-border scenarios, language can be a big problem if several organizations are involved. The predefined fields of scenario data structure could be translated into several languages. Interoperability and a standardized model are required for this.

The presented concept is integrated as part of the HEIMDALL system and has been evaluated and demonstrated throughout the project in operational environment with end users from firefighters, medical service, civil protection, command and control, and police. During a set of four demonstrations, feedback was collected and integrated into the development presented. An interesting topic to be further investigated is the access control; other options for future additional mechanisms for providing access to shared content can be investigated. Such mechanism that can achieve strong consent between the disciplines wishing to share/exchange content is the use of smart contracts and block-chain encryption.

Acknowledgments The HEIMDALL project received funding from the European Union's Horizon 2020 research and innovation program under grant agreement No 740689.

References

Barth, B., et al. Design of a multi-hazard collaborative system for scenario-based response planning. In *Lecture notes in informatics, proceedings, Informatik 2019*, 23–26 Sept 2019.

Chen, J., Arumaithurai, M., Jiao, L., Fu, X., & Ramakrishnan, K. (2011). COPSS: An efficient content oriented publish/subscribe system. In *Seventh ACM/IEEE symposium on architectures for networking and communications systems*.

Flachberger, C., & Gringinger, E. (2016). Decision support for networked crisis & disaster management – A comparison with the air traffic management domain. In *ISCRAM 2016 conference proceedings – 13th international conference on information systems for crisis response and management*, Rio de Janeiro.

Fotiou, N., Marias, G. F., & Polyzos, G. C. (2012). Access control enforcement delegation for information-centric networking architectures. In *ICN'12*, August 17th, 2012, Helsinki, Finland.

Ion, M., Zhang, J., Schuchard, M., & Schooler, E. M. (2013). Toward content centric privacy in ICN: Attribute-based encryption and routing. In *SIGCOMM'13*, August 12–16, 2013, Hong, Kong, China.

OASIS. *Emergency data exchange language situation reporting (EDXL-SitRep) version 1.0*, 6 Oct 2016, available at http://docs.oasis-open.org/emergency/edxl-sitrep/v1.0/edxl-sitrep-v1.0.html. Last accessed 9 Mar 2022.

Pottebaum, J., Schäfer, C., Kuhnert, M., Behnke, D., Wietfeld, C., Büscher, M., & Petersen, K. Common information space for collaborative emergency management. In *Proceedings of the IEEE international symposium on technologies for homeland security 2016*. Waltham, MA, USA.

Seedorf, J., Arumaithurai, M., Tagami, A., Ramakrishnan, K., & Blefari-Melazzi, N. *IETF RFC 8884, "Research directions for using information-centric networking (ICN) in disaster scenarios"*, Oct 2020. https://doi.org/10.17487/RFC8884.

The International Forum to Advance First Responders Innovation (IFAFRI), Statement of Objectives (SOO) for Technologies Related to: The ability to maintain interoperable communications with responders in any environmental conditions, Dec 2018.

A Decade of Netcentric Crisis Management: Challenges and Future Development

Jeroen Wolbers, Willem Treurniet, and F. Kees Boersma

Abstract Information exchange is regarded as a vital component of crisis management, yet organizations continue to struggle with the timely distribution of information across organizational and professional boundaries in a crisis. In this chapter, we reflect on the doctrine of "netcentric operations" in the Netherlands, which has been implemented to enhance the quality and speed of information exchange in distributed crisis management networks. First, we provide an overview of the principal tenets of netcentric operations: self-synchronization, distributed sensemaking, information superiority, transparency, and connectivity. Next, we highlight five key challenges from a decade of operations: (1) how to codify and make sense of information; (2) how to foster goal-directed collaboration; (3) how to enable collaborative decision-making; (4) how to overcome a reluctance to share information; and (5) how to maintain functionality in extensive distributed networks. Finally, we specify future directions to improve connectivity and transparency and reflect on finding an alternative for self-synchronization.

Keywords Crisis management · Information management · Netcentric operations · Command and control · Networks

J. Wolbers
Leiden University, Leiden, Netherlands
e-mail: j.j.wolbers@fgga.leidenuniv.nl

W. Treurniet
Netherlands Institute for Public Safety, Arnhem, Netherlands
e-mail: willem.treurniet@nipv.nl

F. K. Boersma (✉)
Vrije Universiteit Amsterdam, Amsterdam, Netherlands
e-mail: f.k.boersma@vu.nl

H. J. Scholl et al. (eds.), *Disaster Management and Information Technology*, Public Administration and Information Technology 40,
https://doi.org/10.1007/978-3-031-20939-0_5

Introduction

In the past decade, information management is progressively recognized as a cornerstone of effective crisis management (Palen et al., 2007; Reuter & Kaufhold, 2018; Comfort, 2007). In rapidly changing and complex crises that bring forward uncertainty and equivocality, the quest for producing a shared overview through a common operational picture is of primary concern for crisis managers (Wolbers & Boersma, 2013; Boersma & Wolbers, 2021). The challenge of organizing a coherent crisis response requires both situational awareness and collaboration awareness, as a broad range of actors collaborate in multi-organizational networks (Treurniet et al., 2012). In the response network, each organization has different responsibilities and goals, which generates different jurisdictional and functional boundaries (Comfort & Kapucu, 2006). To overcome these boundaries, different systems are developed to enhance the quality of information sharing between response organizations.

A key doctrine that is being implemented worldwide is netcentric operations. It is envisioned that netcentric operations will enable a shared understanding of a crisis situation by linking individuals and their distributed networks through a shared information platform that allows the rapid and timely sharing of information, which in turn leads to better, more informed decisions (Houghton et al., 2008). Yet, the past decade has shown that improving collaboration according to netcentric principles is not that simple. In this chapter, we will discuss the main challenges that were experienced in a decade of netcentric crisis management in the Netherlands and formulate lessons for the future development of a netcentric information management doctrine. We base our analysis on a longitudinal research project on netcentric operations initiated in 2010 (Boersma et al., 2010, 2012; Wolbers & Boersma, 2013; Wolbers, 2016; Treurniet & Wolbers, 2021), combined with a range of studies conducted by the Netherlands Institute of Physical Safety (in Dutch: NIPV), which is responsible for supporting and developing the netcentric information management doctrine in the Netherlands (Treurniet & van Buul, 2013; van Buul et al., 2016; Treurniet et al., 2019a).

The Concept of Netcentric Operations

The concept of netcentric information management primarily originates from developments in military command and control doctrine in both the UK and the USA (Houghton et al., 2006). In the UK, the doctrine of "Network Enabled Capabilities" was developed to improve the collaboration among military branches during expeditionary missions (Ferbrache, 2003). This new paradigm of information sharing was envisioned to improve situational awareness by developing systems to share information between the army, air force, and navy (Endsley, 1995; Houghton et al., 2006). In the USA, a similar development was undertaken, under the name of "Network Centric Warfare." Network Centric Warfare designates "*the conduct of*

Table 1 Key tenets of netcentric operations

	Cognitive	Information	Physical
Military domain	Self-synchronization	Superiority	Connectivity
Civil domain	Distributed sensemaking	Transparency	Connectivity

military operations using networked information systems to generate a flexible and agile military force that acts under a common commander's intent, independent of the geographic or organizational disposition of the individual elements" (Fewell & Hazen, 2003: 2).

The idea is thus that the awareness of the military units is enhanced by sharing accurate and up-to-date information so that the units themselves are able to assess what actions to take in order to contribute to achieving the mission's objective. In that way, increased operational freedom relates netcentric warfare to the concept of "commander's intent," in which subordinates are instructed to understand the larger context of their actions, allowing them to adapt according to their own judgment in a way that is consistent with the aims of the commander (Cowper, 2000). Such local adaptations do not indicate a lack of planning (Dempsey & Chavous, 2013) but indicate that an operation should not be constrained by central command that might prevent improvisation and creativity (Mendonça et al., 2007). Over time, the doctrines of Netcentric Warfare and Netcentric Enabled Capabilities were integrated into netcentric operations, in order to encompass peacekeeping missions in addition to the focus on traditional warfare in collaboration between army, navy, and air force (Hayes, 2007).

Three central principles guide netcentric operations in military doctrine: *connectivity*, *information superiority*, and *self-synchronization* (see Table 1, the row "Military domain"). Connectivity in the network is enhanced as actors can use mobile devices to hook on to a shared information platform that allows units to get an overview of the situation and share new information with each other (Morris et al., 2007). In turn, information superiority is achieved when actors have the most actual information of the battlefield, which provides them with a decisive advantage over their opponent. Self-synchronization is achieved when the actors on the battlefield can engage in decentralized decision-making based on an up-to-date situational awareness. The netcentric platform offers units real-time information on what is happening around them, so that they can make their own informed decisions based on their commander's intent. In turn, higher echelons are able to monitor the progress and intervene whenever necessary. These three tenets thus allow for faster and more agile operations in more autonomy, because the commander is able to monitor and guide the operation on overall progress, instead of getting lost in too many operational details (van Bezooijen & Kramer, 2015). The assumption is thus that a robustly networked force increases the effectiveness of operations (Alberts & Hayes, 2003).

Despite the straightforward doctrine, the actual practice unfortunately turned out not to be that simple. The idea that there is a unified military force is misleading

(Hayes, 2007), especially in civil-military collaboration, where information needs to be shared across a wide network of disparate actors. As the concept of netcentric operations reached the field of crisis management through intensified civil-military collaboration, it turned out that networks are rarely coherent and large differences in goals, structures, and processes remained (Comfort, 2007). Crisis and disaster management in the civil domain requires acting in a network of autonomous organizations under conditions of goal consensus and, thus, is essentially a cooperative endeavor that includes processes of *distributed sensemaking*, *information transparency*, and – like in the Military domain – *connectivity* (Hayes, 2007; Moynihan, 2008) (see Table 1, the row "Civil domain").

A major challenge underlying of the tenet of self-synchronization in the military domain is that the commander's intent is often not that clear in practice, as actors sometimes have problems interpreting what the scope and translation of the intended action are (Thomas et al., 2007). This is also problematic for adopting the idea of mission command in crisis settings, as commander's intent relies on having a clear commander in chief. A key difference between a military network and public safety networks in the civil domain is that multiple organizations are interacting where stakeholders act under principles of autonomy and goal consensus (Comfort & Kapucu, 2006).

At first sight, it seems straightforward that sharing information among key actors results in better awareness during a crisis. Better awareness, in turn, results in agencies developing increasing understanding of their interdependences, thus facilitating better collaboration. However, while the adaptation of the military netcentric warfare approach to the civil domain is promising, the actual reality of netcentric information management in the civil domain turns out to be challenging. A decade of netcentric information management points to a range of key socio-technical and organizational challenges that need to be overcome.

Development and Implementation of Netcentric Information Management

Netcentric information management was introduced in the Netherlands after the Advisory Committee ICT Coordination in Disaster Management published a critical report in March 2005. The report concluded that both the availability and the exchange of information seriously fell short in a range of response operations, such as the Enschede Fireworks Explosion in 2000, the fire in the Schiphol train tunnel in 2001, and a number of hazardous materials incidents in 2002–2004 (ACIR, 2005). A common issue in all these operations was that relevant information was not immediately recorded, not accessible to others, or quickly became distorted and incomplete through ad hoc verbal exchange. Information did not reach the people who needed it. Moreover, it turned out that strategic commanders regularly based their decision-making on outdated operational information. Strategic and tactical level commanders engaged in decision-making on issues that had already been resolved in practice. Miscommunication to the general public easily arose, and important crisis partners were often not involved in the response operation. Accordingly, in June 2005, the Dutch government used the report to initiate a renewed crisis information management system and doctrine: netcentric operations. The implementation of the system and doctrine took place in the following years across three phases. We became involved around 2009 in what would become a longitudinal study of netcentric operations that spanned across the three phases.

Experimental Development (2007–2009)

In the early years, from 2007 to 2009, seven safety regions, the Ministry of Interior Affairs and the Netherlands Organization for Applied Scientific Research (TNO) engaged in the iterative development of a netcentric doctrine, supported by an information system called "Cedric" (Boersma et al., 2010). Cedric was an information system that included all the elements for building a common operational picture. It was comprised of a text and a map section, in which information about the emergency could be represented on a map by using geographical information and symbols. Subsequent versions of the doctrine and the Cedric information system were applied in exercises in which the usability and added value were assessed. This way, the netcentric doctrine and the supporting information system were iteratively developed in conjunction with the field. In various disaster simulations, it was tested what happened if the incident information was shared between response agencies. Safety regions could experiment with netcentric principles in an operational setting and experience the impact of the netcentric doctrine on their work practices.

Early results showed that netcentric operations were initially used in various ways, as several autonomous safety regions adopted their own systems and systematic. Consequently, the netcentric doctrine varied from merely focusing on information sharing, toward an enhanced decision support tool and even a shift in organization culture to a renewed concept of operations. As a response to the fragmentation across safety regions, the ministry established the "Platform Netcentric Operations" as a frontstage network for relevant actors to discuss the features of netcentric work, including its technical standards (Boersma et al., 2012).

Implementation (2010–2012)

A key moment for the integration of the various concepts of netcentric operations in Dutch emergency management sector was the initiation of the Safety Regions Act in 2010. This legal framework that officially installed the safety regions also made it compulsory for each safety region to produce and share a common operational picture within a specific time frame (Safety Region Act 2010, art 2.4.1). Moreover, it legally installed the information manager as a compulsory role to the operational, tactical, and strategic command levels. Taken together, the Safety Regions Act formalized netcentric operations in the Dutch emergency management sector. The implementation of the Safety Regions Act came together in the project "netcentric work" in which the netcentric doctrine was formalized in all 25 safety regions. The project also formalized the information system itself, which to be called the "nationwide crisis management system."

The information system featured a geographical section, in which information could be represented on a map, and a text section with different pages in which all other information from different disciplines could be provided. It was configured in such a way that each emergency management discipline had the opportunity to maintain and share their own part of the common operational picture. A collective main page featured the essence of the common operational picture relevant for all emergency management agencies. New information managers were hired to operate the system during a crisis, who also embody the new information management doctrine in each safety region.

Netcentric Operations in Use (2013–Current)

In 2013, the implementation project was transformed into a regular program netcentric operations, accommodated within the Netherlands Institute of Physical Safety. This program is responsible for the development of the netcentric doctrine and the information system itself. To guide this development, once every 1 or 2 years, the "state of netcentric operations" is drawn up (Treurniet & van Buul, 2013, 2014; van Buul & Treurniet, 2015; van Buul et al., 2016; de Koning et al., 2017; Treurniet et al. 2019a, b). Across these years, a number of recurring trends can be distinguished, such as the inclusion of an increasingly diverse set of crisis partners, the incorporation of preparedness and risk management in addition to the response phase, the development of information-driven command and control processes, and the generic improvement of information system capacities.

Research Approach

This chapter is based on a longitudinal research project into netcentric operations that spans from 2009 to 2019, proving insight into key developments during a decade of netcentric operations. We first became interested in the concept of netcentric operations around 2009, when we learned about the challenges of multidisciplinary collaboration and information sharing between emergency response organizations. We conducted a range of studies into the concept of netcentric operations where we interviewed commanders and policy officers (Boersma et al., 2010, 2012). Subsequently, we were asked by the project managers of netcentric work to study the cultural and organizational characteristics required to develop netcentric operations (Wolbers et al., 2012). Through these studies, we developed our expertise on netcentric operations and followed the progression of the netcentric doctrine across the following years. We continued to develop our knowledge by developing theoretical inferences on the topics of collective sensemaking (Wolbers & Boersma, 2013), netcentric (military) doctrine (Wolbers, 2016), network configurations (Treurniet et al. 2019b), institutional design (Boersma & Wolbers, 2021), and distributed decision-making (Treurniet & Wolbers, 2021).

Parallel to this research effort, the second author was involved in as advisor in the implementation and development process of netcentric operations, resulting in (bi)annual studies into the "state of netcentric operations" (Treurniet & van Buul, 2013, 2014; van Buul & Treurniet, 2015; van Buul et al., 2016; de Koning et al., 2017; Treurniet et al. 2019a). Combined with our intimate knowledge of the netcentric development, we analyzed the recurrent challenges that were identified in these reports. We coded the themes that were mentioned in each report and used those to create categories with recurrent themes across several years. We discussed and renamed the categories together so that they reflected the major issues identified across the years as accurately as possible, which resulted in five key challenges.

Five Key Challenges

After a decade of netcentric work in operational use (2013–2022), we observed that the doctrine of netcentric operations has been employed in a range of emergencies, crises, and disasters in the civil domain in the Netherlands. Information management turned out to be one of the core aspects of netcentric operations, adding value to collective sensemaking and situational awareness (Wolbers & Boersma, 2013), but crisis response evaluations also showed some hard-to-solve challenges. Response organizations in the civil domain (i.e., the fire service, the police, and ambulance services) are often not familiar with each other's operational procedures, routines, and ways of working and sometimes reluctant to share information with other agencies. This makes collaboration based on shared situational awareness hard to achieve. In addition, shared situational awareness in netcentric operations presupposes moving from "just" exchanging information to collaborative decision-making. A complicated factor is that in netcentric operations – depending on the kind of crisis – multiple response agencies and crisis management partners are "added" to the network, as their knowledge and expertise are needed to create an adequate crisis response organization. Finally, it is also the new type of crisis – slow burning, creeping, and protracted (Boin et al., 2020) – that puts a burden on netcentric operations. Such crises ask for a long-term commitment of agencies involved in crisis response and management. Based on our research and our engagement with the highlight, the five most pressing challenges in netcentric crisis management of the last decade have broader implications for the netcentric doctrine:

Maintaining an Adequate Information Position

A recurring challenge in crisis management is how to develop and maintain an adequate information position (Boin et al., 2016). Involved agencies need to stay informed on operational progress of key actors in the response network so that they can develop and coordinate intervention strategies (Deverell et al., 2019; Treurniet et al., 2012; Pfaff et al., 2013). Yet, it turns out that in highly dynamic situations, it is challenging to codify and share relevant information in time (Schakel & Wolbers, 2021; Treurniet & Wolbers, 2021). Efforts to compile a "complete" and factual overview on a common operational picture during a crisis are destined to fail due to a crucial trade-off known as "the variable disjunction of information" (Turner, 1976). By the time information managers have succeeded in bringing together the various perspectives of different actors in a response network, the situation is likely to have changed. Indeed, as Groenendaal and Helsloot (2021) note, evaluations show that crisis managers struggle to identify outdated information or deal with multiple interpretations.

Codifying the different perspectives that emerge as a result of distributed sensemaking is difficult, as presenting information also pertains to reduction and simplification (Wolbers, 2021). Aligning different perspectives and interests under time pressure means that factual information should not only be shared on a syntactic level but also requires an interactive process to negotiate different meanings and interest on a semantic and pragmatic level, in a process that has been labeled "collective sensemaking" (Wolbers & Boersma, 2013; Treurniet & Wolbers, 2021). As time pressure builds, these more advanced levels of information exchange are likely to be sacrificed for the sake of speed. Deviating understanding and contrasting interests are likely to remain unresolved and reappear at a later stage in the operation. The key challenge is transforming information exchange among actors in a distributed network into a collaborative endeavor, in which actors engage in a continuous process of updating and questioning the significance of information to collectively tackle the crisis.

Reluctance to Share Information

In each crisis, a different set of actors is brought together to collaborate in an occasional network. Each time, the composition and structure of the response network are tailored to the specific nature, progression, and scope of the crisis. The occasional nature of the collaboration implies that organizations may not be familiar with each other, or with the concept of netcentric operations (Berlin & Carlström, 2011). When organizations are not familiar with each other, this complicates their collaboration, as actors that lack trust are often reluctant to share information (Comfort & Kapucu, 2006). As such trust – the positive attitude, degree of goodwill, and reliability in the exchange of information between actors (Das

& Teng, 1998) – is a crucial aspect of netcentric collaboration (Hayes, 2007). In occasional collaborations where trust is initially lacking, it is possible to rapidly build trust together during the operation (Beck & Plowman, 2014; Meyerson et al., 1996; Quinn & Worline, 2008). Meyerson et al. (1996) adopted the term "swift trust" to denote how actors manage the vulnerability, uncertainty, and risk inherent in occasional collaborative situations. Swift trust emerges when actors develop a sense of reliability based on the visible actions or professional role execution of partners. Throughout the years of experience with netcentric operations, developing swift trust is a challenge if the netcentric platform (i.e., the technical tool) is the only means connecting the organizations, whereby there is limited room for judging a partners' role execution, or keeping a clear view on what is done with the information that is shared with other agencies.

Moving from Information Exchange Toward Collaborative Decision-Making

Information exchange between crisis response agencies is not a neutral process, as the information that is shared impacts the way crisis managers make sense of the situation and shapes how interpretations and decisions are enacted (Weick, 1988). Yet, in the early years of netcentric operations, the emphasis lied on exchange of factual information to solve the shortcomings noted in critical evaluation reports (ACIR, 2005). Crisis managers soon experienced the limits of this approach that was solely based on the exchange of factual information (Wolbers et al., 2012). The real benefits of netcentric operations emerge when the common operational picture is used to support the process of collaborative decision-making. If actors share their prognoses, intentions, and plans, other organizations and teams in the network can take these into account when making their decisions. As such, the role of a common operational picture in shaping command and control processes across the response network received more and more attention. Still, we note that the effective use of netcentric operations at the strategic level appears to be a consistent problem (Treurniet & van Buul, 2013; van Buul & Treurniet, 2015; Verheul et al., 2021). At the strategic level, the emphasis lies more on a political process of defending and negotiating policy alternatives that reflect various interests. At this administrative level, the process of information sharing is often politicized, which reflects a focus on *information superiority* instead of *transparency* (see Table 1).

Fostering Goal-Directed Collaboration in Larger Response Networks

Netcentric collaboration works fairly well between a limited number of organizations that are used to the concept and are more or less familiar with each other. The initial implementation of netcentric operations in the Netherlands was focused on reaching this level of familiarity in the collaboration between the local emergency services and municipalities. Over time, more and more crisis partners in the periphery of emergency response networks encountered similar information management challenges and decided to implement the netcentric doctrine. This included waterboards, the executive agency of Infrastructure and Water Management (Rijkswaterstaat), drinking water companies, and energy supply organizations. The increase of the number of netcentric crisis partners made it necessary to improve and differentiate the access rights structure and support for dealing with large amounts of data and for linking with other information systems.

Over the past decade, the broader adoption of netcentric operations across occasional partners in the crisis management network triggered a new challenge. How to collaborate with crisis partners that are not working according to a netcentric doctrine or without netcentric information technology? Here we observe a paradox. While netcentric operations is designed to support the occasional collaboration between a diverse set of organizations, the institutionalization of the system draws a sharp line between actors using the system and actors not using the system (Treurniet et al., 2019a). It requires a big investment to adopt the netcentric doctrine, train information managers, and maintain the technology. Netcentric operations are thus less well-equipped to support information exchange and situational awareness in more spontaneous networks.

This problem intensified during the COVID-19 crisis, as collaborations between unfamiliar organizations expanded rapidly, both in number and type. First evaluations show that collaboration in a very extensive organizational network on the basis of a common operational picture is problematic (Verheul et al., 2021). This raises the question whether information exchange through a common operational picture is still feasible in such large networks. There is a risk of information overload (Bharosa et al., 2010), misinterpretation, insufficient evaluation, and validation of the information (Rake & Njå, 2009), but most importantly of an issue of reach and focus. It is challenging to interpret information properly when lacking domain-specific expertise and to reach goal consensus in the network so that information sharing facilitates network governance.

This challenge of reaching goal consensus needs some further elaboration. We argued that achieving information superiority and self-synchronization toward a commander's intent are key tenets of netcentric operations in the military domain. In contrast, the civil domain focuses on achieving a level of transparency, so that all actors are able to attain a shared level of situational awareness. The outcome of netcentric operations in the civil domain is that a collective response can be organized, based on shared awareness across organizations and command levels.

Still, a key quest in the past decade of operational use is how working on the basis of a common operational picture subsequently leads to a coherent, goal-directed collaboration. The governance of civil response networks needs to strike a balance between directive command and the facilitation of different interests across a heterogenous response network (Herranz, 2008; Boersma et al., 2021). This implies that there is no single archetypal network governance approach that matches all strategic orientations of the organizations involved (Kenis et al., 2019).

Setting up a goal-directed netcentric collaboration is thus often a challenge, as actors have different responsibilities and thus ultimately different goals that might even be in direct conflict (Boersma et al., 2021). This is visible in a range of operations across the past decade in the Netherlands, in which different agencies formulated conflicting communication messages, while communities were confronted with a serious threat (Lakerveld & Wolbers, 2020). Different actors in the Dutch response network, such as municipalities, electricity providers, or waterboards, had divergent views on the nature of the threat and required response, which were hard to solve by merely the exchange of information. Without a clear and collective overarching goal adopted across the heterogenous network, achieving goal-directed netcentric collaboration proves to be a hard-to-solve challenge.

Sustaining Collaboration in Protracted Crises and Risk Management

Not only the extensiveness of the organizational network but also the *duration* of the collaboration can be problematic for effective netcentric operations. The challenge in a protracted crisis is to retain goal consensus across time when the pace and intensity of the crisis start shifting. Particularly in periods of relative calmness and stability, it can be difficult to keep each other informed without overloading each other with data and information. At this stage, setting up continuous risk assessment is warranted, as each new event does not necessarily cause an escalation of the crisis. We noted that actors struggle to assess to what extent it is necessary to keep collaborative partners informed of developments inside their own area of expertise. Moreover, longer-term collaboration opens opportunities to transform the common operational picture from a static picture into a form of structured process of data collection and analysis.

In the response to the COVID-19 crisis, we have seen many examples of this as numerous dashboards have been developed in which trends in infections, hospitalizations, deaths, vaccinations, etc., were visualized. Although such dashboards may provide valuable input, it is a pitfall that aspects that are easy to quantify are given too much weight in the decision-making process. Quantifiable input and hard data can easily outweigh qualitative information and values, while the latter may be more important in the longer term. We noted that a key challenge is to retain a balance between the type of information that feeds into prolonged collaborative decision-making cycles (Bosomworth et al., 2017; Curnin & Owen, 2013; Owen et al., 2016). As collaborations stretch over time, the inherent risk is that decision-making cycles can become isolated from outside events or partner organizations. The challenge is how to keep the long-term and short-term decision cycles integrated across time.

Future Developments for Research and Practice

Increasing Connectivity of Netcentric Operations

An important future quest is to develop a way in which new crisis partners that are not working according to netcentric principles can be incorporated into the network or find means for netcentric agencies to share information. Partly this is a problem of connectedness, as not all agencies have access to the netcentric information system, but also it is a question of opening up the practices of information sharing. The risk is that netcentric operations work only for a small set of organizations that are extensively trained, have information managers, and have adopted the netcentric systems. This stands in contrast to the unexpected and transboundary nature of crises that are likely to stretch across domains. In what ways can organizations not using netcentric operations be connected to the network and what minimal requirements are necessary for an effective information exchange that increases both situational and collaboration awareness?

As the network grows, it becomes increasingly difficult to share sensitive information as trust in the occasional network might be compromised. In essence, actors need to weigh what kind of information is shared with other organizations and civil actors in the network. This issue has already been experienced in emergency response operations with information from criminal police investigations and personalized medical information but is likely to play a larger role when response networks become more heterogenous (Schmidt et al., 2018). As such, developing formats, conditions, and strategies for information sharing in a very extensive organizational network on the basis of a common operational picture is a very relevant research area. Contemporary experiences in management of large transboundary crises such as the COVID-19 pandemic, migration, or climate change might provide valuable insights and material for renewed research in this area (Boersma et al., 2022).

Developing an Alternative for Self-Synchronization

Self-synchronization is an important tenet of military netcentric warfare but has not yet found its way into the civil domain. In the military sector, self-synchronization lies at the heart of the netcentric doctrine, meaning that units use the information system to autonomously determine their own cause of action based on the commander's intent. Essentially, information management and command and control doctrine are interwoven and reinforce each other. This enables parallel processing and rapid adaptation to demands in the local context. Still, civil response networks struggle to set a clear overarching intent, due to the heterogenous nature of response networks that often struggle to achieve goal consensus (Moynihan, 2008). A robust alternative for the tenet of self-synchronization has not been found. For the future development of netcentric operations, we need to engage in a quest to determine how units can fit their own objectives into the goals set in the larger heterogenous response network. Advancement does not necessarily lie in more effective information exchange but in ways to interconnect information management and network governance so that more adaptive responses are possible. This entails using situational and collaboration awareness to develop goal consensus, but also feeding operational progress back into the decision-making cycle of crisis command teams and partner agencies.

Our own research into adaptation in emergency response has indicated that incident command should not be regarded as linear process but requires continuous switching between more centralized and decentralized modes of operation (Schakel & Wolbers, 2021). Response networks tend to transition to frontline organizing to maintain situational awareness (Endsley, 1995) and sensitivity to operations (Barton & Sutcliffe, 2009; Weick & Sutcliffe, 2011) or decouple into separate pockets of control to sustain action beyond the capabilities of the larger collective (Wolbers et al., 2018). As the command network decentralizes, its composition, connectivity, and leadership may change during the operation (Schakel & Wolbers, 2021). We thus witnessed a back-and-forth transitioning between tight coupling, loose coupling, and decoupling, which demonstrates the importance of supporting these transitions with an information sharing platform that enables organizations to retain operational functionality in demanding environments.

Balancing Information Transparency with Information Superiority

A key part of military netcentric doctrine is the notion of information superiority to develop a tactical advantage against an opponent. In the civic domain, the challenge is instead to develop a level of transparency across a diverse set of actors in the response network. We noted that achieving transparency is not a goal in itself but helps to develop trust and feeds into achieving goal consensus. The challenge is that the netcentric platform may implicitly function as a means to judge a partner's role execution, feeding into the development of swift trust. Interestingly, the way, type, and amount of information are shared also tells actors belonging to other organizations much about how organizations are performing, what their focus is on, are what might be expected from the collaboration. The netcentric platform is not merely a means for information storage but also a podium to actively judge the progression of the networked collaboration itself. Achieving a level of transparency thus helps actors from different organizations to judge the quality and progression of the collaborative effort.

In contrast, at the political/administrative level, actors in the response network face a different type of interaction, where bureau-politics may feed into the existence of conflicting goals and norms in a crisis situation (Rosenthal et al., 1991). In this type of interaction, actors have benefits of achieving information superiority or framing information in a specific direction to suit their interests. Moreover, actors may decide to whether or not to share information, limit the level of detail, or whether or not to claim authority on providing valid information on a specific topic. In this respect, only having attention for achieving a sufficient level of transparency may obscure important aspects of the bureau-political nature of administrative crisis management (Kalkman & Groenewegen, 2019). For the future development of the netcentric doctrine, it offers value to see in what ways the goal of achieving optimal levels of transparency has to be weighed against the ubiquitous bureau-political dynamics in crisis response networks.

Conclusion

In the past decade, netcentric information management has been developed into a key process for managing crises and disasters. Starting from a quest to improve information exchange among emergency response agencies, the netcentric philosophy has developed into a comprehensive information management doctrine. The core operational concept focuses on developing a common operational picture and simultaneously improving command and control processes by incorporating information managers in command teams. It is worth reflecting on how its original military tenets of self-synchronization, information superiority, and connectivity are being translated into the civil domain through distributed sensemaking and transparency. The doctrine of netcentric operations could mature toward fully fledged decision support but needs to develop ways to support interagency trust, transparency in information sharing, and a more flexible adoption among a diverse set of crisis partners.

Acknowledgments The third author (Kees Boersma) recognizes the support of the H2020 Research & Innovation Programme for this research under Grant Agreement "LINKS – Strengthening links between technologies and society for European disaster resilience", No. 883490

References

ACIR. (2005). *De Vrijblijvendheid Voorbij. Op naar een effectieve multidisciplinaire informatievoorziening bij grootschalig gezamenlijk optreden in onze gedecentraliseerde eenheidsstaat*. ACIR.

Alberts, D. S., & Hayes, R. E. (2003). *Power to the edge: Command and control in the information age*. Office of the Assistant Secretary of Defense: Washington DC Command and Control Research Program (CCRP).

Barton, M. A., & Sutcliffe, K. M. (2009). Overcoming dysfunctional momentum: Organizational safety as a social achievement. *Human Relations, 62*(9), 1327–1356.

Beck, T. E., & Plowman, D. A. (2014). Temporary, emergent interorganizational collaboration in unexpected circumstances: A study of the Columbia space shuttle response effort. *Organization Science, 25*(4), 1234–1252.

Berlin, J. M., & Carlström, E. D. (2011). Why is collaboration minimized at the accident scene? A critical study of a hidden phenomenon. *Disaster Prevention and Management: An International Journal, 20*(2), 159–171.

Bharosa, N., Lee, J., & Janssen, M. (2010). Challenges and obstacles in sharing and coordinating information during multi-agency disaster response: Propositions from field exercises. *Information Systems Frontiers, 12*(1), 49–65.

Boersma, F. K., & Wolbers, J. J. (2021). Institutional design for transboundary crisis management. In *Oxford encyclopedia of crisis analysis*. Oxford University Press. https://doi.org/10.1093/acrefore/9780190228637.013.1610

Boersma, K., Wolbers, J., & Wagenaar, P. (2010). Organizing emergent safety organizations: The travelling of the concept netcentric work in the Dutch safety sector. In *Proceedings of the 7th International ISCRAM Conference* – Seattle, USA, May 2010.

Boersma, K., Wagenaar, P., & Wolbers, J. (2012). Negotiating the trading zone. Creating a shared information infrastructure in the Dutch public safety sector. *Journal of Homeland Security and Emergency Management, 9*(2), article 6.

Boersma, K., Ferguson, J., Groenewegen, P., & Wolbers, J. (2021). The dynamics of power in disaster response networks. *Risk, Hazards & Crisis in Public Policy, 12*(4), 418–433.

Boersma, K., Büscher, M., & Fonio, C. (2022). Crisis management, surveillance, and digital ethics in the COVID-19 era. *Journal of Contingencies and Crisis Management, 30*(1), 2–9.

Boin, A., Stern, E., & Sundelius, B. (2016). *The politics of crisis management: Public leadership under pressure*. Cambridge University Press.

Boin, A., Ekengren, M., & Rhinard, M. (2020). Hiding in plain sight: Conceptualizing the creeping crisis. *Risk, Hazards & Crisis in Public Policy, 11*(2), 116–138.

Bosomworth, K., Owen, C., & Curnin, S. (2017). Addressing challenges for future strategic-level emergency management: reframing, networking, and capacity-building. *Disasters, 41*(2), 306–323.

Comfort, L. K. (2007). Crisis management in hindsight: Cognition, communication, coordination, and control. *Public Administration Review, 67*(s1), 189–197.

Comfort, L. K., & Kapucu, N. (2006). Inter-organizational coordination in extreme events: The World Trade Center attacks, September 11, 2001. *National Hazards, 39*, 309–327.

Cowper, T. J. (2000). The myth of the military model of leadership in law enforcement. *Police Quarterly, 3*(3), 228–246.

Curnin, S., & Owen, C. (2013). Obtaining information in emergency management: a case study from an Australian emergency operations centre. *International Journal of Human Factors and Ergonomics, 2*(2–3), 131–158.

Das, T. K., & Teng, B. S. (1998). Between trust and control: Developing confidence in partner cooperation in alliances. *Academy of Management Review, 23*(3), 491–512.

de Koning, L., van den Brink, P., Treurniet, W., & Suitela, V. (2017). *Staat van netcentrisch samenwerken 2017: Een eerste beeld van de netcentrische samenwerking tussen veiligheidsregio's, GHOR'en en waterschappen*. TNO.

Dempsey, R., & Chavous, J. M. (2013). Commander's intent and concept of operations. *Military Review, 93*(6), 58–66.

Deverell, E., Alvinius, A., & Hede, S. (2019). Horizontal collaboration in crisis management: An experimental study of the duty officer function in three public agencies. *Risk, Hazards & Crisis in Public Policy, 10*(4), 484–508.

Endsley, M. R. (1995). Toward a theory of situation awareness in dynamic systems. *Human Factors, 37*(1), 32–64.

Ferbrache, D. (2003). Network enabled capability: Concepts and delivery. *Journal of Defence Science, 8*(3), 104–107.

Fewell, M. P., & Hazen, M. G. (2003). *Network-centric warfare-its nature and modelling*. Defense Science and Technology Organization: Salisbury System Sciences Lab.

Groenendaal, J., & Helsloot, I. (2021). Why technology not always adds value to crisis managers during crisis: The case of the Dutch nation-wide crisis management system LCMS. In A. Adrot, R. Grace, K. Moore & C. Zobel (Eds.), *Proceedings of the 18th ISCRAM Conference* – Blacksburg, VA, USA, May 2021.

Hayes, R. E. (2007). It's an endeavor, not a force. *The International C2 Journal, 1*(1), 145–176.

Herranz, J. (2008). The multisectoral trilemma of network management. *Journal of Public Administration Research and Theory, 18*(1), 1–31.

Houghton, R. J., Baber, C., McMaster, R., Stanton, N. A., Salmon, P., Stewart, R., & Walker, G. (2006). Command and control in emergency services operations: A social network analysis. *Ergonomics, 49*(12/13), 1204–1225.

Houghton, R. J., Baber, C., Cowton, M., Walker, G. H., & Stanton, N. A. (2008). WESTT (workload, error, situational awareness, time and teamwork): An analytical prototyping system for command and control. *Cognition, Technology & Work, 10*(3), 199–207.

Kalkman, J. P., & Groenewegen, P. (2019). On frontline workers as bureau-political actors: The case of civil–military crisis management. *Administration & Society, 51*(7), 1148–1170.

Kenis, P., Schol, L. G., Kraaij-Dirkzwager, M. M., & Timen, A. (2019). Appropriate governance responses to infectious disease threats: Developing working hypotheses. *Risk, Hazards & Crisis in Public Policy, 10*(3), 275–293.

Lakerveld, J., & Wolbers, J. (2020). *State of the art crisisbeheersing. Fase 2*. Wetenschappelijk Onderzoek- en Documentatie Centrum (WODC).

Mendonça, D., Jefferson, T., & Harrald, J. (2007). Collaborative adhocracies and mix-and-match technologies in emergency management. *Communications of the ACM, 50*(3), 44–49.

Meyerson, D., Weick, K. E., & Kramer, R. (1996). Swift trust and temporary groups. In R. Kramer & T. Tyler (Eds.), *Trust in organizations: Frontiers of theory and research* (pp. 166–195). Sage.

Morris, J. C., Morris, E. D., & Jones, D. M. (2007). Reaching for the philosopher's stone: Contingent coordination and the military's response to Hurricane Katrina. *Public Administration Review, 67*(s1), 94–106.

Moynihan, D. P. (2008). Combining structural forms in the search for policy tools: Incident command systems in US crisis management. *Governance, 21*(2), 205–229.

Owen, C., Brooks, B., Bearman, C., & Curnin, S. (2016). Values and Complexities in Assessing Strategic-Level Emergency Management Effectiveness. *Journal of Contingencies and Crisis Management, 24*(3), 181–190.

Palen, L., Vieweg, S., Sutton, J., Liu, S. B., & Hughes, A. (2007). Crisis informatics: Studying crisis in a networked world. In *Proceedings of the third international conference on E-Social Science* (pp. 7–9).

Pfaff, M. S., Klein, G. L., Drury, J. L., Moon, S. P., Liu, Y., & Entezari, S. O. (2013). Supporting complex decision making through option awareness. *Journal of Cognitive Engineering and Decision Making, 7*(2), 155–178.

Quinn, R. W., & Worline, M. C. (2008). Enabling courageous collective action: Conversations from United Airlines flight 93. *Organization Science, 19*(4), 497–516.

Rake, E. L., & Njå, O. (2009). Perceptions and performances of experienced incident commanders. *Journal of Risk Research, 12*(5), 665–685.

Reuter, C., & Kaufhold, M. A. (2018). Fifteen years of social media in emergencies: A retrospective review and future directions for crisis informatics. *Journal of contingencies and crisis management, 26*(1), 41–57.

Rosenthal, U., Hart, P. T., & Kouzmin, A. (1991). The bureau-politics of crisis management. *Public Administration, 69*(2), 211–233.

Schakel, J. K., & Wolbers, J. (2021). To the edge and beyond: How fast-response organizations adapt in rapidly changing crisis situations. *Human Relations, 74*(3), 405–436.

Schmidt, A., Wolbers, J., Ferguson, J., & Boersma, K. (2018). Are you Ready2Help? Conceptualizing the management of online and onsite volunteer convergence. *Journal of Contingencies and Crisis Management, 16*(3), 338–349.

Thomas, J. A., Pierce, L. G., Dixon, M. W., & Fong, G. (2007). *Interpreting commander's intent: Do we really know what we know and what we don't know*. Army Research Lab.

Treurniet, W., & van Buul, K. (2013). *De staat van de netcentrische crisisbeheersing (TNO 2013 R10515)*. TNO.

Treurniet, W., & van Buul, K. (2014). In TNO (Ed.), *De staat van netcentrische crisisbeheersing – update 2013*.

Treurniet, W., & Wolbers, J. (2021). Codifying a crisis: Progressing from information sharing to distributed decision-making. *Journal of Contingencies and Crisis Management, 29*(1), 23–35.

Treurniet, W., van Buul-Besseling, K., & Wolbers, J. (2012). Collaboration awareness–a necessity in crisis response coordination. In L. Rothkrantz, J. Ristvej & Z. Franco (Eds.), *Proceedings of the 9th International ISCRAM Conference* – Vancouver, Canada, April 2012. ISCRAM.

Treurniet, W., Suitela, V., & van Dijk, E. (2019a). *De staat van netcentrisch werken – update 2018*. IFV.

Treurniet, W., Boersma, F. K., & Groenewegen, P. (2019b). Configuring emergency response networks. *International Journal of Emergency Management, 15*(4), 316–333.

Turner, B. A. (1976). The organizational and interorganizational development of disasters. *Administrative Science Quarterly, 21*(3), 378–397.

van Bezooijen, B., & Kramer, E. H. (2015). Mission command in the information age: A normal accidents perspective on networked military operations. *Journal of Strategic Studies, 38*(4), 445–466.

van Buul, K., & Treurniet, W. (2015). *De staat van netcentrisch werken – Update 2015*. TNO.

van Buul, K., Treurniet, W., & van den Brink, P. (2016). *Eindrapportage staat van netcentrisch werken – update 2016*. TNO.

Verheul, M., van der Vlies, V., Stadhouders, L., Peeters, M., Vlagsma, J., Hylkema, D., & van Engelshoven, E. (2021). *Evaluatie van het Netcentrisch Werken tijdens de eerste maanden van de coronacrisis*. Berenschot.

Weick, K. E. (1988). Enacted sensemaking in crisis situations. *Journal of Management Studies, 25*(4), 305–317.

Weick, K. E., & Sutcliffe, K. M. (2011). *Managing the unexpected: Resilient performance in an age of uncertainty*. John Wiley & Sons.

Wolbers, J. (2016). Enhancing network centric operations doctrine to support civil military cooperation in disaster management. In *NL ARMS Netherlands Annual Review of Military Studies 2016* (pp. 115–131). TMC Asser Press.

Wolbers, J. (2021). Understanding distributed sensemaking in crisis management: The case of the Utrecht terrorist attack. *Journal of Contingencies and Crisis Management*, early view. https://doi.org/10.1111/1468-5973.12382

Wolbers, J., & Boersma, F. K. (2013). The common operational picture as collective sensemaking. *Journal of Contingencies and Crisis Management, 21*(4), 186–199.

Wolbers, J., Boersma, F. K., & De Heer, J. (2012). *Netcentrisch werken in ontwikkeling; een cultuuronderzoek naar multidisciplinaire samenwerking en gezamenlijke operationele beelden in de Veiligheidsregio's*. VU University Amsterdam.

Wolbers, J., Boersma, K., & Groenewegen, P. (2018). Introducing a fragmentation perspective on coordination in crisis management. *Organization Studies, 39*(11), 1521–1546.

Common Operational Picture and Interconnected Tools for Disaster Response: The FASTER Toolkit

Konstantinos Konstantoudakis, Kyriaki Christaki, Dimitrios Sainidis, Ivanka Babic, Dimitrios G. Kogias, Guillaume Inglese, Luca Bruno, Gabriele Giunta, Charalampos Z. Patrikakis, Olivier Balet, Claudio Rossi, Anastasios Dimou, and Petros Daras

Abstract The planning and execution of disaster response missions are complex and multifaceted tasks that need to consider and coordinate personnel and other resources while tracking the progress of the event. Innovative technical tools can both increase situational awareness and provide an interface for information display and mission management. The FASTER project has developed multiple innovative tools for disaster response and integrated them in a common operational picture (COP) aiming to provide a unified dashboard to first responders at multiple levels (commander, team leader, responder, or volunteer). The FASTER COP allows the display of information in easily toggle-able layers and provides a front end to direct both human personnel and unmanned vehicles. Connected tools include wearables for personnel and K9 units for localization, communication, and health

---

K. Konstantoudakis (✉) · K. Christaki · D. Sainidis · A. Dimou · P. Daras
Centre for Research and Technology-Hellas, Thessaloniki, Greece
e-mail: k.konstantoudakis@iti.gr; kchristaki@iti.gr; dsainidis@iti.gr; dimou@iti.gr; daras@iti.gr

I. Babic
Engineering Ingegneria Informatica S.p.A., Belgrade, Serbia
e-mail: Ivanka.Babic@eng.it

D. G. Kogias · C. Z. Patrikakis
University of West Attica, Egaleo, Greece
e-mail: dimikog@uniwa.gr; bpatr@uniwa.gr

G. Inglese · O. Balet
Defense and Security Business Line, CS Group, Le Plessis Robinson, France
e-mail: guillaume.inglese@csgroup.eu; olivier.balet@csgroup.eu

L. Bruno · C. Rossi
LINKS Foundation, Torino, Italy
e-mail: luca.bruno@linksfoundation.com; claudio.rossi@linksfoundation.com

G. Giunta
Engineering Ingegneria Informatica S.p.A., Palermo, Italy
e-mail: Gabriele.Giunta@eng.it

H. J. Scholl et al. (eds.), *Disaster Management and Information Technology*, Public Administration and Information Technology 40,
https://doi.org/10.1007/978-3-031-20939-0_6

tracking; drone applications for automated mapping and emergency supply delivery; AI applications for scene analysis; shared points of interest; a chatbot to collect information from volunteers and citizens; and a mission management module coordinating all of the above. This chapter presents the FASTER COP, its connected tools, the system's architecture, and its use on the field.

Keywords Common operational picture · Situational awareness · Augmented reality · Drone · Unmanned aerial vehicle · Artificial intelligence · Smart textiles · Animal wearable · Gesture recognition · Mission management · Mapping · Computer vision · Disaster response

Introduction

First responders (FRs) often operate in chaotic and risky environments, both for civilian victims and themselves. Situational awareness (SA) is defined as a person's general knowledge about a dynamic environment and comprises three main phases: perception of the relevant elements (or points of interest—POIs), their relation to the operation goals, and projection of the operation environment future states (Endsley, 1995). POIs relevant to response missions can include hazards, victims, entry and exit routes, important equipment, and more. In the course of a response mission, good situational awareness can have a very significant impact on FR safety, the minimization of casualties, and the overall mission's success.

New and emerging technologies are being integrated into the disaster response procedures: drones are being used for search and rescue operations (Grogan et al., 2018) and supply delivery (Jo & Kwon, 2017); augmented reality technology improves situational awareness (Zhu & Li, 2021); mobile and wearable technologies are used for communication (Alsamhi et al., 2021) and health tracking (Kunnath et al., 2012); and artificial intelligence is increasingly used in our everyday life. The use of such technologies in disaster response in the recent past has been piecemeal and fragmented, with each tool providing a single functionality unconnected to the others or the bigger picture. However, a host of unconnected or even incompatible tools is not appropriate for disaster response and mission management, where the unified and concerted use of resources and personnel is of paramount importance.

FASTER[1] is an EU-funded Horizon2020 project providing advanced technologies to improve the safety and efficiency of first responders (FRs). It comprises a group consisting of both leading technical innovators and emergency response organizations; it has developed multiple tools to address a diverse range of challenges related to disaster response, spanning data collection, autonomous vehicles, situational awareness, communications, and mission management.

[1] https://www.faster-project.eu/.

The core of the developed toolkit is the common operational picture (COP), which serves two purposes: firstly, to aggregate information coming from all available sources and present it to the users in a clear and intuitive way, with toggle-able layers and tool-specific tabs, providing an overview of the mission's progress, the position of personnel and resources, and more detailed information on demand, and, secondly, to act as an easy and intuitive user interface for FASTER tools, allowing the COP user to interact directly with drones and Augmented Reality (AR) devices and assign missions and objectives to teams.

In this chapter, we will present the COP itself as well as eight innovative tools connected to it, aiming at increased situational awareness, efficiency, and communication:

1. An **augmented reality app for increased situational awareness**, displaying the user's live position on a minimap and creating, visualizing, and sharing points of interest
2. An **augmented reality drone control application**, sharing the drone's position and status with the COP, creating shared points of interest, controlling unmanned vehicles with gestures, as well as live streaming the drone's camera feed to the COP and the video display in AR
3. An **automated drone mapping tool**, which directs one or more drones to scan a selected area, creates a map from the resulting photographs, and displays it on the COP
4. A suite of **AI scene analysis algorithms** that detect victims, vehicles, and other features of interest in the map or from individual photos
5. A **smart textile framework** that tracks a wearer's position and biometrics and shares them with the COP
6. An **animal wearable** that similarly tracks rescue dogs and posts their position on the COP
7. A framework for **gesture-and-wearable-based communication**, allowing haptic communication within a team or with the COP
8. A **mission management** tool to create and coordinate missions and organize the deployment of resources, including a chatbot application to allow responders and volunteers to accept missions, report their status and activity, and post text and multimedia reports

This suite of integrated, interconnected, and collaborating tools not only provides a unified toolkit for disaster response but also maximizes the added value of each individual tool. Up-to-date maps, resource location and status, and common spatially annotated points of interest increase their operational value when they are shared with team members and presented in context.

The rest of this chapter is organized as follows: Section "Related Work" provides a review on current solutions to common operational pictures for disaster response and other FASTER tool functionalities. Section "Architecture" describes the FASTER architecture and inter-tool communication. Section "Tools" includes a brief overview of the FASTER COP and each of the nine connected and collaborating tools. Section "Operational Use Case Scenario" outlines some of the possible use cases of this toolkit, highlighting the synergies between the tools and the COP. Section "Field Trials" presents both early feedback and plans for upcoming evaluation and piloting events. Finally, Section "Conclusion" summarizes the presented work and outlines future plans.

Related Work

Situational Awareness for Emergency Response

A high level of situational awareness facilitates efficient decision-making and overall performance in dynamic systems such as a crisis situation. It is important to understand the complexity of emergency response in disaster scenarios: different responding agencies, with different roles, are required to operate and collaborate in the same environment to pursue an overarching goal. For example, in a collapsed building, different types of FRs are responsible for different mission objectives: firefighters to assess the damage, identify dangerous spots, and locate and extract trapped victims; paramedics to attend to victims; and police to secure the area.

In such complex scenarios, centralized situation awareness tools provide emergency management teams with a clear perception of the scene, highlighting the relations between the actors involved and environmental factors with respect to time and space. During the large-scale disasters, vast amounts of disaster-related information about affected people, infrastructure, and resources need to be handled and are often geo-localized (reports, tracking, dead-reckoning localization, aerial imagery). Map making and spatial analysis for disaster response have become simpler and more powerful due to geographic information system (GIS) developments in the last 10–15 years. Disaster incidents continue to demonstrate the practical need for GIS in emergency response as well as persistent challenges, such as geospatial data interoperability, sharing, and need for pre-event data-sharing cooperative agreements (Tomaszewski et al., 2015).

A variety of approaches on improving situational awareness for emergency response have been investigated and are available in literature: Van de Walle et al. (2016) investigate how enriching raw incoming information and utilizing a central coordinator for appropriate information distribution among the team members improves situational awareness. The use of crowdsourcing and social media content is another common approach (Pogrebnyakov & Maldonado, 2018; Watson & Rodrigues, 2018; Basu et al., 2016). Many works utilize smartphones and tablets to provide SA tools focusing mainly in localization and mapping during crisis situations. Tashakkori et al. (2015) propose a spatial indoor/outdoor city model with embedded critical information to be used for orienting and navigating inside buildings during emergency situations. Berbakov et al. (2015) propose a smartphone-based indoor positioning system for situational awareness, capable of providing information in environments without GNSS coverage. An Android application for collaborative mapping is suggested by Berbakov et al. (2017). In the studied case, first responders were able to collaboratively create a map of the field and upload multimedia files in order to visually communicate the situation.

Heterogeneous Tools in Emergency Response Service

The proliferation of interconnected mobile devices and the production of cheap but powerful Internet-enabled sensors inside wearable devices (e.g., smartwatches) and/or fabrics (e.g., smart textiles) have allowed for these solutions to be used by common people in their everyday life but, also, to be considered as possible candidates to be used in demanding environments like those where FRs work and operate (Hackett et al., 2019). Following this increasing trend of intermittent connectivity and monitoring or tracking, the probability of taking advantage of the many capabilities introduced by this technology in diverse and demanding environments is being studied. One such environment is the one where FRs have to operate. To this end, there are commercial solutions that are being developed specifically to provide help to the FRs and to facilitate their operations. For example, a Samsung smartwatch[2] is being used by law enforcement agencies (LEA) to increase their connectivity with the operational network and to ensure the needed data can be delivered to the agent without them having to use their hands to interact or communicate.

At the same time, solutions that involve the use of smart textiles, equipped with biometric or environmental sensors, are gaining the trust of interested parties.[3,4] These solutions are specifically designed to meet the strict requirements of the FRs workspace and are accompanied by custom software that allows for storing of the user's data to private cloud solutions where processing, analytics, and visualizations can take place. As an extra service, FRs can retrieve those data to a smartphone. Wearables have also been developed for animals, especially for dogs. There is a number of commercial solutions[5] that have been developed to monitor the dog's location and to extend communications or capture videos of the ongoing operations for later analysis and training.

In emergency management, AR has demonstrated a significant number of conceptual or market-ready applications in emergency response and post-emergency recovery (Zhu & Li, 2021) facilitating SA. Sebillo et al. (2016) used a mapping solution to visualize points of interest in an AR interface for smartphones. In the same direction, Frøland et al. (2020) applied AR for live training to treat severe

[2] Samsung Watch for Public Safety, https://www.samsung.com/us/business/solutions/industries/public-safety/smartwatches-wearables/.

[3] Hexoskin Smart Garments, https://www.hexoskin.com/.

[4] Zephyr Performance Systems, https://www.zephyranywhere.com/system/components.

[5] Elite K9 Harnesses, http://www.elitek9.com/Harness/departments/12/.

wound injuries after disasters. In building evacuation cases, Ahn and Han (2012) introduced an evacuation method using AR with a smartphone. Evacuees were able to see the evacuation route as a rendered path overlaid on top of the building corridors on their smartphone displays. Sharma et al. (2020) explored a different approach for an AR-based application for situational awareness, improving building evacuation. The goal of the application was to help users abandon the building by presenting the fastest evacuation plan in a 3D map where the user's current position was a point on the map and the evacuation route was indicated by arrows.

Architecture

FASTER's disaster response tool suite revolves around a central communications hub, around which the devices, modules, and services comprising each tool are deployed.

Communications

Communication with the COP, as well as inter-tool communication, is implemented through Apache Kafka,[6] a message broker supporting both binary and JSON formats and incurring minimal latency. Kafka's contents are organized into topics, with each tool and functionality using a separate topic to post and receive messages. Hence, the position and status of all connected drones go into one topic, mapping requests by the COP go into a different topic, point of interest coordinates and info into a third topic, and so on. Overall, more than 30 topics are used. Tools, including the COP, have the option to receive all new messages from a given topic, or fast-forward to the latest available message, which can help to reduce latency in cases where previous messages are irrelevant. Individual messages are structured in a JSON format, allowing the inclusion of data (e.g., photos, positioning data, biometric data, etc.) vital to each tool as well as metadata (e.g., user ID or mission ID) that can help organize the receive data.

The architecture supports both online usage, via the Internet, and offline usage on a local network. In the former case, the Kafka broker, the COP back-end and many tool-specific services are hosted on remote servers, while in the latter case, all services run in locally hosted Docker containers. In addition, these two cases can coexist and merged seamlessly using Kafka mirroring, in which data from the local Kafka is copied to the Internet Kafka, and vice versa. This hybrid scenario can make use of Internet-only resources and provide remote COP access to decision-makers

[6] https://kafka.apache.org.

while at the same time benefiting from the lower communication latency of a local network and providing continued functionality in case of a loss of Internet access.

Overall System Architecture

FASTER's architecture, depicted in Fig. 1, is designed to be modular and platform-agnostic. The use of Kafka with specified message structure allows tool interoperability, regardless of the individual hardware and software setup. Most tools, with the exception of mission management, are deployed on the edge: on first responders or other resources (K9 units and drones) on the field. A diverse range of hardware is utilized: augmented reality devices, wearable devices for human FRs and K9 units, and remote controllers with attached smartphones for drones, running a custom Android app.

The COP itself, the mission management tool, as well as tool-specific services are deployed on the cloud and are also connected to Kafka. Users interact with the COP using its web-browser-based front-end interface, usable through any device supporting a browser, logging in with their credentials. Information is organized in layers over an online map and tabs dedicated to each tool. The common operational picture supports simultaneous access by multiple users, regulating the amount of information and privileges available to each through different types of user accounts. This reflects the use of COP by people with different roles and hierarchy position, such as mission coordinators, team leaders, observers, etc.

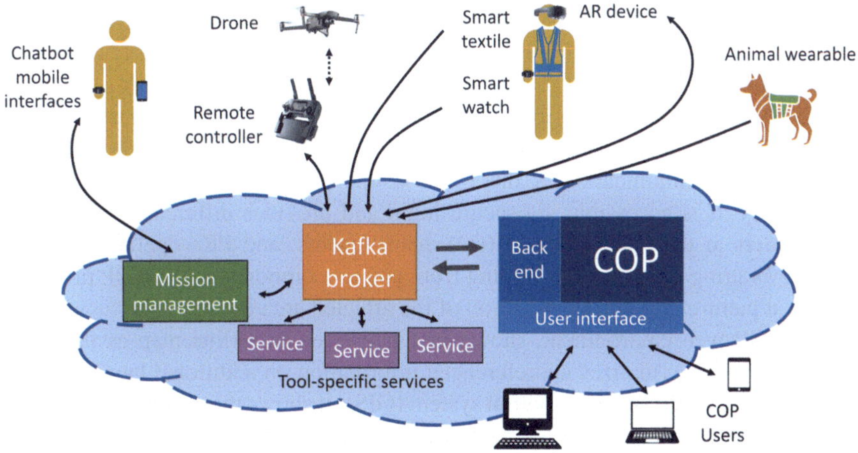

Fig. 1 An overview of the FASTER architecture and communications. A Kafka message broker provides the central communications hub to which all tools are connected. The COP's back end exchanges data with the broker, while users interact with the COP through its web browser-based interface

The architecture's modular design also allows an easy and seamless addition of new tools, or the upgrade of existing ones. Changes made to one tool will not affect the others, and integration with the COP is to a large extent assured as long as the defined message structures are observed. Substantial changes or the addition of new tools will require the definition of new message structures. Due to the use of different Kafka topics, layers, and tabs, these will still not affect the operation of other tools or the overall system.

The next section will present the COP and each of the nine tools connected to it.

Tools

The presented solution encompasses a plethora of interconnected tools developed in the context of a larger project aiming at increasing the safety and efficiency of FRs. The tools are connected with the centralized common operational picture (COP) application where information, visualization, and communication functionalities assist the quick assessment of the situation. In addition, each tool offers a range of other functionalities relevant to disaster response. This section briefly presents each of the contributing tools, their capabilities, and their use cases during disaster response scenarios.

The FASTER Common Operational Picture

The COP is the backbone of the FASTER tool suite and provides both a user-friendly dashboard to aggregate mission-relevant information and an interactive interface for the connected tools.

The COP is a web-based application for improving situational awareness that collects and visualizes data from heterogeneous connected tools. As described in Section "Communications", the COP is operative with or without Internet connectivity. It is accessible via secure login and provides different privileges to commanders at the control center (C2), team leaders, and FRs operating on the field. Leveraging on the inputs coming from project components, the COP provides a detailed picture of a current situation of the affected area in real time.

The COP web environment, shown in Fig. 2, uses an offline map as its background layer and visualizes georeferenced information on additional layers on top. By using the geographic information system (GIS), it shows the current positions of all engaged subjects (e.g., FRs, UxVs, dogs with animal wearables, AR users), the distance between them, their activity status, and other relevant data. Each item on the map is presented with descriptive elements (e.g., color, icon, animation).

A new critical area with its details can be defined on the map by the commander and visualized by all users. Visualization of data from UxVs, such as images and videos, gives a detailed overview of the consequences of the disaster and a better

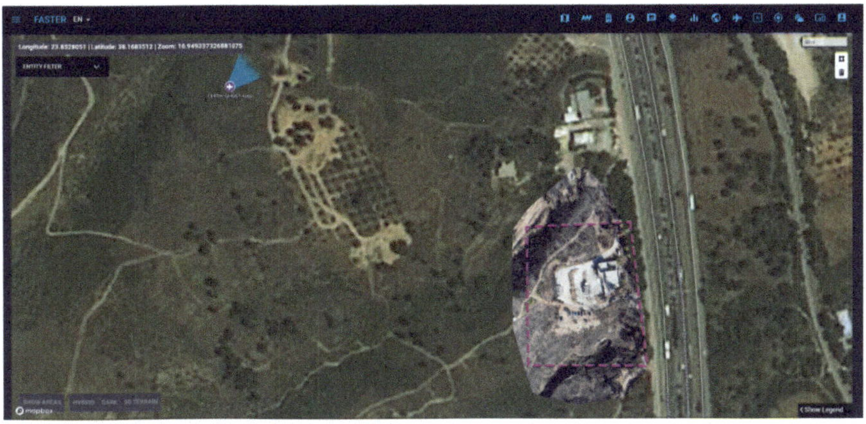

Fig. 2 The COP web environment. The offline map in the background layer forms the canvas on which live information is displayed. Tool-specific icons on the upper right provide additional dialogues, information, and interfaces

starting point for mission planning. With the mission management tool, a user can create a new mission, edit an existing one, assign it to specific team members, change the status, inspect all created missions, and more.

Different tools and features have their own tabs and menus. The following sections describe the connected tools.

Situational Awareness AR App

The situational awareness AR application for HoloLens 2[7] offers targeted situational awareness and real-time collaborative capabilities, enabling FRs to contextually access information previously inaccessible and share geo-localized information with the control center (Fig. 3). The AR system displays immediate threat information, mission information, and multiple geo-localized information as holograms and as objects on an AR minimap. It tries to keep the field of view (FoV) of the user clear by displaying information primarily on demand or on a specific area of the FoV.

The Minimap The application can display the 2D map as a hologram, as shown on Fig. 4, left. On top of the map, the user's position and orientation are indicated with a blue arrow. Other FRs locations are also indicated (with a green dot) along with the shared POIs (displayed as icons on top of the map). Finally, blueprints of buildings are depicted when available.

[7] https://www.microsoft.com/en-us/hololens/hardware.

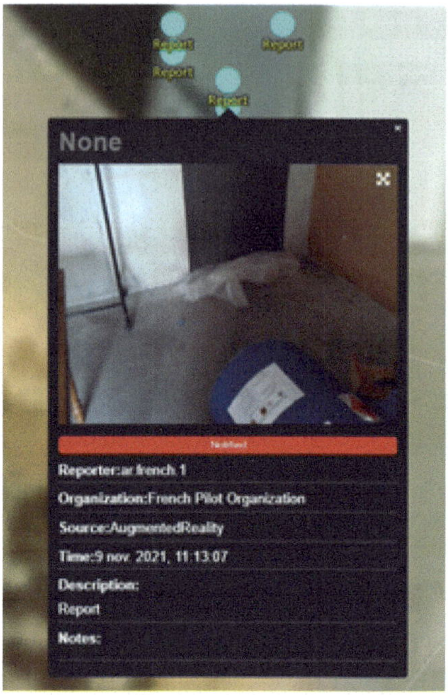

Fig. 3 Report from the AR application, displayed in the COP, showing what could be the origin of a chemical release (use case tested during the France pilot)

Fig. 4 The minimap (left) and POIs (right), as displayed in AR in HoloLens 2. On the minimap, the blue arrow shows the location of the user. The green dot shows another team member, while nearby POIs are also displayed

User Tracking and Georeference The HoloLens 2 is equipped with multiple sensors (cameras, depth, IMU) and can create a spatial map of the environment. Taking advantage of these capabilities, we developed a functionality to match geographical coordinates to the HoloLens space. We used a QR code embedding (latitude and longitude) and placed it at the corresponding position in the real world (aligned to the geographical north). Once the coordinates are retrieved, we can

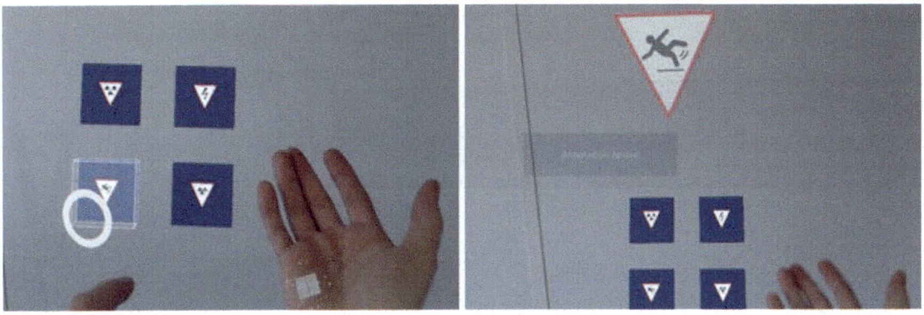

Fig. 5 POI creation from inside the HoloLens app. Left: a menu presents different types of POIs as AR buttons. Right: the POI is added and displayed in front of the user

match the position of objects in the virtual space to a common reference system (WGS84[8]) and track the position and orientation of the user.

Holograms of the POIs The AR application uses geographical tracking capabilities to display holograms of the POIs (Fig. 4, right) in the environment of the user, as a means of hands-free visualization of important information. The application also allows FRs to create and share a POI directly from the field using voice commands or holographic buttons, as shown in Fig. 5.

Report and Distress Message Users can send georeferenced pictures or distress signals to the COP to help operators get a better understanding of what is happening on the field.

UAV Gesture-Control and Extended Vision App

Part of the synergy of tools we developed is an additional AR application for controlling UAVs using hand gestures and voice commands. The rationale behind this approach is that during emergency operations, FRs need to carry various tools and equipment, and being able to control the UAVs without the need of a specialized controller by using only one hand or even voice commands would be useful.

Gesture Control The user of the HoloLens 2 AR app can control the drone using the right or left hand (default is the right hand) performing intuitive palm gestures that simulate the drone movement. Making the hand into a fist corresponds to braking and stopping, while having the palm open and the fingers extended and tilting to the front instructs the drone to move forward. When the user's hands are occupied performing another task, the drone stays in place and waits for the next

[8] https://gisgeography.com/wgs84-world-geodetic-system/.

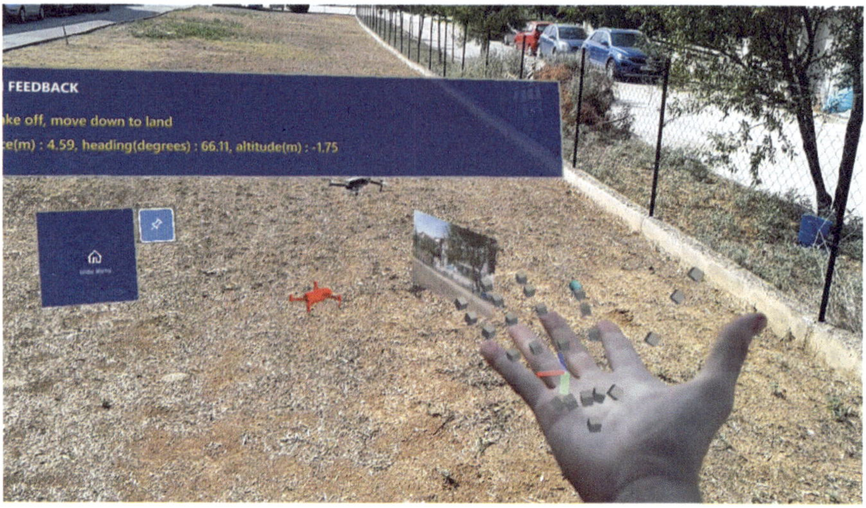

Fig. 6 A capture from a UAV control application. The hand joints displacement error visible in the figure is due to the caption camera position. The AR user can see the virtual joints overlaid on the exact position of the actual joints

command. Additionally, the user can use voice commands to perform high-level tasks, e.g., drone landing/takeoff. In a similar approach, using the other hand, by default the left hand, and by performing similar palm gestures, the user can control the UAV's camera viewing direction and view the video feed inside the HoloLens 2 display. Additional features include a "Periscope" mode, where the drone's viewing direction follows the user's viewing direction. For example, when the user rotates her head to look 10° North, the UAV turns to the exact same direction. This mode allows for a quick and intuitive inspection of the surrounding environment, a feature very useful in search operations.

Extended Vision Two main tools comprise the extended vision functionality: drone tracking and contextualized video feed. In *drone tracking*, a virtual drone object is overlaid on top of the real one so the UAV pilot can have a rough estimation of the UAV's location and direction when flying beyond line of sight. Using a *contextualized video feed*, the user can see the UAV's video feed in the AR app. The video feed can be displayed either in front of the user or on a smaller panel placed in front of the virtual drone. This *contextualized* video feed visualization provides an easily perceivable way to the user to understand what the UAV "sees" and in which direction during flight time. Additionally, the user has the ability to choose between RGB, infrared, and a hybrid mode, suitable for different types of search missions.

Figure 6 shows gesture control and extended vision in first-person view, including the capture of the user's right hand, the red virtual object tracking the drone's position, and the video feed displayed in AR. Near the top, the navigation feedback panel displays information about the currently interpreted gesture command and the drone's heading and distance from the user.

UAV Mapping and AI Scene Analysis

The UAV mapping and AI annotation tool is a combination of tools aiming at creating an up-to-date annotated 2D map of the area of interest. It uses UAVs to obtain high-resolution overlapping aerial photographs of an area at pre-calculated waypoints and combines them to create a true-to-scale orthomosaic representation (2D map). The produced orthophoto is fed through a suit of AI algorithms to detect and annotate objects of interest such as buildings, vehicles, risks, landscape features, victims, and more (Fig. 7 right). Besides 2D maps, the mapping tool also supports 3D maps and thermal (IR) maps when the right equipment is present on active drones (IR cameras).

The tool involves four cooperating modules:

1. The COP (presented in Section "The FASTER Common Operational Picture")
2. The flight path calculation system
3. The UAV interface Android app (presented in Section "UAV Gesture-Control and Extended Vision App")
4. The map generation module
5. The AI annotation group of algorithms

Integration with the COP The COP is the tool's front-end interface, allowing the user to mark the desired area, set mission parameters, and select one or more drones to execute the mission. When all mission parameters are set, the feasibility of the

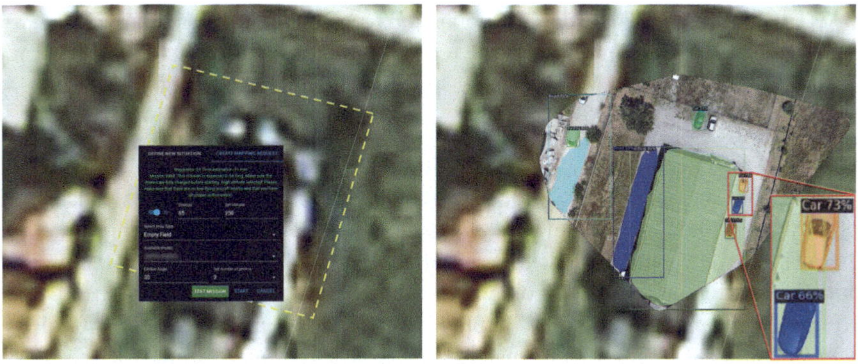

Fig. 7 Mapping and AI annotation. On the left: marking an area for mapping on the COP, setting the mission parameters, and receiving feedback regarding feasibility (in green). On the right: the results of mapping as a layer on the COP map, including AI annotations (zoomed detailed shown in lower right corner)

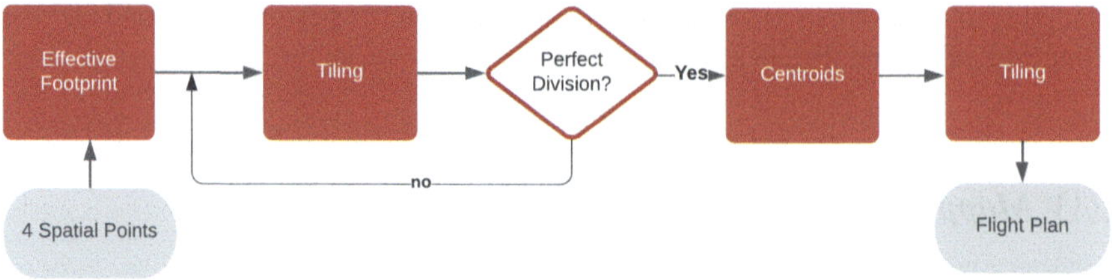

Fig. 8 Path algorithm: Compute effective footprint based on camera parameters. Tile the plane and round up if needed. Compute. Create routes utilizing the centroids of tiles. Split route according to number of drones

mission is evaluated, and, in case of a negative assessment, suggestions to improve the mission's performance are provided; e.g., if the selected area is so large that it would take the UAVs too much time to scan, the user would be warned and prompted to increase the altitude, so that the area can be covered with fewer photographs (Fig. 7 left).

Flight Path Calculation To model the desired area, four spatial coordinates (approximating a rectangle) that represent actual points on the Earth's surface are required. The desired area is divided into rectangles that represent the effective footprint of the drone's camera. As the effective footprint represents the camera's footprint with the overlap factored out, a side-by-side tiling of such rectangles will cover the area of interest with the desired overlap percentage. Since most drones have similar sensor sizes, this method produces accurate results, even though it is not the most effective one. After the division, the centroids of the rectangles are the waypoints of the mission. Finally, the waypoints are distributed to all the available drones, and a mission is created. A schematic overview of this procedure is presented in Fig. 8.

UAV Interface App The Android application receives data through Kafka and generates a corresponding mission for the respective drone. After mission completion, the app collects all photos and forwards them to the map generation system, again through Kafka.

Map Generation Module ODM[9] was chosen as the primary tool for 2D mapping because it is an open-source project that is highly customizable. An exhaustive exploration of how the parameters affect the result was started, both in terms of the quality of the outputs and in terms of time needed to run. Understanding the impact of different parameter sets was a two-step process. Firstly, the theoretical effect of each parameter on the output was considered, and likely default values were identified for different scenarios. After that, thorough testing of the most

[9] https://github.com/OpenDroneMap/ODM.

important parameters was carried out, determining the best parameter combinations for achieving optimal output quality, again in different scenarios.

AI annotation algorithms The orthomosaic map is scanned for different features relevant to disaster response:

- Human figures (victims)
- Disaster areas
- Disaster-related environmental elements (infrastructure, vehicles, environment, etc.)

For this purpose, established AI architectures have been used as a baseline, including Ren et al. (2016), He et al. (2016), and Kirillov et al. (2019). The orthomosaic map is geotagged (i.e., the GPS coordinates of each corner are known, and hence the coordinates of any pixel on it can be inferred by bilinear interpolation); thus, the coordinates of detected features are also known. Therefore, they can be used to generate POIs, as appropriate per mission type. Victims will always generate a POI, and other features, such as fires or vehicles, can be configured to generate POIs when these are relevant to the mission.

UAV Supply Delivery

The FASTER solution also includes the capability of transferring supplies by UAVs to a specified location. For example, if an FR discovers a victim in need of urgent medical attention, they can tag their location with the supply drop POI and have a drone navigate to them automatically, carrying the needed supplies. This may be done in an unsupervised way, where a UAV pre-loaded with a specific type of supply appropriate to the mission flies to the POI on request, or in a semi-supervised way, where the FR requesting the supply drop first communicates their exact need to the COP or the drone operator to attach the requested supplies before sending the drone to fly autonomously to the location.

Smart Textile Framework

The STF is a prototype solution that includes textiles with sensors worn by FRs and a mobile application that collects, displays, processes the generated data, and communicates alerts when certain thresholds are met. The textiles comprise two modules: a biometric module placed on the inside of the FR's uniform and an environmental module placed on the outside of the uniform. A software solution has been developed which collects data from both aforementioned modules and processes them. The solution is designed in a modular way and can be extended with further functionality in the future. Figure 9 displays the user interface for the

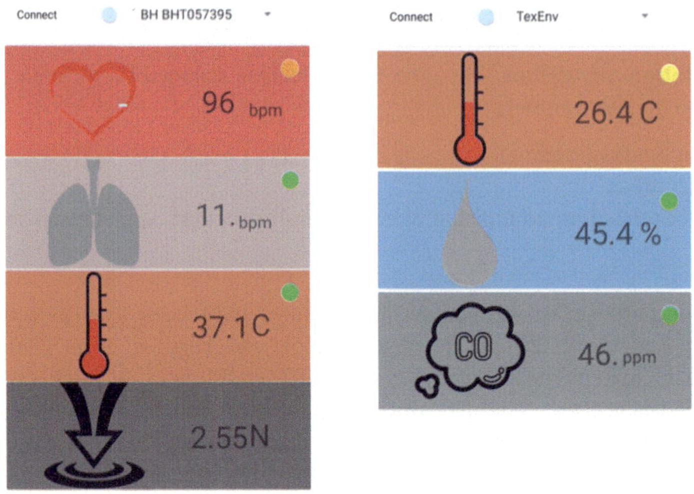

Fig. 9 Information on the STF mobile application. Left: the biometrics tab. Right: the environmental tab

Table 1 Sensors and data types in STF

Feature	Origin	Destination	Data	Format	Communication
Respiration frequency	Biometric module	Application	Sensor data	Raw	External
Body temperature	Biometric module	Application	Sensor data	Raw	External
Heart rate	Biometric module	Application	Sensor data	Raw	External
Force	Biometric module	Application	Sensor data	Raw	External
Temperature	Environmental module	Application	Sensor data	Raw	External
Humidity	Environmental module	Application	Sensor data	Raw	External
CO	Environmental module	Application	Sensor data	Raw	External

mobile application used in the STF. Table 1 summarizes the information that is collected by the two textile modules.

The developed solution is also GDPR compliant. There is no storing of the collected data, since after being visualized on the display they are deleted, and only alerts propagate inside the FASTER ecosystem and are being collected and displayed in the COP (Fig. 10). Regarding the latter, these propagated alerts use a color code to represent the intensity level of the alert based on predefined thresholds for its color/intensity level (Fig. 11).

Fig. 10 STF data displayed in the COP using a color code for GDPR compliance

Fig. 11 Color code and severity representation

MORSE

MORSE consists of an application for smartphones and smartwatches to recognize hand gestures from FRs. The app uses the accelerometer and gyroscope sensors in the smartwatch to feed a trained neural network and recognize predefined hand gestures. The smartwatch application gets FRs' position using GNSS and broadcasts it along with the gesture to nearby FRs. The latter receives haptic feedback at their smartwatches and are aware of the sender's condition. Finally, this information is transmitted to the COP. Given that FRs have received training on using hand gestures for communicating with each other in the field, they have been able to propose a set of hand gestures for use in MORSE coming from airport ground operations.

The selected gestures can be seen in Fig. 12, and they are as follows:

1. "Recommend stop"
2. "Emergency contained"
3. "Recommend evacuation"
4. "Fire indication"

Finally, Fig. 13 displays the user interface of the smartwatch application running the MORSE software displaying the notification of a recorded gesture. This message is received by all the FRs wearing the smartwatch running the MORSE application.

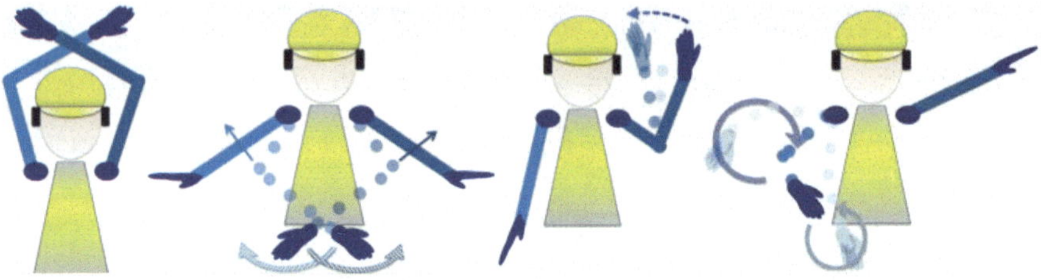

Fig. 12 MORSE recognized gestures

Fig. 13 MORSE UI on the FR's smartwatch

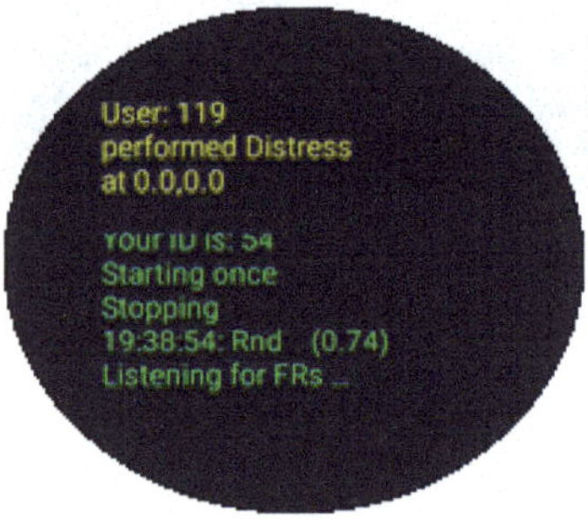

Animal Wearable

The animal wearable is a novel wearable device, aiming to enhance the effectiveness of trained K9 units. The module has been designed to satisfy the defined user requirements. These requirements mainly focus on the shape and dimensions of the wearable in order to be safe of the animals. To address the former, the use of a harness with a small pouch was selected, while for the latter, detachability of each part was included to allow the animal to not get tangled while operating at the field. The primary features/goals of the wearable comprise the ability to:

- Geo-locate the animal unit in real time
- Monitor the motion signals of the animal
- Recognize the animal's activity
- Detect barking (acting as a trigger)
- Record and playback audio
- Capture video or still images

In order to meet the goals, the animal wearable is equipped with artificial intelligence (AI) algorithms to detect when the animal is barking and when specific moves are performed. The monitored animal moves (i.e., K9 dogs for FASTER) have been selected by their trainers and include already trained moves, in order to ensure that the training set and the tests can be completed in the lifetime of the project. The result from the activity recognition and the bark detection process, along with the location of the animal, are all being communicated from

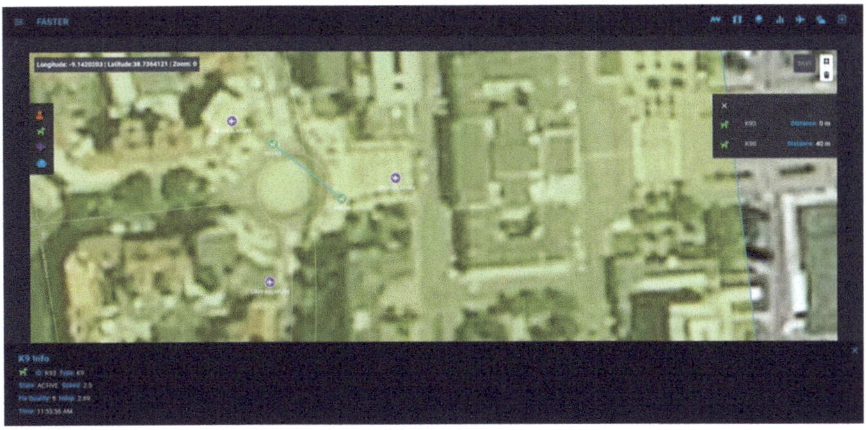

Fig. 14 COP displaying the location of two K9s wearing the animal wearable

the wearable to the custom cloud implementation of FASTER, from where they are being displayed in the COP and in a specially designed mobile application on the trainer's smartphone. Figure 14 illustrates the COP displaying location data between two K9 units.

Mission Management and Chatbot

The main purpose of the mission management module is collecting user-generated content and providing synthetic information to field agents. Its main component is a back-end service that provides data access through a REST API. External services and other components like the Smartwatch Standalone App and the chatbot use the interfaces provided by the mission management back end to insert user-generated content or for data visualization.

The mission management back end organizes users according to permissions and roles, keeping track of each user's status, activity, and—optionally—location. It supports the creation of missions through through the COP, the assignation of specific users to each mission, and the status of the mission. Finally, it files reports submitted by users and routes communication between them.

The FASTER chatbot is the primary means of first responders and volunteers to interact with the mission management module. Its main features are providing an interface for submitting user-generated content (e.g., photos or reports of the disaster area) and providing a way for the decision-makers in the control room to monitor the on-field agent's status, activity, and mission progress.

The FASTER chatbot leverages the possibility of building rich interactions using Telegram custom keyboards and multimedia cards, excluding potential ambiguities.

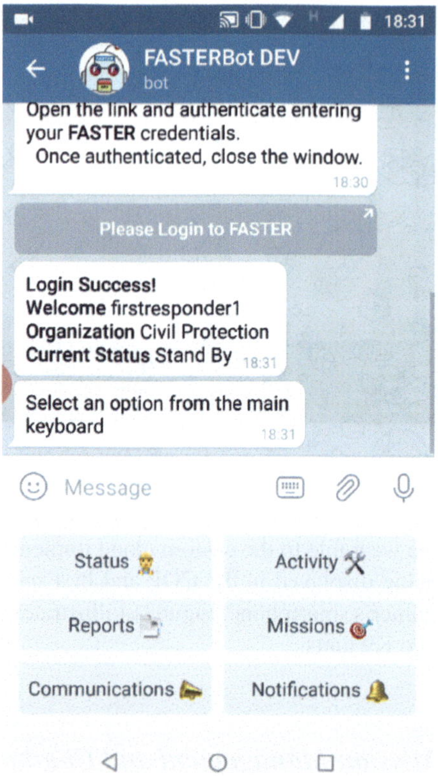

Fig. 15 The chatbot main menu in the mobile app

The bot uses a predefined set of emojis for making menu navigation more intuitive where possible.

The chatbot's main menu, shown in Fig. 15, presents users with the core functionalities: setting their status (Active, Unavailable, In Transit); describing their current activity (e.g., fire prevention, flood barrier, etc.); sending reports containing text, photos, location coordinates, and/or detected hazards; browsing missions created by the COP with options to accept them, abandon them, or mark them as complete; sending messages to specific groups of recipients or broadcast them for all users to see; and browsing notifications generated by all other options or COP actions.

In addition, a custom smartwatch application (screens shown in Fig. 16) was developed for Wear OS. It includes a heartrate measuring function and is able to post an alert in case of abnormality detection. Moreover, it includes support for wrist gesture commands and voice commands, which can drastically improve usability in the adverse and stressful conditions of a response mission.

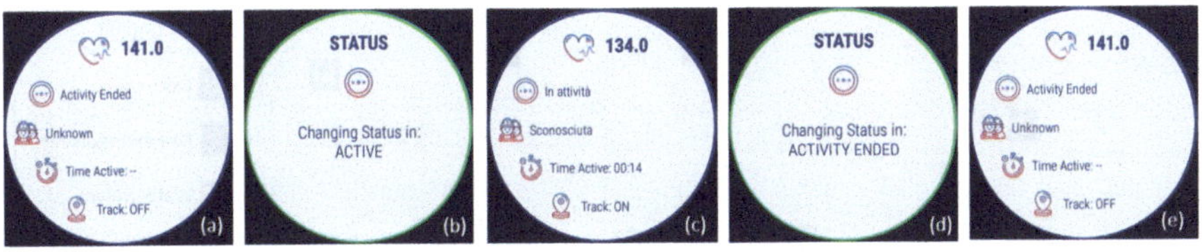

Fig. 16 Smartwatch screens showing status, heartrate, and user interface

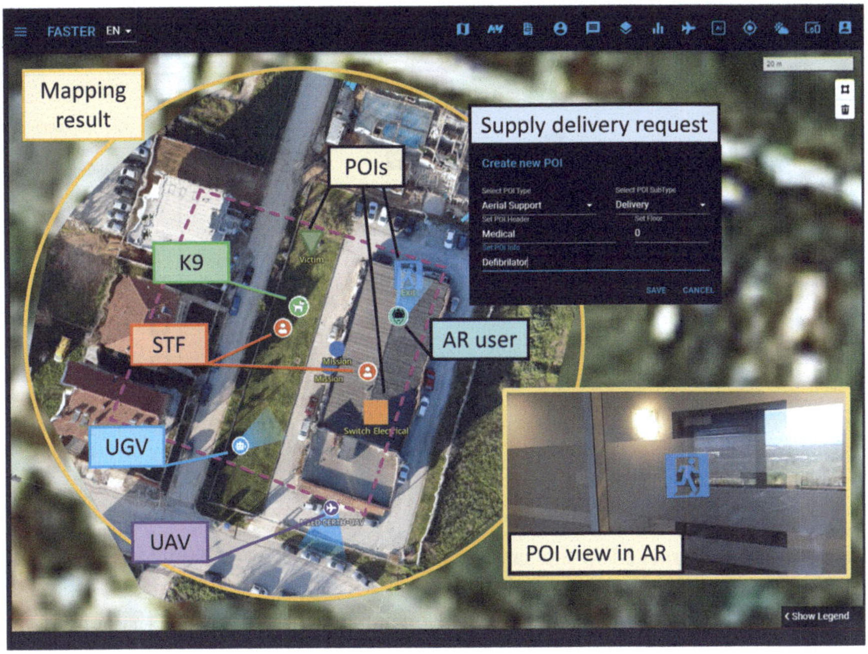

Fig. 17 An overview of the COP and some of the connected tools

Operational Use Case Scenario

The FASTER COP and its suite of connected tools can be used to provide a multilayer, interactive, common operational picture to the mission commander and individual team leaders during a response mission. By visualizing location data of personnel and equipment, mission status, and points of interest, it can aid mission planning, monitoring, and decision-making. Figure 17 shows an overview of some, though by no means all, tools and functionalities.

Personnel equipped with the smart textile vest, the HoloLens, the chatbot, or the smartwatch application can have their positions tracked in real time. This allows team leaders and commanders using the COP to monitor the progress of responders' deployment throughout an area of operation and easily identify proximity to dangerous areas or gaps in the coverage. K9 units and unmanned

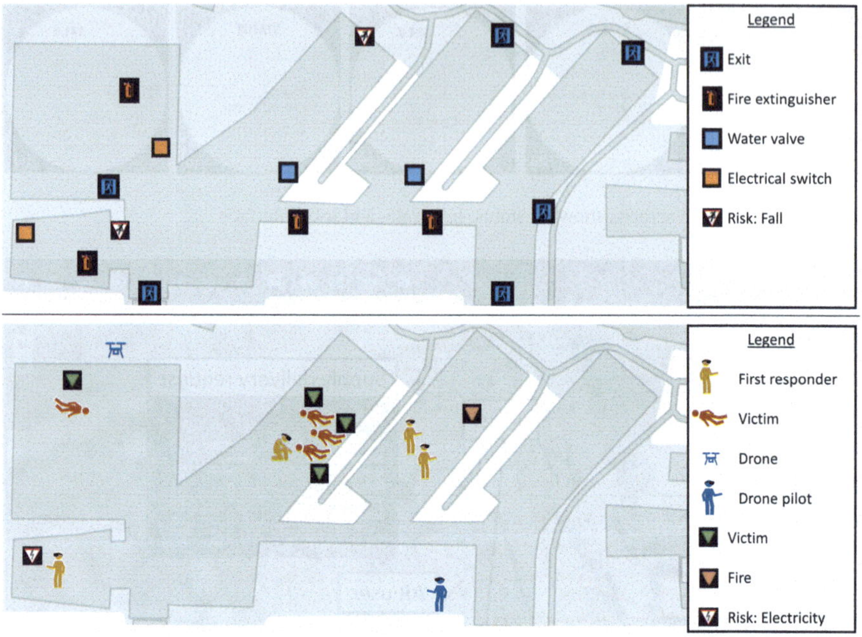

Fig. 18 Points of interest shared between COP users and HoloLens users. Top: static POIs created before mission start. Bottom: POIs discovered during the course of the mission, by first responders or drones

vehicles are also tracked in the same way, with each resource depicted by a type-specific icon.

Points of interest (POIs) can be used to append extra information both on the COP map and in the AR vision of responders, in context with their actual surroundings. Static POIs (Fig. 18, top), like exits, electrical, or other switches whose location is known, can be created before mission commencement and are visible to both the COP users and the holographic displays of appropriately equipped responders. As the mission progresses, the shared pool of POIs will be continuously updated, as victims are located, new risks are identified, and earlier risks are mitigated (Fig. 18, bottom). Drone involvement in the pool of shared POIs allows the swift delivery of supplies to specified locations visible on the map.

While the COP provides an offline satellite map as a background layer, this is of relatively low resolution and, in most cases, weeks or months old. In most disaster response missions, the current state of the area will be drastically different to its usual state, perhaps including destroyed buildings, abandoned cars, blocked roads, and victims. The automated drone mapping tool can provide a high-quality, up-to-date view of the affected area, seamlessly superimposed on top of the COP's offline map, showing the mission commander the true state of the area, with AI scene analysis assistant highlighting important detected features.

Finally, the participation of all personnel, including volunteers, in the integrated mission management through the chatbot and smartwatch apps provides both a clear view of the human resource allocation and a way to crowdsource information about an evolving situation.

In a typical use case scenario, the command team would first use the COP to request a drone mapping of the affected area, in order to get a detailed and up-to-date view of the current state of play. This would be complemented by reports from the ground via the chatbot, including text and images. Equipped with this information, the command team would then mark static points of interest on the COP, gradually building the virtual layer of the field of operations to increase situational awareness. Missions with specific objectives, linked to appropriately skilled FRs, would then be created and continuously updated throughout the mission.

Individual responders or squads would be equipped with wearable tools appropriate for the mission type: HoloLens AR devices for squad leaders or drone pilots, smart textiles for responders operating in dangerous environments or away from teammates, smartwatches for MORSE or chatbot interactions, and animal wearables for K9 units. As squads, individual FRs, dogs, and UAVs move to complete their mission objectives, their location and status are transmitted and displayed in real time on the COP, allowing the command team to take action or to adapt their action plans immediately as the mission unfolds.

With the FRs deployed, more information is added to the COP display, as squad leaders and drone pilots add or remove POIs dynamically, victims are located or evacuated, and hazards detected or neutralized. At regular intervals, new drone mapping missions are requested to update the COP display with the newest state. When responders move beyond the range of conventional communications, RESCUE boxes are deployed, individually or in chains, to provide an alternative mean of communication. Emergency supplies are delivered by drone to exact coordinates, as requested by the COP or a HoloLens-equipped squad leader. The health of personnel and the status of drones are monitored from the COP, allowing the command team to trigger appropriate responses, such as evacuation, assistance, a call for rest, bringing drones home for battery recharge, etc.

Field Trials

Throughout its duration, the FASTER project organized several events (or "pilot" exercises) to demonstrate and evaluate the presented toolkit. Early events focused on testing the deployment of tools outside the lab, showing working versions to FR project partners, identifying bugs and shortcomings, and planning future improvements based on this feedback. These had a marked impact on the development of tools, with design decisions often taken immediately following a piloting event.

Examples of such impact include the decluttering of the AR situational awareness app's display, following feedback from the users that the field of view should be kept mostly clear; displaying additional information not continuously but on

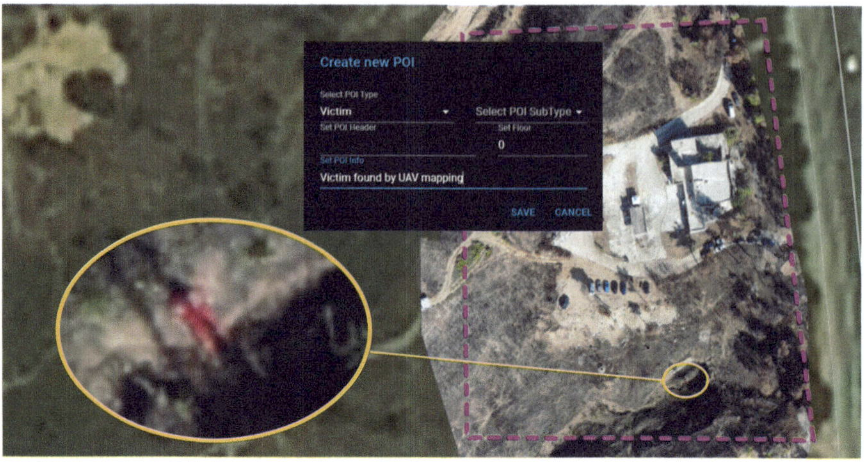

Fig. 19 The results of UAV mapping displayed on the COP. Zooming in, the COP operator can identify a victim laying on the ground and add a label

demand; the repositioning of electronic components in the animal wearable to avoid them snagging in tight spaces; and the total redesign of the UAV gesture-control app, replacing the LeapMotion controller with the HoloLens 2 for gesture acquisition, after the former was observed to underperform outdoors, especially in bright sunlight.

Later pilots, particularly those held in the final 7 months of the project before its conclusion in April 2022, focused on larger-scale demonstrations, evaluation of the completed tools, and deployment in approximations of real operational conditions. Five such pilots were held, increasing in scope and realism as the date approached the project's end:

The first of these final pilots was held in late October 2021 in Athens, Greece. Hosted by the Hellenic Rescue Team of Attica (HRTA), it centered around a scenario of search and rescue following an earthquake, in and around a damaged building. Local HRTA responders were joined by small delegations from the French National Fire Officers Academy (ENSOSP—France) and the Municipality of Grandola (Portugal). The scenario followed a realistic operational procedure, moving through the different phases of search and rescue and involving the FASTER toolkit at key points. Volunteers played the parts of victims, both outdoors and in different points inside the building. The FASTER COP was set up before the start of the mission and aided in the coordination and monitoring of its progress. The automated 2D drone mapping located the outdoor victims as well as a number of vehicles blocking access to the site (Fig. 19). Individual FRs wore the smart textile framework and had their health status and position monitored by the COP. The HoloLens situational awareness app was used extensively, aiding FR navigation by tracking their location on the minimap and visualizing points of interest created by the COP while also allowing the user to tag victims found indoors by dynamically created, additional POIs. The RESCUE box allowed the establishment of communications with rescuers deployed in the basement, where no GSM or Wi-Fi signals could penetrate.

The next testing event took place in early November 2021 at ENSOSP's training facilities in Aix-en-Provence, France. In contrast with other events, it did not follow a scenario, focusing rather on presenting selected tools to local FRs and providing short, hands-on training sessions. More than 20 ENSOSP firefighters participated, training in UAV gesture control and extended vision, 2D mapping using the COP interface, MORSE, and the situational awareness AR app. Trainees' evaluation was positive, indicating that tools were easy to learn and use. However, this event highlighted connectivity as one of the weaker points in the toolkit, as Wi-Fi could not penetrate easily the thick reinforced walls of the ENSOSP test buildings (built to withstand fire). In addition, memory management issues became apparent when testing 2D mapping on lower-end smartphones and tablets, leading to an upgrade of that tool to become both more memory-efficient and robust in case of application crashes.

January 2022 saw a piloting event in Turin, Italy, hosted by the Region of Piedmont. This event featured a large-scale demonstration and evaluation of the mission management and chatbot tool, with over 100 volunteer responders accessing it and contributing to it simultaneously, both at the pilot site and spread out over a large area. The Turin pilot also offered the opportunity to test collaborative 2D mapping with multiple drones, as local FRs contributed their own drones to cover a larger area faster. This event, although held completely outdoors, was also subject to weak communications, in the form of bad Internet connection and multiple overlapping Wi-Fi networks, all of which degraded the performance of tools. Based on these observations, later events followed a strict Wi-Fi channel allocation and hand multiple 4G access points to different mobile broadband providers, to maximize communications speed and robustness.

The penultimate pilot was held in Kajaani, Finland, in March 2022, hosted by the city of Kajaani and its local FRs. Due to intensely low temperatures, this was a mostly indoor event, excepting drone use. It followed a terrorist attack and hostage scenario and included the majority of FASTER tools, including animal wearables, drones, AR situational awareness, smart textiles, mission management, and more, coordinated by the COP. The scenario followed operational procedures for area assessment, victim evacuation, suspect detection and apprehension, and debriefing. Besides local Finnish FRs, it saw the participation of Spanish responders: (SUMMA paramedics and the Madrid municipal police, including drone experts as well as a K9 dog and handler team).

The final pilot took place in Madrid, Spain, in April 2022. Co-hosted by the Madrid municipal police and the Medical Emergency Service of the Community of Madrid (SUMMA 112), it evolved over 2 days: the first day focused on demonstrations and training of individual FASTER tools, with teams of FRs moving from one tool station to the next; the second day saw an operationally realistic, close to real-time deployment of police and paramedic forces, incorporating FASTER tools at specific points for victim detection and extraction. The full FASTER toolkit took part and was evaluated in this exercise, involving more than 50 FRs, including local responders (Madrid police, SUMMA 112, and ERICAM) as well as teams from other countries (HRTA, Greece; Municipality of Grandola, Portugal; ENSOSP, France). In addition to previously tested tools, this pilot also included UAV supply delivery, additional K9 units testing the animal wearable, and both local and global versions of the COP to maintain some functionalities in case of loss of Internet connection.

Conclusion

In the context of the FASTER project, a series of innovative and interconnected tools were developed for improving the efficiency and safety of first responders during emergency and rescue situations. With the FASTER common operational picture acting as the core and the information fusion and visualization module, the various solutions comprising the toolset are designed to offer improved situational awareness, augmented understanding of the situation, unobstructed communication, team monitoring, better cooperation of the different parties involved, and in general more efficient response to emergency situations.

The requirements and the elements of the project were developed in close cooperation between technology parties and first responder organizations in order to ensure that the proposed solutions align with the needs of the people who are actually on the field and deal with such situations. While the various tools differ in technology readiness, with some, such as chatbot, being based on existing market solutions and others, such as UAV gesture control and extended vision app, being proposed as useful prototypes that while functional have not been tested in large-scale and real-world emergency situations, we believe that FASTER proposes a complete ecosystem of tools for technology-based and technology-assisted search and rescue operations.

As the presented tools were developed in the context of a research project, most are not ready for true operational use yet, spanning technology readiness levels[10] of 5–7. Still, with innovative and emerging technologies gradually becoming integrated for everyday use, the FASTER toolkit offers a realistic glimpse of how disaster response might look like in the near future. The FASTER toolkit was based on the close collaboration of researchers and developers with frontline responders and mission coordinators, beginning at the design phase and culminating in the final large-scale piloting exercises. This not only geared the tools towards real FR needs but also served to familiarize responders of different backgrounds, specialization, and country of origin with innovative technologies like augmented reality, artificial intelligence, and autonomous vehicles. Such convergence between two different points of view—researchers' and responders'—is perhaps the most vital element

[10] https://en.wikipedia.org/wiki/Technology_readiness_level.

that will enable the use of new technologies on the field, transforming the future of disaster response and increasing the safety of both citizens and responders.

Acknowledgments The presented work has been supported by the European Commission-funded program FASTER, under H2020 Grant Agreement 833507. The authors would like to thank the whole of the FASTER consortium, in particular the first responder organizations who tested and evaluated the presented tools: the Hellenic Rescue Team of Attica (HRTA, Greece); the French National Fire Officers Academy (École nationale supérieure des officiers de sapeurs-pompiers – ENSOSP, France); the Madrid Municipal Police (Spain) and the Medical Emergency Service of the Community of Madrid (Servicio de Urgencia Médica de la Comunidad de Madrid – SUMMA 112, Spain); the Emergency and Immediate Response of the Community of Madrid (Emergencia y Respuesta Inmediata de la Comunidad de Madrid – ERICAM, Spain); the City of Kajaani (Finland); the Region of Piedmont; and the Municipality of Grandola (Portugal).

References

Ahn, J., & Han, R. (2012). An indoor augmented-reality evacuation system for the smartphone using personalized pedometry. *Human-Centric Computing and Information Sciences, 2*(1), 1–23.

Alsamhi, S. H., Almalki, F. A., AL-Dois, H., Shvetsov, A. V., Ansari, M. S., Hawbani, A., Gupta, S. K., & Lee, B. (2021). Multi-drone edge intelligence and SAR smart wearable devices for emergency communication. *Wireless Communications and Mobile Computing, 2021*. https://www.hindawi.com/journals/wcmc/2021/6710074/

Basu, M., Bandyopadhyay, S., & Ghosh, S. (2016). Post disaster situation awareness and decision support through interactive crowdsourcing. *Procedia Engineering, 159*, 167–173. https://doi.org/10.1016/j.proeng.2016.08.151. https://www.sciencedirect.com/science/article/pii/S1877705816322998. humanitarian Technology: Science, Systems and Global Impact 2016, HumTech2016.

Berbakov, L., Pavkovic, B., & Vrane, S. (2015). Smart indoor positioning system for situation awareness in emergency situations. In *2015 26th International Workshop on Database and Expert Systems Applications (DEXA)* (pp. 139–143). https://doi.org/10.1109/DEXA.2015.44

Berbakov, L., Tripi, F. N., Abad, A. C., Gómez, J. V., & Pavković, B. (2017). Android application for collaborative mapping in emergency situations. In *2017 25th Telecommunication Forum (TELFOR)* (pp. 1–4). https://doi.org/10.1109/TELFOR.2017.8249442

Endsley, M. R. (1995). Toward a theory of situation awareness in dynamic systems. *Human Factors, 37*(1), 32–64. https://doi.org/10.1518/001872095779049543

Frøland, T. H., Heldal, I., Ersvær, E., & Sjøholt, G. (2020). State-of-the-art and future directions for using augmented reality head mounted displays for first aid live training. In *2020 International Conference on e-Health and Bioengineering (EHB)*(pp 1–6). IEEE.

Grogan, S., Pellerin, R., & Gamache, M. (2018). The use of unmanned aerial vehicles and drones in search and rescue operations–a survey. In *Proceedings of the PROLOG 2018–the 4th Edition at the Logistics Institute*, Hull, UK, 28–29.

Hackett, S., Cai, Y., & Siegel, M. (2019). Activity recognition from sensor fusion on fireman's helmet. In *2019 12th International Congress on Image and Signal Processing, BioMedical Engineering and Informatics (CISP-BMEI)* (pp. 1–6). IEEE.

He, K., Zhang, X., Ren, S., & Sun, J. (2016). Deep residual learning for image recognition. In *Proceedings of the IEEE Conference on Computer Vision and Pattern Recognition (CVPR)*.

Jo, D., & Kwon, Y. (2017). Development of rescue material transport UAV (unmanned aerial vehicle). *World Journal of Engineering and Technology, 5*(4), 720–729.

Kirillov, A., Girshick, R. B., He, K., & Dollár, P. (2019). Panoptic feature pyramid networks. In *2019 IEEE/CVF Conference on Computer Vision and Pattern Recognition (CVPR)* (pp. 6392–6401).
Kunnath, A. T., Pradeep, P., & Ramesh, M. V. (2012). Locating and monitoring emergency responder using a wearable device. In *Proceedings of the International Conference on Advances in Computing, Communications and Informatics* (pp. 1163–1168).
Pogrebnyakov, N., & Maldonado, E. (2018). Didn't roger that: Social media message complexity and situational awareness of emergency responders. *International Journal of Information Management, 40*, 166–174. https://doi.org/https://doi.org/10.1016/j.ijinfomgt.2018.02.004. https://www.sciencedirect.com/science/article/pii/S026840121730138X
Ren, S., He, K., Girshick, R., & Sun, J. (2016). Faster R-CNN: Towards real-time object detection with region proposal networks. arXiv:1506.01497.
Sebillo, M., Vitiello, G., Paolino, L., & Ginige, A. (2016). Training emergency responders through augmented reality mobile interfaces. *Multimedia Tools and Applications, 75*(16), 9609–9622.
Sharma, S., Stigall, J., & Bodempudi, S. T. (2020). Situational awareness-based augmented reality instructional (ARI) module for building evacuation. In *2020 IEEE Conference on Virtual Reality and 3D User Interfaces Abstracts and Workshops (VRW)* (pp 70–78). IEEE.
Tashakkori, H., Rajabifard, A., Kalantari, M., & Aleksandrov, M. (2015). Indoor incident situation awareness using a 3d indoor/outdoor spatial city model. In *2015 2nd International Conference on Information and Communication Technologies for Disaster Management (ICT-DM)* (pp 240–245). https://doi.org/10.1109/ICT-DM.2015.7402050
Tomaszewski, B., Judex, M., Szarzynski, J., Radestock, C., & Wirkus, L. (2015). Geographic information systems for disaster response: A review. *Journal of Homeland Security and Emergency Management, 12*(3), 571–602.
Van de Walle, B., Brugghemans, B., & Comes, T. (2016). Improving situation awareness in crisis response teams: An experimental analysis of enriched information and centralized coordination. *International Journal of Human-Computer Studies, 95*, 66–79. https://doi.org/10.1016/j.ijhcs.2016.05.001. https://www.sciencedirect.com/science/article/pii/S1071581916300441
Watson, H., & Rodrigues, R. (2018). Bringing privacy into the fold: Considerations for the use of social media in crisis management. *Journal of Contingencies and Crisis Management, 26*(1), 89–98. https://doi.org/10.1111/1468-5973.12150. https://onlinelibrary.wiley.com/doi/abs/10.1111/1468-5973.12150
Zhu, Y., & Li, N. (2021). Virtual and augmented reality technologies for emergency management in the built environments: A state-of-the-art review. *Journal of Safety Science and Resilience, 2*(1), 1–10. https://doi.org/10.1016/j.jnlssr.2020.11.004. https://www.sciencedirect.com/science/article/pii/S266644962030030X

Intelligent Building Evacuation: From Modeling Systems to Behaviors

Mahyar T. Moghaddam, Henry Muccini, and Julie Dugdale

Abstract Disaster risk management requires new approaches and mechanisms to improve citizens' safety in disasters. The Internet of Things (IoT) is among the technologies that could enhance awareness by providing real-time information. When an emergency happens, building occupants need to be evacuated to safe areas in the shortest possible time. Optimization algorithms could receive humans' mobility data from IoT resources and calculate the best route to follow. The algorithm we present in this chapter formulates and solves a linearized, time-indexed flow problem on a network that represents feasible movements of people at a suitable frequency. We evaluate the performance of the IoT system, including the algorithm, to confirm compliance with real-time use. While the optimization method gives a best case scenario, it does not reflect actual human behavior in evacuation. Humans may stay calm and follow our IoT system's instructions, but they may also have different characteristics and contexts or experience panic attacks, or emotional and social attachment. Thus, we recreate our scenarios with agent-based social simulations, which model occupants as computational agents in an artificial society. The simulations give insights towards a more efficient IoT infrastructure design. We apply our approach to a real location with actual data to prove its feasibility.

Keywords Emergency management · Internet of things · Internet of behaviors · Built environments · Performance · Software architecture · Agent-based

---

M. T. Moghaddam (✉)
University of Southern Denmark, Odense, Denmark
e-mail: mtmo@mmmi.sdu.dk

H. Muccini
University of L'Aquila, L'Aquila, Italy
e-mail: henry.muccini@univaq.it

J. Dugdale
University Grenoble Alps, Grenoble, France
e-mail: julie.dugdale@imag.fr

H. J. Scholl et al. (eds.), *Disaster Management and Information Technology*, Public Administration and Information Technology 40,
https://doi.org/10.1007/978-3-031-20939-0_7

modeling · Human behavior modeling · Social attachment · Simulation · Optimization · Network flow

Introduction

The aggressive and unpredictable nature of hazards requires designing dynamic evacuation plans. Equipping buildings with the Internet of Things (IoT) resources can provide real-time awareness about, e.g., dangerous areas, congestions, and obstacles. IoT infrastructures are mainly composed of sensing, computation, actuating, and network facilities distributed over physical spaces (Muccini & Moghaddam, 2018; Muccini et al., 2018). The way those components are related and combined is specified by software architectures. In the emergency management context, IoT could adopt logic and rules to facilitate occupants' safety by tracking them, detecting bottlenecks, and updating safe evacuation paths.

Essential questions are as follows: (i) How can evacuation be facilitated by showing occupants the quickest path towards safe areas? (ii) How should IoT infrastructures be designed to be able to tackle the contextual and internal changes? (iii) How can dynamic (and sometimes irrational) human behavior be analyzed and considered in designing IoT infrastructures?

A building can be modeled as a network of *nodes* (corresponding to the building's space, organized into suitable square cells) and *arcs* (representing passages between adjacent cells). Such a model can be combinatorial since it could decompose both space (building plan) and time dimension into finite elements: unit cells and time slots. We previously proposed a network flow algorithm (Arbib et al., 2018, 2019b,a) that acts as the decision-maker of IoT-based evacuation infrastructures reacting to environmental events. IoT cameras continuously monitor the cells' occupancy and the flow among them. Collected data are used to create a second acyclic digraph, indexed on time, which models all the feasible transitions between adjacent cells at any given time slot and given the current occupancy status of each cell. Minimizing the total evacuation time then corresponds to solving a mathematical program that, in the final refinement, has the form of a linear optimization problem.

In addition to minimizing evacuation time, IoT architects should establish mechanisms to reduce the system response time by self-adaptive software architectures. Minimizing the response time of IoT-based emergency management systems is critical since endangered people need to receive the routing guide as quickly as possible. In self-adaptive systems, the position of computation could be dynamically changed if a quality issue is perceived. In other words, running the evacuation algorithm on a local server can enhance the performance in specific conditions. However, in a different situation, it may be more efficient to run it on the cloud. An adaptation manager typically performs the adaptation control that comprises the application logic and supervises the managed system (Moghaddam et al., 2021, 2020). We use queuing networks (Arbib et al., 2019a) to test the performance of our IoT system.

Considering human behavior is another crucial factor. In the context of socio-technical IoT (Dugdale et al., 2020) and Internet of Behaviors (IoB) (Moghaddam et al., 2022; Alipour et al., 2021, 2020), humans are immersed in the system, and their behaviors impact the system's quality and functionality. Our vision is that individual (goals, intentions, context, etc.) and social (collective social behaviors, social links, collaborations, etc.) dimensions of software systems are essential elements that must be considered when designing architectures for IoT applications. We propose an agent-based modeling (ABM) approach to model humans and their individual and social behaviors. In this way, we put humans, their context, goals, and safety at the heart of IoT system design while at the same time considering the software quality.

This chapter presents the following contributions:

- A self-adaptive IoT system that adopts an optimization algorithm and tackles the contextual and internal risks
- An ABM that models and simulates human behavior in disaster risk situations
- Applying our dynamic emergency evacuation approach to a real case, an exhibition venue in the Alan Turing Building at the University of L'Aquila, Italy

The chapter is structured as follows. Relevant literature is discussed in Section "Related Work". Section "An Intelligent Infrastructure for Evacuation" proposes the IoT infrastructure and its software architecture. The optimization algorithm for quick evacuation is presented in Section "A Flow Model for Quick Evacuation", and human behavior modeling is defined and developed in Section "Human Behavior Modeling in Evacuation". The application of the model to a real exhibition venue is presented in Section "Application". Lessons learned are given in Section "Lessons Learned", and conclusions are finally drawn in Section "Conclusion".

Related Work

Information technologies are receiving increasing attention in the emergency management domain (Huggins & Prasanna, 2020; Luna & Pennock, 2018). However, the use of IoT for evacuation planning is not widely explored. Some studies (Saini et al., 2022) distribute the processing over different computation layers to form a hybrid architecture (Muccini & Moghaddam, 2018). In those architectures, IoT resources capture the contextual data, and the fog layer analyzes the data and detects an emergency. The cloud layer then facilitates an evacuation algorithm to compute the safe and fast routes. Some studies focus on networking in cloud-based systems (Chung & Park, 2016) to obtain rapid and smooth responses to disasters. In that case, building local wireless disaster information network systems connected to each other delivers information about disaster situations. Some studies (Franchi et al., 2019) focus on fifth-generation (5G) mobile networks to facilitate IoT-based disaster management systems. 5G provides high reliability and performance when the IoT hardware, network infrastructure, and software platforms are natively integrated.

Literature rarely discusses the performance of IoT-based emergency management systems. In general, queuing networks (QNs) provide editors and environments for analyzing the performance of IoT systems (Arbib et al., 2019a). QNs are used as an analytic model for IoT systems (El Kafhali et al., 2018) to reduce the cost of computing resources while guaranteeing performance constraints. QNs also help to predict the system's response time (Huang et al., 2018) and estimate the minimum required processing resources to meet the service level agreement. QNs also model self-adaptive systems by separating the concerns in the environment from infrastructure events analysis (Moghaddam et al., 2020, 2021). For instance, Jung et al. (2008) takes advantage of layered QNs while considering the run-time quality of service (QoS) to automatically generate adaptation policies. Moghaddam et al. (2020) used QNs to model the IoT architectural adaptation and control mechanism. In such systems, functional control elements are in charge of environmental adaptation, and autonomic control elements handle the functional system's architectural adaptation.

Apart from the IoT infrastructure and its quality concerns, a suitable routing algorithm should enable quick evacuation. In the domain of evacuation routing, pioneering work was done by Choi et al. (1988) who modeled a building evacuation problem by dynamic flow maximization where arc capacities depend on flows in incident arcs. Although dating back to the 1980s and limited to a theoretical analysis, the paper provides a good starting point and deserves consideration in the light of the progress done in linear programming solution tools. Chen and Feng (2009) propose a flow control algorithm to compute evacuation paths according to the building plan and the total number of evacuees. The model aims at minimizing total evacuation time while assigning an optimal number of evacuees to each evacuation path. However, as network size increases, the associated problem can no longer be solved in real time. Some researchers (Schloter & Skutella, 2017) base evacuation planning on a transshipment problem, and some (Abdelghany et al., 2014) integrate genetic algorithms with a microscopic pedestrian simulation assignment model. One crucial issue addressed by the recent literature is the ability to find suitable solutions in a short time as required by a practical computational core of a real-time IoT system.

Guiding people based on an optimization algorithm could be desirable, but people may not follow the given guides. For the simulation of human behavior, agent-based social simulations (ABSS) are a good tool (Dugdale et al., 2019). In ABSS, an agent is defined as an autonomous software entity that can act upon and perceive its environment (Ferber & Weiss, 1999). When agents are put together, they form an artificial society, each perceiving, moving, performing actions, communicating, and transforming the local environment, much like human beings in real society. In ABSS, the agents typically represent humans or groups of humans interacting with the environment (Dugdale, 2013). An effective method used to model pedestrian movement in agent-based systems is the social force model (Helbing & Molnar, 1995; Beck et al., 2014). A belief-desire-intention (BDI) agent architecture (Rao et al., 1995) can be used to model the cognitive reasoning of individual human agents. Our simulation environment (PedSim Pedestrian Simulator, 2022) comprises *a 2D/3D map, humans, obstacles, points of interest,* and *IoT resources*. A person can have some points of interest, and they stop when they are sufficiently attracted to this point of interest. When the simulation starts, the simulator generates a routing graph from all obstacles on the map that is automatic and based on run-time situations. The agents find their planned and potential routes from the edges of the route graph.

An Intelligent Infrastructure for Evacuation

An IoT-based emergency evacuation system can collect human and disaster data to be analyzed for further actuation. For such an application, suitable architectures that are automatically adapted based on system and environment dynamics are required. In previous work (Moghaddam et al., 2021; Muccini & Moghaddam, 2018), we proposed three architectural patterns as shown in Fig. 1. The patterns are composed of an *IoT element* layer and one or several *control* layers. The control can be performed locally and/or centrally and remotely. It is here where a centralized cloud and distributed edge and fog can form the *hierarchical* pattern. Thus, the patterns (Moghaddam & Muccini, 2019) characterize *IoT* systems based on their levels of *distribution* and *collaboration* (Muccini & Moghaddam, 2018). Distribution specifies whether data analysis software ought to be deployed on a single node (*centralized*) or on several nodes (*distributed* and *hierarchical)* that are

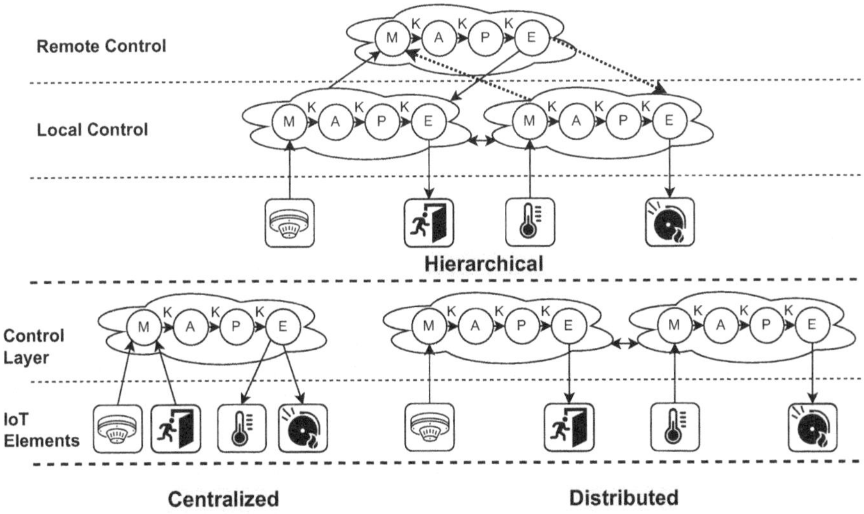

Fig. 1 *IoT* architectural patterns based on control components' composition. The *centralized* pattern comprises processing on a *central local* or *remote* controller. The *distributed* pattern includes the processing on *independent* or *collaborative* controllers. The *hierarchical* pattern contains *independent* or *hybrid* (i.e., with distributed collaborative) controllers

dispersed across the *IoT* system. Collaboration involves interaction among control components to satisfy the goals, requirements, and strategies. This collaboration may appear as a level of information sharing, coordinated analysis or planning, or synchronized execution (Muccini et al., 2018).

Self-adaptation is based on a *MAPE-K* (*monitor, analysis, plan, execute, and comprehensive knowledge*) approach. The *monitor* element aggregates and refines the data to be analyzed and updates the *knowledge* base of the control component. The *analyze* element interprets the monitored data based on the functional goals. The *plan* element builds actuation strategies, and the *execute* element processes the actuation strategies and prepares the type of message to be set to each set of actuators.

For the three patterns mentioned above, the computational component will thus become the central element that will provide evacuation recommendations while inputting situational awareness information. This central computational component has a mathematical logic that is proposed as an algorithm in the following section. In addition to running the algorithm, the presented architectures contain the mechanisms to determine the required architectural adaption based on the intended quality of service satisfaction level. The concept does not rely on any specific tool; thus, practical modeling solutions can be mapped within it. Section "Application" describes the steps taken to map the emergency handling system using this approach to improve its performance indices.

A Flow Model for Quick Evacuation

The following network construction basically follows Choi et al. (1988) and Arbib et al. (2018). The topology of the building to be evacuated is described by a graph $G = (V, A)$ that in Choi et al. (1988) is called a *static network*. Nodes of G correspond to the unit cells i obtained by embedding the building into a suitable grid that will be discussed in Section "Application". In general, cells may have different shapes or sizes: in our work, what is essential is that every cell can be traversed, in any direction, in a single time slot. Cell 0 conventionally represents the outside of the building or, in general, a safe place. Safe places can be disconnected areas, but as their capacity is assumed to be large enough to guarantee safety, we represent them all by a single cell (therefore, what we assume about cells traversing time does not apply to cell 0). The arcs of G correspond to passages between adjacent cells: the passage has full capacity if cells share a boundary that is not interrupted by walls; otherwise, it has a reduced capacity. With no loss of generality, arcs are directed. Let us denote:

T $= \{0, 1, \ldots, \tau\}$, set of unit time slots.

y_i^t = state of cell $i \in V$ at time $t \in T$, that is, the number of persons that occupy i at t: this number is a known model parameter for $t = 0$ (in particular, $y_0^0 = 0$) and a decision variable for $t > 0$.

n_i = capacity of cell i: it measures the maximum nominal amount of people that i can host at any time (in particular, $n_0 \geq \sum_i y_i^0$); this amount depends on cell shape and size; if cells can be assumed uniform, one can set $n_i = n$ for all $i \in V, i \neq 0$.

x_{ij}^t = how many persons move from cell i to an adjacent cell j in $(t, t+1]$: this gives the average speed at which the flow proceeds from i to j.

c_{ij} = c_{ji} = capacity of the passage between cell i and cell j: this is the maximum amount of people that, independently of how many persons are in cell j, can traverse the passage in the time unit (independence from cell occupancy means neglecting system congestion: we will consider this issue later).

The flow model uses an acyclic digraph D with node set $V \times T$ and arc set

$$E = \{(i,t) \to (j,t+1) : ij \in A, t \in T\}$$

Referred to as τ*-time* or a *dynamic network* in Choi et al. (1988), D models all the feasible transitions (i.e., moves between adjacent cells) that can occur in the building in the time horizon T. Transitions are associated with the x-variables defined above, whereas y-variables define the occupancy of each room (and of the building) from time to time. The x- and y-variables are integers and subject to the following constraints:

$$y_j^t - y_j^{t-1} - \sum_{i:ij \in A} x_{ij}^{t-1} + \sum_{i:ji \in A} x_{ji}^{t-1} = 0 \qquad j \in V, t \in T, t > 0 \tag{1}$$

$$0 \leq x_{ij}^t + x_{ji}^t \leq c_{ij} \qquad t \in T, ij \in A \tag{2}$$

$$0 \leq y_i^t \leq n_i \qquad t \in T, i \in V \tag{3}$$

Equation (1) is just a flow conservation law: it expresses the occupancy of cell j at time t as the number y_j^{t-1} of persons present at time $t-1$, augmented by those that during interval $(t-1, t]$ move to j from another cell $i \neq j$ minus those that in the same interval leave cell j for another room $i \neq j$. Box constraints (2), (3) reflect the limited hosting capability of the elements of G.

Maximizing Outflow in a Given Time To model the relation between time and people outflow, we can try to maximize the number of persons evacuated from the building within τ:

$$\max \quad y_0^\tau \tag{4}$$

To find the minimum total evacuation time, we can solve a max flow problem for different τ, looking for the smallest value that yields a zero-valued optimal solution.

To reduce computation time, this optimal τ can be computed by logarithmic search. The method can thus provide the decision-maker with the Pareto frontier of the conflicting objectives $\min\{\tau\} and \max\{y_0^\tau\}$. Linearizing arc capacities, which is quite standard in applications, can be found in our previous work (Muccini et al., 2019). The presented optimization model could result in a quick evacuation. However, people do not always behave in an optimal way, and how this has been taken into account in the simulator is discussed below.

Human Behavior Modeling in Evacuation

The agent-based model for IoT socio-technical systems consists of four classes of agents, *humans, cyber elements, physical space, and IoT resources*, which all are part of the *environment* class. A class is, by definition, a template for an agent. When the model is implemented and the simulator is run, various agents within the same class but with potentially different attributes satisfy the social behavior and contextual heterogeneity. For instance, many human agents with the same attributes are created but with possibly different values for the attributes, thus creating a heterogeneous artificial society.

Environment agents represent the perimeter within which the agents interact with each other. In IoT, the environment could be an indoor or outdoor space containing humans, physical space (including IoT resources), and cyber elements.

Human agents represent occupants and are modeled using the a belief-desire-intention (BDI) architecture. A *belief* represents the agent's own knowledge of events and locations. A *desire* outlines the motivational state of an agent, activities that the agent would like to perform. An *intention* represents the deliberative state of an agent, i.e., a selected desire. Once an intention is chosen, the agent develops a plan to achieve that intention (goal). The agent's decision-making and dynamic path routing are influenced by the desire to avoid congestion and obstacles. Human agents have attributes such as movement speed, perceptive radius, vision, social force (personal and interpersonal radius), and social attachment. This is updated using real geospatial data obtained from the IoT infrastructure.

Physical space agents represent the topology of the space, such as obstacles, walls, doors, passageways, and installed devices. These agents have certain forces and characteristics, such as wall force, passageway, and door flow capacity. The physical space is divided into cells, each containing human agents, and the flow between those cells represents the occupants' mobility.

IoT resources agents are a category of physical space agents that capture human agents' mobility behavior and give human agents instructions. The IoT physical resources include sensors, network facilities, processors, and actuators. IoT resources agents' behavior is in line with their proper functionality, their mobile or static position, and their coverage.

Cyber elements agents represent the software that is run on the IoT resources agents. They provide cyber twins for sensing, network, processing, and actuating and reflect the attributes of physical space agents. Their behavior is specified by their level of functionality and quality.

Application

Our proposed model has been applied to the evacuation of the Alan Turing building, in Italy, which is sometimes used for exhibitions. The building consists of 29 rooms, 4 main corridors, and 34 sets of IoT sensors and actuators. Room sizes vary greatly and, as a consequence, so does the average time for a person to cross them from door to door. The complex building structure, as well as data on people attendance collected during events, made this study case ideal for illustrating a general methodology for system sizing and development. We run various simulations to assess the application of our models on:

- Discovering the optimal evacuation time that results from crowd routing via ideal evacuation paths and comparing it with the evacuation time that derives from static shortest paths (Section "Algorithm Simulations")
- Evaluating the performance of the IoT infrastructure that runs the algorithm (Section "Algorithm Simulations")
- Providing guidelines about human behavior in an emergency (Section "Algorithm Simulations")

Algorithm Simulations

We split each room into unit cells, behaving like a (virtual) square room that can be traversed in a unit time slot. In practice, we embedded the building plan into a square grid as shown in Fig. 2. To decide the cell size, we looked at both the error (areas not covered by cells) introduced by room approximation and the number of nodes in the resulting graph G. The latter is in an inverse proportion of cell size; the former varies irregularly with cell size (for more details, see Arbib et al., 2019b). We considered square cells of 3×3 meters, which led to only 144 nodes (Fig. 3). The selected cell size reduces the largest error for all rooms and facilitates IoT camera monitoring.

Simulation The simulation code was written in the OPL language, and problems were solved by CPLEX version 12.8.0. All experiments were run on a Core i7 2.7 GHz computer with 16Gb of RAM under Windows 10 pro 64-bits. In all tests, we computed the minimum time required for 225 persons, randomly distributed in the building rooms, to reach a safe place. This data comes from an experiment performed in the building during the *researchers' night* event when the IoT system

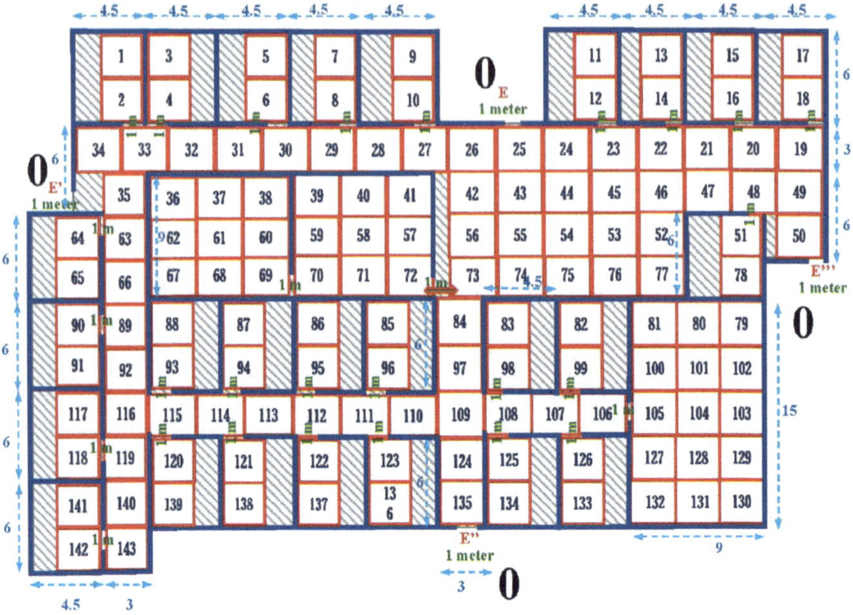

Fig. 2 Plan embedding the Alan Turing building into square grids with a low resolution: 3 × 3 cells. The area that is not covered by cells (error) is shown in gray

recorded the simultaneous presence of 225 people as a peak value. We solved problem (1–4) for $\tau = 1, 2, \ldots$ until a solution of value 225 was found.

To get a reliable model, some parameters such as walking velocity under various conditions, door entrance capacities, and room capacities were set to numbers that reflect reality. We set these model parameters based on empirical observations reported in the literature (Table 1).

Table 2 reports the number of evacuees at each τ and the computation time of each solution step. In terms of evacuation, everyone has reached a safe place in 47.5 seconds; on the other hand, computation requires 1.82 seconds in the worst case and is therefore totally compliant with real-time applications.

This simulation depicts an ideal situation in which human agents autonomously choose the best among all the available routes in the building. Of course, managing such an ideal evacuation is not easy and perhaps unpractical. As a general practice, evacuation is conducted through predetermined routes. Considering this fact, we suppose that the prescribed evacuation routes are the shortest paths from any cell to a safe place. To evaluate this situation, we find the subgraph of G formed by the shortest paths from any cell to 0 (as from a static evacuation map), construct its time-indexed network, and solve the problem (1)–(4) for increasing τ. Evacuating 225 individuals takes, of course, more time: 1 minute and 10 seconds. Thus, compared to

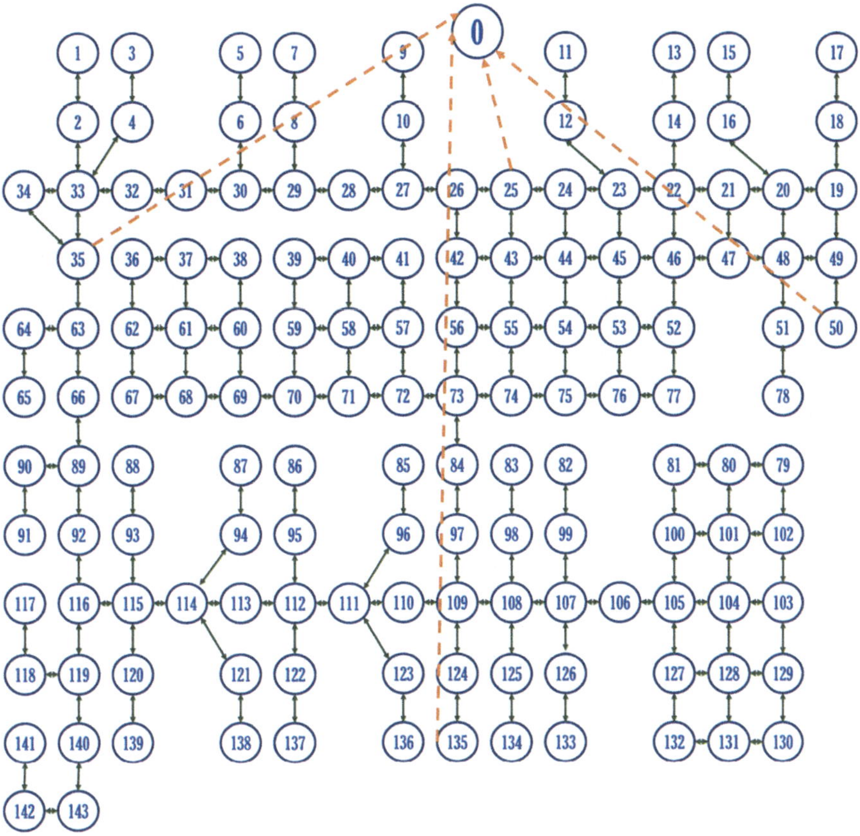

Fig. 3 Network associated with the plan of Fig. 2

Table 1 Evacuation model parameters

Model parameter	Assigned value
Walking velocity	1.2 m/s (Ye et al., 2008a)
Door capacity	1.2 p/m/s (Daamen & Hoogendoorn, 2012)
Cell capacity	1.25 p/m^2 (Matthews, 2015)

the Netflow model we propose, the shortest routes increase, in this case, the optimal evacuation time by 47% (Fig. 4).

Comparing Netflow and the shortest path, there are similar flows for 15 seconds. After that, the shortest paths approach experiences congestion, and evacuation slows down.

Table 2 Evacuation and computation time for 3 × 3 cells with time slots of 2.5 seconds

Tau	Evacuees	CPU time	Tau	Evacuees	CPU time
1	12	0.65 sec	11	132	0.96 sec
2	24	0.50 sec	12	144	1.11 sec
3	36	0.54 sec	13	156	1.18 sec
4	48	0.63 sec	14	168	1.30 sec
5	60	0.65 sec	15	180	1.52 sec
6	72	0.80 sec	16	192	1.40 sec
7	84	0.77 sec	17	204	1.52 sec
8	96	0.89 sec	18	216	1.78 sec
9	108	0.87 sec	19	225	1.82 sec
10	120	1.20 sec			

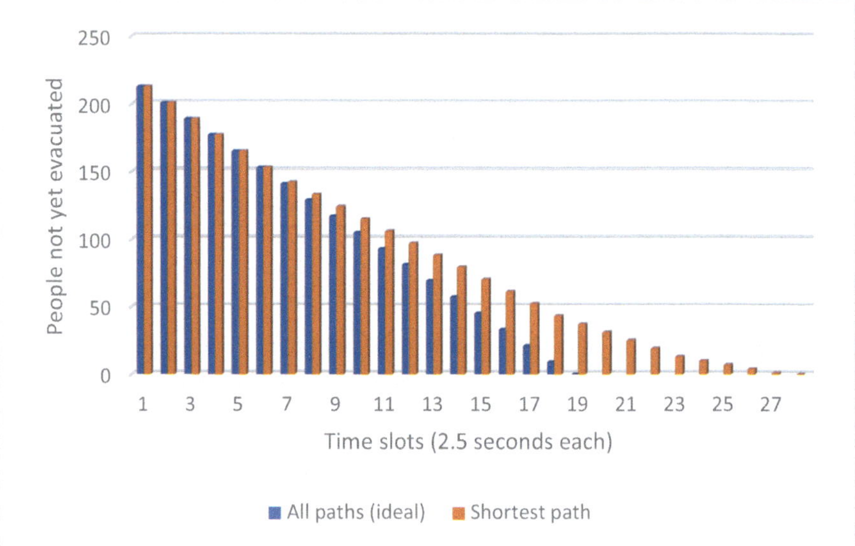

Fig. 4 Ideal vs. shortest paths evacuation

Software Architecture Simulations

In the suggested IoT-based environment for emergency response, CCTV cameras detect people's position and movement and feed them into the running algorithm. The algorithm decides on the actuation set based on the situation. As shown in Fig. 5, additional sets of sensors can be embedded for emergency detection to further enable controllers to decide about normal or critical mode and activate a particular set of actuators. In normal situations, the system shows a 2D representation of the monitored space and the crowd's position and movement. In this mode, the optimal flow algorithm is periodically run to estimate the minimum evacuation time required under current conditions. If an emergency happens, in addition to

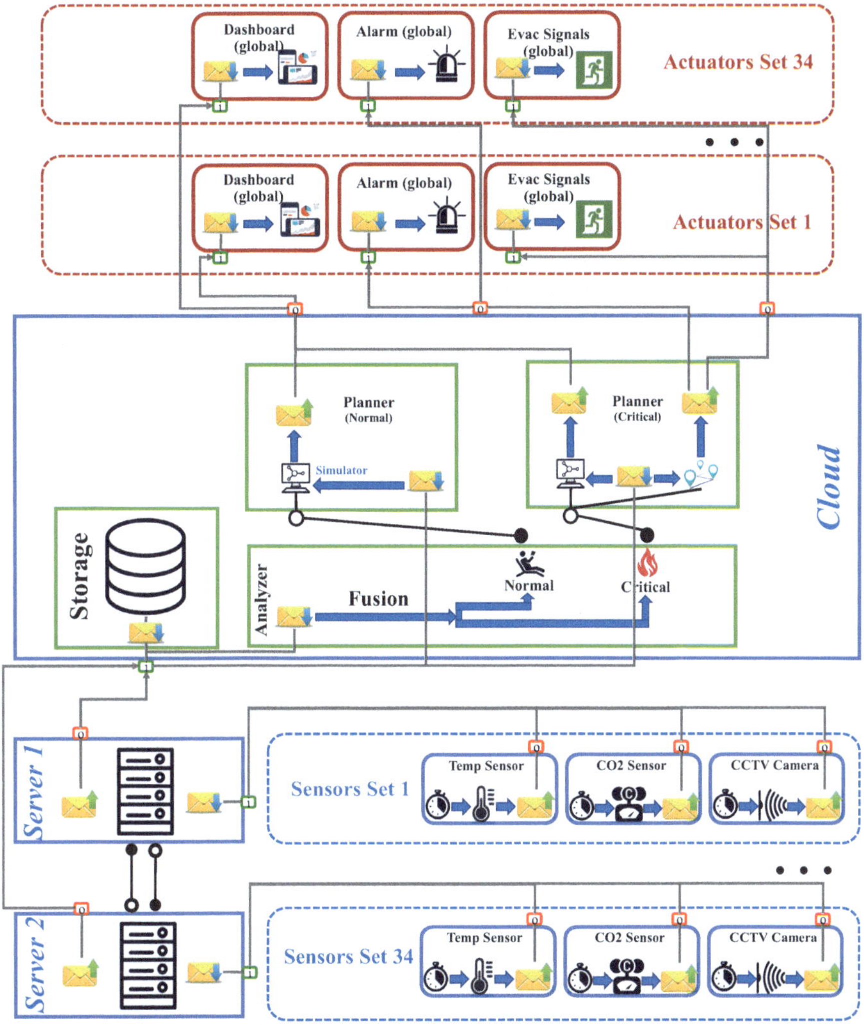

Fig. 5 Software architecture of the IoT-based emergency management system

the dashboard, alarm actuators are activated, and evacuation signs in each area show the best evacuation routes based on the network model described above. Specifying the position of computation (i.e., servers, cloud, or a mix of them) determines the architectural patterns at run time (see Section "An Intelligent Infrastructure for Evacuation", Fig. 1).

In our proposed infrastructure, in addition to the computational delay of the processing components, the sensors take some time to detect people's positions, transmit these data, and display the best evacuation routes. Reducing these delays to a minimum improves the system's functionality since people can follow the

Table 3 Response time for different modes and configurations (seconds)

Pattern	Response time (normal)	Response time (critical)
Centralized	1.2	2.65
Distributed	0.55	1.05
Hierarchical	0.95	1.5

given instructions more quickly, and more individuals will be in a better evacuation position at the subsequent monitoring time-spot. Reducing the delays mentioned above is a function of software architectural patterns, which can be improved by adequately relating the IoT components to one another. Using a probabilistic routing strategy, we modeled the same system with different architectural configurations with QNs. We used JMT (Casale et al., 2009) to model and simulate the QNs. For more information about QN models and service times used for the response time analysis, please see Arbib et al. (2019a).

In our QNs simulation, we assess the response time of the three architectural patterns (presented in Section "An Intelligent Infrastructure for Evacuation") in normal and critical situations. The response time (delay) that is analyzed is the mean time spent from starting the sampling to the time that actuation ends. As shown in Table 3, experimental results show that the distributed pattern minimizes system response time for the normal mode (0.55 seconds). Still, it should be adapted to a hierarchical pattern (1.5 seconds) when an emergency occurs. While the response time associated with the hierarchical pattern is 43% more than distributed (still better than the centralized pattern with a delay equal to 2.65 seconds), our routing algorithm must be run on a single processor.

Human Behavior Simulations

In our agent-based model of the Alan Turing Building, we set the simulation parameters either by using gathered real data or according to the literature. With a real population of 225 occupants in the building, we apply the following parameters:

- *Walking speed*—ranges from 0.7 to 1.2 m/s (Wagnild & Wall-Scheffler, 2013; Tolea et al., 2010).
- *Social force*—0.2 m was used an individual agent's radius by using the *biacromial diameter* in Patil et al. (2017). Thus, agents maintain a certain distance from each other and do not cross through each other. In addition, this eases setting the maximum number of agents per cell, room, and passage flow.
- *Wall force*—0.1 m is the wall force, which means that agents cannot get closer to 0.1m from a wall. The result is that agents do not cling to walls or pass through obstacles.
- Door flow capacity— 1.2 p/m/s, Ye et al. (2008b).
- Cell capacity— 1.25 p/m^2, Daamen and Hoogendoorn (2012).

We use the ***belief-desire-intention*** agent architecture:

- *Belief*—All agents believe that a disaster is happening and that they must seek safety.
- *Desire*—All agents desire or *goal* to reach an exit.
- *Intention*—Since the agents *perceive* their surroundings, they try to find the shortest and/or optimal paths to get to the exit (based on the algorithms).

While the agents have specific points of interest, they could change their target based on some contextual situations such as visible congestion and the intention of their friends or relatives. We set the target switch and abandon time, based on the importance of the agent's point of interest. We ran all the experiments on a *Corei7 2.7 GHz* computer with *16 Gb* of RAM memory under Windows 10 pro *64-bits*. For these simulations, we obtain information regarding the number of visitors who fall under the coverage area of various sensors, the route each agent took, the variation of their velocity, acceleration, stops index, the behavior of each agent (such as obstacle collision avoidance, anticipatory and passive collision avoidance), movement state (e.g., moving and looking), and visiting satisfaction. We also assess the number of visitors who visited a room, their access points, the location of collisions, and any queue length.

We used the historical data to assign different characteristics to human agents regarding age, gender, origin, and physical condition. In fact, each human agent has a profile including vision, maximum speed, and target force that are impacted by their characteristics. We observed various challenges regarding congestion, physical bottlenecks, and grouping. To increase realism, we incorporate social attachment. Congestion is common in emergencies; thus, the agents can form herds, which affect their decisions and movement towards exits. Speed of movement is essential, e.g., a man will walk more slowly to match the speed of a woman (Tolea et al., 2010), and groups of individuals typically move more slowly than a single person (Sarmady et al., 2009). The slow movement of interacting groups can consequently affect evacuation efficiency (Qiu & Hu, 2010). To model such behaviors, groups move at a slower speed than individuals. While these solutions are assessed in the simulation environment, they could provide situational awareness for the stakeholders (managers, operators, and visitors) and show possible movement patterns.

In the next step, we evaluated the optimization algorithms under a realistic situation regarding human behaviors. We considered groups of 3 to 7 agents. This gives an interesting scenario as congestion at exits becomes more pronounced. In this simulation, agents' walking speed varies between 0.7 and 1.2 m/s since the speed of movement depends on other group members and the velocity of the slowest person (Wagnild & Wall-Scheffler, 2013). As shown in Fig. 6, we observed that evacuating 225 agents takes 1 minute and 57.5 seconds with shortest path algorithm and 1 minute and 47.5 seconds with Netflow.

We understood that grouping and attachment slow down evacuation, compared to optimization only. Evacuation time increases with the number of agents because

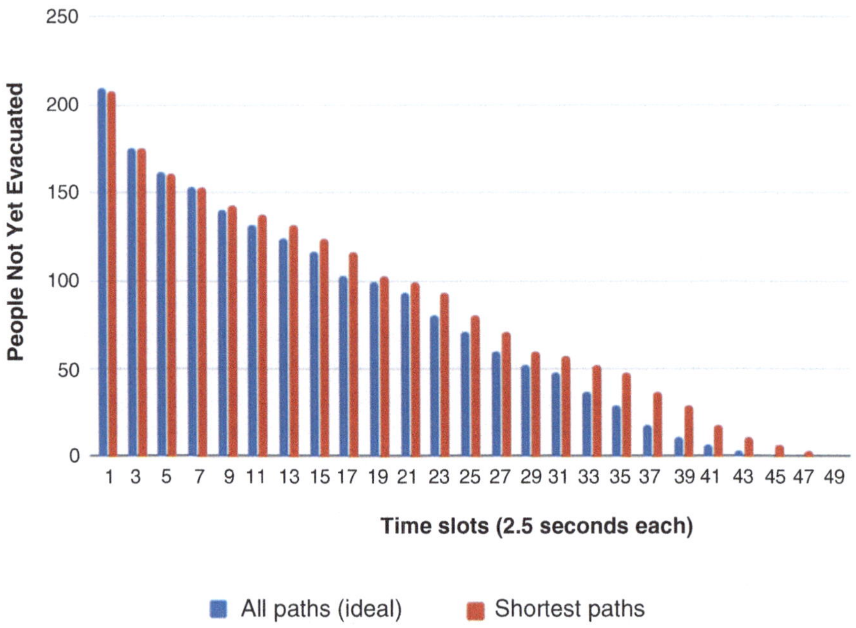

Fig. 6 Netflow vs. shortest path evacuation considering grouping and attachment with 225 agents

socially attached agents will not leave the building without their friends, family, or acquaintances.

Lessons Learned

The discussion of our approach and the results of our evaluation indicate how IoT architects could design an emergency management infrastructure by considering the architecture qualities, algorithm, and human behavior. More specifically, we learned that:

- While the design of a solid software architecture is crucial, its adaptation based on run-time environmental and internal situations could enhance quality.
- The core optimization algorithm for IoT-based emergency evacuation should consider the dynamic flow of people and congestion in order to perform efficiently.
- While an optimization approach is valid, considering realistic human behaviors in emergencies could benefit a solid IoT architectures design.

- Social links and preferences should be seriously considered and modeled within emergency handling systems since they can impact the functionality and quality of the system.
- Simulations enhance situational awareness of occupants, managers, and practitioners and improve their preparedness in case of disasters (Dugdale et al., 2021).

Conclusion

In this chapter, we presented an intelligent IoT infrastructure to handle emergencies. The system gets data from sensors and uses an optimization algorithm to lead people to safe areas as quickly as possible. The response time of the system was also assessed for various architectural patterns. The consideration of human behaviors in such risky situations was addressed by an agent-based modeling approach that gives insights towards a human-oriented design and adaptation of the infrastructure. In future work, the authors will consider more quality attributes such as fault tolerance, availability, and energy efficiency. Moreover, more empirical studies will be performed to get real data to input into simulations. We will explore more the links between human behavior and system behavior in the context of IoT-based emergency management.

Acknowledgments We kindly thank our colleagues Prof. Claudio Arbib and Prof. Paul Davidsson who contributed to the previous version of this chapter. This work is supported by the Innovation Fund Denmark for the project DIREC (9142-00001B) and the VASARI PON R&I 2014–2020 and FSC project.

References

Abdelghany, A., Abdelghany, K., Mahmassani, H., & Alhalabi, W. (2014). Modeling framework for optimal evacuation of large-scale crowded pedestrian facilities. *European Journal of Operational Research, 237*(3), 1105–1118.

Alipour, M., Dupuy-Chessa, S., & Céret, E. (2021). An emotion-oriented problem space for ui adaptation: From a literature review to a conceptual framework. In *2021 9th International Conference on Affective Computing and Intelligent Interaction (ACII)* (pp. 1–8). IEEE.

Alipour, M., Dupuy-Chessa, S., & Jongmans, E. (2020). Disaster mitigation using interface adaptation to emotions: a targeted literature review. In *10th International Conference on the Internet of Things Companion* (pp. 1–15).

Arbib, C., Muccini, H., & Moghaddam, M. T. (2018). Applying a network flow model to quick and safe evacuation of people from a building: A real case. *RSFF, 18*, 50–61.

Arbib, C., Arcelli, D., Dugdale, J., Moghaddam, M., & Muccini, H. (2019a). Real-time emergency response through performant iot architectures. In *International Conference on Information Systems for Crisis Response and Management (ISCRAM)*.

Arbib, C., Moghaddam, M. T., & Muccini, H. (2019b) Iot flows: a network flow model application to building evacuation. In *A View of Operations Research Applications in Italy, 2018*, (pp. 115–131). Springer.

Beck, E., Dugdale, J., Van Truong, H., Adam, C., & Colbeau-Justin, L. (2014). Crisis mobility of pedestrians: from survey to modelling, lessons from lebanon and argentina. In *International Conference on Information Systems for Crisis Response and Management in Mediterranean Countries* (pp. 57–70). Springer.

Bertoli, M., C. G., & Serazzi, G. (2009). Jmt: performance engineering tools for system modeling. In *ACM SIGMETRICS Performance Evaluation Review* (pp. 10–15). ACM.

Chen, P.-H., & Feng, F. (2009). A fast flow control algorithm for real-time emergency evacuation in large indoor areas. *Fire Safety Journal, 44*(5), 732–740.

Choi, W., Hamacher, H. W., & Tufekci, S. (1988). Modeling of building evacuation problems by network flows with side constraints. *European Journal of Operational Research, 35*(1), 98–110.

Chung, K., & Park, R. C. (2016). P2p cloud network services for iot based disaster situations information. *Peer-to-Peer Networking and Applications, 9*(3), 566–577 (2016).

Daamen, W., & Hoogendoorn, S. (2012). Emergency door capacity: influence of door width, population composition and stress level. *Fire Technology, 48*(1), 55–71.

Dugdale, J. (2013). *Human behaviour modelling in complex socio-technical systems: an agent based approach.* PhD Thesis, Université Joseph-Fourier-Grenoble I.

Dugdale, J., Moghaddam, M. T., Muccini, H., & Narayanankutty, H. (2019). A combined netflow-driven and agent-based social modeling approach for building evacuation. In *International Conference on Principles and Practice of Multi-Agent Systems* (pp. 460–468). Springer.

Dugdale, J., Moghaddam, M. T., & Muccini, H. (2020). Human behaviour centered design: developing a software system for cultural heritage. In *Proceedings of the ACM/IEEE 42nd International Conference on Software Engineering: Software Engineering in Society* (pp. 85–94).

Dugdale, J., Moghaddam, M. T., & Muccini, H. (2021). Iot4emergency: Internet of things for emergency management. *ACM SIGSOFT Software Engineering Notes, 46*(1), 33–36.

El Kafhali, S., Salah, K., & Alla, S. B. (2018). Performance evaluation of iot-fog-cloud deployment for healthcare services. In *2018 4th international conference on cloud computing technologies and applications (Cloudtech)* (pp. 1–6). IEEE.

Ferber, J., & Weiss, G. (1999). *Multi-agent systems: An introduction to distributed artificial intelligence* (Vol. 1). Addison-Wesley Reading.

Franchi, F., Marotta, A., Rinaldi, C., Graziosi, F., & D'Errico, L. (2019). Iot-based disaster management system on 5g urllc network. In *2019 International Conference on Information and Communication Technologies for Disaster Management (ICT-DM)* (pp. 1–4). IEEE.

Helbing, D., & Molnar, P. (1995). Social force model for pedestrian dynamics. *Physical Review E, 51*(5), 4282.

Huang, J., Li, S., Chen, Y., & Chen, J. (2018). Performance modelling and analysis for iot services. *International Journal of Web and Grid Services, 14*(2), 146–169.

Huggins, T. J., & Prasanna, R. (2020). Information technologies supporting emergency management controllers in new zealand. *Sustainability, 12*(9), 3716.

Jung, G., Joshi, K. R., Hiltunen, M. A., Schlichting, R. D., & Pu, C. (2008). Generating adaptation policies for multi-tier applications in consolidated server environments. In *2008 International Conference on Autonomic Computing* (pp. 23–32). IEEE.

Luna, S., & Pennock, M. J. (2018). Social media applications and emergency management: A literature review and research agenda. *International journal of disaster risk reduction, 28*, 565–577.

Matthews, D. (2015). *Special event production: The resources.* Routledge.

Moghaddam, M. T., & Muccini, H. (2019). Fault-tolerant IoT. In *International Workshop on Software Engineering for Resilient Systems* (pp. 67–84). Springer.

Moghaddam, M. T., Muccini, H., Dugdale, J., & Kjægaard, M. B. (2022). Designing internet of behaviors systems. In *2022 IEEE 19th International Conference on Software Architecture (ICSA)* (pp. 124–134). IEEE.

Moghaddam, M. T., Rutten, E., & Giraud, G. (2021). Hierarchical control for self-adaptive iot systems a constraint programming-based adaptation approach. In *HICSS 2022*.

Moghaddam, M. T., Rutten, E., Lalanda, P., & Giraud, G. (2020). IAS: an IoT architectural self-adaptation framework. In *European Conference on Software Architecture* (pp. 333–351). Springer.

Muccini, H., Arbib, C., Davidsson, P., & Tourchi Moghaddam, M. (2019). An iot software architecture for an evacuable building architecture. In *Proceedings of the 52nd Hawaii International Conference on System Sciences*.

Muccini, H., & Moghaddam, M. T. (2018). Iot architectural styles. In: *European Conference on Software Architecture* (pp. 68–85). Springer.

Muccini, H., Spalazzese, R., Moghaddam, M. T., & Sharaf, M. (2018). Self-adaptive iot architectures: An emergency handling case study. In *Proceedings of the 12th European Conference on Software Architecture: Companion Proceedings* (pp. 1–6).

Patil, S. S., Jadhav, P. L., Dongare, S. S., & Deokar, R. B. (2017). Correlation of stature to arm span and biacromial shoulder width in young adults of western indian population. *International Journal of Education and Research in Health Sciences, 3*(2), 64–70.

PedSim Pedestrian Simulator (2022). https://www.pedsim.net/, Accessed February 10, 2022.

Qiu, F., & Hu, X. (2010). Modeling group structures in pedestrian crowd simulation. *Simulation Modelling Practice and Theory, 18*(2), 190–205.

Rao, A. S., Georgeff, M. P., et al. (1995). Bdi agents: from theory to practice. In *ICMAS* (Vol. 95, pp. 312–319).

Saini, K., Kalra, S., & Sood, S. K. (2022). Disaster emergency response framework for smart buildings. *Future Generation Computer Systems, 131*, 106–120.

Sarmady, S., Haron, F., & Talib, A. Z. H. (2009). Modeling groups of pedestrians in least effort crowd movements using cellular automata. In *2009 Third Asia International Conference on Modelling & Simulation* (pp. 520–525). IEEE.

Schloter, M., & Skutella, M. (2017). Fast and memory-efficient algorithms for evacuation problems. In *Proceedings of the Twenty-Eighth Annual ACM-SIAM Symposium on Discrete Algorithms* (pp. 821–840). SIAM.

Tolea, M. I., Costa, P. T., Terracciano, A., Griswold, M., Simonsick, E. M., Najjar, S. S., Scuteri, A., Deiana, B., Orrù, M., Masala, M., et al. (2010). Sex-specific correlates of walking speed in a wide age-ranged population. *Journals of Gerontology Series B: Psychological Sciences and Social Sciences, 65*(2), 174–184.

Wagnild, J., & Wall-Scheffler, C. M. (2013). Energetic consequences of human sociality: Walking speed choices among friendly dyads. *PloS one, 8*(10), e76576.

Ye, J., Chen, X., Yang, C., & Wu, J. (2008a). Walking behavior and pedestrian flow characteristics for different types of walking facilities. *Transportation Research Record: Journal of the Transportation Research Board, 2048*, 43–51.

Ye, J., Chen, X., Yang, C., & Wu, J. (2008b). Walking behavior and pedestrian flow characteristics for different types of walking facilities. *Transportation Research Record, 2048*(1), 43–51.

Challenges of Integrating Advanced Information Technologies with 5G in Disaster Risk Management

Dimiter Velev and Plamena Zlateva

Abstract There is a constant increase in the number, intensity, and magnitude of disasters caused by natural phenomena or human activities around the world in recent years. Such disasters adversely affect social relations, economic growth, and sustainable development of the countries. Although many information systems for disaster management try to reduce the possible aftereffects of disasters and assess the damages, they are not always capable of handling the consequences in the right way regardless of the advanced information technologies used. The recent trend toward the integration of advanced IT services becomes more popular with its possible applications in different aspects of life. The aim of this chapter is to investigate the challenges of integrating advanced information technologies with 5G and how this could improve the disaster risk management.

Keywords Natural disaster · IoT · Big data · Cloud computing · 5G · VR · AI

Introduction

In last decades, natural disasters (as earthquakes, landslides, floods, etc.) worldwide have more than tripled, and economic losses have increased more than eight times (United Nations Office for Disaster Risk Reduction (UNISDR), 2015). The monitoring of the natural disasters, the evaluation of their negative impact, and the general risk assessment are decisive steps toward the selection of adequate protective measures.

Natural disaster crises can quickly cross functional, temporal, and even political borders and thus have an effect over multiple regions (Padli et al., 2010). In order

D. Velev (✉)
University of National and World Economy, Sofia, Bulgaria
e-mail: dgvelev@unwe.bg

P. Zlateva
Institute of Robotics – Bulgarian Academy of Sciences & UNWE, Sofia, Bulgaria

H. J. Scholl et al. (eds.), *Disaster Management and Information Technology*,
Public Administration and Information Technology 40,
https://doi.org/10.1007/978-3-031-20939-0_8

to mitigate those increasing negative effects, an increasing number of resources are required, as well as the participation of multiple organizations, which must operate in close coordination in order to minimize human, economic, and ecological losses.

The essence of the successful cooperation is the effective, real-time information exchange between the participating responsible institutions, the ability to quickly make adequate decisions and organize a coordinated response.

It should be noted that advanced information technologies can greatly support achieving such successful cooperation in disaster risk management. Nowadays, many advanced information technologies (as social media, Internet of Things, big data, cloud computing, artificial intelligence, virtual reality, etc.) are being integrated to work together to solve problems related to disaster risk reduction.

The aim of this chapter is to investigate the challenges of integrating advanced information technologies and their applications with 5G and how this could improve the risk management and reduce the negative consequences due to natural disasters.

Current State of ICT Usability for Disaster Management

Organizations are looking for ways to find value in and insight from both structured and unstructured data and from internal and external sources in regard to natural disasters. This is expected to complement but not to replace long-standing information management programs and investments in data warehouses, business intelligence suites, reporting platforms, and relational database experience. The concept of information known as big data is not only managing large volumes of data but also controlling the velocity and variety of data that exists nowadays. The ability to extract data from different sources to perform a specific task and the ability to provide information in real time with the right context are essential.

Currently *social media*, *Internet of Things*, *big data*, *cloud computing*, *artificial intelligence*, and virtual reality are main pillars of information systems for disaster management.

Social Media

The role of social media in the wake of natural disasters is still unclear, but sites like Facebook, Twitter, and YouTube can be of great value when tsunamis, earthquakes, floods, and other natural disasters strike. The functions of social media are as follows (Washington, 2017):

- Provides valuable information to those in a disaster area pre- and post-disaster (via Internet, if available, or SMS updates)
- Drives awareness to those outside the affected areas, generating volunteers and/or donors

- Connects displaced family and friends
- Provides information about unclaimed property, and in worst case scenarios, bodies
- Offers information about aid, centers, and other resources available to those affected

During disasters, social media networks provide an instant view of conditions on the ground.

Generally, social media is used in four ways during a disaster (Afzalan et al., 2013; Rajashree, 2016):

- Sharing information and spreading awareness
- For relief operations – building communities, volunteering, etc.
- For collecting funds
- Monitoring and providing insights to the whole situation

Internet of Things

Internet of Things (IoT) is a network of physical objects or "things" embedded with electronics, software, sensors, and connectivity to enable objects to exchange data with the production, operator, and/or other connected devices (Pethuru & Raman, 2017). The Internet of Things allows objects to be sensed and controlled remotely across existing network infrastructure, creating opportunities for more direct integration between the physical world and computer-based systems, and resulting in improved efficiency, accuracy, and economic benefit. Each thing is uniquely identifiable through its embedded computing system but is able to interoperate within the existing Internet infrastructure. Through IoT, a vast variety of signals can be acquired and measured during disasters which could be used for meaningful interpretation of events.

Big Data

Big data is a broad term for data sets so large or complex that traditional data processing applications are inadequate (Akerkar, 2014; Berman, 2013; Thomas & McSharry, 2015). Challenges include analysis, capture, search, sharing, storage, transfer, visualization, and information privacy (Pedrycz, 2015; Rowan University, 2016). The term often refers simply to the use of predictive analytics or other certain advanced methods to extract value from data and seldom to a particular size of data set. Scientists, practitioners of media and advertising, and governments alike regularly meet difficulties with large data sets in areas including Internet search, finance, and business informatics. Additionally, 11 kinds of big data datasets useful in natural hazards management have been also identified (Innovation Enterprise, 2015; Mongo, 2016):

- Satellite imagery
- Elevation and surface models
- Meteorological data
- Transportation networks data
- Demographics and population density data
- Country and urban borderline data
- Use of land and buildings
- Utility networks
- Critical infrastructures
- Hospitals, schools, and other vulnerable locations and last but not least
- PoI data, which is data practically about any point of interest (PoI) directly or indirectly related to natural hazards management

Cloud Computing

Cloud computing is a model for providing on-demand Internet-based access to a shared pool of virtualized computing resources, including networks, storage, and applications (Bhowmik, 2017). The user of cloud services never has to buy or upgrade computing hardware, not to worry about disaster recovery and significantly simplifying business continuing planning. Cloud computing can provide data-communication-as-a-service solution to emergency management. A cloud computing disaster management system could provide for a dedicated platform to enable users (workers, first responders, local disaster-related nonprofit organizations, volunteers, and local residents) to access information, communicate, and collaborate in real time from all types of computing devices, including mobile handheld devices, such as smartphones and tablets. Such a system could help for the establishment of a community-based, effective, and self-scalable cloud computing environment in which a diverse set of organizations and personnel can contribute their data, knowledge, experience, storage, and computing resources to deal with natural disasters.

The 5G Technology

One of the most significant advances of radio science is the emerging of the 5G technology, although 4G cellular networks have existed for a few years only.

The G in 5G means it is a generation of wireless technology. While most generations have technically been defined by their data transmission speeds, each has also been marked by a break in encoding methods, or "air interfaces," which make it incompatible with the previous generation.

1G was analog cellular; 2G technologies, such as CDMA, GSM, and TDMA, were the first generation of digital cellular technologies; 3G technologies, such as EVDO, HSPA, and UMTS, brought speeds from 200 kbps to several megabits per second; 4G technologies, such as WiMAX and LTE, were the next incompatible leap forward, and they are now scaling up to hundreds of megabits and even gigabit-level speeds (Prasad, 2014; Zander & Mosterman, 2014).

5G is a new network system that has much higher speeds and capacity, and much lower latency, than existing cellular systems. The technologies to be used in 5G are still being defined. 5G networks will use a type of encoding called OFDM, which is similar to the encoding that LTE uses. The air interface will be designed for much lower latency and greater flexibility than LTE.

The new networks can use frequencies as low as old TV channels, or as high as "millimeter wave," which are frequencies that can transmit huge amounts of data, but only a few blocks at a time. 5G may also bring in Wi-Fi as a seamless part of a cellular network or transmit LTE-encoded data over Wi-Fi frequencies, which are called LTE Unlicensed.

The technology 5G networks are much more likely to be networks of small cells, even down to the size of home routers, than to be huge towers radiating great distances. Some of that is because of the nature of the frequencies used, but a lot of that is to expand network capacity (Rodriguez, 2017).

The official 5G standard, known as 5G NR (new radio), will probably be established in 2018 with full commercial implementations in 2020. The goal is to have significantly higher speeds and higher capacity per sector at far lower latency than 4G. The standard bodies involved are aiming at 20 Gbps speeds and 1 ms latency, at which point very interesting applications are to happen.

Main implications of 5G will emphasize on the following (Bizaki, 2017; Varrall, 2016; Wei et al., 2017):

- High capacity – 5G will be required to handle the traffic generated by the expected 28 billion connected devices in 2021. This means that multiple people will be able to stream videos, play games, and use virtual reality without any delays.
- Faster data throughput – Not only will 5G networks have high capacity to handle large amounts of data – they will be able to process that data at speeds never achieved before, such as video-viewing experience will be as smooth as possible.
- High reliability – Within the 5G technology, gaps or lags in connectivity simply will be not acceptable, so entertainment applications will be implemented interruption.

The emerging 5G technology will enable numerous improvements in many industry areas, such as fixed wireless broadband, manufacturing, smart living, health care, transportation, education, media and gaming, virtual reality, Internet by drones (European Commission, 2015; Huawei, 2017; Qualcomm, 2016). Evidently, such a promising technology should have its place in information systems for natural disasters.

Artificial Intelligence

Intelligence concerns the human brain, mind, involvement, logical thinking, understanding, and applicability. In general, intelligence can be well defined as an individual's capability to do things effectively by using own knowledge, interpretation, and insight. The term artificial intelligence (AI) was defined by John McCarthy, a Stanford University emeritus professor of computer science, as "the science and engineering of making intelligent machines," particularly intelligent software program. Artificial intelligence leverages computers and machines to mimic the problem-solving and decision-making capabilities of the human mind. AI combines computer science and large datasets to enable problem-solving (Copeland, 2021).

Various AI domains are defined as follows (Wikipedia, 2021):

- Machine learning teaches a machine how to make inferences and decisions based on past experience by evaluating data.
- Deep learning teaches a machine to process inputs through layers in order to classify, infer, and predict the outcome.
- Neural networks represent algorithms that capture the relationship between various variables and processes the data as a human brain.
- Natural language processing reads, understands, and interprets a language.
- Computer vision identifies an image by decomposing it and studying different parts of the objects.
- Cognitive computing mimics the human brain by analyzing text, speech, and images in a way the human does and tries to give the required output.

Three types of AI are expected to fully develop in time (Advani, 2021):

- Artificial narrow intelligence (ANI) – Existing AI systems solve a single problem in a better manner than a human can, but generally they have narrow (limited) capabilities. They come close to human functioning in specific contexts, surpassing them in many instances, but only excelling in very controlled environments with a limited set of parameters.
- Artificial general intelligence (AGI) is still a theoretical concept, defined as AI which has a human level of cognitive functions, such as language and image processing and reasoning.
- What is artificial super intelligence (ASI) is expected to surpass all human capabilities in the near future. This will include decision-making and taking rational decisions.

Virtual Reality

Virtual reality (VR), which can be described as immersive multimedia or computer-simulated reality, replicates an environment that simulates a physical presence in places in the real world or an imagined world, allowing the user to interact in that world (Fuchs, 2017; Jung & Claudia tom Dieck, 2018). Virtual reality is becoming more and more of an everyday reality.

Seven different concepts of VR – simulation, interaction, artificiality, immersion, telepresence, full-body immersion, and network communication – have been identified (Heim, 1994; McMenemy & Ferguson, 2007). The human body has major senses which allow it to gather information about the world surrounding it, such as sight, hearing, touch, smell taste, pain, balance, and movement. The senses receive information from outside and inside the body. This information must then be interpreted by the human brain. The process of receiving information via the senses and then interpreting the information via the brain is known as perception. When creating a virtual world, it is important to be able to emulate the human perception process, or in other words, the key to VR is trying to trick or deceive the human perceptual system into believing they are part of the virtual world. Thus a perfect feeling of immersion in a virtual world means that the major senses have to be stimulated, including of course an awareness of where we are within the virtual world. To do this, we need to substitute the real information received by these senses with artificially generated information. In this manner, we can replace the real world with the virtual one.

Combining *social media*, *IoT*, *big data*, *cloud computing*, *artificial intelligence*, and *virtual reality* with 5G can be an excellent challenge to the needs and requirements of the government, organizations, and individuals responding to catastrophic disasters. The availability, scalability, cost, speed of communication, and potential security, which offer solutions to current dilemmas within the emergency response and relief work community, are considered. The combined computing services are more readily available for a response to a catastrophic event. Analyzing big data generated through social media can help understand the identity and activity of people in these networks and examine the possibility of recruiting them as volunteers in recovery processes. Big data generated by IoT device could bring up to additional clarification of the damages caused. Since the cloud applications are hosted at geographically dispersed locations, they are not at risk of going down if one of the facilities fails. Cloud computing provides the ability for users to communicate between those in the field with those coordinating efforts outside the field. Artificial intelligence will propose not only a highly efficient data processing but also will offer algorithms for making predictions regarding the real disaster management. Evidently putting together social media, IoT, big data, cloud computing, AI, and VR is a reasonable solution.

Integrating Social Media, IoT, Big Data, Cloud Computing, AI, and VR

All main ICT components used in disaster management, social media, IoT, big data, cloud computing, AI, and VR will get a new meaning and usability in disaster management when integrated with 5G. The new 5G communication technology will enable fixed wireless broadband for a last mile connectivity. For operators, this will lower costs; for residential customers, the network will support multiple video streams at once without delay and will allow smart homes to operate at their smartest – so that families can enjoy more bandwidth than ever before; for disaster management, this will provide immediate connectivity with zero delay when exchanging data, sending messages, delivering relief information, and getting updated scenarios about the affected zones.

Internet and Special Deliveries by Drones

Drones will help spread 5G Internet access to areas that lack connectivity, especially in the cases of disasters. Sets of drones will fly autonomously within close proximity to ensure there are no gaps in signal distribution. More than those, special deliveries can be provided, such as delivering goods, food, and medical supplies. These tasks can become autonomous with such drones, which communicate and adjust their behavior through real-time data inputs and sharing.

Social Collaboration

Social collaboration, enhanced by the use of 5G, will enable users more effectively to participate, comment on, and create content as means of communicating with other users and the public in the cases of catastrophic events, and it will perform the following:

- Allow interactions to cross one or more platforms through social sharing, email, and feeds.
- Involve different levels of engagement by participants who can create or comment or on social media networks.
- Facilitate enhanced speed and breadth of information dissemination.
- Provide for one-to-one, one-to-many, and many-to-many communications.
- Enable communication to take place in real time or asynchronously over time.
- It is device indifferent – it can take place via a computers, tablets, and smartphones.

- The large volumes of data will be efficiently handled by 5G, enabling real-time online events, extending online interactions offline, or augmenting live events online.

Mobile Computing

Mobile computing involves mobile communication, mobile hardware, and mobile software, and it is expecting during disaster communications to be heavily used:

- Mobile communication issues include ad hoc and infrastructure networks as well as communication properties, protocols, data formats, and concrete technologies.
- Mobile hardware includes mobile devices or device components.
- Mobile software deals with the characteristics and requirements of mobile applications.

Having at disposal, the 5G technology will be a guarantee not to have successful implementation of the social collaboration only but also timely and stable processing of data and executing the corresponding computations in critical situations.

Big Data

In today's heavy generation of different types of data from different sources, especially from social collaboration, sensors, transportation, etc., the idea of using 5G could greatly reduce the technical overhead concerning acquisition, storage, and processing of such large volumes of data, i.e., big data. The use of 5G will enhance the rapid and seamless transfer of important data, especially in such sensitive disaster-related events:

- Handling the growing volume of data generated from different sources (sensors, mobile devices).
- The ability to extract data from different sources to perform a specific task and the ability to provide information in real time with the right context are essential. Information is stored everywhere.
- Controlling and managing the acquisition speed of the data and additionally the speed at which the data should be processed and analyzed.
- Social, mobile, and cloud make information accessible, shareable, and consumable at anytime and anywhere. The knowledge to capture the right information and utilize the smaller subsets applicable to a specific company, a product and customers, at a specific point in time, will be critical to new opportunities and for avoiding risks.

Cloud Computing

The evolution toward 5G mobile networks is characterized by an exponential growth of traffic. This growth is caused by an increased number of user terminals, richer Internet content, more frequent usage of Internet-capable devices, and by more powerful devices with larger screens. This implies also the need for more scaling possibilities in mobile networks in order to handle spatially and temporally fluctuating traffic patterns, terminals with different quality requirements, and more diverse services (Koubaa & Shakshuki, 2016; Quek et al., 2017). Current mobile networks are not able to support this diversity efficiently but are designed for peak provisioning and typical Internet traffic. However, not everything could be implemented in the cloud. There are latency, mobility, geographic, network bandwidth, reliability, security, and privacy challenges. Fog computing addresses these gaps by bridging the continuum from cloud to things. It distributes compute, communication, control, storage, and decision-making closer to where the data is originated, enabling dramatically faster processing time and lowering network costs. Fog is an extension of the traditional cloud-based computing model where implementations of the architecture can reside in multiple layers of a network's topology. By adding layers of fog nodes, applications can be partitioned to run at the optimal network level. 5G will immensely enhance the function mechanism of fog computing.

Artificial Intelligence

Different combinations of AI and 5G could be used for disaster management, supporting scores of cameras for environmental monitoring in real time – visual inspection software with deep learning algorithms, used to recognize vehicles behavior, visual inspection of other moving and nonmoving elements, etc., for the purpose of safety, space management, accident control (Kerravala, 2021).

Although many disaster risk reduction approaches today rely on single data streams such as assessing rainfall, temperatures, or vegetation, the integration of 5G with AI will remove the barriers to implementing AI solutions for disaster management, since the data sets will be coming as an integrated input data sets together (AI for Good, 2021). Response time is limited during a crisis. The fast data processing is crucial in all emergency situations. Artificial intelligence can be used to find patterns which are difficult to establish with traditional techniques. Sophisticated algorithms together with a greater amount of data that can be analyzed faster are a great challenge to be applied to disaster management (Mir, 2021).

5G technology will increase the amount of the transferred data in an exponential way due to the massive amount of IoT devices in the environment. Besides that, 5G-based devices are multidimensional in terms of the underlying elements, from location to software version to device type (Kelley, 2021). The integration of all such devices into one system will create new data in large volumes that will be needed by AI models.

Virtual Reality

5G may bring a new challenge in disaster training through virtual and augmented reality. As phones transform into devices meant to be used with VR headsets, the very low latency and consistent speeds of 5G will bring to an Internet-augmented world. The small cell aspects of 5G may also help with in-building coverage, as 5G encourages every home router to become a cell site. The delivery of immersive experiences will need to rely on robust networks. Virtual reality requires near-zero latency so that the motion inner ear senses line up with the created visual environment. Virtual reality also requires high speed and superior content quality, all of which require improved networks with the capacity and sophistication to handle massive amounts of data at lightning-fast speeds. A 5G-backed VR education will have an immense impact for preparing relief operations and trainees because of the following:

- The need for disaster management training is expected to grow over the next decade, mostly due to the effects of global warming. With glaciers melting, sea levels rising, cloud forests drying, and ravaging storms, it is never been more important for institutions to be prepared for the worst.
- Disaster risk reduction and emergency specialists can obtain an invaluable experience from VR environments in which different disaster scenarios could be simulated and the personnel could be trained to respond to critical situations with confidence. A virtual reality simulation of emergency preparedness could provide more varied scenarios and help avoid the hasty, panic-driven thinking which can lead to unnecessary accidents and deaths.
- Interactive VR-based disaster training can be tailored to specific users as well as organizations, based on their resources and hazard vulnerability analysis. VR-based scenarios can be developed for instructional task-focused training in which the program responds to user inputs and provides instant feedback.
- VR-based exercises can also allow an organization to test its emergency response plans in order to assess its effectiveness and in turn identify gaps and areas for improvement. VR-based applications can also facilitate consistent and repeated training over geographical and organizational divides.
- VR applications can be applied individually or to groups allowing participants do work on their own or interact with other users. The VR environment can replicate any real-world settings such as different landscapes, mountains, water resources, buildings, vegetation, winds, complex natural events, and sounds.
- From a cost perspective, VR-based disaster training has significant advantages. From relatively simple tabletop exercises where participants convene in a conference setting for discussion, to more complex full-scale exercises where personnel

and equipment are mobilized, real-life drills and exercises are expensive in both time and resources required.

Conclusion

Advanced pillars of information technologies, such as social media, IoT, big data, cloud computing, artificial intelligence, and virtual reality, can heavily take upon the use of the established 5G technology. Governmental organizations and rescue teams can successfully use 5G-connected drones to aid in emergency and disaster relief efforts, as well as for providing reliable Internet connectivity. The stable Internet connections can allow flawless exchange of messages through online social networks, effective mobile computations, instantaneous acquisition of data from IoT sensors, and reliable and uninterrupted support by cloud environments. Disaster training by means of 5G-backuped virtual reality can help the exchange of large volumes of data of the trainees and the learning management systems. Such 5G real-time communications and sharing of data between the victims of disasters and the responsible personnel will allow relief managers safely dispatch rescue teams, quickly estimate structural damage and destruction levels, and better distribute resources, increasing the speed and effectiveness of search-and-rescue missions.

Acknowledgments The first author thanks the National Science Fund of Bulgaria for the support under the Grant № KP-06-H55/5 from 15.11.2021, titled "Smart risk management for business from adverse events and natural disasters." The work of the second author has been partially supported under the Grant № NID NI 1/2021 titled "Development and use of artificial intelligence in education and economy" financed by the Science Fund of the University of National and World Economy, Bulgaria.

References

Advani, V. (2021). *What is artificial intelligence? How does AI work, types and future of it?*https://www.mygreatlearning.com/blog/what-is-artificial-intelligence/

Afzalan, N., Cowley, J., & Barijough, M. (2013). *From big to little data for natural disaster recovery: How online and on the ground activities are connected?*http://papers.ssrn.com/sol3/

AI for Good. (2021). *A safer, more resilient world: Reducing disaster risks with AI.* https://aiforgood.itu.int/a-safer-more-resilient-world-reducing-disaster-risks-with-ai/

Akerkar, R. (Ed.). (2014). *Big data computing*. CRC Press.

Berman, J. (2013). *Principles of big data – Preparing, sharing, and analyzing complex information*. Morgan Kaufmann.

Bhowmik, S. (2017). *Cloud computing*. Cambridge University Press.

Bizaki, H. K. (Ed.). (2017). *Towards 5G wireless networks: A physical layer perspective*. Wiley.

Copeland, B. J. (2021). Artificial intelligence. *Britannica*. https://www.britannica.com/technology/artificial-intelligence

European Commission. (2015). *5G vision*, 57 p. https://5g-ppp.eu/wp-content/uploads/2015/02/5G-Vision-Brochure-v1.pdf

Fuchs, P. (2017). *Virtual reality headsets – A theoretical and pragmatic approach*. CRC Press.
Heim, M. (1994). *Metaphysic of virtual reality*. Oxford Univer-sity Press.
Huawei. (2017). *5G: A technology vision*. http://www.huawei.com/5gwhitepaper/
Innovation Enterprise. (2015). *Big data in a crisis*. https://channels.theinnovationenterprise.com/articles/
Jung, T., & Claudia tom Dieck, M. (2018). *Augmented reality and virtual reality: Empowering human, place and business*. Springer.
Kelley, B. (2021). *Why 5G needs AI to succeed*. https://www.forbes.com/sites/forbestechcouncil/2021/10/20/why-5g-needs-ai-to-succeed
Kerravala, Z. (2021). *How AI and 5G will power the next wave of innovation*. https://www.zdnet.com/article/how-ai-and-5g-will-power-the-next-wave-of-innovation/
Koubaa, A., & Shakshuki, E. (Eds.). (2016). *Robots and sensor clouds*. Springer.
McMenemy, K., & Ferguson, S. (2007). *A hitchhiker's guide to virtual reality*. A K Peters, Ltd.
Mir, O. (2021). *Can 5G, AI and IoT save us from disasters*. https://www.linkedin.com/pulse/can-5g-ai-iot-save-us-from-disasters-omar-mir/
Mongo, D. B. (2016). *Using big data for humanitarian crisis mapping*. https://www.mongodb.com/blog/post/
Padli, J., Habibullah, M., & Baharom, A. (2010). Economic impact of natural disasters' fatalities. *International Journal of Social Economics, 37*(6), 429–441.
Pedrycz, W. (Ed.). (2015). *Information granularity, big data, and computational intelligence*. Springer.
Pethuru, R., & Raman, A. (2017). *The internet of things – Enabling technologies, platforms, and use cases*. CRC Press.
Prasad, R. (2014). *5G: 2020 and beyond* (Communications and networking). River Publishers.
Qualcomm. (2016). *Leading the world to 5G*. https://www.qualcomm.com/media/documents/files/qualcomm-5g-vision-presentation.pdf
Quek, T. Q. S., Peng, M., Simeone, O., & Yu, W. (2017). *Cloud radio access networks – Principles, technologies, and applications*. Cambridge University Press.
Rajashree, D. (2016). *The role of social media during a natural disaster*. http://simplify360.com/blog/the-role-of-social-media-during-a-natural-disaster
Rodriguez, J. (Ed.). (2017). *Fundamentals of 5G mobile networks*. Wiley.
Rowan University. (2016). *Tips on using social media during a natural disaster*. http://www.newswise.com/articles/tipson-using-social-media-during-a-natural-disaster
Thomas, R., & McSharry, P. (2015). *Big data revolution*. Wiley.
United Nations Office for Disaster Risk Reduction (UNISDR). (2015). *Proceedings of the third UN world conference on disaster risk reduction*, 14–18 March 2015, Sendai, Japan.
Varrall, G. (2016). *5G spectrum and standards*. Artech House.
Washington, C. (2017). *The role of social media during natural disasters*. http://crystalwashington.com/the-role-ofsocial-media-during-natural-disasters
Wei, X., Kan, Z., & Xuemin, S. (Eds.). (2017). *5G mobile communications*. Springer.
Wikipedia. (2021). *Artificial intelligence*. https://en.wikipedia.org/wiki/Artificial_intelligence
Zander, J., & Mosterman, P. J. (Eds.). (2014). *Computation for humanity – Information technology to advance society*. CRC Press.

Part III
CIMS Requirements, Development, and Testing

An Integrated Framework to Evaluate Information Systems Performance in High-Risk Settings: Experiences from the iTRACK Project

Ahmed A. Abdelgawad and Tina Comes

Abstract Evaluation and testing are significant steps in developing any information system. More attention must be devoted to these steps if the system is to be used in high-risk contexts, such as the response to conflict disasters. Several testing methodologies are designed to guarantee that software fulfills technology requirements; others will assure usability and usefulness. However, there is currently no integrated evaluation framework with agreed standards that bring together the three elements: technology requirements, usability, and usefulness. This gap constitutes a barrier to innovation and imposes risks to responders or affected populations if the technology is introduced without proper testing. This chapter aims to close this gap.

Based on a review of evaluation methods and measurement metrics for information systems, we designed an integrated evaluation framework including standard metrics for code quality testing, usability methods, subjective usefulness questionnaires, and key performance indicators. We developed and implemented a reporting and evaluation system that demonstrates our evaluation framework within the context of the EU H2020 project iTRACK. iTRACK developed an integrated system for the safety and security of humanitarian missions. We demonstrate how our approach allows measuring the quality and usefulness of the iTRACK integrated system.

Keywords Evaluation framework · Software quality testing · Requirements engineering · Usability · Usefulness · High risk · Humanitarian disaster

A. A. Abdelgawad (✉)
Department of Information Systems, University of Agder, Kristiansand, Norway
e-mail: ahmedg@uia.no

T. Comes
Faculty of Technology, Policy and Management, TU Delft, Delft, Netherlands
e-mail: t.comes@tudelft.nl

H. J. Scholl et al. (eds.), *Disaster Management and Information Technology*, Public Administration and Information Technology 40,
https://doi.org/10.1007/978-3-031-20939-0_9

Introduction

In the Middle East and other high-risk areas, those who try to aid the most vulnerable are increasingly risking their own lives and safety. The number of humanitarian workers who fall victim to attacks continues to rise, according to the Aid Worker Security Database (Humanitarian Outcomes, 2019). Meanwhile, seeking to maintain access to populations in need, humanitarian organizations in the field are confronted with mounting tensions. Consequently, there is a new role for technology to support operations. Nevertheless, these innovations, particularly information and communication technologies (ICT) used in conflicts, can cause severe risks. These risks range from privacy violations to threatening the lives and safety of those the systems are designed to protect in the first place.

Evaluation and testing are a significant step in the development life cycle of any software system, and it is a vital phase in the quality assurance of ICT systems (Jovanović, 2009). The goal of software evaluation frameworks is to assess the quality and sophistication of the system from different points of view (Boloix & Robillard, 1995). However, thus far, there is no integrated evaluation framework combining testing functionality, quality, and usefulness of the software to assist in humanitarian conflict disasters. Such a framework requires the standards and problems of humanitarian innovation and experimentation to be met (Sandvik et al., 2017), and the context of the problem to be considered. In conflicts, a significant challenge is dealing with sensitive information and organizational barriers to information sharing (Van de Walle & Comes, 2015) and evaluating risks as they emerge (Van de Walle & Comes, 2014). The lack of an integrated framework and commonly agreed standards constitutes a significant barrier to innovation. At the same time, technology introduction without proper testing may impose risks to responders and beneficiaries alike.

Based on a review of evaluation standards and metrics, this chapter compiles and proposes an integrated evaluation framework for ICT systems in humanitarian conflicts. The proposed framework aims at assisting in measuring the quality and usefulness of a system on different levels, from the performance of individual components to the overall system. The Institute of Electrical and Electronics Engineers IEEE defines software system quality as *the degree to which a system, component, or process meets specified requirements* and *the degree to which a system, component, or process meets customer or user needs or expectations* (IEEE Computer Society, 1991). Meanwhile, the International Software Testing Qualifications Board ISTQB defines quality in general as *the degree to which a component, system or process meets specified requirements and user/customer needs and expectations* (ISTQB, 2018). It defines software quality as *the totality of functionality and features of a software product that bear on its ability to satisfy stated or implied needs* (ISTQB, 2018). In sum, the quality of the software is concerned with meeting the specified requirements and user satisfaction. The former is achieved by testing the software system's components individually or together, or the whole system against the requirements in terms of specifications, use cases,

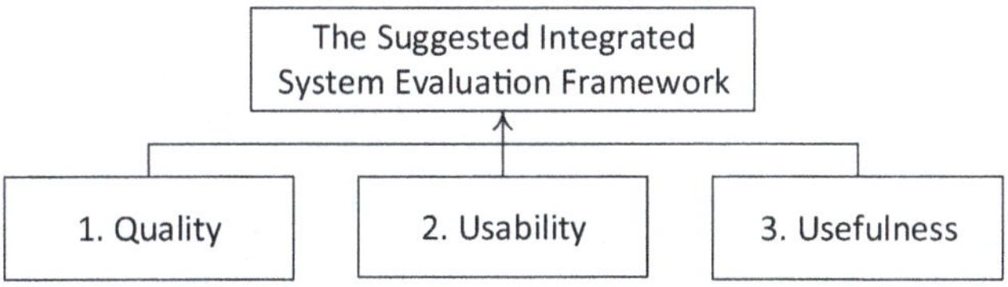

Fig. 1 The proposed integrated system framework

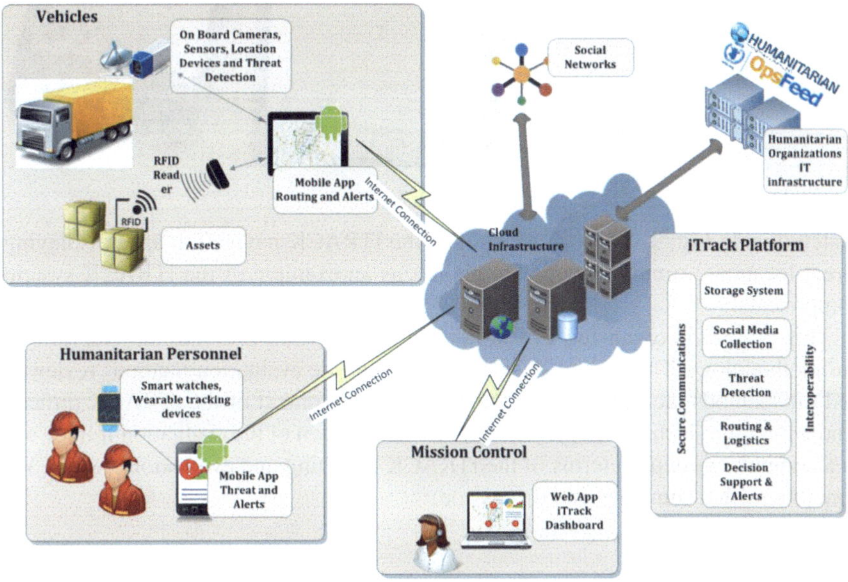

Fig. 2 Conceptual operational representation of the iTRACK system. (Adapted from iTRACK (2022a))

design documents, etc. In contrast, the latter is accomplished by testing the system usability and user satisfaction (Nielsen, 1993).

System usefulness means that *a product, website or application should solve a problem, fill a need or offer something people find useful* (Sauro, 2018a). Based on Fred Davis' usefulness construct, system usefulness is about helping users accomplish job tasks quicker, improving job performance, productivity, and effectiveness, and making the job easier to do in general. Figure 1 shows the pillars of our proposed integrated system evaluation framework.

The evaluation methods reviewed in this chapter and the methods included in our integrated framework are applied in the context of the EU H2020 project iTRACK (https://www.itrack-project.eu). The iTRACK project aims to develop a single open-source integrated system for real-time tracking of both people and assets, in addition to threat detection to support decision-making during civilian humanitarian missions run by humanitarian organizations operating civilian missions (iTRACK, 2018). Figure 2 illustrates the conceptual operational representation of the iTRACK

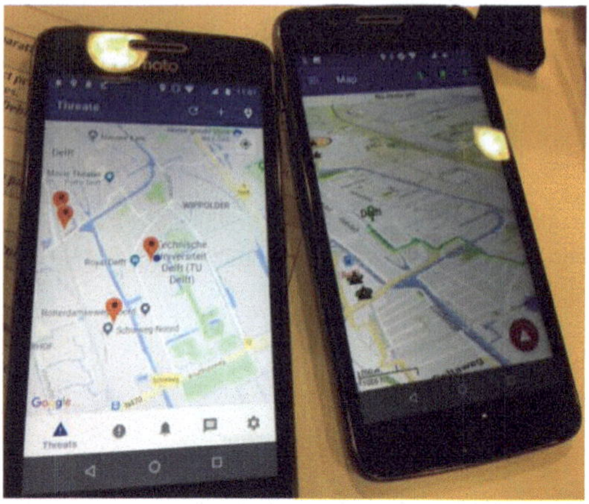

Fig. 3 iTRACK navigation app. (Adapted from iTRACK (2022b))

system, while Fig. 3 shows a snapshot of the iTRACK navigation app (displaying threat locations) running on mobile phones as an example of the iTRACK system components.

This chapter is organized as follows: the next section provides an overview of our methodology. The "Results" section describes the evaluation methods reviewed and the methods included in our framework in the context of the iTRACK project. Under the same section, we present our implementation of the evaluation framework in a computer system in terms of the iTRACK reporting and evaluation system. We conclude with a summary and discussion.

Methodology

To achieve the goal of this chapter, we surveyed relevant sources for "software testing methods" and "technology usefulness instruments" to collect quality and usefulness assessment methods and metrics. Websites of organizations connected to humanitarian conflicts were the target of our initial investigation, such as Aid in Danger, the European Interagency Security Forum EISF, and the United Nations Development Program UNDP. We followed an exploratory approach and used a variety of keywords like: "software testing," "software evaluation," "information system testing," "information system evaluation," "software quality," and "information system quality," sometimes even just using "software" and searched for relevant material in results. This search, however, did not yield sufficient results. To mitigate the situation, we have used the exact search keywords mentioned above and broadened our search circle to include sources like the following:

- International Organization for Standardization ISO (https://www.iso.org/publication-list.html)
- International Electrotechnical Commission IEC (http://www.iec.ch)

- IEEE (https://www.ieee.org)
- ISTQB (https://www.istqb.org)
- Scientific publications (via Google Scholar and others)
- Other sources which are available on the Internet in general

The results of this search were organized under the three pillars of our intended framework: quality, usability, and usefulness. The resulting framework was used to develop the iTRACK reporting and evaluation system.

Results

Framework Description

The quality of software, as indicated previously, is about meeting the specified requirements and user satisfaction. The former is achieved by testing the software system components individually or together and the whole system against the requirements in terms of specifications, use cases, design documents, etc. The latter is achieved via testing the system usability and user satisfaction directly with users and subjectively via questionnaires administered to them. System usefulness can be measured in terms of performance indicators of an individual user, a team, or an organization because of using the system. It can also be subjectively measured by explicitly asking the users to provide their opinions on the system's usefulness.

Our literature review results are compiled under the first two main subsections: "Software Testing and Quality" and "Software Usability." Each of these subsections was concluded by our selected methods and metrics for the iTRACK system. The third main subsection focuses on the usefulness of the iTRACK system.

Software Testing and Quality

Software Testing Methods

All software testing methods are classified under either Black-Box, White-Box, or in-between, i.e., Gray-Box (Jovanović, 2009). The software testing method is decided based on the testers' access to the internal structure of the software system under test (its source code):

- Black-box testing (a.k.a. specifications-based or behavioral testing) is a software testing method in which there is no need to access the source code of the tested item (Black Box Testing, 2018).
- White-box testing (a.k.a. clear-box, glass-box, transparent-box, open-box, code-based testing, or structural testing) is a software testing method to test a software

item with knowledge of its internal structure, design, and implementation (source code) (White Box Testing, 2018a, b).
- Gray-box testing combines the black-box and white-box software testing methods (Gray Box Testing, 2018).

Software Testing Levels

In addition to the testing method, software testing is also conducted on four levels:

- Unit testing level (a.k.a. component, module, program, or structural testing)[1] (Types of Software, 2018) is a typical white-box method testing level. *Unit testing is micro testing which is done by developers to ensure that each and every individual unit of source code performing well enough to match their expectation* (Types of Software, 2018; Müller & Friedenberg, 2011). This testing level is all about answering the question of "did we build it right?".
- Integration testing level aims at examining how units/components/parts of the system work together. The different units/components are tested working together to ensure that interfaces and interactions among them or other parts of the system (e.g., operating system, file system, hardware) are performing well and in compliance with the requirements/specifications (Types of Software, 2018; Müller & Friedenberg, 2011).
- System testing level is a system test concerned with the complete functionality and behavior of the whole system (Müller & Friedenberg, 2011). The environment where this testing level is conducted should resemble the production environment to reduce the environment-specific failures (Müller & Friedenberg, 2011). System testing level *may include tests based on risks and on requirements specifications, business processes, use cases, or other high-level text descriptions or models of system behaviour, interactions with the operating system, and system resources* (Müller & Friedenberg, 2011). This testing level inspects functional and nonfunctional requirements and could be conducted by an independent tester (Müller & Friedenberg, 2011).

Figure 4 shows the relationship between the testing methods and the testing levels.

The iTRACK Software Testing and Quality Assurance

Unit testing has been performed using the tools in the iTRACK development environment. The requirements for the tests were developed in a series of interviews, field research, and simulation tests (Noori et al., 2017). Complete documentation is available on the project website https://www.itrack-project.eu. Successive versions

[1] A structural or an architectural testing aims at knowing what is happening inside the system.

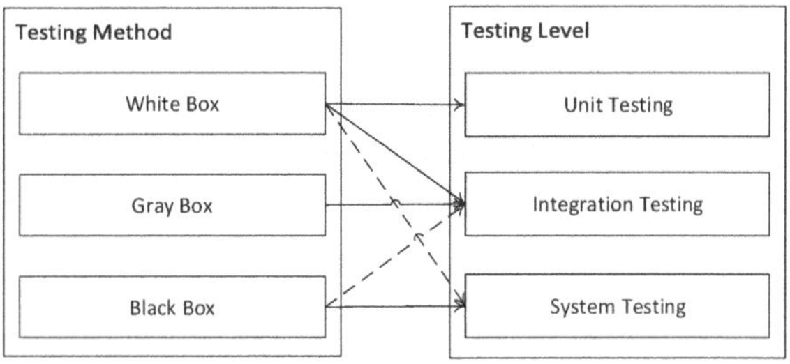

Fig. 4 Testing levels and methods

of the iTRACK corresponding deliverables have reported the resulted testing metrics. One of the metrics reported is the code coverage which is *an analysis method that determines which parts of the software have been executed (covered) by the test suite and which parts have not been executed,* e.g., *statement coverage, decision coverage or condition coverage* (McKay et al., 2016).

In the iTRACK development environment, integration testing for mainly the server-side components was carried out as well. In a simulation exercise in April 2018, another integration testing, including the client-side components, was performed in addition to system-level testing to evaluate end-to-end workflows. Before the final deployment, another system-level testing was conducted. After deployment, other metrics like the numbers and rates of bugs and issues reported, fixes, enhancements, improvements and new features released, and issues reopened (for others, please check (Data, 2018; Issues, 2018)) can indicate the quality of the iTRACK system.

Software Usability

Usability testing level (a.k.a. acceptance testing) is the final testing phase prior to sending the software to the production environment in the market. This level aims at answering the question of "did we build the right thing?". The testing is conducted firstly in the developers' workplace by the internal developers, testers, or users employed for that reason, which is called, in general, alpha testing. Then the testing is conducted at the users' place by the actual users to provide feedback before releasing the system to the market, which is called beta testing (Types of Software, 2018; Müller & Friedenberg, 2011). *The goal in acceptance testing is to establish confidence in the system, parts of the system or specific non-functional characteristics of the system. Finding defects is not the main focus in acceptance testing* (Müller & Friedenberg, 2011).

Acceptance in terms of usability is defined as "a quality attribute that assesses how easy user interfaces are to use. The word 'usability' also refers to methods for improving ease-of-use during the design process" (Nielsen, 2018a). Usability can be measured both objectively by asking users to complete specific tasks and observe them, and subjectively by asking users to fill out questionnaires about the usability of the software system.

Usability Testing Sessions

Usability testing aims at observing users using the tested software under test. A set of users, preferably similar in characteristics to the end users, should be employed and asked to fulfill goal-based tasks using the software; during these testing sessions, usability problems would be observed (Corona, 2019). Observations are made in terms of how users interact with the software. Then the developers will know the required features and understand issues facing the users while working with the software. Accordingly, developers can make improvements.

Usability Evaluation (Testing Metrics)

As mentioned above, the users will be given a set of tasks to complete during the testing session. The following metrics could be calculated:

Learnability

Is a metric for how easy it is for the user to learn using the system (Nielsen, 2018a; EN_Tech_Direct, 2018). Learnability can be measured by measuring if a user becomes faster in performing a task:

$$\text{Learnability} = \frac{T_2 - T_1}{T_1}$$

where T_1 and T_2 are the durations taken by the user to accomplish the same task for the first and the second times, respectively.

Efficiency

Measures how fast a user can accomplish tasks after learning the system (Nielsen, 2018a; EN_Tech_Direct, 2018). Efficiency could be measured by finding the total time saved between the first and the last times doing a specific task using the system.

Effectiveness

Measures how well the users achieve their goals by using the system (EN_Tech_Direct, 2018). Effectiveness could be measured by classifying the accomplishment level of the tasks by different users (in terms of **S** for success, **F** for failure or **P** for partial **S**uccess).

For example:

	Task 1	**Task 2**	**Task 3**	**...**	**Task N**
User 1	F	S	S		PS
User 2	S	S	F		F
...					
User M	F	S	PS		F

Completion Rates

"Often called the fundamental usability metric or the gateway metric, completion rates are a simple measure of usability. It's typically recorded as a binary metric (in terms of **1** for task success and **0** for task failure). If users cannot accomplish their goals, not much else matters" (Sauro, 2018b).

For example:

	Task 1	**Task 2**	**Task 3**	**...**	**Task N**
User 1	1	0	1		1
User 2	0	1	0		1
...					
User M	1	1	1		0

Usability Problems

This measure is about user interface problems that the users encounter during the test. The observer should "describe the problem and note both **how many** and **which users encountered it**. Knowing the probability, a user will encounter a problem at each phase of development can become a key metric for measuring usability activity impact and [return on investment] ROI. Knowing which user encountered it allows to better predict sample sizes, problem discovery rates and what problems are found by only a single user" (Sauro, 2018b).

Observer notes should be based on the **frequency** of the usability problem: "Is it common or rare?", the **impact** of the problem: "Will it be easy or difficult for the users to overcome?", and the **persistence** of the problem: *Is it a one-time problem that users can overcome once they know about it or will users repeatedly be bothered by the problem?* (Nielsen, 2018b).

Errors

"Record any unintended action, slip, mistake or omission a user makes while attempting a task. Record each instance of an error along with a description. For example, 'user entered last name in the first name field'" (Sauro, 2018b). Afterward, the observer can add severity ratings to the errors. Otherwise, categorize these errors. "Errors provide excellent diagnostic information and, if possible, should be mapped to [user interface] problems. Errors are somewhat time-consuming to collect, as they usually require a moderator or someone to review recordings" (Sauro, 2018b). Errors are detected via the observer's notes, for example, "user entered last name in the first name field" (Sauro, 2018b).

Task Time

"**Total task duration** is the de facto measure of efficiency and productivity. Record how long it takes a user to complete a task in seconds and or minutes. **Start task times when users finish reading task scenarios and end the time when users have finished all actions** (including reviewing)" (Sauro, 2018b).

	Task 1	**Task 2**	**Task 3**	**...**	**Task N**
User 1	00:05:30	00:14:30	00:05:30		00:01:30
User 2	00:04:25	00:13:20	00:04:25		00:01:20
...					
User M	00:06:45	00:12:15	00:06:45		00:02:15

Page Views/Clicks

"For websites and web-applications, these fundamental tracking metrics might be the only thing you have access to without conducting your own studies. Clicks have been shown to correlate highly with time-on-task which is probably a better measure of efficiency. The first click can be highly indicative of a task success or failure" (Sauro, 2018b). Page Views/Clicks could be detected by counting the clicks and page views by the system itself.

Expectation

"Users have an expectation about how difficult a task should be based on subtle cues in the task-scenario. Asking users how difficult they expect a task to be and comparing it to actual task difficulty ratings (from the same or different users) can be useful in diagnosing problem areas" (Sauro, 2018b).

Pre-task		1	2	3	4	5	6	7	
How difficult you think Task M will be? - Please explain your choice:	Very easy	○	○	○	○	○	○	○	Very difficult

Task Level Satisfaction

"After users attempt a task, have them answer a few or just a single question about how difficult the task was. Task level satisfaction metrics will immediately flag a difficult task, especially when compared to a database of other tasks" (Sauro, 2018b). For example, was "Task M" easy to do?

Post task		1	2	3	4	5	6	7	
How difficult did you find Task M? • Please explain your choice:	Very easy	○	○	○	○	○	○	○	Very difficult

Single Usability Metric (SUM)

"There are times when it is easier to describe the usability of a system or task by combining metrics into a single score, for example, when comparing competing products or reporting on corporate dashboards. SUM is a standardised average of measures of effectiveness, efficiency of satisfaction and is typically composed of 3 metrics: **completion rates**, **task-level satisfaction** and **task time**" (Sauro, 2018b).

Usability and User Experience Subjective Evaluation

Over the last 30 years, several usability and user-experience subjective questionnaires have been used to assess the usability aspects as well as reliability and validity of software systems. EduTech Wiki collected many of these questionnaires. They can be used for all systems, including websites and mobile apps (Usability and User Experience, 2018).

According to Perlman: "Questionnaires have long been used to evaluate user interfaces ... Questionnaires have also long been used in electronic form ... For a handful of questionnaires specifically designed to assess aspects of usability, the validity and/or reliability have been established ..." (Perlman, 2018). In the following table, we enlist some of the subjective questionnaires resulted from our review.

Questionnaire title	Questionnaire type	Number of items	Sub-scales/construct	Reference
Perceived Usefulness and Ease of Use	7-points scale	12	Perceived usefulness, and perceived ease of use	Davis (1989)
Software Usability Scale (SUS)	5-points scale	10	Usability and learnability	Borsci et al. (2009), Brooke (1996), Sauro (2015) and System Usability Scale (2017)
Standardized User Experience Percentile Rank Questionnaire (SUPR-Q)	11-points scale	8	Usability, trust, appearance, and loyalty	Sauro (2015)
User Experience Questionnaire (UEQ)	7-points scale	26	Attractiveness, perspicuity, efficiency, dependability, stimulation, and novelty	Laugwitz et al. (2006, 2008)

The iTRACK Usability and User Experience Testing

The iTRACK system consists of several packages with different roles in supporting humanitarian aid workers. Based on these roles, a list of usability tasks was prepared. This list compiles the possible iTRACK system features to be tested per the iTRACK system component. Each feature to be tested is provided with a description of its test. The idea, in general, is to find if the participants will be able to fulfill the required tasks with success, partial success, or failure. One of the iTRACK system features is the "threat creation," which, as the name implies, enables users to create a threat report so that other iTRACK system users can be careful. One example of a test activity description for this feature is "create threats on the map, indicate, e.g., threat types, estimated impact, etc."

The metrics mentioned previously in the review will be used whenever suitable to find our usability issues. For our selected usability task example, before doing this task, the participants should answer the following question:

Before Task

How difficult you think this task will be? - Please explain your choice:	Very easy	○ ○ ○ ○ ○ ○ ○	Very difficult

After finishing the task, the participants should log the time they took to complete it and report if the result was success, partial success, or failure. Then answer a question like the one they have answered before the task:

After Task

Task			Log
Task Time			__:__:__
Completion (Success, **F**ailure and **P**artial **S**uccess**)**			o S o PS o F
How difficult did you find this task? - Please explain your choice:	Very easy	○ ○ ○ ○ ○ ○ ○	Very difficult

These *Before* and *After Task* questions will enable calculating most of the usability metrics mentioned in the "Usability Evaluation (Testing Metrics)" subsection of this chapter.

As indicated in the review, many questionnaires could measure different constructs subjectively. Usually, users' time is limited and filled with several activities. To use this limited time efficiently, our team has selected only Davis's Perceived Usefulness and Ease of Use questionnaire and UEQ questionnaires to be administered as subjective usability measures. Davis's Perceived Usefulness and Ease of Use questionnaire is short and assesses the usefulness and ease of use, while UEQ provides more insights into the user's experience. These questionnaires are to be administered to users for each of the iTRACK system components individually to understand the text of the questionnaires within the context of each of these components.

iTRACK Perceived Usefulness and Ease of Use

Instructions:

- Try to respond to all the items.
- For items that are not applicable, use: NA
- Add a comment about an item if needed

Perceived usefulness			**1**	**2**	**3**	**4**	**5**	**6**	**7**		**NA**
1.	Using the iTRACK system in my job would enable me to accomplish tasks more quickly	Unlikely	○	○	○	○	○	○	○	Likely	○
2.	Using the iTRACK system would improve my job performance	Unlikely	○	○	○	○	○	○	○	Likely	○
3.	Using the iTRACK system in my job would increase my productivity	Unlikely	○	○	○	○	○	○	○	Likely	○
4.	Using the iTRACK system would enhance my effectiveness on the job	Unlikely	○	○	○	○	○	○	○	Likely	○
5.	Using the iTRACK system would make it easier to do my job	Unlikely	○	○	○	○	○	○	○	Likely	○
6.	I would find the iTRACK system useful in my job	Unlikely	○	○	○	○	○	○	○	Likely	○
Perceived ease of use			**1**	**2**	**3**	**4**	**5**	**6**	**7**		**NA**
7.	Learning to operate the iTRACK system would be easy for me	Unlikely	○	○	○	○	○	○	○	Likely	○
8.	I would find it easy to get the iTRACK system to do what I want it to do	Unlikely	○	○	○	○	○	○	○	Likely	○
9.	My interaction with the iTRACK system would be clear and understandable	Unlikely	○	○	○	○	○	○	○	Likely	○
10.	I would find the iTRACK system to be flexible to interact with	Unlikely	○	○	○	○	○	○	○	Likely	○
11.	It would be easy for me to become skilful at using the iTRACK system	Unlikely	○	○	○	○	○	○	○	Likely	○
12.	I would find the iTRACK system easy to use	Unlikely	○	○	○	○	○	○	○	Likely	○

iTRACK UEQ

Instructions: For each of the following items, mark one box that best describes the iTRACK system.

		1	2	3	4	5	6	7	
1.	annoying	○	○	○	○	○	○	○	enjoyable
2.	not understandable	○	○	○	○	○	○	○	understandable
3.	creative	○	○	○	○	○	○	○	dull
4.	easy to learn	○	○	○	○	○	○	○	difficult to learn
5.	valuable	○	○	○	○	○	○	○	inferior
6.	boring	○	○	○	○	○	○	○	exciting
7.	not interesting	○	○	○	○	○	○	○	interesting
8.	unpredictable	○	○	○	○	○	○	○	predictable
9.	fast	○	○	○	○	○	○	○	slow
10.	inventive	○	○	○	○	○	○	○	conventional
11.	obstructive	○	○	○	○	○	○	○	supportive
12.	good	○	○	○	○	○	○	○	bad
13.	complicated	○	○	○	○	○	○	○	easy
14.	unlikable	○	○	○	○	○	○	○	pleasing
15.	usual	○	○	○	○	○	○	○	leading edge
16.	unpleasant	○	○	○	○	○	○	○	pleasant
17.	secure	○	○	○	○	○	○	○	not secure
18.	motivating	○	○	○	○	○	○	○	demotivating
19.	meets expectations	○	○	○	○	○	○	○	does not meet expectations
20.	inefficient	○	○	○	○	○	○	○	efficient
21.	clear	○	○	○	○	○	○	○	confusing
22.	impractical	○	○	○	○	○	○	○	practical
23.	organized	○	○	○	○	○	○	○	cluttered
24.	attractive	○	○	○	○	○	○	○	unattractive
25.	friendly	○	○	○	○	○	○	○	unfriendly
26.	conservative	○	○	○	○	○	○	○	innovative

The iTRACK System Usefulness

System usefulness is about how the system is helping users in accomplishing their job tasks quicker; improving their job performance, productivity, and effectiveness; and, in general, making doing their job easier, in other words, the enhancement in performance of the users doing their jobs as a result of using the system (Davis, 1993). In predicting the actual system use, Davis found that system usefulness is 1.5 times more important than ease of use or usability (Sauro, 2018a; Davis, 1993).

The iTRACK system aims to improve the security and efficiency of civilian humanitarian missions. Using the iTRACK system is expected to enhance the performance of its users. In the following subsections, we will describe the metrics that we think would be useful in assessing the performance of the iTRACK system

*M*ission	***M, i***	***M, t***	***M, o***
*P*hase	***P, i***	***P, t***	***P, o***
*T*ask	***T, i***	***T, t***	***T, o***
	*i*ndividual	*t*eam	*o*rganisation

Fig. 5 Indicator measurement levels granularity (arrows go toward higher levels of aggregations)

components, the usage of these components, in addition to the performance of the individuals, teams, and overall organization because of using the iTRACK system.

A humanitarian mission could be divided into three phases: (1) planning, (2) executing, and (3) response and recovery. Each of these phases has different tasks according to the mission on the one hand and the threat/attack this mission is facing on the other hand. These tasks are performed by individuals who could be part of one team or gathered from different teams. Accordingly, an indicator could be on the highest resolution scale, i.e., measuring the performance of an individual working on one task. It could be scaled up to the case in which this individual is working through an entire phase or a whole mission. The same principle applies when the indicator is scaled up from an individual to a team or an organization. Figure 5 shows indicator measurement levels granularity that we have used while composing the performance indicators in the following subsections.

Usage Indicator of the iTRACK System

Individual Usage per System Component

Usage indicator ui_i: how many times an individual uses (open to look for or check anything) one of the iTRACK system components per time unit, therefore ui_i is measured in [times/hour].

Team Average Usage per System Component

Usage indicator ui_t: the average number of times of all individuals who belong to a team t use one of the iTRACK system components per time unit:

$$\mathrm{ui}_t = \frac{\sum_{i \in t} \mathrm{ui}_i}{|t|}$$

ui_t is measured in [times/hour], where $|t|$ is the number of all individuals who belong to the team t.

Organization Average Usage per System Component

Usage indicator ui_o: the average number of times of all individuals who belong to an organization o use one of the iTRACK system components per time unit:

$$\mathrm{ui}_o = \frac{\sum_{i \in o} \mathrm{ui}_i}{|o|}$$

ui_o is measured in [times/hour], where $|o|$ is the number of all individuals who belong to the organization o.

Coordination Indicator Using the iTRACK System

Reaction Time to Messages

The iTRACK system provides users with the ability to exchange text messages. The value of this indicator is based on how long it takes a user to react because of a message she/he has received on average. Indicators like replying to the message or performing an action because of the message content could be insightful. However, aside from being hard to measure, there are cases where a message does not need a reply or an action to be performed. For simplicity, reaction to a message could be considered as opening or reading this message (marking it as read). For example, during the first task of the planning phase PT_1, the time passed between receiving a certain message x by an individual until reading it is $\mathrm{rmt}_x^{\mathrm{PT}_1}$. Accordingly:

- For an individual, the total reaction time to all messages during this task is $\mathrm{rmt}_{\mathrm{total}}^{\mathrm{PT}_1} = \sum_{x \in \mathrm{PT}_1} \mathrm{rmt}_x^{\mathrm{PT}_1}$, and the average is $\mathrm{rmt}_{\mathrm{average}}^{\mathrm{PT}_1} = \frac{\sum_{x \in \mathrm{PT}_1} \mathrm{rmt}_x^{\mathrm{PT}_1}}{|\{x : x \in \mathrm{PT}_1\}|}$.
- For an individual, the total reaction time to all messages during all tasks of the whole planning phase is $\mathrm{rmt}_{\mathrm{total}}^{P} = \sum_{x \in P} \mathrm{rmt}_x^{P}$, and the average is $\mathrm{rmt}_{\mathrm{average}}^{P} = \frac{\sum_{x \in P} \mathrm{rmt}_x^{P}}{|\{x : x \in P\}|}$. Similarly, $\mathrm{rmt}_{\mathrm{total}}^{E}$ and $\mathrm{rmt}_{\mathrm{average}}^{E}$ and $\mathrm{rmt}_{\mathrm{total}}^{R}$ and $\mathrm{rmt}_{\mathrm{average}}^{R}$ can be calculated.
- For an individual, the total reaction time to all messages during the whole mission is $\mathrm{rmt}_{\mathrm{total}}^{\mathrm{mission}} = \sum_{x \in M} \mathrm{rmt}_x^{M}$ or $\mathrm{rmt}_{\mathrm{total}}^{P} + \mathrm{rmt}_{\mathrm{total}}^{E} + \mathrm{rmt}_{\mathrm{total}}^{R}$, and the average is $\mathrm{rmt}_{\mathrm{average}}^{\mathrm{mission}} = \frac{\sum_{x \in M} \mathrm{rmt}_x^{M}}{|\{x : x \in M\}|}$.

If the indicator is to be calculated for a team or an organization, the value can be calculated as the average of averages of all individuals who belong to that team or that organization.

Time-Saving Using the iTRACK System

This indicator requires two different entities (two individuals, two teams, or two organizations) to execute the same task. One of these entities uses the iTRACK system, while the other does not. Otherwise, a comparison can be conducted between the performance of the same entity in the current time and the last time this entity performed the same task, phase, or mission to measure the **learnability**. A comparison can also be conducted between the performance of the entity in the current time and the first time this entity performed the same task, phase, or mission to measure the **efficiency** (this answers questions like: how are we doing compared to the first time we have used the iTRACK system? and what is our overall trend using the iTRACK system?).

Individual Time-Saving Indicator

Let $\text{ts}_i^{\text{PT}_1}$ denotes the individual's time saved per task PT_1. Therefore, $\text{ts}_i^{\text{PT}_1}$ is the difference between the time elapsed by an individual (using the iTRACK) and the time elapsed by another individual (not using the iTRACK) – otherwise, the past reading of the time elapsed by the same first individual – executing the same task PT_1. Accordingly, the individual's time saved for all tasks during the whole planning phase is $\text{ts}_i^P = \sum_{x \in P} \text{ts}_i^x$; similarly, we can calculate the individual's time saved during the execution phase ts_i^E, and the individual's time saved during the response and recovery phase ts_i^R. Furthermore, the individual's time saved during the whole mission is $\text{ts}_i^M = \text{ts}_i^P + \text{ts}_i^E + \text{ts}_i^R$.

Team Average Time-Saving Indicator

For the task PT_1, the average time saved across individuals who belong to a team t performing this task is $\frac{\sum_{i \in t} \text{ts}_i^{\text{PT}_1}}{|t|}$. The same equation can be applied for a phase (e.g., P) and a whole mission, i.e., $\frac{\sum_{i \in t} \text{ts}_i^P}{|t|}$ and $\frac{\sum_{i \in t} \text{ts}_i^M}{|t|}$, respectively.

Organization Overall Average Time-Saving Indicator

For an organization o, the average time saved across all individuals who belong to this organization during the task PT_1, the phase P, for example, or the whole mission can be calculated by $\frac{\sum_{i \in o} \text{ts}_i^{\text{PT}_1}}{|o|}$, $\frac{\sum_{i \in o} \text{ts}_i^P}{|o|}$, and $\frac{\sum_{i \in o} \text{ts}_i^M}{|o|}$, respectively.

In general, the time saving related to specific tasks like loading trucks and completing deliveries. can be separately considered independent indicators.

Cost Saving Using the iTRACK System

The cost could be calculated as the actual cost of executing the task(s), phase(s), or mission(s) per an individual, team, or organization, which is challenging to be done quickly. Otherwise, it can be taken as the average cost per the time unit for an individual during executing task(s), phase(s), or mission(s) multiplied by her/his time elapsed executing this/these task(s), phase(s), or mission(s), respectively. The same approach can be applied to a team or an organization by summing the cost of the individuals who belong to this team or organization, respectively.

Like the time-saving indicator, this requires two entities (individual/team/organization) to execute the same task for comparison. One entity uses the iTRACK system, while the other does not. Otherwise, the comparisons can be conducted between the performance of the entity in the current time and the last time the entity performed the same task, phase, or mission to measure the **learnability**. The comparisons can also be conducted between the performance of the entity in the current time and the first time this entity performed the same task, phase, or mission to measure the **efficiency**. Like the time-saving indicators, cost saving for specific tasks like loading trucks and completing deliveries can be separately considered independent indicators on their own.

The iTRACK Usefulness Subjective Evaluation

Several questionnaires can subjectively assess the system's usefulness from the users' viewpoint. For example, from the reviewed questionnaires that cover usefulness in the "Usability and User Experience Subjective Evaluation" subsection of this chapter:

- Davis' Perceived Usefulness and Ease of Use
- CSUQ/PSSUQ
- USE

To subjectively measure the usefulness of the iTRACK system or one of its components, as mentioned earlier, Davis' Perceived Usefulness and Ease of Use questionnaire could be used, as it has been very well accepted and used for a long time (as it is part of the Technology Acceptance Model TAM) (Müller & Friedenberg, 2011). Considering the limited time of the users testing the iTRACK system, another reason to select Davis' is that it is shorter than the others.

System Implementation

System Overview

The iTRACK reporting and evaluation system are a web system implementation of the proposed integrated system framework that monitors different indicators concerning the iTRACK system and its users during different missions and presents these indicators. The web system was designed to serve the iTRACK system users by giving them indicators about the system performance and their performance. Figure 6 shows the context diagram or level zero workflow diagram (a.k.a. data flow diagram) of the iTRACK reporting and evaluation system. The main external entities in addition to the "User" are the "Database" on "MySQL Server" and the

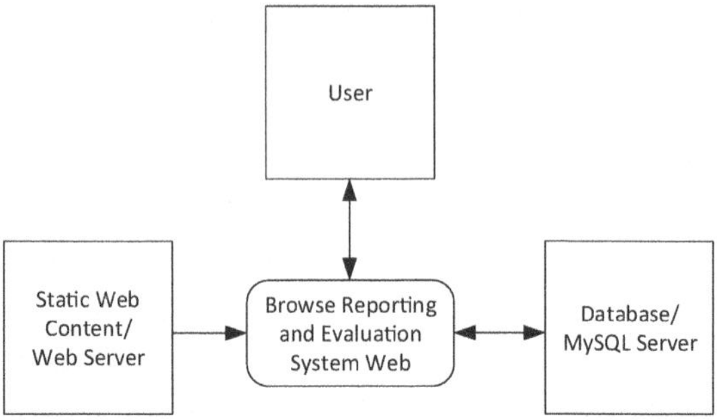

Fig. 6 Context-level workflow diagram of the iTRACK reporting and evaluation system

"Static Web Content" on the system's "Web Server." The database has several tables related to the users and system management and the main tables, which the system uses to store indicator-related data. Communication between the primary process of browsing the "Web Server" entity and other entities is two ways in all cases except with the "Static Web Content" entity, taking into consideration that the "User" entity can edit data in the "Database" entity when conducting system management.

The iTRACK reporting and evaluation system source code is available at https://github.com/ahgawad/iTRACK-Reporting-and-Evaluation-System, under GNU General Public License v3.0. The iTRACK reporting and evaluation system is web-based[2] and was built using common standard web technologies such as HyperText Markup Language (HTML), Cascading Style Sheets (CSS), and JavaScript (W3Techs, 2016) on the client-side. The iTRACK reporting and evaluation system uses Python/Django web-service framework on the server-side. Python programming language is popular among data scientists. According to the KDNuggets software poll in 2016, Python came in the second position after R with a share of 45.8%, with +51% growth over 2015 (R, Python Duel, 2017). Such popularity is reflected in the availability of several Python packages commonly used in developing scientific/data science applications like ours.

System's Graphical User Interface

The iTRACK reporting and evaluation system is a web-based system that provides different views corresponding to different functionalities. The system provides a *User view* for the users and an *Admin view* for the administrators to maintain the system's database. Figure 7 shows the components of the iTRACK reporting and evaluation system. The primary view is the *User view* which shows the iTRACK development indicators, the users' survey inputs and results, and the users' performance indicators, including standard operating procedures (SOP)/policies

[2] With proper installation, the system can be used offline on a PC or within a local area network.

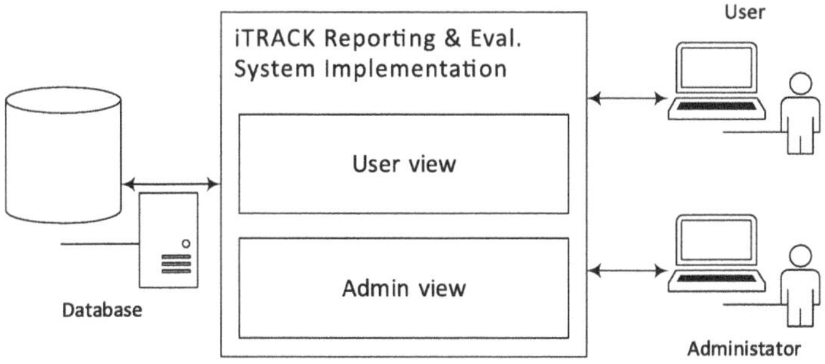

Fig. 7 Components of the iTRACK reporting and evaluation system implementation

compliance surveys inputs and results.[3] On the other side, the *Admin view* presents a tool for the system's administrators to add new development indicators, add new iTRACK future system components, add users' surveys, and add new SOPs/policies performance indicators in addition to users' accounts management. In addition to describing the system's graphical user interface, this section works as a user manual and guide on how to use the system.

User View

The iTRACK reporting and evaluation system has a main/instructions page. The primary/instructions page is shown in Fig. 8. Menus on the navigation bar at the top of this page and all other pages also work as an entry point to all system functionalities. In addition to the Home menu, which refers to this specific first page, the menus are:

- Development Indicators menu item refers and guides the user to the development indicators page.
- User Surveys menu item which takes the user to either:
  - Users Surveys Show page
  - Users Surveys Entry page
- Performance Indicators menu item which guides the user to one of four options which are as follows:
  - Performance Indicators Load sub-menu item which allows users with the correct permissions to load the performance logs generated by the iTRACK system to the iTRACK reporting and evaluation system

[3] Based on the best practices of the UN and other humanitarian organizations, the iTRACK project introduced a set of standard operating procedures (SOPs) and policies to support humanitarian missions.

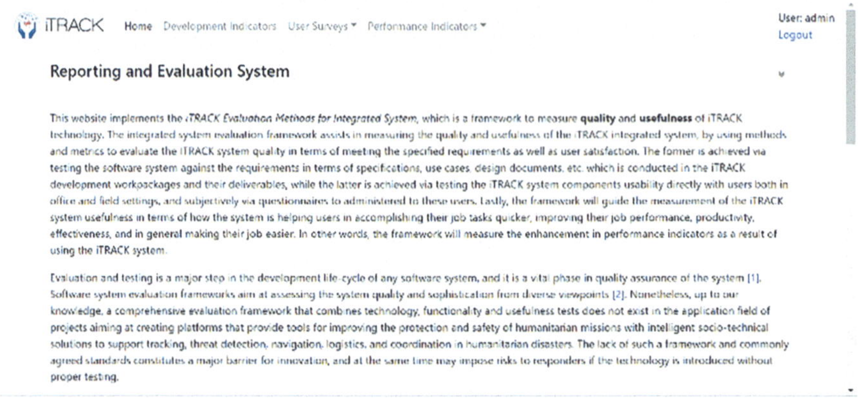

Fig. 8 The main and instructions page

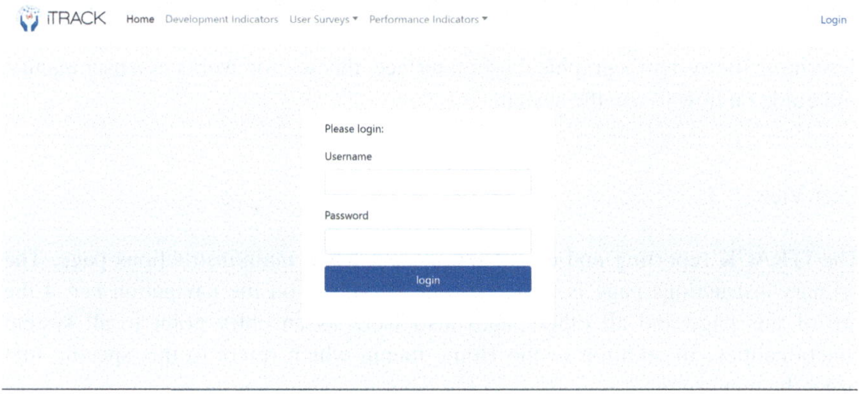

Fig. 9 Login page

- Performance Show sub-menu item which guides the user to show the results of the performance indicators logged by the iTRACK system components
- SOP Entry sub-menu item which enables a user with proper permissions to fill the SOPs/policies compliance survey for a particular mission
- SOP Show sub-menu item which allows a user to see the SOPs/policies compliance report

In general, the user view is possible to be accessed by users with proper permissions. These permissions can be set in the admin view by a system administrator (Fig. 9 shows the login page to the admin view).

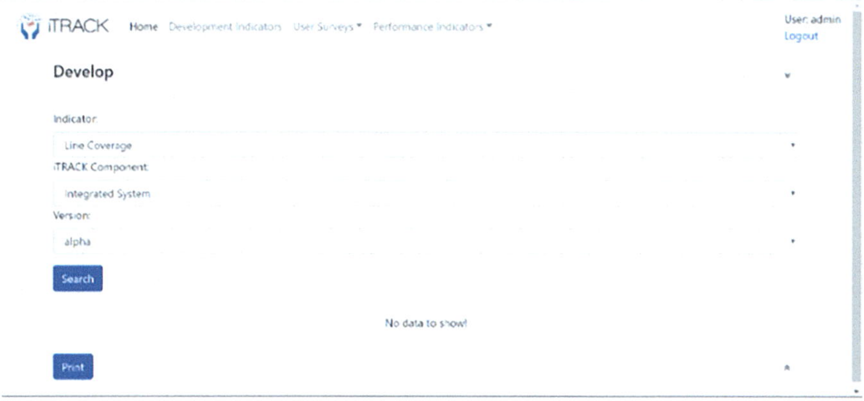

Fig. 10 The page of the development indicators (select indicator and component)

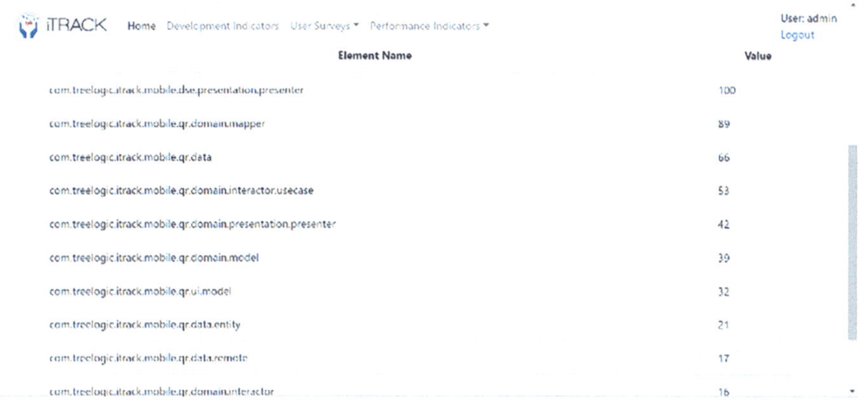

Fig. 11 The page of the development indicator (indicator values)

Development Indicators Page

Any logged-in user can view the development indicators on the Development Indicators page. The system is not limited to any of the development indicators, tested software components , or software versions presented on this page shown in Fig. 10 (Fig. 11 shows the indicator values). With future extensibility in mind, new development indicators, tested software components, and software versions can be added via the admin view.

Users' Surveys Entry Page

The users' survey page enables the logged-in user to fill one of the user surveys available in the iTRACK reporting and evaluation system for any tested software components. The user can select the survey, component name, and version, as shown

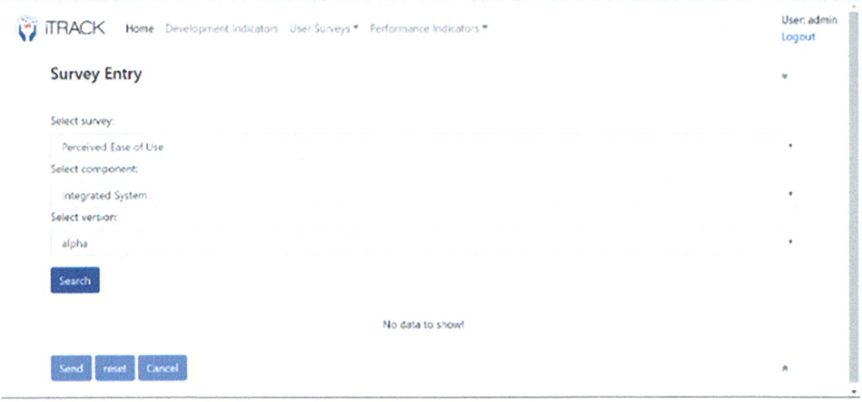

Fig. 12 The page of the user surveys input (select survey)

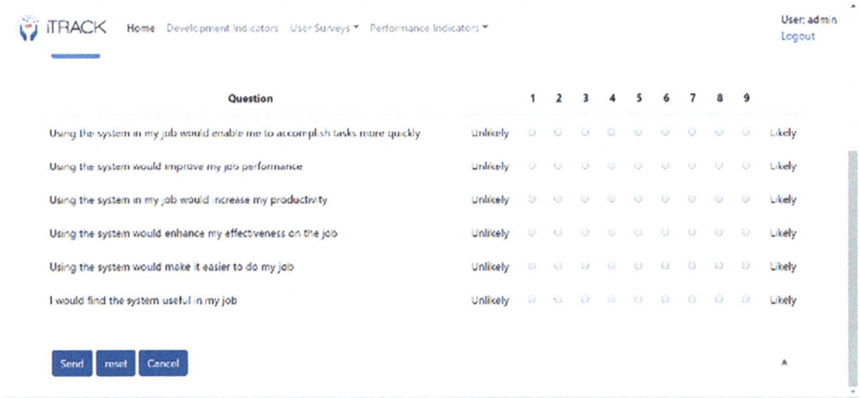

Fig. 13 The page of the user surveys input (survey to fill)

in Fig. 12. Pressing the Search button retrieves the selected survey from the system and shows it on the same page as shown in Fig. 13. The system will not allow the user to answer the same survey for the same combination of a tested software component and version more than one time.

Users' Surveys Results Page

The user-surveys results page displayed in Fig. 14 allows the user to see the collective results of a specific user survey for a particular combination of a tested software component and version for the team(s) she/he is a member of. If the user is an administrator, she/he will be able to see a collective result for the whole organization. The user might be interested in seeing more recent results or even older ones; the system allows the user to select a starting and ending date, which

Fig. 14 The page of the user surveys results (select survey)

Fig. 15 The page of the user surveys results

will be used to retrieve survey answers answered in between. The system retrieves the results from the database and shows them in the form of a diverging stacked bar chart (as shown in Fig. 15).

Performance Indicators Load Page

Software components log several indicators according to their design. The iTRACK reporting and evaluation system allows an administrator to upload any tested software component's log file (if prepared in the correct format, see the GitHub repository referred to earlier in the "System Overview" subsection for more information). Figure 16 shows the Performance Indicator Upload page, in which the administrator can provide the path of the log file. As soon as the log file is selected, the system parses and views it, as demonstrated in Fig. 17. If the selected file has

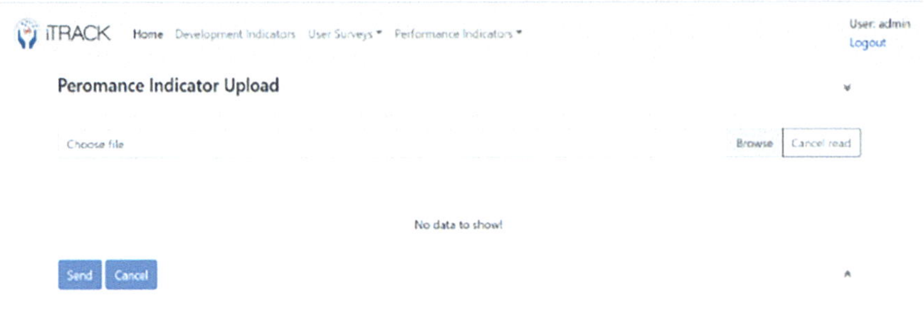

Fig. 16 The page of the performance indicators upload

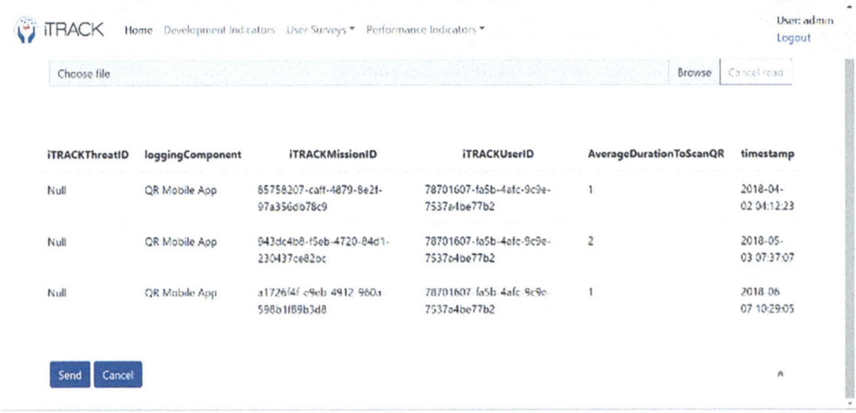

Fig. 17 The page of the performance indicators upload

any lines with formatting errors, they will not be parsed. The administrator can then upload the logs to the server of the iTRACK reporting and evaluation system. The system saves only new records and ignores any repetitions.

Performance Indicators Show Page

As described earlier, the tasks are performed by individuals. These individuals could be part of one team or grouped into different teams. Therefore, if an indicator is on the highest resolution (i.e., measuring the indicator's value for one individual working only on one task), it could be scaled up to this individual working through an entire phase or even the whole mission. The same principle applies when scaling up from an individual to a team or the whole organization. In the system, to view performance indicator results, the iTRACK reporting and evaluation system allows a user with administrative privileges, as shown in Fig. 18, to select:

- The user(s) to whom the performance indicator values belong, otherwise select an entire team

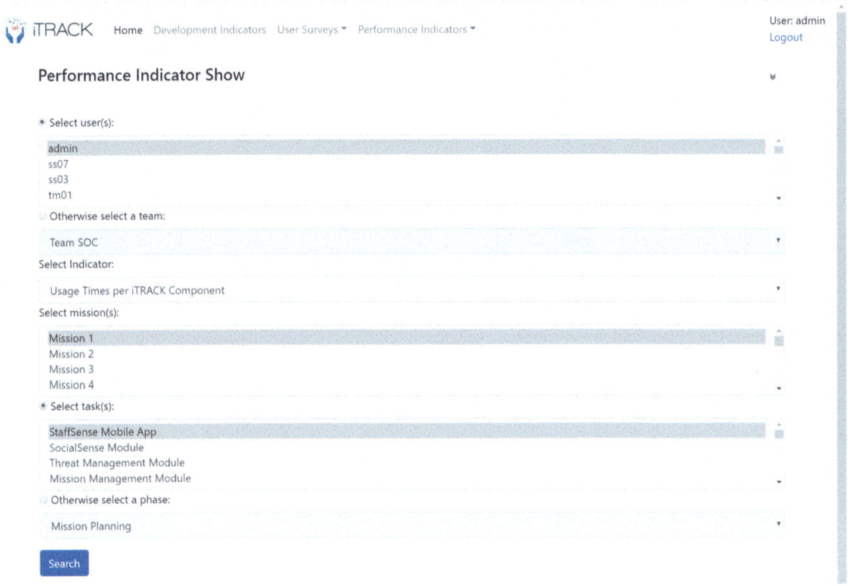

Fig. 18 The page of the performance indicators (select indicator)

- The indicator itself
- The mission(s) in which the performance indicator values have been captured
- The task(s) in which the performance indicator values have been captured, otherwise a whole phase

As shown in Fig. 19, the system shows detailed results concerning the iTRACK performance indicator for the selected parameters. To facilitate human readability, the results include textual comments about the indicator values, including some essential descriptive statistics like the general trend of the indicator, maximum value and its date, minimum value, and its date. In addition, the system presents a chart plotting the values of the indicator, including the linear trend.

SOPs/Policies Entry Page

The iTRACK technology is supposed to help humanitarians act according to the SOPs and policies. A logged-in user can fill the SOPs/policies compliance survey for a mission she/he is the leader of (otherwise, if she/he is an administrator), as shown in Fig. 20.

The user will be able to fill out a survey for the selected mission to assess the compliance of the staff of this mission with the SOPs and policies. Figure 21 shows a snapshot from the SOPs/Policies Entry page with SOPs and policies checkboxes list. The figure also shows an example of an error message that will appear if the

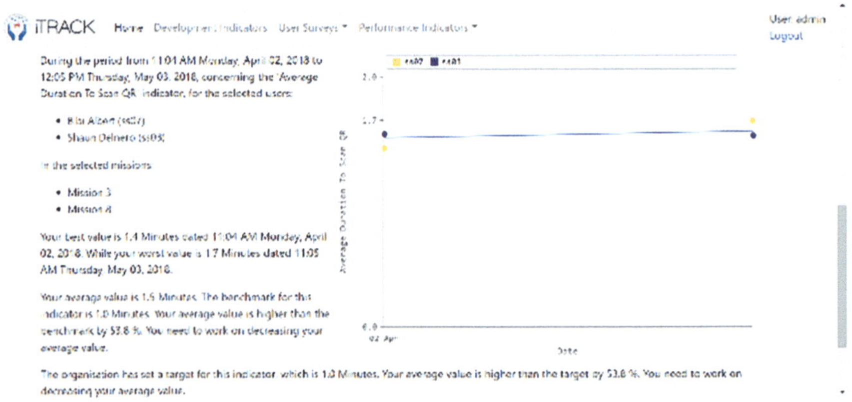

Fig. 19 The page of the performance indicators (human-readable textual results)

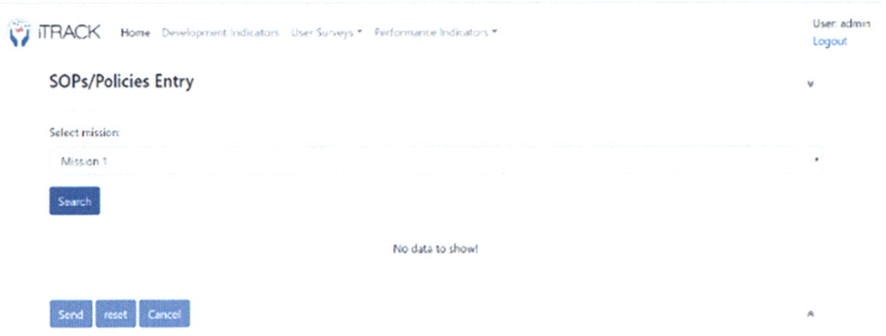

Fig. 20 The page of the SOPs/policies input (select mission)

user tries to check an SOP dependent on other SOPs that have not been checked yet or uncheck an SOP dependent on other SOPs that are still checked.

SOPs/Policies Show Results Page

A logged-in user with the correct permissions to view the SOPs/policies survey results for particular mission(s) can use the SOPs/Policies Show Results page shown in Fig. 22. The page allows the user to select a mission or more to view the results. The system accordingly shows the detailed results concerning the compliance with SOPs/policies of the selected mission(s), as shown in Fig. 23. The results are grouped under SOPs/policies tags. To also facilitate human readability, these results contain textual comments showing the SOPs/policies the team has not complied with. In addition, the system presents a chart showing the values of the SOPs/policies compliance indicator.

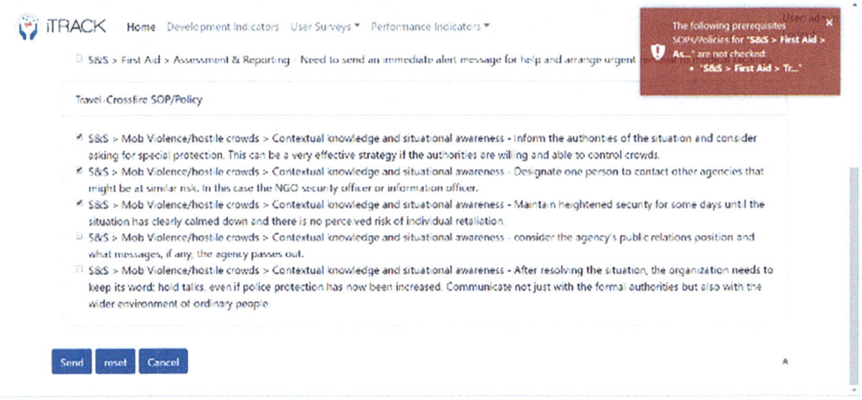

Fig. 21 The page of the SOPs/policies compliance entry (fill the survey with error messages)

Fig. 22 The page of the SOPs/policies results (select mission(s))

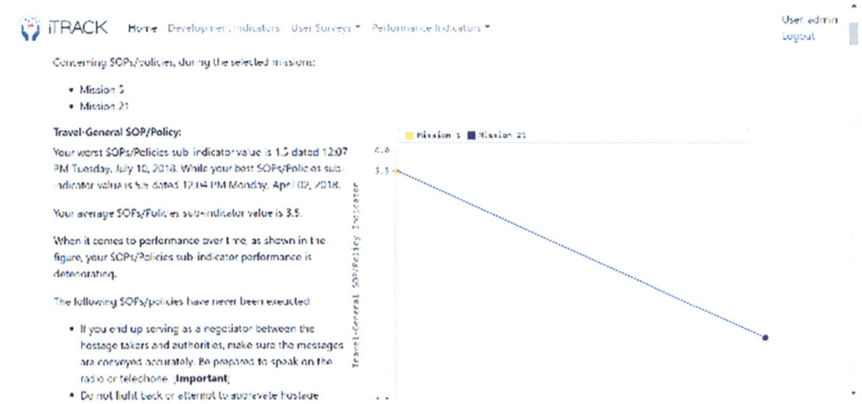

Fig. 23 The page of the SOPs/policies results (human-readable textual results)

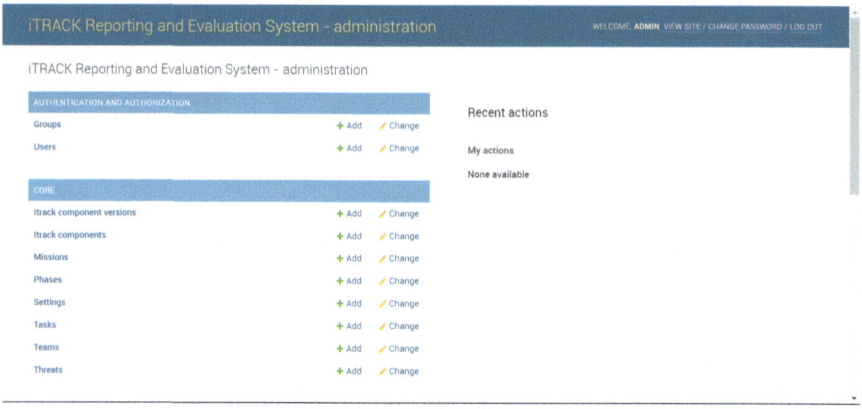

Fig. 24 The admin view for logged-in users

Administration View

The administration view could be viewed as a database management system for the underlying database of the iTRACK reporting and evaluation system. In this view, a user with proper administrator credentials can add, edit, and remove records from the different tables related to all indicators and results shown in all views of the *User view* mentioned earlier. This will keep the database updated with new and correct records. Figure 24 shows the page that will appear by calling the *Admin view* after passing the username and password authentication page.

As an example of the related admin pages, the previously mentioned set of performance indicators was added to the iTRACK reporting and evaluation system. Nonetheless, an administrator can add a new/edit/delete one or more performance indicators. As shown in Fig. 25, a performance indicator can be defined by:

- Adding an indicator name
- Adding the indicator's unit of measurement
- Deciding if the indicator is an average or an absolute value
- Deciding if the indicator uses a normal or inverted scale
- Deciding if the indicator is related to user performance or related to the performance of a technical component (e.g., the "Threat Detection")
- Adding the indicator's whereabouts (which is the name used for this indicator in the log file generated by the software components)

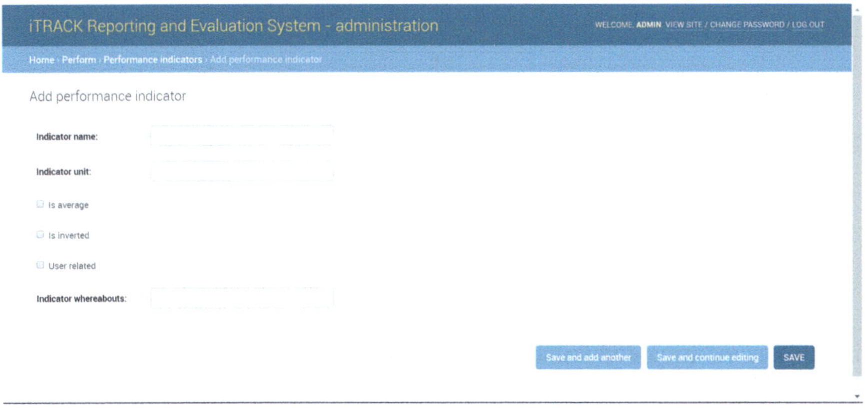

Fig. 25 The page to add a new performance indicator in the admin view

Summary and Discussion

Evaluation and testing are significant steps in developing software, but they are critical if innovation is used in highly sensitive contexts such as humanitarian conflicts. It is a vital phase in quality assurance of the system in terms of assessing the system quality and sophistication from diverse viewpoints. Nonetheless, an integrated evaluation framework that combines technology, functionality, and usefulness tests does not exist. This chapter presents metrics that were developed to help measure the quality and usefulness of a system and apply them to the case of the iTRACK system, a tracking and monitoring system for humanitarian conflicts.

This chapter reviewed the adequate evaluation methods and metrics to compile this integrated evaluation framework to assist in measuring the quality and usefulness of the iTRACK system. We have indicated that the software system quality is assessed in terms of software testing. We have introduced different software testing methods and levels used in software testing in general.

The usability of the iTRACK system is assessed separately, either via the system usability testing directly with users or via questionnaires administered to them. Moreover, for users to find any system useful, this system should solve a problem they face, fill a need, or offer them something. System usefulness is about helping accomplish job tasks quicker; improving job performance, productivity, and effectiveness; and making it easier to do the job. To measure the usefulness of the iTRACK system, we have proposed several performance indicators, in addition to subjectively recognizing the users' opinions about the usefulness of the system.

The iTRACK integrated system evaluation framework has been reviewed by several iTRACK project partners that belong to academia and software development, and their notes were taken into consideration in the final version. Figure 26 shows the pillars and details of the final framework.

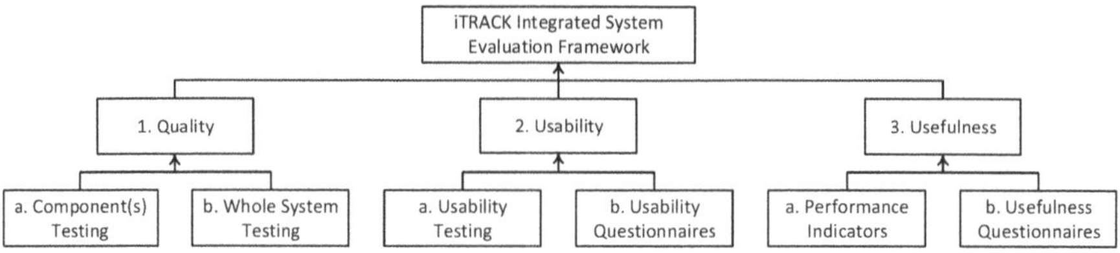

Fig. 26 iTRACK integrated system framework

The chapter also presents the iTRACK reporting and evaluation system that implements the proposed framework. A detailed look at graphical user interface design and functionalities was provided. The iTRACK reporting and evaluation system was developed with extensibility in mind. Extensibility is in terms of the system's capability of allowing its administrators to add new development indicators, performance indicators, surveys, SOPs, etc.

In April 2018, the iTRACK project conducted a simulated environment exercise. This exercise is an example of applying the iTRACK integrated system evaluation framework, as it was the first iTRACK system testing with users. During this exercise, participants tested the ready iTRACK system components. The participants were asked to complete specific tasks using the iTRACK system. The suitable usability and usefulness metrics and questionnaires proposed in this chapter were used during the exercise. The iTRACK reporting and evaluation system was used during the exercise. Some development results, like code coverage, were included in the iTRACK reporting and evaluation system as examples of the development indicators. The results of the questionnaires collected during the exercise were included in the iTRACK reporting and evaluation system as examples of users' surveys as well. Finally, some performance indicators were randomly generated for presentation purposes instead of actual results for privacy reasons. Results of the mission's SOPs/policies surveys were randomly generated and included in the system for presentation purposes as well.

For future work, the framework still requires more testing with the iTRACK system as well as other systems. For the iTRACK, the selected set of indicators and surveys was reviewed by the iTRACK partners as mentioned above. However, other systems will inevitably require other indicators. Our integrated framework and our reporting and evaluation system implementation facilitate extensibility in that sense by design. Accordingly, new development indicators, performance indicators, surveys, etc., could be easily added to the framework and the reporting and evaluation system based on the choices and needs of the target system. The reporting and evaluation system is available as an open source to facilitate further design changes or specific project adaptation requirements.

Acknowledgments This work is carried out as part of the iTRACK project, funded by the European Union's Horizon 2020 research and innovation program under grant agreement No 700510.

References

Black Box Testing, http://softwaretestingfundamentals.com/black-box-testing/. Last accessed 16 Mar 2018.

Boloix, G., & Robillard, P. N. (1995). A software system evaluation framework. *Computer, 28*, 17–26. https://doi.org/10.1109/2.476196

Borsci, S., Federici, S., & Lauriola, M. (2009). On the dimensionality of the system usability scale: A test of alternative measurement models. *Cognitive Processing, 10*, 193–197. https://doi.org/10.1007/s10339-009-0268-9

Brooke, J. (1996). SUS-A quick and dirty usability scale. In *Usability evaluation in industry* (Vol. 189, pp. 4–7). Taylor & Francis.

Corona, A. *What is usability and why should i care?*https://digitalconference.yale.edu/what-usability-and-why-should-i-care. Last accessed 14 Feb 2019.

Data, N. *13 essential software development metrics to ensure quality*, https://blog.usenotion.com/13-essential-software-development-metrics-to-ensure-quality-219cfc264ed1. Last accessed 19 Nov 2018.

Davis, F. D. (1989). Perceived usefulness, perceived ease of use, and user acceptance of information technology. *MIS Quarterly, 13*, 319–340. https://doi.org/10.2307/249008

Davis, F. D. (1993). User acceptance of information technology: System characteristics, user perceptions and behavioral impacts. *International Journal of Man-Machine Studies, 38*, 475–487. https://doi.org/10.1006/imms.1993.1022

EN_Tech_Direct. *Usability test report for mobile applications part ii: When the perfect combination of smart phone & music application*, http://www.technical-direct.com/en/usability-test-report-for-mobile-applications-part-ii-when-the-perfect-combination-of-smart-phone-music-application/. Last accessed 19 Feb 2018.

Gray Box Testing, http://softwaretestingfundamentals.com/gray-box-testing/. Last accessed 17 Mar 2018.

Humanitarian outcomes: Aid worker security database, https://aidworkersecurity.org/. Last accessed 14 Feb 2019.

IEEE Computer Society (Eds.). (1991). *IEEE standard glossary of software engineering terminology*. Institute of Electrical and Electronics Engineers.

Issues, https://docs.gitlab.com/11.6/ee/user/project/issues/index.html. Last accessed 19 Nov 2018.

ISTQB Glossary, http://glossary.istqb.org/. Last accessed 25 Apr 2018.

iTRACK Project – iTRACK, http://www.itrack-project.eu/. Last accessed 29 Jan 2018.

iTRACK: D8.1–Market analysis, https://www.itrack-project.eu/media/articles/files/iTRACK_WP8_D8.1_Market_Analysis_and_technology_foresight_FINAL.pdf. Last accessed 30 Jan 2022a.

iTRACK: D9.5–Final conference brief, https://www.itrack-project.eu/media/articles/files/D9.5%20%E2%80%93%20Final%20Conference%20Brief.pdf. Last accessed 30 Jan 2022b.

Jovanović, I. (2009). Software testing methods and techniques. *The IPSI BgD Transactions on Internet Research, 5*, 30–41. http://tir.ipsitransactions.org/2009/January/Paper%2006.pdf

Laugwitz, B., Schrepp, M., & Held, T. (2006). Konstruktion eines Fragebogens zur Messung der User Experience von Softwareprodukten. In H. M. Heinecke & H. Paul (Eds.), *Mensch und Computer 2006*. Oldenbourg Wissenschaftsverlag. https://doi.org/10.1524/9783486841749.125

Laugwitz, B., Held, T., & Schrepp, M. (2008). Construction and evaluation of a user experience questionnaire. In A. Holzinger (Ed.), *HCI and usability for education and work* (pp. 63–76). Springer Berlin Heidelberg. https://doi.org/10.1007/978-3-540-89350-9_6

McKay, J., Hamburg, M., & ISTQB Glossary Working Group (Eds.). (2016). *Standard glossary of terms used in software testing: Version 3.1*. International Software Testing Qualifications Board.

Müller, T., & Friedenberg, D. (2011). *ISTQB WG foundation level: ISTQB certified tester-foundation level syllabus*. International Software Testing Qualifications Board.

Nielsen, J. (1993). *Usability engineering*. Morgan Kaufmann.

Nielsen, J. *Usability 101: Introduction to usability*, https://www.nngroup.com/articles/usability-101-introduction-to-usability/. Last accessed 14 Mar 2018a.

Nielsen, J. *Severity ratings for usability problems: Article by Jakob Nielsen*, https://www.nngroup.com/articles/how-to-rate-the-severity-of-usability-problems/. Last accessed 1 Apr 2018b.

Noori, N. S., Wang, Y., Comes, T., Schwarz, P., & Lukosch, H. (2017). Behind the scenes of scenario-based training: Understanding scenario design and requirements in high-risk and uncertain environments. In T. Comes, F. Bénaben, C. Hanachi, M. Lauras, & A. Montarnal (Eds.), *Proceedings of the 14th ISCRAM conference* (pp. 948–959). Albi, France.

Perlman, G. *User interface usability evaluation with web-based questionnaires*, http://garyperlman.com/quest/. Last accessed 7 Mar 2018.

R, Python Duel As Top Analytics, Data Science software – KDnuggets 2016 Software Poll Results, https://www.kdnuggets.com/2016/06/r-python-top-analytics-data-mining-data-science-software.html. Last accessed 5 Dec 2017.

Sandvik, K. B., Jacobsen, K. L., & McDonald, S. M. (2017). Do no harm: A taxonomy of the challenges of humanitarian experimentation. *International Review of the Red Cross, 99*, 319–344.

Sauro, J. (2015). SUPR-Q: A comprehensive measure of the quality of the website user experience. *Journal of Usability Studies, 10*, 19.

Sauro, J. *Measuring usefulness*, https://measuringu.com/usefulness/. Last accessed 30 Mar 2018a.

Sauro, J. *10 essential usability metrics*, https://measuringu.com/essential-metrics/. Last accessed 8 Mar 2018b.

System usability scale. (2017). https://en.wikipedia.org/w/index.php?title=System_ usability_scale&oldid=805142158

Types of software testing for dummies, https://www.360logica.com/blog/types-of-software-testing-for-dummies/. Last accessed 6 Mar 2018.

Usability and user experience surveys, http://edutechwiki.unige.ch/en/Usability_and_user_experience_surveys. Last accessed 7 Mar 2018.

Van de Walle, B., & Comes, T. (2014). Risk accelerators in disasters. In *International conference on advanced information systems engineering* (pp. 12–23). Springer.

Van de Walle, B., & Comes, T. (2015). On the nature of information management in complex and natural disasters. *Procedia Engineering., 107*, 403–411.

W3Techs. *W3Techs – Extensive and reliable web technology surveys*, https://w3techs.com/. Last accessed 26 Nov 2016.

What is a White Box Testing? http://www.softwaretestingclass.com/white-box-testing/. Last accessed 17 Mar 2018a.

White Box Testing, http://softwaretestingfundamentals.com/white-box-testing/. Last accessed 16 Mar 2018b.

Rural First Responders and Communication Technology: A Mixed Methods Approach to Assessing Their Challenges and Needs

Kerrianne Buchanan, Yee-Yin Choong, Shanée Dawkins, and Sandra Spickard Prettyman

Abstract Although new technology may benefit rural first responders to help them serve their communities, to date little is known about what communication technology problems rural first responders most need addressed and what future technology they desire. This chapter explores communication technology problems and needs of rural first responders in the USA based on data from semi-structured interviews with 63 rural first responders and survey responses from 2698 rural first responders. Data from both the interviews and the survey come from rural first responders representing four disciplines: Communications Center & 9-1-1 Services, Emergency Medical Services, Fire Service, and Law Enforcement. Analysis of both qualitative and quantitative data is used to identify the problems rural first responders experience with communication technology and the technology needs they identify as most important moving forward. Their greatest problems were with reliable coverage/connectivity, interoperability, information technology (IT) implementation and cost of technology, and physical ergonomics. Rural first responders' greatest need was to address the problems they experience with current communication technology, but they were interested in new technology that leverages real-time access to information and location tracking. Implications for researchers and developers of public safety communication technology are discussed.

Keywords Communication technology · First responders · Public safety · Rural communities · Usability

K. Buchanan · Y.-Y. Choong (✉) · S. Dawkins
National Institute of Standards and Technology, Gaithersburg, MD, USA
e-mail: kerrianne.buchanan@nist.gov; yee-yin.choong@nist.gov; shanee.dawkins@nist.gov

S. S. Prettyman
Culture Catalyst, LLC, Chicago, IL, USA
e-mail: sspretty50@icloud.com

H. J. Scholl et al. (eds.), *Disaster Management and Information Technology*, Public Administration and Information Technology 40,
https://doi.org/10.1007/978-3-031-20939-0_10

Introduction

Rural Environments and Incident Response

First responders in public safety disciplines, namely, Communications Center & 9-1-1 Services (COMMS), Emergency Medical Services (EMS), Fire Service (FF), and Law Enforcement (LE) personnel, respond to emergency incidents to serve and protect their communities. These professions face many dangers and difficulties. First responders in rural communities encounter unique challenges by nature of the rural areas they serve. To better understand these challenges and how to mitigate them, rural areas have been a topic of research in the USA (Ricci et al., 2003; Tiesman et al., 2007) and in countries around the world (Aftyka et al., 2014; Birdsey et al., 2016; Hang et al., 2004; Jennings et al., 2006). Many studies focus exclusively on rural emergency response (O'Meara et al., 2002; Gamache et al., 2007; Oliver & Meier, 2004; Ramsell et al., 2019; Reddy et al., 2009; Roberts et al., 2014).

A commonality across studies above is that rural first responders are tasked to serve small communities that span wide landmasses. This can lead to longer ambulance response times in rural areas as supported by studies (Aftyka et al., 2014; Jennings et al., 2006). According to the US Census Bureau's definition, rural areas comprise 97% of the US's landmass, but only 19.3% of the population (Ratcliffe et al., 2016; US Census Bureau Rural America, 2022).

Rural first responders also respond to incidents resulting from the unique terrain of the area. Some rural areas are impacted by seasonal weather, experiencing high rates of sporting injuries during certain seasons, such as skiing in winter (Birdsey et al., 2016). There are also high rates of injuries during times of the year with more severe weather, such as monsoons (Hang et al., 2004). Injury hospitalization and death percentages are often higher in rural than urban areas (Tiesman et al., 2007; Coben et al., 2009). Unfortunately, rural areas are often served by rural first responders with small staffs that rely on volunteers or community workers who often have less experience and training (Gamache et al., 2007; Roberts et al., 2014).

Rural Barriers to Technology

Environmental features make incident response different for rural first responders relative to their urban and suburban counterparts. Rural first responders also face challenges in utilizing the proper equipment to respond to incidents. Communication technology, such as radios, cell phones/smartphones, and mobile data terminals (MDTs), are some of the most important tools first responders use in incident response, allowing them to obtain information about incidents and coordinate the appropriate response (Choong et al., 2018). Unfortunately, rural first responders face two primary barriers that prevent them from accessing and using communication technology.

First, rural areas tend to lack the infrastructure needed to implement the latest communication technology (Federal Communications Commission, 2020). This lack of infrastructure results in a lack of broadband access in many rural areas (Federal Communications Commission, 2020) and slow broadband speeds in some areas (Meinrath et al., 2019; Vogels, 2021) that may ultimately prevent rural first responders from accessing and using technology for incident response. Moreover, the costs for buying, installing, and maintaining broadband infrastructure are high in rural areas (Strover, 2001; Yankelevich et al., 2017), sometimes due to the impact of natural geographic barriers (e.g., mountains) and harsh weather conditions on equipment (Pötsch et al., 2016; Surana et al., 2008).

Second, some studies suggest that people in rural areas are reticent to adopt new technology. Despite many rural areas gaining more access to broadband infrastructure, the urban-rural broadband adoption gap continues to persist (Dickes et al., 2010; U.S. Department of Commerce Economics and Statistics Administration and the National Telecommunications and Information Administration, 2010; Whitacre, 2008). Some studies suggest demographic disparities between rural and urban areas are related to these lower adoption rates (Whitacre, 2008). Another study finds that broadband adoption in rural areas is predicated on individuals' prior experience, expected outcomes, and self-efficacy when using the internet (LaRose et al., 2007). Relatedly, studies examining non-internet users found that their primary reason against adopting broadband in their homes was that they did not have any interest or need for broadband (U.S. Department of Commerce Economics and Statistics Administration and the National Telecommunications and Information Administration, 2010). This was the top reason for both rural and urban households. However, a larger share of rural households than urban had this belief. These studies suggest that people in rural areas may not adopt technology because the benefits of new technology are not made clear to them (Dickes et al., 2010; LaRose et al., 2007), possibly preventing rural first responders from utilizing tools that would help them during incident response.

Opportunities to Address Barriers

New legislation has created opportunities for mitigating these challenges by developing new technology specifically for first responders. The US Middle Class Tax Relief and Job Creation Act of 2012 (Public Law 112-96, 2012) (Middle Class Tax Relief and Job Creation Act, 2012) provided funding and dedicated broadband to establish the Nationwide Public Safety Broadband Network (NPSBN). While NPSBN development is in progress, this network will improve broadband access for first responders by supplementing land mobile radio (LMR) with Long-Term Evolution (LTE) solutions. In addition, the Public Safety Communications Research (PSCR) program at the National Institute of Standards and Technology (NIST) is leading a coordinated, multidisciplinary research effort to facilitate the LMR to LTE transition (National Institute of Standards and Technology (NIST), 2022).

The public safety research and development community has focused on developing new communication technology for first responders to operate with the new network. By improving broadband access and developing new communication technology, rural first responders can better share critical information during emergencies and disasters (Comfort et al., 2004) as well as use new capabilities such as those that improve location information (Weichelt et al., 2019) and assist with providing care to people in remote locations ahead of ambulance arrival (e.g., telehealth (Ricci et al., 2003)).

The NPSBN is poised to help address rural first responders' need for broadband infrastructure. However, solutions are needed to ensure that rural first responders will adopt new communication technology. Recent studies have emphasized adoption as a critical consideration when developing new technology for rural first responders and communities (Weichelt et al., 2019; Gasco-Hernandez et al., 2019). These studies including those from the NIST PSCR program (Choong et al., 2018) emphasize that technology showing great promise to help first responders must be developed with the context and needs in mind for first responders to adopt its use. The concept of including users of technology in technology development is central to human factors research and user-centered design (International Organization for Standardization, 2019). By understanding the user, a developer can design technology with the users' needs in mind (Hackos & Redish, 1998). Ultimately, this improves the usability of a product, increasing its efficiency, effectiveness, and satisfaction to the user (International Organization for Standardization, 2019). Therefore, rural first responders must be directly included in research so that technology meets their needs within their context of use.

Relevant Research on Rural First Responders

To date, most studies that focused on rural first responders examined their unique context of use. Studies examining the context for rural emergency and healthcare workers have found that rural emergency responders rely on community workers and volunteers (Roberts et al., 2014; Greene et al., 2019), feel overburdened (Oliver & Meier, 2004; Iversen et al., 2002), have fewer resources and equipment (Oliver & Meier, 2004; Greene et al., 2019; Pilemalm, 2018), and serve wide, remote, and geographically diverse areas (Oliver & Meier, 2004; Greene et al., 2019; Iversen et al., 2002). However, fewer studies have investigated how rural first responders perceive, interact with, and use communication technology.

The studies that have assessed rural first responders' perceptions and use of communication technology has focused broadly on emergency and healthcare professionals, including nurses, emergency department workers, and EMS personnel (O'Meara et al., 2002; Reddy et al., 2009) as well as community citizens, volunteers, and organizations (Ramsell et al., 2019; Pilemalm et al., 2013). These studies find that emergency, healthcare, and volunteer personnel are hindered by their communication devices due to the lack of interoperability between the numerous devices they use (O'Meara et al., 2002; Reddy et al., 2009) and connectivity problems (Reddy et al., 2009) from a lack of infrastructure (O'Meara et al., 2002; Pilemalm et al., 2013). Recently Ramsell et al. (2019) found that usability and interoperability are important for semiprofessional emergency responders and community volunteers when using a smartphone application supporting communication during incident response.

Gaps in Past Studies

Past studies have provided important insights. However, they have two important gaps. First, the studies that have assessed rural first responders' perceptions and use of communication technology are largely specific to healthcare professionals and EMS personnel. It is unclear if these same problems transfer to other types of rural first responder disciplines, or if other disciplines have different problems with communication technology. Second, many of these studies examined limited types of technology, focusing largely on network coverage and mobile devices (e.g., smartphones) rather than on other communication technology more broadly such as radios, MDTs, and body cameras. More studies are required to identify useful functionalities beyond networks and smartphones and instead assess needs broadly across communication technology for rural first responders.

The "Voices of First Responders" Research

Our research is part of the user interface/user experience portfolio which is one of several major portfolios of NIST's PSCR program (National Institute of Standards and Technology (NIST), 2017). Our research focuses on conducting research in human factors and user interfaces to understand important components for successful deployment and adoption of new communication technology. With this research goal, we conducted an exploratory, sequential, mixed methods study, *Voices of First Responders*, to understand the experiences of first responders. In this chapter, we specifically discuss our findings regarding the communication technology problems and needs of rural first responders across four disciplines (i.e., COMMS, EMS, FF, and LE). In this way, our study addresses gaps in prior research and builds off prior studies (Oliver & Meier, 2004; Greene et al., 2019; Iversen et al., 2002) to understand rural first responders' context of use. Focusing on hearing the voices of rural first responders is important as historically their perspectives have been left out of research about rural environments (Chambers, 1994). Insights from this study can help developers to identify what shortcomings in current technology need to be addressed as well as where to invest future resources in developing technology for rural first responders. By ensuring solutions that are tailored to work within the unique environments in which rural first responders operate, rural first responders may be more eager to adopt and use new communication technology.

Method

We conducted an exploratory, sequential, mixed methods study with two phases. This type of design is often used when a measure or instrument is not currently available; when the variables are not known (e.g., the technology needs and problems of first responders); and/or when exploring a particular phenomenon such as public safety communication. In Phase 1 of the study, we conducted 193 qualitative interviews with first responders across the USA to comprehensively explore their experiences with communication technology. Findings from Phase 1 were then used to design the Phase 2 quantitative survey instrument. The use of a large-scale, nationwide survey provided for greater representation from first responders across the country. There were 7182 total survey responses. This allowed for the ability to confirm, clarify, and expand on the findings from Phase 1 of the study.

This chapter focuses specifically on data and analysis of rural first responders in the study. Of the 193 interviews in Phase 1 of the study, 63 of them were with rural first responders (32.64%). In Phase 2 of the study, 2698 of the 7182 responses were from rural first responders (37.68%).

Both phases of the study were approved by NIST Research Protections Office. All data were collected anonymously. Full methodological details related to study design, data collection, and data analysis can be found in relevant reports for the in-depth interviews (Choong et al., 2018) and for the survey (Greene et al., 2020).

Phase 1: Interviews

A semi-structured interview instrument was developed that focused on two high-level areas: (1) understanding first responders' contexts of work and (2) identifying first responders' perceptions of and experiences with technology. To understand context of work, the instrument included questions and follow-up probes related to job tasks and routines, relationships with people they work with or for, and characteristics of the environment they work in. Questions about technology focused on what technology they use, what problems they have encountered, and what technology they wish they had for their jobs. The interview instrument was developed iteratively through a process with a literature review, pilot interviews with first responders, and feedback from first responders and human factors subject matter experts.

A demographic questionnaire was also developed to identify participant characteristics (i.e., discipline, years of service, area, location, gender, and age) to ensure interview data reflected the diversity of first responders. Additionally, we asked two questions related to technology experience and adoption to better understand first responders' familiarity with technology. For these two questions, participants could select as many options as were applicable to their own experiences.

Purposeful, convenience, and snowball sampling were used to recruit first responders for the Phase 1 interviews. Five of the ten Federal Emergency Management Agency (FEMA) (2020) regions in the USA were represented in the sample.

Prior to the interviews, participants were informed they could withdraw at any time, skip any question as needed, and decline to be audio recorded. They also completed a demographic questionnaire. Interviews lasted approximately 45 minutes. Recorded interviews were transcribed, de-identified, and assigned an interview number.

Phase 1: Participant Characteristics

Sixty-three rural first responders participated in Phase 1 consisting of 18 COMMS participants, 6 EMS participants, 19 FF participants, and 20 LE participants. Table 1 displays the number of participants across rural first responder disciplines by gender, age, and total years of service. The sample was less representative of female first responders than male first responders, with female first responders comprising only 13 participants, though this was consistent with low proportions of female responders in FF and LE disciplines nationally (Fahy et al., 2021; Crooke, 2013). Relatedly, the larger number of females in our COMMS sample was consistent with gender demographics for the discipline nationally (U.S. Bureau of Labor Statistics,

Table 1 Rural interviewee demographics by disciplines

		COMMS	EMS	FF	LE	Total
Gender	Female	10	1	0	2	13
	Male	8	5	19	18	50
Age (years)	18–25	1	1	3	2	7
	26–35	2	1	3	5	11
	36–45	5	2	6	4	17
	46–55	8	1	5	8	22
	56–65	2	1	1	0	4
	Over 65	0	0	1	1	2
Total years of service	1–5	2	3	3	3	11
	6–10	3	0	4	3	10
	11–15	4	1	2	2	9
	16–20	1	1	2	3	7
	21–25	1	0	5	7	13
	26–30	3	0	2	2	7
	Over 30	3	1	1	0	5
	No response	1	0	0	0	1

Table 2 Interviewees' experience with technology and technology adoption

	Rural (%)[a]	Overall dataset (%)[a]
Technology experience		
I can do all things that I want to do with technology without help from others	17.46	18.85
I can do most things that I want to do with technology and only need help occasionally	65.08	71.20
I have some knowledge about how technology works but often need to ask for help to perform more advanced activities – such as to configure the privacy settings on my cell phone	15.87	10.99
I have limited experience using technology, and I don't know much about how technology works	3.17	1.05
Technology adoption		
I try the latest technologies as soon as they come out	17.46	19.90
I follow technology trends	28.57	38.22
I let others work out the kinks first	39.68	39.27
I wait until my old technology dies	12.70	8.38
I only adopt new technologies when it's required	7.94	5.24

[a]The percentages do not sum to 100% since participants could select more than one option

2019). A majority of the sample was between 36 and 55 years old and had a wide range of total years of service.

Table 2 displays rural first responders' experiences with using and adopting technology compared to responses from the overall dataset. Although nearly 83% indicated they could do most or all things with technology with some assistance, 19.04% indicated they had limited knowledge or needed help with technology. In looking at experience adopting new technology, nearly 40% mentioned they let others work out the kinks. Although 28.57% said they follow technology trends, nearly 20.64% either adopt new technology when theirs has died or it becomes required. Thus, rural participants self-report having slightly less experience with and knowledge about technology, and they adopt technology slightly later than participants in the overall dataset.

Phase 1: Qualitative Analysis

As part of the qualitative analysis process, transcripts were coded. Coding refers to assigning categories to participants' responses as a way to reduce the dataset so that it can be analyzed to find patterns and themes. The multidisciplinary research team first created an a priori coding list to be used for the initial coding of five randomly chosen transcripts from the entire Phase 1 dataset (Choong et al., 2018). These five transcripts were independently coded by all team members, and then the research team met to review their coding to ensure the codes were applied in consistent ways and to discuss and resolve any disagreements in coding. This provided the opportunity to revise codes and operationalize how each should be applied, ultimately resulting in a finalized code list. The researchers coded all remaining transcripts using the final code list. The data associated with each code were extracted into separate files so that the relationships within and among the codes could be explored and themes identified.

This chapter specifically focuses on codes related to communication technology problems and needs and the context of use rural first responders operate within. First, to identify communication technology problems and needs, we reanalyzed responses initially coded into the "problem: technology" or "wish list" codes by further classifying responses into more specific categories and subcategories (Dawkins et al., 2019). This resulted in 18 technology problems and 15 "wish list" categories. These categories and their corresponding subcategories were created for the larger research study to identify the needs and requested functionalities that were most important to first responders (Dawkins et al., 2019). Two researchers independently identified the categories and subcategories for each response, with one researcher categorizing the problems and the other categorizing the needs. The research team then met to discuss, operationalize, and finalize the classifications. Here coding categories were examined only for the subset of the data with rural first responders. Second, to identify the rural context of use for problems and needs, we identified themes about the rural context from the extracted data (see Greene et al., 2019).

Phase 2: Survey

In Phase 2, we developed a survey instrument that was distributed to first responders across the USA. The survey instrument was developed iteratively using findings from Phase 1 interview data, reviews from subject matter experts (first responders from all four disciplines) and survey experts, and survey pilots with first responders. Two major categories of questions were used in the final survey instrument: the first section focused on experiences with technologies for day-to-day incident response and the second section focused on large-scale events (major disasters or large planned events such as football games or concerts). The overall survey structure and flow were largely similar across the four disciplines: all began with a section on demographics, followed by a section on use of technology[1] for day-to-day incident response (including questions on apps/software), problems with technology, and

[1] For those respondents who chose the response option that they did not have a particular device, those devices were piped forward to the futuristic technology section of the survey. In that section, a list of futuristic technology that might be useful for their job was presented. The list included both a preset list of emerging technologies plus those devices they selected "do not have" earlier.

Fig. 1 Major survey components and flow

perceived usefulness of futuristic technology. The survey concluded with a section on the use of technology in major disasters or large events (Fig. 1).

The surveys for EMS, FF, and LE were similar, although the types of devices and apps/software asked about were somewhat different for each discipline, along with the technology problems experienced. The survey for COMMS varied slightly more, due to the different nature of their working environment. For example, COMMS respondents were asked questions about call centers and Next Generation 9-1-1 (NG 9-1-1), a digitally based 9-1-1 system (National Highway Traffic Safety Administration's Office, 2021). Since they were asked these additional questions, they were not asked questions about specific problems with technology but were instead asked about information problems they experience. This was done in order to respect the time it took to take the survey. More detailed descriptions of survey logic, branching, and all questions can be found in the relevant report (Greene et al., 2020).

The target population for this survey was first responders in the USA, including COMMS, EMS, FF, and LE. Three different types of outreach occurred during survey dissemination: (1) emails sent to a general sample from an online database purchased from a national public safety directory and data firm (database includes first responder departments/agencies in all 50 states and the District of Columbia); (2) via previous points of contact within the public safety community; and (3) through a variety of different public safety organizations. Individuals contacted were asked to forward the request to as many of their personnel as possible, as well as to colleagues from other departments/agencies. To have broad representation, the goal was to reach as many departments and agencies as possible and through them to reach first responders.

Phase 2: Participant Characteristics

Overall, there was a total of 7182 completed survey responses. Of these, 2698 responses were from rural first responders (37.68%). Of these 2698 responses, 23.68% were from COMMS, 18.12% from EMS, 33.06% from FF, and 25.13% from LE. This was the only question that required a response on the survey; participants could choose not to answer any of the other questions. In general, demographic variables of interest showed good variability and were similar to the demographics of the overall study. Male respondents represented 78.34% of the rural responses and females represented 21.66% of those who responded ($n = 2668$). As shown in Fig. 2, all age groups were represented in the responses, with the majority of participants between 46 and 55 years of age (33.65%). Less than 6%

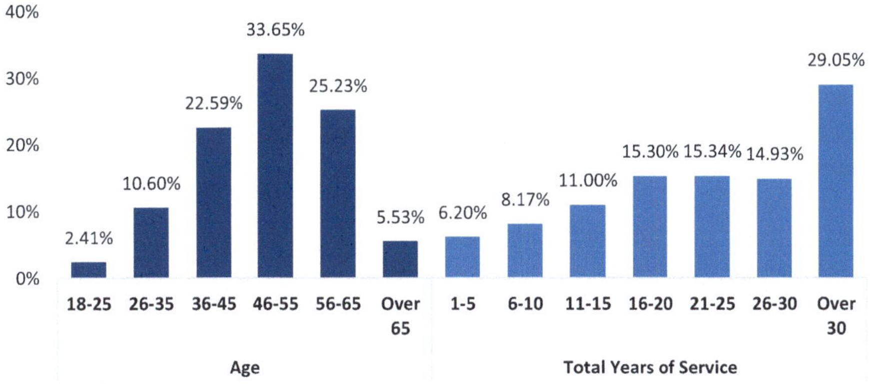

Fig. 2 Rural survey respondents' age and total years of service

of participants were 25 or younger or 66 or older. Almost half of the participants who responded had between 16 and 30 years of experience working in public safety (45.57%).

Phase 2: Data Analysis

While the survey covered a broad range of questions and first responder demographics, the analysis in this chapter presents descriptive statistics focused on rural first responders, specifically their problems with technology, and futuristic technology they would like to have or think would be useful. Additionally, most survey sections included questions with open-ended fields. Open-ended survey responses were analyzed by sorting, counting, and/or coding responses to identify similarities, differences, and/or patterns in the data. Thus, the survey data provides quantitative evidence to support themes identified from Phase 1 interview data.

Results

Results present both qualitative and quantitative data. The qualitative results present themes using direct quotes given by rural first responders. The quantitative results present percentages of first responders who provided each survey response.[2] Throughout this section, qualitative data from both the interviews and open-ended survey questions are illustrated with exemplar quotes that are representative of the dataset as a whole. Each quote is in indented text and followed by a reference to the participant in parentheses, including their discipline (i.e., COMMS, EMS, FF,

[2] Full data and sample sizes are available at https://publicsafety.nist.gov/analyzer.html.

or LE), area (R = Rural), and participant number (e.g., 001). Interview quotes are identified by the prefix "INT" and the use of dashes to separate participant information (e.g., INT-LE-R-048). Quotes from the open-ended survey responses do not have a prefix and separate participant information by colons (e.g., LE:R:8193). Because participants were anonymous, identifiers are not tied back to a specific participant.

Technology Problems

Technology problems are presented below in two sections. First, we discuss the qualitative findings for the five important problem areas: connectivity/coverage, interoperability, IT implementation and cost of technology, physical ergonomics, and reliability. Where applicable, survey results are presented to support each of these main themes. Predominately, results from the surveys for EMS, FF, and LE are used to support the themes, as each survey for these disciplines included specific questions about device problems. Second, we present qualitative findings for problems specific to each of the four disciplines with supporting survey results.

Technology Problems Across Disciplines

Coverage Many rural first responders discussed the problems with dead zones and lack of bandwidth or coverage for both radios and smartphones, as evidenced by the following interview quote:

> ... we're in some kind of a remote location and sometimes you know we don't get cell service either. I mean we do have a co-op up here, a telephone co-op and that's been so much better now but it's not perfect either and so we've got some areas too where it's a little more difficult even with a cell signal. (INT-LE-R-046)

Some discussed dead zones in buildings or other structures, but many mentioned dead zones specific to rural terrain (e.g., mountains) that limit communication technology.

> We have that technology in the field when we don't have a cell signal which in the mountains here is soon as you get north of town 5 miles you start losing signal. You don't get it back until you're like two spots on [town/city redacted] and then not until you're down on the valley floor. (INT-FF-R-046)

> In a rural area, radio coverage is severely hampered by distance and cell phones experience regular, known dead zones. Our CAD system for text message dispatching through our county regularly fails – messages aren't transmitted fully or at all for periods of time. (EMS:R:504)

This finding is supported by the survey results, as a majority of rural first responders from EMS, FF, and LE had radio and smartphone coverage problems at least "sometimes" (i.e., selecting survey response "always," "most of the time," or "sometimes"). Evidence suggests coverage problems are pervasive: 30.00% of EMS, 34.33% FF, and 25.69% of LE participants experienced radio coverage

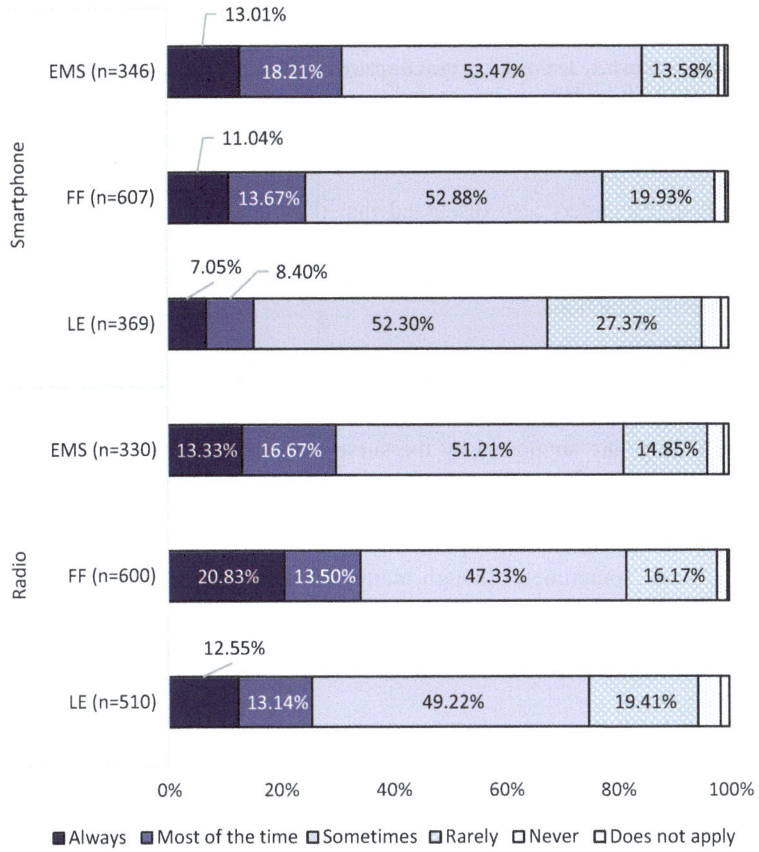

Fig. 3 Radio coverage problems for EMS, FF, and LE

problems "always" or "most of the time." Although the percent of rural first responders who experienced smartphone coverage problems were comparable to those who experienced radio coverage problems for EMS, fewer FF and LE survey participants reported smartphone coverage problems compared to radio coverage problems. Figure 3 shows the percentages of radio and smartphone coverage problems for EMS, FF, and LE.

Taken together, results suggest that coverage problems occur frequently for rural first responders. The dead zones and lack of coverage unfortunately often result in rural first responders being unable to rely on their communication technology during incident response.

Interoperability Communication across disciplines, areas, and jurisdictions is vital to first responders' incident response and coordination efforts, and this communication is especially important for rural first responders who often cover a wide area. Rural first responders described difficulties with communicating among disciplines across rural areas and also during situations where they must work with other jurisdictions.

> ... I mean, I can't call [county name redacted], call on the cell phone. I can't call [another county name redacted]; we don't have their frequencies available, so it would all have to be relayed from us to here to County, to their dispatch to their officer and then back to the state again ... (INT-LE-R-060)

> Biggest problem is interoperability. In 17 years I've heard a lot of plans and big talk; NO ACTION. (EMS:R:936)

Rural first responders also discussed that the numerous devices they use are not well integrated. As described in the following interview quote, lack of device interoperability can result in first responders carrying too many devices that each perform specific functions.

> I think my biggest gripes are that e-ticketing machine and just the fact that it's not well thought-out for the application. I don't think there's any reason why it couldn't be done on the phone that I already carry or the computer that's already in the car. (INT-LE-R-018)

These findings are supported by the survey data: rural EMS, FF, and LE first responders experienced problems with device interoperability for radios, MDTs, laptops, tablets, and computers (Fig. 4). The highest percentage of EMS, FF, and LE survey participants had interoperability problems with their radios, MDTs, and laptops at least "sometimes," though many also reported issues with tablets and computers.

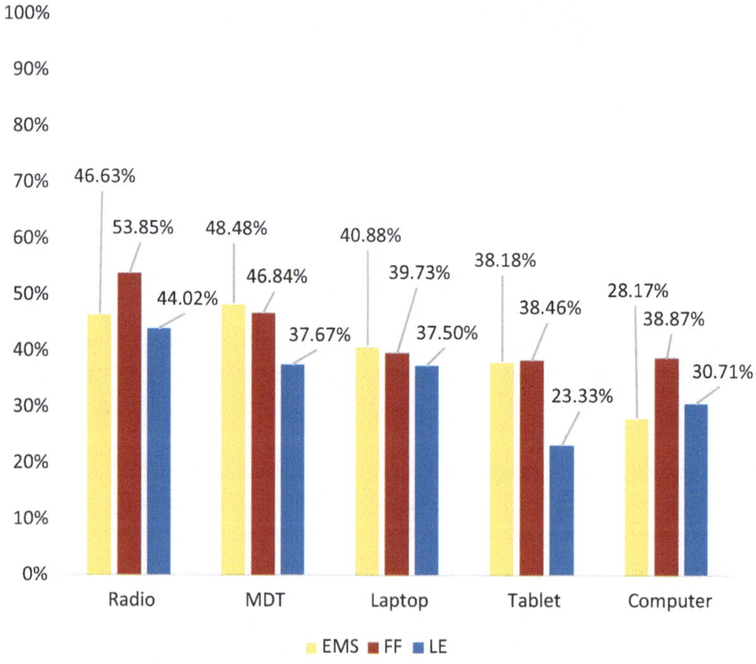

Fig. 4 Interoperability problems occurring at least sometimes for EMS, FF, and LE

Our findings suggest that devices' interoperability problems often result in unreliable communication during incident response. Lack of device interoperability may also have the unintended consequence for rural first responders, such as physical and cognitive burdens from carrying multiple devices that all perform different but related functions.

IT Implementation and Cost of Technology Rural first responders described problems implementing and installing communication technology. One reason mentioned in the interviews was that some updates require access to the latest technology or the use of broadband speeds to which many rural first responders do not yet have access.

Rural first responders often discussed these issues with implementation as being related to a broader issue of funding.

> We try to stay updated but with tight budgets and changing technology and software and govt requirements with no funding for requirements it's not easy for volunteer depts. radios are something we just can't keep updates on not to mention purchasing new ones. (EMS:R:3437)

> Technology is great, but, the cost is out of hand a lot of times and small centers like mine cannot buy the latest and greatest. Needs to be more affordable. (COMMS:R:231)

Results show that cost is often a prohibitor for rural first responders in accessing, training for, updating, and replacing communication technology. Problems with the price of devices were also pervasive across devices for EMS, FF, and LE survey participants (Fig. 5). Over 50% of survey respondents in each of these disciplines

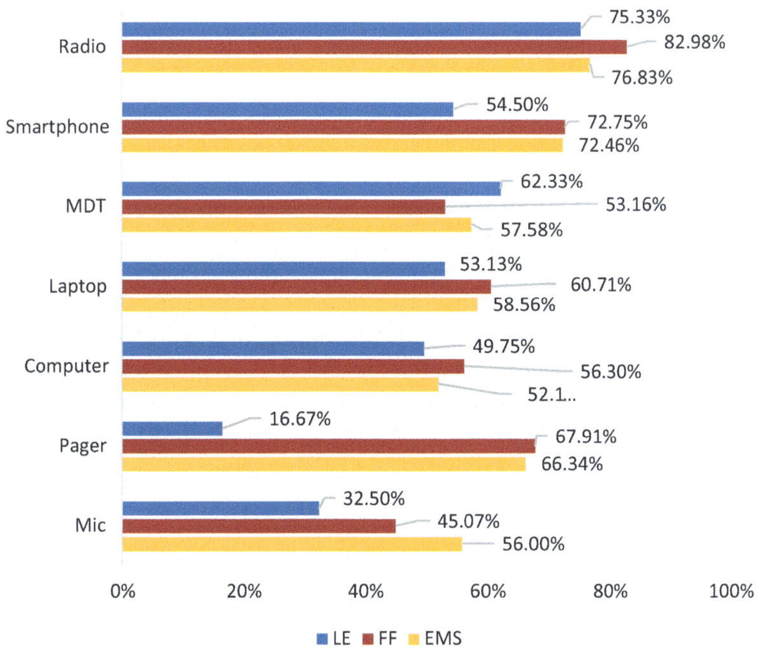

Fig. 5 Device price problems occurring at least sometimes for EMS, FF, and LE

had price problems at least "sometimes" with radios, smartphones, MDTs, laptops, and computers. The device with the highest reported price problems was radio, with over 75% of rural first responders in each discipline reporting they had price problems with radios at least "sometimes." Rates of having price problems were generally consistent across EMS, FF, and LE, except for pagers in which rural EMS and FF first responders had comparatively higher rates of having these problems than LE. However, this is likely due to LE having low rates of using pagers in the survey data (597 LE participants out of 648 who answered the pager frequency of use question (92.13%) did not have a pager).

This suggests that rural first responders do not just have issues purchasing devices specific to the first responder discipline such as MDTs and radios; rather, they have problems purchasing all kinds of communication technology, even more common communication technology such as laptops and computers. They also are unable to quickly replace broken or old technology. When rural departments cannot purchase the communication technology they need, rural first responders may have to rely on unreliable, outdated, and poorly functioning technology during incident response.

Physical Ergonomics Physical ergonomics problems encompass a wide range of topics, with some related to the number, size, and weight of devices, and others related to physical aspects of devices such as robustness, battery life, comfort, and safety concerns. Rural first responders discussed problems with devices' robustness in rural environments. Rural first responders must have durable equipment to meet the challenges of the incidents they respond to and the environments they work within, as they often encounter difficult terrain such as mountains or rivers.

> One of the issues that we see is that the equipment that's being issued is not rugged enough... police officers were out there in the sun, we're out there in the freezing cold, in the rain, they're getting in and out of their police units so they equipment needs to be more rugged... Or you're in the middle of a rainstorm, and a tree falls on the people's house and you're trying to get them out, you're trying to rescue them, and your radio doesn't work because it got wet. It needs to be able to function in any type of environments. (INT-LE-R-053)

Survey results support that durability is a frequently experienced problem for rural EMS, FF, and LE first responders across many devices. For all three disciplines, the largest number of first responders reported having problems with durability at least "sometimes" for smartphones (EMS, 50.00%; FF, 46.12%; and LE, 38.15%) and laptops (EMS, 48.07%; FF, 46.43%; and LE, 31.88%). Durability problems differed between the disciplines for the other devices: more EMS and FF survey participants reported problems at least "sometimes" with the durability of their tablets (EMS, 41.82%; FF, 42.31%; and LE, 23.33%), MDTs (EMS, 45.45%; FF, 35.44%; and LE, 24.65%), and pagers (EMS, 27.32%; FF, 34.22%; and LE, 16.67%).

Many also discussed having battery issues with their devices, and this was supported in the survey data. The majority of the participants from each discipline had battery problems at least "sometimes" with their smartphone (EMS, 67.91%; FF, 66.21%; and LE, 59.00%) and radios (EMS, 59.24%; FF, 65.47%; and LE,

56.55%). Problems at least "sometimes" were also common for laptops (EMS, 60.77%; FF, 54.46%; and LE, 46.25%). Between 40% and 50% of EMS and FF survey participants also reported having battery problems at least "sometimes" for their pagers (EMS, 51.22%; FF, 52.67%; LE, 16.67%) and tablets (EMS, 45.45%; FF, 43.59%; LE, 16.67%).

These results suggest that communication technology can cause ergonomics challenges when technology is not developed with rural conditions in mind. Communication technology may work well in optimal conditions, but rural first responders often encounter temperatures, altitudes, and distances their communication technology was not designed to withstand.

Reliability A major theme across interview and survey data was that communication technology is often unreliable. In fact, this came up often in the interviews when many rural first responders described past experiences in which their communication technology did not work in the way it was intended to.

> We have the [inaudible] MDTs, but I think we would call it a failed technology... We spend more time wasting time trying to keep that thing working than we do doing our job. So we've given up on it... (INT-FF-R-019)

Although the survey did not explicitly ask about devices' reliability, survey participants reported reliability issues in the open-ended survey questions. Often rural first responders commented on the unreliability of their radios, but many also wrote about experiences with unreliable laptops, pagers, body cameras, and desktops.

> Due to our rural and remote location we are forced to use mobile repeaters, and they are less than reliable. Also, due to the restrictions of narrow-band radios and the low power output of the ones our agency can afford, actually reaching our dispatch center (which is several miles away) is hit-and-miss at best. There are higher-powered radios available, we just cannot afford them, and it seems that when the Federal government mandated the switch to narrow-band transceivers, it exacerbated an already bad situation for small and rural agencies like ours. (LE:R:8193)

> Interoperability with radios and software would be great, but is still not widely adopted. Being forced to use a person cell/tablet sucks when the network coverage is basically non-existent ([vendor redacted]). Cell coverage maps are absolutely unreliable and not a true indication of coverage (ALL carriers)... (EMS:R:2428)

As described in the open-ended survey response quotes, often problems with reliability were the result of other problems with connectivity, interoperability, implementation, and/or physical ergonomics. Thus, when one of these problems occurs, it often results in poor reliability, with rural first responders being unable to trust on their devices to keep them safe and perform their duties.

Technology Problems Specific to Each Discipline

Although many problems were common across all disciplines, each rural first responder discipline experienced unique problems specific to their job requirements and context of use. The discipline-specific data presented here were emphasized within a discipline but were not unique to that discipline.

Communications Center and 9-1-1 Services Rural COMMS personnel experience unique problems by nature of the environment they work within. COMMS personnel do not respond on-scene; they instead take emergency calls and dispatch first responders to the scene. A major problem for rural COMMS personnel was technology's inability to track callers' locations. In the interviews, rural COMMS personnel discussed the difficulty in locating callers during 9-1-1 calls, as some rural areas did not have addresses. Some also discussed that this problem can be exacerbated when there is an increase in seasonal tourists who are unfamiliar with the area and cannot easily identify their location when calling 9-1-1.

> …Location information sometimes is difficult to get from a cell phone. And again, we have a lot of visitors here. And they never know where they're at. Had no clue. (INT-COMMS-R-002)

> Many phone providers CAN NOT provide good location information for their callers, if at all. We have one company that transfers calls to use from the other end of our state – which would be about an 8-hour response time. (COMMS:R:421)

This is supported in the survey data with the information problems rural COMMS personnel experienced (Fig. 6). Over a fourth of COMMS survey, participants (28.15%) had problems "always" or "most of the time" with tracking a caller's location from a cell phone, and an additional 61.01% experienced this problem "sometimes." Another common problem was the inability to receive accurate and complete information when dispatching first responders to the scene. Over 90% of rural COMMS personnel had problems with callers providing inaccurate or missing

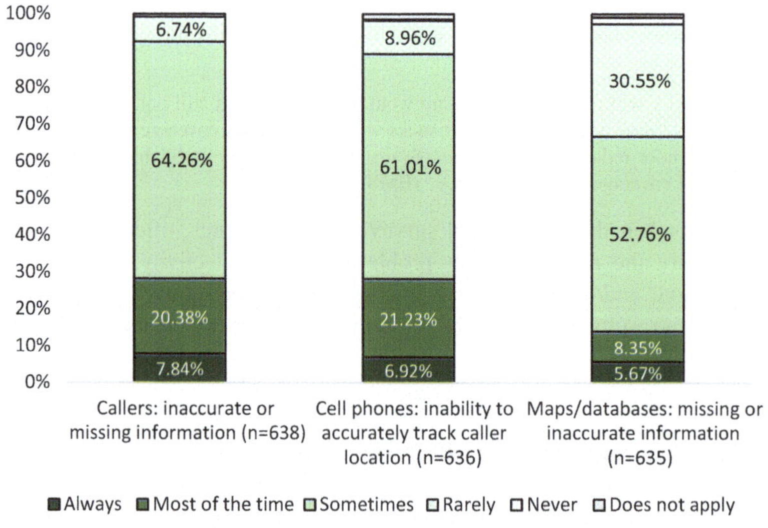

Fig. 6 Caller, cell phone, and map/database information problems for COMMS

information at least "sometimes." Problem with maps and databases providing accurate information at least "sometimes" was also common for nearly two-thirds of COMMS personnel.

Although they saw benefits to technology, rural COMMS personnel were often wary of both new technology and significant changes to existing systems. Many responses expressed trepidation for receiving text messages, pictures, and videos as well as using NG 9-1-1. COMMS personnel expressed concerns over seeing graphic or inappropriate images in texts as well as needing to slow down their response time to communicate via text with callers.

> ...I have speculation, but I really don't know how's that going to impact and if that's going to take too much time. I don't know if it's going to slow things down or quicken it, I don't know. I know it's a technology that the millennials love and it's easy for them, but it may not be necessarily easy for us. I don't understand how a video would be better than a text or a call. (INT-COMMS-R-020)

> Texting takes considerably more time to communicate than voice communications, delaying the processing and response to emergencies. (COMMS:R:1668)

Survey results indicated that more COMMS personnel received texts at their call centers (46.38%) than pictures and videos (8.52%). The majority of COMMS personnel believed there were benefits to receiving texts (74.60%) and pictures/videos (51.81%). However, 17.14% were unsure that texts would be beneficial and 28.98% were not sure that pictures and videos would be helpful. Similarly, survey results showed that nearly three out of four COMMS personnel thought NG 9-1-1 would be helpful, and only 5.5% believed it would not be helpful. However, 20.13% were unsure about NG 9-1-1's helpfulness, suggesting some COMMS personnel are also wary about this new technology.

Taken together, these results suggest COMMS responders are open to changes in technology for receiving information and dispatching first responders, but some are concerned about potential negative impacts and new challenges that may come with new technology.

Emergency Medical Services Rural EMS personnel mentioned a variety of problems, especially with writing patient reports and sending them to hospitals. They were often frustrated by how difficult their systems were to use. In fact, EMS personnel sometimes spent more time writing a report than they needed to and in some cases had to rewrite their reports. This is supported by survey results, as 45.45% of rural EMS survey participants had problems with report writing on tablets at least "sometimes." Nearly a fifth experienced this problem "always" or "most of the time." This unreliability was often due to problems with devices connecting to the internet or with device software crashing.

> ...It took 2 to 3 times as long to do your report which when you have a day where you only have 2 calls it's not that big of a deal because you have plenty of down time to get that report done but when you're running back to back calls and you're on a second call and you haven't even gotten to finish your first report it's very frustrating and they shut down a lot especially when these things depend on internet and we are so you get out here somewhere and then the information the things that you need won't load... (INT-EMS-R-019)

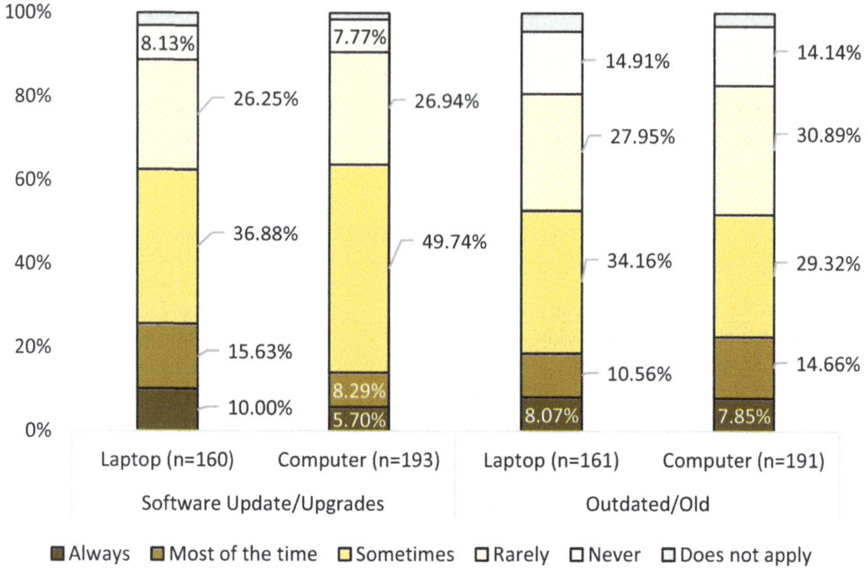

Fig. 7 Problems with old and outdated devices and software updates/upgrades for EMS

Internet connectivity and software crashes were frequently reported by rural EMS survey participants. A majority of EMS participants had internet connectivity problems at least "sometimes" with their laptops (81.48%) and tablets (79.55%), and of those, nearly a third of these problems were experienced "always" or "most of the time" (laptops: 32.72%; tablets: 29.55%). Fewer rural EMS survey participants reported internet connection problems with their computers, with 49.49% having problems connecting their computer to the internet at least "sometimes" and only 9.18% having these issues "always" or "most of the time." A majority of rural EMS survey participants reported having problems at least "sometimes" with their laptops (53.42%) and computers (47.42%) crashing, with fewer rural EMS participants indicating this problem occurred "always" or "most of the time" for computers (7.22%) than laptops (14.29%).

EMS personnel discussed that reliable and usable technology was expensive, causing some departments to opt for outdated solutions. In some cases, EMS personnel discussed using pencil and paper for report writing rather than computers. Nearly half of the rural EMS survey participants indicated they experienced problems with their laptops and computers being old or outdated at least "sometimes" (Fig. 7). Moreover, problems updating or upgrading laptops and computers occurred at least "sometimes" for over 60% of rural EMS survey participants. One in four had these problems "always" or "most of the time" with laptops.

Not only did rural EMS first responders often have difficulties with their laptops, computes, and tablets reliably working, but when they did have these issues, finding a solution was difficult.

> What happens when it doesn't work? What happens when we have trouble with it? Who fixes it? Because I can't just call downstairs to IT, okay? I've got a contractor that does our IT because we don't have an IT department. They're budgeted two days a week, maybe. (INT-EMS-R-008)

As in the interview quote above, some mentioned that their departments do not have dedicated IT staff and experts to fix common problems. Ultimately, the lack of support often results in rural EMS first responders spending considerable time and resources fixing their systems or finding alternate solutions.

Fire Service Rural FF personnel had difficulty with mics and radios during incident response. They had problems hearing their radios when there was external sound caused by fire and alarms, and their mics picked up breathing and other sounds that made communications hard to hear.

> ...we have handhelds, walkie talkies and they are hardest thing to hear when you are in a fire... (INT-FF-R-055)

Rural FF survey participants also frequently experienced problems with the audio quality of their radios and mics: 77.22% experienced problems with radios and 66.67% experienced problems with mics at least "sometimes." For some rural FF survey respondents, these problems were more frequent, with 22.95% experiencing audio quality problems "always" or "most of the time" for radios and 15.69% experiencing these problems with mics.

Many rural FF participants also expressed that their technology was outdated.

> ...When a fire is paged out here they may page out the appropriate response it may or may not go out over the radio. We have somewhat of an outdated underfunded antiquated communications here in our county. (INT-FF-R-049)

Problems with old and outdated technology were a common experience across numerous devices for rural FF survey participants (Fig. 8).

Nearly one in five rural FF first responders experienced these problems "always" or "most of the time" with their computers, laptops, MDTs, mics, pagers, and thermal image cameras (TICs). This rate was even higher for radios, with nearly one in four having old and outdated radio problems "always" or "most of the time."

Law Enforcement The use of body cameras is specific to LE personnel in their day-to-day work. Rural LE personnel expressed physical challenges securely attaching their body cameras to their uniforms, and many also mentioned that they spend significant time and effort storing and uploading the cameras' information.

> It can add quite a bit of time because for the most part the upload time is the real time... I think the longest recording I have was probably about 3 hours which it breaks it up into thirty minute intervals but it took almost 2 ½ or 3 hours for that one video to upload then I had 10 other ones that I had to upload so the upload speed is absolutely horrible. (INT-LE-R-045)

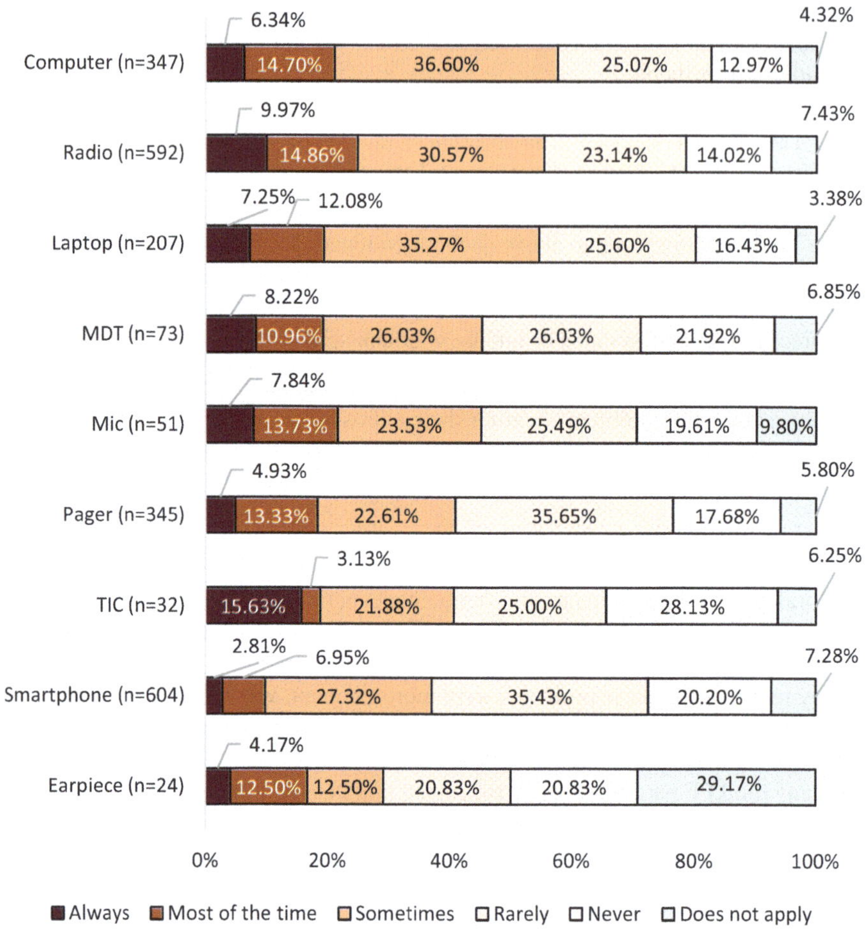

Fig. 8 Problems with old or outdated devices for FF. TIC = thermal image camera

Survey results also revealed problems with body cameras (Fig. 9). The most common problems with body cameras were with the price (at least "sometimes": 66.30%; "always" or "most of the time:" 48.32%) as well as with physical ergonomics challenges. Some problems were the same issues common across first responders and devices, as many rural LE respondents had problems at least "sometimes" with body camera battery (61.37%) and durability (45.45%). Other problems that occurred at least "sometimes" were more specific to the body camera, such as placement (58.13%), size (44.83%), and likelihood of falling off (39.09%). Problems at least "sometimes" with the using recorded data (37.07%), video transfer/storage (35.23%), turning the camera on and off (34.49%), and video quality (25.29%) occurred less frequently.

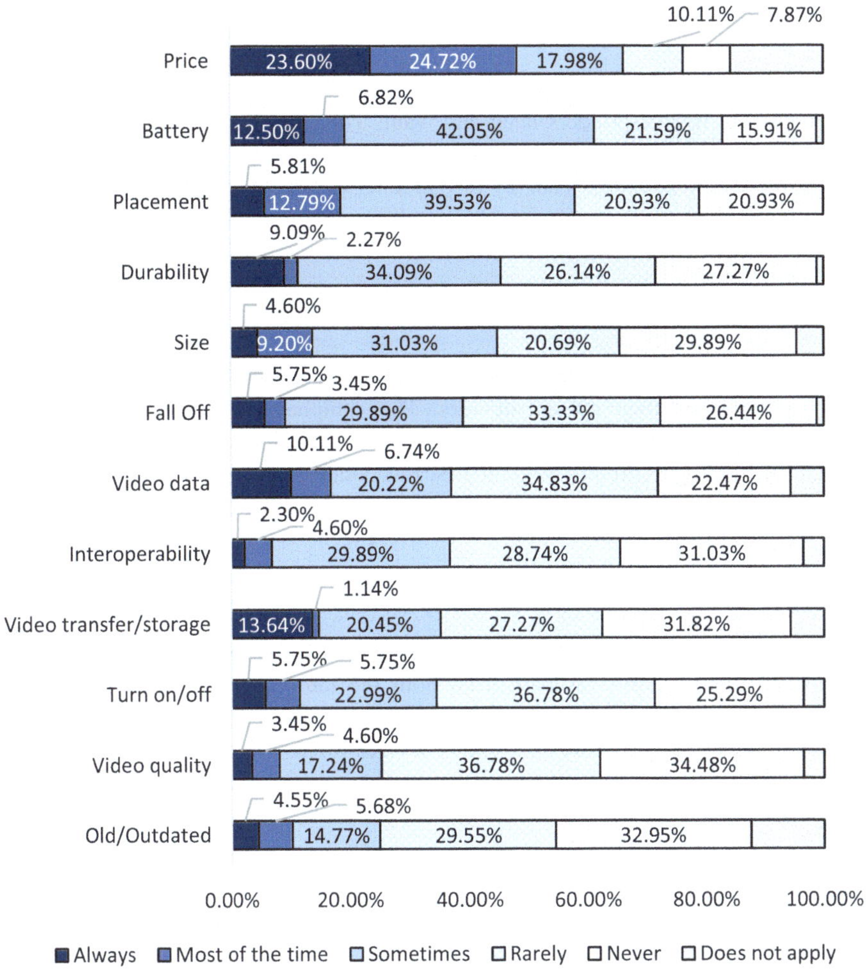

Fig. 9 Problems with body cameras for LE

Rural LE personnel mentioned challenges using devices that were bulky, too numerous, and/or not reliable. These ergonomics challenges were often specific to the equipment they use, such as e-ticketing devices. Survey results support that rural LE first responders often had issues with the size and weight of their devices. Nearly 40% had problems at least "sometimes" with the size of their MDTs (42.42%) and radios (39.41%), and nearly 30% had problems at least "sometimes" with laptop weight (29.25%). Tablet size and weight were the least common problem for rural LE participants, with less than 10% of rural LE survey participants having these problems at least "sometimes."

Technology Needs

This section presents data from interviews and the survey related to the types of technology first responders need and want. This includes technology that first responders do not currently have and "futuristic" technology. Figure 10 shows the list of futuristic technologies survey respondents were able to choose from and the percentages of respondents from each discipline who selected the various items.

Improving Current Technology

Overarchingly, rural first responders wanted greater reliability, functionality, and interoperability of their current devices. They emphasized that they need their current problems fixed and therefore wanted a strong focus on improving basic and current technology. Ultimately, rural first responders want to be able to trust the technology that they use, eliminating unnecessary burdens, disruptions, and stress they experience as a direct result of their current technology.

> Instead of new stuff it would be good to know that the tools we already use would work better rather than getting new stuff. We already can't afford things. (FF:R:5506)

Rural first responders most wanted to have radios and smartphones that work consistently and reliably, as data from both the interviews and the open-ended survey responses identify these devices as some of the most important tools for rural first responders. Because they use these devices often and need to rely on them, many expressed a need for improvement in these devices, especially in ensuring better coverage in rural areas.

> You want your radios to work and you want your cell phones to work all over the county. I mean that's pretty much it. (INT-LE-R-048)

> Cellular/internet coverage that reaches all areas of my fire district. Also cheap plans available to public safety. (FF:R:2118)

With access to wider coverage, rural first responders could improve the efficiency and effectiveness of communication with their team members, transmit information to other responders and hospitals, and maintain a lifeline in dangerous situations. Fixing problems and providing greater reliability for current communication devices could encourage usage and reduce frustration.

Data support that rural first responders had a stronger need for their current technology to be improved rather than for development of entirely new technology. Some rural first responders believed new technologies could disrupt their work or make it harder, making them less efficient and effective.

> None of these sound particularly useful and some could be disruptive to our normal work processes in dispatch. If one of the items listed was increased staffing then I would've happily checked that box. (COMMS:R:1545)

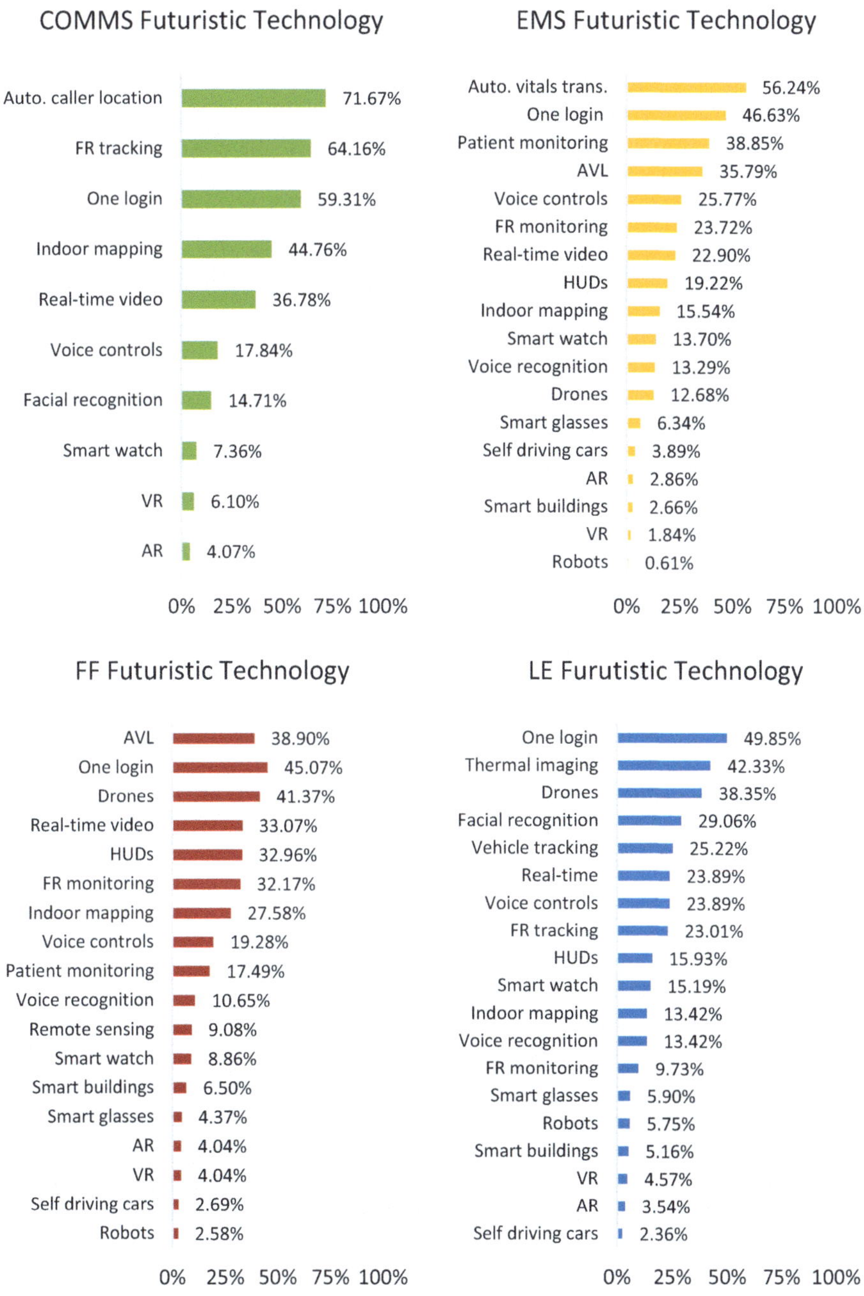

Fig. 10 Futuristic technology needs. Note: AR, augmented reality; auto., automatic; AVL, automatic vehicle location; FR, first responder; HUD, heads-up display; vital trans., transmission of vitals; VR, virtual reality

The survey results provide support that advanced technology is of less interest to rural first responders. Many of the futuristic technologies listed were selected by a low percentage of survey respondents as being important for their day-to-day work. In fact, many of the most futuristic technologies in the list were selected by 10% or less of survey respondents (Fig. 10). For example, "AR (augmented reality)" and "VR (virtual reality)" were in the bottom four items selected by respondents from all four disciplines; neither was selected by more than 7% of respondents from any discipline. "Robots," "self-driving vehicles," "smart glasses," and "smart buildings" were some of the other items selected by low percentages of respondents across disciplines.

Although rural first responders did not believe many advanced technologies would benefit them, there was one item from the futuristic list of technologies that rural survey respondents across disciplines chose. The item "one login (instead of many different usernames and passwords)" was in the top three items checked rural respondents from all four disciplines (COMMS, 59.31%; EMS, 46.63%; FF, 45.07%; and LE, 49.85%), demonstrating its importance to this population.

The open-ended survey responses also indicated that having only one login would be of tremendous benefit for rural first responders.

> One login would be at the top of everybody's list here. It is ridiculous the number of passwords and log-ins that have to be used and waste the time of first responders in their preparation and continuous log-in status. (LE:R:5075)

Rural first responders believed that having one login that works across platforms would improve the usability of many of their devices, increase interoperability, and ultimately save time and lead to less frustration.

Overall, these results suggest that advanced technology was not always perceived as the right answer to the problems rural first responders face. Instead, rural first responders overwhelmingly wanted improvement of current technology and believed that would be most helpful.

Location Information

Responses from rural first responders in interviews and on the survey show the importance of location information for their day-to-day work. While location information technologies were identified by all four disciplines as useful for day-to-day work, there were differences among the disciplines, due in large part to the fact that different disciplines saw different lists of futuristic technologies on the survey. For example, the top two futuristic items chosen by COMMS survey respondents were "automatic caller location" (71.67%) and "first responder tracking" (64.16%). Qualitative data also show that accurate caller location was a top priority for COMMS personnel, as was being able to track the first responders they dispatch to the field.

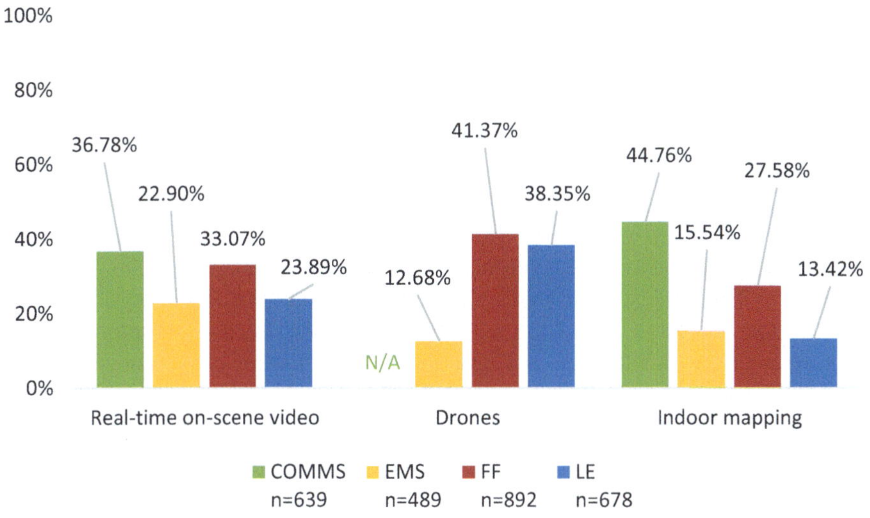

Fig. 11 Real-time information

> Location is number one. We can dispatch. We can do anything else in the world with that call if we have the location. But getting that location is just paramount. We can't do anything if we don't get a location. (INT-COMMS-R-016)

"First responder tracking" was checked by 23.01% of LE survey respondents as well. Over 25% of respondents from EMS, FF, and LE identified "Automatic vehicle location" as something they think would be useful in their day-to-day work (EMS: 35.79%; FF: 38.90%; and LE: 25.22%).

Real-Time Information

Rural first responders also indicated, in interviews and on the survey, they were interested in access to real-time information (Fig. 11).

For example, high numbers of survey respondents across disciplines identified real-time on-scene video as a technology they would find useful in their day-to-day work (COMMS, 36.78%; EMS, 22.90%; FF, 33.07%; LE, 23.89%). This is supported by interview and open-ended survey data as well.

> Being able to be live at a scene would be a huge tool to have as a dispatcher. The same with receiving pictures that could help with cases. (COMMS:R:9199)

> Or that there's the ability that that camera would be tied to the MDC so that I could push a button, take a picture, and transmit that without sitting here and opening an email, figure out who's working today, who's going to get this email... (INT-FF-R-008)

Additional items that garnered relatively high percentages from first responders in all four disciplines are indoor mapping and voice controls. These items had relatively high percentages across the four disciplines, suggesting they are important technologies for public safety in rural communities.

Drones appeared as one of the items in the futuristic list of technology on the survey for three of disciplines (EMS, FF, and LE). Large percentages of FF (41.37%) and LE (38.35%) selected this item, which may indicate that FF and LE rural first responders can envision possibilities for the use of drones in their day-to-day work. A lower percentage of EMS respondents (12.68%) chose drones as beneficial. This may be because EMS first responders work more specifically with patients and medical issues and may not find drones beneficial due to the nature of their work.

Several discipline-specific items had high percentages of first responders who thought they would be useful in their day-to-day work. For EMS, more than half of respondents (56.24%) selected "automatic transmission of patient vitals and information to the hospital" and nearly 40% also thought "health/vitals monitoring of patients" would be useful (38.85%). Over 40% of LE respondents chose "thermal imaging" (42.33%) and over 30% of FF respondents checked "heads-up displays" as potentially helpful for their day-to-day work. These technologies provide specific functions and support for their particular area of public safety and are of tremendous importance to the disciplines that use them.

Discussion

Rural first responders experienced problems with their communication technology, especially lack of connectivity, interoperability, reliability, and the cost of communication technology. Our results are consistent with studies that have examined both rural (O'Meara et al., 2002; Reddy et al., 2009; Greene et al., 2019; Pilemalm et al., 2013) and urban and suburban first responders (Dawkins et al., 2019) and further support that the manifestation and impact of these problems are unique to the rural context of use. Rural first responders in the study often experienced situations in which their devices were not suited to rural contexts. Devices were often unreliable due to challenges connecting in rural dead zones, traversing long distances, and enduring through extreme weather and terrain. Often these challenges were exacerbated by funding limits. When these issues are compounded, rural first responders must do their jobs without proper equipment. This places a significant burden on rural first responders during incident response.

Technology has the potential to decrease these burdens by increasing the amount of information available to rural first responders and decreasing time spent on tasks. However, in many cases, technology was an added burden, both mentally and physically to the day-to-day tasks of rural first responders. Thus, it is unsurprising that when rural first responders were asked what new technology would benefit them, they wanted their current problems fixed rather than entirely new communication technology. However, this does not mean that rural first responders were uninterested in new or futuristic technology. For example, rural first responders saw more utility for technology to improve access to location and real-time information. These findings are consistent with prior studies with urban and suburban first responders (Choong et al., 2018) and underscore the need for developers to address problems but also anticipate first responders' need for information.

The subsections below highlight four major areas that researchers and developers should consider as they improve and develop communication technology for rural first responders. Research and development in these areas are likely to benefit all first responders, but we specifically discuss how each area can be addressed in light of the rural context of use to improve the communication technology experiences of rural first responders.

Better Coverage and Connectivity

The lack of broadband infrastructure and geographic dead zones is largely unique to rural areas. Most rural first responders in this study relied on communication technology to communicate, and when these devices were unable to connect, rural first responders had no way to coordinate with other responders in the area or acquire new information. Although broadband coverage has been improving (Federal Communications Commission, 2020), some areas still have slow speeds (Meinrath et al., 2019; Vogels, 2021). Researchers and developers should carefully consider the communication technology they develop for use in rural areas; until broadband access and speed are improved, some devices may not work as intended or at all. Therefore, researchers and designers should continue to consider how to increase coverage and connectivity of communication technology in rural areas.

Durable and Reliable Devices

Rural first responders need devices that are durable and robust to conditions experienced by all first responders as well as to the extreme weather and terrains unique to the rural context of use. In addition to the environment, developers should also consider the additional distance and time rural first responders need for incident response in rural areas. Technology must be suited to long travel times and have long-lasting batteries for such journeys. Batteries should also be developed to be easily charged, while rural first responders are traversing long distances.

Improved Interoperability Both for Communicating Across Agencies, Across Devices, and Across Platforms

Rural first responders need devices that are both externally and internally interoperable. Because rural first responders often coordinate incident response across wide distances with many disciplines, areas, and jurisdictions, it is essential that the devices they are using can easily facilitate these connections. Devices must also be internally interoperable, working effectively and efficiently together to support first responders' needs during incident response. Improving internal interoperability may decrease the amount of time to transmit information and may also reduce the burden, frustration, and confusion of using multiple devices.

Affordable Devices That Are Easy to Fix and Inexpensive to Train on

Researchers and developers must consider existing barriers for rural first responders to implement communication technology. Rural first responders in this study had limited budgets that precluded them from replacing technology. Often, they had problems with the price of numerous devices and were also unable to update or upgrade their current devices. Additionally, our results suggest rural first responders often have few resources for technical support when they encounter problems with their technology. Therefore, rural first responders would benefit from affordable technology that can endure for a long period of time, have low training burden, and be simple to update.

Conclusion

Research and development are needed to continue to improve and understand the communication technology of rural first responders. Efforts should be focused on reducing current problems and tailoring communication technology to be better suited to the rural context of use. We also encourage research in several areas. First, future studies are needed to move beyond self-report and begin to use scenario-based assessments (Pilemalm, 2018) to elucidate problems experienced during incident response and highlight technology that works well in rural environments. Second, research is needed to understand the adoption of communication technology in rural areas, as our study suggests that rural first responders are hesitant to adopt new technology. Research is needed to understand both facilitators and barriers to adoption. Third, research using human factors and user-centered design is needed to ensure rural first responders are included in the research and development of communication technology made for them. This can ensure that technology will reflect the experiences, wants, and needs of rural first responders as well as focus on alleviating the burdens currently caused by technology.

By continuing to study the communication technology experiences of rural first responders, technology can be developed and improved for this population. This could shift how rural first responders view, adopt, and use communication technology. Rural first responders may transition away from viewing communication technology as a problem and burden and instead view communication technology as a trusted tool for more effectively and efficiently protecting and serving their communities.

Acknowledgments NIST would like to thank the many first responders, public safety personnel, and public safety organizations who graciously gave their time and input. We also would like to thank the larger NIST PSCR Usability Team for their efforts: Susanne Furman, Kristen Greene, Kevin Mangold, Brian Stanton, Michelle Steves, and Mary Theofanos.

References

Aftyka, A., Rybojad, B., & Rudnicka-Drozak, E. (2014). Are there any differences in medical emergency team interventions between rural and urban areas? A single-centre cohort study. *Australian Journal of Rural Health, 22*(5), 223–228. https://doi.org/10.1111/ajr.12108

Birdsey, M., Islam, M. R., & Barmare, A. (2016). Sporting injuries, seasonal trend and impact on rural Australian hospitals: Implications and recommendations. *Australian Journal of Rural Health, 24*(6), 402–408. https://doi.org/10.1111/ajr.12278

Chambers, R. (1994). The origins and practice of participatory rural appraisal. *World Development, 22*(7), 953–969. https://doi.org/10.1016/0305-750X(94)90141-4

Choong, Y., Dawkins, S., Furman, S., Greene, K. K., Prettyman, S. S., & Theofanos, M. F. (2018). *Voices of first responders – Identifying public safety communication problems, findings from user-centered interviews, phase 1, volume 1* (NISTIR 8216). National Institute of Standards and Technology. https://doi.org/10.6028/nist.Ir.8216

Coben, J. H., Tiesman, H. M., Bossarte, R. M., & Furbee, P. M. (2009). Rural–urban differences in injury hospitalizations in the U.S., 2004. *American Journal of Preventive Medicine, 36*(1), 49–55. https://doi.org/10.1016/j.amepre.2008.10.001

Comfort, L. K., Ko, K., & Zagorecki, A. (2004). Coordination in rapidly evolving disaster response systems: The role of information. *American Behavioral Scientist, 48*(3), 295–313. https://doi.org/10.1177/0002764204268987

Crooke, C. (2013). Women in law enforcement. *Community Policing Dispatch, 6*(7) https://cops.usdoj.gov/html/dispatch/07-2013/women_in_law_enforcement.asp. Accessed 11 April 2022.

Dawkins, S., Choong, Y.-Y., Theofanos, M. F., Greene, K. K., Furman, S., Steves, M., & Prettyman, S. S. (2019). *Voices of first responders – Examining public safety communication problems and requested functionality, phase 1, volume 2.1* (NISTIR 8245). National Institute of Standards and Technology. https://doi.org/10.6028/nist.Ir.8245

Dickes, L. A., Lamie, D. R., & Whitacre, B. E. (2010). The struggle for broadband in rural America. *Choices, 25*(4) http://www.jstor.org/stable/choices.25.4.09. Accessed 12 April 2022.

Fahy, R., Evarts, B., & Stein, G. P. (2021). *US fire department profile 2019*. National Fire Protection Association (NFPA). https://www.nfpa.org/-/media/Files/News-and-Research/Fire-statistics-and-reports/Emergency-responders/osfdprofile.pdf. Accessed 12 April 2022.

Federal Communications Commission. (2020). *2020 Broadband deployment report*. Federal Communications Commission. https://www.fcc.gov/reports-research/reports/broadband-progress-reports/2020-broadband-deployment-report. Accessed 11 April 2022.

Federal Emergency Management Agency (FEMA). (2020). *Regions*. https://www.fema.gov/about/organization/regions. Accessed 21 September 2020.

Gamache, S., Hall, J. R., Ahrens, M., Penney, G., & Kirtley, E. (2007). *Mitigation of the rural fire problem: Strategies based on original research and adaptation of existing best practices*. FEMA. https://www.hsdl.org/?view&did=483058. Accessed 11 April 2022.

Gasco-Hernandez, M., Zheleva, M., Bogdanov, P., & Gil-Garcia, J. R. (2019). Towards a socio-technical framework for bridging the digital divide in rural emergency preparedness and response: Integrating user adoption, heterogeneous wide-area networks, and advanced data science. In *Proceedings of the 20th annual international conference on Digital Government Research, Dubai, United Arab Emirates* (pp. 362–369). Association for Computing Machinery. https://doi.org/10.1145/3325112.3325217

Greene, K. K., Dawkins, S., Theofanos, M. F., Steves, M., Furman, S., Choong, Y.-Y., & Prettyman, S. S. (2019). *Voices of first responders – Examining public safety communication from the rural perspective phase 1, volume 3* (NISTIR 8277). National Institute of Standards and Technology. https://doi.org/10.6028/nist.Ir.8277

Greene, K. K., Dawkins, S., Prettyman, S. S., Konkol, P., Theofanos, M. F., Mangold, K., Furman, S., Choong, Y.-Y., & Steves, M. P. (2020). *Voices of first responders—Nationwide public safety communication survey methodology: Development, dissemination, and demographics, phase 2, volume 1* (NISTIR 8288). National Institute of Standards and Technology. https://doi.org/10.6028/NIST.IR.8288

Hackos, J. T., & Redish, J. (1998). Chapter 2: Thinking about users. In *User and task analysis for interface design* (pp. 23–50). Wiley.

Hang, H. M., Byass, P., & Svanström, L. (2004). Incidence and seasonal variation of injury in rural Vietnam: A community-based survey. *Safety Science, 42*(8), 691–701. https://doi.org/10.1016/j.ssci.2003.12.001

International Organization for Standardization. (2019). *Ergonomics of human-system interaction – Part 210: Human-centred design for interactive systems*. ISO 9241-210.

Iversen, L., Farmer, J. C., & Hannaford, P. C. (2002). Workload pressures in rural general practice: A qualitative investigation. *Scandinavian Journal of Primary Health Care, 20*(3), 139–144. https://doi.org/10.1080/028134302760234573

Jennings, P. A., Cameron, P., Walker, T., Bernard, S., & Smith, K. (2006). Out-of-hospital cardiac arrest in Victoria: Rural and urban outcomes. *Medical Journal of Australia, 185*(3), 135–139. https://doi.org/10.5694/j.1326-5377.2006.tb00498.x

LaRose, R., Gregg, J. L., Strover, S., Straubhaar, J., & Carpenter, S. (2007). Closing the rural broadband gap: Promoting adoption of the Internet in rural America. *Telecommunications Policy, 31*(6–7), 359–373. https://doi.org/10.1016/j.telpol.2007.04.004

Meinrath, S. D., Bonestroo, H., Bullen, G., Jansen, A., Mansour, S., Mitchell, C., Ritzo, C., & Thieme, N. (2019). *Broadband availability and access in rural Pennsylvania*. The Center for Rural Pennsylvania. https://www.rural.palegislature.us/broadband/Broadband_Availability_and_Access_in_Rural_Pennsylvania_2019_Report.pdf. Accessed 11 April 2022.

Middle Class Tax Relief and Job Creation Act of 2012, Public Law 112-96, 126 Stat. 156. (2012). http://www.gpo.gov/fdsys/pkg/PLAW-112publ96/pdf/PLAW-112publ96.pdf. Accessed 21 September 2020.

National Highway Traffic Safety Administration's Office of Emergency Medical Services National 911 Program Next Generation 911. https://www.911.gov/issue_nextgeneration911.html. Accessed 23 February 2021.

National Institute of Standards and Technology (NIST). (2017). *PSCR portfolio for user interface/user experience*. https://www.nist.gov/ctl/pscr/research-portfolios/user-interfaceuser-experience. Accessed 11 April 2022.

National Institute of Standards and Technology (NIST) Public Safety Communications Research Division. https://www.nist.gov/ctl/pscr. Accessed 11 April 2022.

O'Meara, P., Burley, M., & Kelly, H. (2002). Rural urgent care models: What are they made of? *Australian Journal of Rural Health, 10*(1), 45–50. https://doi.org/10.1111/j.1440-1584.2002.tb00008.x

Oliver, W. M., & Meier, C. A. (2004). Stress in small town and rural law enforcement: Testing the assumptions. *American Journal of Criminal Justice, 29*(1), 37–56. https://doi.org/10.1007/BF02885703

Pilemalm, S. (2018). Participatory Design in emerging civic engagement initiatives in the new public sector: Applying PD concepts in resource-scarce organizations. *Association for Computing Machinery (ACM) Transactions on Computer-Human Interaction, 25*(1), Article 5. https://doi.org/10.1145/3152420

Pilemalm, S., Stenberg, R., & Andersson Granberg, T. (2013). Emergency response in rural areas. *International Journal of Information Systems for Crisis Response and Management, 5*(2), 19–31. https://doi.org/10.4018/jiscrm.2013040102

Pötsch, T., Schmitt, P., Chen, J., & Raghavan, B. (2016). Helping the lone operator in the Vast Frontier. In *Proceedings of the 15th ACM workshop on hot topics in networks, Atlanta, GA* (pp. 1–7). ACM. https://doi.org/10.1145/3005745.3005757

Ramsell, E., Granberg, T. A., & Pilemalm, S. (2019). Identifying functions for smartphone based applications in volunteer emergency response. In Z. G. Franco, J. J. González, & J. H. Canós (Eds.), *Proceedings of the 16th international conference on Information Systems for Crisis Response and Management (ISCRAM 2019), Valencia, Spain, 2019* (pp. 1044–1056). Linköping University.

Ratcliffe, M., Burd, C., Holder, K., & Fields, A. (2016). *Defining rural at the U.S. Census Bureau.* https://www.census.gov/library/publications/2016/acs/acsgeo-1.html. Accessed 11 April 2022.

Reddy, M. C., Paul, S. A., Abraham, J., McNeese, M., DeFlitch, C., & Yen, J. (2009). Challenges to effective crisis management: Using information and communication technologies to coordinate emergency medical services and emergency department teams. *International Journal of Medical Informatics, 78*(4), 259–269. https://doi.org/10.1016/j.ijmedinf.2008.08.003

Ricci, M. A., Caputo, M., Amour, J., Rogers, F. B., Sartorelli, K., Callas, P. W., & Malone, P. T. (2003). Telemedicine reduces discrepancies in rural trauma care. *Telemedicine Journal and E-Health, 9*(1), 3–11. https://doi.org/10.1089/153056203763317602

Roberts, A., Nimegeer, A., Farmer, J., & Heaney, D. J. (2014). The experience of community first responders in co-producing rural health care: In the liminal gap between citizen and professional. *BMC Health Services Research, 14*(1), 460. https://doi.org/10.1186/1472-6963-14-460

Strover, S. (2001). Rural internet connectivity. *Telecommunications Policy, 25*(5), 331–347. https://doi.org/10.1016/S0308-5961(01)00008-8

Surana, S., Patra, R., Nedevschi, S., Ramos, M., Subramanian, L., Ben-David, Y., & Brewer, E. (2008). Beyond pilots: Keeping rural wireless networks alive. In *5th USENIX symposium on networked systems design and implementation, San Francisco, California* (pp. 119–132). USENIX Association.

Tiesman, H., Zwerling, C., Peek-Asa, C., Sprince, N., & Cavanaugh, J. E. (2007). Non-fatal injuries among urban and rural residents: The National Health Interview Survey, 1997-2001. *Injury Prevention, 13*(2), 115–119. https://doi.org/10.1136/ip.2006.013201

U.S. Bureau of Labor Statistics. (2019). *HOUSEHOLD DATA ANNUAL AVERAGES 11: Employed persons by detailed occupation, sex, race, and Hispanic or Latino ethnicity*. U.S. Bureau of Labor Statistics. https://www.bls.gov/cps/aa2019/cpsaat11.htm. Accessed 11 April 2022.

U.S. Census Bureau Rural America. https://mtgis-portal.geo.census.gov/arcgis/apps/MapSeries/index.html?appid=49cd4bc9c8eb444ab51218c1d5001ef6. Accessed 12 April 2022.

U.S. Department of Commerce Economics and Statistics Administration and the National Telecommunications and Information Administration. (2010). *Exploring the digital nation: Home broadband internet adoption in the United States*. Department of

Commerce. https://www.ntia.doc.gov/report/2010/exploring-digital-nation-home-broadband-internet-adoption-united-states. Accessed 3 November 2020.

Vogels, E. A. (2021). *Some digital divides persist between rural, urban and suburban America*. Pew Research Center. https://www.pewresearch.org/fact-tank/2019/05/31/digital-gap-between-rural-and-nonrural-america-persists/. Accessed 12 April 2022.

Weichelt, B., Heimonen, T., Pilz, M., Yoder, A., & Bendixsen, C. (2019). An argument against cross-platform development: Lessons from an augmented reality app prototype for rural emergency responders. *JMIR mHealth and uHealth, 7*(3), e12207. https://doi.org/10.2196/12207

Whitacre, B. E. (2008). Factors influencing the temporal diffusion of broadband adoption: Evidence from Oklahoma. *The Annals of Regional Science, 42*(3), 661–679. https://doi.org/10.1007/s00168-007-0178-7

Yankelevich, A., Shapiro, M., & Dutton William, H. (2017). Reaching beyond the wire: Challenges facing wireless for the last mile. *Digital Policy, Regulation and Governance, 19*(3), 210–224. https://doi.org/10.1108/DPRG-01-2017-0002

Designing Well-Accepted IT Solutions for Emergency Response: Methods and Approaches

Erion Elmasllari and Isabella Kirk

Abstract This chapter introduces system designers, usability engineers, interaction designers, system analysts, architects, requirements engineers, and project managers to a variety of methods that highly increase both the quality of IT solutions for emergency response and their acceptance among emergency responders. The methods are applicable for solutions at any level of the emergency response hierarchy and for any kind of disaster, but their relevance is highest when the intended solution addresses response frontlines and chaotic, abrupt extreme events such as earthquakes, floods, large-scale accidents, terror attacks, and fires.

Keywords IT system quality · CIMS quality assessment · CIMS usability · Minimum requirements · Evaluation methods · Prototyping · User centered design (UCD) · Participatory design (PD) · Requirements specification · Testing methods · Usability engineering · Specificity of CIMS

Problem Statement and Intended Audience

Despite both academia and industry having supplied a plethora of research and commercial IT-based tools for emergency response,[1] and despite responders'

---

[1] Emergency response has long been a darling of academic research and a test bed of new IT technologies, with, e.g., more than 111 academic articles and systems for electronic triage alone (Elmasllari & Reiners, 2017). Complete frameworks for emergency-related IT systems have been proposed by Turoff et al. (2004); Ganz et al. (2013); Adler et al. (2011); and Elmasllari (2018a), whereas industry giants such as Oracle, ESRI, and Raytheon have offered commercial solutions, respectively Oracle LEADERS (Lightweight Epidemiological Advanced Detection & Emergency Response System), ESRI ArcGIS, and Raytheon Emergency Patient Tracking System.

E. Elmasllari (✉) · I. Kirk
Factorsixty GmbH, Zürich, Switzerland
e-mail: erion@elmasllari.com; research@factorsixty.com

H. J. Scholl et al. (eds.), *Disaster Management and Information Technology*, Public Administration and Information Technology 40,
https://doi.org/10.1007/978-3-031-20939-0_11

increasing demand for tools to better manage and coordinate emergency response interventions, the actual adoption of IT-based tools, especially in the front lines, is lagging and the attitude of emergency responders to them is negative (Paul et al., 2008; Orthner et al., 2005; Adler et al., 2012; Ammenwerth et al., 2006; Elmasllari & Reiners, 2017).

Schmitt et al. (2007); Wu (2009); and Jennings et al. (2017) have noted several technology-intrinsic hindrances to acceptance of IT, whereas Elmasllari (2018b) and Elmasllari and Reiners (2017) have identified 12 kinds of problems that drive responders' negative attitude toward IT-based solutions, as well as six acceptance dimensions that determine how likely a given IT solution is to be accepted or rejected by emergency responders. The overwhelming majority of the problems and grounds for rejection stem from the mismatch between what emergency responders need and what IT systems have actually offered them. This mismatch is not simply "lacking functionality," but rather an inability of the IT solution to properly fit itself in the workflows of emergency responders, whether because of missing functionality, too much functionality, bad usability, or a variety of other shortcomings of the solution.

The mismatch between what users need and what IT systems offer them is a classic in the IT industry (see Fig. 1). It arises from missing or wrong requirements, which, in turn, are caused by the use of inappropriate or insufficient methods for eliciting and understanding user needs during system specification and development. Our research in Elmasllari (2018b) and Elmasllari and Reiners (2017) has shown that 5 out of the 6 acceptance dimensions could be fulfilled and 8 of the 12 causes of the negative attitude could be completely avoided simply by using the correct analysis and development methods.

Given the above, there is a clear need to introduce system designers (an umbrella term we will use for analysts, developers, requirements engineers, interface/interaction designers, and project managers) to tried-and-true methods for eliciting user needs and developing IT solutions for emergency response. We present in this chapter a minimal set of techniques that, both in our experience and according to state of the art practice, can guide designers toward IT solutions that get positively accepted and embraced by emergency responders. Rather than a detailed tutorial on the recommended methods, we aim to give a short introduction to each of them and focus instead on how to fine-tune it for usage in the emergency response context.

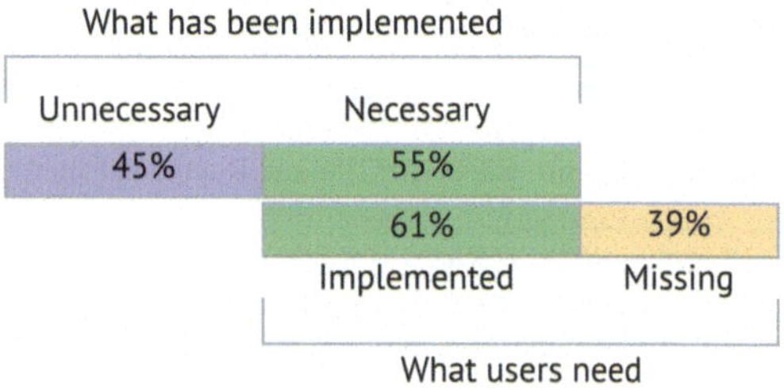

Fig. 1 The mismatch between user needs and IT system implementation. (Diagram based on The Standish Group (1995); Fowler (2002))

Interested readers can find further details about each method in the respective cited works or recommended reading.

Our method suggestions are based on our decade-long, hands-on experience researching and developing various complex socio-technical systems in the fields of emergency response, security in large events, work in dangerous factory environments, etc. The methods we propose were all successfully used in the research and development of 10 different IT-based systems in all areas of emergency response. By the end of development all systems passed rigorous tests by real users in realistic conditions. At least four systems have become commercially available, while the rest reached technology readiness levels of 7 or 8 ("Prototype demonstration in operational environment," "Actual system completed and qualified through test and demonstration").

Fundamental Considerations on Emergency Response Systems

IT solutions used in emergency response are fundamentally different from typical business software and present many pitfalls for the unwary designer, analyst, or developer tackling them for the first time. A short introduction to *complex systems* will help highlight these differences.

Simon (1962) defines complex systems as "made up of a large number of parts that interact in a non-simple way" and where "system properties and behavior are hard to infer based on the properties of the parts." Note that the word "system" here does not mean a "computer system," but rather any aggregation of parts, processes, and elements that work and interact together.

Complex systems are not merely "big and complicated." They have particular characteristics and behaviors that make them special:

1. The properties and behavior of a complex system are hard to infer, even when the properties and behavior of each part or component are known in detail (Simon, 1962). The system can exhibit emergent behavior, i.e., it can behave in ways that were never explicitly designed and may even be undesirable.
2. Complex systems cannot be studied or designed using a reductionist approach, such as decomposing the system top-down in parts and studying or designing each part separately. The true characteristics of a complex system only emerge when its parts are brought together.
3. The behavior of a complex system is nonlinear: tiny changes can lead to large differences in the outcome (Waldrop, 1993).

Complex *socio-technical* systems (CSTSs) are a kind of complex system where one or more of the parts are humans or organizations. The social and technical aspects are equally important in a CSTS; people and technology are very tightly interconnected, especially regarding the social, communication, and interaction aspects. CSTSs emerge over time and organize themselves without being under the full control of any singular entity (Holland, 1995).

Finally, complex *adaptive* systems are complex systems that adapt and organize themselves without being deliberately managed or controlled by anyone (Holland, 1995). They are intrinsically resilient, which means they will behave in such a way as to sustain their operation under all conditions (Hollnagel, 2013) and resist *external* efforts to change the system.

When considering that every emergency response effort involves a large number of people, organizations, tools, rules, the environment, physical world, etc., and that all these parts interact and influence each other, it can be shown that emergency response itself is a complex socio-technical system with a very strong adaptive element (Elmasllari, 2018a). The traditional software engineering approach of "splitting the problem top-down into parts, solving the parts, then combining the solution modules" clashes thus directly against point 2 above. As a result, traditionally developed solutions either do not match responders' needs and get rejected, or they exhibit undesired emergent behavior, undermining both the designer's (or engineer's) capability to understand the system and the responders' trust in it.

Because emergency response is a complex socio-technical adaptive system, and because complex adaptive systems are resilient against external efforts, it follows that any efforts to *impose* a new tool or technology on emergency responders will be met with resistance and rejection.[2] The best illustration for this effect is the failed introduction of the London Ambulance Service's dispatch tool, which was sabotaged by the emergency responders themselves (SW Thames, 1993; Shapiro, 2005). The implication is that successful, well-accepted IT solutions for emergency response must arise from within, i.e., must be developed by the responders themselves.

An Opposing View

Through our research and development work, we have noticed that it is better to treat IT solutions for emergency response as complex systems in their own. A possible objection to this view is that, in practice, commercial suppliers address only single aspects of emergency response, such as "logistics management" and "communications." Software for these aspects is simple, well-known, and very similar to standard business software, so why should it be treated as a complex system and why should suppliers pay special attention during its development?

This objection underestimates the ways in which IT integrates into the emergency response effort:

(continued)

[2] This includes cases when the technology is purchased or commissioned by the "higher-ups" of an emergency response organization and mandated on the other members or employees.

- Except for the tiniest software, IT solutions typically have different functions or modules (=parts), which will very likely interact with multiple different responders and systems (=other parts and interactions), often in unforeseen or improvised ways (=even more interactions). In effect, you start with a CSTS (the emergency response effort) and add more parts and interactions to it (your IT solution). It should be clear that, in the resulting complex system, there is no real boundary between the supposedly simple IT solution and the rest of the emergency response effort.
- What matters for acceptance is the view from the responders' side, i.e., how a given IT solution fits inside the emergency response effort. Ensuring that a (supposedly simple) IT solution "plays well" within this CSTS requires the same methods as if the IT solution were a complex system on its own. You are thus better off treating it as such from the beginning and choosing the appropriate design and development methods accordingly.

The correct way to design IT solutions for emergency response was outlined already by SW Thames (1993) and Shapiro (2005), who recommended that when designing emergency systems in the future:

- The emergency response context and users need to be studied very carefully.
- Emergency professionals' trust in the system needs to be earned, otherwise they will distrust and/or sabotage systems imposed on them.
- Emergency-related IT systems must be designed with constant and wide participation from the users.

While the above recommendations are correct, they are too high level to be used in practice. The next sections will present concrete methods on how to tackle each of those recommendations: how to study the emergency response context, how to involve users, and how to design IT systems that easily gain the responders' trust for successful adoption in the emergency response practice.

High-Level Approaches and Paradigms

Only two commonly used development paradigms match the recommendations from SW Thames (1993). We present these paradigms shortly below; an in-depth view is provided by Norman and Draper (1986); Ritter et al. (2014); Ehn (2008); Shapiro (2005).

User-Centered Design

User-Centered Design (UCD) is a design and development paradigm that puts the user at the center of the designers' attention (Norman & Draper, 1986; Norman, 1988). The system is designed to fit the user, instead of expecting the user to "learn" the system or adapt to it.

The UCD paradigm first analyzes the context: the capabilities, characteristics, tools, and goals of the user, as well as the physical, social, and regulatory environment within which the system is to work (see Fig. 2). This analysis is then expressed as user needs and requirements and, in a third step, implemented in a prototype to be tested with actual users in realistic conditions. The test insights are used in a new iteration, deepening the understanding of the context, clarifying the requirements, and making better prototypes until all user needs and expectations are fulfilled and the system can be successfully used in the intended environment.

UCD does not draw a distinction between the technological part and the social part of the system, but considers both of them holistically (Ritter et al., 2014). With UCD, the development effort cannot stray too far from users' needs; the resulting systems tend to match the users' workflow, capabilities, and needs extremely well. These qualities make UCD appropriate for the complex, critical, and change-sensitive systems related to emergency response.

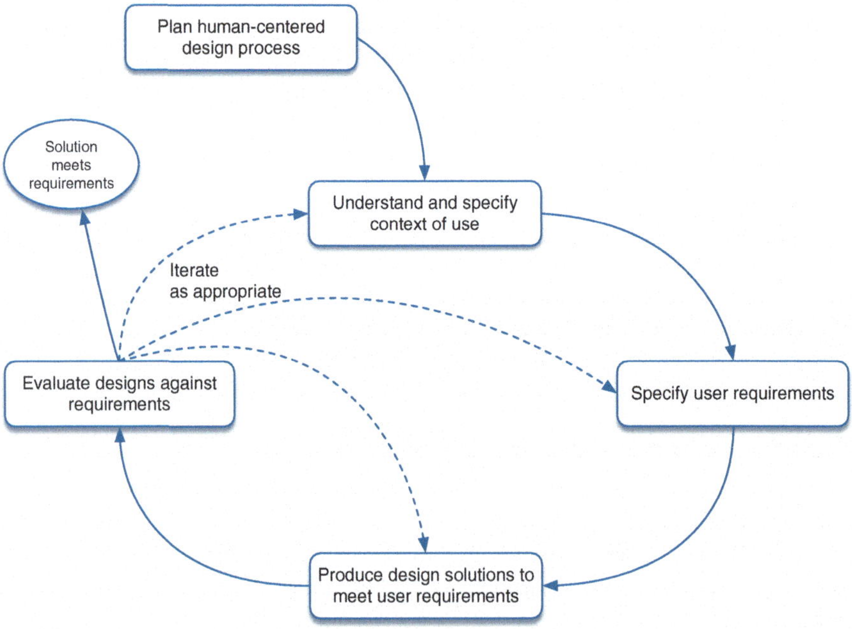

Fig. 2 The user-centered design process for interactive systems. (Source: ISO9241-210 (2008))

UCD also has some drawbacks, but these can be easily avoided by Participatory Design (see section "Participatory Design"):

- UCD was meant for human-machine interaction, but the dominant interaction today is human-human, mediated by machines.
- When users are put at the center, they become unaware of how the system itself interacts with the world and what is necessary to make the system work (Slavin, 2016). As a result, they can neither change the system, nor repair it, nor can they judge the ethical aspects of using the system.
- Users do not live isolated from other technology, nor do they keep a coherent set of beliefs and preferences (Visciola, 2003). A pure-UCD development can waste time catching-up with shifting preferences and technology fashions.

Participatory Design

Participatory Design (PD) keeps UCD as its foundation, but postulates that, because the system affects how users work, users themselves should take part in designing that system. For emergency response this means that the system design team must include actual emergency responders.

PD is ideally suited to emergency response. The responders' mistrust against IT can be entirely overcome by letting them shape the new solutions. This way the solutions will match their needs and way of working and will have "arisen from within" the emergency responder collective, as opposed to being "forced upon them." The responders who participate in the design effort also become the initial, most vocal supporters of the new product. Such social proof leads to much higher acceptance rates than mandatory usage, as reported by Venkatesh and Davis (2000).

Methods for Design and Development

The following methods have been the most effective, in our experience, for the design and development of complex systems in emergency response. For ease of reference, we have grouped them below by the UCD step in which they are typically used (see Fig. 2). As we only provide an overview of each method, readers are encouraged to consult Hollnagel (2013); Rasmussen et al. (1994); and Endsley (2011) for further details. Suggestions on how to combine the proposed methods for maximum efficiency under a limited budget can be found in Elmasllari (2018a).

Methods for Analyzing the Context of Use

Methods for context analysis can be broadly organized into two categories: analytic methods, whose basis is the analysis of formal documents and other available data, and ethnographic methods, whose basis is the interaction with users and their environment. Analytic methods are good at finding out the "formal" context, or how things should be done "by the book," but ignore the actual ways in which responders work in the real world. Ethnographic methods are good at finding out how things are really done on the ground (i.e., the informal context), but they are blind to the rules, requirements, and processes that responders neglect or circumvent. Analytic and ethnographic methods must always be used together, because only then can all user needs and requirements toward a tool or system be identified.

The Four Types of User Needs

Rasmussen (1983) reports four types of user needs, each of which requires different methods and degrees of effort to identify.

Explicit needs, such as "We need a stretcher to carry victims" are easily recalled and expressed by users when you ask them about their tasks and workflow.

Observable needs are not usually mentioned explicitly by the responders, because they tend to be obvious and self-explanatory to them, e.g., "The stretcher must have a handle." These needs are readily identifiable to an observer using the appropriate methods.

Users cannot express *tacit needs* accurately in words. They may say, for example, "The handle of the stretcher feels wrong," but may not be able to describe how exactly it can "feel right."

Users are not even aware of having *latent needs*, so you can't uncover them by asking or observing the user. Latent needs include, for example, convenience, lower task load, and meaningfulness of a task or interaction.

Analytic Methods

Document analysis focuses on written documents and rules, for example, laws, standards, process descriptions, and codes of conduct. These are necessary for understanding the limits of what would be an acceptable solution. *Literature research*, instead, learns from existing research and production efforts, i.e., from the experience, insights, and mistakes of others. This is used to find inspiration and to quickly prune infeasible solutions. Both methods should be used together in order to identify new solutions and approaches and to ensure these don't conflict with existing rules.

Ethnographic Methods

As "work-to-rule" labor strikes prove, following the rules of a job to the letter is a sure way to slow an organization down or to stop it completely. It is only thanks to informal behavior and overlooking some rules that organizations—especially emergency response organizations—can function at all. This is why it is crucial to understand this informal behavior, for which the ethnographic methods below have proven very useful.

The study of incident reports and emergency response case evaluations straddles the border between analytic and ethnographic methods. It is obviously similar to document analysis, but, due to the detailed nature of incident reports, a good amount of ethnographic information is included. These reports do a great job of teaching system designers about behaviors and actions that led to failure in the past and should be avoided in the future. The reports, however, contain little detail about current behaviors and actions, as by definition these have not (yet) caused failures or incidents. To get detailed knowledge of how responders currently work, what problems they face, and how they tackle emergency response, it is necessary to use one of the following methods.

Observation methods (participant and nonparticipant observation) are based on observing users as they go about their work. Behavior and movement patterns, tools, and interactions among users are noticed and documented. A *nonparticipant observer* tries to not influence the users' actions in any way. In *participant observation*, the observer takes part in the process as a guest and can ask questions, can experience the same physical and emotional environment, can listen to the communications more closely, and can achieve a holistic understanding of the users and their context. Participant observation is good for finding out latent and tacit needs, whereas nonparticipant observation uncovers the observable needs. Participant observation is one of our favorite techniques, because it helps designers touch the reality of emergency response and viscerally understand the harsh constraints of this domain. In addition, participant observation helps create a rapport with the responders, paving the way for mutual trust and collaboration.

Observation-based methods have two drawbacks: (i) the observer's own background and emotions may influence how they *interpret* the observed events and (ii) the results may be tightly related to the individual responder being observed, i.e., they may be non-generalizable. Both of these drawbacks are compensated by combining observations with the following methods.

Interviews can be anywhere from informal and spontaneous to formal, with a list of questions known in advance to the subject. Two techniques, *semi-structured interviews* and *contextual inquiries*, have been especially useful for understanding the context of emergency response.

Semi-structured interviews are built around a list of questions drafted before the interview, based on document research, prior knowledge of the context, or standardized question sets, e.g., DAkkS (2010). The order of the questions is not important. Indeed, it is expected that the discussion will branch off; responders should not be forced to answer questions fully, at once, or in a certain order. An experienced interviewer will know when and how to steer the discussion back on topic. In case of doubt, especially when mutual trust and rapport has not been achieved yet, it is better to listen to a few off-topic stories than to break rapport by urging the responder to only answer your questions.

Contextual inquiries are a variation of an interview that is appropriate for tacit needs, i.e., needs that cannot be verbalized. The responder is interviewed in his or her work environment, while working. The researcher or designer becomes an "apprentice," asking questions and learning how to do the work. The needs and behaviors that responders take for granted because of their experience will become obvious and explicit to the researcher who is struggling to learn. As a beneficial side effect, contextual inquiries help establish trust and rapport with responders, who feel more at ease "teaching an apprentice" than being interviewed.

Interview-based methods require a skilled interviewer (Hamill, 2016). Even so, interview transcripts and summaries should always be validated with the responders, so that they can correct misunderstandings. To maximize the amount of useful data, the responders that are interviewed should be carefully chosen to have as diverse fields of expertise as possible, but they should also span all levels of experience. It is counterproductive to interview responders at only one level of experience, as each level has different needs which must all be found out and accounted for.

Affinity diagramming is a method in which keywords that come up during discussions, interviews, observations, and other activities are first written on post-it notes, then grouped on a whiteboard according to similarity and other relatedness criteria. This helps identify central and peripheral topics as well as their relative importance. We have had very good results organizing affinity diagramming "workshops," where we invite several emergency responders *from various backgrounds* and let them group the post-its. Because of the participants' different backgrounds and viewpoints, the sorting and grouping stimulates discussions about how the topics influence their work and how they really relate to each other. The discussions provide much more domain detail than can be inferred by interviews and observations alone.

Event Storming is a newer method that promises to be useful for collaboratively exploring and understanding complex domains (Brandolini, 2013). Its roots appear similar to affinity diagramming, but it starts from domain-specific *events* instead of keywords. A structured discussion process is then used to understand and document the domain in minute detail, in a way that is suitable both for developing software and for communicating with nontechnical people. We believe Event Storming has the potential to extend or replace affinity diagramming and to provide a better understanding of emergency responders' work and needs.

Participatory Design Methods

The methods presented below require the participation of responders in the design and development team and help elicit expertise and ideas from the responders themselves. For further approaches beyond this minimal set of methods, see Klann (2007).

A focus group is a discussion with a small group of participants, which centers ("focuses") on certain topics and questions of interest to the designer or developer. Focus groups have an inherent advantage over interviews, because they highlight important points better. When conducting an interview, the designer may not recognize some points as important, but those same points will stimulate such lively discussion, related thoughts, and experience exchanges in a focus group, that they cannot be missed.

Our experience using the focus group technique with emergency responders showed that it is best to invite responders from different backgrounds and response organizations, but they should have the same experience level and be at the same hierarchy level within the respective organizations. Differences in background ensure that the discussed topics will be new or unfamiliar to some of the participants. The needs that are tacit or latent for the experts of one field will be explicit—hence easy to speak and describe—for participants from the other fields. The other two conditions, having the same experience level and being at the same hierarchy level, are necessary so that participants can discuss as equals and are not shy to express their thoughts in front of higher-status peers.

Just like interviews, focus groups require a skilled moderator. The knowledge achieved from focus groups should be verified by testing a prototype or by administering questionnaires to a larger group of users. Academic literature points out that people in focus groups tend to give "socially desirable" answers and avoid controversial topics, but in our experience, front-line emergency responders were not noticeably prone to this problem.

Sandbox sessions are discussions where participants use play figures and toys to enact and explain their part, role, or view of a complex activity. LEGO® Minifigures, action figures, dolls, play-dough, wooden cubes, cars, and generally any toy from a child's sandbox can also be used here. This method provides a window into the responders' knowledge without any particular verbal or memory skills (which other methods require). Sandbox sessions are very useful and easy with emergency responders, because they commonly use play figures to plan exercises and are not shy to use them in a sandbox session as well. When working with responders from different countries and languages, sandbox sessions lower the language barriers and allow responders to participate who would otherwise have been excluded.

Methods for Specifying Requirements

While we have successfully used both "The Working Model for Usability Engineering" by Geis and Polkehn (2018) and "The Volere template" by Robertson and Robertson (2018) to distill requirements from the context analysis, we find that the exact process of extracting requirements is not as important as identifying the user needs correctly and doing the context analysis properly in the first place. Furthermore, our experience with different development teams has shown that each team has its own, often deeply ingrained and formalized methods for requirements engineering. As long as those methods are correct, we see little advantage in switching to another method; the cost and delays from the changeover often offset the benefits.

That said, user requirements in UCD subtly differ from traditional, system-centered requirements. UCD user requirements describe what the user must be able to do at the system once it's implemented, not how the system must implement the needed functionality. Compare, for example, the user-centered requirement. "At the system the user must be able to input his identity" and the system-centered requirement "The system must have a text-box for the username." The distinction between the two is powerful: whereas system-centered requirements define one single solution (the text-box), user-centered requirements define the outcome but allow for multiple solution possibilities (text-box, voice, fingerprint, etc.). We have found that the model from Geis and Polkehn (2018) does a much better job of forcing the designers to think in user-requirement terms and to understand the core of what the user needs. Despite a steeper learning curve at the beginning, it ultimately opens up more design opportunities that would otherwise be missed.

Methods for Prototyping

In addition to being required by the UCD process, prototypes give users and designers a concrete implementation to focus discussion on, help to avoid misunderstandings about system scope and features, allow a more "visual" and "hands-on" approach to discussion, and allow testing physical actions with the system. Prototypes are indispensable when designing solutions for emergency response.

Scenarios are the simplest prototypes; they are just a high-level, textual description of how a proposed tool can be used to fulfill a certain task. *Storyboards* do the same job as scenarios, but are presented as a drawn comic strip. Whereas scenarios encourage verbal thinking, storyboards encourage visual thinking and can present spatial and physical-size relationships much better, e.g., the size or handling of the tool or system. Both methods invite critique and feedback from users and help understand domain requirements better. We have successfully used both scenarios and storyboards in our work with emergency responders, but we found these techniques to be most useful in the first iterations of the process, for presenting initial ideas. For later iterations we found that observation, focus groups discussions with a rough prototype, and contextual inquiry worked much better.

Interface sketches, wireframes, and physical prototypes make ideas concrete and graspable, both physically and figuratively speaking. They set a baseline for discussion between users and developers, they help train users, and, when created via participatory design, they make users accept and advertise the system to their peers instead of opposing it. Prototypes can (and should) be created at various levels of fidelity, from simple sketches on paper, to mock-ups of interfaces and devices with simple materials (wood, plastic, baked play-dough), to partially implemented IT systems. The level of fidelity depends on the phase of development (earlier = lower fidelity) and on the questions for which developers need answers (rough estimates = lower fidelity; detailed questions and interactions = higher fidelity).

Scope and Life-Span of a Prototype
It is crucial to see the prototype as a throw-away item and use the least amount of work and energy necessary to produce it. The only features implemented in the prototype should be the ones you need for getting an answer to specific questions about the domain and user needs.

The prototype should look unfinished, cheap, temporary, and open to criticism; if it "looks finished" or "looks too good," responders will withhold negative feedback in order to be nice, but they will reject your product when you bring it to market.

New tools must earn the responders' trust before they can be accepted; misuse and abuse is part of their acceptance process. Never let your prototypes become an exhibition piece, displayed but untouchable. Find creative ways of breaking the ice; make responders interact with your physical and software prototypes in both desired and unusual ways, including breaking or destroying them! The aim is for responders to become familiar with the prototype's limits and capabilities. Only then will they be open to giving it—and your solution—detailed attention, trust, and honest, constructive feedback.

Methods for Evaluation

The Scenario Walk-through method is the cheapest, easiest method to evaluate the design of a tool or system. One or two responders or emergency response experts enact a typical task with the tool and note difficulties or inconsistencies during usage. The evaluation is usually done in a lab or office, not necessarily in the real environment where the system will be used. It is crucial that the experts have extensive and practical knowledge of the emergency response domain, because only someone who can put themselves in the responders' shoes can identify meaningful difficulties with the proposed design.

Prototype workstations are stands in a simulated "fair," where all the developed prototypes are shown and "pitched" to small, multidisciplinary groups of domain experts and users. The experts and users listen to the pitches, can ask questions, and can play with the prototypes if they wish. Finally they give feedback and critique the proposed system, pointing out both positive features to be kept and problems to be solved. The "prototype workstations" method is more intensive than simple scenario walk-throughs, but it delivers much more feedback and can point out many more problems, thanks to its multidisciplinary approach and higher number of participants.

User testing is a very wide and complex topic on which entire books have been written. It is impossible to even scratch the surface of this topic here, so we will instead defer the details to the books by Rubin et al. (2011) and Goodman et al. (2012). That said, we have very successfully used—and overcome the limitations of—the "user testing with thinking aloud" method.

User testing with thinking aloud is a classic user testing method in which users verbalize their thoughts out loud while working with the prototype. This allows the system designer or analyst to notice discrepancies between the user's mental model (i.e., how the user expects the prototype to work) and the actual implementation (i.e., how the prototype actually works). The method is great when testing rough, early stage prototypes, or perhaps in a tabletop or other low-intensity exercise. The method is inappropriate in task-loaded, realistic emergency scenarios or when the user needs to work fast, because the user's behavior, speed, and actions will be noticeably hindered by having to think aloud. Because the front lines of emergency response are such a task-loaded, extreme stress environment, user testing with thinking aloud is not appropriate for testing in the front lines of realistic emergency response exercises. In such cases we have had very good results by doing a silent, nonparticipatory observation during the exercise itself, followed by a *retrospective review* immediately after it. During the silent observation phase we let responders work with the prototype and pay attention to their actions, face expressions, and level of frustration. Immediately after the exercise we chat with the responder to "review in retrospect" what went on, focusing on the difficulties they had with the task or the prototype. Video recordings, if available, are very useful as a memory aid for the responder.

The Necessity of User Testing Under Realistic Conditions

The complex behavior and failure modes of a complex system arise from the interplay between its elements. These include the users (responders as well as other users), tools (both your prototype system and other tools they use), tasks (what users have to do), and the environment (the kind of emergency, weather, intervention rules, terrain, etc.). By the above reasoning, to properly test a new IT solution for emergency response, the *actual users* must *use* it in the *actual context* to do their *actual job*. This is called "user testing under realistic conditions" and is the single most important of all evaluation methods when designing for emergency response. It is also the most expensive, because it requires testing in a realistic emergency or disaster scenario (e.g., response exercise). A tabletop exercise will not be enough. The pain, suffering, destruction, and chaos that one typically faces in a crisis area create high levels of stress that alter the responders' behavior, memory, and mental ability, thus directly impacting the way they use the prototype and the errors that occur. The only way to uncover these errors is to let responders use the prototype under realistic stress conditions, not on a comfortable chair in a tabletop exercise.

Test With Responders Who Don't Know Your Solution
Using the Participatory Design paradigm means that some emergency responders will be part of your system design team. It is tempting to test the prototypes mainly (or only) with these responders: it is cheaper, quicker, and they are available all the time. This kind of testing is guaranteed to give wrong results, because the responders who are part of your team, or who have had extended exposure to your solution, know it too well and want it to succeed—it is their creation as much as yours! For this reason, testing should always involve responders from outside the development team, who are not familiar with your solution.

Idiosyncrasies, Challenges, and Pitfalls of Designing IT Systems for Emergency Response

Most of our discussion so far has focused on two things: (i) the awareness that emergency response is a complex system, and (ii) the necessity for particular methods and adjustments to correctly find out and validate the user needs within this CSTS. Designing IT systems for the emergency response domain, however, presents a few other hurdles and challenges that are intrinsic to the design process itself, independently of the methods used.

Conflicting Interaction Paradigms

Paramedics, emergency responders, soldiers, and other persons in high-stress emergency environments report that "in an emergency you don't rise to the occasion. You instead fall to the level of your training and can only do the things you know so well as to do them in your sleep."[3] The aim of training for crisis response is exactly this: ingrain behaviors so deep that they can be done automatically, without conscious thought, "in one's sleep" (Marx, 2019).

As a corollary to the above, processes, communication flows, interaction paradigms, and tools used for managing an emergency have to remain stable over relatively long periods of time, otherwise (i) they can't be ingrained deeply enough, and (ii) deeply learned behaviors would become useless or even counterproductive every time a process or paradigm changes. Thus, the tacit need of responders to

[3] This sentence was quoted to us multiple times in different versions. We recommend the paper by Rasmussen (1983) for a detailed analysis of the different drivers of human behavior and automatisms.

work without conscious thought has a price for the system designer: IT systems may need to use familiar technologies and older interaction paradigms instead of state-of-the-art ones. (The aim is to minimize mental switches between "old" and "new" tools, and not have to remember each tool's interaction quirks.) This should not be treated as a blanket statement, however, but only as an invitation to pay attention to this tacit need, involve responders in the choice of interaction paradigms, and heavily test the latter in realistic conditions.

Mismatched Understandings of the System Boundary

Usability engineering practice as well as the formal ISO9241 standard make a clear distinction between a product or system and the context in which it is used (ISO9241-210, 2008). From the designer's point of view, the "system boundary"—the imaginary border around your product—typically includes only the product's interface, backend, and hardware. Everything else is deemed to be part of the context, external to the product. As an example, a network switch would be seen as "the system," whereas the electric power supply and the rack or truck in which the switch gets mounted would be considered "context."

From the point of view of the emergency responder, however, all elements that work together to complete one logical task are seen as one single large system. The responder would mentally lump together the network switch, the electrical power supply, and the rack or truck into a "communication center." The system boundary according to the user is thus much wider than the boundary according to the designer.

This discrepancy affects the development of IT solutions for emergency response in three ways (Elmasllari, 2019):

- It may hide important use cases (e.g., "repair/restore communications" instead of simply "reset the network switch").
- It may give rise to usability problems and inconsistencies that do not exist in isolation, but arise when several products are used together. For example, the power supply for the network switch looks like the power supply for the signal amplifier mounted on the same rack, but has twice the voltage and burns the amplifier.
- It may lull the designer into thinking her product is a single, simple IT system, with well-defined behaviors and interfaces, whereas in reality the system—as seen by the user—is complex and has unforeseen emergent behaviors.

The antidote to these three problems is, unsurprisingly, keeping them in mind while performing a proper and detailed context analysis using the methods from section "Methods for Design and Development". We have found contextual inquiry and participant observation particularly useful in giving designers a detailed, visceral feeling of the emergency response mindset and problems.

Usability Testing Hurdles

We highlighted user testing under realistic conditions as a crucial and unavoidable step in designing IT solutions for emergency response. However, depending on the concrete IT solution being developed and the kind of emergencies it is intended for, it may be infeasible or even illegal to simulate emergency conditions that are "realistic enough." The chance of users being hurt or traumatized during a too-realistic simulation may be ethically unacceptable. Usability engineers should design the scenarios and amount of user testing so as to compensate for these limitations.

Human-Computer Interaction Versus Machine-Mediated Human-Human Interaction

Many IT products not only enable, but are the main or only channel over which human-human interaction and communication happen during a task. Yet, usability engineers typically see themselves as "optimizing the interaction between human and system," "optimizing the interface," or "making products easy to use." Rarely do usability engineers look beyond human-computer interaction and onto the *human-human interaction* that their products enable and mediate, even though this human-human interaction will be deeply affected by the product. A simple usability problem at the human-computer level, e.g., difficulty or sluggishness when composing a message, may break the human-human interaction in critical ways. This is very costly—even unforgivable—in emergency response. Designers and usability engineers should holistically analyze and support the human-human interaction mediated by their product.

Conclusion

While there is no doubt that IT can revolutionize emergency response, practitioners have made it clear that IT tools and systems being offered to emergency responders are not satisfactory and helpful enough to be widely accepted. Existing research has confirmed that the causes of rejection lie with the IT systems themselves (Paul et al., 2008; Orthner et al., 2005; Adler et al., 2012; Ammenwerth et al., 2006; Elmasllari & Reiners, 2017; Elmasllari, 2018b). We posit that the root of the problem lies in the wrong or insufficient context and requirements analysis, stemming from usage of development methodologies that are not suitable for the emergency response domain.

To correct the problem and to increase the acceptance of IT solutions in emergency response, we presented several approaches and concrete methods which we have successfully used in designing for emergency response and other complex systems. Far from providing a detailed tutorial on any particular technique or method, we offer an overview of each of them together with their drawbacks, our critique on them, and our experience on when and how they could be best used and adjusted in the emergency response domain. Our target audience: system designers, architects, developers, analysts, requirements engineers, usability engineers, and project managers are invited to take advantage of these methods and to further their proficiency and practical knowledge about them.

In addition to the provided methods and suggestions, we strongly recommend that all system designers should participate in at least one crisis exercise in the domain for which they are designing, e.g., firefighting and rescue. Such exercises will suffice to ground the system designers to the realities of the emergency response domain and inspire them towards solutions that fit into the work and needs of emergency responders.

As a special characteristic of emergency response, we argued that the response effort is a complex, adaptive, socio-technical system, in which a reductionist, top-down mindset and system architecture, as is typical in software engineering, is counterproductive. Instead we advocate for awareness of how the complex socio-technical nature of emergency response impacts IT solutions, and for always including emergency responders as part of the team designing such solutions.

References

Adler, C., Krüsmann, M., Greiner-Mai, T., Donner, A., Chaves, J. M., & Estrem, A. V. (2011). IT-supported management of mass casualty incidents: The e-triage project. In *Proceedings of the 8th International ISCRAM Conference*, Washington, DC, USA.

Adler, T., Jakob, L., & Krüsmann, M. (2012). Die Einführung neuer Technologien im Rettungsdienst – Akzeptanzforschung mit GABEK® dargestellt am Projekt e-Triage. In *GABEK V: Werte in Organisationen und Gesellschaft* (pp. 307–324). StudienVerlag.

Ammenwerth, E., Iller, C., & Mahler, C. (2006). IT-adoption and the interaction of task, technology and individuals: A fit framework and a case study. *BMC Medical Informatics and Decision Making, 6*(1), 1–13. https://doi.org/10.1186/1472-6947-6-3

Brandolini, A. (2013). URL https://www.eventstorming.com/

DAkkS. (2010). *Leitfaden usability* (71 SD 2 007 A1 ed.). DAkkS.

Ehn, P. (2008). Participation in design things. In *Proceedings of the tenth anniversary conference on Participatory Design 2008, PDC '08* (pp. 92–101). Indiana University.

Elmasllari, E. (2018a). *A framework for the successful design and deployment of electronic triage systems*. PhD thesis, RWTH Aachen, Germany.

Elmasllari, E. (2018b). Why IT systems for emergency response get rejected: Examining responders' attitude to IT. In *Proceedings of the 15th ISCRAM conference* (pp. 994–1002). Rochester Institute of Technology.

Elmasllari, E. (2019). Usability engineering in life-critical contexts. In *Keynote at the Congress of Medical Software and Device Development, MedConf 2019*, Munich, Germany.

Elmasllari, E., & Reiners, R. (2017). Learning from non-acceptance: Design dimensions for user acceptance of e-triage systems. In *Proceedings of the 14th ISCRAM Conference*, ISCRAM, Albi, France, pp. 798–813.

Endsley, M. R. (2011). *Designing for situation awareness: An approach to user-centered design* (2nd ed.). CRC Press.
Fowler, M. (2002). *The xp 2002 conference.* https://martinfowler.com/articles/xp2002.html
Ganz, A., Schafer, J., Yu, X., Lord, G., Burstein, J., & Ciottone, G. R. (2013). Real-time scalable resource tracking framework (DIORAMA) for mass casualty incidents. *International Journal of E-Health and Medical Communications (IJEHMC), 4*(2), 34–49.
Geis, T., & Polkehn, K. (2018). *Praxiswissen user requirements.* Dpunkt.verlag.
Goodman, E., Kuniavsky, M., & Moed, A. (2012). *Observing the user experience: A practitioner's guide to user research* (2nd ed.). Morgan Kaufmann Publishers Inc.
Hamill, H. (2016). *Interview methodology.* https://doi.org/10.1093/OBO/9780199756384-0105
Holland, J. H. (1995). *Hidden order: How adaptability builds complexity.* Perseus Books.
Hollnagel, E. (2013). *Resilience engineering in practice: A guidebook.* Ashgate Publishing, Ltd.
ISO9241-210. (2008). *ISO9241-210: Ergonomics of human system interaction.* ISO.
Jennings, E. A., Arlikatti, S., Andrew, S. A., & Kim, K. (2017). Adoption of information and communication technologies (ICTs) by local emergency management agencies in the United States. *International Review of Public Administration, 22*(2), 193–210. https://doi.org/10.1080/12294659.2017.1323481
Klann, M. (2007). Playing with fire: User-centered design of wearable computing for emergency response. In J. Löffler & M. Klann (Eds.), *Mobile response* (pp. 116–125). Springer Berlin Heidelberg.
Marx, D. (2019). *Entscheidungsprozesse, workshop on emergency response at the "Rettmobil 2019"*, Fulda, Germany.
Norman, D. (1988). *The psychology of everyday things.* Basic Books.
Norman, D. A., & Draper, S. W. (1986). *User centered system design; New perspectives on human-computer interaction.* L. Erlbaum Associates Inc..
Orthner, H., Mishra, N., Terndrup, T., Acker, J., Grimes, G., Gemmill, J., & Battles, M. (2005). Information infrastructure for emergency medical services. In *AMIA annual symposium proceedings* (p. 1067). American Medical Informatics Association.
Paul, S. A., Reddy, M., Abraham, J., & DeFlitch, C. (2008). The usefulness of information and communication technologies in crisis response. In *AMIA annual symposium proceedings* (pp. 561–565). American Medical Informatics Association.
Rasmussen, J. (1983). Skills, rules, and knowledge; signals, signs, and symbols, and other distinctions in human performance models. *IEEE Transactions on Systems, Man and Cybernetics, SMC-13*(3), 257–266. https://doi.org/10.1109/TSMC.1983.6313160
Rasmussen, J., Pejtersen, A. M., & Goodstein, L. P. (1994). *Cognitive systems engineering.* John Wiley & Sons, Inc..
Ritter, F., Baxter, G., & Churchill, E. (2014). User-centered systems design: A brief history. In *Foundations for designing user-centered systems: What system designers need to know about people* (pp. 33–54). Springer.
Robertson, J., & Robertson, S. (2018). *Volere requirements specification template* (Technical report). Atlantic Systems Guild.
Rubin, J., Chisnell, D., & Spool, J. (2011). *Handbook of usability testing: How to plan, design, and conduct effective tests.* Wiley. https://books.google.ch/books?id=l_e1MmVzMb0C
Schmitt, T., National Research Council, Rao, R. R., & Eisenberg, J. (2007). *Improving disaster management: The role of IT in mitigation, preparedness, response, and recovery.* National Academy Press.
Shapiro, D. (2005). Participatory design: The will to succeed. In *Proceedings of the 4th decennial conference on critical computing: Between sense and sensibility, CC '05* (pp. 29–38). ACM. https://doi.org/10.1145/1094562.1094567
Simon, H. A. (1962). The architecture of complexity. *Proceedings of the American Philosophical Society, 106*(6), 467–482. http://www.jstor.org/stable/985254
Slavin, K. (2016). Design as participation. *Journal of Design and Science.* https://doi.org/10.21428/a39a747c. https://jods.mitpress.mit.edu/pub/design-as-participation

SW Thames. (1993). *Report of the inquiry into the London Ambulance Service* (Technical report). South West Thames Regional Health Authority, London, UK.

The Standish Group. (1995). *Chaos report* (Technical report). The Standish Group.

Turoff, M., Chumer, M., de Walle, B. V., & Yao, X. (2004). The design of a dynamic emergency response management information system (DERMIS). *Journal of Information Technology Theory and Application (JITTA), 5*(4), 3.

Venkatesh, V., & Davis, F. D. (2000). A theoretical extension of the technology acceptance model: Four longitudinal field studies. *Management Science, 46*(2), 186–204. https://doi.org/10.1287/mnsc.46.2.186.11926

Visciola, M. (2003). Reflections on the User Centered Design (UCD) perspective in research on wireless applications. *Ubiquity, 2003*(April), 1. https://doi.org/10.1145/777947.772542

Waldrop, M. M. (1993). *Complexity: The emerging science at the edge of order and chaos*. Simon and Schuster.

Wu, P. F. (2009). User acceptance of emergency alert technology: A case study. In *Proceedings of the 6th International ISCRAM Conference*, ISCRAM, Gothenburg, Sweden.

Mobile Device-to-Device Communication for Crisis Scenarios Using Low-Cost LoRa Modems

Jonas Höchst, Lars Baumgärtner, Franz Kuntke, Alvar Penning, Artur Sterz, Markus Sommer, and Bernd Freisleben

Abstract We present an approach to enable long-range device-to-device communication between smartphones in crisis situations. Our approach is based on inexpensive and readily available microcontrollers with integrated LoRa hardware that we empower to receive and forward messages via Bluetooth, Wi-Fi, or a serial connection by means of a dedicated firmware, called *rf95modem*. The developed firmware cannot only be used in crisis scenarios but also in a variety of other applications, such as providing a communication fallback during outdoor activities, geolocation-based games or broadcasting of local information. We present two applications to show the benefits of our approach. First, we introduce a novel device-to-device LoRa chat application that works on both Android and iOS as well as on traditional computers like notebooks using a console-based interface. Second, we demonstrate how other infrastructure-less technology can benefit from our approach by integrating it into the DTN7 delay-tolerant networking software. Furthermore, we present the results of an in-depth experimental evaluation of approach consisting of (i) real-world device-to-device LoRa transmissions in urban and rural areas and (ii) scalability tests based on simulations of LoRa device-to-device usage in a medium-sized city with up to 1000 active users. The firmware, our device-to-device chat application, our integration into DTN7, as well as our code fragments of the experimental evaluation and the experimental results are available under permissive open-source licenses.

Keywords LoRa · Disaster communication · Device-to-device communication

J. Höchst (✉) · A. Penning · A. Sterz · M. Sommer · B. Freisleben
Department of Mathematics and Computer Science, University of Marburg, Marburg, Germany
e-mail: hoechst@mathematik.uni-marburg.de

L. Baumgärtner · F. Kuntke
Department of Computer Science, Technical University of Darmstadt, Darmstadt, Germany

H. J. Scholl et al. (eds.), *Disaster Management and Information Technology*, Public Administration and Information Technology 40,
https://doi.org/10.1007/978-3-031-20939-0_12

Introduction

The functionality of today's smartphones and other mobile devices highly depends on the availability of telecommunication infrastructures, such as Wi-Fi or cellular technology (e.g., 3G, 4G, 5G). However, there are situations in which no communication infrastructure is available, e.g., in remote areas (Gardner-Stephen, 2011), in the agricultural sector (Elijah et al., 2018), as a result of disasters (Manoj & Baker, 2007), or due to political censorship (Liu et al., 2015). Furthermore, in countries with less evolved infrastructures, e.g., due to low population densities or due to economic reasons, cellular networks often cannot be used at all or cannot be established in an economically feasible manner. In this case, low-cost communication technologies would give people the possibility to communicate with each other (Kayisire & Wei, 2016). However, while modern infrastructure-independent technologies do exist, these are often only accessible to advanced users due to regulations, high costs, or technical complexity. To make these technologies accessible to a broad user base, they need to be integrated into devices already known to users.

We propose to use LoRa wireless technology as a communication enabler in such situations. LoRa (long range) is a long-range and low-power network protocol designed for the Internet of Things (IoT) to support low data rate applications (Hornbuckle, 2010). It consists of a proprietary physical layer, using the chirp spread spectrum (CSS) in the freely usable ISM bands at 433, 868, or 915 MHz, depending on the global region. The additional MAC layer protocol LoRaWAN is designed as a hierarchical topology. A set of gateways is receiving and forwarding messages of end devices to a central server that processes the data. While LoRa itself has to be licensed by the Semtech company and implemented in specific hardware, it is independent of LoRaWAN and can thus be used in a device-to-device manner.

In this chapter, we present an approach to equip existing mobile devices with LoRa technology, by distributing small System-on-a-Chip (SoC) devices supporting multiple Radio Access Technologies (RATs). There are several commercially off-the-shelf microcontroller units (MCUs) available that support Wi-Fi, Bluetooth, and LoRa. We propose to use these low-cost devices to upgrade existing smartphones, laptops, and other mobile devices for long-range infrastructure-less communication. To reach this goal, we present a custom firmware for Arduino-SDK compatible boards, called *rf95modem*. Existing mobile devices can be connected to a board through a serial connection, Wi-Fi, or Bluetooth. As a general solution, we propose to use modem AT commands as an interface for application software. This interface can then be exposed through different communication channels and used by application software without requiring LoRa-specific device drivers. Since these boards are cheap and do not require laying new cables or setting up communication towers, these boards can either be distributed to people living in high-risk areas beforehand or handed out by first responders during the event of a crisis. We further formulate possible applications for the daily usage of these devices to incentivize people buying and using these devices during nonemergency times, such as geolocation-based games or broadcasting of local information, so that they are available and ready to use when an emergency occurs.

To demonstrate the functionality of our implementation, we first present a cross-platform mobile application for device-to-device messaging. This re-enables basic infrastructure-less communication capabilities in disasters. Second, we present an integration of our implementation into a disruption-tolerant networking (DTN) software. Although the low data rates of LoRa are not sufficient to support multimedia applications, sensor data, e.g., in agricultural applications or environmental monitoring, as well as context information for further DTN routing decisions can be transmitted through the LoRa channel. To illustrate the benefits of our approach, the developed device-to-device messaging app as well as our DTN integration are tested through experimental evaluations in an urban and a rural area. Furthermore, to demonstrate the feasibility but also the limitations of this approach, we simulated and evaluated a scenario with up to 1000 users.

To summarize, we make the following contributions:

- We present a novel free and open-source modem firmware implementation for LoRa-enabled MCUs, featuring a device-driver-independent way of using LoRa via serial, Bluetooth LE, and Wi-Fi interfaces.
- We present a novel device-to-device LoRa chat application for (i) Android and iOS smartphones and (ii) traditional computers.
- We present a freely available and open-source integration of long-range communication into a delay-tolerant networking software.
- We experimentally evaluate the proposed approach by conducting field tests in an urban environment as well as in a rural area and perform energy measurements of multiple devices.
- We demonstrate the scalability of our approach by simulating and evaluating large application scenarios with up to 1000 users.
- The presented rf95modem software,[1] the device-to-device chat application,[2] the integration into DTN7,[3] the experimental evaluation code fragments,[4] and the results as well as the evaluation code of the scalability test[5] are freely available.

This chapter is organized as follows. Section "Related Work" discusses related work. Section "Design" presents the design of approach to enable device-to-device communication between smartphones using LoRa. Implementation issues are described in section "Implementation". Section "Experimental Evaluation" presents the results of our experimental evaluation. Section "Conclusion" concludes this chapter and outlines topics for future work.

[1] https://github.com/gh0st42/rf95modem/, MIT License.

[2] https://github.com/umr-ds/BlueRa, MIT License.

[3] https://github.com/dtn7/dtn7-go, GNU General Public License v3.0.

[4] https://github.com/umr-ds/hoechst2020lora

[5] Will be released with the final version of the chapter.

Related Work

Augustin et al. (2016) experimentally evaluated the foundations of LoRa. The authors built a LoRa testbed and conducted different tests including receiver sensitivity and network coverage. LoRa's Chirp Spread Spectrum (CSS) modulation technique allows users to decode the received signals from -120 to -125 dBm, depending on the spreading factor (SF). The network coverage was examined in a suburb of Paris using SFs of 7, 9, and 12, based on different test locations. With SF7 and SF9, distances of 2.3 km were reached with less than 50% packet loss. Using SF12, the packet delivery ratio at the highest distance of 3.4 km was 38%.

Bor et al. (2016) investigated the current LoRaWAN protocol and proposed an alternative MAC layer to be used with LoRa, making use of multi-hop communication. Wixted et al. (2016) evaluated the properties of LoRaWAN for wireless sensor networks, demonstrating reliable usage of LoRa up to 2.2 km in an urban scenario.

Baumgärtner et al. (2018) proposed to use LoRa for environmental monitoring. In the included LoRa evaluation, ranges of 4.6–6.5 km with the base station placed on a high building were achieved depending on the antenna and the frequencies in use. Furthermore, the concept of a unified radio firmware was introduced, but only limited functionality was implemented and evaluated.

Long-range peer-to-peer links were investigated by Callebaut et al. (2019). The authors showed experimentally that with an increased SF, the received signal strength (RSS) did not change, but the signal-to-noise ratio (SNR) was increased, proving the better decoding ability. Distances of up to 4 km in line of sight and 1 km in forested terrain were achieved.

Deepak et al. (2019) created an overview of wireless technologies for post-disaster emergency communication. They identified three disaster network scenarios: congested network, partial network, and isolated network. In isolated networks, the user devices have to deploy a new network to provide temporal wireless coverage. This could be achieved with drone-assisted communication or mobile ad hoc networks (MANETs). The advantage of the latter is high redundancy: a failure of individual nodes is not necessarily mission critical.

Lieser et al. (2017) analyzed multiple disaster scenarios to highlight the main communication issues that occurred. The depicted scenarios are based on unavailable or broken communication infrastructures. In particular, the authors proposed an architecture that incorporates delay-tolerant MANETs to be independent of any fixed infrastructure. Additionally, the authors focused on communication tools that ordinary civilians can use, since civilians typically do not possess their own dedicated communication facilities, in contrast to disaster relief organizations.

By analyzing 49 crisis technology articles that focus on mobile apps in disaster situations, Tan et al. (2017) illustrated that disaster communication is shifting away from authority-centric approaches toward approaches that integrate and engage the public. The authors argued that supporting on-site collaboration (e.g., by chatting) is the main purpose of mobile apps for disaster situations.

According to Kaufhold et al. (2018), the widespread use of smartphones provides opportunities for bidirectional communication between authorities and citizens. The authors developed the app 112.social for communication between authorities and citizens during emergencies. The authors argued that further research in the area of infrastructure-less technologies for emergency communication apps is required to provide new opportunities.

Sciullo et al. (2018) presented an infrastructure-less solution for emergency communication by combining LoRa modules with smartphones. In their approach, the LoRa transceiver was hooked directly to the smartphone via USB to achieve higher communication ranges compared to conventional wireless transmission technologies (e.g., Wi-Fi). Thus, only Android devices work with this approach, and the solution is tightly coupled to the emergency communication app provided by the authors. Olteanu et al. (2013) used an USB dongle to access ZigBee nodes through an Android app. These USB-connected devices were later also identified by Sciullo et al. (2020) as being problematic and tackled through the addition of an extra Bluetooth bridge. This setup is still tailored to the provided emergency application of the authors and has higher complexity, bill of materials, and energy consumption compared to our approach.

Berto et al. (2021) are investigating LoRa-based mesh networks that implement peer-to-peer communication between nodes and extend node reachability through multi-hop communication. The evaluation is based on a hardware/software prototype in a real-world scenario, and the scaling of the approach is not investigated further.

Mekiker et al. (2021) propose a LoRa-based radio and relay protocol allowing real-time application traffic on point-to-point and multi-hop connections. The proposed Beartooth Relay Protocol (BRP) aims to extend mobile applications functionality beyond infrastructure coverage areas. An evaluation of the approach is performed using a real scenario, but the crucial test of the scalability of the approach is not part of the work.

Design

In this section, the design goals of the proposed approach are discussed. First, general principles of using LoRa on smartphones are covered. Second, design goals of a generic LoRa modem firmware are presented. Third, requirements for a device-to-device chat application are examined. Finally, thoughts on integrating LoRa into disruption-tolerant networking are presented.

Enabling LoRa on Smartphones

To extend smartphones and other common devices by infrastructure-less communication technologies, a generic interface must be designed. While these devices offer a variety of communication technologies, only few are shared across different categories of devices. Ethernet and USB may be available on most devices including laptops and routers, but smartphones can utilize these connections only using special adapters, if at all. However, all of the mentioned devices offer Wi-Fi and/or Bluetooth interfaces. Furthermore, the used approach should be based on low-energy solutions, since in the described scenarios power supply may be limited or not available. In the following, we present a modem firmware, called rf95modem, for LoRa MCUs that can enable access to the LoRa hardware through other communication channels.

Modem Firmware

Figure 1 shows how different devices can be connected to a modem board. There are several commercial off-the-shelf microcontroller boards available that include a LoRa transceiver and thus can be used for the proposed functionality. With our approach, we aim to support the majority of these boards by providing a hardware abstraction layer across all of them. Thus, the provided implementation supports a wide variety of available boards, e.g., the LilyGO TTGO LoRa series,[6] Adafruit's Feather 32u4 and M0 boards[7] or the Heltec Automation Wi-Fi LoRa 32, and Wireless Stick (Lite).[8] Some of these boards only provide LoRa and a serial interface via USB, but others also provide Wi-Fi and Bluetooth. The modem firmware is supposed to be controllable through AT commands similar to classic modems or various smartphones. Thus, no specific device drivers are needed to send and receive data via the rf95modem firmware. Finally, the firmware should be flexible enough and easily configurable to only ship the code actually needed for the device and the scenario in which it is used.

[6] http://www.lilygo.cn/pro.aspx?FId=t3:50003:3, Xing Yuan Electronic Technology Co., Ltd., LongGang, Shenzhen, China.

[7] https://www.adafruit.com/product/3178, Adafruit Industries, LLC, 150 Varick Street, New York 10013, USA.

[8] https://heltec.org/proudct_center/lora/lora-node/, Heltec Automation, Longtan Industrial Park, Chengdu, China.

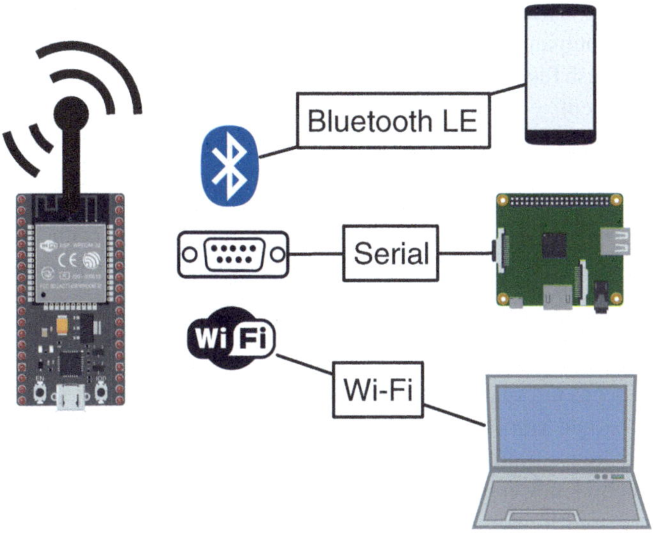

Fig. 1 ESP32-based modem board and its connection options for smartphones, single-board computers, and laptops

Incentivizing LoRa Usage

An important challenge in establishing emergency networks is the availability of hardware and software to users when an emergency happens. If users find themselves in an emergency situation with an infrastructure failure, they either have to wait until the infrastructure is restored; they are equipped with new technology, e.g., from the emergency services; or they can use existing and already known devices and technologies. The latter case has the clear advantage that rudimentary communication and, in particular, emergency calls are possible without involving third parties. For the technology presented here to have an impact, it is necessary for users to be able to use it meaningfully outside of a crisis, to gain experience with it, and to avoid the need for elaborate steps in the event of a crisis. In this section, we outline some use cases where LoRa-based communication is helpful in everyday life and can get users to familiarize themselves with LoRa technology.

A strong use case for LoRa outside of emergency communication is outdoor activities, in which people are in areas of bad or completely missing cellular coverage. While in skiing areas cellular networks are built due to commercial interest, many activities depending on less infrastructure suffer from a missing communications infrastructure. Using LoRa communication among the participants of a group or even among different groups in the same area can be very useful for coordination, e.g., if a part of the group separates and looks for food, water, or firewood. Even in the case of unintentional separation, e.g., if the group gets lost while canoeing, this infrastructure-free communication can be helpful to find each other again. There are several commercially available products that support the case for a companion device offering infrastructure-free communication, such as GoTenna[9] MeshTastic,[10] or Beartooth.[11]

A second incentive for using LoRa is gamification, e.g., by deploying beacons through volunteers in certain locations. Beaconing can be implemented as a service on already existing LoRa infrastructure, such as on LoRa gateways or even on weather stations or other IoT devices. The goal of the game would be to collect as many beacons as possible and thus prove that a player has actually visited the locations. To make cheating in the game more difficult and to introduce another component for the competition of different players, the beacons are generated and signed based on a timestamp.

A third use case for LoRa in everyday life is a public message board that is enhanced by local information. Important information of the city, e.g., for visitors but also for people who live in the city can be announced via LoRa, e.g., local weather recordings, traffic information, or information in potentially dangerous situations, such as power outages, fires, or terrorist attacks. The inherent property of a location-based limitation allows effective and efficient distribution of location-based information and can also be used for marketing purposes.

A Device-to-Device Messaging Application

To enable communications in rural areas or in situations after disasters, mobile applications play an outstanding role for various reasons and support a variety of communication technologies like cellular, Wi-Fi, and Bluetooth. Therefore, we designed a mobile application to support off-grid communication in the scenarios mentioned above. In particular, in crisis situations, it is important that users do not first have to familiarize themselves with new paradigms or UI/UX concepts and are not confronted with technical terms that are incomprehensible to laypersons. Therefore, our application should use Bluetooth Low Energy (BLE) as the primary connection technology. Bluetooth is widely accepted as a technology to create one-to-one connections and exchange data between the involved peers, whereas Wi-Fi is usually used to access information from a central place. Therefore, the Bluetooth paradigm fits better to the given scenario. Additionally, Bluetooth is more energy efficient compared to Wi-Fi, which makes it the appropriate technology to use in this case. To further reduce barriers in app usage, our app should automatically connect to nearby modem devices without any further actions required by the user. This increases the chances of instant access to the communication infrastructure in cases of emergencies. The app should also be able to receive messages in the background,

[9] https://gotenna.com

[10] https://meshtastic.org

[11] https://beartooth.com

e.g., when the user leaves the application. Additionally, the user should not worry about using a specific mobile device. It is therefore crucial to provide a platform-independent application that is usable on the most popular mobile platforms iOS and Android.

To get people in contact as fast as possible without prior exchange of IDs, usernames, or alike, the application should follow a public message board paradigm, similar to Twitter, where users can post short messages to a publicly visible channel. Here, users can send messages visible for all and ask for help or provide status information. This approach gives users easy and fast access to a communications method. Users should have an easy and fast way to find new channels and create channels for specific topics. Finally, users should be presented with a common and familiar look and feel including accessibility features so that no one is excluded.

Disruption-Tolerant Networking

For crisis scenarios, DTN is a technology to enable infrastructure-less communication using an emergency infrastructure in conjunction with existing devices of users (Baumgärtner et al., 2016; Lieser et al., 2017). DTNs benefit from a large number of devices storing and forwarding messages to other devices when they become available. Today, end user-focused DTNs are mostly based on ad hoc Wi-Fi and Bluetooth, since these are available in the mobile devices used by the users. Due to slow data rates and duty cycle restrictions introduced by regulation, LoRa in DTNs is not suited for larger data transmissions, such as multimedia content, but is helpful to transmit context information or small messages. LoRa can be used to connect different local clouds of people, where smaller messages available inside the cloud can be transmitted to another cloud. Modern DTN routing algorithms use context information to reduce overheads introduced by unnecessary transmission (Graubner et al., 2018). We propose to add LoRa to existing delay- and disruption-tolerant networks to enable larger spatial low-bandwidth coverage, in order to propagate small messages and context information. To facilitate the use of LoRa in DTN networks, an exemplary integration should be implemented that can use LoRa via Bluetooth, Wi-Fi, or a serial connection and thus is available on mobile devices and static nodes added in crisis scenarios.

Implementation

In this section, our implementations of the rf95modem firmware, the device-to-device messaging application, and the integration into disruption-tolerant networking software are presented.

Modem Firmware

Since a rf95modem should be controlled by AT commands over all of its available connection mechanisms, handling such commands is an essential part of the implementation. Therefore, this functionality is shared across all supported hardware platforms and connection mechanisms, as shown in Fig. 2. Here, the software components are displayed in blue, while the rest represents the underlying hardware modules. For interaction with users and software, the serial device interface, usually accessible via USB, is always active. Furthermore, the in-/output functions may also be hooked to the Bluetooth Low Energy or Wi-Fi modules we developed, if enabled at compile time. Any output is mirrored to all enabled interfaces that can be used simultaneously.

To achieve optimal results on various hardware platforms and configurations, all features and hardware configurations can be set using build flags. For example, the SPI pin configuration and the underlying CPU architecture must be configured, as well as the base LoRa frequency. Currently, we support ESP32-based boards with RF95-compatible LoRa transceivers as well as some Cortex M0 and ATmega32u4-based boards, such as the ones produced by Adafruit for the Feather line of devices.

For the ESP32 boards, we provide a Wi-Fi mode featuring two different ways of communication that can be used in parallel. In both cases, an access point is opened by the device itself for modem users to connect to. The first mode is UDP-based and just broadcasts the modem output to the local network and interprets incoming AT commands via datagram packets. This is especially useful if many local devices want to listen on incoming transmissions. The second mode is the TCP exclusive mode. Here, a single TCP connection is accepted that can then control the model similarly to a serial interface. Since the ESP32 boards also feature Bluetooth, they can be used to announce a BLE characteristic for interaction with the rf95modem. This interface acts similarly to the others by interpreting strings received via a write characteristic as AT modem commands. The output is shared via a notify characteristic to which devices can subscribe. BLE is supposed to have a payload limit of 20 bytes, and thus splitting the serial output into smaller chunks is necessary.

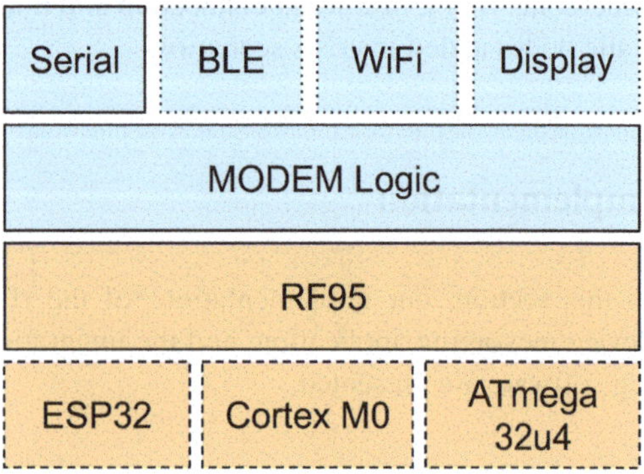

Fig. 2 Overview of the rf95modem architecture

Our tests on various platforms, e.g., iPhones and Raspberry Pis, have shown that sending much larger packets via BLE is often also possible and much more efficient. Therefore, sending overlong frames via BLE can optionally be activated during runtime via a specific AT command. Finally, there is also a software module to support OLED displays as they are pretty common on TTGOs and Heltecs ESP32 devices. If enabled at compile time, these can be used to display status information such as the current frequency, packets received, and number of packets transmitted, which can be used for debugging or providing statistical information at a glance without the need for special hardware or software.

Since all board-specific features can be configured at compile time, the firmware can be custom-tailored to fit even very resource-limited devices. Enabling all features at once results in a large firmware, which requires more flash memory and a custom partition layout, but still works on the most common ESP32 boards. Due to the fact that all output is mirrored between the interfaces, one can easily use two interfaces in parallel, e.g., debugging the BLE communication via an attached serial cable. The firmware is completely written in C/C++ using the Arduino SDK and PlatformIO as a build system.

A Device-to-Device Messaging Application

To satisfy the requirements of the messaging application, we provide two different approaches. First, we provide a console-based user interface for traditional computers, as shown in Fig. 3.[12] Second, for the mobile version of the application (BlueRa), we used the Flutter UI toolkit.[13] Flutter allows developers to create platform-independent apps for both major mobile operating systems, iOS and Android, using the same code base.

Figure 4 gives a simplified overview of the components of the app. The top block shows the UI classes. The application starts at the home screen, which contains a path to the settings, a list view of the available channels and a path for joining to new channels or to create channels. On the left, users can change their usernames or manage the app's Bluetooth connection, each in their own screens (the username settings screen is not shown in the figure). When the app's route heads over to the JoinChannelScreen, a list of available channels that the user has not joined yet is presented. Additionally, this screen enables the user to create new channels. The final screen is the chat screen itself, where the user can see a history of the messages in this particular channel as well as a text field for creating and sending new messages.

[12] https://github.com/gh0st42/rf95modem-rs

[13] https://flutter.dev

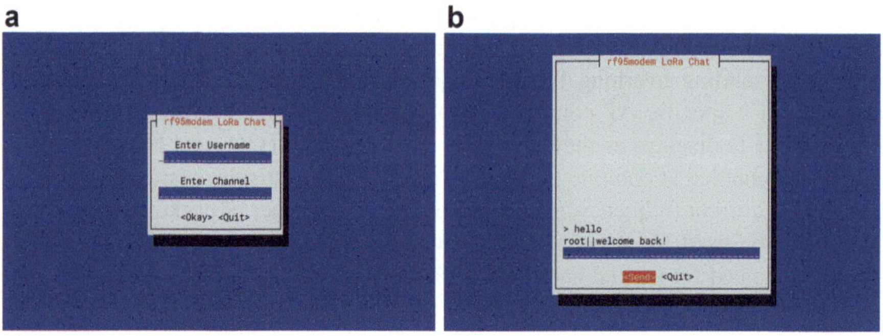

Fig. 3 Console-based rf95modem LoRa chat example. (**a**) Login screen. (**b**) Chat interface

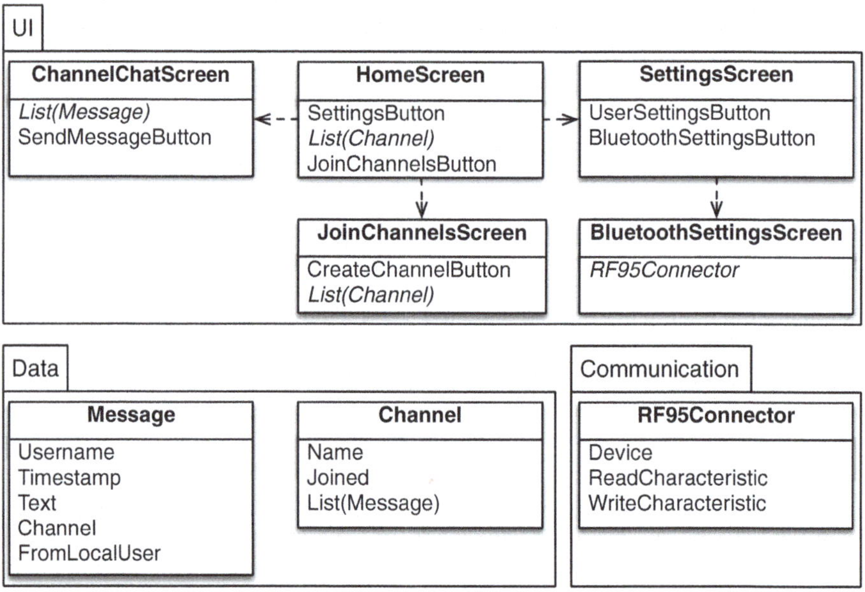

Fig. 4 Overview of the components of the app

Figure 5 shows the chat screen for the announcements channel. Using this common chat UI/UX, the user gets a familiar look and can start messaging immediately, without the need of getting familiar with a special UI.

As indicated by the Channel module in Fig. 4, a channel has a name, an indicator whether the local user has joined this channel and a list of messages. A message, on the other hand, contains the name of the user who sent this message, a timestamp, the text itself, the channel name, and an indicator whether the message was sent from the local user.

The connection to the rf95modem device is implemented in its own module, RF95Connector. This module holds the device ID and Bluetooth connection state,

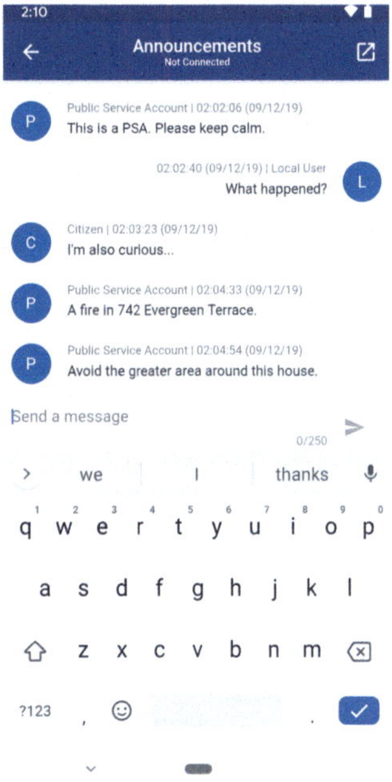

Fig. 5 Screenshot of the chat screen for the announcements channel

as well as the read and write characteristics for the serial communication service. Additionally, this module also implements data and message handling. When sending a new message, all required data are serialized to the appropriate format and sent to the modem using the write characteristic. Furthermore, a receive listener gets notified, as soon as new data is available in the read characteristic. The received data is parsed, and the internal channel and message database is updated. If the channel of the received message is already present, the message is appended to the channel's message list. Otherwise, a new channel in the local database is created with the received message. This new channel will be presented in the JoinChannelScreen, so that users can join this channel if they want to.

We use a simple communication protocol for sending and receiving messages. The message is encoded using the Concise Binary Object Representation (CBOR) format, which allows only a small overhead for encoding the message. A message encoded according to this scheme requires an additional five byte overhead for the CBOR encoding, which is comparatively low. Every message sent contains the channel name the message belongs to, the sending user's name, the message itself, and, optionally, the position of the sending user. Channel and username and the message are encoded as strings, and the location is encoded in the form of two single precision floats. Using single precision floats reduces GPS accuracy to roughly 3 m,[14] which is sufficient for estimating a user's location. To make use of the location being sent with every message, we added a map view showing the last

[14] https://sites.google.com/site/trescopter/Home/concepts/required-precision-for-gps-calculations

received message of every user in a channel on the map. This gives an overview of where the communication partners were last seen, e.g., so that first responders can quickly use this information to coordinate a mission.

Disruption-Tolerant Networking

To use LoRa in disruption-tolerant networking, we have extended the DTN7 implementation[15] introduced by Penning et al. (2019). Within the DTN context, the communication interface for bundle exchange between nodes is called convergence layer. We have implemented the convergence layer interface provided by DTN7 to achieve LoRa support.

To integrate rf95modem's serial link into DTN7, we have first developed a library,[16] written in the Go programming language. This library's main task is to provide Golang typical interfaces for writing and reading data streams through rf95modem. Furthermore, status information of the modem can be read and reconfigured.

Until now, DTN7 only had support for unicast convergence layers, while the transmission of LoRa packets corresponds to a broadcast. Since most broadcast technologies are similar in structure, we first developed a generic broadcasting convergence layer, the Bundle Broadcasting Connector (BBC). Its simplified implementation model is shown in Fig. 6.

The main component of the BBC package is the connector that implements DTN7's convergence layer interfaces for both sending and receiving bundles. The connector itself communicates with a modem, which is an interface implemented in rf95modem-go and a mock object for testing. Each modem reports its MTU such that transmissions can be fragmented accordingly.

With regard to transmissions, the BBC makes a distinction between incoming and outgoing ones. Both types have an identifier and can determine whether they have finished. If a bundle should be sent via our BBC, an outgoing transmission with a new identifier will be generated. This identifier is derived from the node. Every node is initialized with a random identifier, which is then incremented for each transmission. The payload is the xz-compressed bundle. As long as the transfer is not completed, the connector requests a new fragment. Its length including headers must not exceed the modem's MTU. This is then handed to the modem, which broadcasts it via LoRa in our case.

The network protocol specification of a fragment is shown in Fig. 7. A fragment itself consists of a header of two bytes, followed by the payload. In the header, the identifier of the transmission is referenced next to a sequence number. Each fragment contains the incremental sequence number of its predecessor. Thus, lost

[15] https://github.com/dtn7/dtn7-go

[16] https://github.com/dtn7/rf95modem-go

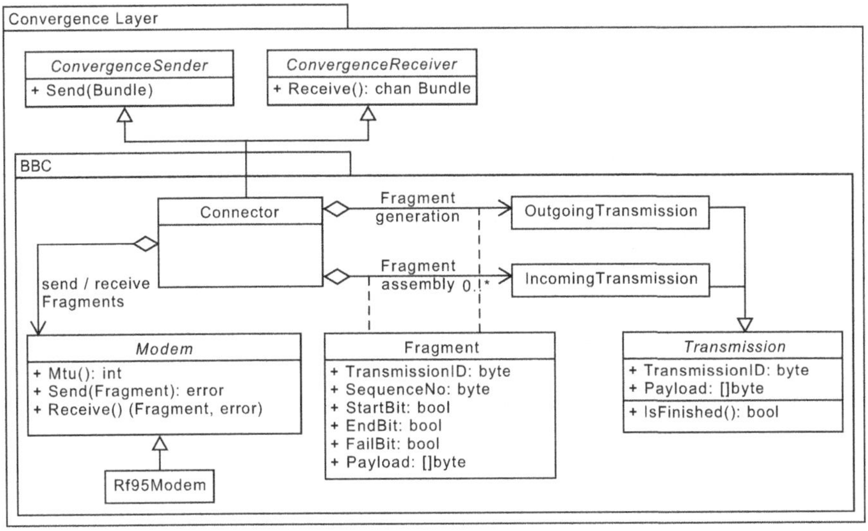

Fig. 6 Simplified implementation model of the Bundle Broadcasting Connector

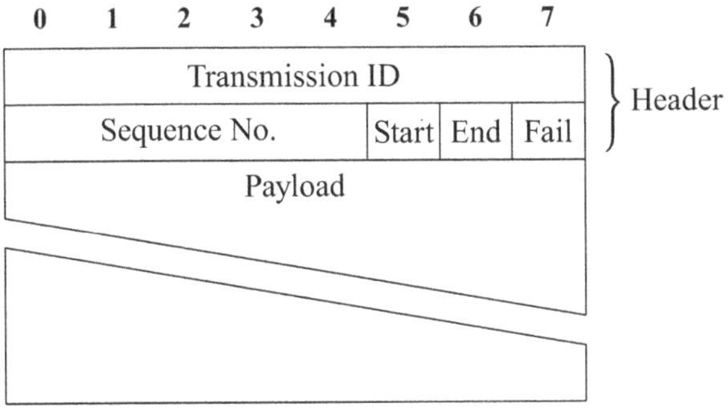

Fig. 7 Protocol specification of a fragment

fragments can be detected in advance. In addition, the header has three flags. The start bit indicates the beginning of a new transmission, while the end bit indicates its end. A failure bit is set for status packets that imply the absence of fragments.

When receiving fragments, the modem forwards them to the connector. This checks whether the transmission identifier is already known. If this is the case, the fragment is added to the incoming transmission. Otherwise, a new incoming transmission is created. Once the transmission is finished, the entire payload is extracted and decompressed. The resulting bundle will be passed back to DTN7's logic. However, if a reception error occurred, e.g., due to a skipped sequence number, a status packet is sent. This packet is equal to the last fragment, except that the failure bit is set and the payload is empty. Reception of such a packet by the sender marks the transmission as faulty. As a result, DTN7 will re-trigger the transmission at a later time.

Experimental Evaluation

In this section, LoRa protocol properties are discussed, and the presented implementations are evaluated through experiments.

LoRa in Device-to-Device Scenarios

LoRa as a long-range protocol is limited in terms of bandwidth, since the resilient encoding scheme introduces some overhead and a duty cycle needs to be followed to fairly use the shared medium. To understand the limitations of LoRa communication, some application-oriented examples are discussed.

Figure 8 shows the payload sizes compared to the airtime required for sending with different spreading factors (SF), where the coding rate is set to 4/5. The presented SF and channel bandwidth examples are taken from the EU standards (LoRa Alliance, 2018). The message length of LoRa is limited depending on the SF to limit the airtime each individual message requires. The highest SFs are limited to a payload of 51 bytes. Using SF9, the payload can go up to 115 bytes, and in the fastest SFs 8 and 7, messages can contain up to 222 bytes. SF12 packets, with the maximum payload of 51 bytes, take up to 1.92 seconds airtime, while 222

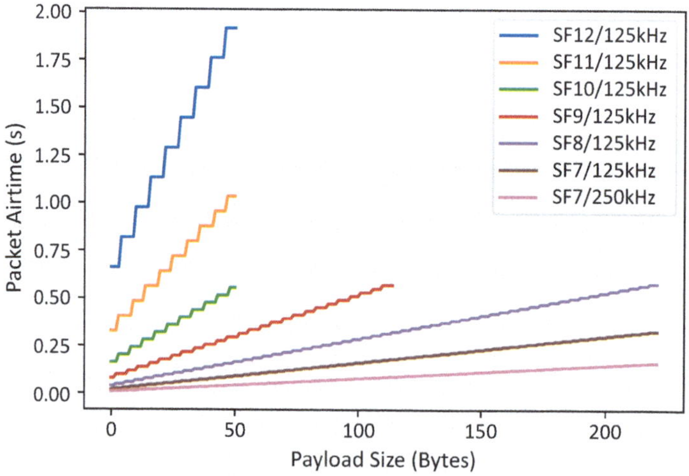

Fig. 8 Exemplary packet airtime in different LoRa profiles

bytes in SF7/250 kHz only take 0.16 seconds. When using LoRa for emergency communication, different profiles can be used to model, e.g., the importance of messages. Public service announcements of governmental institutions, including messages of rescuers, can be sent in more resilient configurations, while chats of users helping each other in emergency situations can be limited to smaller areas, to cope with the limitations of the protocol.

Device-to-Device Smartphone Communication

We evaluated our proposed infrastructure-less LoRa communication via real-world tests that cover two scenarios: (a) city area communication and (b) rural area communication.

The motivation for scenario (a) is communication demands in disaster situations. By having a low-cost companion device that extends the infrastructure-less communication range of our everyday devices could be a real benefit for such scenarios. However, the inherent characteristics of cities, e.g., the high density of buildings, are a major problem for each wireless technology.

Scenario (b) is motivated by the fact that some rural areas, also in industrial countries, are still not covered by mobile networks (GSM, 3G, 4G, 5G). The expectations of the tests in the rural areas therefore differ, since regions without obstacles might easily get good coverage, while areas with many trees might suffer from worse connections.

Experimental Setup

For the conducted tests, we used one fixed and one mobile station. The fixed station consists of a laptop logging the incoming messages. Figure 9 shows the mobile station, consisting of a smartphone in combination with a Heltec Wireless Stick driven by a powerbank. The default antenna was replaced by a +3dBi model, connected via SubMiniature version A (SMA). The antennas of each station were 1.5 m above the ground, in order to model realistic usage in device-to-device scenarios.

First, we selected one exemplary region for each of our two considered scenarios. The fixed station was then placed in the middle of the selected area and started listening for incoming messages. For reproducibility and accuracy, we scripted message generation and sending on the mobile station, such that every 15 seconds one message including a GPS position was sent via Bluetooth LE and broadcasted by the companion device. The mobile station was then moved away from the static station until no message could reach its counterpart anymore. To observe a realistic model of device-to-device communication, the mobile station was moved in multiple directions. The tests in both scenarios were repeated using two LoRa profiles provided by rf95modem: (a) medium range: bandwidth: 125 kHz, Cr: 4/5,

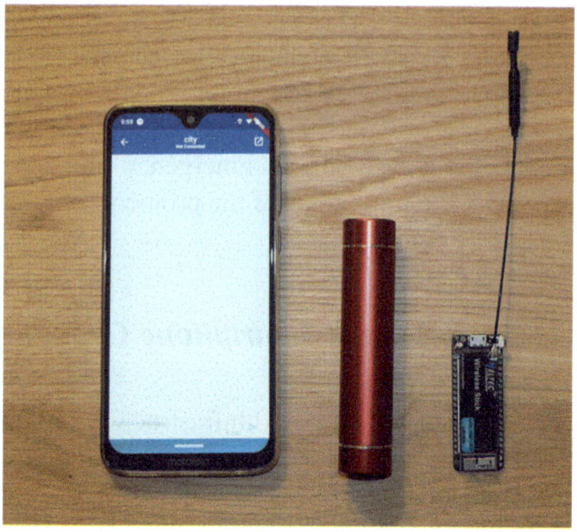

Fig. 9 Mobile station: smartphone, powerbank, and Heltec wireless stick

Table 1 Maximum distances achieved in the different areas and tested LoRa profiles in the conducted experiments

Scenario	Mode	Maximum distance (km)
City	(a) Medium range	1.09
Rural area	(b) Long range	2.89
	(a) Medium range	1.31
	(b) Long range	1.64

SF7 and (b) long range: bandwidth: 125 kHz, Cr: 4/8, SF12. Due to the simplicity of our test procedure, we did not get the maximum possible distances of our exemplary regions, but two real-world setups, with distances that work even with the simple out-of-box experience of the rather low-cost Heltec wireless sticks.

Results

By analyzing the logs of the smartphone applications that transmit GPS locations of each sent message, we were able to calculate the distances of reliable communication setups between all participants for each scenario.

Table 1 shows the maximum distances of the conducted tests. For the medium-range configuration, 1.09 km in the city area and 1.31 km in the rural area could be achieved. With the rather high data rate of 5.47 kbps, the mode is a good choice in dense areas, where a larger amount of messages might occur, and airtime is limited. In the long-range profile, 1.64 km could be achieved in the rural area, while in the city scenario, some messages could be transmitted from 2.89 km range.

Figure 10 shows the results of the conducted tests in the city area. The orange dots denote the medium-range profile, while the red dots show the successful transmissions in the long-range profile. In the size of the markers, the received signal strength indicator (RSSI) is visualized. The larger the marker, the better the RSSI is. Note that in LoRa, a higher SF enables a higher chance of successful decoding

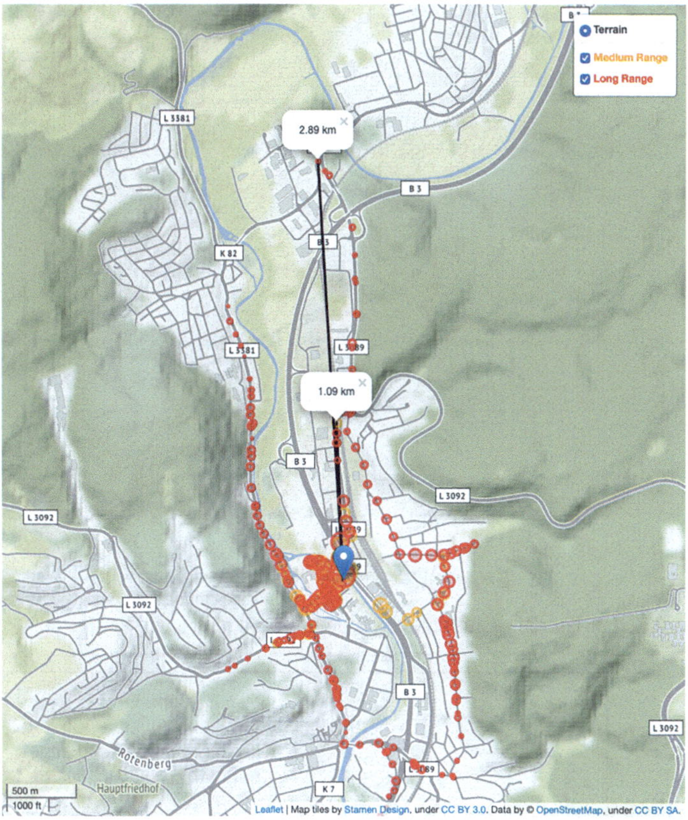

Fig. 10 Successful LoRa transmissions in the city area

under worse RSSI values. In the presented results, it is evident that LoRa works well as long as no obstacles are in the way. The maximum distance in the city area was achieved in the valley going through the city. Even though obstacles, such as buildings, were in the way, the signal could reach the other peer well. When moving behind a hill, such as in the western or eastern parts of the presented map, the signal was not able to penetrate the obstacle.

In Fig. 11, the successful LoRa transmissions of the rural area are presented. As expected, the transmission range in the forested area is worse compared to the unforested area. In the presented example, the northern part of the map consists of a forested area, while the southern part is mostly not forested. From the plot, it can be observed that in the non-forested valley area, RSSI is high, and all LoRa messages are successfully transmitted in both modes. When forested areas and hills are in the line of sight, the RSSI worsens and quickly becomes unavailable. In long-range mode, transmission in forested places improves and messages are successfully transmitted through up to 600 m of forested area.

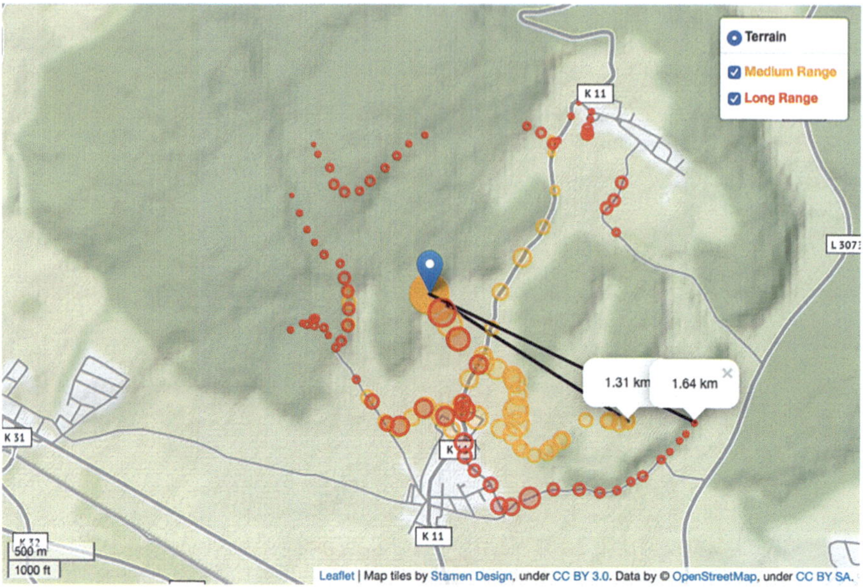

Fig. 11 Geo-positions of successful LoRa transmissions in a rural area

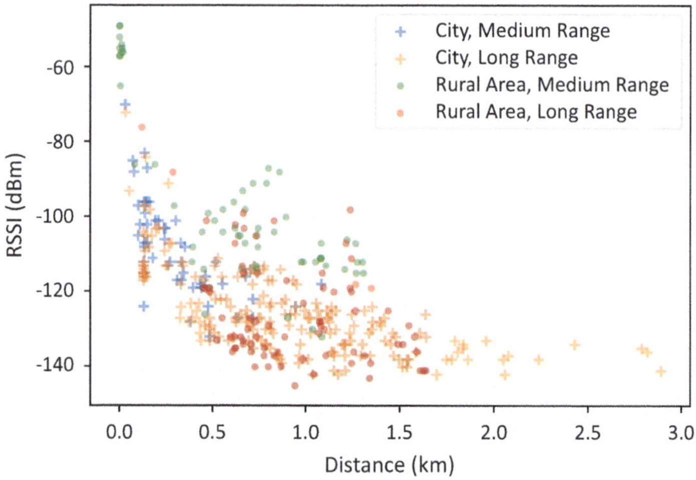

Fig. 12 Received signal strength indicator in relation to transmission distance in the proposed device-to-device scenario

In Fig. 12, the observed RSSI values in relation to the distances are presented. With the long-range profile, signals with RSSI values of up to -140 dBm can be decoded successfully, while in the medium-range profile, the limit is around -130 dBm.

In general, this shows that LoRa is a viable option to enable device-to-device communication in crisis scenarios, where infrastructure is destroyed or temporarily not available. The different profiles of LoRa can be used to limit communication to a certain area and therefore allow higher data rates or cover a larger area and therefore reach out to more people.

Interfacing Emergency Networks

When transmitting data over a disruption-tolerant network, an overhead is generated. This is caused by the additional metadata that a DTN bundle carries, e.g., the sender, receiver, or other blocks of information. In addition, there is now a second overhead for the fragmentation header of the BBC. Due to the small size of a LoRa packet, it is advisable to examine the total size of a transmission and the number of fragments. The benefits or costs of the xz compression should also be considered.

For our evaluation, we created two types of payload data: randomly distributed data and the lorem ipsum placeholder text. The respective payloads were generated in the sizes of the power of two, from 21 to 211. For this purpose, the 445 byte long lorem ipsum text was shortened or repeated accordingly. This payload was wrapped into a DTN packet, sent from dtn://source/ to dtn://destination/ with an additional age block to set the lifetime to 1 hour. The LoRa maximum payload can be up to 251 bytes in size, as instructed by rf95modem in our test configuration.

The overhead of a DTN bundle is 77 bytes without compression. In Fig. 13, the final transmission size and the number of required fragments are shown for the two characteristics of the payload data and its size. It is noticeable that for a random payload, the transmission size is slightly larger. However, the number of fragments is almost always the same. Furthermore, user data is usually not randomly distributed. This is where the advantage of the compression comes into effect, as

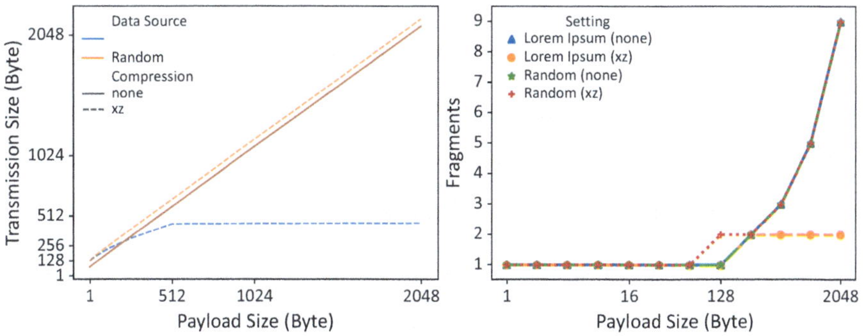

Fig. 13 Total transmission size and amount of fragments for different payloads

it becomes evident especially in the low number of fragments with compressed payloads.

We also carried out a small field test. For this purpose, three DTN nodes were installed, each equipped with a rf95modem for 868 MHz in the short-range profile: 500 kHz, Cr: 4/5, SF7. The nodes were positioned so that only one node had direct radio contact with the other two. Every time a packet is forwarded in a DTN, some metadata is updated, e.g., the previous node to specify the last relaying node. To verify the packet forwarding, we inspected the previous node from the received packet. If this value does not match the packet's sender, it was successfully forwarded. To perform this evaluation, we prepared three nodes, n0, n1, and n2. n1 was positioned in the midpoint; further n0 and n2 were not supposed to have direct contact. Outgoing from n0, packets were sent addressed to n2. These should be transferred from n0 to n1 first and forwarded from n1 to n2 afterward. We then sent DTN packets with a small payload so that they fit into a single LoRa packet. As a result, we observed situations where the previous node was adjusted accordingly. In such a case, the roundtrip time took 1.7 seconds from initiating the transmission to receiving the acknowledgment of reception.

Energy Considerations

While the energy consumption of smartphones is a well-studied field and battery lifetimes of these devices are up to some days, the companion devices studied in this chapter are not evaluated that well. Thus, we measured multiple devices targeted by the proposed firmware in terms of energy usage in different energy states, namely, receiving, sending, and deep sleep. From these measurements, the required battery capacities can be inferred.

The energy consumption was measured using an ODROID Smart Power Meter[17] connected to the microUSB connector of the board and supplied 5 V.

In Table 2, the average energy consumption of the listed boards is presented. Since the boards need to be online to receive messages from other boards, the receiving mode has the highest impact on energy consumption.

The power consumption of the measured boards when receiving data shows a broad variance, e.g., from about 72 mW for the Adafruit Feather 32u4 LoRa board up to 723 mW for the TTGO T-Beam v0.7 board. While sending data, the required power differences become more balanced. When deployed in sensor networks, the deep sleep power consumption becomes important. Four of the tested boards require 49–76 mW in this mode, while one board requires below 1 mW. The values for deep sleep are likely caused by powering the boards through the micro-USB connection, which requires a transformation to the voltage required by the microprocessors.

[17] https://www.hardkernel.com/shop/smart-power/

Table 2 Energy consumption in receiving, sending, and deep sleep modes of rf95modem compatible boards

Board	Receiving (mW)	Sending (mW)	Deep sleep (mW)	Additional features	Price (€)
TTGO T-Fox 27 dB	392	1771	61	Wi-Fi, BLE, OLED, RTC	20
TTGO T-Fox 20 dB	400	902	61	Wi-Fi, BLE, OLED, RTC	20
TTGO LORA ESP32	404	782	68	Wi-Fi, BLE	15
TTGO LORA32 V2.0	393	689	57	Wi-Fi, BLE, OLED, SD	20
TTGO LORA32 V2.1_1.6	387	785	57	Wi-Fi, BLE, OLED, SD	20
Heltec Wireless Stick	391	923	76	Wi-Fi, BLE, OLED	12
Adafruit Feather 32u4 LoRa	72	648	49	–	35
Adafruit Feather M0 LoRa	95	697	<1	–	35
TTGO T-Beam v0.7	723	1125	393	Wi-Fi, BLE, GPS	20

Also, most boards contain a serial to USB converter, which cannot be turned off when powered via USB.

To put these numbers into perspective, we assume a powerbank with a capacity of up to 20,000 mAh. Such powerbanks are widespread and used by smartphone users to recharge their phones. This capacity at 3.3 volts relates to 66 Wh and thus can power the TTGO and Heltec hardware for more than 160 hours. The maximum receiving time can be achieved using the Feather 32u4 LoRa board with more than 900 hours of receiving time.

Scalability

When speaking of LoRa, the question regarding usability with respect to large networks and radio interference arises. As mentioned earlier, LoRa, or more precisely any protocol in the same frequency band, must follow a strict duty cycle of 1% with respect to time. This is mainly to allow for fair use of the radio spectrum and to reduce collisions of packets leading to data loss. In an emergency scenario with users sending messages in an uncontrolled and unrestricted manner, however, it is hardly possible to enforce any such limitation. Thus, in this section, we investigate the limitations of LoRa with respect to three aspects: (a) how many active users can be in the network before rendering it unusable due to too many collisions, (b) how many people can be reached in which distance (i.e., how far do LoRa packets travel), and (c) what can be done to circumvent saturated networks with respect to practical applicability.

Experimental Setup

To perform large-scale tests with a high number of devices sending data using LoRa, we rely on the NS-3 network simulator (Henderson et al., 2008). NS-3 allows us to simulate a high number of users using different physical layer implementations as well as a variety of path loss and propagation models. However, currently, NS-3 does neither support LoRa as the physical layer nor the LoRaWAN data link layer. Thus, we use the LoRaWAN plugin for NS-3 presented by Magrin et al. (2017). By omitting the data link layer implementation and sending data directly to the physical layer, the used LoRaWAN plugin can also simulate the LoRa physical layer without the LoRaWAN data link layer, which emulates the usage of our proposed application.

Due to the duty cycle requirements of LoRa, one main goal of this test is to explore how our system performs under different amounts of network traffic. Furthermore, it is more likely that such a LoRa communication application as proposed in this chapter is reaching its limits in urban environments than in rural areas due to the different population densities. Thus, we modeled a city including suburban areas of 10 km $\times$ 10 km. We assume a population of 100,000 inhabitants,

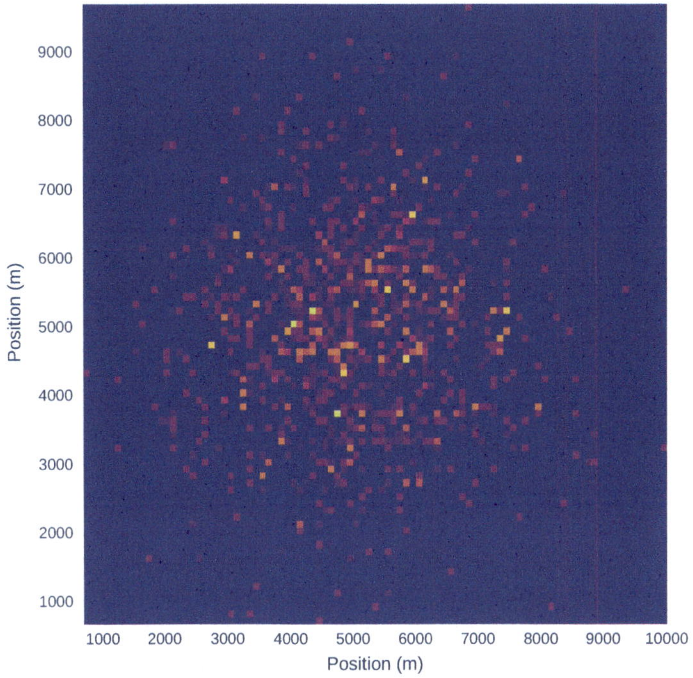

Fig. 14 User distribution

whereas their distribution follows roughly a normal distribution on both sides of the square, where the mean is set to the center (5000) and the standard deviation to 1000. This results in a population distribution that is densest at the center of our hypothetical city and decreases with higher distances. Figure 14 visualizes this distribution. Each cell in the grid represents a 100 by 100 m^2, where an empty cell is blue and a more crowded cell gets brighter. We used this distribution since it roughly resembles the distribution of a city: many people live and spend their time in the city center, while the outer areas of a city, i.e., the suburbs, are populated less densely. Regarding the number of users, we assume that realistically at most 1% of the population would use such an application. Thus, we simulated scenarios of 100 (0.1% of the population), 500 (0.5% of the population), and 1000 users (1% of the population). Finally, we modeled three different user behaviors: users sending only a few messages (3), e.g., because they are currently helping others or because they are busy doing other things during an emergency. On the other end, we modeled users sending many messages (50), e.g., because they are actively searching for people. Finally, an average user was modeled to send 10 messages. During a simulation, each user sends the specified number of messages during the simulation period of 1 hour, where the time a user sends its messages is uniformly distributed across the entire simulation time.

Table 3 Experimental configurations

Parameter	Values
Simulation time	1 hour
Area	10 km × 10 km
Seed	35,039
Repetitions per configuration	5
Base frequency	868.0 MHz
Users	100, 500, 1000
Messages per user	3, 10, 50
LoRa configurations (SF, BW, Payload)	1. SF7, 250 kHz, 222 bytes 2. SF7, 125 kHz, 222 bytes 3. SF7, 125 kHz, 51 bytes 4. SF9, 125 kHz, 51 bytes 5. SF12, 125 kHz, 51 bytes

The next parameter set refers to the LoRa parameters. For the base frequency, we used 868.0 MHz since it is predominantly and almost exclusively used in Europe. Furthermore, to test the capabilities of different LoRa settings and their effect on both the maximum transmission distance and interferences under high loads, we used five different configurations: (1) SF7 with a bandwidth of 250 kHz using a payload size of 222 bytes; (2) SF7, 125 kHz, and 222 bytes payload; (3) SF7, 125 kHz, and 51 bytes payload; (4) SF9, 125 kHz, and 51 bytes payload; and (5) SF12, 125 kHz, and 51 bytes payload. These payload sizes were chosen as they are both the maximum payload size of a LoRa packet for the given configuration (except configuration 4.) and, at the same time, also provide a good reference size for typical short messages. Table 3 summarizes these parameters.

Furthermore, each experiment was repeated five times, to cope with side effects due to unfortunate randomness, e.g., during user positioning. Finally, as the experiments require randomness for distributing the users within the simulation area and selecting sending times within the simulation time, we used a starting seed of 35,039 and incremented this number for every iteration of the 5 simulation repetitions resulting in 805 overall simulation runs.

Applicability and Limitations

Since LoRa is intended to be used as a low-bandwidth technology, one of the primary questions one needs to ask when considering feasibility is at what point will traffic saturate the network.

In Fig. 15, each plot represents one distinct simulation parameter set, as described in the previous section. Each row containing three figures shows results for different messages per user, and each column represents a different number of users. Within each figure, each bar on the x-axis shows a different LoRa configuration with respect to SF, bandwidth, and payload, and the y-axis shows the percentage of attempted

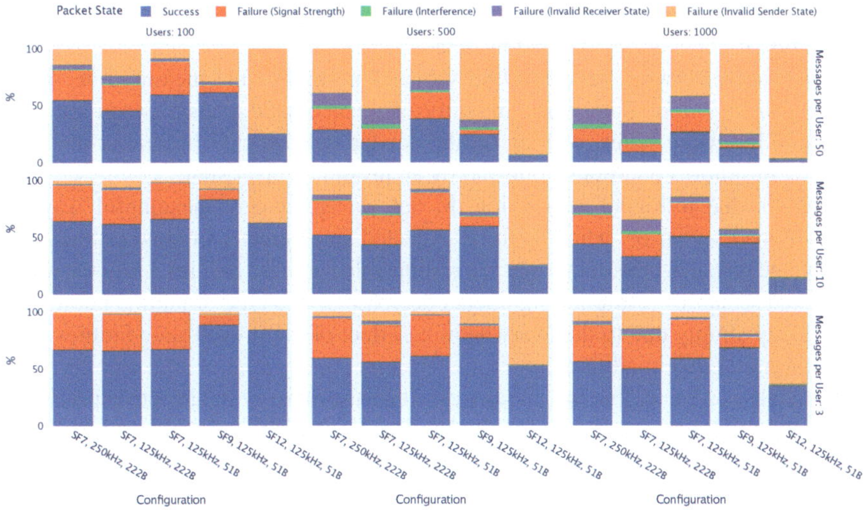

Fig. 15 Transmission results

transmissions which resulted in one of five states. Note that due to the broadcast nature of LoRa, a single transmission will lead to $n - 1$ reception events (where n is the number of users) with potentially different results:

- *Success* represents successful transmissions, i.e., a user received the packet and was able to successfully decode it.
- *Failure (signal strength)* represents users being unable to receive a packet because the signal attenuation due to path loss was too high.
- *Failure (interference)* is an unsuccessful reception due to multiple, simultaneous transmissions interfering with each other.
- *Failure (invalid receiver state)* means that the receiving LoRa module was in a state in which it was unable to receive the packet. This occurs since LoRa modules cannot simultaneously transmit and receive data.
- *Failure (invalid sender state)* is a packet reception that did not occur because the packet was not sent at all. This can be due to either one of two reasons. One possible reason is the sender being in receive mode when the packet was meant to be sent. Since LoRa modules cannot send data while they are receiving, this results in a failure. The other possible reason for this failure mode is that a LoRa module can only send a single packet at once; thus, if one tries to send a second packet while the first is still being transmitted, the sending fails.

It can be observed that with increasing load, be it due to a higher number of users, or more packets sent per user, or both, the probability that a packet will be received successfully decreases. While an increase in messages seems to impact delivery somewhat more strongly than an increase in users, the difference seems comparatively small. However, as either, or both, load factors increase, the delivery probability quickly drops to or below 50%.

Interference between senders plays virtually no part in the measured decrease of the delivery ratio. Rather, the majority of unsuccessful transmissions are due to invalid hardware states, with an invalid sender state quickly becoming the vast majority of failure conditions, followed by an invalid receiver state.

Failures due to signal attenuation do not change in any meaningful way in between load scenarios, which is to be expected since greater or smaller loads do not change physical constraints that are responsible for these failures. Only the most congested scenarios result in a significant decrease of this type of failure, but this is most likely simply due to the overwhelming effect of the invalid state failures that overpower all other conditions.

The only parameter that has a major effect on the delivery range is the spreading factor, with SF9 having already greatly decreased signal strength failures, and SF12 effectively eliminating them altogether. However, the tradeoff of higher spreading factors is obvious, since they are the most susceptible to state failures as the load increases. Comparing the three rightmost columns, which are identical except for different SFs, it becomes obvious that any spreading factor greater than seven is infeasible for our use case with respect to the ratio of successfully received packets compared to failed transmissions. Higher spreading factors increase the time it takes to send the same amount of data. Transmitting a 222 bytes large packet using SF7 and 125 kHz bandwidth takes roughly 370 ms, whereas sending 51 bytes using SF12 requires about 2800 ms airtime, i.e., 7.6 times more. This also increases the likelihood of the LoRa module being occupied in the sending state where it can neither receive packets nor accept new packets for transmission. The fact that sending takes longer in SF12 explains this observation.

Figure 16 is generated from the same data as Fig. 15 but shows the total number of events rather than the percentage-based normalized values in Fig. 15. The differences in load that are separating the simulation scenarios can be best understood when having this view on the data.

To summarize, it can be seen that the probability of successfully delivering a packet is highly susceptible to network congestion. To cope with this challenge, we need to find mitigations that allow us to prevent saturating the LoRa band, one of which we are going to present in the following section.

While congestion may be the principal issue in the way of real-world feasibility, transmission distance is another. Since LoRa messages are single-hop broadcasts, if two users are too far apart for direct transmission, they can effectively not communicate. Therefore, we have to answer the question of how far LoRa packets get depending on the experimental configuration.

Figure 17 shows the reception events in their spatial distribution, where the meaning of the colors of the packet states is the same as in the above figures. Note that in Fig. 15 (transmission ranges), the failure (invalid sender state) is not shown because packets that could not be sent do not have any location information and thus no distance associated. Furthermore, the x-axis denotes the LoRa configuration, where every group of boxes is associated with one LoRa configuration, and the

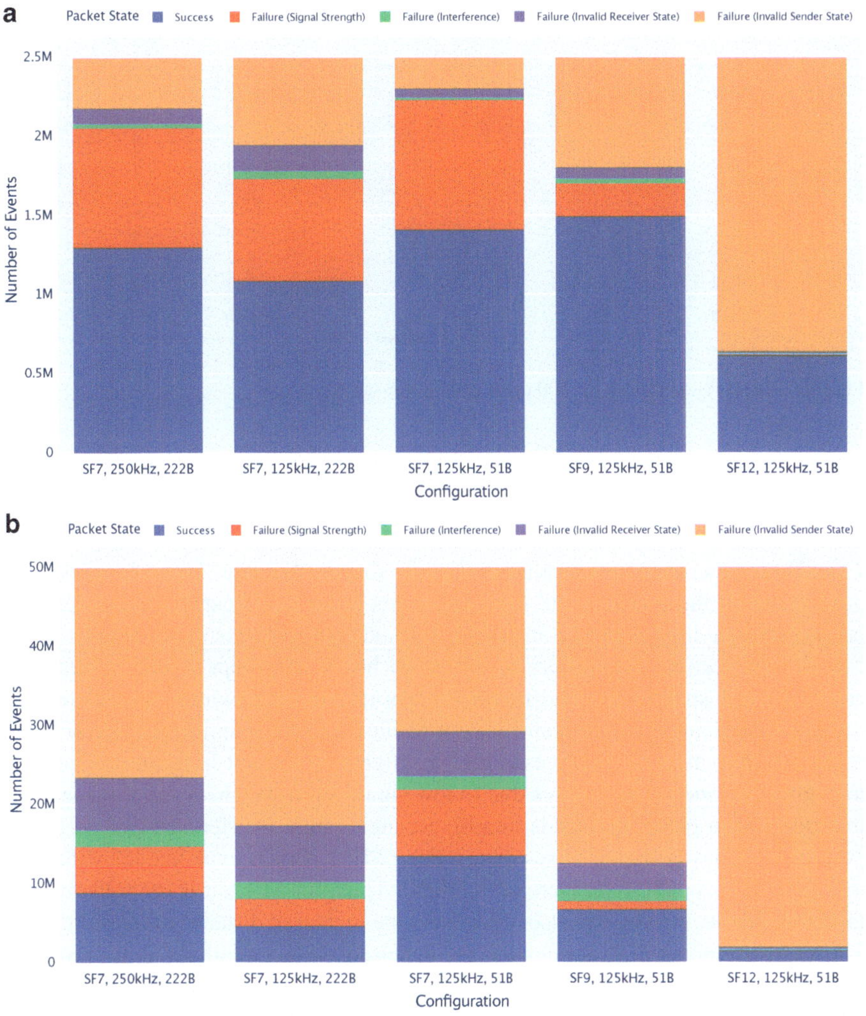

Fig. 16 Transmission results (absolute). (**a**) 10 messages per user, 500 users. (**b**) 50 messages per user, 1000 users

y-axis denotes the distance in meters that a packet traveled between sender and receiver.

One insight of the evaluation is that the general results of the distance evaluation do not depend on the load of the network, i.e., they are largely independent of how many users are sending in the network and how many packets each user sends. Thus, Fig. 17 only shows distances of packets for a single number of users (500) and a single configuration for the messages per user (10). SF, bandwidth, and payload are set as discussed previously. As can be seen in Fig. 17, the configured bandwidth

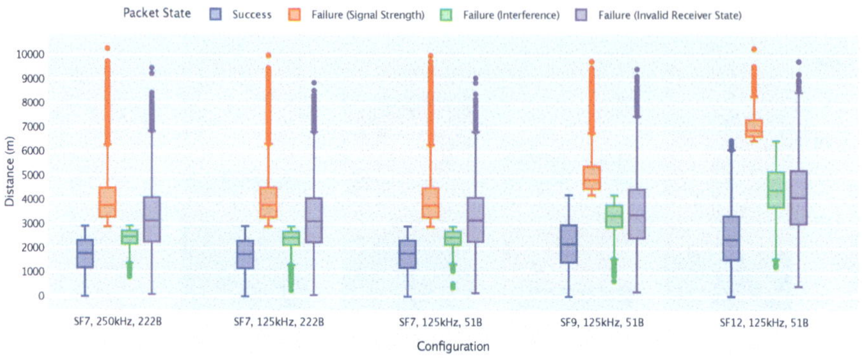

Fig. 17 Transmission ranges for 500 users and 10 messages per user

and packet payload do not affect the distance of a transmitted packet. The first three groups show SF7 but with different bandwidths and payloads. The distance of successful transmissions, however, does not change. With a lower bandwidth of 125 kHz interferences occur after a slightly shorter distance, but only visible in outliers, while the quartiles and medians do not differ significantly. The difference between the payload with SF7 and 125 kHz bandwidth with respect to interferences can also be seen in the outliers of the green boxes of groups 2 and 3. Here we can see that a smaller payload results in less interference, which is validated by the above evaluation of the transmission results. The most influential factor with respect to transmission distances is the SF. Higher SFs result in farther successful transmissions and fewer failures due to low signal strength. However, this increase in transmission range also leads to a bigger area where interference can occur, as evident in the last group of boxes representing SF12. This is explainable by the fact that higher SFs result in an increased airtime. Thus, for SF12, it is more likely that interferences occur, which is also reflected in the increased distance of interferences. The same argument also applies for an increased range of failures due to invalid receiver states. The longer the transmission takes, the higher is the probability that a user is currently in the sending state and not able to receive an incoming packet across all distances.

In summary, these results show that LoRa is able to cover a large area of a city. Users are able to reach other users within a radius of up to 2.9 km for SF7, 4.2 km for SF9, and 6.4 km for SF12. Due to interferences in the ranges around 2.4 km (SF7), 3.3 km (SF9), and 4.4 km (SF12) on the average, the usable radius is about 1.7 km, 2.2 km, and 2.5 km, respectively. However, it must be noted that the average transmission range is a result of our user distribution. With a different geographic distribution of users, the mean transmission range also changes due to interferences in different distances, but not the maximum. These results show that LoRa and especially our approach are suitable to provide emergency communications with respect to the communication range. With this transmission range, people in affected areas can communicate, coordinate themselves, and ask for help with a high chance

Table 4 Experimental configurations for additional edge-case tests

Parameter	Values
Users	100
Messages per user	1, 10, 20, ..., 200
LoRa configurations (SF, BW, payload)	SF7, 125 kHz, 222 bytes (cf. 2.) SF9, 125 kHz, 115 bytes SF12, 125 kHz, 51 bytes (cf. 5)

to reach first responders that might not be in proximity but are still able to receive messages due to the high LoRa transmission range.

Building LoRa Communities

As a result of the issues discussed in the previous section, a single LoRa channel is of limited use to a city public, such as for the distribution of public information or emergency messages. Luckily, the different international frequency bands available for LoRa provide us with a way to implement multiple, non-interfering channels, which can be used for better practical usability in a scenario as ours. In addition to these separately usable frequencies, chirp spread spectrum modulation has the advantage that the spreading factors are orthogonal, which means that messages sent with one spreading factor do not interfere with the transmission of messages from another spreading factor.[18] Following the LoRa Alliance's definition of 8 channels in the 868 MHz band and the common spreading factors 7–12, a total of 48 independent channels are available. These channels can be used by different communities and institutions, whereby the channel distribution is either agreed upon in advance or negotiated among the users at a central coordination channel.

To get an impression of the usability of a single channel, we performed additional simulations in which the channel was used by 100 users with different message rates (1–200 messages per user and hour). For this experiment series, we used spreading factors 7, 9, and 12, and their respective maximum message lengths. A summary of the updated values used for these tests can be found in Table 4.

Figure 18 shows the experimental results of the proposed experiment in a community of 100 people. As already indicated in the previous experiments, the rate of successfully delivered messages is limited by the range, especially in smaller spreading factors. For SF7, 27.6–33.2% of the messages are lost due to low signal strength, while SF9 incurs 6.3–9.9% loss. When using spreading factor 12, the transmission time of the packets is so high that a successful transmission is no longer possible even with a low number of messages per user. The capacity limit of the channel can be derived by determining the intersection of the successful

[18] https://semtech.my.salesforce.com/sfc/p/#E0000000JelG/a/2R0000001Rbr/6EfVZUorrp oKFf-vaF_Fkpgp5kzjiNyiAbqcpqh9qSjE

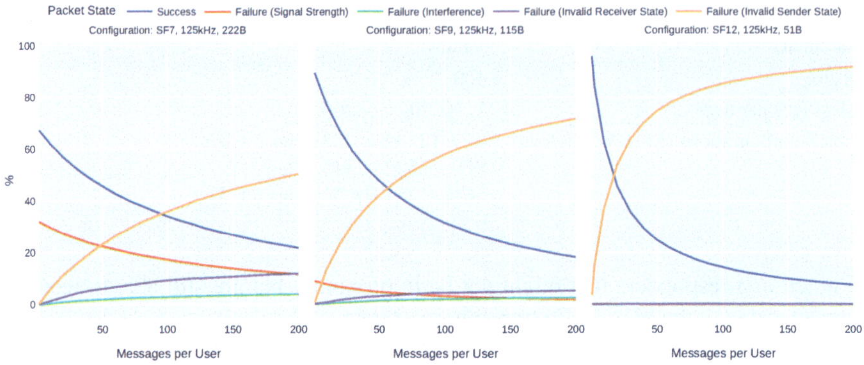

Fig. 18 Message receiving performance for different spreading factors and variable messages per user for a community of 100 users

deliveries and the transmission prevented by simultaneous reception, i.e., invalid sender state. Following this scheme for 100 users, a SF7 channel has a capacity of 90,222-bytes messages and a SF9 a capacity of around 60,115-bytes messages, and a SF12 channel is limited to around 2051-bytes messages. These metrics, alongside with the range benefits and drawbacks of individual spreading factors, can help communities to decide about a configuration to establish useful communication.

Conclusion

In this chapter, we presented an approach to facilitate long-range device-to-device communication between smartphones in crisis situations. Our approach relies on inexpensive microcontrollers with integrated LoRa hardware that we enabled to receive and forward messages via Bluetooth, Wi-Fi, or a serial connection. We developed a dedicated firmware, called *rf95modem*, to provide this functionality not only in crisis situations but also in several other applications, such as providing a communication fallback during outdoor activities, geolocation-based games, or broadcasting of local information. To illustrate the practical relevance of our approach, we implemented a novel device-to-device LoRa chat application for iOS, Android, and laptop/desktop computers. Furthermore, we integrated LoRa using *rf95modem* into the disruption-tolerant networking software DTN7. Our experimental evaluation based on real-world device-to-device LoRa transmissions in urban and rural areas, as well as scalability tests based on simulations of LoRa device-to-device usage with up to 1000 active users, showed that our approach is technically feasible and enables low-cost, low-energy, and infrastructure-less communication. All software implemented as part of our work and the results of the experimental evaluation are released with this chapter under permissive open-source licenses.

There are several areas of future work. For example, to efficiently use LoRa and its limited bandwidth in crisis scenarios, a frequency plan for users and first responders should be created. Such a plan can be integrated into the emergency communication app, and the plan could be presented to the user. Furthermore, while the presented energy evaluation provides a basic model, further measurements with the board-specific connection options should be conducted and evaluated in field tests.

Acknowledgments This research work has been funded by the Deutsche Forschungsgemeinschaft (DFG), the German Federal Ministry of Education and Research (BMBF), and the Hessian State Ministry for Higher Education, Research and the Arts (HMWK) in the National Research Center for Applied Cybersecurity ATHENE (BMBF, HMWK), the Collaborative Research Center (SFB) 1053 – MAKI (DFG), the LOEWE Research Center emergenCITY (HMWK), and the LOEWE Project Nature 4.0 (HMWK).

References

Augustin, A., Yi, J., Clausen, T., & Townsley, W. (2016). A study of LoRa: Long range & low power networks for the internet of things. *Sensors, 16*(9), 1466.

Baumgärtner, L., Gardner-Stephen, P., Graubner, P., Lakeman, J., Höchst, J., Lampe, P., Schmidt, N., Schulz, S., Sterz, A., & Freisleben, B. (2016). An experimental evaluation of delay-tolerant networking with serval. In *2016 IEEE Global Humanitarian Technology Conference (GHTC)* (pp. 70–79). IEEE.

Baumgärtner, L., Penning, A., Lampe, P., Richerzhagen, B., Steinmetz, R., & Freisleben, B. (2018). Environmental monitoring using low-cost hardware and infrastructureless wireless communication. In *2018 IEEE Global Humanitarian Technology Conference (GHTC)* (pp. 1–8). IEEE.

Berto, R., Napoletano, P., & Savi, M. (2021). A LoRa-based mesh network for peer-to-peer long-range communication. *Sensors, 21*(13), 4314.

Bor, M., Vidler, J., & Roedig, U. (2016). LoRa for the internet of things. In *Proceedings of the 2016 international conference on embedded wireless systems and networks. EWSN '16* (pp. 361–366). Junction Publishing.

Callebaut, G., Leenders, G., Buyle, C., Crul, S., & Van der Perre, L. (2019). LoRa physical layer evaluation for point-to-point links and coverage measurements in diverse environments. *arXiv preprint arXiv:1909.08300.*

Deepak, D. C., Ladas, A., Sambo, Y. A., Pervaiz, H., Politis, C., & Imran, M. A. (2019). An overview of post-disaster emergency communication systems in the future networks. *IEEE Wireless Communications, 26*(6), 132–139.

Elijah, O., Rahman, T. A., Orikumhi, I., Leow, C. Y., & Hindia, M. N. (2018). An overview of Internet of Things (IoT) and data analytics in agriculture: Benefits and challenges. *IEEE Internet of Things Journal, 5*(5), 3758–3773.

Gardner-Stephen, P. (2011). *The serval project: Practical wireless ad-hoc mobile telecommunications*. Technical report. Flinders University, Adelaide, South Australia.

Graubner, P., Lampe, P., Höchst, J., Baumgärtner, L., Mezini, M., & Freisleben, B. (2018). Opportunistic named functions in disruption-tolerant emergency networks. In *ACM international conference on computing frontiers 2018 (ACM CF 2018)*. ACM.

Henderson, T. R., Lacage, M., Riley, G. F., Dowell, C., & Kopena, J. (2008). Network simulations with the ns-3 simulator. *SIGCOMM Demonstration, 14*(14), 527.

Hornbuckle, C. A. (2010). *Fractional-N synthesized chirp generator*. United States Patent US7791415B2, Semtech Corp (May 2007).

Kaufhold, M. A., Rupp, N., Reuter, C., Amelunxen, C., & Cristaldi, M. (2018). 112.Social: Design and evaluation of a mobile crisis app for bidirectional communication between emergency services and citizens. In *26th European conference on information systems: Beyond digitization – Facets of socio-technical change, ECIS 2018*.

Kayisire, D., & Wei, J. (2016). ICT adoption and usage in Africa: Towards an efficiency assessment. *Information Technology for Development, 22*(4), 630–653.

Lieser, P., Alvarez, F., Gardner-Stephen, P., Hollick, M., & Boehnstedt, D. (2017). Architecture for responsive emergency communications networks. In *2017 IEEE Global Humanitarian Technology Conference (GHTC)* (pp. 1–9). IEEE.

Liu, Y., Bild, D. R., Adrian, D., Singh, G., Dick, R. P., Wallach, D. S., & Mao, Z. M. (2015). Performance and energy consumption analysis of a delay-tolerant network for censorship-resistant communication. In *Proceedings of the 16th ACM international symposium on mobile ad hoc networking and computing* (pp. 257–266). ACM.

LoRa Alliance. (2018). *LoRaWAN regional parameters v1.0.3*. LoRa Alliance.

Magrin, D., Centenaro, M., & Vangelista, L. (2017). Performance evaluation of LoRa networks in a smart city scenario. In *2017 IEEE international conference on communications (ICC)* (pp. 1–7). IEEE.

Manoj, B. S., & Baker, A. H. (2007). Communication challenges in emergency response. *Communications of the ACM, 50*(3), 51–53.

Mekiker, B., Wittie, M. P., Jones, J., & Monaghan, M. (2021). Beartooth relay protocol: Supporting real-time application streams with dynamically allocated data reservations over LoRa. In *2021 International conference on computer communications and networks (ICCCN)* (pp. 1–9). IEEE.

Olteanu, A.-C., Oprina, G.-D., Tapus, N., & Zeisberg, S. (2013). Enabling mobile devices for home automation using ZigBee. In *2013 19th international conference on control systems and computer science* (pp. 189–195). IEEE.

Penning, A., Baumgärtner, L., Höchst, J., Sterz, A., Mezini, M., & Freisleben, B. (2019). DTN7: An open-source disruption-tolerant networking implementation of Bundle Protocol 7. In *International conference on ad-hoc networks and wireless* (pp. 196–209). Springer.

Sciullo, L., Fossemo, F., Trotta, A., & Di Felice, M. (2018). LOCATE: A LoRa-based mObile emergenCy mAnagement sysTEm. In *2018 IEEE global communications conference (GLOBECOM)* (pp. 1–7). IEEE.

Sciullo, L., Trotta, A., & Di Felice, M. (2020). Design and performance evaluation of a LoRa-based mObile emergenCy mAnagement sysTEm (LOCATE). *Ad Hoc Networks, 96*, 101993.

Tan, M. L., Prasanna, R., Stock, K., Hudson-Doyle, E., Leonard, G., & Johnston, D. (2017). Mobile applications in crisis informatics literature: A systematic review. *International Journal of Disaster Risk Reduction, 24*, 297–311.

Wixted, A. J., Kinnaird, P., Larijani, H., Tait, A., Ahmadinia, A., & Strachan, N. (2016). Evaluation of LoRa and LoRaWAN for wireless sensor networks. In *2016 IEEE SENSORS* (pp. 1–3). IEEE.

Digitalized Cross-Sector Collaboration for an Effective Emergency Response: Emerging Forms of Network Governance

Sofie Pilemalm and Kayvan Yousefi Mojir

Abstract Digitalization has transformed the public sector and ICT has enabled the pooling of emergency response resources. Here, we explore and compare three cases of cross-sector collaboration: co-location, co-use of resources, and semiprofessionals as first responders. Identified opportunities include shared facilities and equipment and a positive attitude toward the new collaboration. Challenges include undefined roles, responsibilities, difficulties in prioritizing among ordinary and new tasks in resource-strained organizations, and lack of legislation and agreements. Reported needs are related to improved training and joint exercises and to trauma support and basic supplies, e.g., blankets, reflective vests, and warning triangles. ICT suggestions included, e.g., systems for errand handling, joint assessment of information, status and acknowledgment of available and dispatched resources, and smartphone-based dispatch management. The emerging collaborations can be seen as hybrid forms of government and network governance. Network governance may thus support the development of their institutional aspects but needs to be complemented with practical elements relating to the emergency response context. We also argue that ICT as a key factor enabling collaborations must receive more attention in network governance, which is currently the case.

Keywords Emergency response · Digitalization · Information and communication technology · Cross-sector collaboration · Network governance

---

S. Pilemalm (✉)
Department of Science and Technology, Linköping University, Linköping, Sweden

Department of Information Systems, University of Agder, Kristiansand, Norway
e-mail: sofie.pilemalm@liu.se

K. Y. Mojir
Swedish School of Library and Information Science, University of Borås, Borås, Sweden
e-mail: kayvan.yousefi_mojir@hb.se

H. J. Scholl et al. (eds.), *Disaster Management and Information Technology*,
Public Administration and Information Technology 40,
https://doi.org/10.1007/978-3-031-20939-0_13

Introduction

In recent decades, the public sector across the world has had to deal with increasing challenges, natural disasters, increased socioeconomic gaps, urbanization with depopulation of rural areas, aging populations, migration streams, war, and terrorism (e.g., Haddow et al., 2013). This has taken place against a background in which the sector has often experienced substantial financial cutbacks and resource shortages. In early 2020, the ongoing Covid-19 pandemic struck globally, both putting an increased pressure on emergency response organizations and through its enormous costs and further contributing to strained public sector budgets. Emergency response organizations, at the same time, have to deal with the increasing frequency of extraordinary events, crises, and catastrophes, e.g., due to climate change, and must continue to respond to everyday frequent emergencies, for example, traffic accidents, fires, drownings, heart failures, and criminal actions. This puts a tremendous strain on contemporary response organizations and will continue to do so in a financially strained environment and a context of scarce personnel resources.

One way to cope with these societal developments is to create cross-sector collaborations combining resources from different sectors, including private organizations, various public organizations, nongovernmental organizations, and civil citizens. Cross-sector collaboration has been applied in a range of areas, for example, addressing climate change, environmental protection, tackling poverty, natural resource management, bridging the educational achievement gap, and crisis and emergency management (Agranoff, 2007; Agranoff & McGuire, 2010; O'Leary & Bingham, 2009; Bryson et al., 2006; Vigoda, 2003). As for emergency response, using security officers in the USA to assist in life-threatening emergencies is one example (Valenzuela et al., 2000). Patton (2007) listed several possible groups that are helpful in completing and strengthening local capacity to deal with emergencies; for example, subject-matter experts, community-based organizations, social service agencies, civic groups, private businesses, and media organizations. In Sweden, groups such as guard companies, nurses, taxi drivers, and civil volunteers have been engaged in various collaborations with the municipal rescue services, the national alarm center, and the police (e.g., Pilemalm & Yousefi Mojir, 2020; Pilemalm, 2020; Ramsell et al., 2017).

Cross-sector collaborations have been studied from various perspectives and employing different theories, including network governance coproduction, policy networks, and new public management (e.g., Pestoff et al., 2013; Agranoff, 2007; Carlsson, 2000). "Network governance" and "cross-sector collaboration" are terms that are actually sometimes used interchangeably in the research literature (e.g., Agranoff, 2007; Jones et al., 1997). From a theoretical perspective, it is thus possible to see the emergency response collaborations as an emerging form of network governance, i.e., autonomous partners engage in addressing a common issue or problem, insufficient professional first-response resources, and joint delivery of public services through horizontal networking and the sharing of resources (Klijn & Koppenjan, 2012; Jones et al., 1997). Network governance does assume or explicitly include ICT as a key factor enabling the collaborations. There are, however, studies that focus on the relation between ICT and network governance (e.g., Loukis et al., 2016). There are also studies that argue that perspectives taken from the information systems (IS) research field are increasingly needed to complement policy science and public administration at a general level (Melin & Wihlborg, 2018; Janowski et al., 2012; Dawes, 2009). In our previous research, we argue that emerging governance forms are rather enabled by governments' digitalization and access to ICT and argue that more focus should be given to the ICT artefacts themselves (Pilemalm & Yousefi Mojir, 2020; Yousefi Mojir & Pilemalm, 2016).

In the domain of emergency response/cross-sector collaboration, most studies have focused on such aspects as medical issues (Weisfeldt et al., 2010), economics (Weinholt & Andersson Granberg, 2015), technological improvement (Jaeger et al., 2007), or on the general effect of the collaborations (Drezner et al., 2009), mainly in relation to large-scale emergencies and ad hoc organization. Our own research has also included accidents on a smaller scale and includes collaboration opportunities, challenges, and the need for support as well as on the related business and development processes (e.g., Yousefi Mojir and Pilemalm., 2016; Yousefi Mojir & Pilemalm, 2014; Pilemalm et al., 2013). However, to enable the development of more systemized knowledge and general conclusions, it seems crucial to compare various collaborative initiatives, identify similarities and differences, and relate them to factors such as steering mechanisms, policy analysis, and juridical matters and to basic needs for training, equipment, and ICT support. Also, there are scarce, if any except our own, studies that explicitly connect network governance and emergency response to the digitalization/ICT perspective. Finally, it should be of interest to connect the application domain to theory and a broader public sector perspective where ICT is used to enable and sustain cross-sector networks in pursuit of societal goals.

Study Aim and Objectives

In this study, we focus and cross-compare three cases of cross-sector collaboration and the pooling of resources from different professions in day-to-day Swedish emergency response in order to as follows:

- Identify similarities and differences regarding opportunities, challenges, and needs for support in terms of organization, legal matters, training, and ICT artefacts
- Perform an analysis under the theoretical lens of network governance to place the collaborations in a wider emergency response/public sector context and assess the theory's usefulness when developing and implementing future emergency response cross-sector collaborations

The study thus takes place within the Swedish emergency response system (ERS) but should also be of interest to similar emerging cross-sector collaborations and public sector network contexts. Specifically, it may apply to emergency response in other countries since many basic tasks and goals of first response are similar and, thus, they have the same basic needs. From a theoretical point of view, the results may be useful to researchers generally interested in the interplay between digitalization, public sector governance, and networks, with a specific focus on network governance in emerging emergency response cross-sector collaborations and on ICT artefacts.

Background

In this section, we first describe the emerging trends in public sector cross-sector collaboration with specific focus on the emergency response study context. Then we provide an overview of network governance.

Emerging Trends in Public Sector Cross-Sector Collaboration

In this study, we define cross-sector collaboration as a process in which different autonomous actors from different societal sectors (e.g., the public sector, private sector, nonprofit sector) or even within the public sector (e.g., healthcare, emergency response, social care) attempt to create a new joint setting. This, by establishing new ways of sharing information, resources, and capabilities and to collaborate in response operations to achieve shared goals, i.e., saving lives and minimizing environmental damage.

Greater efficiency, reduced bias, higher quality of services, and improved organizational accountability are some examples of the perceived benefits of cross-sector collaboration (e.g., Alford & O'Flynn, 2012; Brinkerhoff, 2002). Meanwhile, several studies also argue that achieving collaboration is difficult (Bryson et al., 2006; Greve & Hodge, 2005; Huxham & Vangen, 2000). Identified challenges include distrust, managerial complexity, cultural conflict, power imbalances, risk of dependence, and lack of incentive for collaboration (Babiak & Thibault, 2009; Gazley & Brudney, 2007; Young, 2000). The perceived increase in cross-sector collaboration in recent years seems to be closely related to digitalization and accessible ICT that supports communication, information sharing, decision-making, and so on, However, this has not been the focus of previous research. There are a few recent exceptions, but they take a different perspective than this study, e.g., in cross-sector collaboration for developing artificial intelligence (Mikhaylov et al., 2018).

In relation to emergency response, cross-sector collaboration has mainly focused on large-scale crisis management; for example, in the role of nonprofits in natural disasters (Chatfield & Reddick, 2018; Simon & Angela, 2007) and the ongoing Covid-19 pandemics (Arslan et al., 2020). Meanwhile, cross-sector collaborations have started to emerge in relation to frequent small accidents, not least in Sweden. Here, public sector challenges also include the continuing depopulation of rural areas, specifically in the country's northern parts, and a corresponding rapid growth of cities, to which recent immigration has contributed. This, in combination with the previously mentioned challenges, has led to difficulties in providing continuous high-quality public service delivery and in maintaining or reducing response times (e.g., Pilemalm, 2018; Yousefi Mojir & Pilemalm, 2016). To address these issues, new constellations and cross-sector collaboration forms have been developed and successively implemented. Examples include municipal rescue services and elderly care nurses being dispatched together on some medical alarms, "while waiting for the ambulance" (Swedish abbreviation: IVPA). Another is when various occupations, e.g., nurses/care staff, taxi drivers, technicians/caretakers, and guard companies, receive basic training in first response and are dispatched on certain alerts if they are close to an emergency site to provide first response while waiting for the professional response resources (Yousefi Mojir et al., 2018). This study reports from three different examples of cross-sector collaboration in emergency response that have emerged in the past decade as follows:

- *Co-location* of professional response actors and nonprofit organizations in the Safety House in Östersund.
- *Co-use of resources* and collaboration between the rescue services, the social care unit, and the technical division in Nyköping municipality.
- Collaboration of the municipal rescue services with home care personnel, fire services day personnel, guards, and technicians in Norrköping municipality, in a study called *semiprofessionals*.

Cross-Sector Collaboration as Network Governance

Emerging trends in cross-sector collaboration can thus be discussed and studied from various perspectives and employing various theories. In this study, we have chosen to focus on network governance. Network governance is primarily described as a phenomenon referring to horizontal collaboration between autonomous actors with shared interests, leading to collective service delivery or decision-making. Its core assumption is that the network consists of autonomous actors who interact to make policies and perform service delivery in a horizontal pattern without any clear top-down governing mechanism. Collaboration is rather based on mutual interests or contracts (Jones et al., 1997). There have also been attempts to theorize around the term to explain under what conditions networks emerge, thrive, and have advantages (e.g., Jones et al., 1997). As mentioned, the terms have sometimes been used interchangeably in the research literature (e.g., Agranoff, 2007). However, here we distinguish between them and consider network governance as a broad perspective for collaboration (including also citizen engagement). It includes identified key factors, theoretical components, and subcategories, as described below. Cross-sector collaboration is considered as a phenomenon, process, and instantiation of network governance.

Network governance is usually categorized into three major types (Antivachis & Angelis, 2015). *Participant networks governance* is based on meetings and shared interests, an equal basis for all participants, and is markedly decentralized. *Lead organization governance* occurs when an organization undertakes the lead role in the coordination of members. *Network administration organization* has a distinct and external governance entity that is not a member of the network. Network governance usually includes several key factors, for example, trust, conflict, institutional rules, collaboration, and decision-making, which can either promote or hinder the network, sometimes depending on their prevalence or absence (Klijn & Koppenjan, 2014).

Thus far, network governance theory or perspectives have been applied mainly when studying public administration, interorganizational relationships, new public management, public-private partnerships, stakeholder and citizen involvement, network societies, horizontal interactive decision-making, and public sector innovation, with no explicit connection to ICT (e.g., Pestoff et al., 2013; Agranoff & McGuire, 2010; O'Leary & Bingham, 2009; Carlsson, 2005). However, Loukis et al. (2016) have pointed out that the relationship between network governance and technology is bidirectional. In their preface to a special issue aimed to contribute to the investigation and understanding of the relationships between ICT and network governance, they write that "evolutions in IT enable the development of new types of network collaborations and governance, whereas governance of collaboration networks is critical for the development of complex IT infrastructures" (p.7). They argue that network governance should be conceptualized as socio-technical processes that are directly shaped by the involved actors when tackling complex and dynamic contemporary challenges. Even if the word "enabled" is thus used here, the chapter of the special issue rather focuses on relations. For instance, Sun and Wallis (2012) examine the geographic concentration of the e-business sector of China and analyze factors that influence it. Jacobson (2016) focuses on the relationships between technology/ICT and the National Justice Network of the USA, over a 40-year perspective, and concludes that this network remained successful because the network organization was able to make governance changes in response to new technologies. Janowski et al. (2012) described how organizations and sectors increasingly must work through networks claiming that the new paradigm increasingly relies on IT to connect the actors and to build, manage, and sustain relationships between them. Janssen and Estevez (2013) describe a new wave of "i-Government," transcending traditional public sector organizational boundaries and relying on recent developments in technology. In conclusion, we see how previous research surfaces the ICT aspect. At the same time, we miss studies of the type where digitalization or ICT is seen as key factor, component of the organizational or institutional types exemplified and where ICT needs are identified to enable specific network governance types.

Since the emerging emergency response cross-sector collaborations are new and emerging, we have not found any studies focusing on cross-sector emergency

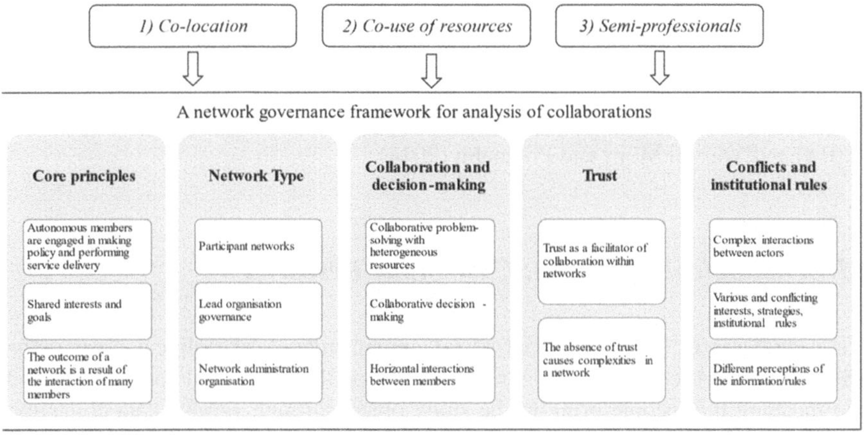

Fig. 1 A network governance framework for analysis of cross-sector collaboration

response from a network governance perspective. Meng et al. (2016) studied the governance of an emergency/crisis management network developed by a government agency and using social media but do not refer to this as cross-sector collaboration. Therefore, in this study, we will apply network governance as a theoretical lens for the cross-case comparison analysis. We reviewed about 20 scientific articles about network governance to formulate an analytical framework. The articles were from the past four decades and their focus was on how network governance has been defined and been used in research. Since network governance stems from different research disciplines with various application areas, we created a network governance framework which contains the core principles and those key factors that seem relevant for the analysis of the collaboration forms in this study. It will be used to explore the cross-sector collaborations, and in what sense, they may be seen as network governance forms and, thus, whether the theory is usable when analyzing and developing future emergency response collaborations. We have chosen to include the identified relevant key factors in Fig. 1 (Jones et al., 1997; Powell, 1990; Klijn & Koppenjan, 2014; Weber & Khademian, 2008). Other key factors were identified but not included in the framework since they did not seem applicable to the current study. An example is "network management" (Peters et al., 2017), which focuses on the internal mechanism of networks. Another is "network performance" (Klijn & Koppenjan, 2014), which can only be assessed over the long term, not where the networks do not yet exist or are new (Peters et al., 2017). Also, we have not included ICT in the framework since it does not recur in the existing literature (as a key factor), but we will pay explicit attention to ICT in relation to the chosen key factors.

Methods and Material

In this section, we briefly describe the study methods. For a more detailed description of the methods applied in the separate cases, see Yousefi Mojir et al. (2018) and Yousefi Mojir and Pilemalm (2014).

Methodological Approach: Case Study Research

Case studies seek to study actual social, organizational, or political phenomena (Stake, 2000). Accordingly, the case is understood through social construction and the meaning that people bring to the study object through various data collection methods. Case study research may include a single case or stretch over several case studies, relating to the same or similar phenomena, thus allowing for comparisons and conclusions on the transferability of the study results. Our study is carried out as a triple qualitative case study revolving around the same overall phenomenon: cross-sector collaboration in emergency response as an instantiation of public sector network governance.

In the study, we focus specifically on three cases involving the following:

- *Co-location* of professional response actors (e.g., the municipal rescue services and the police) and nonprofit organizations (e.g., the Swedish Church) in the Safety House in Östersund, northern Sweden.
- *Co-use of resources* and collaboration between the rescue services, the social care unit, and the technical division in Nyköping municipality, middle Sweden.
- Collaboration of the municipal rescue services with home care personnel, fire services day personnel, guards, and technicians in Norrköping municipality, middle Sweden, in a study where *semiprofessionals* were engaged as first responders.

This study is a further development and comparison of the separate cases presented in Pilemalm and Yousefi Mojir (2020) with an extended analysis and update. The co-location case also has been reported in Yousefi Mojir and Pilemalm (2014) and the semiprofessional case in Yousefi Mojir et al., 2018. It should be noted that this is a qualitative study where the overall phenomenon explored is emergency response cross-sector collaboration. This means that we have not replicated the research design exactly in each different case (since they stem from different projects). However, we have used similar approaches for data collection in each case, relying mostly on interviews, workshops, and a framework as a template for data collection and data analysis. Therefore, the results from each separate case are not entirely comparable to the other cases. Rather, we try to identify key factors that either reoccur through the cases or that stand out in a specific case to be able to provide a knowledge base whose transferability can be tested by future research, as similar initiatives emerge. Finally, it should be noted that there may be a risk of potential cross-contamination of case 2 and 3 since they are somewhat similar, and the involved municipalities are comparatively adjacent in time and place (the municipalities are situated about 50 km from the other). However, we deem the risk as low, except for the potential bias in the analysis performed by the researchers, which is present in all qualitative research. The co-location case is an own initiative from within the municipality, while the case of semiprofessionals is a research project and no municipality initiative. At the time of the study, initiatives in Sweden where largely local with little or no knowledge on what took place in other communities.

Interviews and Focus Groups

Interviewing is one of the most used techniques for data collection in qualitative methods and case study research. In focus group interviews, it is possible to ascertain collective views on a particular phenomenon from a group of people who have interests, experience, or knowledge concerning the topic in question (Myers, 2009). In all the cases, interviews lasting between 60 and 90 min were conducted with representatives from groups including project management, the municipal rescue services, and the SOS Alarm and national alarm center. Additional focus groups of similar length were held in the third case. They included 13 representatives from four selected groups of semiprofessionals, including both operative personnel and the managerial level from each respective group (Table 1).

Scenario-Based Future Workshops

Jungk and Müllert (1987) developed the original concept of future workshops as a technique allowing participants to reflect upon their current work situation and develop innovative ideas to enhance it. It has since been applied in various formats and application areas, not least as part of participatory design (Schuler & Namioka, 1993). In our study, full-day and half-day scenario-based future workshops were held in all three cases and involved representatives from the municipalities, the rescue services, SOS Alarm, social care units, and various semiprofessional groups (Table 1). In all cases, some of the workshop participants had also been involved in the interviews/focus groups. While future workshops is a design technique rather than a method, it can be used for qualitative data collection, e.g., by asking about the current situation, challenges, and future needs and documenting the data, as in our case.

Experiment and After-Action Review

In the case of semiprofessionals, an additional experiment was arranged (Table 1). A car accident was simulated and two semiprofessionals, along with the rescue

Table 1 The three cases and data collection involved in each case

Case	Interviews	Focus groups	Future workshop	Experiment/AAR
Safety House, Östersund	Four interviews with the project manager, police representative, fire and rescue services representative, and Swedish Defense representative	–	One workshop with eight participants from the police, the municipalities, the fire services, and the Swedish Defense	–
Co-use in Nyköping	Three interviews with representatives from fire services, social care unit, and facility services	–	One workshop with ten participants from the fire services, the social care unit, and the technical division/facility services	–
Semiprofessionals in Norrköping	–	4 focus groups with a total of 13 representatives from guard company, home care personnel, facility services, and fire services day personnel	One workshop with eight representatives from the fire services, the municipality, the police, and the healthcare sector One workshop with four representatives from the fire service day personnel and the fire services	Experiment/AAR with two semiprofessionals (fire services day personnel), one representative from the fire services, and two representatives from the ambulance services

services and the ambulance services, were sent on the response. The experiment had several purposes (e.g., measuring response times) but for this study, we observed the semiprofessionals arriving at the incident site about 15 min before the professional resources providing first response. We then held an after-action review (AAR) with all the participants. AAR is a debriefing/learning method, originating in the military domain that aims to capture and reflect upon the strengths and weaknesses of past events to improve future situations (Bolton, 2016).

Data Analysis

A data analysis approach based on thematic analysis was applied in each case. All the interviews and focus groups were audio-recorded and transcribed. The future workshops and experiment/AAR were documented using post-it notes, memory notes, and audio-recording of the AAR. The thematic analysis evolved in an iterative process around themes that were successively identified as relevant to the emerging collaborations. A conceptual framework including the categories *type/role*, *attitude*, *training*, *background*, *task and responsibility*, *availability/accessibility*, *incident type*, *communication method*, *information technology*, *emergency supplies*, *organizational structure*, *leadership*, *costs/benefits*, *environment*, and *regulations* and *legal issues* was used as support (Yousefi Mojir & Pilemalm, 2016). Opportunities, challenges, and related needs were then identified in relation to each theme. In the subsequent cross-case comparison, network governance was applied. A network governance analysis was first performed for each case, but only the cross-case comparison is displayed in this study. The authors of the study have been involved in all the cases, in data collection and data analysis, and in the network governance analysis. Two additional researchers were involved in the case of the semiprofessionals.

Results and Analysis

In this section, we first describe the three cases and then present the identified themes with their associated opportunities, challenges, and needs in each case. We also characterize the cases as various forms of cross-sector collaboration and relate them to the core principles of network governance and relevant key factors.

Co-location in Safety House in Östersund Jämtland is a sparsely populated province in mid-Sweden with a population of about 112,000. This population triples during the summer season because of tourism. The "Safety House" building is in the province capital, the city of Östersund. Both professional response organizations and other organizations supporting or having strategic responsibilities for response operations reside at the Safety House. Examples include the municipal rescue services, the police, SOS Alarm, the Swedish Defense, the church, and several authorities, for example, the city council and the county board of Jämtland, the prison and probation service and the customs. The co-location arrangement, at the time of the study, was designed to improve alarm management in order to reduce the dispatch time of professional response resources. This, by improving collaboration between actors, allows actors to quickly gain a common understanding of the emergency and creates a platform and citizen-centered service for shared information management and the dissemination of information to the public. The main characteristic of the Safety House is the interorganizational collaboration among professional response organizations. However, they also include elements of cross-sector collaboration. This, since that the defense sector and nonprofit sector (the Church) and other organizations not typically working with first response (e.g., the customs) are part of the co-location. Also, it aims to involve civil citizens.

Relating this to the *core principles of network governance*, the organizations are still autonomous in the new setting and have their own organizational rules. They share interests and goals, i.e., reducing response time, providing a more effective response, and reaching a shared understanding of the situation. Therefore, it is possible to consider the collaborations as an instantiation of network governance in the form of *participant networks governance* (Antivachis & Angelis, 2015). This is also reflected in that the participant organizations have received no regulation of mandates, no joint or common training or equipment. Rather they are supposed to build their network collaboration on routines existing in their respective organization. The same goes for ICT applications. Those in use at the time of the study (2012) included mostly stationary (non-portable) tools, for example, an alarm management system and a map system. Communication between actors took place via e-mail, telephone, and mobile phones. Some actors also had RAKEL, which is a shared radio-based platform for communication among response organizations. The ICT applications had not been designed specifically for the new collaboration/co-location setting but were basically the same as those actors were using before entering this collaboration, also when they were shared/used for collaborative purposes.

Co-use of Resources in Nyköping Municipality Nyköping is a municipality in the middle of Sweden, about 100 km south of the capital, Stockholm, and with a population of approximately 55,000. In Nyköping, the fire and rescue services, the social care division, and the municipality facility services are co-located in the new fire station. They also share certain vehicles, equipment, and technologies in order to reduce costs. Both personal security alarms and automatic fire alarms are located at the fire station to be managed more efficiently by social care operators. At the time of the study (2014), the fire services still performed the response operations, but they sometimes requested support or information from the co-located actors, such as exact addresses or keys to buildings. As the collaboration progressed, the facility services were also expected to become more involved in the project and the related alarms (e.g., water damage to streets, elevators breaking down in the municipality's properties), and the social care night patrols were planned to be dispatched on some medical alarms.

Nyköping municipality displays public sector cross-sector collaboration as its main characteristic, focusing on the pooling of resources. Even if it also embraces the vision of creating a safer society with its citizens in focus, the collaboration was mainly based on economic motives and efficient use of resources. From a network governance perspective, it is also possible to see the collaboration as a form of *participant networks governance*, even though the division of tasks is somewhat more pronounced than in the case of the Safety House. But also, in Nyköping, there were no top management mechanism or mandate to control the collaboration. Rather, none of the organizations had priority over others, and they collaborated in a network governance pattern when necessary. Certain equipment was shared but not accompanied by common training. Also, the involved actors did not have ICT applications developed specifically for the new collaboration but used the existing systems of alarm management, with separate systems for each organization. For communication they used e-mail, telephone, and mobile phones.

Cooperative Use of Resources in Norrköping Municipality Norrköping is a municipality in south Sweden with about 140,000 inhabitants. Here, emergency response cross-sector collaboration is not yet established, but between 2015 and 2017, a project was carried out in preparation for the collaboration. It was supported by participation from the municipality and its fire and rescue services and was based on the concept of the cooperative use of resources. The project was intended to identify, train, equip, dispatch, and evaluate potential resources, *semiprofessionals*, who included facility services, taxi drivers, security guards, fire services day personnel, and eldercare personnel. Semiprofessionals' primary jobs are not first response, but they have competence (e.g., medical) or equipment that is useful and they often patrol the community, thus being closer to emergency sites than professional response resources. Semiprofessionals will be alerted simultaneously with the fire services and are free in certain, but far from all, decision-making at an emergency site. They are also restricted in performing certain actions to protect their own safety (e.g., smoke diving, managing explosive material) or by the law (e.g., giving medicine to victims).

The Norrköping study explores the recent trend in cross-sector collaboration of using entirely new occupations as first responders, and it also involves various groups from the private sector (security guard companies) in the collaboration. Potential groups of semiprofessionals have their own organizations and associated rules. Their regular tasks are sometimes, but not always, like those of first response. The fire services and semiprofessionals share interests in saving lives and helping others in emergencies. In network governance terms, it is possible to view the collaboration as being of the type "lead organization governance" (Antivachis & Angelis, 2015). However, as we will discuss later, it probably makes more sense to consider it as a *hybrid form of network governance and more hierarchical government forms*. This, since the semiprofessionals will receive their training and guidelines from the fire services. Their actions are thus influenced by the fire services' regulation mandate in a top-down manner, and they are not to be considered as independent and autonomous actors in the new collaboration. Training is also provided in a top-down manner rather than joint training among rescue services and semiprofessionals. At the time of the study, semiprofessionals did not have any ICT tools to support the emerging collaboration. There was also no fixed method for communication between actors. However, the project aimed to develop a mobile app prototype for the semiprofessionals to enable them to receive alerts and be dispatched to the incident site.

Theme: Responsibility, Availability, and Attitude

Several *opportunities* related to *the use of heterogeneous resources and competencies* (Jones et al., 1997) can be identified in our studies. The interviewees and participants in the *Safety House* Future Workshop all confirmed the potential of their new work environment, and the shared facilities enable more comprehensive collaboration, exchange of information, and collective solutions. In network governance terms, the co-location of actors was thus deemed to facilitate *communication*, *collective problem-solving*, and *horizontal collaboration* (Powell, 1990; Klijn & Koppenjan, 2014), all designed to gain a shared understanding of emergencies.

In Nyköping, the interviewee from the fire services saw their organization as resource intensive but not adequately utilizing current resources:

> We pay 33 part-time firefighters in four municipalities, but we do not use them in an efficient way compared with the police, who have six resources in the same area.

Similarly, the interviewee from the social care division pointed out that their 30 staff often work on patrol and can, for example, help the police to report an event or hand keys to the rescue services. The interviewee from the facility services mentioned providing lifting assistance and intervening in incidents of damage to properties, streets, parks, and ports. Participants in the Future Workshop argued that municipal alarms can be managed completely from within the joint alarm center, including camera surveillance and burglar alarms. Thus, actors at the new fire station in Nyköping municipality also pooled their resources and competencies to help each other. However, in this case it seemed that economic motivations in terms of cost reduction played a more important role than the collaboration itself.

In Norrköping, the interviewees were in general positive about the potential new role of semiprofessionals, regarding it as both individual development and an organizational bonus. Except for home care, they agreed that, if they received an alarm, most of the time they would be able to interrupt their current tasks and leave within about 5 min. Opportunities included being on patrol during daytime (home care) or at night (security guards) and the pooling of cars. Potential tasks at the emergency site included stopping simple bleeding, performing heart and lung rescue, calming down shocked people, dispersing onlookers, extinguishing smaller fires, putting warning triangles on the road, and putting injured individuals in the recovery position. The opportunities identified in the study, from a network perspective, are thus most notable in relation to the pooling of resources, since the number of potential semiprofessionals is much higher than that of professional resources and they are spread across the entire municipality. This implies that creating a network by involving them would create a pool of huge capacity and resources to use in emergency response and might promote collective problem-solving.

The major identified *challenges* in all three studies were ambiguities in actors' roles, responsibilities, and tasks in response operations. Actors at the *Safety House* had joint meetings to manage emergencies and made decisions based on mutual discussions. However, representatives at the Future Workshop identified a lack of clarity as to who/which response organizations can command the others and said that there is no available documentation concerning related decision-making. This can be related to network government incentives for democratic *decision-making* (Klijn & Koppenjan, 2014), indicating ambiguities and a need for greater formalization in the new setting.

In Nyköping, the representative from the fire services expressed concerns as to:

> Who is responsible (and for what) when performing a response operation with the social care division or other actors? How many new tasks can one take on while simultaneously doing the regular work?

It is also somewhat unclear as to who is responsible for the joint work environment when the fire station is shared, raising primarily financial and management questions. In the Nyköping fire station, actors did not interfere in each other's work but took decisions together in certain situations as needed. But nevertheless, there were sometimes conflicts in decision-making, about budget allocation, and management processes that could potentially become an obstacle to collaborations/networking.

In Norrköping, similar concerns about ambiguities when prioritizing among ordinary and "first-response" task were expressed, both by the interviewees from the facility services and the home care personnel:

> [...] while fixing a big water leak at a school [...], we might receive an alarm about an accident nearby. To leave the school would lead to very big damage but of course if it was a matter of life and death, you'd need to attend to it [the accident] first. But there can be complications.

> You may think that it's easy to interrupt a stroll [to go and help others in an accident], but it's not possible to just leave an elderly person [client] in the street and walk away.

The semiprofessionals also expressed uncertainty and sometimes fear about acting as first responders, not being able to manage the situation, making a wrong decision, and putting people's lives in danger (e.g., moving a person with a neck injury). The interviewees from fire services day personnel also claimed that being semiprofessionals might be stressful, knowing that at any moment you might suddenly receive an alarm. This may prevent people from being able to perform their new tasks correctly and be harmful to themselves or others. Relating the challenges of semiprofessionals to network governance democratic decision-making, their autonomy is more restricted than in the other studies. They cannot replace and do not have the same scope for action as the fire services in emergencies over who administrates the collaboration and who has decided the range of semiprofessional tasks and responsibilities. In some critical situations, they need to wait for professionals. At the same time, this has the consequence that semiprofessionals must choose their main tasks and thus may not act as first responders if they come into a situation where they need to prioritize.

As to *needs*, all actors at the *Safety House* Future Workshop saw the need to formulate and document the roles and responsibilities of actors and the hierarchy of different actors and command structures. In Nyköping, the needs similarly concerned roles, responsibilities, priorities, and tasks, for example, having a reasonable workload in the new setting, clear mission goals, and related established knowledge among the different parties. In Norrköping, the identified needs again concerned clearly defined expectations and responsibilities for the semiprofessionals, including defined tasks at the emergency site; but also, that there should be supported to help them handle potential stress, and emotional or psychological consequences. Interviewees from the fire services day personnel said they would feel safer if two semiprofessionals worked together. The interviewees from the facility services claimed that a higher salary might encourage some personnel to take part in emergency response, while the other groups felt this would not be a good way to motivate people. Again, taking the network governance perspective, some of the main identified *conflicts* in network governance include conflicts of interests and strategy, perceptions of information and problems by members, and institutional rules, mostly because of the lack of a formal governing mechanism (e.g., Klijn & Koppenjan, 2014; Weber & Khademian, 2008). The studies display similar challenges but in various forms and degrees. However, they share the need for steering mechanism to govern the emerging collaboration.

Theme: Organizational Aspects: Laws, Regulations, and Work Environment

As to *opportunities*, all *Safety House* participants agreed that regular formal and informal meetings and social contacts between actors had increased their knowledge about each other's organizations, their tasks, and skills. This knowledge might lead to better trust between actors and was considered an important factor in collaborations:

> The fact that the Safety House has done it this way [to share facilities] has resulted in me knowing people in all the sections available here, including SOS, the police and ambulance services. I know exactly who I should call if I need to collaborate with someone.

The interviewees from the police and the fire and services emphasized the positive role of receiving feedback about completed response operations in the aftermath meetings from the respective actors who had participated. In the Nyköping Future Workshop, all participants believed that shared cars and premises had reduced costs and created better communication between actors. They also said that the centralization of municipal alarms had worked well and that essential money could be saved in this way. *Trust* is usually discussed as a key factor, a central coordination mechanism, and a facilitator (e.g., mutual interests and goals) or hindrance (e.g., inhibiting information exchange) for collaboration within networks (Klijn et al., 2010). According to the results, the co-location of actors in the Safety House and the new fire station in Nyköping seems to have increased trust between actors because they have better opportunities (e.g., informal meetings, nearby offices) to get to know each other. In Norrköping, the interviewees saw no need to change their current work setting, if the numbers of alarms are relatively few and, according to the management-level interviewees, there is no formal organizational obstacle, regulation, or law to prevent them from acting as semiprofessionals in emergencies:

> Of course, if there is an accident or injury where we can help, surely, we can dispatch our resources, it is possible for us and it does not feel strange at all to me.

As to *challenges*, in the *Safety House*, the issue of information confidentiality was identified as a major problem that inhibited the sharing of information (e.g., pictures, movies, documents) between different actors:

> We [the fire services] have a confidentiality rule, the county council has another confidentiality rule [regarding ambulance services] that's a bit stricter than ours, SOS has its confidentiality and the police its own. Here, we have at least four different confidentiality laws that steer collaborations.

Other reported challenges included very limited and informal feedback on their work and response operations. In Nyköping, the interviewee from facility services said that privacy is not a problem for them because they generally deal with alarms in which the information does not need confidentiality. The interviewee from the social care division on the other hand saw confidentiality as a key problem, and the participants in the Future Workshop agreed that it is a common problem when different actors collaborate and share information. Furthermore, the difficulty of calculating the costs and benefits of the emerging collaborations was emphasized both by the interviewee from fire services and by participants in the Future Workshop:

> It's very difficult to calculate costs and benefits. It's mostly in theory that you can do it.

In other words, when insufficient information exchange, inhibiting a shared understanding of situations, or preventing resource sharing occurred at Safety House and in Nyköping, this did not seem to have to do with a lack of trust between parties but more with confidentiality matters.

In Norrköping, there was a perceived lack of clarity as to what the consequences would be, not least in terms of insurance coverage, if a semiprofessional is harmed at an emergency site or unintentionally harms another person, for example, a victim. Several representatives also pointed out that there are not any particular laws at the organizational or national level concerning these new cross-sector collaborations. From a network governance perspective, the identified ambiguity in supportive laws and the lack of insurance can be related to conflicting, or even absent or insufficient, institutional rules. From an ethical point of view, some interviewees from home care and the fire services day personnel were not comfortable with being continuously positioned by a dispatch system. Interviewees from facility services and the fire services day personnel claimed that traffic rules are not clear when they are driving their car to save somebody's life. For example:

> I think it's a bit stressful [. . .] You know that you're on your way [to help a dying person] but you can't exceed the speed limit.

As regards *needs*, those identified at the *Safety House* were related to the secrecy issues and concerned aspects like the identification and handling of legal issues and potential obstacles. The police and fire services also noted the necessity of involving other actors, such as the municipalities and the County Administrative Board, in regular meetings. All participants pointed out the need to involve other actors who have local knowledge and may be used as volunteer resources, for example, the nonprofit organization "Missing People," the Swedish National Home Guard, and civil citizens. Another need identified by all Future Workshop participants was a steering group to handle internal feedback and questions from the authorities and citizens, thus once more emphasizing the need for steering mechanisms:

> Now we've grown, developed and we're so complex that we need an official group/function that can drive issues . . . we can't answer all development queries and feedback internally because of the limited resources we have. It's an obstacle to development. (Police representative)

In Nyköping, as well as the perceived need to address the secrecy issues, the participants in the Future Workshop argued that they should revise decision-making methods because decisions are based on old principles and agreements, thus again addressing the need for improved decision-making and steering mechanisms. An important example is how to allocate money and budgets to the co-located organizations. They also pointed out the lack of a forum where involved actors can sit down and talk about what they can do together, answer various issues, and discuss new ideas and ways of interacting.

As to Norrköping, the identified needs concerned clarification of roles, tasks, and responsibilities and legal and ethical aspects such as what semiprofessionals are allowed to do, how they should deal with alarm information, and what kind of insurance they need. Again, this can be related to ambiguities in, or the absence of, adequate institutional rules. The interviewees from facility services mentioned the need for a system by which they can inform their managers that they have left their current workplace. Similarly, their manager said that they need to know the number of resources and time their employees should spend as semiprofessionals. The interviewees from home care and the fire services day personnel also said that it is important that other people inside the organization know about semiprofessionals' responsibilities. Otherwise, they might be questioned by their colleagues, for example, if they fail to do something or if the people they tried to help die. In network governance terms, this can be related to a lack of culture within their organization about being semiprofessionals. Semiprofessionals mentioned their trust both in each other and in relation to the professional response organizations. At the same time, some of them did not have full trust in taking part in the collaborations due to ambiguities in the involved goals and how to prioritize between first-response tasks and ordinary tasks. The home care personnel thus expressed a need to create *internal trust* in their own organization/employer, rather than among the network participants, so as not to create internal suspicion about their new assignment.

Theme: Training and Emergency Supply

As to *opportunities*, at the *Safety House*, the interviewees from the police and the fire services mentioned that they had gained basic knowledge about each other's organizations, the new collaborations, and information exchange through work-related education and feedback exchange between actors and informal meetings. This had led to increasing trust between actors and facilitated collaborations. In Nyköping, the participants in the Future Workshop said that staff in social care and facility services receive "municipal training" in risk management, fire, and healthcare and learn how to act in different situations. In the case of the Norrköping semiprofessionals, most of the interviewees said that they had received some training in heart and lung rescue and some also in basic firefighting as part of their current employment contract. Interviewees from home care knew that some of the home care personnel had training as assistant nurses. Security guard interviewees pointed out that they had been trained, to some extent, to act as first responders. Interviewees from the fire services day personnel mentioned that a few of them have previously worked as firefighters or fire engineers. Regarding equipment, all the interviewees except home care said that they have cars with equipment, for example, first aid kits and fire extinguishers. Home care interviewees said that they have digital keys with which they can easily open their clients' apartment doors.

As regards *challenges*, the *Safety House* interviewees from the police and fire services mentioned the difficulties of applying the knowledge they had gained about the new collaboration to their practical work. As an example, the police are trained in information confidentiality and what should or should not be shared with others. However, in their daily routines, the personnel did not exchange sufficient information about response operations because of the false understanding that all information is confidential. Thus, from a network governance perspective, the lack of training can once again be related to insufficient knowledge about relevant institutional rules and information handling, rather than not trusting each other.

In Nyköping, the interviewee from the fire services and the Future Workshop participants agreed that there is currently no dedicated training focusing on the cooperative use of resources or co-location of actors. In Norrköping, the semiprofessional interviewees mentioned the difficulties of applying previous training because they had forgotten it, had not repeated it, or would not dare to use it in real situations. The manager of facility services claimed:

> [...] it's fresh the first year; however, then you start to forget. [...] we have training in CPR and similar types every four years but, as I said, it's not sufficient if we're expected to help in this way.

Even though all the interviewees acknowledged that they had already received some training, this was not always true for other employees working in their organization. Regarding equipment, interviewees from the security guards and facility services said that their cars did not have much space to locate additional emergency supplies. The manager interviewees said that some equipment (e.g., defibrillators) is expensive and additional training is needed to use it properly.

In terms of related *needs,* in the *Safety House* Future Workshop, methods for transferring theoretical training/knowledge about the new collaboration into practice in terms of simulations and exercises were requested. Regarding confidentiality, there was a need for regular education to inform people about the correct handling of information and correct restrictions on information exchange between actors:

> We thought it [confidentiality] was a bigger problem than it really is. We received training and could find good ways to not break the confidentiality rules while communicating. (Project manager)

In Nyköping, training about the new roles was requested by the fire services:

> You should also receive training and knowledge about each other's roles to be able to have a better interaction. As an example, when actors have shared tasks, sometimes an actor may not intervene in an emergency because the actor may think that another actor is going to intervene and solve the problem and that is because roles and responsibilities are not clear.

The interviewee from facility services also believed that education is sometimes important when, for example, responding to alarms. However, this interviewee did not think the training for new tasks had the same importance for them:

> In many cases and situations, it is handwork that is needed.

The interviewee from the social care division and the Future Workshop participants believed that training for alarm management and the categorization of alarms is central when invoking on-call resources. Joint training can also be a part of creating consensus about the new collaborations and the benefits of, for example, creating common interests and goals within the networks. As to hands-on equipment supporting the collaboration, the interviewee from the fire services mentioned RAKEL,[1] mobile phones, computers, and physical offices as most important. In Norrköping, the training needs of the semiprofessionals concerned updated training in heart and lung rescue and basic fire extinguishing at least once a year and practical exercises with the professional resources. The interviewee from the fire services day personnel also mentioned a need for training on traffic rules to act appropriately in traffic accidents, in managing shocked persons and injured

[1] RAKEL is the Swedish national digital communications system used by the fire services and others in the fields of civil protection, public safety and security, emergency medical services and healthcare (www.msb.se, 2013).

relatives, and familiarity with routines relating to professional resources. The fire day personnel representatives highlighted more advanced training on managing suicide cases and traffic accidents, as well as how to use the alarm management systems and perform risk assessment. In terms of equipment, their needs were basic and concrete and included dedicated smartphones for receiving alarms, blankets, reflective vests, warning triangles, pocket breathing masks, warning lights, defibrillators, extinguishing grenades, and car chargers for mobile phones.

Theme: Information Technology and Communication

As to *opportunities*, at the *Safety House* both interviewees and workshop participants claimed that real-life face-to-face communication before a response operation often leads to a more accurate interpretation of an incident and that relying solely on digital data, such as emails and digital records, may not be as effective. On the other hand, both at the Safety House and in Nyköping, most respondents emphasized the usefulness of the RAKEL communication system by which they could talk to each other using a shared platform, individually or in groups. The RAKEL coverage in the Safety House area is more extensive in comparison with the generally limited coverage of mobile phones in forests and mountains. In Nyköping, the social care unit argued that the use of RAKEL has already shortened the response time for the personal security alarms and has simplified the positioning of night patrols. The interviewee from the fire services mentioned email and telephone as the main communication methods for sending response operation reports. However, all the semiprofessionals in Norrköping emphasized their preference for using smartphone-based solutions for receiving alarms, communicating with others, and taking photos of the emergencies. Interviewees from home care and the security guards said that they already receive work-related alarms concerning urgent events on their mobile phones and would prefer to continue using the same devices. The security guards also already had extra equipment for communication, such as handheld PCs.

As regards *challenges*, not all actors at the *Safety House* had RAKEL since it is expensive and not affordable/prioritized by some organizations, which thus have to rely on mobile phones. In Nyköping, the facility services said they do not have RAKEL because it is too expensive. Also, in Norrköping, the semiprofessionals claimed that, in a purely mobile phone-based system, network coverage might be inadequate in some areas such as forests, rural areas, and the basements of buildings. For example, the interviewee from facility services said:

> [...] one problem can be when you are in the basement of buildings or are working in some underground centers [...] and there is no mobile phone coverage. This can be a problem since you spend a lot of time there, at least I often work in underground centers.

The Safety House interviewees from the fire services and the police mentioned that it was difficult to access other actors' information (e.g., their position or their status) or their information about an incident. Regular meetings and face-to-face conversations are not deemed sufficient in larger emergencies involving more information and many response actors. Difficulties with information exchange were discussed in the Future Workshop because actors might not know exactly what kind of information is needed by other actors. The interviewee from the fire services mentioned difficulties in viewing and browsing information from the incident site due to the absence of more sophisticated ICT, especially mobile tools. Moreover, not having sufficient communication channels to exchange information with the public had inhibited one of the main aims of the Safety House, to provide a citizen-centered service. In Norrköping, several semiprofessional representatives pointed out that more comprehensive information systems are not an important part of their current job and that they do not have their own system (e.g., an alarm management system or positioning system) that can be used in their new tasks.

As to *needs,* those identified at *Safety House* included a shared platform for communication and data exchange in response operations that would facilitate a shared understanding of a situation and an information system that provides a facility for actors to share maps and other visual and spatial information. The interviewee from the Swedish Defense also mentioned the potential usefulness of an integrated system for exchanging information with other actors located physically outside the Safety House. The interviewee from the fire services mentioned the need for sophisticated portable tools to view, analyze, and disseminate information, for example, portable digital maps. Participants in the Future Workshop suggested a document management system to both facilitate incident information seeking and learning from previous experiences (feedback). In Nyköping, the most important identified needs included a joint alarm management system, IT support displaying the geographical location, and a map of the emergency site. Others concerned digital channels to the public and support to extract relevant statistics from existing data. A future shared platform for accessing information was deemed important. Being able to document directly in the night patrol using IT was a key requirement of the social care division. In the Future Workshop, participants thought that a joint forum for thoughts and ideas could simplify the development of new collaborations.

As regards the semiprofessionals in Norrköping, all the interviewees emphasized the need to talk to the alarm center and the professional resources in case they need to receive more information. They also requested a dedicated ICT application for receiving alarms that could be integrated with their current mobile phones. The system should provide short but precise information about the type of incident, its location, a brief description of the incident, a navigation function, and information about when professional resources would arrive. The interviewees from home care mentioned the possibility to easily send information (video, photos, text) relevant to emergencies to the alarm center or the fire services. Interviewees from the fire services day personnel and home care highlighted the need for an acknowledgment function by which semiprofessionals can inform others that they are at the emergency site and for a function by which they can inform the alarm center whether they are available. In the Future Workshop, an additional set of functions were identified, including to support report back after the response operation, to automatically inform their employers about interrupting their current task, and a status function by which a semiprofessional can inform others (e.g., the alarm central) when he or she is on the way, has arrived, or needs extra help. Quick checklists about what a semiprofessional should do in a specific emergency were also identified as helpful.

Network Governance Analysis Summary

The results and analysis indicate that emerging forms of collaboration in Swedish emergency response in many respects resemble but also differ from more traditional network governance patterns and display a hybrid form of governance and government. A main finding is that all three studies uncovered a distinct need for steering mechanisms, the clearing of responsibilities, and agreements – much more distinct than has been reported in network governance based more on informal, dynamic interactions among members. In the cross-case comparison, it was also notable that this need increases with the cross-sector character of the collaboration and the heterogeneity of the involved actors. The Safety House, which is currently more of an interorganizational than a pure cross-sector collaboration, most resembles traditional network governance structures based on shared interests. The Nyköping municipality's ongoing cross-sector collaboration also resembles network governance in many respects but is more based on economic incentives than shared interests and displays a larger complexity in terms of power, responsibilities, and task prioritization. The semiprofessionals in Norrköping, who embrace cross-sector collaboration both within the public sector itself and with the private sector, involving entirely new occupation groups as first responders, display the most complexity and can be characterized as the most hybrid form of governance and government. Their cross-sector collaboration takes place in a more hierarchical decision-making pattern than a pure network governance structure. An additional explanation for the complexity and substantial need for steering mechanisms is that, here, the collaboration concept has not yet been implemented and thus the tasks are not defined.

More specifically, the cross-sector collaborations fit comparatively well into an overall network governance framework in terms of institutional perspectives, most notably in the identified themes 1 and 2. This includes the key factors of *shared interests*, *collaboration between heterogeneous autonomous actors*, *democratic decision-making*, *the importance of trust*, and *related conflicts in collaborations and institutional rules*. An example is when complexities in interactions between members of the Safety House relate to difficulties in decision-making in emergencies due to ambiguities about responsibilities and conflicts of opinion. In Nyköping municipality, related questions arose, such as "who is the main body responsible for the new shared environment?," and it was also possible to discern conflicts around the new budget allocation. A third example is when institutional rules in Norrköping are not only unclear but also do not yet actually exist; agreements are not yet written, and existing laws are insufficient.

At the same time, there are also concrete key factors that enable – or hinder – emergency response cross-sector collaboration, which falls outside the network governance institutional perspective. They are notable above all in relation to themes 3 and 4. One of these factors is the obvious need for training and joint exercises, discernible in all cases. Another is the need for basic equipment, relating specifically to the assignment of first response and thus most visible in the case of the semiprofessionals. While Nyköping municipality spoke mostly about a need for office equipment, and basic equipment was available at the Safety House, the semiprofessionals requested checklists, reflective vests, fire extinguishers, and defibrillators, among other things. The semiprofessionals also mentioned fear and stress as a potentially key factor hindering collaboration and requested trauma support. Finally, ICT support should be considered a prerequisite/key factor for the emerging cross-sector collaborations, even though this is not part of previous identified network governance key factors. This, at the time of studies, included GPS, mobile applications, and decision-support systems for dynamic resource allocation, dispatching the new resources as ICT enablers of the collaborations. Others, for instance, RAKEL and mobile solutions, could work both as facilitators (if existing and working) or hindrances (if too expensive and with insufficient coverage).

The cross-case network governance analysis is summarized in Table 2.

At a more general level, it is notable that besides the absence of regulations of mandates, joint training, and new ICT to support the new collaboration in each case/collaborative space, within the time frame of the study, there was no inventory or reinforcement of structures, equipment, and ICT solutions across networks. We will return to this in the discussion section together with how the network governance collaborations have evolved over time, not the least in a digitalization perspective.

Discussion

In this section, we first discuss the results in light of the emerging need for emergency response cross-sector collaborations and digitalization/ICT as an enabler. We then discuss the potential usefulness of network governance perspectives when analyzing and developing these emergency response collaborations. Finally, we discuss potential transferability of study results to wider public sector cross-sector collaboration contexts.

Table 2 Comparison between network governance and emerging forms of collaboration in the three cases

<table>
<tr><th>Network governance (NG)</th><th>Co-location</th><th>Cooperative use</th><th>Semiprofessionals</th></tr>
<tr><td rowspan="2">Core principles</td><td colspan="3">Similarities NG:
Heterogeneous actors with shared interests
Collaboration between independent organizations with their own rules</td></tr>
<tr><td>Differences to NG:
Present need for steering mechanism for command/control and decision-making</td><td>Differences to NG:
Present need for steering mechanism for decision-making and budget allocation</td><td>Difference to NG:
Existing hierarchical control of semiprofessionals' actions</td></tr>
<tr><td rowspan="2">Collaboration and decision-making</td><td>Similarities to NG:
Collaborative action and problem-solving
Democratic decision-making</td><td>Similarities: to NG:
Democratic decision-making
Resource sharing and collaboration in certain alarms</td><td>Similarities: to NG:
Collaborative action and problem-solving</td></tr>
<tr><td>Differences to network governance:
N/A</td><td>Differences to NG:
Visible focus on cost reduction which is not a common factor in NG</td><td>Differences to NG:
Limited decision-making by semiprofessionals</td></tr>
<tr><td rowspan="2">Trust</td><td colspan="3">Similarities to NG:
Facilitator of collaboration
Can reduce institutional complexities</td></tr>
<tr><td colspan="2">Differences to NG:
Potential lack of trust stems mostly from ambiguity, conflicts, and lack of training in institutional rules about confidentiality, not from a lack of respect for each other's interests</td><td>Differences to NG:
"Internal trust" not discussed in network governance</td></tr>
<tr><td rowspan="2">Conflicts and institutional rules</td><td>Similarities to NG:
Ambiguities in responsibilities and conflicts in opinions and strategies
Institutional rules/laws as obstacles</td><td>Similarities to NG:
Ambiguities in institutional rules, most appearing in budget allocation and the prioritization of tasks</td><td>Similarities to NG:
Complexities/conflicts, e.g., ambiguities in responsibilities, and how to prioritize between tasks
Institutional rules/laws as obstacles</td></tr>
<tr><td colspan="2">Differences to NG:
Visible factors such as "fear" and "motivation" may cause conflicts, not discussed in NG literature
Prevalent ethical challenges not discussed in NG literature</td><td>Differences to NG:
Visible factors such as "fear" and "motivation" may cause conflicts, not discussed in NG literature
Prevalent ethical challenges not discussed in NG literature</td></tr>
</table>

Emerging Emergency Response Cross-Sector Collaborations and New Research Needs

Public sector cross-sector collaborations are global trends (e.g., Johnston & Finegood, 2015; Jones et al., 2015; Grudinschi et al., 2013; Alford & O'Flynn, 2012; Agranoff & McGuire, 2010; O'Leary & Bingham, 2009; Bryson et al., 2009). In the past decades, they have become important to emergency response (e.g., Barsky et al., 2007; Venema et al., 2010; Waugh & Streib, 2006), not the least in Sweden (e.g., Weinholt & Andersson Granberg, 2015; Pilemalm et al., 2013). Natural large-scale disasters, man-made incidents, and the ongoing pandemics have become increasing threats to our society and will continue to be so. At the same time, regular accidents on a smaller scale will continue to occur and public sector resources available for emergency response will likely decrease. In Sweden, the municipal rescue services, for example, expect further cut in budgets, aggravated by the Covid-19 economic effects. This combination means that the professional emergency response organizations responsible for delivering essential services are often placed under extreme pressure while having to meet increased demands for efficiency. Cross-sector collaborations are thus likely to grow. As we will discuss below, since the time of this study, above all the collaboration type of using semiprofessionals as first responders has expanded to many Swedish municipalities. Since the trend is comparatively recent, corresponding research is needed. However, emergency response studies are seldom *explicitly* connected to cross-sector collaborations. Furthermore, they are fragmented and focus a specific topic (e.g., techniques, human elements, teamwork, exercises). This study contributes to an overview and a more comprehensive picture, by providing knowledge from three different cases in Swedish cross-sector collaboration emergency response and identifying common opportunities and challenges, as a starting point for future research.

Cross-Sector Collaboration as Network Governance: Capturing the Institutional Perspectives But Missing Out on Digitalization and ICT

This chapter contributes to the analysis and development of future cross-sector collaborations to help ensure that network governance key institutional factors for progress are enabled and hindrances reduced. In retrospect, we deem the network governance perspective useful in that it helped us to identify the key institutional factors relevant for emergency response cross-sector collaborations. Such identification is crucial as starting point for developing and improving the collaborations. At the same time, the studied collaborations are generally more formalized than pure network governance dynamic patterns because they are more tightly coupled with the respective organizations' own contexts. This, in turn, requires more formalization and steering mechanisms of the collaboration form that is usually the case in network governance networks. In other words, hierarchical governing mechanisms and regulations may need to supplement network governance mechanisms for cross-sector collaborations. This notion is supported if we return to the various cases in 2021, several years after respective study was performed. At the Safety House, things much remain the same as in 2012, with the same organizations participating using the same shared facilities, equipment, and technical systems but with no new development. The citizen platform has not been realized even though this should a rather straightforward process if using social media. Perhaps this can be attributed to lack of steering. The same goes for co-use at Nyköping municipality which still relies on collaboration and joint handling of incoming alerts between the rescue services and social care. The technical division was never further integrated in the co-use, i.e., did not take on new tasks or providing new equipment. This may have several explanations but, again, lack of formalization and steering of the collaboration might have contributed. On the other hand, other actors, for example, authorities and security offers, have been co-located at the fire station, implying some similarity with co-location at the Safety House. As a hybrid network government form of using semiprofessionals as first responders, this is the cross-sector collaboration type that has expanded most rapidly in the past few years. There are currently numerous municipalities using semiprofessionals, both in urban and rural settings. Norrköping will start in 2022. The most common group is security guards, but we also see some municipality rescue services engaging in collaboration with the home care night personnel (the night personnel is not so occupied as the day personnel making prioritization of tasks easier). Since the time of the study, it is possible to see an increased steering and regulation of this collaboration forms. This is in terms of agreements between employers where the ordinary employer usually takes the responsibility for work environment and insurance and sometimes through own training programs. Nevertheless, it is still possible to see it as a hybrid network governance form, since it is the rescue services who have the mandate/decision-making right at the incident site. In conclusion, we believe that network governance in its current form may well be used but is not sufficient when capturing the institutional aspects of emergency response cross-sector collaborations. Complementary perspectives, including theories from policy networks (Carlsson, 2000) and new public management (Gruening, 2001), may be used to address the potential need for hierarchical governing mechanisms and regulations.

In our study, we also identified a need for *internal trust*, which has rarely been discussed in network governance (to our knowledge and the overview of network governance literature in relation to this study), which rather focuses on trust among network organization (e.g., Jones et al., 1997; Klijn & Koppenjan, 2014). This is not surprising given the nature of many network collaborations. However, including internal trust, i.e., trust from managers and colleagues in the ordinary organization, seems crucial when new occupations are to be involved in first response and thus must switch among work tasks, role, and organizational "belonging." Actors in all three studies seem having achieved this internal trust, which is likely to enhance the prospects for collaboration. There are also key factors or practical needs in the collaborations that cannot be captured solely by using a network governance perspective, most notably in the case of the semiprofessionals, but that must be addressed when developing the collaborations. For example, basic equipment and training/exercises play a specific role, given the emergency context.

Somewhat more surprisingly, we have not found any descriptions of network governance including ICT as an explicit key factor, in our literature overview, even though ICT support should play an important role, not only in emergency response but also in any contemporary network governance context. When digitalization or ICT is in focus, it is rather from a perspective focusing *relations* between organizations and ICT (e.g., Sun et al., 2016; Loukis et al., 2016). There are a few studies also embracing ICT as an enabler, e.g., the Janowsky et al. (2012) meta-study of 12 cases on various networks all being enabled by ICT. In the background section, it is argued that ICT as a *key factor* should be included as part of future network governance theory and that this is of special importance when analyzing emerging response cross-sector collaborations, which are indeed time-critical and involve attempts to save lives. The study results support this claim. In all cases, digitalization and ICT are or will be crucial for the network cross-sector collaborations, which we will elaborate on below.

ICT as an Enabler of Emergency Response Cross-Sector Collaborations

Some of the organizational needs and challenges identified in this study are in line with the previous literature. Studies on Swedish emergency response highlight difficulties in building trust and legitimacy, in gaining a shared understanding of incidents and insufficient categorization of responsibilities, ambiguities about actors' needs, uncertainty in communication, and a lack of incentives when involving other resources and creating networks (e.g., Yousefi Mojir & Pilemalm, 2016; Pilemalm et al., 2013; Berlin & Carlström, 2011; Palm & Törnqvist, 2008). When it comes to ICT, in the area of emergency response, the need for proper and optimized positioning of both professional resources and volunteers for faster response has been demonstrated in several technically oriented studies (e.g., Matinrad et al., 2019; Leknes et al., 2017; Andersson Granberg and Värbrand, 2007). Turoff et al. (2004) further identifies the needs for systems training, accessing vital, up-to-date, and correct information, and the free exchange of information.

However, we believe that (also) when taking the cross-sector collaboration perspective, it is important to view and handle ICT as a key factor – enabler or hindrance of collaboration. This is also something that has been highlighted by Yousefi Mojir and Pilemalm et al. (2016). This becomes clear, not the least, when taking a linear time perspective. The study illustrates the fast evolution of technological development. Whereas the Safety House and Nyköping municipality express future needs for mobile solutions, in Norrköping (2016–2017) the mobile solutions are already in place and part of the user's own existing applications or requested. The perceived ICT enablers such as GPS, mobile applications, and decision-support systems for dynamic resource allocation for dispatching exist – for professional response resources. The major challenge, identified in the study, not the least in the case of semiprofessionals, lies instead in reconfiguring this ICT. This implies to add cross-sector functions in line with identified needs and according to proper organizational structures and matters of confidentiality, agreements, and laws, when integrating the new technologies into dispatch of new resources. At the time of writing (late 2021), digitalization permeates society, has become something of a buzzword, and the ICT for Swedish emergency response has further developed (e.g., Pilemalm & Yousefi Mojir, 2020; Pilemalm, 2020, 2022; Matinrad et al., 2019). An example is commercial app solution for dispatching volunteers as first responders (another emerging collaboration form referred to as "digitalized coproduction") (Pilemalm, 2020). At the same time, it tends to act as a barrier or hindrance for the cross-sector collaboration forms in this study. For instance, no new technology has been developed at the Safety House or in Nyköping and the civil citizen platform was never realized. In our study, several respondents spoke good about RAKEL, but, in several initiatives involving semiprofessionals as first responders, the semiprofessional express frustration over limitations with this audio-based technology. They await a joint app solution currently under development by the Swedish public safety answering point (PSAP). However, this app has been under development for 5 years, with no release (Pilemalm, 2021). All this also serve as illustrations of how ICT – as a key factor – can become a hindrance for the emerging collaboration/network governance forms.

Network Governance, Cross-Sector Collaboration, and Information Systems: Implications for Research and Practice

Relating the study to a larger public sector perspective, studies highlighting the significant role of networks, information sharing and resources, private sector partnering, and public sector cross-sector collaborations have been discussed under different names, including network governance, new public management, public-private partnerships, and e-government, as a potential solution to many public challenges (Agranoff, 2007; Waugh & Streib, 2006). That digitalization/ICT thus far has not been included as network governance key factors might have to do with that it is usually applied from a public management or public administration perspective. Here, we want to relate to the discussion by Loukis et al. (2016) arguing "that network governance should be conceptualized as an evolving socio-technical process shaped by actors and aimed at tackling complex and dynamic contemporary challenges" and to the Gil-Garcia et al. (2018) macro-level claims about the need to bridge the research disciplines of IS and political science, reflecting the recent proposed merging of digital government and public administration research. It also has been proposed that public policymaking and project management in the field of IS can be balanced and thereby reach a more sustainable outcome at this juncture (Melin & Wihlborg, 2018).

In relation, we suggest that network governance analysis of, for example, cross-sector collaborations could benefit from combinations of approaches and perspectives taken from the IS research field. One example is the *socio-technical ensemble view* which conceptualizes IS as a *package of people, tasks, devices, artefacts, and policies*, and focuses on the interactions between people and technology, whether during construction, implementation, or use in social contexts (Orlikowski & Iacono, 2001). The socio-technical ensemble view is a perspective rather than a theory, and while it has some overlaps with network governance, it is broader in scope while remaining at a more abstract level and providing concepts, rather than explaining how to use them. Socio-technical ensembles may thus be used as a point of departure to ensure that aspects such as tasks, devices (here: equipment), and ICT artifacts are included and combined with network governance. This, to concretize and focus the key institutional aspects that were central to, but mainly unsolved in, the emerging emergency response collaborations. In relation, it would be possible to argue that network governance is rather descriptive and explanatory, while this study is mainly exploratory. However, we believe that it is a necessary first to explore whether a theory or perspective is suitable to address a certain phenomenon (here: emergency response cross-sector collaboration), and if it is, in the next step see to it that associated key factors are handled in the collaborations.

We believe that it is equally important to translate these macro-level perspectives to concrete cross-sector collaborations, in other words, taking a more pragmatic perspective. In relation to practical IS development, the need for interdisciplinary design teams for the cross-sector collaborations, including political science and juridical perspectives, has been suggested (Yousefi Mojir & Pilemalm, 2016). Our study points in the same direction.

Study Transferability and Limitations

The study is a triple case study on cross-sector collaboration in first response to small-scale, frequent emergencies in Sweden spanning from 2012–2017. As noted in the analysis section, there were, at the time, no transfer of lessons identified, e.g., in terms of equipment inventory, need for joint regulations of mandates, and joint ICT support across the cases. This is not surprising, given that cross-sector collaboration in emergency response was a new phenomenon and that two of the cases differed in both character and space (co-location and co-use) and the third case (semiprofessionals) was a research project. Nevertheless, since all cases pointed at similar needs, this is something that should be, and is, to some extent, addressed by current emergency cross-sector collaborations. In terms of network governance, the cases in the study (co-location, co-use, semiprofessionals) have been viewed as instantiations of a hybrid form or specific governance regime, i.e., emerging when occupations that previously did not work together perform joint collaborations. Of course, it is a limitation of study that only three cases were included. It is difficult to say whether they are transferable to similar emerging governance regimes, nationally and internationally. However, since the time of the study, in particular the concept of using semiprofessionals as first responders has expanded and been implemented in various municipalities, as discussed above. Recent related studies of this cross-sector collaboration or hybrid network governance form in Swedish emergency response point at similar present key factors (e.g., the need for steering mechanisms, mandate, trust, work agreements, task prioritization, ICT as facilitator or hindrance) (Pilemalm, 2020, 2022). This indicates the transferability of the study findings at a national level. As for international applicability, more research is needed. Possibly, the emerging network forms with identified key factors are most applicable to countries with similar decentralized structures, regulations for confidentiality, and legal systems as in Sweden where, for instance, the decision to engage in cross-sector collaborations resides at the local level (e.g., with involved municipal rescue services). On the other hand, other more hands-on aspects of the emergency response cross-sector collaborations (e.g., resources deployed, main tasks, lifesaving goals, basic needs for equipment, training, and ICT support) should be similar in many countries.

Also, as to the potential transferability of the study results in a wider perspective, they specifically refer to emergency response of frequent accidents. But it is also of interest to comparing scale, i.e., routine accidents versus large-scale crises and catastrophes. Quarantelli (2000) argues that, despite both quantitative and qualitative differences between everyday emergencies and large-scale disasters, research and development work in both types of emergencies can learn from each other. Large-scale crises are more demanding in terms of resources and more unpredictable than small, frequent accidents. The infrastructure and services in a society may become unavailable, and response operations generally involve a huge number of actors from different sectors, regions, and even countries, in the form of “mega communities” (Kleiner & Delurey, 2007). Nevertheless, similar resources, ICT and IS, and equipment are often deployed. Also, we know that people (e.g., semiprofessionals) who are trained in, and have some experience of providing, first response in routine emergencies will be better prepared to act in large-scale crisis management, especially if they have already learnt how to use the technology employed. At a more general level, while various public sector cross-sector collaborations have different aims, there are also similarities because the actors are from different sectors and have to collaborate within the frame of their respective organizations. In relation, clarification of the roles, practices, interests, and duties of involved partners is always necessary. For example, Bryson et al. (2006) argue for the complexity of the interaction between actors and the need for continuous trust building between them. Also, in a healthcare cross-sector collaboration involving both the public and private sectors, trust was found to be a key success factor (Johnston & Finegood, 2015). Therefore, other parts of the public sector are likely to benefit from parts of the results and can adapt them or use them as inspiration for their own cross-sector collaboration development. Of course, some sectors are more like emergency response than others. One potential example of the former is healthcare, in which dealing with patient care (compared with victim care) might include similar medical tasks, where the ambulance services are often involved and where the same laws and regulations sometimes apply.

Conclusions and Future Work

Cross-sector collaborations are highly relevant to emergency response, in a society where crises occur frequently and where at the same time emergency response organizations need to continue their day-to-day first response in a resource-strained public sector. To our knowledge, this is the first study juxtaposing and comparing the opportunities, challenges, and needs from several cases of emergency response cross-sector collaboration, and this should be seen as the study's major contribution. The major opportunities identified included shared facilities and equipment and a positive attitude toward the new assignment/collaboration. Major challenges included the undefined roles, responsibilities, and tasks of new actors in response operations, difficulties in prioritizing among ordinary tasks and new tasks in resource-strained organizations, and a lack of legislation, routines, and insurance. Needs are related to improved and repeated training and joint exercises and to trauma support and basic supplies, including blankets, reflective vests, warning triangles, and pocket breathing masks. ICT suggestions included improved shared communication platforms, systems for errand handling, joint assessment of information, status, and acknowledgment of available and dispatched resources, and smartphone-based alarm management. The study's cross-comparison network governance analysis suggested that emergency response cross-sector collaborations can be characterized as a hybrid form of government and network governance, especially when new occupations are brought in to act as first responders. In retrospect, it seems that these hybrid forms will continue to grow in importance. In Sweden, since the time of the study, the concept of semiprofessionals has expanded to several municipalities and the needs for steering identified in the study have been addressed by agreements among employers, insurances, and new training programs. However, it is still the rescue services who has the mandate at the incident site.

In the study, we also argue that previous network governance research when taking the digitalization or ICT perspective focuses its relations to governance at institutional or macro-level. Here, the study provides a theoretical contribution in arguing for the explicit inclusion of ICT as a *key factor* in network governance, complementing the institutional key factors. In relation, we discuss the potential benefits of combining network government analyses with perspectives from the IS field, for example, the socio-technical ensemble view.

Some possible directions for future work include exploring the potential co-use of new resources in ordinary accidents and large-scale crises. From a wider public sector perspective, studies should also include the development of effect measures, methods, and cost-benefit models to evaluate emerging cross-sector collaborations. As to the connection of network governance and emergency cross-sector collaboration, future work may also incorporate other related theories, for example, public administration, new public management, and policy networks theory. Also, the connection between the fields of IS and policy science research in areas of public policymaking is interesting to explore, because they must both be involved in future cross-sector collaborations. This also calls for method studies on how to carry out IS development in an interdisciplinary manner. Finally, in line with the study limitations outlined above, it would be, if possible, of great interest to compare the emerging cross-sector collaborations/network governance forms to similar initiatives in emergency response in other countries.

References

Agranoff, R. (2007). *Managing within networks: Adding value to public organisations*. Georgetown University Press.

Agranoff, R., & McGuire, M. (2010). *Collaborative public management: New strategies for local governments*. Georgetown University Press.

Alford, J., & O'Flynn, J. (2012). *Rethinking public service delivery: Managing with external providers*. Palgrave Macmillan.

Andersson Granberg, T., & Värbrand, P. (2007). Decision support tools for ambulance dispatch and relocation. *Journal of the Operational Research Society, 58*(2), 195–201.

Antivachis, N. A., & Angelis, V. A. (2015). Network organisations: The question of governance. *Procedia - Social and Behavioral Sciences, 175*, 584–592. https://doi.org/10.1016/j.sbspro.2015.01.1241

Arslan, A., Golgeci, I., Khan, Z., et al. (2020). Adaptive learning in cross-sector collaboration during global emergency: Conceptual insights in the context of COVID-19 pandemic. *Multinational Business Review, 29*(1), 22–42. https://doi.org/10.1108/MBR-07-2020-0153

Babiak, K., & Thibault, L. (2009). Challenges in multiple cross-sector partnerships. *Nonprofit and Voluntary Sector Quarterly, 38*(1), 117–143. https://doi.org/10.1177/0899764008316054

Barsky, L., Baumann, J., Torres, M., et al. (2007). Managing volunteers: FEMA's urban search and rescue programme and interactions with unaffiliated responders in disaster response. *Disasters, 31*(4), 495–507. https://doi.org/10.1111/j.1467-7717.2007.01021.x

Berlin, J. M., & Carlström, E. D. (2011). Why is collaboration minimised at the accident scene? A critical study of a hidden phenomenon. *Disaster Prevention and Management: An International Journal, 20*(2), 159–171. https://doi.org/10.1108/09653561111126094

Bolton, F. (2016). Use of the after-action review to improve learning. *Assessment Update, 28*(2), 3–15. https://doi.org/10.1002/au.30051

Brinkerhoff, J. M. (2002). Government–nonprofit partnership: A defining framework. *Public Administration and Development, 22*(1), 19–30. https://doi.org/10.1002/pad.203

Bryson, J., Crosby, B., & Stone, M. (2006). The design and implementation of cross-sector collaborations: Propositions from the literature. *Public Administration Review, 66*, 44–55.

Bryson, J., Crosby, B. C., Stone, M., & Saunoi-Sandgren, E. (2009). Designing and Managing Cross-Sector Collaboration: A Case Study in Reducing Traffic Congestion. Washington, DC: IBM Center for the Business of Government. Available at: http://www.businessofgovernment.org/sites/default/files/Designing and Managing.pdf (accessed October 2017).

Carlsson, L. (2000). Policy network as collective action, Policy Studies Journal, 28, (3), 502–520 https://doi.org/10.1111/j.1541-0072.2000.tb02045.x

Carlsson, L. (2005). Policy network as collective action. *Policy Studies Journal, 28*(3), 502–520. https://doi.org/10.1111/j.1541-0072.2000.tb02045.x

Chatfield, A. T., & Reddick, C. G. (2018). All hands on deck to tweet #sandy: Networked governance of citizen coproduction in turbulent times. *Government Information Quarterly, 35*(2), 259–272. https://doi.org/10.1016/j.giq.2017.09.004

Dawes, S. (2009). Governance in the digital age: a research and action framework for an uncertain future, *Government Information Quarterly, 26*(2), 57–264. https://doi.org/10.1016/j.giq.2008.12.003

Drezner, J. R. A., Heistand, J., Bloomingdale, M., et al. (2009). Effectiveness of emergency response planning for sudden cardiac arrest in United States high schools with automated external defibrillators. *Circulation, 120*(6), 518–525.

Gazley, B., & Brudney, J. L. (2007). The purpose (and perils) of government-nonprofit partnership. *Nonprofit and Voluntary Sector Quarterly, 36*(3), 389–415. https://doi.org/10.1177/0899764006295997

Gil-Garcia, J. R., Dawes, S. S., & Pardo, T. A. (2018). Digital government and public management research: Finding the crossroads. *Public Management Review, 20*(5), 633–646. https://doi.org/10.1080/14719037.2017.1327181

Greve, C., & Hodge, G. (Eds.). (2005). *The challenge of public–private partnerships: Learning from international experience*. Edward Elgar.

Grudinschi, D., Kaljunen, L., Hokkanen, T., et al. (2013). Management challenges in cross-sector collaboration: Elderly care case study. *The Innovation Journal, 18*(2), Article 7.

Gruening, G. (2001). Origin and theoretical basis of New Public Management. *International Public Management Journal, 4*(1), 1–25. https://doi.org/10.1016/S1096-7494(01)00041-1

Haddow, G., Bullock, J., & Coppola, D. P. (2013). *Introduction to emergency management* (5th ed.). Butterworth-Heinemann.

Huxham, C., & Vangen, S. (2000). Ambiguity, complexity and dynamics in the membership of collaboration. *Human Relations, 53*(6), 771–806. https://doi.org/10.1177/0018726700536002

Jacobson, D. (2016). How and why network governance evolves: Evidence from a public safety network. *Electron Markets, 26*, 43–54.

Jaeger, P. T., Shneiderman, B., Fleischmann, K. R., Preece, J., et al. (2007). Community response grids: e-government, social networks, and effective emergency management. *Telecommunications Policy, 31*(10–11), 592–604. https://doi.org/10.1016/j.telpol.2007.07.008

Janowski, T., Pardo, T. A., & Davies, J. (2012). Government information networks – Mapping electronic governance cases through public administration. *Government Information Quarterly, 29*(1), 1–10. https://doi.org/10.1016/j.giq.2011.11.003

Janssen, M., & Estevez, E. (2013). Lean government and platform-based governance – Doing more with less. *Government Information Quarterly, 30*(1), 1–8. https://doi.org/10.1016/j.giq.2012.11.003

Johnston, L., & Finegood, D. (2015). Cross-sector partnerships and public health: Challenges and opportunities for addressing obesity and noncommunicable diseases through engagement with the private sector. *Annual Review of Public Health, 36*(1), 255–271. https://doi.org/10.1146/annurev-publhealth-031914-122802

Jones, C., Hesterly, W. S., & Borgatti, S. P. (1997). A general theory of network governance: Exchange conditions and social mechanisms. *The Academy of Management Review, 22*(4), 911–945. https://doi.org/10.5465/amr.1997.9711022109

Jones, D. M., Lyle, D., Brunero, C., McAllister, L., Webb, T., & Riley, S. (2015). Improving health and education outcomes for children in remote communities: A cross-sector and developmental evaluation approach. *Gateways: International Journal of Community Research and Engagement, 8*(1), 1–22. ISSN: 1836-3393.

Jungk, R., & Müllert, N. R. (1987). *Future workshops: How to create desirable futures*. Institute for Social Inventions.

Kleiner, A., & Delurey, M. (Eds.). (2007). *The megacommunity way: Mastering dynamic challenges with cross-boundary leadership*. Booz Allen Hamilton.

Klijn, E., & Koppenjan, J. (2012). Governance network theory: Past, present and future. *Policy and Politics, 40*(4), 587–606. https://doi.org/10.7564/14-CGN8

Klijn, E., & Koppenjan, J. (2014). Complexity in governance network theory. *Complexity, Governance and Networks, 1*(1), 61–70.

Klijn, E., Edelenbos, J., & Steijn, B. (2010). Trust in governance networks: Its impacts on outcomes. *Administration and Society, 42*(2), 193–221. https://doi.org/10.1177/0095399710362716

Leknes, H., Skorge Aartun, E., Christiansen, M., & Andersson Granberg, T. (2017). Strategic ambulance location for heterogeneous regions. *European Journal of Operational Research, 260*(1), 122–133. https://doi.org/10.1016/j.ejor.2016.12.020

Loukis, E., Janssen, M., Dawes, S., & Zheng, L. (2016). Evolving ICT and governance in organisational networks – Conceptual and theoretical foundations. *Electronic Markets, 26*(1), 7–14. https://doi.org/10.1007/s12525-015-0210-1

Matinrad, M., Andersson Granberg, T., Ennab Vogel, N., & Angelakis, V. (2019). *Optimal dispatch of volunteers to out-of-hospital cardiac arrest patients*. Proceedings of the 52nd Hawaii International Conference on System Sciences (HICSS) Hawaii, USA, pp. 4088–4097.

Melin, U., & Wihlborg, E. (2018). Balanced and integrated e-government implementation: Exploring the crossroad of public policy-making and information systems project management processes. *Transforming Government: People, Process and Policy, 12*(2), 191–208. https://doi.org/10.1108/TG-12-2017-0080

Meng, Q., Zhang, N., Zhao, X., Li, F., & Guan, X. (2016). The governance strategies for public emergencies on social media and their affects: A case study based on the microblog data. *Electron Markets, 26*, 15–29. https://doi.org/10.1007/s12525-015-0202-1

Mikhaylov, S. J., Esteve, M., & Campion, A. (2018). Artificial intelligence for the public sector: Opportunities and challenges of cross-sector collaboration. *Philosophical Transactions of Royal Society A, 376*, 21–28. https://doi.org/10.1098/rsta.2017.0357

Myers, M. D. (2009). *Qualitative research in business and management*. SAGE Publications Ltd.

O'Leary, R., & Bingham, L. (2009). *The collaborative public manager: New ideas for the twenty-first century*. Georgetown University Press.

Orlikowski, W. J., & Iacono, C. S. (2001). Research commentary: Desperately seeking the 'IT' in IT research – A call to theorizing the IT artifact. *Information System Research, 12*(2), 21–134. https://doi.org/10.1287/isre.12.2.121.9700

Palm, J., & Törnqvist, E. (2008). Governing the sea rescue service in Sweden: Communicating in networks. *Journal of Risk Research, 11*(1), 269–280. https://doi.org/10.1080/13669870801939449

Patton, A. (2007). Collaborative emergency management. In W. L. Waugh & K. Tierney (Eds.), *Emergency management: Principles and practice for local government* (pp. 71–85). ICMA.

Pestoff, V., Brandsen, T., & Verschuere, B. (Eds.). (2013). *New public governance, the third sector, and co-production*. Routledge.

Peters, D., Klijn, E. H., Stronks, K., & Harting, J. (2017). Policy coordination and integration, trust, management and performance in public health-related policy networks: A survey. *International Review of Administrative Sciences, 83*(1), 200–222. https://doi.org/10.1177/2F0020852315585061

Pilemalm, S. (2018). Participatory design in emerging civic engagement initiatives in the new public sector: Applying PD concepts in resource-scarce organisations. *ACM Transactions on Computer-Human Interaction (TOCHI) - Special Issue on Reimagining Participatory Design, 25*(1), Article 5. https://doi.org/10.1145/3152420

Pilemalm, S. (2020). Volunteer co-production in emergency management in rural areas – using civil citizens and semi-professionals as first responders. *e-Journal of e-Democracy (JEDEM) special issue, 12*(1), 61–86.

Pilemalm, S. (2021). Digitalized co-production: Using volunteers as first responders. *Proceedings of the Eighth International Conference on eDemocracy & eGovernment (ICEDEG)*, 25–32. http://urn.kb.se/resolve?urn=urn:nbn:se:liu:diva-179286

Pilemalm, S. (2022). *Barriers to digitalized co-production: the case of volunteers as first responders*. Accepted to the 19th international conference of information systems (ISCRAM). Tarbes, France.

Pilemalm, S., & Yousefi Mojir, K. (2020). ICT enabled cross-sector collaboration in emergency response: emerging forms of public-sector network governance. *International Journal of Emergency Management, 16*(3), 249–280. https://doi.org/10.1504/IJEM.2020.113936

Pilemalm, S., Stenberg, R., & Andersson Granberg, T. (2013). Emergency response in rural areas. *International Journal of Information Systems for Crisis Response and Management, 5*(2), 19–31. https://doi.org/10.4018/jiscrm.2013040102

Pilemalm, S., Lindgren, I., & Ramsell, E. (2016). Emerging forms of inter-organizational and cross-sector collaborations in e-government initiatives – Implications for participative development of information systems. *Transforming Government People Process and Policy, 10*(5), 603–636.

Powell, W. W. (1990). Neither market nor hierarchy: Network forms of organisation. In B. M. Staw & L. L. Cummings (Eds.), *Research in organisational behavior* (pp. 295–3369). JAI Press.

Quarantelli, E. L. (2000). *Emergencies, disaster and catastrophes are different phenomena. Disaster Research Center preliminary paper* (Vol. 304). University of Delaware: Disaster Research Centre.

Ramsell, E., Pilemalm, S., & Andersson Granberg, T. (2017). *Using volunteers for emergency response in rural areas – Network collaboration factors and IT support in the case of Enhanced Neighbours*. Proceedings of the 14th international conference on information systems for crisis response and management. Albi, Occitanie Pyrénées-Méditerranée, France, ISCRAM association, pp. 985–995.

Schuler, D., & Namioka, A. (Eds.). (1993). *Participatory design: Principles and practices*. Lawrence Erlbaum Associates.

Simon, A., & Angela, L. (2007). The role of nonprofits in disaster response: An expanded model of cross-sector collaboration. *Public Administration Review, 67*(1), 125–142. https://doi.org/10.1111/j.1540-6210.2007.00821.x

Stake, R. E. (2000). Case studies. In N. K. Denzin & Y. S. Lincoln (Eds.), *The SAGE handbook of qualitative research* (2nd ed., pp. 119–150). SAGE Publications, Inc.

Sun, J. H., & Wallis, L. A. (2012). The emergency first aid responder system model: Using community members to assist life-threatening emergencies in violent, developing areas of need. *Emergency Medicine Journal: EMJ, 29*(8), 673–678.

Sun, Y., Kuang, X., & Sun, D. (2016). The geographic concentration of China's e-business enterprises: Where they gather and why. *Electron Markets, 26*, 31–42.

Turoff, M., Chumer, M., van de Walle, B., & Yao, X. (2004). The design of a dynamic emergency response management information system (DERMIS). *Journal of Information Technology Theory and Application (JITTA), 5*(4), Article 3: 1–Article 3:35.

Valenzuela, T. D., Roe, D. J., Nichol, G., Clark, L. L., Spaite, D. W., & Hardman, R. G. (2000). Outcomes of rapid defibrillation by security officers after cardiac arrest in casinos. *New England Journal of Medicine, 343*(17), 206–209. https://doi.org/10.1056/NEJM200010263431701

Venema, A., Groothoff, J., & Bierens, J. (2010). The role of bystanders during rescue and resuscitation of drowning victims. *Resuscitation, 81*(4), 434–439. https://doi.org/10.1016/j.resuscitation.2010.01.005

Vigoda, E. (2003). *Managing collaboration in public administration: The promise of alliance among governance. Citizens, and businesses*. Praege.

Waugh, W., & Streib, G. (2006). Collaboration and leadership for effective emergency management. *Public Administration Review, 66*, 131–140. https://doi.org/10.1111/j.1540-6210.2006.00673.x

Weber, E. P., & Khademian, A. M. (2008). Wicked problems, knowledge challenges, and collaborative capacity builders in network settings. *Public Administration Review, 68*(2), 334–349. https://doi.org/10.1111/j.1540-6210.2007.00866.x

Weinholt, A., & Andersson Granberg, T. (2015). New collaborations in daily emergency response: Applying cost-benefit analysis to new first response initiatives in the Swedish Fire and Rescue

Service. *International Journal of Emergency Services, 4*(2), 177–193. https://doi.org/10.1111/j.1540-6210.2006.00673.x

Weisfeldt, M. L., Sitlani, C. M., Ornato, J. P., Rea, T., et al. (2010). Survival after application of automatic external defibrillators before arrival of the emergency medical system: Evaluation in the resuscitation outcomes consortium population of 21 million. *Journal of the American College of Cardiology, 55*(16), 1713–1720. https://doi.org/10.1016/j.jacc.2009.11.077

Young, D. R. (2000). Alternative models of government-nonprofit sector relations: Theoretical and international perspectives. *Nonprofit and Voluntary Sector Quarterly, 29*(1), 149–172. https://doi.org/10.1177/F0899764000291009

Yousefi Mojir, K., & Pilemalm, S. (2014). *Emerging communities of collaboration: co-location in emergency response systems in Sweden*. Proceedings of the 2014 information systems for crisis response and management conference (ISCRAM). Pennsylvania State University, USA, pp. 548–555.

Yousefi Mojir, K., & Pilemalm, S. (2016). Actor-centred emergency response systems: a framework for needs analysis and information systems development. *International Journal of Emergency Management, 12*(4), 403–420.

Yousefi Mojir, K., Pilemalm, S., & Andersson Granberg, T. (2018). Semi-professionals: Emergency response as an additional task in current occupations. *International Journal of Emergency Services, 8*(2), 86–107. https://doi.org/10.1108/IJES-11-2017-0059

Defining Common Information Requirements for Supporting Multiagency Emergency Operations

Kristine Steen-Tveit and Bjørn Erik Munkvold

Abstract Effective response in complex emergency events requires establishing shared situational awareness among the agencies involved, through sharing relevant information and building a common operational picture (COP). However, despite its acknowledged importance, developing effective practices for such information sharing proves to be challenging. A basis for this is identifying what information is critical to share and also defining a well-functioning structure for this.

Based on interviews with Norwegian emergency management stakeholders, this study investigates common information requirements for emergency management services and presents an example of a framework for structuring the sharing of critical information and building a COP. The study identified eight common information requirement categories for managing extreme weather scenarios. The focus on common information needs and a process for structured information sharing contributes to a more holistic perspective on cross-sectoral operations than in current practice.

Keywords Situational awareness · Common operational picture · Information sharing · Common information requirements · Multiagency emergency operations

Introduction

Climate change results in an increase in extreme weather events (Stott, 2016), such as floods, landslides, large-scale forest fires, and damaging storms. Emergency management related to such events tends to be complex because of cascading effects, threatening human survival, and causing damage to property and critical infrastructure. These events often hit critical functions in society, such as roads, elec-

K. Steen-Tveit (✉) · B. E. Munkvold
Centre for Integrated Emergency Management (CIEM), Department of Information Systems, University of Agder, Kristiansand, Norway
e-mail: kristine.steen-tveit@uia.no; bjorn.e.munkvold@uia.no

H. J. Scholl et al. (eds.), *Disaster Management and Information Technology*, Public Administration and Information Technology 40,
https://doi.org/10.1007/978-3-031-20939-0_14

tricity, and telecommunications. Operational response to natural disasters requires coordination with organizations beyond the regular emergency management services that handle crises on a daily basis. In addition, the first hours of a disaster are complex and chaotic, and emergency management in this phase is crucial for the outcome. These operations require effective collaboration and information sharing in order to reach common goals, such as saving lives and reducing damage. Because of several heterogeneous information needs among the organizations involved, it is challenging to determine what information needs to be shared (Bharosa et al., 2010), which represents a bottleneck for collaborative efforts. The literature on multiagency crisis management emphasizes the importance of a common operational picture (COP) for the purpose of collaborating and sharing information (e.g., Bunker et al., 2015). The COP is intended to support the actors' development of shared situational awareness (SA) (Comfort, 2007; Endsley, 1995a). However, there is still a need for more in-depth analysis of what information elements need to be shared in such a COP for supporting multiagency operations in different contexts and what structure could be applied as the basis for this information sharing.

This chapter defines common information requirement categories for multiagency crisis management as a basis for establishing a COP during extreme weather events. Moreover, it presents a structure for sharing this information based on current practice among Norwegian first responders. The study focuses on managing extreme weather scenarios in the acute phase and is based on data collection in first responder agencies (fire and rescue, police, and medical services) and municipalities. The findings presented is thus intended to contribute to more systematic and effective information exchange in multiagency emergency response.

The next section presents a brief summary of relevant research and practice related to the concepts of SA and COP. This is followed by a description of the research approach, comprising qualitative interviews and a web-based survey. The findings from the data analysis are then presented and discussed, with conclusion and implications in the final section.

Related Research

Situational Awareness and Common Operational Picture

Collaboration is emphasized as a critical success factor in complex emergency management operations (e.g., Berlin & Carlström, 2014; Kapucu, 2008), such as multiagency management of extreme weather scenarios. However, information sharing among emergency response organizations also implies several challenges due to different disciplinary traditions, work practices and culture, lack of understanding of mutual information needs, and limited interoperability for the technology support (e.g., Bharosa et al., 2010; Comfort, 2007; Munkvold et al., 2019; Wolbers & Boersma, 2013; Steen-Tveit & Munkvold, 2021).

Situational awareness is considered a key element in emergency management (e.g., Cak et al., 2019; Dilo & Zlatanova, 2011; Endsley, 1995a). SA is defined as "the perception of elements in the environment within a volume of time and space, comprehension of their meaning, and projection of their status in the near future" (Endsley, 1995a, p. 287). This definition refers to three hierarchical levels of SA. Level 1 SA is the first step in achieving SA and involves a perception of the relevant elements and the related attributes and dynamics connected to the specific information. For example, a firefighter would perceive the size of the fire, topography, wind direction, and color of the smoke. Furthermore, the elements in level 1 SA provide the actor with an understanding of the situation in terms of what the different elements mean in relation to the agent's professional goals. This gives a holistic picture based on the elements in level 1 SA and the professional's ability to form patterns with that information, which leads to level 2 SA (Endsley, 1995a). At this level, the firefighter would understand that the wind direction, location, and topography indicate certain features about the situation. Some professional experience is required to be able to relate the elements in level 1 SA to the relevant goals and thus achieve level 2 SA. Level 3 SA is the highest form of SA, which involves the ability to project the future status of the situation. For instance, based on the two previous SA levels, the firefighter understands that the fire might spread to a populated area. The accuracy of the projection depends on the degree of the two lower levels of SA (Falkland & Wiggins, 2019). SA is associated with cognitive capabilities such as attention, perception reasoning, and working memory (Cak et al., 2019).

Scholarly articles present the concept of COP differently, for example, as an information system that enables information to be presented in a visual form (Luokkala et al., 2017), a continuously maintained description of a situation (Norri-Sederholm et al., 2017), a display of relevant operational information (Karagiannis & Synolakis, 2016), or a checklist of the characteristics in a certain situation within a geographical area (Wolbers & Boersma, 2013). Whether the COP is a process, a product, or an operating environment remains undefined.

Regardless of the different characteristics, an identification of the common information needs in particular scenarios is a required basis for building a COP. However, as long as the different organizations are characterized by different disciplines, tasks, goals, and working modes, a COP still cannot guarantee that stakeholders will achieve a common situational understanding. These differences might result in a diverse operational understanding of the COP. For a successful outcome, the actors involved must have the same awareness of what is going on (Berggren & Johansson, 2010), and a comprehensive COP supports building a common situational understanding. However, it is important to avoid an "all information to all people" approach (She et al., 2019), which will result in information overload through dissemination of redundant and irrelevant information (e.g., Ben Lazreg et al., 2018; Laakso & Palomäki, 2013). Humans have limited capacity to hold information available for processing, referred to as the working memory (Lauria et al., 2019). Thus, information overload complicates decision-making and creates simplified mental models (Van den Homberg et al., 2018).

Borglund (2017) acknowledged the COP as a selection of the important parts of the information available to actors. Based on this, the COP is the result of both static and available dynamic information analyzed by the different actors involved and thus their SA. They must then decide what information needs to be shared and what is irrelevant to the collaborating parties. By further drawing on the COP concept, Berggren and Johansson (2010) suggested that the COP is a geospatial representation of the operational area and that it consists of units and fields of significance. In emergency management, this could mean visualizing the location of all the units involved, the areas of interest, evacuation spots, and the different types of resources. This is supported by Johansson et al. (2013) who argue for the relevance of the ability to localize objects in the terrain of emergency management.

There are different ways in which the organizations involved can share information in order to build a COP, one option is to communicate via technology, such as a geographic information system (GIS). A GIS uses custom symbols to display relevant operational information, such as location, topography, infrastructure, and different resources (Karagiannis & Synolakis, 2016). However, many emergency management services do not have access to a common GIS interface because they use different support technologies with lacking interoperability (Opach et al., 2020). This means that they must share geographical information verbally. Several studies have addressed the difficulty of information sharing among the various actors, whereby the collection of relevant and verified information from different sources in the environment must be shared with the collaborating services (e.g., Luokkala et al., 2017; Seppänen et al., 2013; Steigenberger, 2016).

The SA of the involved actors is a basic component for the outcome of agency-specific tasks and goals but is also a central source in establishing the COP. The involved organizations require their own SA elements; however, even if the team members hold different roles in the operation, there is often an overlap in what information they need (Endsley, 1995b; Sorensen & Stanton, 2016). Such shared SA elements must be communicated among the involved stakeholders and require knowledge on what information the team members should not keep individually. This can be briefly illustrated by the first responders' communication with each other and their respective command and control centers (CCC). As Fig. 1 shows, the three first response agencies (police, fire and rescue, and medical services) need

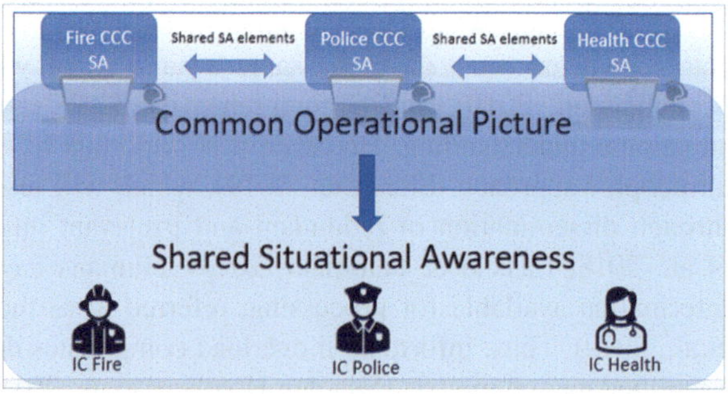

Fig. 1 Agencies' SA and communication of shared SA elements to create a COP and shared situational awareness

to build SA and communicate the shared SA elements with each other in order to establish a COP. The sharing of the common SA elements constituting the COP enables the stakeholders to develop shared situational awareness, implying that the involved stakeholders "understand a given situation in the same way" (Perla et al., 2000, p. 17).

Current Information Sharing Practice

First responders have a long tradition of collaborating on the emergency site. The first responder to arrive at the incident site provides other stakeholders with a "window report" in the Norwegian Public Safety Network, which is a common platform for collaborative communication. For the first response agencies, the features of the information they receive can have major consequences for the outcome of the operation (Schroeder et al., 2018). They rely on information that reflects the situation they are handling (Liang & Gao, 2010). There is no univocal standard for this kind of window reporting, but the essence is to provide knowledge on, for example, position, resources, and scope (Solberg et al., 2018). An example of such a reporting structure is the Gothenburg Window (Fig. 2) used by the Swedish Police (Borglund, 2017). This provides information about *place* (location), *direction* (short description of what is going on), *resources* (summary of operative units on site), and *trend* (status quo and, for instance, if the situation is escalating or calming down).

Recently, the Norwegian CCCs for police, fire and rescue, and medical services implemented new procedures for common questioning of callers in nine different cross-sectoral scenarios (Dreyer, 2019). However, this strategic way of information sharing is limited to internal use for the first responder services and does not include other external organizations involved in emergency management. In joint operations, where organizations besides the first responders are participating, the need for information sharing includes other actors besides the operational units and their associated CCCs. For example, in extreme weather events, municipalities play a central role as they are tasked with safety at the local level and are thus an important part of the emergency management system (Civil Protection Act, 2010; Regulation on municipal emergency duty, 2011). A Norwegian project called

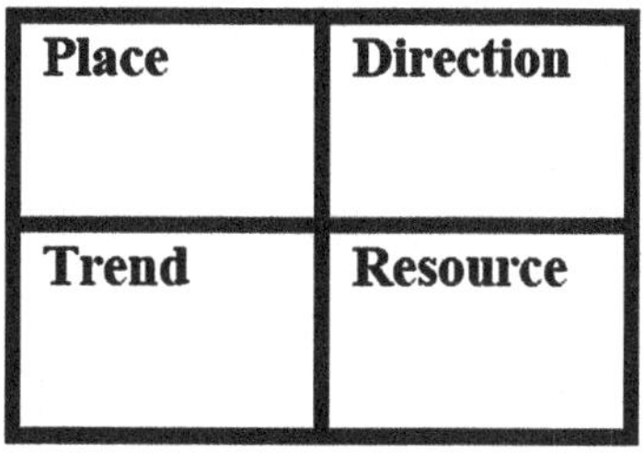

Fig. 2 The Gothenburg Window (Borglund, 2017)

OPSAM (Operation Center for Collaboration and Preparedness) (Fredheim, 2017) has demonstrated the need for an efficient and streamlined information sharing process between first responders and the municipalities. Other international studies have shown that there is a lack of shared protocols for communication between agencies (e.g., Bunker et al., 2015). A functional information sharing process can contribute toward building a COP between the operational units, with their associated CCCs, the municipalities, critical infrastructure providers (e.g., energy sector, road services), and other relevant organizations that must also act within their areas of responsibility. Cross-sectoral processes simplify communication, as exemplified by the structured "window report" procedure for mutual information sharing with prioritized content.

Research Method

As there exist few established procedures for information sharing between the emergency response organizations focused, an exploratory study was conducted to identify common information requirements related to extreme weather events and to investigate a possible information sharing structure based on the window report. The study involved two rounds of data collection, described in the following.

Data Collection on Information Requirements

The first round of data collection involved semi-structured interviews with nine experts from first response agencies and municipalities. In addition, a survey was sent to six experts, including two first responders and four representatives from three additional stakeholders that can be characterized as support organizations as they are not responsible for handling the crisis themselves. Table 1 specifies the interviewees and survey respondents in the first round of data collection.

The informants from the first response organizations were either recruited by their leaders following a request from the first author or contacted directly based on existing relations. The interviews were conducted in the informants' workplace. Several of the informants from the first response agencies demonstrated their working process by means of a tour and gave an introduction to their information systems as well as how and when these were used. In addition, the first author could also build upon 10 years' previous work experience as a medical emergency dispatcher, which resulted in good rapport with the interviewees.

The interviews lasted between 45 min and 1 h and were based on a semi-structured interview guide. The interview guide focused on the informants' work practices related to complex events requiring multiagency collaboration, using a forest fire scenario as example. The questions were related to the structures or procedures used to collect information on the emergency, with whom and how they share

Table 1 Overview of respondents for first round of data collection

Organization	Role	Data collection
Fire and rescue services A	Emergency dispatcher	Interview
Fire and rescue services A	Shift leader	Interview
Fire and rescue services B	Professional development	Survey
Police services	Emergency dispatcher	Interview
Police services	Emergency dispatcher	Interview
Medical services A	Head of section, acute medical Communication services	Interview
Medical services B	Professional development in acute medical communication services	Survey
Municipality A	Emergency coordinator	Interview
Municipality B	Emergency coordinator	Interview
Municipality C	Emergency coordinator	Interview
Municipality D	Emergency coordinator	Interview
Municipality E	Head of the preparedness section	Survey
Ministry of Justice and Public Security	Director	Survey
County governor	Assistant director	Survey
Civil defense	Head of district	Survey

information, and their specific information requirements. In addition, the informants were asked about their experiences and opinions regarding the construction of a COP and the achievement of a common situational understanding. The main purpose was to learn about the organizations' processes for information sharing and identify common information requirements. All interviews were recorded and transcribed in full.

In order to collect further common information requirements intended for extreme weather scenarios, experts in several emergency management organizations were contacted. These informants received a link to a web-based survey with descriptions of storm and flood scenarios and were asked to write their information requirements in the specified fields. The informants represented first responders as well as municipalities and support organizations. The information requirements from the support organizations were collected in order to identify possible differences between their requirements and those of the first response organizations.

The data from both the interviews and the survey were coded and analyzed in NVivo (QSR International). The answers were categorized based on the focused scenarios (e.g., flood, storm, and forest fire) and were further classified into information requirement categories using an inductive method. For example, when an informant said, "which area is affected by the forest fire," this was classified into the information requirement category "location." Similarly, roads, energy grid, and networks were classified under "critical infrastructure." Finally, the information requirements were compared, and the common requirements were determined and described.

Table 2 Overview of respondents for the second round of data collection

Organization	Role
Fire and rescue services A	Emergency dispatcher
Fire and rescue services B	Incident commander
Medical services A	Emergency dispatcher
Medical services A	Incident commander
Medical services A	Incident commander
Police services A	Emergency dispatcher
Police services B	Incident commander
Police services B	Incident commander

Data Collection on Information Sharing Structure

In the second round of data collection, interviews of eight first responders were conducted for investigating how information sharing could be supported by using a window report structure such as the Gothenburg Window (Fig. 1). Both emergency dispatchers and incident commanders were included, as they are the key actors in window reporting (see overview of respondents in Table 2). The questions focused on the respondents' experience with the use of window reports, what information these reports should ideally include, and possible variation in this between the different first response organizations. The data analysis was conducted in NVivo and included codes such as "window report content", "window report sharing structure", and "views and differences between the organizations."

Some of the interviews were conducted physically, while some had to be conducted online due to the Covid-19 pandemic. The informants were either recruited by their leaders following a request or contacted directly based on existing relations.

Results and Discussion

This section presents the results from the data analysis related to common information requirements and structure for information sharing and discusses the implications of this.

Common Information Requirements

From the data collected, eight common information requirement (IR) categories for sharing were identified, as presented in Table 3. The information requirement categories contain static and dynamic information. The static information remains the same throughout the incident, for example, the origin of a fire will remain the

Table 3 Common information requirement categories

Information requirement category		Description	Static/dynamic information
IR 1	Location	Exact area for coordination point or meeting place. In addition, topography, terrain, and exact scope	Static
IR 2	Critical infrastructure	Essential assets such as transportation systems, water supply, electricity, and telecommunications	Static and dynamic
IR 3	Information on possible victims	Whether there are people involved who are – or are at risk of being – injured, threatened, or dead because of the situation; vulnerable groups that might be in the affected area	Dynamic
IR 4	Evacuation possibilities	Whether evacuation is required now or in the future, where the possibilities are and the approximate number of people	Dynamic
IR 5	Resources	All operations units from the first responders involved, and the collaborative organizations' resources, such as power generators and water supply. Other available resources, such as tractors and buses	Dynamic
IR 6	Weather forecast	Current weather at affected locations and weather forecasts	Dynamic
IR 7	Critical buildings	Hospitals, evacuation center, and schools	Static
IR 8	Situational development	Expert assessment on how the situation can develop	Dynamic

same, while the location of an operative resource is changing. However, elements in critical infrastructure such as roadblocks can be both static and dynamic as they either can be permanent or eliminated/moved.

In the following, the information requirement categories are introduced in more detail.

Location (IR 1) includes information on the scope and exact position of the important locations. This can be the coordination point for the incident commanders from the first response agencies, a meeting place for operations units, and support organizations or representatives from the municipality. The organizations interviewed did not have access to the same GIS interface, which sometimes results in spending a considerable amount of time explaining locations to the collaborative organizations. As stated by one informant, "If we could see the positions in the map instead of describing (. . .) then you would know exactly where to go." According to another, "Now, everyone is searching for position (. . .) where it has happened, separately." This lack of information sharing relating to the position was specifically stated in the interviews. And the possible benefit was documented by two of the first response agencies that actually had the possibility of sending the GIS position to each other. Both organizations pointed to the major advantage of this feature and underlined its time-saving functionality: "It [shared position in GIS] saves us a lot of time when you don't have an exact address." This indicates that a common GIS interface would be beneficial for creating a COP concerning emergency locations, as emphasized by all the informants. Location information also concerns the type of terrain and topography of the area. To address the different needs related to this information, a scaling of the details on the map could solve the issue of information overload. This information is also important when assessing and mapping the possible impacts of the scenarios.

Critical infrastructure (IR 2) concerns critical societal infrastructure such as transportation systems, water supply, and telecommunications. One informant described how they coordinated the bus transportation in a storm scenario by using a real-time GIS solution: "We knew a lot of trees would break (. . .) but the public transport must go on. We then called in the bus company, and they have a real-time view of all their busses. This was incredibly useful because when a tree fell over the road, the coordination of the bus could adapt to the situation." In this case, the overview of the transport systems and access to information on obstacles enabled the organization to maintain its responsibility in a crisis situation. Critical infrastructure is also important for sharing information regarding different challenges in an area, and several of the informants highlighted the importance of mapping and taking early actions concerning vulnerable groups, such as old, sick, and disabled people. Many people need electricity for medical reasons, home care, and special measures. While this is the responsibility of municipalities in many scenarios, it might result in tasks that need to be solved by first responders. One informant illustrated the despair of not having the overview: "In X scenario, 40,000–50,000 people had no electricity (. . .) and we didn't know how many patients have received a COPD apparatus [breathing apparatus] that needed to be refilled (. . .). How should we know this? They [the patients] were sitting and calling someone and worrying about the electricity being gone. So, this was just chaotic, so to speak." This illustrates how the responsibility of municipalities fuses with that of first responders if the patients' condition worsens because of sustained power outages and if measures are not implemented in time.

Information on possible victims (IR 3) is important for several reasons. First, the first responders must prepare medical treatments and search and rescue operations for victims, both according to the scope of the incident and relating to specific conditions such as burns and trauma injuries. These are resource-demanding operations that require great effort from several stakeholders. Second, this is important information concerning the evacuation process. Third, during disasters, an important task is to keep people informed. The extent of damage, especially when it comes to injuries, is of great interest to the public.

Evacuation possibilities (IR 4) is connected to IR 3 but also concerns the total number of people affected, including victims and next of kin. In addition, the need for evacuation is not exclusively for injured people but also involves situations where people need to evacuate from their homes. IR 4 also considers the need for staff in the evacuation situation. IR 1 relates to this category in the sense that the location of the evacuation spot or center must be determined.

Resources (IR 5) includes several aspects, as presented by the informants. For instance, resources can be the operational units (e.g., vehicles) of the first responders involved. Another category of resources has to do with different supplies, aid, and support that can be used when needed. An overview of available resources can help organizations mobilize measures while also considering resource adequacy vis-à-vis the situation at hand. One informant explained resources like this: "Available resources, who, what, where? Are there other resources besides ours we can take advantage of? That's the first thing."

Weather forecast (IR 6) is crucial for planning the next steps of the operation. For instance, wind direction, rainfall, and wind speed are important information elements in preventing and handling the consequences of extreme weather.

Critical buildings (IR 7) includes information on important buildings such as building plans, materials, storage, and hazardous materials, both to support handling the operation and preventing damage. Examples of such buildings include nursing homes, hospitals, and evacuation centers, all of which are connected to IR 4.

Situational development (IR 8) is an interconnected information requirement category, which concerns weather forecast (IR 6), possible victims (IR 3), and resources (IR 5). In addition, this category covers other projections on how the situation might develop. According to an informant, "How we comprehend the situation, if it's a threatening situation posing a danger for others involved." In the "window report" structure, IR 8 can be seen as an information category in itself because it covers information that needs to be shared among all the involved actors.

Our findings from the analysis of the different information requirements corroborate previous research (e.g., Bunker et al., 2015) stating that it is not possible to operate with a single COP, as it must consider all the organizations involved and their need for an operational picture. Information overload here becomes an issue, in addition to the fact that the consideration of all information needs would require a COP that is difficult to build and maintain. Some of the information requirements presented in Table 3 may therefore apply with different levels of detail for the different organizations, in addition to their agency-specific information requirements for supporting their individual tasks and goals.

The Window Report Structure for Information Sharing

While the actors involved in multiagency operations each have some agency-specific goals, collaboration is a critical success factor in the achievement of common goals. In order for this collaboration to be successful, it is crucial that the common information requirements are shared with the relevant stakeholders and not remain within the agencies or individual actors (Sorensen & Stanton, 2016). A study on building SA in a fire emergency response demonstrated the importance of information collection for this, especially information items from the emergency site (Li et al., 2014). Thus, the "window report" structure should not be limited to a fraction of the organizations involved; it should include all relevant levels of the cross-sectoral collaboration. Today, the structure is mainly designed for information sharing between first responders and is perceived as a well-known structure for information sharing where elements are distributed within the multiagency network, appearing as an effective and prioritized structure. During the data collection for this chapter, several of the actors referred to the window structure when asked about how they build a COP, e.g., "I really like what we call the "window report" in the common call group, the first actors on the scene – what do they observe? This is important for us in the CCC because we do not have any visual picture of the situation." This structure for information sharing among the relevant agencies can therefore be seen as the foundation of the COP and shared SA.

Several informants still pointed to the need for improved structure for such window reporting. One informant argued that "ideally, one should follow a pattern for this type of situation reporting" (emergency dispatcher, Police), and another said, "It must be structured with short, concise, and time-critical information" (emergency dispatcher, Fire). Interestingly, there were differences in the results between the emergency dispatchers and the incident commanders regarding the window report structure. The emergency dispatchers called for more structure in the window reports provided by the incident commanders, while the incident commanders were reluctant toward this. For example, one incident commander stated that "You feel like you want to start doing something, then you have to talk [in the common call group] and there will be a delay" (incident commander, Police). Nevertheless, all the informants reported that there is a need for an improvement in the window reporting structure. The results indicated that the difference between the incident commanders' and emergency dispatchers' views can be explained by the possible additional workload from such "procedure-based tasks" for the incident commanders who already have several urgent tasks they must perform at the incident scene. However, the lack of information in the window report may also result in additional inquiries from the CCC: "We often have to ask for information (. . .) but sometimes we know that they [the incident commanders] have an insane workload" (emergency dispatcher, Police). Taking this into account, a streamlined structure might save time for all the stakeholders involved. An incident commander suggested that "if we could implement a procedure-based window structure reporting (. . .) into our certification, then I'm very in favor of it. But it has to be learned, people have to try it before they have to do it in real events" (incident commander, Health).

When asking the informants about the ideal content of a window report, four categories emerged: *location*, *status quo*, *resources*, and *projection*. These categories can be associated with the categories in the Gothenburg Window, however, they are more descriptive for the content in the categories. For example, location corresponds to place (but appears to be more specific with including coordinates), status quo

(1) Location		(2) Status Quo	
Information requirement	Receiving organization	Information requirement	Receiving organization
IR 1	All organizations	IR 3	First responders Municipality
		IR 2	All organizations
Information requirement	Receiving organization	Information requirement	Receiving organization
IR 5	All organizations	IR 6 & IR 8	All organizations
IR 7 & IR 4	First responders Municipality		
(3) Resources		(4) Projection	

Fig. 3 A window report structure for sharing common information

relates to direction, projection relates to trend, while the resources category appears the same.

Based on the data from the interviews, first responders are familiar with the "window report" structure, which arguably depicts a relevant procedure for information sharing. The common information requirement categories can be placed in the window and serve as a structure for indicating what information must be shared and to whom (Fig. 3).

Location is the first square in the window report and must be accurately communicated, with no room for errors. Incorrectly communicated information regarding location can have critical consequences, such as resources being delayed. An exact position in a common GIS would obviously be effective. Further, the stakeholders need to confirm that the location is accurate: "we must confirm that it is the address that the others also have received, that there is a common understanding of the location. Also, possibly if the road is slippery before the incident scene, for example, obstacles or something" (incident commander, Health).

Status quo functions as a confirmation of the emergency event itself. For example, an emergency dispatcher states that "we often experience that the first information [i.e., from the bystander that reported the emergency by calling the emergency number] does not correspond to reality at all" (emergency dispatcher, Police). Status quo involves SA because it is a short objective description of the situation. Because a "window report" is a first impression description, the status quo should mainly consist of level 1 SA elements, whereby the actor describes the situation in an objective way and distributes the elements in the environment to the collaborative organizations. This could relate to victims (IR 3), information about whom should be presented in an objective manner such as whether or not there are injuries. There are several pitfalls in projecting the status of patients, and injuries must be evaluated by medical personnel. Critical infrastructure (IR 2) represents issues concerning closed roads or other dynamics of the environment that could impact the operation and should be presented in the status quo square.

In the *resources* square, the first stakeholder on the incident scene must provide an update on the resources. An incident commander states that "we must inform what resources are alerted and coming, and we need a good feedback from health and fire as well, what resources they have sent" (incident commander, Police).

The last square in the window is *projection*, where information requirements 6 and 8 should be presented. These requirements are interconnected in the sense that the weather forecast needs to be shared, and the consequences need to be predicted. IR 8 can also be interpreted as an analysis of the previous information requirements.

Conclusion

This study has identified eight information requirement categories common for first responders and other organizations involved in emergency management, which are necessary for building a COP and shared situational awareness when handling extreme weather scenarios. One can argue that the COP is the result of preparation and a structured working methodology. This preparation consists of knowledge regarding each other's operational modes and the common information requirements that need to be shared during an operation. The working methodology consists of how to share the relevant information. This chapter presents the "window report" structure as an example of how to effectively share both static and dynamic operational information (i.e., location, status quo, resources, and projections). Together, the common information requirement categories and the window report structure can contribute to more systematic and effective information sharing practices in multiagency emergency operations.

While our study has focused on common information requirements for handling extreme weather events, this also has relevance for other crisis scenarios. The "window report" structure would here serve as a template for which information categories need to be shared and with whom, in different types of crises. Further research is needed on how to integrate this mode of operation in the work practices of the organizations involved in the joint response and on developing technology support infrastructure that allows for effective and seamless information sharing.

Acknowledgments This study was made possible through the engaged participation of several emergency management stakeholders in Norway. The authors would like to thank all the informants for their time and assistance. The findings, arguments, and conclusions in this chapter are the result of the authors' understanding. The study was partly funded by a grant from the Research Council of Norway (the INSITU project, grant # 295848).

References

Ben Lazreg, M., Chakraborty, N. R., Stieglitz, S., Potthoff, T., Ross, B., & Majchrzak, T. A. (2018). Social media analysis in crisis situations: Can social media be a reliable information source for emergency management services? In *Proceedings of the 27th international conference on information systems development (ISD 2018), Sweden.*

Berggren, P., & Johansson, B. J. (2010). Developing an instrument for measuring shared understanding. In *Proceedings of the 7th international conference on information systems for crisis response and management, (ISCRAM 2010), USA.*

Berlin, J. M., & Carlström, E. D. (2014). Collaboration exercises - the lack of collaborative benefits. *International Journal of Disaster Risk Science, 5*(3), 192–205.

Bharosa, N., Lee, J., & Janssen, M. (2010). Challenges and obstacles in sharing and coordinating information during multi-agency disaster response: Propositions from field exercises. *Information Systems Frontiers, 12*(1), 49–65.

Borglund, E. A. (2017). The role of artefacts in creating a common operational picture during large crises. In *Proceedings of the 14th international conference on information systems for crisis response and management (ISCRAM 2017), France.*

Bunker, D., Levine, L., & Woody, C. (2015). Repertoires of collaboration for common operating pictures of disasters and extreme events. *Information Systems Frontiers, 17*(1), 51–65.

Cak, S., Say, B., & Misirlisoy, M. (2019). Effects of working memory, attention, and expertise on pilots' situation awareness. *Cognition, Technology & Work, 22*, 1–10.

Civil Protection Act. (2010). *The Act on Municipal Emergency Preparedness, Civil Protection Measures and the Civil Defense, LOV-2010-06-25-45.* Retrieved from https://lovdata.no/dokument/NL/lov/2010-06-25-45#KAPITTEL_5.

Comfort, L. (2007). Crisis management in hindsight: Cognition, communication, coordination, and control. *Public Administration Review, 67*, 189–197.

Dilo, A., & Zlatanova, S. (2011). A data model for operational and situational information in emergency response. *Applied Geomatics, 3*(4), 207–218.

Dreyer, K. (2019). *Innføring av Felles trippelvarslingsrutiner (Implementation of triple alert routines)*. Retrieved from https://kokom.no/innforing-av-felles-trippelvarslingsrutiner/

Endsley, M. R. (1995a). Toward a theory of situation awareness in dynamic systems. *Human Factors, 37*(1), 32–64.

Endsley, M. R. (1995b). A taxonomy of situation awareness errors. *Human Factors in Aviation Operations, 3*(2), 287–292.

Falkland, E. C., & Wiggins, M. W. (2019). Cross-task cue utilisation and situational awareness in simulated air traffic control. *Applied Ergonomics, 74*, 24–30.

Fredheim, H. (2017). *A new model for crisis management, OPSAM (Operation center for collaboration and preparedness). Final report from project on Concept for Holistic Crisis Management.* Oslo police, Oslo Municipality, Bærum Municipality, Asker Municipality and Oslo University Hospital.

Johansson, B. J., Hellgren, C., Oskarsson, P.-A., & Svensson, J. (2013). Supporting situation awareness on the move- the role of technology for spatial orientation in the field. In *Proceedings of the 10th international conference on information systems for crisis response and management (ISCRAM 2013), Germany.*

Kapucu, N. (2008). Collaborative emergency management: Better community organising, better public preparedness and response. *Disasters, 32*(2), 239–262.

Karagiannis, G. M., & Synolakis, C. E. (2016). Collaborative incident planning and the common operational picture. In *Proceedings of the international conference on dynamics of disasters* (pp. 91–112). Springer.

Laakso, K., & Palomäki, J. (2013). The importance of a common understanding in emergency management. *Technological Forecasting and Social Change, 80*(9), 1703–1713.

Lauria, M. J., Ghobrial, M. K., & Hicks, C. M. (2019). Force of habit: Developing situation awareness in critical care transport. *Air Medical Journal, 38*(1), 45–50.

Li, N., Yang, Z., Ghahramani, A., Becerik-Gerber, B., & Soibelman, L. (2014). Situational awareness for supporting building fire emergency response: Information needs, information sources, and implementation requirements. *Fire Safety Journal, 63*, 17–28.

Liang, S., & Gao, Y. (2010). Real-time notification and improved situational awareness in fire emergencies using geospatial-based publish/subscribe. *International Journal of Applied Earth Observation Geoinformation, 12*(6), 431–438.

Luokkala, P., Nikander, J., Korpi, J., Virrantaus, K., & Torkki, P. (2017). Developing a concept of a context-aware common operational picture. *Safety Science, 93*, 277–295.

Munkvold, B. E., Radianti, J., Rød, J. K., Opach, T., Snaprud, M., Pilemalm, S., & Bunker, D. (2019). Sharing incident and threat information for common situational understanding. In *Proceedings of the 16th international conference on information systems for crisis response and management (ISCRAM 2019), Spain.*

Norri-Sederholm, T., Joensuu, M., & Huhtinen, A.-M. (2017). Ensuring information flow and the situation picture in Public Safety Organisations' Situation Centres. In *Proceedings of the 16th European conference on cyber warfare and security (ECCWS 2017), Ireland.*

Opach, T., Rød, J. K., Munkvold, B. E., Radianti, J., Steen-Tveit, K., & Grottenberg, L. O. (2020). Map-based interfaces for common operational picture. In *Proceedings of the 17th international conference on information systems for crisis response and management (ISCRAM 2020), USA* (pp. 276–294).

Perla, P., Markowitz, M., Nofi, A., Weuve, C., Loughran, J., & Stahl, M. (2000). *Gaming and shared situation awareness*. The Defense Advanced Research Projects Agency, DARPA. Retrieved from: https://apps.dtic.mil/sti/pdfs/ADA390137.pdf.

QSR International. What is NVivo. Retrieved from https://www.qsrinternational.com/nvivo/what-is-nvivo

Regulation on municipal emergency duty. (2011). *Regulation on municipal emergency duty, FOR-2011-08-22-894*. Retrieved from https://lovdata.no/dokument/SF/forskrift/2011-08-22-894.

Schroeder, J. M., Manz, D. O., Amaya, J. P., McMakin, A. H., & Bays, R. M. (2018). Understanding past, current and future communication and situational awareness technologies for first responders. In *Proceedings of the fifth cybersecurity symposium, ID, USA.*

Seppänen, H., Mäkelä, J., Luokkala, P., & Virrantaus, K. (2013). Developing shared situational awareness for emergency management. *Safety Science, 55*, 1–9.

She, M., Li, Z., & Ma, L. (2019). User-defined information sharing for team situation awareness and teamwork. *Ergonomics, 62*, 1–41.

Solberg, S., Halvorsen, J., Urdal, A., Sørsdal, L., Aasgaard, M., Parnemann, O. P. and Eggertsson, Y. (2018) Handbook for search and rescue: System descriptions, principles and values, level 1,.

Sorensen, L. J., & Stanton, N. A. (2016). Keeping it together: The role of transactional situation awareness in team performance. *International Journal of Industrial Ergonomics, 53*, 267–273.

Steen-Tveit, K., & Munkvold, B. E. (2021). From common operational picture to common situational understanding: An analysis based on practitioner perspectives. *Safety Science, 142*, Article 105381.

Steigenberger, N. (2016). Organizing for the Big One: A review of case studies and a research agenda for multi-agency disaster response. *Journal of Contingencies and Crisis Management, 24*(2), 60–72.

Stott, P. (2016). How climate change affects extreme weather events. *Science, 352*(6293), 1517–1518.

Van den Homberg, M., Monné, R., & Spruit, M. (2018). Bridging the information gap of disaster responders by optimizing data selection using cost and quality. *Computers & Geosciences, 120*, 60–72.

Wolbers, J., & Boersma, K. (2013). The common operational picture as collective sensemaking. *Journal of Contingencies and Crisis Management, 21*(4), 186–199.

Part IV
CIMS Assessment, Evaluation, and Data Management

A Commercial Cloud-Based Crisis Information Management System: How Fit and Robust Is It in Response to a Catastrophe?

Beth M. Nolan and Hans Jochen Scholl

Abstract Professional disaster response management is supported by the so-called Crisis Information Management Systems (CIMS), which help capture, update, organize, share, and keep incident-relevant information, contribute to situational awareness, maintain a common operating picture, initiate and manage resource requests, assign tasks, and track progress among a host of other functionality needed in the coordination and direction of response units. One of the most widely proliferated CIMS is a commercial system known under its product name of WebEOC, which as the name indicates is a Web-based system. While WebEOC provides a large range of functionality, it has not been researched how robustly and appropriately this system fares when incidents of large scope, scale, and duration require the collaboration and coordination of multiple response agencies across both jurisdictional boundaries and different governmental levels. This study establishes technical and nontechnical challenges that WebEOC-supported responders face when responding to larger-magnitude incidents. The study confirms in some detail a previous congressional investigation on the subject. WebEOC appears to not scale effectively when used in multi-jurisdictional and multilevel settings, which introduces additional vulnerabilities to the response itself.

Keywords Crisis Information Management Systems (CIMS) · WebEOC · CIMS scalability and reliability

Introduction

For many years, first disaster and emergency responders in the United States as well as in other countries have been using WebEOC, a commercial and, as the product name suggests, Web-based commercial off-the-shelf system (COTS)

B. M. Nolan · H. J. Scholl (✉)
University of Washington, The Information School, Seattle, WA, USA
e-mail: bethmnol@uw.edu; jscholl@uw.edu

H. J. Scholl et al. (eds.), *Disaster Management and Information Technology*, Public Administration and Information Technology 40,
https://doi.org/10.1007/978-3-031-20939-0_15

crisis information management system (CIMS) to plan, organize, and manage their respective responses in the context of an Emergency Operations Center (EOC). WebEOC is seen by quite a few responders in the United States as the quintessential and undisputed de-facto standard, and some jurisdictions are promoting and even requiring the use of this particular COTS by local government partners. While any standardized system provides various identifiable and measurable advantages such as compatibility of messages, protocols, data, interfaces, and usages, a system built for and used by first responders across all hazards and incident sizes must be able to also scale over a large range of incidents from a small local event such as a single building afire to a major national catastrophe of the magnitude of Hurricane Katrina and even larger. With scale, scope, and duration (Fischer, 2003) of an incident increasing along all three of these dimensions, the response becomes more complex and exponentially more complicated. WebEOC has demonstrated its effectiveness and versatility in the response to smaller incidents and, in particular, when supporting a WebEOC-trained single incident management team (IMT) that is operating under the National Incident Management System/Incident Command System (NIMS/ICS) structure. However, larger incidents and less aligned command structures along with less WebEOC-trained response teams appear to present quite different challenges.

In this study, the informational, (inter-)operational, functional, and human actor-related scalability of WebEOC is investigated using the case of a large-scale exercise, which was conducted in June 2016 in the Pacific Northwest of the United States. The so-called Cascadia Rising 2016 exercise simulated a magnitude 9 megathrust of the 700-milelong Cascadia subduction zone (CSZ), which stretches some 70 miles offshore from Oregon to the Canadian province of British Columbia. CSZ megathrust ruptures have occurred in the past with a certain regularity every 320–360 years in this area, and the resulting earthquakes and subsequent tsunamis have devastated and reshaped the coastal zones of what is now Oregon, Washington State, and British Columbia. Unlike with the last occurrence of a CSZ megathrust in the evening of January 26, 1700, the affected areas are nowadays far more densely populated, which upon the next reoccurrence will predictably lead to greater loss of human life and property damage than during earlier incidents.

Response units on federal, state, county, and municipal levels in Idaho, Oregon, and Washington state engaged in the four-day exercise to test the level of preparedness and readiness for this particular response situation. The large-scale exercise involving 23,000 participants quickly surfaced what many first responders and public officials had anticipated. As the 2017 state's after action report (AAR) bluntly states with regard to Washington state's critical infrastructures and lifelines, "Cascadia Rising demonstrated that Washington is currently not a resilient state" (Anonymous, 2017, p. 5). And, with regard to response units' readiness, the report concluded that the "state's current planning framework and approach to disaster response is not suitable to a catastrophic-scale incident" (Anonymous, 2017, p. 6). The AAR also emphasized that a CSZ megathrust would create "an extreme response environment demanding state interagency activities well beyond current operational practice" (Anonymous, 2017, p. 5). Since incidents of this magnitude not only overwhelm local capabilities and capacities but rather also transgress multiple jurisdictional boundaries, the cross-jurisdictional coordination of response efforts is of the essence. Interagency activities on state, interstate, county, and local levels as well as with the federal level require coordination and communication infrastructures, of which WebEOC is an important part in quite a number of jurisdictions.

This research does not intend to provide a comprehensive functional and overall performance assessment of WebEOC; it rather focuses on information gathering, verification, and dissemination, most of which is organized via the so-called boards within WebEOC resembling electronic ledgers, which first responders access and populate with information to establish situational awareness and a common operating picture as a prerequisite to an effective and coordinated response effort. Nevertheless, this study arrives at the conclusion that WebEOC is not sufficiently scalable nor sufficiently interoperable on a large scale, for example, when used in responding to catastrophic incidents involving multiple and multilevel jurisdictions. While the study casts light on how over the years WebEOC slowly but surely grew into its current de-facto standard position without ever having been subjected to a formal scrutiny and evaluation of fitness for such immense mission scale, the authors understand that they enjoy the luxury of hindsight, and therefore they are reluctant to criticize federal, that is, FEMA, and state responders for their settling in favor of a tool that was available in times of need and at that time appeared to perform reasonably well in service for the so-called garden variety of incident responses. Beyond the lack of scalability and interoperability of WebEOC, the study identifies additional issues with depending on this particular commercial tool and rather proposes to develop and maintain as bedrock of disaster response management an open-source, twenty-first century technology-ready, and NIMS/ICS-conforming CIMS at national level, which can be downloaded, implemented, and used by any jurisdiction in the nation, ideally free of charge.

The second co-author was an ex ante exercise planner, active participant, and ex post results analyst, and partial findings were published before (Scholl et al., 2018). Further investigations were conducted into how some of the information and communication technology (ICT used interchangeably with IT)-related issues previously discovered could be further analyzed and addressed, in particular, with regard to the use of WebEOC. This latter part of the investigation was carried out by the first co-author at the city of Seattle's implementation of WebEOC at the Office of Emergency Management.

The manuscript is organized as follows: In the next section, related works in the academic literature and represented in government documents regarding WebEOC are reviewed. Then, research questions are presented, and the methodology is detailed. The findings are given for each research question before they are discussed in the next section. Concluding remarks and directions for future research are presented at the end.

Related Work

Context of WebEOC's Emergence as a De-Facto US Standard

With the Homeland Security Act of 2002 as legislative and administrative response to the 9/11 attacks, the federal government of the United States established the Department of Homeland Security (DHS) in late November of 2002, which for the purpose of better coordination and avoidance of unnecessary reduplication of efforts joined together multiple federal agencies chartered with various homeland security-related missions under one roof and at cabinet level (Thessin, 2003). Shortly after it was formed, the Federal Emergency Management Agency (FEMA) was also integrated into DHS, and exactly a year later the National Incident Command System (NIMS), which defines a standardized incident command structure and a set of practices, was also established (Anonymous, 2008). Interestingly, just prior to these major administrative adjustments and without the apparent involvement of FEMA, but rather "in response to numerous requests from state and local public safety agencies" (Hart, 2002, p. [ii]), the National Institute of Justice (NIJ) as a research arm of the Department of Justice (DOJ) had released a 50-page report on "Crisis Information Management Software (CIMS) Feature Comparison" (Hart, 2002). The "bulk of the research" was carried out by Camber Corporation of Huntsville, Alabama, a private defense contractor (Hart, 2002, p. [ii]). The feature comparison covered 27 "categories" and comprised a total of 106 "features."

The report emphasized that since the needs of states and other jurisdictions differed, the compared products would satisfy each agency's respective needs differently. The authors explicitly cautioned that there was "no best product" and "no perfect fit" (Hart, 2002, p. 8) but rather suggested that agencies in their decisions should consider the respective budgets, system environment, scale of operation, sophistication of operation, discipline to implement, and political considerations (Hart, 2002, p. 9). Consequently, rather than recommending any one system, the authors provided a downloadable spreadsheet containing an evaluation matrix covering the aforementioned categories and features, which agencies then could use for their individual evaluations. The report also explained that features might be of different weight, and it introduced a scale from 0 to 5, with "0—of no importance to the user whether or not the feature is provided, 1—possibly useful, 2—nice to have, 3—important, 4—very important, 5—extremely important" (Hart, 2002, p. 42), which users of the evaluation matrix would then input to tailor the evaluation criteria to their individual needs.

Among the ten systems, whose "features" were compared, WebEOC in its version 5.3 was included. While the report as pointed out refrained from providing any explicit recommendation for any particular product or vendor, it was noticeable that by a margin of 8.5% and a sum of 102 (of 106) of the reported unweighted scores, WebEOC was found the most "feature"-rich software product in the comparison, which may or may not have influenced decision-makers' perception in the aftermath.

However, while nothing was wrong with feature-oriented investigations like this one when used for an initial "environmental scan" and orientation of what was out there, no feature comparison test would allow for any final assessment of versatility and practical viability of any software system, which was not the stated purpose of the study, but it rather was produced in response to requests for guidance from numerous state and local jurisdictions.

Feature tests can neither substitute for real-world performance tests nor for real-world use tests, nor for system and network load and stress tests, and it must be remembered to keep the perspective; for a study in 2002, incidents of the magnitude of Hurricanes Katrina (2005), Sandy (2012), Maria (2017), and the Covid-19 pandemic (2020–2021) affecting multiple states and territories were not among the then considered "normal" scale, scope, and duration parameters of a disaster yet.

However, a few assessments in the 2002 NIJ report still perplex the later reader, for example, remarks found in the summary of WebEOC 5.3 reading "Easy to use, WebEOC Users are often trained in under 15 minutes" (Hart, 2002, p. 32) along with granting full credit for feature-related questions such as "Is the interface user friendly?" (Hart, 2002, p. 34); whereas later AARs, for example, the CR16 City of Seattle AAR [ref] reported that only 28% of respondents were able to gain "situational awareness" from the system, and 51.4% of respondents requested more training for using WebEOC, although the city had required and provided specific WebEOC training to all exercise participants shortly before the exercise was conducted. Furthermore, WebEOC 5.3 received full credit on questions for features such as "Does the server application software support and provide robust performance in a multi-site, mid-tier user environment? (Hart, 2002, p. 34). From practical real-world performance reports of even higher versions of WebEOC (Scholl et al., 2018), it is unclear how the 2002 investigators could have ever arrived at these particular conclusions. Also, with regard to secure network operations, the report appears to assess WebEOC's 2002 readiness fairly optimistically, to say the least, and even more so, since the investigators found out by themselves that the product was unable to identify and alert for any suspicious activity.

After the 9/11 attacks of 2001, disaster responses in the United States have been typically organized along the principles and practices as defined in the National Incident Management System (NIMS) with the Incident Command System as one of its important core building blocks (Anonymous, 2008). As the 2008 core document explicitly states, "NIMS is not an operational incident management or resource allocation plan. NIMS represents a core set of doctrines, concepts, principles, terminology, and organizational processes that enables effective, efficient, and collaborative incident management" (Anonymous, 2008, p. 3). It is deliberately designed for scaling relative to the magnitude of an incident and the type of the hazard. In order to establish and maintain a unified command, multiagency coordination systems are formed, which "includes a combination of facilities, equipment, personnel, and procedures integrated into a common system with responsibility for coordination of resources and support to emergency operations" (Anonymous, 2008, p. 65). The larger the scale, scope, and duration of an incident, the more vertical and horizontal communication and coordination are needed. The

NIMS architects and planners clearly foresaw that interoperability of systems, their reliability, scalability, and portability would be key with regard to communication and information management:

> It is essential that these communications systems be capable of interoperability, as successful emergency management and incident response operations require the continuous flow of critical information among jurisdictions, disciplines, organizations, and agencies...
>
> Communications and information systems should be designed to be flexible, reliable, and scalable in order to function in any type of incident, regardless of cause, size, location, or complexity. They should be suitable for operations within a single jurisdiction or agency, a single jurisdiction with multiagency involvement, or multiple jurisdictions with multiagency involvement. Communications systems should be applicable and acceptable to users, readily adaptable to new technology, and reliable in the context of any incident to which emergency management/response personnel would be expected to respond (Anonymous, 2008, p. 24).

All that notwithstanding, in the first decade of the twenty-first century, a number of states and other jurisdictions appear to have gone ahead and gradually settled on implementing and using WebEOC as their premier emergency management platform. However, it was not before August of 2012 that FEMA finally jumped on the WebEOC bandwagon and established this particular COTS for their own operations (Kelly, 2014, p. 6).

In order to meet the specified requirements outlined above starting in 2005, the "Standards and Technology Branch" of the National Integration Center within FEMA launched an initiative under the title "National Incident Management System Supporting Technology Evaluation Program (NIMS STEP)," which promoted data and networking standards for commercial incident management products to become compatible with the concepts of NIMS (Anonymous, 2010b, p. E1). In September of 2010, the program published a detailed guide, which made the test procedures and application requirements transparent to COTS vendors (Anonymous, 2010b). COTS vendors were invited to have their systems tested and quasi certified, and quite a number of emergency management systems have gone through this assessment and testing process.

In parallel, the DHS "System Assessment and Validation for Emergency Responders" (SAVER) program also published an "Incident Decision Support Software Application Note" (Anonymous, 2010a), which again cited the system selection criteria of the aforementioned 2002 NIJ report and acknowledged the work of the NIMS STEP initiative. One would expect that a system of the importance of WebEOC would have gone through the STEP evaluation; however, for reasons unknown such report is not findable, and the nimsstep.net website along with the Responder Knowledge Base website (rkb.us), which at one point in time contained 777 test reports, had been taken off the Web for good. Furthermore, the STEP initiative itself, which had meanwhile been brought under the purview of FEMA's Preparedness-Technology, Analysis, and Coordination (P-TAC) Center, was apparently ended somewhat abruptly but without much fuss in September of 2013 (Anonymous, 2015, p. 17).

While it is unclear what led to the program's termination, a couple of years earlier, FEMA had come under heavy scrutiny and harsh criticism regarding its information technology strategy and practices. The Information Technology Audits Unit of DHS submitted a devastating assessment of the agency's information technology readiness, which bluntly stated that "existing information technology systems do not support disaster response activities effectively," that the agency was "challenged to establish an effective approach to modernize its information technology infrastructure and systems" and also "does not have a complete, documented inventory of its systems to support disasters." Furthermore, "program and field offices continue to develop information technology systems independently of the office and have been slow to adopt the agency's standard information technology development approach," and moreover, "systems are not integrated, do not meet user requirements, and do not provide the information technology capabilities agency personnel and its external partners need to carry out disaster response and recovery operations in a timely or effective manner" (Deffer, 2011, p. 1). Four years later, the follow-up audit report stated that "FEMA has struggled to implement effective agency-wide IT governance," and its "IT environment has evolved over time to become overly complex, difficult to secure, and costly to maintain." Furthermore, the report found that the agency's IT systems were "not sufficiently integrated" and did "not provide personnel with the data search and reporting tools they need," and finally as a result, end users engaged "in inefficient, time-consuming business practices" (McCauley, 2015, p. 24).

Interestingly, this update report already elaborated on WebEOC, which as mentioned above was introduced into agency-wide FEMA operations only 3 years earlier, which in turn was anteceded by the highly critical 2011 audit of FEMA IT operations. It though came to the conclusion that just like other applications, FEMA WebEOC was "not integrated with the WebEOC used by state emergency operation centers" and stated that "FEMA regions rely on an inefficient manual process to update the FEMA WebEOC with information from the state centers about ongoing disasters." The report then summarized that this process could "cause delays in providing disaster assistance" (McCauley, 2015, p. 22). This observation is in line with the abovementioned 2014 report of the DHS Inspector General, in which it was stated that the WebEOC implementation had presented serious challenges to FEMA in terms of lack of functional and use training and by the "absence of apparent policies and procedures" along with integration problems and "duplication with active redundant systems" (Kelly, 2014, pp. 6–7). In stark contrast, in a presentation in the fall of 2014 on "FEMA's Capability Development After Katrina," FEMA's Office of Response and Recovery director of operations maintained that "WebEOC was [the ~ insertion by authors] correct choice for FEMA's Crisis Management System," that the system was "intuitive" and "new features or changes" could be learned "within minutes," and that "19 other Federal Departments and Agencies, 40 States, hundreds of cities/counties" also used WebEOC for emergency management (Farmer, 2014, slide 18).

At one point along the way though, FEMA must have decided that for security reasons, it was too risky and unsafe to directly connect FEMA WebEOC with the state, territory, and tribal WebEOC sites, which in the aftermath created a considerable dilemma for response coordination between states and FEMA (Scholl et al., 2018). As a workaround, FEMA "had provided every state with FEMA WebEOC accounts, so state users could submit resource requests directly to FEMA" (Spicer et al., 2019, p. 14), and in cases when this would not work, the requests and exchanges would be presented on paper and manually inputted by FEMA personnel in a time-consuming and error-prone fashion. Without particularly mentioning WebEOC again, the audit criticized FEMA's overall approach to building the agency's information technology infrastructure by stating, "FEMA developed systems without adequate business cases or adherence to systems development life cycle guidance. Consequently, systems were developed in silos without attention to overlap, duplication, or the need for integration with other systems" (McCauley, 2015, p. 22).

The FEMA administrator concurred with every single recommendation made in the audit by the DHS Office of Inspector General, however, the responses remained remarkably vague (McCauley, 2015, p.22). Two years later on July of 2017, in an accompanying report to the DHS Appropriations Bill (H.R. 5634), the Committee of Appropriations stated in no uncertain language, "FEMA's Emergency Operations Center (EOC) is not electronically interconnected with state EOCs, relying instead on an inefficient manual process that can cause delays in providing disaster assistance. The Committee expects FEMA to implement policies, procedures, and activities necessary to improve interconnectedness between FEMA and state EOCs, and directs FEMA to report on its progress not later than 180 days after the date of enactment of this Act" (Carter, 2017, p. 67).

On May 29, 2018, during his short 19-month tenure at the federal agency, the then FEMA administrator, Brock Long, formally responded on behalf of FEMA to the congressional request (Long, 2018). The response reemphasized the practice of providing the state, territory, and tribe EOCs only with FEMA WebEOC accounts rather than directly connecting these jurisdictions' WebEOC and non-WebEOC systems to the FEMA WebEOC systems. The report argued that "system interconnections with every state/territory to WebEOC would be costly, complex, and would increase FEMA's exposer [sic!] to cybersecurity risk significantly" (Long, 2018, p. ii). Building and maintaining such "seamless and secure connectivity to the state/territory systems... would cost approximately $3 million annually and would increase FEMA's vulnerability to security risks" (Long, 2018, p. 4). And, in conclusion, downplaying the redundancy, extra work, and error proneness of this much-criticized arrangement, FEMA argued that "[c]ybersecurity threats and cost make interconnectivity between WebEOC and all state EOCs impractical, considering the marginal gains that interconnectivity would achieve" (Long, 2018, p. 6). In other words, contrary to the NIMS principles for communication and information management and also in opposition to its own initial concurrence regarding the identified problems, in 2018 FEMA took a 180-degree turn on its position and course and rather rebuffed and outright ignored the requests from both the DHS Inspector General and the House Committee of Appropriations.

While it was not explicitly mentioned, the 2015 McCauley report appeared to have included WebEOC in the assessment that FEMA's information systems landscape had emerged in an ad-hoc fashion without proper case evaluation and long-term planning of scalability and security requirements. Before this backdrop, the reported interoperability and security problems are unsurprising.

Academic Literature on the Uses and Effectiveness of WebEOC

So far, academic scrutiny into the use and effectiveness of ICTs in disaster response management, in general, and of WebEOC, in particular, has not yet created a full plate of reports that would help better understand particular needs, effective practices, and specific technological and other challenges relative to the scope, scale, and duration of a given disaster. The ten-scale categorization scheme of disaster response scenarios, the so-called Fischer Scale, provides a handle for studying the various response needs in terms of inflicted disruption and degree of necessary adjustment along increasing scale, scope, and duration of a given disaster (Fischer, 2003). The Fischer Scale distinguishes, for example, a DC-1 category incident (everyday emergency, such as a single residential home afire), from a DC-4 category incident (massive disruption in a town, such as the November 2018 wildfire that consumed major parts of the township of Paradise, CA, with 85 civilian deaths and 11,000 homes burned to the ground), from a DC-7 category incident (partial disruption and adjustment in a large city, for example, the 9/11 attacks on New York City), and from a DC-10 category incident (a simultaneous massive disruption and adjustment on society level, for example, after a massive and widespread nuclear attack from a foreign enemy). Please note that the other categories not enumerated here all define gradually increasing scopes, scales, and durations of disasters between those mentioned above.

It is intuitively clear that the management of responses of lower categories involves fewer complexities than the one of higher categories on the Fischer Scale. However, this has immediate consequences also regarding the potential task fitness and purpose-related effectiveness of ICTs relative to the category of the disaster. What may work very well in less complexity-prone categories such as DC-1 to DC-3 may not work well for more complex categories such as DC-4 to DC-6, and vice versa, let alone the even higher categories. Both vertical and horizontal intra- and interagency coordination are "at the very heart of effective and efficient disaster management" and while for various reasons the pre-networked ICT status of coordination was suboptimal, expecting from technology to overcome these barriers might be naïve and actually exacerbate the situation, for example, in terms of information overload (Quarantelli, 1997, p. 101). As early as 1976, Turner had already observed that the larger a disaster response becomes organizationally, the larger the number of messages and with it the opportunity for communication breakdowns (Turner, 1976, p. 394). However, for higher disaster categories, more interagency coordination and collaboration is required, which heavily relies on "the ability of these information systems to communicate, to exchange information, to share services and to coordinate their behaviors" (Truptil et al., 2008, p. 584). Unfortunately, so far, case studies on the uses and the effectiveness of ICTs in disaster response do not make the critically important distinctions à la Fischer regarding scale, scope, and duration. Most studies rather present cases of lower disaster categories, which may have little, if any, significance for higher disaster categories.

When it comes to WebEOC-specific studies, academic reports show fairly mixed results regarding ease of use, functionality, and effectiveness. An older study on a county's use of WebEOC during a relief and support mission for supporting the response to an earthquake in a neighboring overseas country lauded the COTS's flexibility to create boards interactively as needed, which then could be accessed via the Web from any place where and when needed including granting response partners access to the system (Nikolai et al., 2010). The study also reported that responders familiarized themselves quickly with the functionality and operated it without any problems. The report, however, also found that responders experienced that some information was hard to find in WebEOC, the integration with geographical information systems was missing, and the installation had no protection against system failure via backup systems (Nikolai et al., 2010). While this relief and support mission was part of a response to an earthquake, which had all characteristics of a DC-9 category incident on the ground, the response coordination itself was more similar to an incident in a DC-2 or DC-3 category. A study conducted 8 years later still reported that first responders had difficulty finding relevant information inside WebEOC, for example, regarding requests, which then required the use of additional information channels (phone or face-to-face) in order to get to the correct information or to the request followed up upon (Aros & Gibbons, 2018, p. 70). Yet, another study found that certain definitions such as "significant event" varied between different versions of WebEOCs making tracking across various implementation impossible (Ganji et al., 2019). As a study conducted in Western Australia documented, some of these known problems appear to have been addressed to some extent by a better interconnected and networked version of WebEOC referred to as WebFusion, which allowed the managing of state incidents, state activities, and situation reports so that all responding state agencies could maintain a high-level overview of the response (Hanson & McDougall, 2018). However, in the state of Queensland, Australia, WebEOC-based sharing of information was not as easily negotiated and only partially established among participating agencies (Whelan & Molnar, 2018, p. 96).

With the aim of better private-public response collaboration, business communities implemented WebEOC portals in Hawaii and Louisiana that integrated to some degree with governmental EOCs that used the same COTS (Levy & Prizzia, 2018a, b). Another study used WebEOC logs for ex-post spatial and cluster analyses of civic participation (Jung, 2018). Interestingly, a Japanese study stated that WebEOC was introduced in Japanese EOCs mainly on grounds that it had been adopted by "most states in U.S.A." (Inoguchi et al., 2014, p. 396), in other words, if the COTS was already used all over the United States, it ought to be good enough for Japan, which presents an interesting conclusion. The National Disaster Organizations of the Caribbean were somewhat less enthusiastic, stating, "several expressed concern or uncertainty about certain aspects of the implementation, particularly with regard to security of the remotely stored data, and reliability of access during emergencies" (Levius et al., 2017, p. 110). Another comparative study on various CIMS found WebEOC lacking in functionality when it came to (automatic) document summarization and information recommendation (Li et al., 2017). One of WebEOC's characteristic features is its customizability (Misra et al., 2020), which in part may explain the wide variety of experiences reported in the studies referenced above. The study reports that the tool (WebEOC) tended to shape the response process rather than the response process shaped the use of the tool (Misra et al., 2020, p. 10).

Academic research had been foundational to establishing the principles for communication and information management as laid out in the NIMS core document of 2008 (Anonymous, 2008, p. 24). In 2004, Turoff and friends had formulated the main requirements for what they had called a "dynamic emergency response management information system (DERMIS)" (Turoff et al., 2004b): A DERMIS has to (a) be "extremely easy to learn via training and exercises because it is consistent with the task requirements," (b) be "useable by people who will have an understanding of their roles and responsibilities in an emergency environment," (c) "focus on a concise and self-evident design demanded by the small screen orientation and the need to minimize learning," (d) "allow the individual users a high degree of tailoring, filtering, and focusing of the interface tailored to their specific roles and responsibilities," (e) "serve to support planning, evaluation, training, exercises, and system updating and maintenance between crisis events," (f) "allow the operation of the response function without the need for a single operational physical center except for the operation and backups for the computer hardware and software acting as a server and distributed resource databases for this operation," and (g) "be designed as a structured communication process independent of the nature of a particular crisis" (Turoff et al., 2004b, p. 12). In a follow-up contribution, the authors emphasized the need for ICT systems integration across databases, document systems, and communication systems in order to attain the flexibility necessary for responding to any size and any kind of incidents. They explicitly warned that "[i]f these are different incompatible systems, it will represent a huge waste of resources and opportunity. What would be worse is if they were inconsistent and actually produced conflicts and uncertainties that could very well confound a crisis. Inconsistencies in processes, policies, and technologies that exist across different organizations seem to be one of the causes of many major response problems in recent events" (Turoff et al., 2004a, p. 19).

While foundational requirements for disaster ICT systems in technical terms comprise interoperability, flexibility, reliability, scalability, and portability, such systems become most effective once they support what some authors have called the "human infrastructures" (Robinson et al., 2015). Across agencies and jurisdictions, responders' interpersonal familiarity, mutual trust, confidence, expertise, and capabilities, the capacity of collaboration and the proven track record thereof were found key elements of successful and effective collaboration in large-scale responses and exercises (Robinson et al., 2015). The "human infrastructure" perspective closely relates to and ties in with the aforementioned "information perspective" and the notion of information infrastructures relating to human actors' information needs, information behaviors, and inter-actor information flows, which guided this study as outlined below (Scholl & Chatfield, 2014; Scholl & Patin, 2014).

In summary, the academic literature had helped develop the principles and requirements for disaster response ICT systems, which the NIMS core document echoed. The academic literature on the uses and effectiveness of WebEOC as a lynchpin tool for first responders presents a mixed picture, in which the effectiveness and functionality appear to be more sufficient for lower categories on the Fischer Scale than for categories higher than DC-3.

Research Questions

Based on the identified problems in the various bodies of related work presented above regarding the uses, functionality, and effectiveness of WebEOC, this study set out to produce insights regarding the following two research questions:

Research Question #1 (RQ#1): What are specific challenges regarding the *uses, functionality,* and *effectiveness of WebEOC* in response scenarios of higher Fischer Scale categories (requiring simultaneous coordination of multiple agencies, multiple jurisdictions, and multiple levels of government)?

Research Question #2 (RQ#2): What are architectural, informational, and scalability-related limitations of WebEOC in the context of response scenarios of higher Fischer Scale categories?

Methodology

Theoretical Lens

As an important element of responders' information infrastructure, WebEOC emerged as an object of this study, although not exclusively, along with other elements of these information infrastructures, which helped assume situational awareness and managerial coordination and interagency collaboration. The "information perspective" as a theoretical lens regarding any given socio-technical phenomenon views information and communication technologies (ICTs) as facilitators of human information needs, information behaviors, and information flows. Human actors', in this case, the responders', information behavior and the information flows between them depend on formal and informal, organizational, technological, and social elements among others forming these "information infrastructures" (Scholl & Chatfield, 2014; Scholl & Patin, 2014). In disaster management, when looking at the technological elements, ICTs such as WebEOC have assumed important roles as building blocks of information infrastructures (Chua et al., 2007; Kapucu, 2006) by providing high-quality, mission-critical, timely, and actionable information to responders in typically fast and dynamically changing environments (Kapucu, 2006; Kapucu et al., 2010; Turoff, 2007). On the downside, ICTs such as WebEOC have also been found contributing to information overload, work overload, and other stressors to responders in disaster responses (Endsley, 2015; Quarantelli, 1997). As a consequence, rather than in terms of a technical feature-for-feature evaluation, in this study WebEOC has been viewed in the context of existing and emerging information infrastructures as an element and building block during a simulated response, and in a follow-up investigation in terms of the needs for specific information, which first responders regularly seek during a response to a major disaster.

Instrument and Coding Scheme

Based on the theoretical lens, that is, the conceptual framework of resilient information infrastructures (RIIs) (Scholl & Patin, 2014) a semi-structured interview protocol was devised upfront, which covered five topical areas of (1) management and organization, (2) technology, (3) information, (4) information infrastructure, and (5) RIIs/resiliency. The instrument administered was a shortened and adjusted version of the instrument used in a previous study (Scholl et al., 2017; Scholl & Carnes, 2017). A total of 25 interview questions plus respective probes were incorporated.

Sample

The sample was purposive (Ritchie et al., 2003) and included responders from eight different groups: the (1) City Emergency Operations Centers, (2) County Emergency Operations Centers, (3) Washington State Emergency Management Division, (4) WA State Agencies, (5) Health Districts, (6) Regional Aviation, (7) Washington State National Guard, and (8) Federal Emergency Management Agency (FEMA), region X. A total of 17 individuals were interviewed. Furthermore, after action reports (AARs) from 23 agencies from all 8 responder groups were collected and analyzed.

Data Collection

Interviews were conducted in person between September 2016 and March 2017 and lasted between 33 and 107 min. Two interviews were conducted via Skype videoconferencing. All interviews were audiotaped, transcribed, and coded for analysis by at least two coders. During the interview, notes were also taken, and participant interaction was observed and recorded. Moreover, besides the 23 after action reports, other documents such as press interviews were collected, reviewed, and coded as appropriate.

Data Analysis and Coding

The initial codebook, which was based on the aforementioned conceptual RII framework, contained 6 category codes (1 for each topical area) and 141 subcategory codes. Additional codes were inductively introduced during data collection, in individual coding sessions, and inter-coder sessions (Glaser, 1999; Glaser & Strauss, 1967; Strauss & Corbin, 1998; Urquhart et al., 2010). Since a codebook in a hybrid approach of deductive and inductive analyses (Fereday & Muir-Cochrane, 2006) is designed to be open to extension, it ultimately encompassed 176 subcategory codes in the 6 main categories.

At least two researchers coded each transcript and document by means of a cloud-based software tool for qualitative and mixed-method data analyses (Dedoose main versions 7 and 8, dedoose.com). The coded data were compared one by one and demonstrated high inter-coder reliability.

When analyzing the code frequency table, "technology" as a main cluster code produced 1111 occurrences and 5135 co-occurrences with other codes in 1771 excerpts. As a sub-code in the "technology" code cluster, the code "WebEOC" produced 68 occurrences in 65 excerpts; however, the sub-code also produced 725 co-occurrences with other sub-codes and codes in a total of 266 excerpts, which has served as the main basis for this analysis.

For the most part, these excerpts were between two and three paragraphs in length. They were clustered by responder teams and then analyzed for emerging concepts in a grounded fashion. Recurring concepts and main themes were identified and labeled through keywords and key phrases. All excerpt clusters were concept analyzed by at least two analysts, in most cases by three analysts, as well as by the principal investigator. The coded concepts were checked for inter-analyst validity and a convergence of interpretation was found. Converging concepts were identified and transferred to the "canvas" of a cloud-based mapping tool (CMAP, version 6.03). After reconciling the remaining inter-analyst discrepancies in interpretation as much as appropriate, the reconciled concepts were also transferred to the canvas. The concept clusters were inspected and sorted into topical "bins" or "buckets," in which chronological, logical, and other noncausal relationships were identified. Whenever evidence from the data supported it, relationship links between concepts were established, which were not interpreted as causal links.

Research Team and Processes

The research team consisted of the principal investigator (PI) and 32 research assistants (RAs), both for-credit and voluntary. The PI and RAs worked individually and in small teams to transcribe, code, and conceptually/contextually analyze, and map the concepts. The research team met weekly in person or online and communicated via the research project site and the project listserv as well as via individual face-to-face and group meetings. All weekly meetings were streamed and recorded, which kept the whole research team in sync over extended periods of time.

Follow-Up Investigation

Based on the results from the first phase of this study, a follow-up study (phase 2) was conducted, which purposefully focused on one of the longest maintained and most advanced implementations of WebEOC in the Pacific Northwest at the city of Seattle's Emergency Operations Center. The city's EOC had been a major participant in the CR16 exercise and has also been known for its record of support and collaboration with neighboring jurisdictions on all levels. Before this background, the phase-2 study intended to find out how data and information collected in WebEOC in the course of a response could be sifted, consolidated, and used for intelligence in ways not available through the standard implementation of the COTS. The follow-up investigation was carried out in fall of 2019 and early 2020. As had surfaced in both the literature and in the first phase of this study, responders found it hard to pull together information from within WebEOC. The phase-2 investigation particularly focused on the potential of data analytics and business intelligence capabilities of WebEOC and on how the reported informational problems could be addressed. This particular part of the study was carried out by the first author.

Findings

Ad Research Question #1 (RQ#1)

"What are specific challenges regarding the uses, functionality, and effectiveness of WebEOC in response scenarios of higher Fischer Scale categories (requiring simultaneous coordination of multiple agencies, multiple jurisdictions, and multiple levels of government)?"

Challenges Regarding *WebEOC Uses* During CR16

Agencies used WebEOC for logging responders' presence/absence (i.e., reporting to duty), task assignment and tracking, as well as information gathering, storing, and sharing. An important part of the information gathering task was the creation of damage reports and the respective updates of the infrastructure status. Agencies also relied on the product for resource requesting and resource tracking, shelter management, as well as for scheduling meetings and for creating situation reports.

WebEOC allows for quite some flexibility in how a responder organization sets up and organizes the areas of use. While this tailoring of the product via parameter and component configuration allows for a good fit for intra-jurisdictional operations, the variability of individual implementations appears to become more of a liability once vertical and horizontal actions need to be taken. What works reasonably well, in the case of a smaller incident of types DC-2 and DC-3 inside a jurisdiction, appears to be more challenging when it comes to inter-jurisdictional coordination of action organized through WebEOC. But even inside the same organization, the configuration of "boards," which serve as important organizational components inside WebEOC for a range of tasks and purposes, if changed on the fly or not kept consistent with previous configurations, can create serious challenges. As one state agency reported,

> The Task Manager Board on WebEOC disappeared prior to the exercise and was not able to be utilized. This board is used to track internal resource requests and assignments. The inability to use this board led to the inability to consistently track this information. (Quote #01)

And, furthermore, as a result of this reconfiguration of WebEOC,

> Throughout the exercise information was posted on the wrong boards on WebEOC. For example, road and bridge closures were being documented in the Activity Log rather than the road and bridge closure tabs in the WSDOT Infrastructure Board. (Quote #02)

In particular, if other state agencies and outside EOCs on county and city levels are given access to state EOCs, changes in configuration can lead to tremendous consistency and information tracking problems.

But other use challenges emerged also due to inconsistent organizational and configurational setups of WebEOC. While the flow of information and request of resources follows a hierarchical path from the local or municipal level through the county level to the state level (and vice versa), some larger municipalities such as cities can directly interact with the state level, for which these so-called tier-I and tier-II jurisdictions can use an account of their own at the state WebEOC. However, again, this organizational setup did not appear to be completely and correctly understood on all sides. As one city responder explained,

> We have been told that if we want to order anything, we have to put it in Web EOC to the Resource Tracker, which we did. And we taught our people how to do it. And then I started questioning why we didn't get, it's been assigned, or what's not coming. And so, I called the State, and I said, "What's going on?" And they said, "Well, we don't get anything from you". "And I said, "Why are you not getting anything from us?" Well, you have to go to the

> County and then the County sends it to us. I said, "You and the County don't talk to each other. How is it going to get to you?" And so, by law, we're entitled to go directly to the State, but the State prefers to work with the County, so all of our resource requests went into a black hole, and nobody addressed them. (Quote #03)

In the absence of consistency of uses across WebEOC implementations and with widely varying WebEOC configurations, it appears that reduplication of work has occurred in quite a number of jurisdictions. As one city official shared,

> If we constantly create things that work best for us internally, and then create another workload to make it for the county level and for the state level, make it functional for them, I see that us as a hindrance actually. Because it gives me double duties that I don't have time for. We haven't used anything other than WebEOC. (Quote #04)

The same responder also echoed what others had said when mentioning the monitoring of several WebEOC accounts (own, county, and state) simultaneously, which as stated created not only an extra burden but also confusion.

In summary, WebEOC supports many important use cases that matter to first responders. However, when the magnitude of the incident transcends multiple jurisdictional boundaries, the flexibility and configurability of the COTS fosters organizational inconsistencies, which lead to numerous complications. The fact that lower-level jurisdictions are requested to operate WebEOC accounts at the next higher one or two governmental levels complicates matters for first responders at all levels and highlights that organizational interoperability at system level is not attained.

Challenges Regarding *WebEOC Functionality* During CR16

While the 2002 technical feature study (Hart, 2002) touched on several functional areas important in first response situations such as "user friendliness" in terms of interface and operations, incident and event logging, planning, operations, and resource management, it appears that the testers had worked on the assumption of the "regular case" of responses in the DC-1 to DC-4 categories of emergencies, since functionalities, which would support complex inter-jurisdictional coordination and unified command as typical in large-scope, large-scale, and long-duration incidents, were not included in the feature list. Over the years, WebEOC has gone through a number of revisions, which among other areas improved the user experience by means of a more intuitive graphical user interface (GUI). However, the COTS's basic "board"-based architecture, which logs every entry in a sequential fashion, did not change. As a result, in DC-7+ incidents, the WebEOC nodes on the respective next higher governmental level become inundated with information, which makes the receiving end practically unable to cope with the overall information load. While the official FEMA after action report suggested that the cascading access of lower-level jurisdictions to the higher-level jurisdictions' WebEOC systems "provided external partners visibility on the latest operational updates," in reality the situation presented itself differently. As one FEMA official bluntly put it, WebEOC

> doesn't meet the need for what we need for Cascadia. It was very clear, they've made some enhancements, over the years. You know, bumped up how quickly it can respond to users in the system, made it the end user ease of state, ease of use for the interface much better, but the reality is that you have so much information so many resources coming in, and if you were to take that for just one state, you know, it's overwhelming in itself, but if you start multiplying that for Washington, Oregon, then Idaho has an indirect impact, right, because people are starting to migrate that way, the system quickly becomes overwhelmed. (Quote #05)

While the downlinks might have worked to some extent, the respective uplinks certainly did not, and jurisdictions were taken by surprise, as a director of a County Emergency Management Department remarked,

> I think what we didn't expect, there were the State experienced issues with WebEOC. WebEOC, the technical term I think is, 'crashed'. So, we did not expect that to happen. (Quote #06)

However, one manager at a major city EOC presented a rationale for the widespread WebEOC system slowdown, overrun, and even outright crashing, from which it did not recover, by sharing:

> We just had too many, you know, there are 21 counties out of 39, and 18 EOCs open–at the county level and some of the city EOCs open–making requests. It just brought it to its knees (Quote #07)

Some counties were never able to establish a connection to the state WebEOC when they tried to place requests on the state's Resource Tracker system. As another county responder put it:

> The State was too overwhelmed with what they were doing. But at the same time, they didn't practice that or simulate what that interaction would look like during that exercise. (Quote #08)

And a senior executive at the State's Emergency Management Division conceded that using the WebEOC-typical boards such as the activity boards in various sections (operations, planning, logistics, finance, and admin) in sequential and chronological fashion would make things rather complicate, when he described that WebEOC

> would basically allow you to chronologically track events. But, that in itself is not helpful in sharing information, sharing situational awareness, or sharing a common operating picture, because I do not want to have to read through a thread of 200 events from the previous shift to get an idea of what the current situation is. (Quote #09)

Besides WebEOC other information systems, for example, specialized and professional-grade geographic information systems (GIS) such as ArcGIS were in widespread use among first response organizations. Although WebEOC had its own mapping component, the integration and interoperation with professional-grade GIS was lacking, which led to a number of complications and duplications of efforts. As the FEMA AAR states critically (also referring to incompatibilities of WebEOC versions and configurations):

> different versions, configurations, and implementations of these systems introduced varying functionality, a lack of compatibility, and different interfaces for the user, all of which lead to varying representations of incidents, tasks, resource requests, and related data. As a result,

> the exchange of information between systems of different versions and functionality became a cumbersome task. (Quote #10)

In summary, from a functional perspective, while WebEOC supported many, if not most, basic response tasks and activities, it did so in ways that suit smaller responses better than larger and more complex responses. While in a smaller-scope, smaller-scale, and shorter-duration response the sifting through and manual scanning of sequential log files and boards may be practical, in larger and more complex responses the absence of sophisticated and automated filtering, sorting, and aggregating tools is a functional lack. Most importantly, for larger incident responses, the foundational functionalities of a backbone response system include high-load and high-demand resiliency, compatibility, and interoperability (among WebEOC implementations and with professional-grade special function systems such as ArcGIS). WebEOC apparently misses out on these foundational functionalities.

Challenges Regarding *WebEOC Effectiveness* During CR16

Before the backdrop of the aforementioned challenges in uses and functionalities of WebEOC, in part the challenges in effectiveness of WebEOC for larger incident responses must be seen as results of the former. Other parts may be related to organizational rigidities and statutory requirements, which, however, are not alleviated by using WebEOC. A case in point is the resource request process in a disaster. While much of the focus in any response lies on the operations and planning efforts, which the public perception of a disaster response only amplifies, far less visibly the logistics and financial efforts play equally important roles for effective and successful responses. Disaster responses are multimillion and even billion-dollar expenditures of taxpayer monies, for which meticulous accountability is mandated by laws and statutes. Resource requesting, therefore, is a nontrivial undertaking: on the one hand, the response has to be swift and correctly targeted; on the other hand, the requested resources need to be requested, approved, and appropriated in a timely fashion without compromising scrutiny and accountability. Responders, hence, need tools that serve equally well both parts of the equation. If any tool in an incident response becomes the bottleneck in one way or another, the entire effort can be seriously hampered. In 2014 during the response to the Oso/SR530 landslide disaster, Washington state and FEMA region X had previously experienced the resource request problematic in the context of WebEOC (Scholl & Carnes, 2017). Back then the Oso/SR530 landslide had been declared a national disaster by the president. It was rated between DC-4 and DC-5 on the Fischer Scale. The response involved a total of 119 agencies from all levels of government, and it reached a degree of complexity, which already gave responders at all levels a clear view of what might happen, once incidents of an even larger magnitude were at hand (Scholl et al., 2017; Scholl & Carnes, 2017). As a lesson learned, Washington state then standardized the resource request procedure and its related forms (Lombardo et al., 2014). However, as seen in the previous section, despite these improvements the backbone system (WebEOC) would not carry the load. Reflecting on the CR16 exercise experience, a FEMA official bluntly shared her observations regarding the current resource request mechanisms:

> Knock on wood we don't have a lot of disaster in this area that require our emergency operations to stand up and to work through a lot of these resource requests. For example, the Oso landslide, when that happened, I was part of that response. In the EOC was a very small group but even that as an event, which if you look from a federal perspective and our support of that, the federal role is pretty small. The state, it was within the State's capability to respond and support that. But even though the federal government, FEMA region X, stood up, there was a few resources that we asked that we struggled with, getting it in, getting it in the system, getting the proper approvals, you know, you can't sign anything, in some cases you can't sign with just pen and ink, you got to go into the system, you have to e-sign, you have to do an e-signature, and you got to pass it on, and that's got to match up to our other systems such as financing, and contracting. And it becomes just a muddy mess. (Quote #11)

When whatever system is used for the resource requesting procedure in the response to a catastrophic incident becomes unavailable, stalled, or turns out too cumbersome, responders may practically tend to abandon the electronic procedures and the paper trails as aggravating diversions and irritating deflections from the main tasks, as another FEMA responder pointed out:

> In a real-world event, we would bypass some of that stuff, and we would just focus on life saving. Cascadia happened. Look, all the minutiae for right now, it doesn't matter. Let's focus on life saving, let's get the life-saving teams here, let's start getting commodities such as food and water, ordered up and headed this way. But the details of actually getting it into a system of tracking, probably is not going to be as efficient as just perhaps doing verbals and getting resources on the way. And then trying to sort through that mess later on. (Quote #12)

And another highly experienced responder outlined that in routine responses, like DC-1 through DC-3/DC-4, one may enjoy the luxuries of time and sufficient numbers of responders as well as good connectivity, so that systems could readily be used for information collection, resource requesting, and by-the-book documentation in a routine fashion, which, however, would be illusory in a catastrophic incident, and he added:

> There's not even a chance that people are going to look at our current information technology platforms that we've got now to be able to transmit. I do see that if people can get through and communicate with one another, even if it's from coworker to coworker in an emergency management realm, you may be lucky to be able to push through a text message, right. So, though we have this grandiose idea that, oh, we've got these emergency management-based platforms, Web-based platforms, we'll be able to do this, that, and the other, it may not come down to that. It may come down to if you can get a signal through somebody, and you're transmitting a text message – just a few words at a time, that perhaps, could be where it's at. (Quote #13)

In other words, besides WebEOC's observed instability and breakdown when interconnecting with a certain, not necessarily very high number of other WebEOC nodes, or as a single node, when accessed by too many sides simultaneously, the responders' arguments are that absent basic connectivity and with vastly degraded communication capabilities as typical for catastrophic incidents, responders' reliance on a system like WebEOC would be a fallacy.

Any large-scale exercise suffers from what is known as "artificialities." The real-world catastrophic incident can only be simulated to a certain extent. During the CR16 exercise, however, among the known and much criticized artificialities, at which a number of interviewees pointed with some disgruntlement, was the assumption that electric power and with it high-speed Internet connectivity would still be readily available. Some jurisdictions simulated a shutdown of power and systems for a number of hours but then relatively quickly returned to "normal" operations with reliance on uninterrupted interconnectivity. Ironically, this highly questionable assumption fully exposed WebEOC's low-threshold breaking points, which in hindsight might be viewed as a blessing in disguise and an asset of CR16 lessons.

Besides the connectivity problems with WebEOC, some jurisdictions reduplicated information stored on WebEOC accounts also on local systems such as spreadsheets and SharePoint just for the purpose of a local backup or for the convenience to work with more familiar tools locally. However, besides the inherent problem of maintaining consistency with data and information, which are concurrently updated in different databases, the transfer of data from WebEOC to other systems was not an easy undertaking. As the AAR of the Washington State Department of Transportation (WSDOT) reveals:

> The capability to export data from WebEOC boards to an Excel spreadsheet was not functioning properly. The export option only allowed one page of data to be exported at a time rather than the entire board, making the process time consuming. This was especially challenging for making updates to the ArcGIS Online map, which requires data from the WebEOC board to be exported to and Excel spreadsheet for each entry. (Quote #14)

The same report also highlights the problems of rapid influx and large volume of new data entries and subsequently changing status information on infrastructure assets, tasks, and resources as is common in large-scale incident responses. As these entries were recorded on sequentially organized boards in WebEOC, the report bemoans the ineffectiveness of so doing:

> The information received in the EOCs on infrastructure status was changing rapidly throughout the exercise. Information was being updated on the respective boards on WebEOC, but it was difficult to quickly determine, which entries were updated. The only way to currently identify the updates is by the date/time stamp on each entry. It was identified that there needs to be a visual cue to alert EOCs, when an entry has been updated to ensure that critical information is not missed. (Quote #15)

In summary, unlike what some interviewees have called "routine disasters," the nature of catastrophic incident responses is different from the former. As the catastrophic incident response unfolds, the volume of incoming information rapidly increases despite the fact that initially the means of communication might be substantially degraded. Whatever systems are used to effectively support responders under these particular circumstances, they need to be fit to the specific tasks, upward and downward scalable, non-distracting, able to contain information overload, and easy to use to maintain the effectiveness of the response effort. The findings suggest that WebEOC would not effectively support a large-scale, large-scope, long-duration, that is, catastrophic incident response.

Ad Research Question #2 (RQ#2)

"*What are architectural, informational, and scalability-related limitations of WebEOC in the context of response scenarios of higher Fischer Scale categories?*"

With the findings regarding RQ#1 in hand, the research team was interested in determining whether or not the identified shortcomings of WebEOC would be addressable and curable and, if so, how. For that purpose, one of the most advanced and sophisticated WebEOC implementation at the city of Seattle EOC was further investigated. The researchers were given access to the system so to navigate independently, and notes on the system hierarchy were developed. While this portion of the investigation was more technical in nature, it nevertheless produced important insights on the potential expandability, scalability, or reformability of WebEOC.

Technical Foundations Used for WebEOC

The system is built on the so-called .NET stack of technologies, which was introduced by Microsoft in the early 2000s and would initially require a Windows server environment. Since open-source stacks such as LAMP presented formidable competition to Microsoft's development environment, over time the .NET stack of development tools became more of an open-source platform itself, which would not require Windows as server operating system (Ismail, 2019). The .NET stack supports programming languages such as C# and JavaScript, and WebEOC users can use the latter for individually adding functionality to the system, which, on the one hand, adds to flexibility and tailorability, but, on the other hand, it is also the source for incompatibilities among WebEOC implementations. WebEOC can be hosted on local and in-house servers as well as on servers in the cloud. In the former case, it provides response units with utmost control over their system as long as this remains operational, and in the latter case response units depend on high-bandwidth and uninterrupted connectivity with cloud servers. Either case presents major challenges of its own to continued operations in disasters of greater magnitude (greater than DC-6) once physical infrastructures and the power grid are significantly degraded along with heavily impaired high-bandwidth connections.

Hierarchy Design

The city of Seattle's WebEOC platform was divided into four primary modules, each residing a step below in the hierarchy from the previous module. An incident had to be first created in the "Incident Overview." This module then stored high-level identifying information of the incident, a concise summary, and the emergency management team's immediate actions. Once the incident overview was created, "EOC Objectives" were developed to guide the emergency management team's next steps for addressing the incident. Objectives were intended to be brief, broad, and having actionable tasks to accomplish the goal. "Tasks" defined how an objective was envisioned to be achieved. "Actions" were then created to address how a task would be accomplished through the use of specific and measurable activities.

Limitations with the Current System Architecture

While navigating through the city of Seattle's WebEOC platform, in addition to interview notes from the city of Seattle's WebEOC administrator, several significant platform and data integrity and quality issues were identified and stood out. For example, the level of detail provided by responders for each incident was found inconsistent throughout the COTS. Based on a sample set of incidents, far from all events have an incident overview, objectives, tasks, and actions created, clearly defined, and updated throughout the incident life cycle. Inside each module, data values were not always entered or updated. Fields were intentionally created to be non-required, and text field data types were commonly assigned to allow for responder flexibility upon entering data. While flexibility is an important enabler for responders, data fields were extremely difficult to build reports on or to determine any trends in analysis. Additionally, if a field was left blank, ambiguity was created leaving the viewer wondering if the information was simply not available at the time or if the responder chose to not update.

Navigating through the hierarchy was found to not be a straightforward undertaking. An incident first had to be selected using a drop-down menu at the top. Modules were then listed in another drop-down menu to the left with no indication of each module's hierarchy in the application. When inside a task or action, a pop-up box appeared leaving the previous screen blurred out in the background. While this helped better distinguish hierarchy levels, there was, however, no exit button that prompted the responder back to the previous hierarchy. Overall, the structure was found anything but intuitive for responders navigating through the system hierarchy.

Data Analysis Based on WebEOC-Based Information

With regard to using information increasingly accumulating inside WebEOC boards and databases in unfolding incident response, a business intelligence-type current state analysis was conducted on the city's WebEOC implementation and its SQL server database to assess data analysis capabilities. During this current state analysis, the following areas were analyzed and researched: data quality, data storage, data access to stakeholders, data usability, automations, metrics, and KPIs as well as data visualizations.

Data Integrity and Quality

An event or incident was found the highest hierarchical structure in the city's WebEOC implementation. Unique identifiers were created for incident names as well as tasks and actions allowing each hierarchy to be uniquely identified. Various metadata elements were captured automatically for future reporting capabilities. While not used at the time, the ability to implement a tagging system for grouping incidents by specific keywords was found a potential benefit to text-based reporting.

As previously mentioned, most fields were not required upon entering an incident, and many data types were hence not adequately defined. While allowing for flexibility in knowledge of the incident information available at the time, this would invariably lead to producing inconsistent results and findings when analyzing data. A data dictionary was not in place to assist responders in proper definitions of fields or business terms. However, a quick PDF guide had been established to assist in navigating the platform.

Data Storage and Accessibility to Stakeholders

WebEOC data was found stored residing on top of an SQL server database going back until the year 2005. The SQL server itself was located in a large SQL cluster in the city's data center, which was self-hosted. The server was physical and not cloud-based located in the city of Seattle.

First responders and other stakeholders were enabled to view WebEOC-based data from the front-end if they did not have permissions or the technical expertise to access the SQL server. The front-end interface allowed its users to conduct simple analysis tasks such as sorting, filtering, and keyword searches. However, responders were not enabled to export data for analytical purposes to a CSV or Excel file, which could only be performed via JavaScript commands making further analysis fairly cumbersome.

Data Usability and Automations/Workflows

In the SQL server database, tables were created and established directly through the WebEOC application interface (API). However, significant limitations were in place that did not allow the database to function as a standard relationship model. Table names were automatically created, and these table names did not directly correspond to the module hierarchies outlined in the WebEOC front-end interface.

For example, the "Tasks" table was imported into the SQL server as "Table_880" without the ability to rename. In addition, field links between tables were not intuitive and did not correspond to respective field names in WebEOC. For example, the "Task" table linked to the "Objective" table through a foreign key reference column (FK_Table_877), and not "ObjectiveID."

As previously mentioned, all data was fed into the SQL server through the WebEOC API. Beyond the SQL server, no automations nor workflows were built to transform data. SQL views were not designed for business groups to interpret relevant data.

Metrics, Key Performance Indicators (KPIs), and Data Visualization

The only report available to responders in WebEOC was the aforementioned "Resource Tracker." The module was used to help group records by field names in a table structure. Simple data visualizations such as pie charts were also present. The Resource Tracker was found hand-coded in JavaScript making it difficult to update, change, or add new features. Outside the Resource Tracker, no additional metrics, KPIs, or data visualizations were in place to help responders understand whether or not they were meeting their goals or how they were trending. Some metrics were created and available, but not formally established or enforced. The city used an informational and data collection scheme labeled "Essential Elements of Information" by which reporting requirements for stakeholders were determined at the beginning of an incident. Some of the requirements were measurable, but others were not. KPIs were not formally established.

In summary, when looking at the architectural and database-related underpinnings of WebEOC, it becomes obvious why the commercial product may serve responders reasonably well as long as they are well versed and trained in its use and as long as only smaller incidents are the focus of the response. The larger the incident, the larger becomes the amount of incoming data, with which the tool has to cope, in particular, with regard to vetting and distilling raw data into consistent, concise, and actionable information. The COTS, however, appears to not be designed for large-scale incident responses and the respective massive data influx.

Discussion

In this section, first the technical and more WebEOC-specific aspects are discussed before other more general and nontechnical considerations are presented with regard to the requirements and options for tools and systems intended to be used in large-scale, large-scope, and long-duration incident responses.

Technical Considerations for WebEOC Implementations

As a reminder, the WebEOC implementation at the city of Seattle's Office of Emergency Management and its EOC served as the unit of observation for the technical assessment of the COTS. Other implementations of the same COTS may be configured differently; however, responders in the Pacific Northwest region regard Seattle's implementation as one of the most advanced, which is why it was chosen for this particular portion of the investigation.

As mentioned, WebEOC relies on XML code and for customized extensions on JavaScript code for its overall functionality and SQL database access. XML and JavaScript allow for interpreting browser-embedded code line by line at runtime. While scripting technologies like XML and JavaScript afford great flexibility and easy modifiability, the "interpreter" of code has a long-standing reputation for relatively slow execution compared with compiled and runtime-ready programs such as C++ compiled code. Depending on the tasks at hand, compiled programs may execute between 4 and 400 times faster than scripted, that is, real-time interpreted code programs. When considering the design of high-throughput inter-operated transactional systems, an interpreter-based architecture would rather not be a preferred design choice, which seems to indicate that WebEOC was never built with these architectural considerations in mind. Rather the design choice obviously favored flexibility over scalability and high-speed performance.

However, while WebEOC provides EOCs and other response units great flexibility, this very characteristic not only fosters incompatibilities as already discussed above but rather also leads to a great variety of architectural structures and interface implementations, which may serve the needs of a given response unit, or even inside the same response unit a specific incident type, but which adds to the complexity and nonintuitiveness of the tool. A redesign of the architectural structure might allow for a more intuitive and standardized structure as well as increased data quality and analysis capabilities.

Following Turoff et al. (2004b, p. 20), for example, the system directory and the navigation modules "should provide a hierarchical structure for all the data and information currently in the system." By redesigning the directory and navigation of modules in this way, it would allow for a natural progression through an incident response. A clearer structure would likely also decrease the frequency for WebEOC trainings. The more intuitive and easy to use a platform or tool, the more easily and more frequently responders can be expected to adopt them.

A standardized structure would also prompt easier accessibility and navigation to responders from other agencies or organizations who do not normally use the tool. Collaboration and sharing of findings are vital to any emergency management response. While standardization of WebEOC implementations and configurations across agencies in the region would likely be a longer-term goal, it should strongly be considered if WebEOC was decided to remain the backbone of incident responses in the region.

Furthermore, as pointed out before, the boards in WebEOC act like a log file and document retention tool rather than a reliable source of live incident updates. As also described above, this made it difficult and almost impossible for incoming responders to fully understand a complex incident response in all its various aspects, for example, after a shift change. However, not only during shift changes a fully updated and consolidated common operating picture along with incident action plans (IAPs) need to be made readily available to the next shift. But rather also before, during, and after an incident response, the incident commanders and the various IMT/EOC sections need to be able to perform ad-hoc analyses of both historical and current data. While WebEOC stored a plethora of data, it was found providing little to interpret, action off, and make findings available. Yet, in an incident response, data have to be instantly accessible for analysis, and most importantly, these data need to be trustworthy and consistent. Business intelligence techniques should therefore be considered to help transform data from various sources into meaningful information that allows for effective decision-making and response improvements during an unfolding incident response.

In this context, the existing WebEOC SQL server database structure as found in Seattle's implementation was not utilized to its full potential. Tables were simply exported from WebEOC, attribute names were found not intuitive, and relationship links were difficult to identify. By implementing a multidimensional data model, the city would drastically improve data accessibility, quality, and future reporting needs. Fact and dimension tables could be created from the data exports. Entity grains and primary and foreign key relationships should be put in place and enforced. Views of the data could then be created off the dimension and fact tables for responders and analysts to answer specific questions and develop reports and data visualizations.

Along with restructuring the existing database to fit the needs of the organization, a data dictionary should be established. Table and field names should be identified with corresponding definitions to help users navigate the data warehouse. The data dictionary has to define key relationships between entities to assist in linking data for further analysis. Most importantly, this way data integrity would be improved. Responders would be instructed to refer to the data dictionary when entering information directly in the tool, as well as during SQL script creation to fulfill reporting needs. Data analysis tools along with data visualization tools, which use the data collected throughout the incident response, could further enhance responders' analytical capabilities during and after a response.

From a technical perspective, while WebEOC provides quite some flexibility for configuring incident-related "logging boards" even within short periods of time during an unfolding incident, the sequential nature of the boards along with the lack of effective sorting, filtering, consolidating, and searching capabilities makes the boards cumbersome to handle in more complex incident response situations. Ad-hoc data analyses and visualizations of larger amounts of data appear to be among tasks not easily accomplishable within the current architectural design of the COTS. Moreover, this COTS does not scale well for high-speed transactional interoperation requirements, for example, when exchanging graphical datasets and high-resolution images. The discussed performance issues, hence, pertain to a combination of architectural, organizational (e.g., sequential boards), and interoperational system characteristics, the sum of which contributes to the system's degradation under increasing load.

Undoubtedly, the vendor (Juvare) has tried to address the concerns raised here and elsewhere in the past few years. The application program interface (API) of WebEOC has been improved so to connect more readily to other popular applications such as geographic information systems, spreadsheets, and other systems in real time. Also, the data import function appears to be capable of handling a relatively large number of datasets from spreadsheets and other input formats. Also, Juvare Exchange is claimed to facilitate "communication and collaboration across public, private, and healthcare sectors, as well as geographical and jurisdictional borders, in a single real-time dashboard" (https://www.juvare.com/juvare-exchange/ accessed 07/06/2020). However, functionality features do not provide evidence of practical and robust scalability in a major incident response with dozens and hundreds of separately working WebEOC nodes. It is worthwhile to remember that WebEOC in the early 2000s won the first "checkbox-list-of-features" test. As responders have learned since, functional features alone, however, do not provide the necessary proof that a system can reliably and robustly work under increasing load and stress, which is needed in the case of an unfolding catastrophe and is therefore a basic requirement for a scalable national CIMS. Given the built-in architectural performance limitations of its component parts, it is highly unlikely that an intra-jurisdictional "dashboard" integrating many nodes based on Juvare Exchange would perform satisfactorily under duress. It further needs to be seen whether or not FEMA would be willing to lift its current security, safety, and performance concerns for the new Juvare Exchange architecture and integrate directly with state and other jurisdictions. Without the complete, safe, and smooth integration of the resource request and fulfillment hierarchy from local municipality through all necessary intermediaries at county and state levels to the federal government, the response to a catastrophe will remain crippled by design and from the outset. Securing and safeguarding the resource request and fulfillment process could be supported by technologies such as distributed ledger technologies (DLT) and Blockchain, as an example of a DLT, which maintain the integrity and immutability of records and hence effectively guard against fraud and falsifiability.

Nontechnical Considerations Regarding the Use of WebEOC for All Incident Categories

When looking beyond the technical side of the equation, it appears that in the absence of well-crafted federal- and state-level ICT strategies for responses to all categories of disasters in terms of scope, scale, and duration, over the years WebEOC became a rather circumstantial, opportunistic, and unplanned success (for the vendor). This particular COTS served the needs of response units in lower category routine incident responses relatively well, but its scaling-up capabilities, let alone the breaking points when scaling up, were never tested. This research suggests that the breaking points occur relatively soon somewhere before or in the middle of the spectrum of disaster categories, that is, when multiple agencies interconnect or when too many requestors access a WebEOC node concurrently.

It is remarkable that WebEOC apparently was never subjected to nor passed FEMA's NIMS STEP evaluation for fitness. As a reminder, the NIMS STEP program evaluated the compatibility of commercial products along with the inherent scalability requirements of NIMS. Interestingly, the NIMS STEP evaluation program itself was discontinued for no identifiable reason almost at the same time when FEMA embraced WebEOC as its internal ICT platform for managing federal-level disasters, that is, disasters of higher categories. Moreover, despite the well-articulated DHS-internal and congressional criticisms of its lack of strategy in the ICT realm at the same time, FEMA appeared to have rather hastily and still absent a strategic ICT approach adopted WebEOC without further scrutiny and assessment. As a result, FEMA is using a commercial system, which has demonstrated its unfitness to task and to scale when involved as backbone in responding to DC-5+ category disasters.

In this particular context, the practice of not directly interoperating with lower-level government agencies and their respective WebEOC implementations but rather providing these agencies with FEMA WebEOC accounts instead indicates that no load and operational assessments were made before the COTS was introduced at federal level. Had such assessments been made, it would have immediately become clear and discovered that selecting WebEOC as the federal disaster management backbone would necessarily push the federal disaster response toward "[c]ybersecurity threats and cost" that "make interconnectivity between WebEOC and all state EOCs impractical" (Long, 2018, p. 6). This would have undoubtedly disqualified WebEOC as a candidate for the considered purpose.

The NIMS doctrine and its set of practices were designed with the knowledge of the enormous range and types of hazards, which necessitates upward and downward scalability of organizational and procedural settings, which can span multiple levels of governmental and cross multi-jurisdictional boundaries in higher disaster categories (DC-5 to DC-10). Before this backdrop, it is perplexing how the requirements for CIMS interoperability, which were formulated with unmistaken clarity, and the detailed characteristics of scalability and reliability for multilevel real-time cross-jurisdictional integration laid out in the 2008 NIMS core document (Anonymous, 2008) could have been ignored in FEMA's 2012 selection process. Moreover, this was done against the explicit warnings already formulated in the 2011 Deffer report of the DHS-internal Information Technology Audits Unit (Deffer, 2011), which expressed deep concerns about FEMA's nonstrategic and ineffective approach to the selection of various CIMS and their lack of serving the purpose particularly with regard to integrating with external partners. Instead of solid integration and smooth interoperation of systems, the choice of WebEOC at federal level has led to a cumbersome and ineffective bottleneck, which rather complicates the response to a higher-category disaster than simplifying it. Based on the findings of this study,

FEMA's square rebuff of the DHS-internal and congressional insistence on change of approach and reform of practices can hardly be considered the last word on the matter.

Besides the COTS's demonstrated ineffectiveness in complex higher-category disaster response situations, FEMA's 2012 pro-WebEOC decision along with similar decisions on state, county, and municipality levels, has increasingly produced what in both economics and in the realm of high technology is called *path dependency*. In the absence of known alternatives, jurisdictions on all levels of government have jumped on the WebEOC bandwagon and created for themselves a potential costly lock-in situation. However, it is not only the dependency on a single COTS but rather also the dependence on a single vendor, regardless of size, which makes this arrangement highly problematic. A Reagan-era argument holds that government is inefficient and frequently mismanaged (Peters, 1994) and also has capacity limitations (Milward, 1994). As a consequence, it has been argued that, for example, government-run system developments are inferior to commercial ones, since market forces regularly produce better products and superior services more quickly (Osborne, 1993). However, this argument fails, when only one product or one service is available from one vendor, and this very vendor does not face any competition. A lock-in of this particular type with an unfit tool in an area of highest strategic importance and national safety is not only undesirable but potentially rather costly in terms of both material damages and loss of lives.

While it is understandable that responders reached for using tools and instruments that effectively supported their tasks, in the context of disaster response, a one-product-from-vendor approach created the aforementioned potentially dangerous lock-in situation with regard to safety as well as economically and with respect to the vendor's viability. For the lack of alternatives and through promotion on part of state and federal agencies, the WebEOC lock-in also displays elements of self-reinforcement (Vergne & Durand, 2010).

Furthermore, in high technology, lock-ins are known for stifling innovation (Arthur, 1989). In economics, lock-ins foster monopolistic pricing schemes and other moral hazards. Moreover, one-vendor dependency carries the problematic of uncertainty regarding the vendor's future intention and direction, continued managerial soundness, and financial stability among others. Lock-in costs can be defined as opportunity costs for switching to a situation that overcomes path dependency, that is, lock breaking. For disaster responses in the United States in order to escape the WebEOC/Juvare path dependency, this would mean to promote and fund the creation of a more powerful and more capable disaster response management system, which is reliable, scalable, vertically and horizontally interoperable, robust, secure, etc. along the NIMS core document specifications.

Overcoming the path dependency could be accomplished either by a competitive innovation setup for commercial vendors or by using government internal resources, or simultaneously one could proceed on both avenues. In two 2006 articles, the sourcing mix for technology initiatives in government was deliberated, and sourcing decisions were found to be influenced along three dimensions: (1) strategic importance, (2) resource availability, and (3) frequency of change (Scholl, 2006;

Scholl & Carlson, 2006). Two decision scenarios emerged as clear-cut: outsourcing (i.e., procuring and using COTS) would be preferred in cases of (1) little or no strategic importance, (2) little or no own resource availability, and (3) low frequency of change, whereas insourcing (i.e., in-house development) would be the chosen approach in cases of (1) high strategic importance, (2) high availability of internal capabilities and resources, and (3) a dynamically changing environment, where own control is essential (Scholl, 2006, pp. 87–88).

One can easily argue that, in particular, higher-category disaster responses are of enormous strategic importance to the nation. With regard to frequency of change, that is, number of occurrences and types of higher-category disasters but also with regard to technological advances that need to be continuously integrated into any CIMS used for that purpose, the overall situation is dynamic rather than static. And finally, with regard to availability of capable and trained resources, agencies on all government levels in the United States employ a plethora of ICT-related talent and expertise. Following the decision matrix would favor insourcing, that is, in-house building the CIMS used for NIMS-based response management. If funded and built on federal level, the necessary NIMS-oriented standardization of procedures, protocols, forms, and data structures would be implementable. State, county, and municipal jurisdictions would be supported in implementation and training. Development and maintenance costs would be offset by savings from overcoming the lock-in within a calculable and relatively short time. Outsourcing in government has been promoted rather on ideological than economic grounds (Scholl, 2006). In practice, however, it has been shown that government internal ICT resources can rather favorably and conveniently compete both technically and cost-wise with commercial vendors (Scholl et al., 2014).

Another widely used argument for outsourcing ICTs was Carr's 2003 line of reasoning that "IT doesn't matter," since ICTs were portrayed as commodities, which were easily replaceable by other commodities of the same kind (Carr, 2003). While at first glance this so-called car fleet argument may somewhat hold when referring to hardware such as general-purpose microprocessors, laptops, routers, etc. or other garden-variety software packages such as word processors and presentation tools, it certainly does not hold for highly sophisticated algorithmic tools or specialized hardware components. In the absence of a lock-in, an organization can easily switch from a car fleet from vendor one to a car fleet from vendor two, which is not the case with non-commodity highly sophisticated algorithmic tools.

With regard to both classic arguments favoring outsourcing, it is informative to observe what organizations, in general, consider to be outsourceable and what not: for their strategic advantage, for example, both Amazon and Walmart heavily rely on their highly sophisticated in-house built and maintained logistics systems; these systems are among the most securely guarded systems of expertise and advantage. Likewise, in the public sector, nobody would entrust the defense of the country to a contracted mercenary military since the mission is considered too critical and too strategic to leave it to outsiders. However, the exact same arguments can be advanced for the core crisis information management system of the country, which needs to be under full control of the respective disaster response agencies in terms of its architecture, source code, intensity and direction of development, licensing, distribution, and training. No local municipality should be left without proper CIMS support because they can simply not afford to purchase a pricey initial and update COTS licenses from a commercial vendor.

In catastrophic disaster responses, the requirement for CIMS scalability, however, is more complex and more dynamic than obvious at first sight. While some disasters have patterns of steady increase of scope and scale until contained, for example, certain landslides, wildfires, landfalls of hurricanes, or pandemics, other catastrophic disasters strike on a large scale and scope at once, for example, megathrust earthquakes, tsunamis, or large volcanic or meteoric incidents. While the response and with it, the CIMS scales up in the case of the former, in case of the latter the response and the CIMS are severely stifled and degraded from the first moment onward. The CIMS architecture and the overall response organization have to take this important difference into account. Scalability means both upward and downward scalability.

In case of the latter, a CIMS has to still function on the basis of low bandwidths, as one responder said, for example, with snippets of text messages only. Also, paper and pen-based messaging over radio or even via messengers on foot might become the only available means of communication for responders at times. As long as electrical power is available, some communications can be maintained via professional radio or HAM radio, cell phones, as well as via satellite phones and satellite-based Internet. However, this will occur within greatly degraded information and communication infrastructures, and CIMS support under such conditions will be sparse and highly challenging. Moreover, if the degradation of critical infrastructures in a catastrophic disaster including the complete knockdown of the power grid as the most important backbone will not be fixable for weeks and months, then this scenario requires a comprehensive backup plan and the testing of its feasibility.

Such backups might include the regular flying in of recharged batteries for all kinds of equipment including flying in and out laptop computers as well as data storage and communication devices. Handwritten messages and reports can also be collected and flown to data entry centers, which operate in nearby areas, in which the critical infrastructures are intact. In coastal areas such nearby intact infrastructures can, for example, be vessel based. However, the detailed investigation of such extreme scenarios and its necessary CIMS-related adjustments goes beyond the scope of this study. For the purpose of this study, it is important to point out that CIMS scalability is not only simply a one-directional upward-oriented undertaking but rather also needs to include dynamic downward scalability mechanisms, which account for and cope with massive degradation of infrastructures and CIMS operability.

The CR16-related AAR of the Washington National Guard (WANG), when reporting and reflecting on the use of WebEOC-based exchanges with state and federal partners during the exercise, echoes many findings of this study. The National Guard has its own CIMS called DAART for "DOMOPS (Domestic Operations) Awareness and Assessment Tool," which appears to be functionally robust and interoperable. Based on the experience of serious challenges with interorganizational system interoperation and exchanges with state partners and FEMA, the WANG AAR recommends:

> Further evaluation is required for SA <situational awareness>, KM <knowledge management, insertion by authors> and tracking systems in order to identify the current 'best option' for movement forward. Standardization across all echelons of response requires heavy weighting in the decision criteria for that selection. A nationally maintained system that allows access to national, state, and local EMs for SA development, sharing of information, and knowledge management, should receive strong consideration. A current potential solution is the DAART system offered by National Guard Bureau (NGB). (Quote #16)

While without further study, it is unclear at this point whether or not the DAART system would satisfy the aforementioned load, interoperability, and scalability requirements along the NIMS guidelines; the call for standardization and national maintenance of a future core national CIMS is substantiated also by this investigation.

Conclusion and Future Research

The object of this study has been to determine the fitness to task and effectiveness of WebEOC, a widely used commercial off-the-shelf (COTS) Crisis Information Management System (CIMS), when it comes to disasters of greater magnitudes as defined in the ten-category Fischer Scale (Fischer, 2003). Based on findings from a simulated megathrust response (Cascadia Rising) representing a category DC-9 catastrophe conducted in June of 2016, WebEOC was found unfit to purpose and highly ineffective in supporting a multi-jurisdictional and multilevel responses. While this particular commercial CIMS appears to support the so-called garden-variety or routine emergency responses, that is, small-scope, small-scale, and short-duration responses up to Fischer Scale DC-4, reasonably well, beyond the DC-5 category, it appears to become increasingly dysfunctional when massive interoperation and collaboration of numerous response units is the norm.

Part of these functional deficiencies and vulnerabilities of WebEOC can be directly related to its particular technical architecture with interpreted code at runtime, ledger-type sequential entry logging, and its cloud-based service. Based on a relative strength of this particular commercial CIMS, that is, its configurability and tailorability, however, other nontechnical problems arise: each WebEOC configuration is different from any other unless jurisdictions in an entire geographical area or even nationwide agree on standards of configuration and implementation. Yet, even with standardized configurations, the architecture appears to be vulnerable to too many concurrent access requests, which in the case of Cascadia Rising led to nonresponsiveness and outright crashing of the state WebEOC system. While the state meanwhile migrated its system to a powerful cloud system, it remains still to be tested whether or not this switch would cure the problem under a real catastrophic incident.

Yet, before criticizing the vendor of WebEOC for the CIMS's obvious deficiencies and failures, one has to note that the tool's ascent to its current status of de-facto standard has occurred slowly and incrementally. While it serves the lower-category incident types reasonably well, it fails to do so for the higher-category types. Absent a robust test and evaluation scenario, which covers the full range of incident responses in terms of scale, scope, and duration, WebEOC slipped into its current status rather uncontested. The tool's demonstrated unfitness for higher-category incident responses represents a late and now costly discovery, which could have been prevented if FEMA, the federal lead agency, had performed full-range load and functional tests. However, as said earlier, the luxury of hindsight makes such judgments rather easy. Yet, the minimum requirements and standards for a scalable, operationally flexible, interoperable, secure, and robust CIMS were already defined during the years when NIMS was introduced. When in 2002 state and other local agencies were asking the federal government for guidance in their CIMS decision-making processes, FEMA appears to not have been involved in any recognizable part when the DOJ NIJ guidance was crafted. Furthermore, in terms of ICT governance, FEMA has a long and documented track record of lacking a consistent and strategically oriented approach including CIMS (Carter, 2017; Deffer, 2011; McCauley, 2015), which further made possible the gradual proliferation of a number of incompatible and limited tools including WebEOC into response units all over the United States.

Still, the case of WebEOC stands out, since despite internal audit and congressional audit warnings at the time, FEMA hastily and without any publicly documented selection process adopted WebEOC for its own operations. Shortly after this decision was made, it became obvious and received the immediate attention of the respective congressional oversight committee that WebEOC was unfit for interagency operations and not hardened against cyberattacks. Instead of reconsidering its problematic adoption of WebEOC, FEMA imposed a slow, cumbersome, and costly workaround for state agencies. It is important to remember that, for example, resource requests from states, which cannot immediately be handled by FEMA as result of the WebEOC setup, can be extremely costly including the loss of lives. It is therefore troubling that the former short-term FEMA director in 2018 outright declined the reconsideration and change of this much-criticized setup and use of WebEOC.

Since its introduction in the 2000s, the federal NIMS doctrine and its good-practices framework have not been assessed based on experiences in responses to the higher disaster categories (DC-8 to DC-10). However, for the record, unless full attention is paid to the particular needs and requirements for NIMS-conforming and capable CIMS, their potential uses, necessary large-scale robustness, upward and downward scalability, and secure interoperability under extreme circumstances, the nation will be far less ready to cope with disasters of that magnitude than necessary. Such state of affairs is dangerous.

It therefore appears essential and urgent that a national initiative be created that helps define an appropriate and effective national CIMS architecture, the procedural and protocol standards, the performance and interoperability metrics, and the maintenance and distribution policies so that every unit can use the same CIMS for its response management at affordable operating costs. Such undertaking could take on several formats such as a federal government-led project, a private-public consortium, and an academic-practitioner partnership project among others, all of which would be designed to maintain the response community's strategic control over the resulting CIMS.

A national CIMS architecture for the twenty-first-century responses to incidents of all scales, scopes, and durations also needs to include and take advantage of collecting data from social media in real time. Such raw and unvetted data can be put to scrutiny via artificial intelligence (AI)-based algorithms that help responders separate noise from valuable and potentially actionable information leading to improved situational awareness more quickly. Similar AI methods need to be incorporated for sensory and video data collectable from Internet of Things (IoT) devices.

Future research will be directed to further that particular goal of helping create a twenty-first-century, robust, scalable, and interoperable CIMS architecture.

References

Anonymous. (2008). *National incident management system* (FEMA P-501). https://www.fema.gov/pdf/emergency/nims/NIMS_core.pdf

Anonymous. (2010a). *Incident decision support software application note: System assessment and validation for emergency responders (SAVER)*. U.S. Department of Homeland Security. https://www.dhs.gov/sites/default/files/publications/IDSS_AppN_0810-508.pdf

Anonymous. (2010b). *National incident management system supporting evaluation program (NIMS STEP): Guide* [Report]. U.S. Department of Homeland Security. https://www.hsdl.org/?view&did=693929

Anonymous. (2015). *Common alerting protocol alert origination tools technology guide: System assessment and validation for emergency responders (SAVER)*. U.S. Department of Homelad Security—Science and Technology. https://www.dhs.gov/sites/default/files/publications/Alert-Protocol-TG_0215-508.pdf

Anonymous. (2017). *Washington state 2016 Cascadia rising exercise after action report catastrophic earthquake and tsunami scenario* [After-action report]. W. S. EMD. https://www.google.com/search?client=safari&rls=en&q=Washington+State+2016+Cascadia+Rising+Exercise+After+Action+Report+Catastrophic+Earthquake+and+Tsunami+Scenario&ie=UTF-8&oe=UTF-8

Aros, S. K., & Gibbons, D. E. (2018, December 9–12). Developing an agent-based simulation model of the use of different communication technologies in inter-organizational disaster response coordination. In *Proceedings of the 2018 winter simulation conference (WSC)*, Gothenburg, Sweden.

Arthur, W. B. (1989). Competing technologies, increasing returns, and lock-in by historical events. *The Economic Journal, 99*(394), 116–131.

Carr, N. G. (2003). IT doesn't matter. *Harvard Business Review, 81*(5), 41–49.

Carter, J. (2017). *Department of Homeland Security Appropriations Bill, 2017* (H.R. 5634), Issue. https://www.congress.gov/114/crpt/hrpt668/CRPT-114hrpt668.pdf

Chua, A. Y. K., Kaynak, S., & Foo, S. S. B. (2007). An analysis of the delayed response to Hurricane Katrina through the lens of knowledge management. *Journal of the American Society for Information Science and Technology, 58*(3), 391–403. https://doi.org/10.1002/asi.20521

Deffer, F. (2011). *Federal Emergency Management Agency faces challenges in modernizing information technology* (OIG-11-69). D. o. H. Security https://www.oig.dhs.gov/assets/Mgmt/OIG_11-69_Apr11.pdf

Endsley, M. R. (2015). Situation awareness misconceptions and misunderstandings. *Journal of Cognitive Engineering and Decision Making, 9*(1), 4–32.

Farmer, R. A. (2014). *FEMA's capability development after Katrina* [Presentation]. Institut de Seguretat Pública de Catalunya Barcelona. https://recercat.cat/handle/2072/249951?show=full

Fereday, J., & Muir-Cochrane, E. (2006). Demonstrating rigor using thematic analysis: A hybrid approach of inductive and deductive coding and theme development. *International Journal of Qualitative Methods, 5*(1), 80.

Fischer, H. W. (2003). The sociology of disaster: Definitions, research questions, & measurements continuation of the discussion in a post-September 11 environment. *International Journal of Mass Emergencies and Disasters, 21*(1), 91–107.

Ganji, A., Savelli, S., Haselkorn, M., Wilson, T., & Dailey, D. (2019, May 19–22). Cause and effect: A qualitative analysis of obstacles to information sharing during a regional disaster exercise. In *16th international conference on information systems for crisis response and management (ISCRAM 2019)*, Valencia, Spain.

Glaser, B. G. (1999). The future of grounded theory. *Qualitative Health Research, 9*(6), 836–845. https://doi.org/10.1177/104973299129122199

Glaser, B. G., & Strauss, A. L. (1967). *The discovery of grounded theory; strategies for qualitative research*. Aldine Pub. Co.

Hanson, P., & McDougall, C. (2018, November 5–7). Enabling collaborative and resilient emergency management efforts: DFES and Western Australia's adoption of a common operating picture. In *1st international conference on information systems for crisis response and management Asia Pacific (ISCRAM Asia Pacific 2018)*, Wellington, New Zealand.

Hart, S. V. (2002). *Crisis information management software (CIMS) feature comparison report*. D. o. Justice. https://www.ncjrs.gov/pdffiles1/nij/197065.pdf

Inoguchi, M., Tamura, K., Horie, K., & Hayashi, H. (2014, November 17–20). Implementation of web-based system for building damage assessment on online network: Case studies of Typhoon MAN-YI (1318) and Typhoon WIPHA (1326) in Japan. In *Proceedings of the 2014 IEEE Asia Pacific conference on circuits and systems (APCCAS)*, Ishigaki, Japan.

Ismail, K. (2019, January 18). JAMstack vs. LAMP Stack vs. MEAN vs .NET: Tech stacks compared. *CMS Wire,* 1–7. https://www.cmswire.com/digital-experience/jamstack-vs-lamp-stack-vs-mean-vs-net-tech-stacks-compared/

Jung, K. (2018). Mapping community diversity and e-participation in emergency management: Evidence from WebEOC in the city of San Francisco. *International Journal of Emergency Management, 14*(3), 275–290. https://doi.org/10.1504/IJEM.2018.094238

Kapucu, N. (2006). Interagency communication networks during emergencies. Boundary spanners in multiagency coordination. *American Review of Public Administration, 36*(2), 207.

Kapucu, N., Arslan, T., & Collins, M. L. (2010). Examining intergovernmental and interorganizational response to catastrophic disasters: Toward a network-centered approach. *Administration & Society, 42*(2), 222–247. https://doi.org/10.1177/0095399710362517

Kelly, J. V. (2014). *FEMA's initial response to the Colorado flood*. https://www.hsdl.org/?view&did=755887

Levius, S., Safa, M., & Weeks, K. (2017). Use of information and communication technology to support comprehensive disaster management in the Caribbean countries. *Journal of Information Technology Case and Application Research, 19*(2), 102–112.

Levy, J., & Prizzia, R. (2018a). Building effective emergency management public-private partnerships (PPP) for information sharing. In A. J. Masys (Ed.), *Security by design: Innovative perspectives on complex problems* (pp. 375–401). Springer. https://doi.org/10.1007/978-3-319-78021-4

Levy, J., & Prizzia, R. (2018b). Customizing web-EOC crisis management software to facilitate collaboration and increase situational awareness: Advances in business resource center (BRC) design for business continuity management. In A. J. Masys (Ed.), *Security by design: Innovative perspectives on complex problems* (pp. 291–316). Springer. https://doi.org/10.1007/978-3-319-78021-4

Li, T., Xie, N., Zeng, C., Zhou, W., Zheng, L., Jiang, Y., Yang, Y., Ha, H.-Y., Xue, W., & Huang, Y. (2017). Data-driven techniques in disaster information management. *ACM Computing Surveys (CSUR), 50*(1), 1–45.

Lombardo, K., Boggs, J., Boudreau, J., Chiles, P., Erickson, J., Gerstel, W., Montgomery, D., Shipman, L., Radcliff-Sinclair, R., Strachan, S., Sugimura, D., & Trimm, B. (2014 of Conference). SR 530 landslide commission final report. In Conference name, conference location. http://www.governor.wa.gov/documents/SR530LC_Final_Report.pdf

Long, B. (2018). *Web emergency operations center (WebEOC) interconnectivity: Fiscal year 2017 report to congress* [Fiscal year 2017 report to congress]. F. E. M. Agency. https://www.dhs.gov/sites/default/files/publications/FEMA%20-%20Web%20Emergency%20Operations%20Center%20%28WebEOC%29%20Interconnectivity.pdf

McCauley, S. F. (2015). *FEMA faces challenges in managing information technology*. https://www.oig.dhs.gov/assets/Mgmt/2016/OIG-16-10-Nov15.pdf

Milward, H. B. (1994). Nonprofit contracting and the hollow state. *Public Administration Review, 54*(1), 73–77.

Misra, S., Roberts, P., & Rhodes, M. (2020). The ecology of emergency management work in the digital age. *Perspectives on Public Management and Governance*, 1–18. https://doi.org/10.1093/ppmgov/gvaa007

Nikolai, C., Becerra-Fernandez, I., Johnson, T., & Madey, G. (2010). Leveraging WebEOC in support of the Haitian relief effort: Insights and lessons learned. In *7th international conference on information systems for crisis response and management (ISCRAM 2010)*.

Osborne, D. (1993). Reinventing government. *Public Productivity & Management Review, 16*(4), 349–356.

Peters, B. G. (1994). Managing the hollow state. *International Journal of Public Administration, 17*(3–4), 739–756.

Quarantelli, E. L. (1997). Problematical aspects of the information/communication revolution for disaster planning and research: Ten non-technical issues and questions. *Disaster Prevention and Management, 6*(2), 94–106.

Ritchie, J., Lewis, J., & Gillian, E. (2003). Designing and selecting samples. In J. Ritchie & J. Lewis (Eds.), *Qualitative research practice: A guide for social science students and researchers* (pp. 77–108). Sage Publications. http://www.loc.gov/catdir/toc/fy037/2002109391.html

Robinson, J. J., Maddock, J., & Starbird, K. (2015, May 24–27). Examining the role of human and technical infrastructure during emergency response. In *12th international conference on information Systems for Crisis Response and Management (ISCRAM 2015)*.

Scholl, H. J. (2006). Electronic government: Information management capacity, organizational capabilities, and the sourcing mix. *Government Information Quarterly, 23*(1), 73–96.

Scholl, H. J., & Carlson, T. S. (2006). Sourcing decisions in electronic government and the knowledge transfer problem. In R. Traunmüller (Ed.), *Knowledge transfer for eGovernment: Seeking better eGovernment solutions* (Vol. 20, pp. 69–81). Trauner Verlag.

Scholl, H. J., & Carnes, S. L. (2017, May 15–19). Managerial challenges in early disaster response: The case of the 2014 Oso/SR530 landslide disaster. In *Proceedings of the 14th ISCRAM conference*, Albi, France.

Scholl, H. J., & Chatfield, A. T. (2014). The role of resilient information infrastructures: The case of radio Fukushima during and after the 2011 eastern Japan catastrophe. *International Journal of Public Administration in the Digital Age (IJPADA), 1*(2), 1–24.

Scholl, H. J., & Patin, B. J. (2014). Resilient information infrastructures: Criticality and role in responding to catastrophic incidents. *Transforming Government: People, Process and Policy, 8*(1), 28–48.

Scholl, H. J., Jurisch, M., Scholl, M. C., & Krcmar, H. (2014). Building sound foundations for smart city government: The case of Munich, Germany. *International Journal of E-Planning Research, 3*(4), 1–22. https://doi.org/10.4018/IJEPR

Scholl, H. J., Ballard, S., Carnes, S., Herman, A., & Parker, N. (2017, January 4–7). Informational challenges in early disaster response: The massive Oso/SR530 landslide 2014 as case in point. In *50th Hawaii international conference on system sciences (HICSS-50)*, Waikoloa, Hawaii. http://hdl.handle.net/10125/41458

Scholl, H. J., Hubbel, K., & Leonard, J. (2018, November 5–7). Communications and technology challenges to situational awareness: Insights from the CR16 exercise. In *Proceedings of the 1st ISCRAM Asia-Pacific conference*, Wellington, NZ.

Spicer, S., Lowe, A. M., Cho, G., & Walton, M. (2019). *Disaster response: FEMA and the American Red Cross need to ensure key mass care organizations are included in coordination and planning* [Report to congressional requesters] (GAO-19-526). https://www.gao.gov/assets/710/701499.pdf

Strauss, A. L., & Corbin, J. M. (1998). *Basics of qualitative research: Techniques and procedures for developing grounded theory* (2nd ed.). Sage Publications.

Thessin, J. (2003). Department of homeland security. *Harvard Journal on Legislation, 40*(2), 513–536.

Truptil, S., Bénaben, F., Couget, P., Lauras, M., Chapurlat, V., & Pingaud, H. (2008). Interoperability of information systems in crisis management: Crisis modeling and metamodeling. In K. Mertins, R. Ruggaber, K. Popplewell, & X. Xu (Eds.), *Enterprise interoperability III: New challenges and industrial approaches* (pp. 583–594). Springer. https://doi.org/10.1007/978-1-84800-221-0

Turner, B. A. (1976). The organizational and interorganizational development of disasters. *Administrative Science Quarterly, 21*(3), 378–397.

Turoff, M. (2007). Emergency response information systems: Emerging trends and technologies. *Communications of the ACM, 50*(3), 29–31.

Turoff, M., Chumer, M., Hiltz, S. R., & Klashner, R. (2004a). Assuring homeland security: Continuous monitoring, control & assurance of emergency preparedness. *JITTA: Journal of Information Technology Theory and Application, 6*(3), 1–24.

Turoff, M., Chumer, M., Van de Walle, B., & Yao, X. (2004b). The design of a dynamic emergency response management information system (DERMIS). *JITTA: Journal of Information Technology Theory and Application, 5*(4), 1.

Urquhart, C., Lehmann, H., & Myers, M. D. (2010). Putting the 'theory' back into grounded theory: Guidelines for grounded theory studies in information systems. *Information Systems, 20*(4), 357–381. https://doi.org/10.1111/j.1365-2575.2009.00328.x

Vergne, J. P., & Durand, R. (2010). The missing link between the theory and empirics of path dependence: Conceptual clarification, testability issue, and methodological implications. *Journal of Management Studies, 47*(4), 736–759.

Whelan, C., & Molnar, A. (2018). *Securing mega-events: Networks, strategies and tensions.* Palgrave Macmillan. https://doi.org/10.1057/978-1-137-59668-0

Practitioners' Perceptions of Fitness to Task of a Leading Disaster Response Management Tool

Hans Jochen Scholl and Eric E. Holdeman

Abstract Crisis Information Management Systems (CIMS) have been used in emergency and disaster response management for decades. However, while these systems have emerged and improved over time, they still appear to provide lower efficacy when incidents become more complex and, in particular, when used in the context of multi-jurisdictional responses to large and growing incidents and extreme events. Most CIMS like E Team, Veoci, or WebEOC are commercial off-the-shelf systems (COTS), which allow for and also require from emergency response units the customization of the application to their own specific needs. This survey-informed study took a look at practitioners' experiences with one of the most widely used CIMS, that is, WebEOC. The results were mixed at best and confirm other studies, which pointed at WebEOC's lack of scalability, interoperability, network security, and ease of use. The study concludes that in the face of ever more frequent incidents of greater magnitude, the case for developing and deploying securely interoperable and scalable CIMS is compelling and has to be addressed.

Keywords Disaster response management · Coordination of emergency responses · Information and communication technologies (ICTs) · Crisis Information Management Systems (CIMS) · WebEOC · National Incident Management System (NIMS) · Incident Command System (ICS) · Commercial off-the-shelf systems (COTS)

H. J. Scholl (✉)
University of Washington, Seattle, WA, USA
e-mail: jscholl@uw.edu

E. E. Holdeman
Eric Holdeman Associates, Puyallup, WA, USA
e-mail: ericholdeman@ericholdeman.com

H. J. Scholl et al. (eds.), *Disaster Management and Information Technology*,
Public Administration and Information Technology 40,
https://doi.org/10.1007/978-3-031-20939-0_16

Introduction

Contemporary commercial Crisis Information Management Systems (CIMS), it has been suggested (Hanson & McDougall, 2018; Levy & Prizzia, 2018a), support emergency managers and responders relatively well when used in response to smaller, everyday, and geographically isolated incidents. When, however, multiple jurisdictions and different levels of government agencies need to coordinate their responses, they appear to exhibit limitations and rigidities in terms of interoperability, scalability, reliability, network security, and ease of use. Unfortunately, not only when different vendors' systems have to interact but rather also when the same system such as WebEOC has to scale up to meet the needs of a more demanding multilevel and multi-jurisdictional context (Scholl, 2019), this experience of constraints and lack of scalability seems to be commonplace (Cawley, 2020; Prasanna & Huggins, 2016).

As discussed elsewhere, given the wide range of incidents in terms of scale, scope, and duration (Fischer, 2003) spanning from local emergencies such as leaks of hazardous materials or a building afire to large-scale, large-scope, and long-duration catastrophes such as the Indian Ocean earthquake and tsunami of 2004, the Galveston hurricane of 1900, or the East Japan earthquake and tsunami of 2011, the coordination, integration, and scalability of operations is essential to the effectiveness of the response (Anonymous, 2008, 2013). In the United States, the National Response Framework (NRF) and the National Incident Management System (NIMS) with its Incident Command Structure (ICS) were designed exactly for the purpose of providing a common terminology and a framework of principles, practices, and processes, which would be scalable, flexible, and comprehensive enough to guide responders of any discipline along the whole spectrum of possible disasters (ibid.). While these response frameworks entail a certain degree of organizational standardization, the information management portion of the framework and its supporting information and communication technologies (ICTs), that is, the CIMS would have to carry the burden, as the NIMS/ICS planners anticipated:

> Communications and information systems should be designed to be flexible, reliable, and scalable in order to function in any type of incident, regardless of cause, size, location, or complexity. They should be suitable for operations within a single jurisdiction or agency, a single jurisdiction with multiagency involvement, or multiple jurisdictions with multiagency involvement. Communications systems should be applicable and acceptable to users, readily adaptable to new technology, and reliable in the context of any incident to which emergency management/response personnel would be expected to respond (Anonymous, 2008, p. 24).

By the time, these guidelines were formulated, CIMS such as WebEOC were already in use at all levels of government across the United States, and although WebEOC was still far from having become a kind of de-facto standard, a rather wide variety of non-interoperable CIMS was already in use around the country. This, however, began to slowly change when in 2012 the US Federal Emergency Management Agency (FEMA) also adopted WebEOC for their internal use (Kelly, 2014). Yet, only a few years into FEMA's use of this particular CIMS, it became evident that for security and performance reasons, the WebEOC implementation at FEMA would not interoperate with State, Territory, or Tribal WebEOC sites forcing both FEMA and the respective agencies into tedious, error-prone, and time-consuming double work for necessary data exchanges (McCauley, 2015). It immediately follows that during responses to larger incidents, when the coordination and collaboration between and among agencies, both vertically and horizontally, are badly needed, such bottlenecks would be counterproductive and costly. This study's intent was to find out, document, and analyze how practitioners experience their work with WebEOC during a response with the aim of better understanding the efficacy and usefulness of this commercial CIMS along the entire spectrum of emergencies and disasters.

The publication is organized as follows: first, related work on WebEOC in the academic literature is reviewed. Next, research questions and the methodology are detailed. Then, the findings for each research question are presented followed by a discussion of the findings. Finally, concluding remarks and directions for future research are presented.

Related Work

While professional response organizations in the United States have chosen from and implemented a wide range of COTS CIMS for the purpose of supporting their respective response operations, WebEOC appears to have become the most proliferated CIMS (Cawley, 2020; Delaney & Kitchin, 2020). Interestingly, in academic research, although CIMS are at the core of modern information management in emergency response, they have not yet systematically been assessed and evaluated in terms of their efficacy over the entire spectrum of incident responses. As a recent study suggested, "the role of information management tools used in <emergency management>... needs further investigation," which according to the authors required to include "studying differences between centralized control and distributed participation; incorporating multiple incident data into a visually informative form for decision-makers (e.g., hazardous conditions); and improving designs suitable for updating information in a timely manner" (Son et al., 2020, p. 10). Nevertheless, some research, even with regard to WebEOC, has been conducted while the overall picture has remained spotty. The first well-known quasi-academic comparison of contemporary CIMS was conducted as early as 2002 by the Hart study, which was sponsored by the Department of Justice's National Institute of Justice (NIJ). The study performed a 106 "features" comparison of then-contemporary CIMS, among which WebEOC scored highest with 102 desirable "features" identified (Hart, 2002).

A number of WebEOC-related studies went down a similar pathway, when investigating features (such as "boards") and their relative usefulness in incident responses (Delaney & Kitchin, 2020; Nikolai et al., 2010; Li et al., 2017; Barnett et al., 2021; Sánchez & Sánchez, 2020). Some studies took a high-level descriptive approach without concerning themselves with any technology or feature details (Barnett et al., 2021; Wukich, 2020). WebEOC was also found as a unifying connecting link in private-public partnerships between business communities and government agencies (Levy & Prizzia, 2018a, b).

While studies like the former portrayed WebEOC's versatility, others emphasized more critical findings. Around the time that the NIMS/ICS designers detailed their recommendations regarding necessary interoperability, interconnectivity, and scalability requirements for CIMS (as quoted in the introduction), academic research also came to similar conclusions (Prasanna & Huggins, 2016; Truptil et al., 2008). Along these lines, WebEOC was found incomplete in terms of the availability of needed information (Aros & Gibbons, 2018) also with regard to information sharing between and among different agencies (Whelan & Molnar, 2018). During a multi-jurisdictional response to a major landslide disaster, WebEOC implementations at Federal level (FEMA) and State levels were found unable to interoperate in most basic ways for security concerns on either side (Scholl et al., 2017). Similarly, in the simulation of a catastrophic incident, that is, under artificial exercise conditions when no damage of critical infrastructure had actually occurred or was even assumed under the simulated scenario, the interoperation and information sharing between a State-operated WebEOC site and two-dozen county WebEOC sites broke completely down under the sheer load of requests (Scholl et al., 2018).

Besides these serious load-related issues, other reports found a lack of automatic information summarization technologies implemented in WebEOC (Li et al., 2017), which made it hard for responders to see the forest for the trees, once an incident response began growing, so that information had to be manually aggregated on paper to be useful (Kedia et al., 2020). The latter study also found "poor interoperability" within the network infrastructure (Kedia et al., 2020, p. 9) resulting in poor information sharing exacerbated by ineffective ex ante staff training and unaddressed communication gaps.

Other studies found that in order to make good use of WebEOC, the incident response had to accommodate to the "tool" rather than that the tool accommodated to the demands and needs of the response (Misra et al., 2020). The same study also reported that WebEOC's customizability, while giving the respective agency the flexibility to tailor the tool to its specific needs, by so doing it also sacrifices standardization and compatibility with other WebEOC implementations. Many agencies, particularly resource-poor ones, may even have great difficulty with setting up WebEOC in a tailored fashion (Prasanna & Huggins, 2016; Misra et al., 2020).

When analyzing the efficacy of a particular CIMS in response to an incident, scale, scope, and duration of this particular incident present the first benchmarks to consider. As mentioned in the introduction, a CIMS, which performs reasonably well in the response to incidents of small scale, small scope, and short duration, may not perform as well when scale, scope, and duration of the incident increase, let alone when catastrophic proportions are reached. However, few studies such as Son et al. on CIMS efficacy have taken this consideration into account. When, for example, taking Fischer's scale (Fischer, 2003), which categorizes emergencies and disasters in a range from "DC (for disaster category) 1" to "DC 10" with "DC 1" standing for an everyday local and small incident and "DC 10" representing a catastrophe of extraordinary magnitude and annihilation, it appears intuitively evident that a CIMS has to be extremely scalable to cover this enormous range.

In summary, the efficacy of existing CIMS, and especially, WebEOC, in emergency and disaster response management is understudied; therefore, it has remained an open question of whether or not current CIMS, and here, WebEOC, are fit to task, in particular, when it comes to larger and dynamically growing incidents toward the upper end of the Fischer scale.

Research Questions and Methodology

Research Questions

As the literature review illustrated the gap of understanding with regard to the efficacy of CIMS, and specifically WebEOC, in practical disaster response management is wide. Moreover, it will be a potentially lifesaving and likely disaster-mitigating contribution if this known gap in understanding could be narrowed. It also appears that the most important stakeholders, that is, disaster responders, would bring firsthand practical experience to the table, when it comes to the efficacy of WebEOC, which leads to the following two research questions:

Research Question #1 (RQ #1):
How do professional emergency responders perceive the efficacy and fitness to task of WebEOC in emergency response management?

Research Question #2 (RQ #2):
What specific, if any, concerns regarding WebEOC (and its use) do professional emergency responders express in emergency response management?

Data Selection and Analysis

Instrument Owed to the paucity of research on the subject and the concurrent absence of a guiding theoretical framework, the inquiry had to be of exploratory nature. For this purpose, an online (Google Forms) 14-question survey was devised. All questions except the last were either single- or multiple-choice questions. The first two questions established demographics (affiliation, WebEOC licensing status). The next 11 questions queried about use and performance aspects of WebEOC. The last question was free format and open ended, which gave participants an additional opportunity to enter their own observations in a narrative.

Sample The intention of the researchers was to reach out and receive feedback from both the managerial and professional levels of disaster responders around the country. As a reminder, this inquiry did not seek to statistically test any hypotheses regarding the usefulness of WebEOC in disaster response. It rather intended to explore the perception of usefulness of WebEOC on part of professional disaster responders who had gained practical experience with this particular CIMS, which suggested a convenience sample was to be used (Ritchie et al., 2003). As a long-term practitioner and a leader in the field, the second author has run a regular and well-respected blog for several years, which is read by a large audience of response professionals. In order to attract responses, the survey was attached to an opinion editorial that the second author posted on his blog site (Holdeman, 2020). The tone of the blog was critical toward WebEOC, which was hoped to prompt professional responders into reacting and taking the survey, either for reasons of strong disagreement or for the opposite.

Data Collection The vast majority of the data were received and collected within 2.5 weeks after the publication of the opinion piece. Very few responses were entered weeks after the publication. A total of 83 responses were received, and 48 respondents also took the time to enter a narrative, some of which was extensive and rich. Half of the respondents were county-level responders, 26.3% State-level responders, 13.1% municipal government-level responders, just under 5% Federal-level responders, 2.4% other governmental institution-level responders, and 3.6% were nongovernmental organization-based responders. The vast majority of responders (72.6%) represented organizations that had active WebEOC licenses, and 17.9% of responders represented organizations that previously held a WebEOC license.

Data Analysis and Coding Data were analyzed in an open-coding approach (Corbin & Strauss, 1990; Fereday & Muir-Cochrane, 2006), in which tentative concept labels were attributed to chunks of texts and their particular attributes. The concept labels were connected with regard to their relationships to each other in an axial-coding exercise (Charmaz, 2006) and compared to the results of the 11 single- and multiple-choice survey questions for plausibility, consistency, and further explanation.

Neutrality/Impartiality This research has not been funded nor otherwise supported by any commercial or other vested interest.

Findings

In the following the findings are presented in the order of the research questions. The findings from both the single-/multiple-choice questions and the free-format narratives are integrated in each findings subsection.

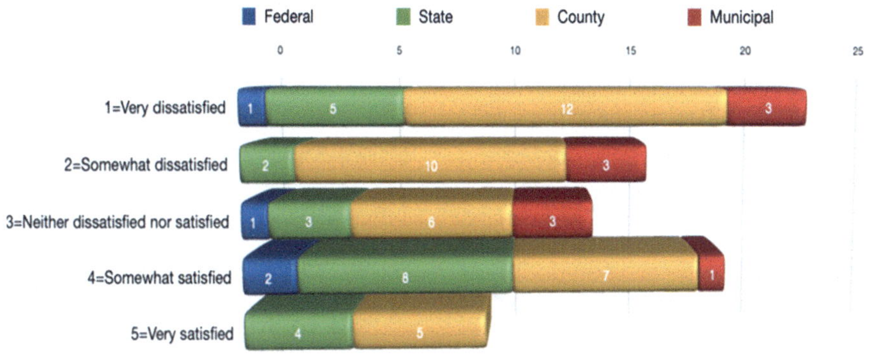

Fig. 1 WebEOC user satisfaction/dissatisfaction per government level

Ad Research Question 1 (RQ #1) (How do professional emergency responders perceive the efficacy and fitness to task of WebEOC in emergency response management?)

The first survey question attempted to establish the overall satisfaction or dissatisfaction of survey respondents with WebEOC. Without undue speculation it was assumed that responders' satisfaction or dissatisfaction with WebEOC would largely correspond to the system's perceived efficacy and fitness to task. It was found that 33.7% of respondents were either very satisfied or at least somewhat satisfied whereas a majority of respondents (53%) across all groups were either very dissatisfied or somewhat dissatisfied, while 18.1% of respondents fell into neither camp. In other words, with only about one third of respondents expressing satisfaction of some kind with the system, WebEOC's efficacy and fitness to task in emergency and disaster response management appears to be called into question for the most part. However, based on the demographic and other data derived from the survey, it was possible to provide sharper contours and more granular detail for painting this mostly unfavorable overall picture of WebEOC performance in US emergency and disaster response management.

As Fig. 1 shows when breaking down the distribution of satisfaction and dissatisfaction along government levels, WebEOC-related satisfaction is strongest at Federal and State levels, whereas on county and municipal levels, dissatisfaction prevails. It is noteworthy, though, that while the survey produced only four responses from the Federal level, the four responses were widely spread with regard to the degree of satisfaction, and no Federal-level response indicated the highest level of satisfaction with WebEOC.

Taking county and municipal levels together, overall dissatisfaction with WebEOC was more than twice as frequent as was overall satisfaction with the tool. Among the variables, which might influence the degree of satisfaction or dissatisfaction, the authors suspected "frequency of use," "ease of use," "functionality," and "degree of customization" (see Table 1). Upon inspecting the percent values, one might tend at first sight to associate, for example, far more

Table 1 WebEOC user satisfaction/dissatisfaction relative to other factors

Variable values (Variables: frequency, ease of use, functionality, and customization)	Very or somewhat dissatisfied (%)	Very or somewhat satisfied (%)
Daily use	17.9	60.7
Weekly use	28.2	14.3
Monthly use	15.4	14.3
Infrequent use	38.5	10.7
Very complicated	37.5	0.0
Somewhat complicated	32.5	37.0
Neither complicated nor easy	20.0	22.2
Somewhat easy	10.0	29.6
Very easy	0.0	11.1
Basic functions	26.3	17.9
Advanced functions	73.7	82.1
No/little customization	28.2	11.1
Some customization	25.6	25.9
Substantial customization	25.6	33.3
Extensive customization + add-ons	20.5	29.6

Table 2 WebEOC customization per government level (%)

Degree of customization	Federal (%)	State (%)	County (%)	Municipal (%)
Little or no customization	0.0	13.6	25.6	30.0
Some customization	0.0	18.2	23.1	50.0
Substantial customization	100.0	22.7	30.8	20.0
Extensive customization/add-ons	0.0	40.9	20.5	0.0
Not sure	0.0	4.5	0.0	0.0
Totals	*100.0*	*100.0*	*100.0*	*100.0*

frequent, that is, "daily use" with higher degrees of satisfaction; as Table 1 shows, only 17.9% of "somewhat or very dissatisfied" respondents indicated that they used WebEOC on a daily basis, while, in contrast, outright 60.7% of "somewhat or very satisfied" respondents suggested they used the system on a daily basis. One might argue that more frequent use leads to, or, at least, illustrates higher degrees of satisfaction. However, regression analyses on all independent variables specified above and their combinations did not produce any statistically significant prediction of the dependent variable (satisfaction/dissatisfaction).

Despite this particular finding, it is noteworthy that WebEOC customization is the greater the higher the level of government (see Table 2). For the Federal level, substantial WebEOC customization was reported in all cases; on State level, customization is over 82% with half of this attributed to "extensive customization with add-ons." On county and municipal levels, customization of WebEOC is also found in or slightly above 70% the responses; however, on the municipal level no "extensive customization with add-ons" is reported.

Table 3 WebEOC functionality usage per government level (%)

Functionality	Federal (%)	State (%)	County (%)	Municipal (%)
1 = Basic functions	0.0	0.0	30.8	70.0
2 = Advanced functions	100.0	100.0	66.7	30.0
3 = Not sure	0.0	0.0	2.6	0.0
Totals	*100.0*	*100.0*	*100.0*	*100.0*

Table 4 Usage of WebEOC mapping per government level (%)

Usage of WebEOC mapping	Federal (%)	State (%)	County (%)	Municipal (%)
Mapping never used	75.0	22.7	48.7	60.0
Mapping rarely used	0.0	27.3	20.5	40.0
Not sure	0.0	9.1	2.6	0.0
Mapping regularly used	25.0	22.7	17.9	0.0
Mapping key functionality	0.0	18.2	10.3	0.0
Totals	*100.0*	*100.0*	*100.0*	*100.0*

With regard to functionality, again the higher the government level the more the advanced functionality of WebEOC is employed. At municipal level, overwhelmingly basic functionality of WebEOC is adopted, which illustrates an enormous gap of sophistication and experience between the local level and even the next higher level (county), let alone the State and Federal levels (see Table 3).

One of the most important, if not *the* most important task in emergency management is gaining and maintaining *situational awareness (SA),* which is the prerequisite for developing and also maintaining a *common operating picture (COP).* Fully developed and vetted SA/COP are at the core of any effective and successfully targeted response to any incident (Anonymous, 2008, 2010a). In this particular context, the detailed geographic location of incident-related information is essential. Many response units employ highly specialized geographic information systems (GIS) such as the Environmental System Research Institute's ArcGIS. However, WebEOC also comprises a mapping component of its own and affords some GIS record integration with ArcGIS, although the WebEOC mapping component lacks the sophistication of ArcGIS.

As Table 4 demonstrates, WebEOC-based mapping is rarely if ever used at municipal level, and also at Federal level its usage is relatively low, which in this latter case is most likely attributable to the use of more powerful GIS at Federal level. But on county and State levels, this particular mapping functionality is never or rarely used in almost 70%, or almost 50%, of the cases, respectively. Similar to the Federal level, it is likely that both county and State responders utilize more powerful and more specialized tools like ArcGIS instead. As before, a major gap in functionality utilization and, consequently, sophistication with regard to WebEOC-based generation and preservation of SA/COP appears to exist between municipal levels of government and higher levels.

Table 5 Intra-/extra-jurisdictional connectivity per government level (%)

Connectivity	Federal	State	County	Municipal
Not connected (intra-jurisdictional)	75.0%	15.0%	23.7%	22.2%
Some connected (intra-jurisdictional)	25.0%	65.0%	57.9%	66.7%
All connected (intra-jurisdictional)	0.0%	20.0%	18.4%	11.1%
Totals (intra-jurisdictional connectivity)	*100.0%*	*100.0%*	*100.0%*	*100.0%*
Not connected (extra-jurisdictional)	75.0%	10.5%	30.8%	0.0%
Some connected (extra-jurisdictional)	25.0%	36.8%	43.6%	88.9%
All connected (extra-jurisdictional)	0.0%	52.6%	25.6%	11.1%
Totals (extra-jurisdictional connectivity)	*100.0%*	*100.0%*	*100.0%*	*100.0%*
Upstream log-in	n/a	40.9%	27.8%	33.3%
No upstream log-in	n/a	59.1%	72.2%	66.7%
Totals (upstream log-in connectivity)	*n/a*	*100.0%*	*100.0%*	*100.0%*

Problems with connectivity have been a known WebEOC characteristic, which encompass network load issues, connection security issues, slow or no responses, connection failures, among others (Whelan & Molnar, 2018; Scholl et al., 2017, 2018, 2019; Misra et al., 2020). The survey instrument is distinguished between same-jurisdiction connections (including resource requesting and tracking) and cross-jurisdictional connections (also, including resource requesting and tracking). Since most respondents were believed to be nonexperts on ICT network-related matters, a control question was included that prompted for the type of establishing connections to WebEOC systems in other jurisdictions (upstream log-in for access). For example, FEMA does not allow for their WebEOC implementation to directly interoperate with States' WebEOC implementations. Rather, State responders have to remotely log on to the FEMA system via a secure connection, where an account for them is maintained. Many States act likewise with their lower-ranking jurisdictions. If upstream log-in is provided as a connectivity mechanism, then in all likelihood there is no other connectivity mechanism established in that particular direction. It is obvious that this type of interoperation is anything but seamless and has to be seen as an inelegant work-around. As Table 5 shows, Federal-level respondents confirmed that most of their WebEOC implementations do not connect to other systems. In contrast, a majority of State, county, and municipal respondents corroborate that most of their WebEOC implementations interoperate in some fashion with other WebEOC systems, both intra-jurisdictionally and extra-jurisdictionally. The highest numbers of upstream log-in access were found at State level (40.9%) followed by municipalities (33.3%) and counties (27.8%). However, that means that in most cases no upstream log-in appears to exist or to be used.

When looking at the narratives in survey responses, only a single highly positive comment stood out from a State-level responder who reported on a decade-long experience also praising the cost-benefit ratio of WebEOC. Unfortunately, the responder did not give more details, for example, regarding the use of the system across emergencies of different magnitudes or regarding the coordination with other agencies. Another State responder stated that all lower-level jurisdictions log on to their State WebEOC system during an incident response, so that the incident is dealt with from a unified SA/COP perspective. Another State responder referring to an identical log-in from remote setup between the State and lower-level jurisdictions, however, remarked that the system was "clunky" and not easy to use, and unlike the other two respondents who were very satisfied with WebEOC, this respondent was somewhat dissatisfied. Some county respondents noted that their upstream log-in setup was a one-way street only for sharing State information downstream. Interestingly, WebEOC's mapping functionality was mentioned in the narrative responses only twice: despite one county respondent's overall dissatisfaction with WebEOC, this individual was highly appreciative of the integration of ArcGIS and WebEOC, which allowed for importing some data from WebEOC into ArcGIS (sic!). Another respondent who was neither satisfied nor dissatisfied with WebEOC had not come across this integration functionality and rather urged for GIS integration. Although mildly satisfied with WebEOC, but implicitly acknowledging the system's problems, one Federal responder stated:

> Big Tech could solve this easily; look at the interoperability within Apple or Google apps – maps, sharing, email, messaging, browsing are instinctively linked. Imagine what they could do if given the task to package existing apps into an EM layer (quote #1—from survey responses).

In summary, dissatisfaction with WebEOC among survey respondents was found much stronger and more outspoken than satisfaction thereof, and, in particular, the "very dissatisfied" outnumbered the "very satisfied" by a margin of more than two to one in the responses. When analyzing, which (independent) variables might have influenced these particular outcomes, neither "frequency of use" nor the "functionality used" (basic or advanced), nor the "degree of customization," nor "ease of use" were found predictors for satisfaction or dissatisfaction on part of the respondents. Furthermore, WebEOC mapping was relatively sparsely used, and certainly not as a core function, but rather as an add-in, which was connected to a more powerful GIS. Finally, overall WebEOC connectivity was only moderately implemented with States most highly engaged. Given the relatively high levels of dissatisfaction in the perception of responding practitioners, WebEOC's fitness to task appears to be debatable, and it appears that the reasons for this dissatisfaction are multifold.

Ad Research Question 2 (RQ #2) (What specific, if any, concerns regarding WebEOC (and its use) do professional emergency responders express in emergency response management?)

Respondents expressed most of their concerns in the open-ended narrative at the end of the survey. However, one multiple-choice survey question was geared at eliciting potential concerns regarding moving away from WebEOC. Nine choices were given including one "other" as shown in Table 6 below. The respondents marked a total of 222 choices or on average 2.7 per respondent. It appears that no single concern stood out above all others with the exception of "budgetary concerns" with 33.3%, which was most pronounced on Federal level than on any other government level followed equally with 16.7% each by concerns regarding

Table 6 Concerns and obstacles perceived (when switching from WebEOC—in %)

Concerns/obstacles	Federal (%)	State (%)	County (%)	Municipal (%)
State standard	0.0	20.6	18.8	18.2
No known alternative	0.0	16.2	15.8	21.2
Budgetary concerns	33.3	11.8	10.9	6.1
New system might not be working	0.0	4.4	6.9	9.1
Changing means going outside the norm	16.7	7.4	9.9	18.2
Difficult adoption of a new system	16.7	16.2	6.9	12.1
Institution deeply invested	16.7	13.2	10.9	9.1
Internal stakeholders deeply invested	16.7	8.8	9.9	6.1
Other	0.0	1.5	9.9	0.0
Totals	*100.0*	*100.0*	*100.0*	*100.0*

"going outside the norm" (sic!), "difficulty of adopting a new system," and both the institution and its internal stakeholders too "deeply invested" into the status quo with WebEOC.

In lower-ranking jurisdictions, the implicit or explicit de facto standardization on WebEOC as the emergency and disaster management system represented the most highly cited concern with 20.6%/ at State, 18.8% at county, and again 18.8% at municipal levels. Furthermore, at municipal level a higher-ranking concern with 21.6% was the absence of a "known alternative" to WebEOC. Since only very few "other" concerns were specified, the first eight choices in this multiple-choice question on the subject must have covered the prevailing concerns and perceived obstacles fairly comprehensively.

On the municipal level, respondents' concerns revolved around the perceived high cost of changes in system versions, system administrators, and when adding functionality by coding and recoding. Some municipal responders felt that WebEOC was oversized for their respective needs, while others bemoaned the absence of mobile versions. Quite a number of municipal responders decried the perceived lack of ease of use and straightforward task-relevant functionality. Said one respondent:

> Having used both <another system> and WebEOC, I have found WebEOC is clunkier and less user friendly. <The other system> is easier to build what is needed by the user. (quote #2—from survey responses).

And another municipal respondent explained:

> WebEOC is designed for large agencies not the majority of EM offices with one or two staff (quote #3—from survey responses).

County respondents also criticized that WebEOC's lack of intuitiveness and ease of use, which they felt, did not take into account the relatively modest ICT savviness of average emergency responders, in particular, in the more typical case that responders would not use the system frequently enough to maintain familiarity. Like respondents on municipal level, the county respondents also expressed dissatisfaction with WebEOC's lack of functionality and unintuitive user interface. In this context, some respondents used explicit language to illustrate their personal frustration with WebEOC ("It sucks." "Terrible old system that has become a failure." "Outdated and obtuse system that wastes an agency's limited resources." "Lots of money spent. Still doesn't work." "After using WebEOC for numerous large and small emergencies and disasters over the past years, I give WebEOC functionality and 'usability' a grade of C/C-."). Respondents on this government level also pointed at compatibility and interoperability problems, which emanated in part from a lack of standards set and followed in WebEOC implementations resulting in a wide variety of organizationally incompatible implementations. Some of these incompatibilities could be attributed to different needs at different levels of government. As one county respondent shared,

> Local EOCs who have adopted WebEOC as their software of choice in this State are buying and operating their WebEOC systems independently (State and local WebEOC systems do not interface with each other). If the locals buy their own WebEOC system, they tailor boards also to their respective EOC needs and unfortunately all the boards do no match each other at all the respective EOC levels (quote #4—from survey responses).

On State level, the concerns of lower-ranking jurisdictions were echoed regarding the lack of "ease of use" and "functionality" as well as the high cost of maintenance including extensive training needs for coping with WebEOC's complexity. Frustration with WebEOC was also expressed on this level in no uncertain terms ("WebEOC is very clunky." "<WebEOC> has outlived its usefulness and should be trashed."). As mentioned while for States "interconnectivity" exists via secure upstream single-user log-in onto FEMA's WebEOC implementation (and not, as manifest, via a bidirectional State-WebEOC-to-FEMA-WebEOC interoperation protocol), this type of interconnection is limited in capacity and bidirectionality, which creates unpleasant bottlenecks and redundancies, in particular, in the resource request process, which employs the so-called resource request forms (RRFs). As a State respondent explains,

> Throughout our response in various disasters, missions could easily get lost as hundreds of mission requests flowed into WebEOC in a short period of time. This was problematic and challenging. We created alerts if missions were time sensitive or not updated in a timely fashion. Having no interface between our State and FEMA's WebEOC platform is problematic and time consuming as we submit RRF's, we have to submit paper RRFs to FEMA which defeats the purpose of WebEOC (quote #5—from survey responses).

Another respondent summed up the experience with WebEOC this way:

> The biggest problem with WebEOC is that emergency managers all too often have to manage WebEOC instead of using it as a tool (quote #6—from survey responses).

On Federal, respondents did not leave comments except for one (see quote #1 above). However, this respondent also highlighted the high licensing cost and the limitations ("single channel") of WebEOC.

In summary, respondents from all levels of government were critical with the relatively high cost of licenses for using and maintaining WebEOC. In particular, a dearth of functionality, a deficit in true interoperability, and a lack of ease of use were criticized on all levels of government. The terms "clunky" and "outdated" were used repeatedly.

Discussion, Future Research, and Concluding Remarks

General Observations

CIMS differs from other and, particularly, non-mission critical information management systems in at least two ways: (1) With regard to their specific purpose, and even more so, with respect to their centrality in the overall critical information infrastructure, CIMS must be resilient, that is, robust, resourceful, redundant, and rapid (in operational usability and response time) (Anonymous, 2008; Scholl & Patin, 2014). The findings of this study along with those of earlier academic reports, however, suggest that WebEOC would not qualify as a resilient CIMS along these lines, at least not in terms of robustness nor rapidity. It rather appears to slow down in response time and even to break down under only moderate loads, which apart from security and network safety concerns also explains the lack of true multiway interconnectivity (with FEMA presenting the most prominent example). Interconnectivity is at the core of any system's scalability. If interconnectivity is limited, then scalability is limited. With limits in scalability, the respective CIMS can only be reasonably and safely used in responses to relatively small-scale incidents. (2) CIMS are supposed to be extremely easy to understand and use (Anonymous, 2008; Turoff et al., 2004), since under the typically increasingly stressful circumstances of an incident response, professional responders have no time nor do they have the stomach for struggling with idiosyncrasies and peculiarities of any given CIMS. The respective CIMS has to support the response seamlessly and without putting additional burdens on its users. However, WebEOC reportedly appears not to be in this category of seamless CIMS. Paraphrasing one respondent's words, when using WebEOC in more complex incident responses, rather frequently, the tail appears to be wagging the dog.

In a nutshell, in terms of flexibility, reliability, scalability, and ease of use, WebEOC does not appear to meet the CIMS standard requirements formulated in the basic NIMS document of 2008 (Anonymous, 2008, p. 24) according to this study's findings.

The Need for a Widely Accepted, Resilient, and Scalable CIMS

In a recent study on the subject, Son and colleagues performed a meta-analysis of the literature (Son et al., 2020) and confirmed earlier insights regarding resiliency in emergency management that highlighted factors including "collective sensemaking," "team decision-making," and "interaction and coordination" (p. 10), all of which heavily rely on the availability and proper functioning of a capable and robust CIMS as a prerequisite. As has been shown elsewhere, it does not suffice that a system can actually perform certain operations under certain circumstances. It rather also matters what the respective system's overall performance expectancy is, which is colored by past and present experiences from a human agent's (and here professional responder's) perspective (Prasanna & Huggins, 2016). If human agents who have to perform together as a coordinated group grow increasingly frustrated with a system's expected performance, then the acceptance of using such a system plummets, which seems to be the case with WebEOC among numerous responders on all level of government. In other words, if WebEOC's reputation among a large group of responders is turning unfavorable through lived and repeated negative experience, then the impact on the adoption and use of the system in the larger community of responders becomes problematic through the social influence of the disenchanted group. Conversely, if a CIMS satisfies the performance expectations of a group of human agents, then the system's adoption and use is strongly and more widely supported also through the group's social influence. As seen in the findings, some responders suggested alternative COTS CIMS, while still others preferred a national initiative and a system standardized and centrally supported for all levels of government at affordable cost. The idea of using cloud-based services and existing standard tools for such undertaking might also be a viable path, which deserves study and evaluation.

It has been argued elsewhere that scalability is not only an upward affair but rather also includes downward capabilities in case that power and networking capabilities are completely lost for an extended period of time and low-tech solutions have to be employed temporarily. While these incident scenarios might still be rare, incidents of larger magnitude will undoubtedly encompass situations, in which, on the one hand, multi-jurisdictional collaboration and coordination of the response is badly needed, while, on the other hand, major portions of the critical (information) infrastructure are destroyed or degraded to an extent, which makes such coordination and collaboration extremely difficult. CIMS redundancy then means that critical functions in such scenarios need to be performable elsewhere. It also requires logistical support for equipping responders on the ground who have limited or no direct connectivity with updated stand-alone CIMS from remote sites via appropriate means of physical transportation.

Limitations of the Study

WebEOC is a CIMS predominantly used in the United States. The results reported here may be different for other CIMS in other countries. Also, software systems undergo relatively frequent revisions. This study did not discriminate between respondents reporting on the most recent version as opposed to older versions of this particular COTS. As a result, experiences with newer versions of WebEOC might have produced more favorable results. However, the convenience sample still reports on "what is currently out there;" yet, a large random or systematic sample might have produced more accurate results. While the number of respondents (83) who fully took the survey cannot be called small, it nevertheless was not large enough to produce highly robust results, which would lend themselves subject to elaborate statistical analyses. The study attracted participation by attaching the Web survey to a subject matter blog widely read by practitioners in emergency management. This particular blog entry on WebEOC was highly critical of the system, which might have primed and incentivized more respondents with negative than positive views to also share their own mainly negative views on WebEOC. Therefore, besides the sampling situation also from this latter perspective of potential bias, no claim of results-based generalizability can be made. Furthermore, when testing for predictors for the dependent variable (satisfaction/dissatisfaction) via regression analysis, none of the independent variables was found as outcome predictors. This might change in case of a larger and systematic sample. While these limitations are acknowledged, the study nevertheless was able to document in detail considerable dissatisfaction with WebEOC on part of practitioners on all levels of government who gave ample comments in support of their views. The study, hence, represents a broader exploratory step than previous studies also geared at better understanding the current problem space involving WebEOC.

Concluding Remarks and Future Research

It has been the object of this exploration to identify and document practitioners and system users' perceptions of fitness to task of WebEOC, the leading CIMS in the United States. This study contributes to the understanding of challenges and potential pitfalls when using commercial-off-the-shelf systems (COTS) in the context of emergency and disaster response management. While WebEOC appears to have some support among practitioners (mainly on Federal and State levels), a far larger number of practitioners on all levels of government was found to be highly critical of the system with respect to its perceived high cost, difficult maintenance, low performance, insufficient functionality, limited interoperability, and weak scalability. Since CIMS are the backbone of effective all-hazard and all-magnitude incident responses, these findings, which are supported by other studies, have to prompt further research, since they suggest a serious vulnerability in the nation's capacity to effectively cope with emergencies and disasters, which can have adverse consequences for lives and assets.

Future research therefore needs to focus on how CIMS can be devised that meet the long established criteria and performance benchmarks (Anonymous, 2008, 2010b) and what obstacles must be cleared in order to implement them.

References

Anonymous. (2008). *National incident management system*. FEMA P-501, FEMA.
Anonymous. (2010a). *National incident management system supporting evaluation program (NIMS STEP): Guide*. Report, Federal Emergency Management Agency.

Anonymous. (2010b). *Incident decision support software application note: System assessment and validation for emergency responders (SAVER)*. U.S. Department of Homeland Security.

Anonymous. (2013). In Homeland Security (Ed.), *National response framework* (p. iv/48). FEMA.

Aros, S. K., & Gibbons, D. E. (2018). Developing an agent-based simulation model of the use of different communication technologies in inter-organizational disaster response coordination. In *Proceedings of the 2018 Winter Simulation Conference (WSC)* (pp. 68–79), Gothenburg.

Barnett, D. J., et al. (2021). An analysis of after action reports from Texas hurricanes in 2005 and 2017. *Journal of Public Health Management and Practice, 27*(2), E71–E78.

Cawley, K. S. (2020). *Assessing the impact of age and experience on the perceived ease of use of crisis information management software*. Northcentral University ProQuest Dissertations Publishing.

Charmaz, K. (2006). *Constructing grounded theory: A practical guide through qualitative analysis* (p. xxiii/207). Sage Publications.

Corbin, J. M., & Strauss, A. (1990). Grounded theory research: Procedures, canons, and evaluative criteria. *Qualitative Sociology, 13*(1), 3–21.

Delaney, A., & Kitchin, R. (2020). Progress and prospects for data-driven coordinated management and emergency response: The case of Ireland. *Territory, Politics, Governance, 8*(6), 1–16.

Fereday, J., & Muir-Cochrane, E. (2006). Demonstrating Rigor using thematic analysis: A hybrid approach of inductive and deductive coding and theme development. *International Journal of Qualitative Methods, 5*(1), 80.

Fischer, H. W. (2003). The sociology of disaster: Definitions, research questions, & measurements continuation of the discussion in a Post-September 11 environment. *International Journal of Mass Emergencies and Disasters, 21*(1), 91–107.

Hanson, P., & McDougall, C. (2018). Enabling collaborative and resilient emergency management efforts: DFES and Western Australia's adoption of a common operating picture. In *Proceedings of the 1st international conference on information systems for crisis response and management Asia Pacific* (*ISCRAM Asia Pacific 2018*) (pp. 75–82), Wellington, New Zealand.

Hart, S. V. (2002). *Crisis information management software (CIMS) feature comparison report*. National Institute of Justice.

Holdeman, E. E. (2020). Use of WebEOC is insanity defined. In *Emergency management: Disaster zone*. Government Technology. 27 Aug.

Kedia, T., et al. (2020). Technologies enabling situational awareness during disaster response: A systematic review. *Disaster Medicine and Public Health Preparedness, 16*, 1–19.

Kelly, J. V. (2014). *FEMA's initial response to the Colorado flood*. U.S. Department of Homeland Security, Office of Inspector General.

Levy, J., & Prizzia, R. (2018a). Customizing web-EOC crisis management software to facilitate collaboration and increase situational awareness: Advances in Business Resource Center (BRC) design for business continuity management. In A. J. Masys (Ed.), *Security by design: Innovative perspectives on complex problems* (Advanced sciences and technologies for security applications) (pp. 291–316). Springer.

Levy, J., & Prizzia, R. (2018b). Building effective emergency management public-private partnerships (PPP) for information sharing. In A. J. Masys (Ed.), *Security by design: Innovative perspectives on complex problems* (Advanced sciences and technologies for security applications) (pp. 375–401). Springer.

Li, T., et al. (2017). Data-driven techniques in disaster information management. *ACM Computing Surveys (CSUR), 50*(1), 1–45.

McCauley, S. F. (2015). *FEMA faces challenges in managing information technology*. Office of Inspector General, Department of Homeland Security.

Misra, S., Roberts, P., & Rhodes, M. (2020). The ecology of emergency management work in the digital age. *Perspectives on Public Management and Governance, 3*(4), 305–322.

Nikolai, C., et al. (2010). Leveraging WebEOC in support of the Haitian relief effort: Insights and lessons learned. In *Proceedings of the 7th international conference on information systems for crisis response and management (ISCRAM 2010)* (pp. 1–5).

Prasanna, R., & Huggins, T. J. (2016). Factors affecting the acceptance of information systems supporting emergency operations centres. *Computers in Human Behavior, 57*(April), 168–181, 1 Apr 2016..

Ritchie, J., Lewis, J., & Gillian, E. (2003). Designing and selecting samples. In J. Ritchie & J. Lewis (Eds.), *Qualitative research practice: A guide for social science students and researchers* (pp. 77–108). Sage Publications.

Sánchez, C. E., & Sánchez, L. D. (2020). Case study: Emergency Department response to the Boston Marathon bombing. In D. W. Callaway & J. L. Burstein (Eds.), *Operational and medical management of explosive and blast incidents* (pp. 363–367). Springer.

Scholl, H. J. (2019). Overwhelmed by brute force of nature: First response management in the wake of a catastrophic incident. In I. Lindgren et al. (Eds.), *Electronic government: Proceedings of the 18th IFIP WG 8.5 International Conference, EGOV 2019* (pp. 105–124). Springer.

Scholl, H. J., & Patin, B. J. (2014). Resilient information infrastructures: Criticality and role in responding to catastrophic incidents. *Transforming Government: People, Process and Policy, 8*(1), 28–48.

Scholl, H. J., et al. (2017) Informational challenges in early disaster response: The massive Oso/SR530 landslide 2014 as case in point. In *Proceedings of the 50th Hawaii international conference on system sciences (HICSS-50)* (pp. 2498–2508), Waikoloa, Hawaii.

Scholl, H. J., Hubbel, K., & Leonard, J. (2018). Communications and technology challenges to situational awareness: Insights from the CR16 exercise. In *Proceedings of the 1st ISCRAM Asia-Pacific Conference* (pp. 1–15). ISCRAM.

Scholl, H. J., Hubbell, K., & Leonard, J. G. (2019). Information sharing and situational awareness: Insights from the cascadia rising exercise of June 2016. In *Proceedings of the 52nd Hawaii international conference on system sciences (HICSS-52)* (pp. 1–11).

Son, C., et al. (2020). Investigating resilience in emergency management: An integrative review of literature. *Applied Ergonomics, 87*(n/a), 1–16.

Truptil, S., et al. (2008). Interoperability of information systems in crisis management: Crisis modeling and metamodeling. In K. Mertins et al. (Eds.), *Enterprise interoperability III: New challenges and industrial approaches* (pp. 583–594). Springer.

Turoff, M., et al. (2004). The design of a dynamic emergency response management information system (DERMIS). *JITTA: Journal of Information Technology Theory and Application, 5*(4), 1.

Whelan, C., & Molnar, A. (2018). Organising across boundaries: Communication, coordination and conflict. In C. Whelan & A. Molnar (Eds.), *Securing mega-events: Networks, strategies and tensions* (pp. 91–122). Palgrave Macmillan.

Wukich, C. (2020). More monitoring, less coordination: Twitter and Facebook use between emergency management agencies. *Journal of Homeland Security and Emergency Management, 17*(3), 1–29.

From Digital Public Warning Systems to Emergency Warning Ecosystems

Dario Bonaretti and Diana Fischer-Preßler

Abstract Digital public warning systems (PWS) are platforms for multichannel emergency communication. Advancements in PWS technological infrastructure—API gateways, among all—transformed them into modular and open systems, thus lowering the barriers for outside actors for (a) integrating national PWS with each other, thereby constituting emergency warning *ecosystems*, and (b) intersecting emergency warning ecosystems with other data ecosystems (e.g., healthcare, supply chain) to provide emergency-related digital services. This chapter introduces a model of the warning process along four phases, that is, activate, represent, dispatch, and counteract. It furthermore explains how the warning process is supported by the PWS and how warning ecosystems can help provide richer representations of emergencies.

Keywords Digital platform · Public warning · Warning apps

Introduction

Since around 2010, public administrators have strived to leverage the pervasiveness of smartphones for emergency warnings via mobile apps (see Tan et al., 2017 for a review). As it became more apparent to policymakers that mobile-enabled emergency warning helps build resilient societies, significant public resources were invested in developing the digital infrastructure to enable emergency warning. Some European countries developed national digital platforms for emergency

D. Bonaretti (✉)
Nova Southeastern University, Fort Lauderdale, FL, USA
e-mail: dbonaret@nova.edu

D. Fischer-Preßler
University of Bamberg, Bamberg, Germany
e-mail: diana.fischer-pressler@uni-bamberg.de

H. J. Scholl et al. (eds.), *Disaster Management and Information Technology*,
Public Administration and Information Technology 40,
https://doi.org/10.1007/978-3-031-20939-0_17

communication. The German PWS, for instance, is called *MoWaS,*[1] which stands for "Modular Warning System." MoWaS is an example of a digital public warning system (PWS) that allows storing crisis-related information and dispatching it to national and regional warning apps (e.g., Katwarn, Nina), as well as multichannel dispatching through channels such as cell broadcast service, radio, and teletext.

Technological advancements—API gateways, among all—enabled to modularize the infrastructure of PWS. Moreover, the worldwide governance of emergency communication standards, such as the adoption of the Common Alerting Protocol (v1.2),[2] enabled integrating PWS into supranational warning systems, like Google Alerts. Compliance with international data standards and modularity enables the emergence of digital ecosystems (Jacobides et al., 2018). These ecosystems enhance with emergency response functionalities even nonemergency digital products or services. For example, smart home systems connected with PWS could automate counteractions that have traditionally required human intervention, such as closing shutters upon receiving a thunderstorm alert. As long as a PWS provides open API access, independent developers may also contribute new warning apps or integrate emergency response functionalities in non-emergency warning apps.

For PWS and emergency data ecosystems to thrive, they must provide accurate and timely digital representations of emergencies. To achieve that, it is necessary to adopt a process perspective of public warning and to focus on the four steps of leveraging digital representations in emergency management: activating, representing, dispatching, and counteracting. This chapter explains the digital warning process along those four steps, the technology supporting each step, and the involved users. We then provide an outlook on how future ecosystems for emergency warning could be developed.

Digital Emergency Warning Process

Authorities shall provide digital representations of emergencies by considering four IT-dependent steps of the warning process: *activate*, *represent*, *dispatch*, and *counteract*. Adopting a process perspective of public warning that cuts across these four steps is critical to uncover opportunities for leveraging digital data in emergency communication. For example, the question of whether technology such as unmanned aerial vehicles (UAVs) could serve as sensors to *activate* the PWS shall be complemented by reflecting on whether UAVs imagery can *represent* the event and provide structured and standardized digital representations to be *dispatched* through digital channels and, finally, whether those representations

[1] https://www.bbk.bund.de/DE/Warnung-Vorsorge/Warnung-in-Deutschland/Warnmittel/MoWaS/mowas_node.html, accessed February 10th, 2022.

[2] http://docs.oasis-open.org/emergency/cap/v1.2/CAP-v1.2-os.doc, accessed February 10th, 2022.

can be transformed in actionable information for the recipients of the warning to *counteract*. Therefore, the role of technology shall be considered across all four steps of the model in Fig. 1.

Activation (Step 1)

Activation is the first step in the warning process. In this step, crisis-related information from human or technological sensors is received by the authority in charge of dispatching the warning. This information can be collected *on-ground* or *remotely* and through *opportunistic* or *dedicated* sensors as we summarized in Table 1.

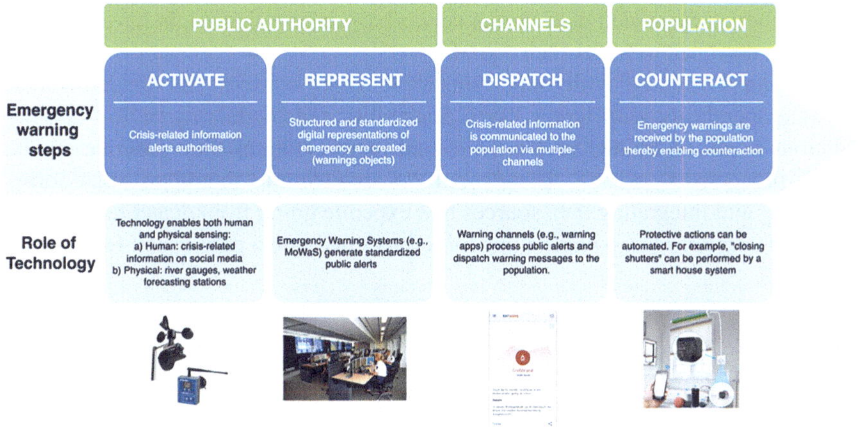

Fig. 1 The four phases of the warning process

Table 1 Forms of emergency-related data collection

	Opportunistic	Dedicated
On-ground	Smartphone apps such as MyShake leverage a network of smartphones to issue earthquake alerts.	Emergency numbers (911) are dedicated communication channels to collect human-sensed emergency information.
Remote	Data from weather stations can be used for detecting wildfires. A weather station can fulfill an emergency warning function even if it was not originally designed for that.	Smart river gauges constitute networks of physical sensors that are designed to track water levels and flood risk.

On-ground sensing requires human presence in the endangered area. It may occur opportunistically via smartphones. For instance, the app MyShake[3] issues earthquake alerts by using smartphones' built-in sensors to detect oscillations. Sensing is *opportunistic* because it does not require user involvement (other than for installing the MyShake app) and because it relies on technology—the network of built-in oscillators on mobile phones—that was not originally designed for detecting earthquakes. Alternatively, an individual may directly call the emergency number and verbally communicate emergency-related information, thereby using a dedicated technology for sensing disasters.

Remote sensing, instead, refers to collecting emergency-related information using physical sensors, such as a system for water level monitoring. Similarly to on-ground sensing, remote sensing can occur opportunistically as well. For example, weather stations can be used for early detection of wildfires thanks to their air quality monitoring capabilities. In fact, the proliferation of IoT technology offers unprecedented scalability to architectures of physical sensors and opportunities to collect emergency-related data from a network of sensors that might have not been originally designed to fulfill such a goal.

A major challenge with opportunistic sensing, however, is standardization and interoperability with larger PWS. Scalability and modularity of IoT sensing solutions might be limited unless the digital representations they generate can be swiftly processed by a PWS. Therefore, PWS architectures should prioritize forms of sensing and integrating data sources that expedite going from detecting a hazard to creating *digital representation* thereof to be turned into a public alert (step 2).

Representation (Step 2)

Representation is about creating standardized, high-fidelity digital representations of an emergency. Such representations are used for creating public warning to be dispatched through different warning channels. The standardization and fidelity of digital representations depend on two main questions (summarized in Table 2). The first concerns the origin of digital representations and whether they are "born digital" or not. A flood simulation model (e.g., LISFLOOD[4]), for instance, provides born digital representations of flooding hazards. Similarly, water index measures such as those obtained by the European system Copernicus[5] through Sentinel-1 satellite imagery are born digital representations of past precipitations.

Non-digital representations are also common in emergency management. In-person reading of river gauges, for example, constitutes non-digital data (see Fig. 2);

[3] https://myshake.berkeley.edu/

[4] https://www.un-spider.org/index.php/links-and-resources/gis-rs-software/lisflood-model-jrc, accessed February 10th, 2022.

[5] https://www.copernicus.eu/en/copernicus-services/emergency

Table 2 Types of emergency-related data feeds

	Structured data	Unstructured data
Born-digital data	Imagery from multispectral satellites allows delineating flooded areas.	Social media feeds may supply representations of emergencies, although emergency-relevant attributes need to be extracted from text, videos, and pictures.
Non-digital data	Ground survey methods such as an in-person reading of river gauge offer structured, human-sensed information.	Emergency calls are unstructured verbal representations of emergencies. It is the 911 telecommunicator who translates the data in structured form and interacts with the caller to ensure all relevant information is gathered.

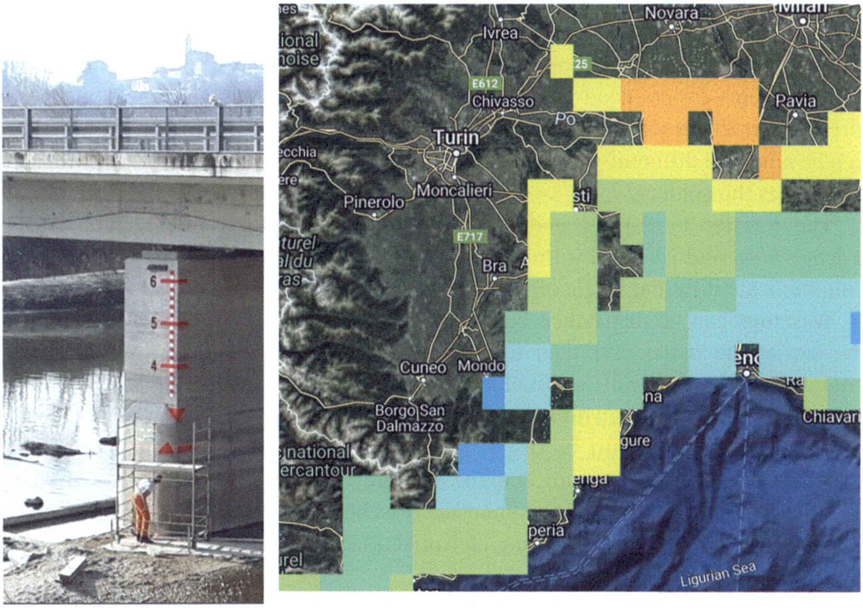

Fig. 2 On the left, a new crest-stage gauge is built by the Tanaro River, Liguria (Italy). On the right is a representation of the soil water index for the same region from Copernicus

likewise, emergency calls are verbal representations of an emergency. Data that is not born digital can be converted into digital form, but the process inevitably results in compression and loss of information.

Secondly, emergency-related data can be provided in *structured* or *unstructured* form. Flood simulation models, for instance, can produce shapefiles of simulation maps. In fact, born-digital and structured data are the easiest data source to integrate in a PWS. However, processing unstructured digital data is sometimes necessary to represent certain events more accurately, timely, or comprehensively. Emergency managers are increasingly investing resources in deciphering emergency-related information that is unstructured and high volume, such as social media posts. In 2016, the American Red Cross launched its Digital Operations Center (Markenson & Howe, 2014) to monitor and engage on social media platforms. However, the richness of digital representations from unstructured data shall be weighed against data cleansing and data integration costs.

Dispatch (Step 3)

Once digital representations of emergencies are created, the PWS can dispatch a public warning via relevant warning channels such as warning apps, TV, or sirens. During dispatching, emergency-related information about event type, description, or location is enriched with recommendations for actions. Public warnings are typically XML messages that are rendered by the channels into warning notifications that recipients experience (e.g., a notification from a warning app, the sound of a siren, a text-to-speech message on the radio). Thus, even the same public warning can be rendered differently by two emergency warning apps depending on how each app parses the content.

The decision to dispatch and what recommendations to provide shall consider *when*, *whom*, and *where* to warn and the extent to which each channel is suitable to communicate different levels of emergency-related information.

Warnings can be dispatched before, during, or after an emergency. Intuitively, the earlier the better, although more lead time does not automatically increase compliance. Paradoxically, individuals who are warned too much in advance may be less likely to comply with recommendations for actions (Hoekstra et al., 2011). Similarly, a warning must be dispatched to a relevant area. Too many irrelevant warnings may increase warning fatigue and decrease compliance because of what is commonly known as cry wolf syndrome (Fischer-Pressler et al., 2021). However, for dynamic and chaotic events (e.g., terrorist attacks), it is not always clear how to define such an area.

The impact of emergencies evolves over time and space. The same event, for instance, can affect some areas worse than others and requires location-specific recommendations for action. People may also need to be alerted despite not being in the immediate hazard area so that they know to avoid it. For example, in case of a fire at a chemical plant, a warning is likely dispatched within the immediate and protective response areas, but highly volatile chemical compounds—depending on the wind strength and direction—might affect a larger area where the impact initially was considered negligible. Should that precautionary area be included in the initial fire warning?

Table 3 summarizes the four functions of emergency warning: preparation, response, precaution, and support. Choosing to support one or all of these four functions shall inform (a) what channels to integrate in the PWS architecture and (b) what channels of those available to activate depending on the emergency. To fulfill

Table 3 The four functions of emergency warning by time and space

	Before	During/after
Disaster area	*Preparation*. Warning in the area of the disaster shall enable preparation. For example, before a hurricane, the population shall be reminded to stock food supplies, electric generators, gas, etc.	*Response*. The population shall receive actionable information to guide protective counteraction.
Precautionary area	*Precaution*. While no countermeasure might be required to people outside the disaster area, they may still need to be warned not to approach it.	*Support*. Authorities can direct people who were not directly affected about how to help victims of a nearby disaster.

any of the warning functions, dispatching must consider *time* (Shall the warning be dispatched before or during/after the disaster?) and *space* (Shall the warning be dispatched to the immediate area of the emergency or a larger one?). Not all channels can aptly fulfill all four functions.

Cell broadcasting, for example, makes targeting a specific geographic area easier than social media. Cell broadcasting is a standard for emergency warning in the USA and several European countries. In fact, a unified European warning service is planned to be launched in Europe.[6] The text messages can be received by any phone within the broadcasting range independent of their carrier and the operating system. For the end user, a cell broadcast message looks similar to an SMS, although the sender is a cell tower rather than someone's device. The warning is displayed simultaneously on all devices within the range of the tower. This represent a more effective channel than actual SMS warning, which may require keeping an up-to-date list of contacts to reach out to and may have limited capacity, in the order of a few hundred SMS per second, meaning that depending on the number of recipients, some might receive delayed SMS warnings. Not requiring any installation or opting in, the main benefit of cell broadcasting is to offer high penetration rates. As individuals are not required to download any software on their phones, resistance toward installing apps due to privacy concerns and the like is not an issue.

Social media is also a mostly mobile warning channel (e.g., Twitter usage is 80% mobile).[7] The rapidity with which information and *misinformation* alike propagate on social media has pushed public authorities to engage with them, albeit sometimes reluctantly. Emergency communication on social media platforms puts extreme pressure on public authorities as they compete for the population's attention against countless social media accounts that might not prioritize sharing accurate and verified information. However, research shows they are effective for *supporting* by enabling coordination among volunteers (Leong et al., 2015).

[6] https://www.etsi.org/deliver/etsi_ts/102900_102999/102900/01.03.01_60/ts_102900v010301p.pdf, accessed January 13th, 2022.

[7] https://developers.google.com/web/showcase/2017/twitter, accessed January 13th, 2022.

Warning apps allow users to opt in for location tracking, so they will receive warnings based on their current location. Moreover, users may subscribe to receive warnings for a certain region of interest regardless of their current position (Fischer-Pressler et al., 2020). Finally, warning apps can provide much richer representations of emergencies than text messages as they enable sharing interactive content such as maps and links to external resources. However, apps are software applications that must be downloaded by a smartphone user to receive notifications about emergencies via push notification. Users may not install them unless they believe the benefits from installing the app offset costs (Fischer-Pressler et al., 2021).

Counteraction (Step 4)

Counteraction concerns the response of the population upon receiving the warning message. Traditionally, the goal of public warnings is to provide the endangered population with information to enable adequate protective actions. Therefore, warning systems have been developed with a strong focus on eliciting compliance with the recommendations for actions such as preparing (e.g., stocking up essentials), shelter in place, or evacuating. They primarily fulfill a *protective* function. By providing richer representations of emergencies (e.g., interactive maps) than traditional warning channels, however, PWS can fulfill an *informative* function on top of a protective one. Moreover, such functions can be carried out by individuals or business organizations, as summarized in Table 4.

When Reuter et al. (2017) investigated the drivers of warning app use in Germany, they discovered that personal safety is not the only—and perhaps neither the most important—driver for using warning apps. People living in a generally safe area may not feel pressured to install a warning app on their smartphones. They might, however, install warning apps to stay up-to-date about emergencies, out of curiosity (Fischer-Pressler et al., 2020), or to learn about emergencies that can possibly endanger their loved ones. Therefore, individuals can leverage the

Table 4 The four types of counteractions by entity and function

	Protective function	Informative function
Individual response	Protective function. Warning information shall enable the recipient to take a prompt and effective protective action (e.g., "shelter in place").	Informative function. Warning information can provide emotional relief to victims of a disaster or to people who worry about loved ones in an affected area.
Business response	Business continuity planning and disaster recovery function. Warning information shall enable data-driven, dynamic business, continuity planning, and disaster recovery.	Business intelligence function. Organizations can take weather-dependent strategic initiatives, such as weather-dependent marketing.

Fig. 3 An example of weather-based marketing by Duracell during Hurricane Lane, a tropical cyclone that affected Hawaii in August 2018 (Duracell, 2018)

informative function of PWS as an emergency may not directly impact the recipient of a warning, but their loved ones—perhaps living far away. In that case, the recipient may gain emotional relief from staying up-to-date about the status of other individuals affected by the emergency.

Similarly, organizations can also leverage representations for business continuity planning or resuming operations in the aftermath of a disaster. Moreover, alongside planning how to continue operating, emergency-related digital data might offer value-generating opportunities on their own. For example, let us consider products with inherent weather sensitivity such as batteries; AccuWeather Inc.[8] (https://www.accuweather.com/), a provider of weather forecasting services, claimed they increased customer engagement of a battery company by leveraging weather-triggered custom content during category 4 and 5 hurricanes (see Fig. 3).

[8] https://advertising.accuweather.com/for-advertising/cpg-success-story/, accessed January 13th, 2022.

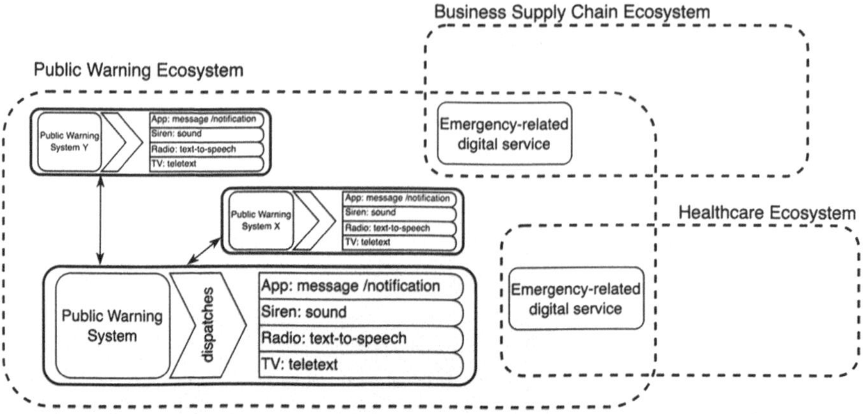

Fig. 4 Intersections among digital data ecosystems

Next-Generation Public Warning Systems

To address the population's rising expectations about the informativeness of public emergency communications, PWS must create and enable access to rich digital representations of emergencies. Among all warning channels, warning apps will benefit the most from richer representations because of their inherent ability to both warn (through push notification) and inform (through hypertext). Moreover, open and common standards in emergency-related data management enable multiple national PWSs to interact within a public warning *ecosystem*. Such an ecosystem might not have a single owner, unlike national PWS, which is controlled by national authorities. The rise of a public warning ecosystem, for instance, around the shared open standard CAP v1.2 enabled developing supranational emergency-related digital services like Google Public Alerts,[9] now seamlessly integrated into the Google Search and Google Maps experience.

Furthermore, once accurate digital representations of an emergency are available in the PWS, broader opportunities to offer *emergency-related digital services* arise at the intersection between the public warning ecosystem and other data ecosystems (see Fig. 4). A public warning ecosystem can be integrated with other platforms or data ecosystems to develop new emergency-related digital services. Weather tracking and forecasting capabilities, for instance, are essential for risk management in supply chain systems and to mitigate supply chain disruption during disasters. In marketing, managers can temporarily reorient advertisement campaigns based on weather-related disasters, as we discussed in section "Counteraction (Step 4)".

[9] https://crisisresponse.google/, accessed February 10th, 2022.

Conclusions

In this chapter, we discussed how the fundamental challenge for PWS is collecting and dispatching digital representations of hazards so that the population can cope with emergencies. Technological progress has enhanced the PWS ability to collect and redistribute digital representations of emergencies through an increasing number of connected devices and sensor networks; mobile phones alone provide manifold opportunities to detect emergencies, deliver warnings, and even automate some responses to emergencies. Moreover, PWS are becoming key enablers of an emergency data ecosystem where digital representations of emergencies enable both individuals and companies to pursue different value appropriation opportunities beyond protective counteracting strictly speaking. Novel opportunities for emergency-related digital services arise at the intersection between the emergency data ecosystems and other ecosystems (e.g., supply chain, healthcare data, marketing), calling for policymakers to invest in PWS as a way to foster societal resilience.

References

Duracell, [Duracell]. (2018). *When severe weather strikes, you need a power you can trust. Make sure to stock up on the #1 trusted battery brand for hurricane lane*. August 24, 2018. https://publish.twitter.com/?query=https%3A%2F%2Ftwitter.com%2FDuracell%2Fstatus%2F1033081428362358785&widget=Tweet

Fischer-Pressler, D., Bonaretti, D., & Fischbach, K. (2020). Effective use of mobile-enabled emergency warning systems. In *Proceedings of 28th European Conference on Information Systems (ECIS)*. Marrakech, Morocco.

Fischer-Pressler, D., Bonaretti, D., & Fischbach, K. (2021). A protection-motivation perspective to explain intention to use and continue to use mobile warning systems. *Business & Information Systems Engineering, 64*, 1–16.

Hoekstra, S., Klockow, K., Riley, R., Brotzge, J., Brooks, H., & Erickson, S. (2011). A preliminary look at the social perspective of warn-on-forecast: Preferred tornado warning lead time and the general public's perceptions of weather risks. *Weather, Climate, and Society, 3*(2), 128–140. https://doi.org/10.1175/2011WCAS1076.1

Jacobides, M. G., Cennamo, C., & Gawer, A. (2018). Towards a theory of ecosystems. *Strategic Management Journal, 39*(8), 2255–2276.

Leong, C. M., Ling, S. L., Pan, P. R., & Kaewkitipong, L. (2015). ICT-enabled community empowerment in crisis response: Social media in Thailand flooding 2011. *Journal of the Association for Information Systems, 16*(3), 174.

Markenson, D., & Howe, L. (2014). American red cross digital operations center (DigiDOC): An essential emergency management tool for the digital age. *Disaster Medicine and Public Health Preparedness, 8*(5), 445–451.

Reuter, C., Kaufhold, M., Leopold, I., & Knipp, H. (2017). Katwarn, Nina, or Fema? Multi-method study on distribution, use, and public views on crisis apps. In *Proceedings of 25th European Conference on Information Systems (ECIS)*. Guimaraes, Portugal.

Tan, M. L., Prasanna, R., Stock, K., Hudson-Doyle, E., Leonard, G., & Johnston, D. (2017). Mobile applications in crisis informatics literature: A systematic review. *International Journal of Disaster Risk Reduction, 24*(September), 297–311. https://doi.org/10.1016/j.ijdrr.2017.06.009

The Role of Ontologies and Linked Open Data in Support of Disaster Management

Anacleto Correia, Pedro B. Água, and Mário Simões-Marques

Abstract An increasing number of disasters, of natural and anthropogenic origin, enhance the importance of the current role played by disaster management (DM) decision support systems regarding the actions at the different phases of the DM cycle. Disaster management is known for the heterogeneity of domain's concepts, the kind of resources deployed for disaster response, and the complexity of the information that needs to be shared among the several organizations participating in a catastrophe scenario. The adoption of common ontologies enables information sharing among them. An exploratory systematic review of ontologies was developed to collect references of already proposed ontologies for the realm of DM, and to identify underexplored topics, and research gaps, which may hamper the semantic alignment of DM decision support systems. Further to this, the goal of the study is to envision a potential evolution of DM decision support systems toward better decision-making processes along the DM cycle, specifically, concerning the synergistic role toward interoperability and collaboration of fusing data and automatically extracting information from the several available distributed sources using Ontologies and Linked Open Data as tools.

Keywords Linked data · Disaster management · Knowledge representation · Ontology · PRISMA

Introduction

An increasing number of disasters (of natural and anthropogenic origin) has affected the world population and challenged disaster relief organizations, highlighting the importance of disaster management (DM) decision support systems. In fact, the gaps and opportunities related with exploiting information technology (IT) tools in

---

A. Correia · P. B. Água · M. Simões-Marques (✉)
CINAV – Escola Naval, Instituto Universitário Militar, Alfeite, Almada, Portugal

H. J. Scholl et al. (eds.), *Disaster Management and Information Technology*, Public Administration and Information Technology 40,
https://doi.org/10.1007/978-3-031-20939-0_18

support of DM have been thoroughly addressed in the literature (e.g., by Simões-Marques (2017) and Sahil and Sood (2021)). It is often pointed that DM success largely depends on successfully collecting, integrating, and processing information from the disaster scenarios, in order to make better decisions, for example, regarding the prioritization of lines of action and the allocation of resources. Due to the complexity of decision-making in disaster situations, intelligent decision support systems are of utmost importance, particularly when conducting disaster response operations. The information required by such systems encompasses both elicited knowledge regarding the domain and the specific context and raw data from historical and current operational actions. DM decision support systems, besides relying on daily activities operational data and resources management, are deeply based on information provided by large and diverse collections of sensors as well as data provided by communities of volunteers made available from Linked Open Data (LOD) (Bizer et al., 2009). This information is critical to effectively support the collaboration and cooperation of disaster response teams that converge to an affected area coming from different origins (countries, languages, and cultures), with the aim of providing humanitarian assistance to the affected population. Preferably, the different response entities must effectively and efficiently share information within the scope of such incidents. To achieve the interoperability among their distributed systems, they must be able to communicate and use a kind of lingua franca of the DM domain.

Given the complexity of DM, ontologies can provide a framework in which categories and relationships among the concepts can emerge (Galton & Worboys, 2011). Therefore, ontologies as a formal representation of incidents and response assets and actions are useful to ensure that data are structured in a meaningful way, fit for DM purposes, and even suited to machine processing. However, since there are several and disparate proposals on DM ontologies, this work raises the research question: how can we coherently make available ontological contributions on DM, integrating DM information systems from different organizations and taking advantage of data provided from Linked Open Data?

The answer to the research question relies on building an ontological architecture for DM. A first step is to identify instances and adequate types of DM ontologies which can be adapted, reused, and refactored to be the modules or building blocks of the sought ontological architecture. Hence, to attain the answer, one has to review the ontologies published in recent years to fulfill the several requirements of DM. Therefore, this chapter addresses a literature review on DM ontologies and incident response together with their intended specificities. The Preferred Reporting Items for Systematic Reviews (PRISMA) method (Liberati et al., 2009) was used as a formal tool and guideline for data collection for the literature review. The chosen data set consists of ontologies published in the last 50 years. The analyzed sample includes papers from journals published on relevant scientific databases and meeting specific query constraints. For each of the retrieved ontologies it was identified: (i) the type of emergency management they cover, (ii) the methods and techniques used, and (iii) the contributions for the foreseen DM ontological architecture. The previously published systematic reviews on disaster management identified did not target the scope of the current work since they covered topics such as (i) social media-based crisis communication (Bukar et al., 2020), (ii) explore the extent to which sharing and reuse of disaster management knowledge is in line with FAIR (findable, accessible, interoperable, and reusable) principles (Mazimwe et al., 2021), and (iii) investigating the extent to which semantic web is used in disaster management systems (Dirgahayu & Setiaji, 2020).

As a result of the research gap identified on the systematic review, this chapter proposes an architecture of ontologies, supported by Linked Open Data, for DM decision support systems that could provide functionalities, such as the elicitation, coding, and representation of the domain knowledge, the storage of semantic data from multiple sources and formats, as well as the treatment and retrieval of information according to suitable methods and algorithms. Ontologies and Linked Open Data are methods for semantic data representation and storage that offer a basis for the semantic integration of the decision support processes applied to DM, specifically supporting the activities of the teams that cooperate in disaster response operations.

This chapter is organized as follows: in order to clarify the DM context the next section introduces some terminology; Section "Decision Support Systems and Disaster Management" describes the functionalities expected from DM decision support systems; Section "Literature Survey" presents a systematic review conducted to survey the literature addressing DM ontologies; Section "Ontologies for Disaster Management" overviews the main contributions made on ontologies for DM, as well as potential platforms for sharing data through the web; and Section "Linked Open Data in Disaster Management" describes a proposal of common architecture for DM decision support systems. The last section offers some conclusions.

Disaster Management and Related Terms

In order to promote a better understanding of DM context, some concepts are introduced following the terminology defined in association with the monitorization of the Sendai Framework for Disaster Risk Reduction 2015–2030 implementation (UNDRR, 2022). From the presented definitions becomes evident the difference between terms that look alike but are significantly different (e.g., disaster management vs. disaster risk management).

Disaster is "a serious disruption of the functioning of a community or a society at any scale due to hazardous events interacting with conditions of exposure, vulnerability, and capacity, leading to one or more of the following: human, material, economic and environmental losses, and impacts."

Hazardous event is "the manifestation of a hazard in a particular place during a particular period of time."

Disaster risk is "the potential loss of life, injury, or destroyed or damaged assets which could occur to a system, society, or a community in a specific period of time, determined probabilistically as a function of hazard, exposure, vulnerability, and capacity."

Hazard is "a process, phenomenon or human activity that may cause loss of life, injury or other health impacts, property damage, social and economic disruption, or environmental degradation." The origin of hazards may be natural (predominantly associated with natural processes and phenomena), anthropogenic or human-induced (induced entirely or predominantly by human activities and choices, not including armed conflicts and other situations of social instability or tension), or socionatural (associated with a combination of natural and anthropogenic factors, including environmental degradation and climate change).

Exposure is "the situation of people, infrastructure, housing, production capacities and other tangible human assets located in hazard-prone areas."

Vulnerability is "the conditions determined by physical, social, economic and environmental factors or processes which increase the susceptibility of an individual, a community, assets or systems to the impacts of hazards."

Disaster risk reduction is "aimed at preventing new and reducing existing disaster risk and managing residual risk, all of which contribute to strengthening resilience and therefore to the achievement of sustainable development."

Disaster risk management is "the application of disaster risk reduction policies and strategies, to prevent new disaster risks, reduce existing disaster risks, and manage residual risks, contributing to the strengthening of resilience and reduction of losses."

Disaster management is "the organization, planning, and application of measures preparing for, responding to, and recovering from disasters."

In summary, the main focus of this work is to contribute to the preparedness for disaster response operations, through the proposal of a common architecture for disaster management intelligent decision support systems, meant to facilitate inter-agency cooperation.

Decision Support Systems and Disaster Management

The scope and objectives of the decision support systems for managing disasters and coordinating activities are contingent on the DM cycle phases (mitigation, preparedness, response, and recovery) they are meant for. More than 100 Commercial off-the-shelf (COTS) (Capterra, 2022), open source (Groen, 2022), and academic (Correia et al., 2018; Scherp et al., 2012) solutions are proposed, aimed at the creation and sharing of a common understanding of the DM processes and requirements (Turoff et al., 2011).

The *mitigation phase* requires functionalities that include (i) gathering relevant information that would be used for risk assessment and for setting strategies to prevent disasters and/or mitigate their effects, through repositories supported by knowledge bases, databases, geographic information systems (GIS), mobile and web-based apps, which store risk reduction and response plans, current and historical data (e.g., weather, river floods) and maps; (ii) disaster risk assessment and management tools, including vulnerability analysis models, policies definition, which encompass data analysis methods (e.g., machine learning and decision analysis) and intelligent systems aimed at increasing resilience through disaster risk reduction.

The *preparedness phase* requires a wide range of functionalities from DM decision support systems, including the development, availability, and/or implementation of: (i) knowledge/databases containing information related to vulnerabilities and response plans, available resources (local, national, regional, and global), skills and contacts of trained personnel, inventory of hazardous materials, etc.; (ii) mobile devices with GPS and build-in cameras, for collecting, updating, and publishing real-time multimedia georeferenced data, as well as GIS for advanced spatial analysis, enhancing the decision-making process; (iii) monitoring and warning systems, supporting human decision-making through a network of sensors (land, sea, air, space) feeding complex predictive models based on simulation and physical models which provide an advanced alert for specific kind of disasters (e.g., tsunami, hurricane, volcanic eruptions); (iv) training applications, ranging from live simulations to constructive simulations involving synthetic environments (e.g., virtual reality and augmented reality) for generating realistic exercise scenarios (field or tabletop) and collecting data for training and evaluation purposes, risk assessment; (v) command and control (C2) tools and infrastructures offering a common operating picture (COP) and situational awareness which allows an effective decision-making and resource management through user-friendly interaction interfaces (e.g., dashboards with real-time visualization of key performance indicators); (vi) modeling and simulation modules to answer "what-if" scenarios about the real systems and investigate the consequences of complex and uncertain phenomena (e.g., outbreak dissemination, evacuation modeling, fire propagation, flooded area); and (vi) intelligent systems, with suitable human-computer interfaces, supported by artificial intelligence (e.g., machine learning, data mining algorithms), and multicriteria techniques for analyzing data and automatic advise on actions to tackle complex scenarios.

The *response phase* requires the extension of the abovementioned C2 functionalities providing communication and information sharing among disaster managers from different origins, supporting the cooperation and coordination of multiple teams engaged on the disaster response operation. These requirements go far beyond the day-to-day needs of interoperability among the local emergency response agencies and can be enabled by technologies such as XML and web services.

The *recovery phase* is a longer-lasting continuation of the response phase, presenting many of the requirements from the previous phase, usually engaging a different set of actors and operating conditions. The information recorded during the disaster response operation provides valuable feedback – regarding, for instance, the incidents and victims identified, the resources engaged, and the actions taken – allowing an assessment of the *dos and don'ts* that support the gathering of lessons learned, which will allow new iterations of the DM cycle feeding the *mitigation* and *preparedness* phases, and contributing to improve disaster resilience and to better disaster response operations.

However, a common criticism is that disaster response organizations operation is stovepiped due to the lack of interoperability and integration of the proprietary systems used. Even when the internet protocols are used to enable exchange of information among C2 systems, often the solution only addresses the network specificities and not the semantics of domain data. Despite efforts, such as the one promoted by the OASIS consortium, supporting the EDXL-DE (OASIS, 2022) to increase interoperability and openness of data in disasters response, the proposal seems to be simplistic and short in providing semantic interoperability among DM support systems (Scherp et al., 2012).

Since ontologies describe what data means and the properties to be used to characterize and link distinct data, they are key to overcome this problem. This gives the data a strong but flexible foundation for interoperability that can be adapted as the data set grows and the requirements evolve. Therefore, the stovepipes' trap could be tackled with solutions based on ontologies that could provide semantically rigorous specifications, amenable of integrating heterogeneous applications and systems in an unambiguous way.

Literature Survey

This section summarizes the systematic review on ontologies to DM done based on the PRISMA method (PRISMA, 2022; Page et al., 2021). The review started by choosing the bibliographic repositories, the inclusion and exclusion criteria for the papers, as well as the search and analysis processes over the identified papers.

For eliciting relevant references, 11 electronic databases were searched (i.e., Web of Science, ProQuest, Scopus, IEEE Xplore, Springer Link, Emerald Publishing, Taylor & Francis Group, Wiley Online Library, ACM Digital Library, SciELO, and JSTOR) retrieving exclusively peer-reviewed journal articles (therefore excluding other kind of documents, e.g., book chapters, conference proceedings, technical reports), published in English, in the period from 1970 to 2021. Therefore, a query was built with a composition of terms and Boolean operators chosen for finding relevant articles by titles, abstracts, or keywords. The query included the disjunction of the terms such as "disaster," "emergency," "catastrophe," "calamity," "accident," "crisis," or "urgency" in conjunction with the words "ontology" and "taxonomy" that were included. The wildcard * (meaning one or more characters) concatenated to each term of the string enabled the extension of the search to the derivatives of each term (e.g., disaster* retrieves also terms such as disasters or disastrous). Thus, journal articles selected for analysis were the ones compliant with the search string in their titles, abstracts, or keywords.

The elicitation of the records was performed in January 2022, and a spreadsheet was filled for each of the following fields: title, abstract, keywords, authors' names and affiliations, journal name, and year of publication. Two independent reviewers screened and assessed the records' titles and abstracts. Subsequently, the screening process was consolidated by applying the eligibility criteria. All articles referring to an ontology/taxonomy, general or tailor-made, for an overall or specific type of disaster were included. Consensus among the reviewers' team allowed to resolve the disagreements raised by any reviewer regarding the records extracted from the digital repositories. The eligibility criteria excluded articles about ontologies not directly related with DM (e.g., safety, security, risk) or approaching DM with techniques other than ontology (e.g., relational schemas, business process models).

For the eligible records, the spreadsheet was further filled with the bibliographic details considered as PRISMA checklist essential items (except for items 12–27, given the exploratory nature of the current stage of the work). The selection proceeded with a pilot test on 50 randomly selected papers to refine and code the extracted items. Finally, the abstracts of the remaining bibliographic records were carefully reviewed.

In summary, the search allowed the retrieval, in total, of 1885 bibliographic records. From the retrieved records, 90% were excluded, after screening the titles, considering that they did not meet the eligibility criteria. The remaining records were assessed in more detail based on their abstracts. Of these, 25% were discarded since they were duplicates retrieved from different electronic databases. From the remaining 143 records, 50 were randomly chosen for abstract screening and refining the coding process. The remaining were subsequently treated based on this process. As a result, another 18 records were excluded for not meeting the eligibility criteria. At the end, the selection was limited to 104 bibliographic records (6% of the total retrieved records) for the coding process and full reading articles. Figure 1 shows a flowchart of this systematic review based on the PRISMA checklist.

The relevant articles were codified according to predefined categories and further analyzed regarding:

(i) *Specific type of disaster addressed by the ontology* – most of the proposals (65%) applied to all kind of hazards, followed by others targeting only one kind of disaster: floods (8%), health care (5%), meteorological events (3%), trail (3%), pollution (2%), earthquakes (2%), geological events (2%), and aviation incidents (2%). Only one proposal addressed each one of the following hazards: chemical, railroad, critical infrastructures, hurricanes, fires, water pollution, solid waste, and metro, either originated by natural causes or anthropogenic.

(ii) *Focus of the approach* – the goals were the understanding of the situational/emerging knowledge (22%), elicitation of the DM domain knowledge (18%), interoperability among involved actors (12%), joint use of robots/IoT devices (6%), understanding of the disaster mechanisms (5%), data gathering from crowdsourcing (5%), study of accident cases (5%), hazard risk estimation (5%), and structure of communication's alert (3%). Facets less considered, with only two proposals (2%), were related to scenarios' definition, requests, and responses in the context of a disaster, disaster's scene visualization, social media coverage, emergency websites presentations, emergency plan guide-

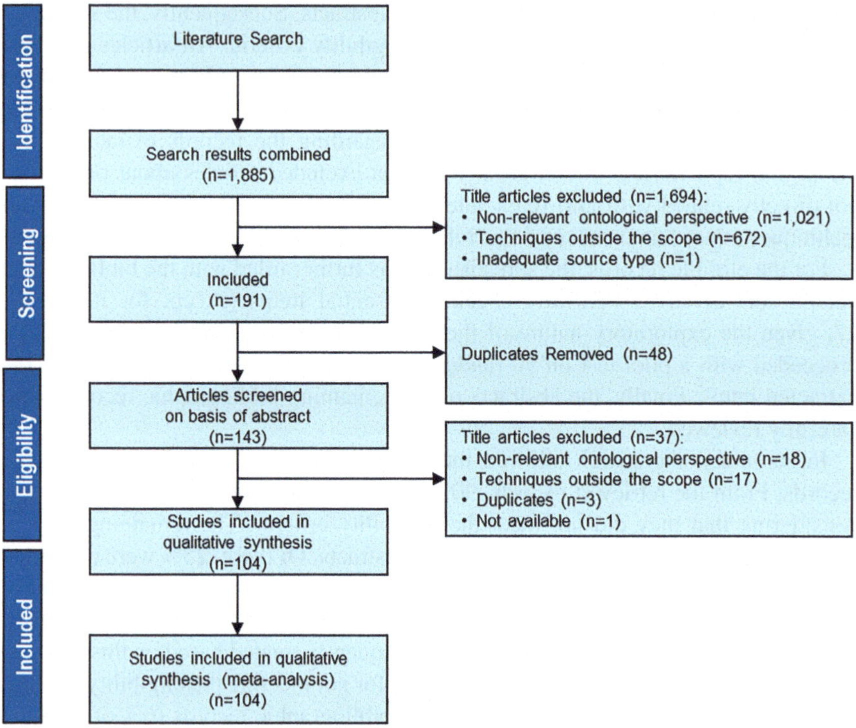

Fig. 1 Flowchart of study selection process

lines, and disasters cascading events. Less frequent occurrences, with only one article, were proposals related with agent-based approaches, environmental impact measurement, management of resources' life cycle, patients' triage, organizations' communication and cooperation, location definition, geospatial data sharing, uncertainty management, vulnerabilities' awareness, and mobile solutions usage.

(iii) *Core methods and techniques adopted* – the more often applied with DM ontologies were the use of semantic web components (59%), machine learning and natural language processing (9%), and taxonomies (6%). Less mentioned, with only two (2%) articles for each topic, were the references to tools for assessment, simulation/analysis, collaboration, process model, IoT integration, knowledge graph, hybrid reasoning, and data integration. With only one proposal (1%) were the techniques such as fuzzy logic description, case-based reasoning, rule-based reasoning, correlation, disambiguation, interlocking of institutional worlds, geotagging, and ontologies' fusion.

(iv) *Major findings and contributions* – the ones claimed by the proposals were new models and artifacts (95%). Also present, in smaller numbers, are new concepts (2%), theory (1%), and infrastructure (1%).

(v) *Type of outcome* – the outcomes are fundamentally on knowledge elicitation, consolidated by ontologies (95%) and, with less contribution, assessment tools (3%), as well as the contribution for DM domain's innovation and improvement.

(vi) *Geographic specificity* – most of the research (96%) did not apply to any specific region, although some targeted Europe (2%), North America, and South America.

This systematic review highlights the intense research done on DM ontologies for the last decade. In fact, the period from 2011 to 2021 was the most fruitful regarding proposals of DM ontologies, representing 93% of proposals' short list identified in the last 50 years. Nevertheless, it is important to note that some topics remain largely underexplored, evidenced by fewer publications by researchers, and others that clearly constitute research gaps that should be overcome. A recognized gap is the absence of the joint use of ontologies and linked data (Bizer et al., 2009) for dealing with scattered and freely available heterogeneous open data, as well as the lack of interoperability among the systems of organizations converging to disasters' scenes. The different sources and data formats, as well as the disparate vocabularies used on disaster situations, make ontologies and Linked Open Data a grounded basis for the semantic integration of DM processes.

Ontologies for Disaster Management

As highlighted by the systematic review, several proposals were suggested for dealing with DM, situational awareness, and situation theory. Examples are the AOUCKP (Segev, 2008), CONON (Wang et al., 2004), O3SERS (Di Maio, 2007), SAWA (Matheus et al., 2005), SC (Lin, 2008), SO (Yau & Liu, 2006), SOUPA (Chen et al., 2005), and STO (Kokar et al., 2009). However, many of these ontologies were typically developed in an ad hoc manner and lack expressiveness for supporting relevant properties – such as mereological, causal, and correlation relationships – and have different representations and interpretations for the same concepts (Scherp et al., 2012). Hence, they fall short of benefiting from the formal semantics already defined in foundational ontologies (aka upper ontologies), such as BFO (BFO, 2022; Grenon & Smith, 2004), DOLCE (Gangemi et al., 2002), GFO (Herre & Heller, 2022), OpenCyc (Cycorp, 2022), PROTON (Jain et al., 2011), Sowa Ontology (Sowa, 2022), and SUMO (Niles & Pease, 2001; Pease et al., 2002). Moreover, some of them do not follow a pattern-oriented approach that would allow them to structure the complex problem of a specific model into smaller, reusable units, which is the design basis for a sound architecture.

For the sake of attaining strong bedrocks, every proposed ontology must be aligned with foundational ontologies, which provide a high-level and abstract vocabulary of concepts and relations that are amenable to be extended for several knowledge domains. Besides formal definitions of world's fundamental concepts, a foundational ontology also provides axioms that can be used and extended. A precise alignment of concepts defined in an ontology with the high-level concepts of a foundational ontology would also allow, if required, the future extension of the derived ontology. That is why more sound DM ontologies rely its formal bases in foundational ontologies, such as DOLCE (Gangemi et al., 2002) or SUMO (Niles & Pease, 2001; Pease et al., 2002). This is an effective choice since those ontologies have already proved to provide a good design and modeling approach for different core ontologies (Scherp et al., 2012). However, the use of different foundational ontologies for different disaster management ontologies also brings problems of overlap and redundancies among proposed ontologies, if not inconsistencies and even ontological classification errors.

With the introduction of the ISO/IEC 21838 (ISO, 2022), based on the experience of BFO (BFO, 2022; Grenon & Smith, 2004), it is expected that this upper ontology becomes the referential hat for other mid-level ontologies. These, on the other hand, will coherently be extended by domain ontologies, ensuring the ontological architecture semantic alignment. These were the steps previously followed by the Gene Ontology (GO) (GO, 2022), built upon the upper ontology of Basic Formal Ontology (BFO) (BFO, 2022; Grenon & Smith, 2004).

Hence, ISO/IEC 21838 (ISO, 2022), as an upper ontology, is able to define domain neutral terms, with high level of formalism, required for any ontology that extend it. The mid-level ontologies, based on the ISO/IEC 21838 ontology, will be able to provide terms that will be applied to multiple domains' ontologies. Some examples of mid-level ontologies that could play this role are, for instance, IAO (Smith et al., 2022), EMMO, AFO, and IOF.

The mid-level layer can, thus, provide the abstraction for DM domain-level ontologies by sharing more specifically related terms with domain-level ontologies, increasing the potential for reuse that ISO/IEC 21838 does not allow. The DM ontologies built following this hierarchical architecture and the FAIR (findable, accessible, interoperable, reusable) principles (Wilkinson et al., 2016) will therefore contribute for better information sharing between information systems (Cummings & Stacey, 2017).

Linked Open Data in Disaster Management

The main goals of DM decision support systems are to provide improved situational awareness through an as clear as possible perception of the environment, improved understanding of the meaning of the most relevant elements, enhanced foresight about their status in chosen areas at a future time, and understanding on how decisions may impact goals. A clear situation awareness may be provided through a well-defined COP. The COP provides a unique and combined representation of relevant information and a framework in which a collaborative planning can take place. Although providing a unified view of a situation, the COP should also enable different perspectives on it, depending on an actor's role, for instance, a data

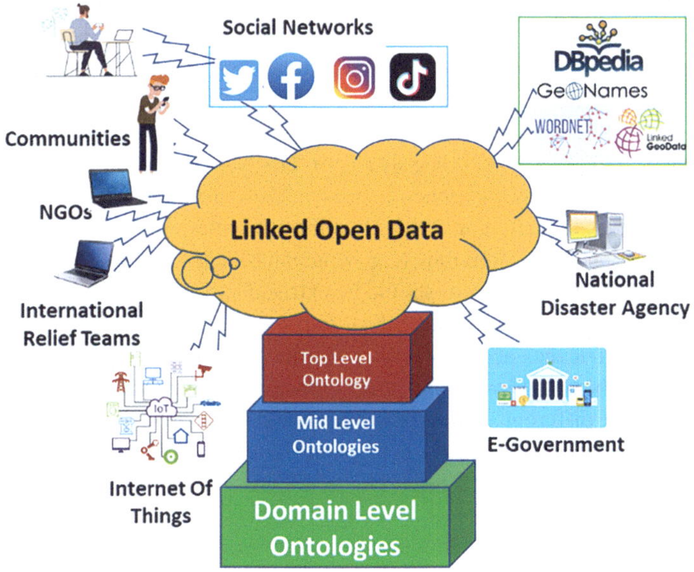

Fig. 2 The architecture for cooperative DM decision support systems

entry user, a member of a search and rescue team, a logistical manager, a medical staff member, or a C2 coordinator/disaster manager. For each of these actors, an optimized user interface should be provided to ensure the adequate usability of this holistic DM support system.

One can expect that the future generation of DM decision support systems (Fig. 2), besides relying on daily activities operational data and resources management, will be deeply based on information provided by large and diverse collections of sensors as well as data provided by communities of volunteers made available at LOD. For instance, although geospatial information has been created traditionally by government agencies and commercial companies, the widespread availability of smartphones with GPS and cameras, and apps enabling fine-resolution satellite imagery and maps, has allowed volunteers to collect and compile useful geospatial data to be integrated and disseminated through social media, web blogs, and the OpenStreetMap (OSM), enabling applications which make them available to the LOD. The degree of trustfulness of such crowdsourced data should be evaluated and criteria defined to ensure data reliability, namely, when faced with time-critical events where other factors should also be considered, such as spatial-temporal proximity, domain knowledge, skills, and prior experience of the source agent regarding the reported situation.

Furthermore, during disaster *mitigation* and *preparedness* phases, identification and collection of data regarding vulnerable places as well as assets, including population and infrastructure facilities, plays an important role. Early identification and digital transformation of data of such vulnerable infrastructures requires complex activities from governmental organizations involving diversified and heterogeneous data sources, many of them paper based. Hence, a well-developed information gathering system including population densities, geographical areas, and disaster historical data should be made available in preparing for disaster occurrences and their consequences. The gathered data should be related to repositories – such as the DBpedia, WordNet, LinkedGeoData, or GeoNames – in the LOD cloud to increase the data relations and generate more useful information. Evacuation routes can be modeled and inserted at OSM. Data from monitorization or alerts regarding earthquakes or volcanos' activities (e.g., epicenter/location point, depth, intensity, date/time), in vulnerable regions, should be extracted and updated from time to time in the LOD. Weather data forecasting destructive forces such as heavy wind and rain or storms and hurricanes at the observed stations with date and time from forecast stations can also be uploaded via the LOD application programming interface (API).

Data lying on different data stovepipes should be shared and interlinked with other related sources. Such sharing is essential for efficient management of disaster events. Consequently, there is a need to extend DM solutions in order to step out of their stovepipes and respond to the challenge of data integration, so that the COP can effectively provide a truly unified view (Galton & Worboys, 2011). The web of data is a way to break old stovepipes and link everyone and everything and make data and services potentially smarter. LOD provides a bridge to enhance the potential of using disaster data gathered by different organizations and individuals using DM systems or any other mechanism in distinct application. Linked data browsers allow users to navigate between different data sources via Resource Description Framework (RDF) links. Therefore, DM users can initiate their data transverse in one data source and then be in motion through a potentially endless web of data consisting of RDF triples. So, in this way not only humans but machines or computers can also utilize the information which is shared as LOD (Silva et al., 2011).

Acknowledging the increasing importance of the LOD's role for disaster management allows the envisioning of a future DM decision support systems architecture, as depicted in Fig. 2. However, as previously mentioned, for an effective data collection automation and coordination of data sources in time-critical situations, the architecture should be grounded on ontologies. The ontologies will play a role in the integration between human-sourced and artificial sensor-sourced information. The top-level ontology ISO/IEC 21838 (ISO, 2022) should support several derived mid-level ontologies, in a domain agnostic way enabling extension for domain ontologies amenable to support the domain of DM-specific ontologies.

According to a systematic review from Mazimwe et al. (2021), a total of 69 ontologies exist that encompass all the phases of the disaster management cycle: risk assessment (hazard, vulnerability, and risk analysis), prevention and mitigation, preparedness and early warning, response, and recovery (e.g., POLARISC (Elmhadhbi et al., 2018), SEMA4A, OntoCity, SOFERS, SOKNOS). These DM domain-level ontologies should be refactored to comply with mid-level ontologies, which in their turn, should extend ISO/IEC 21838.

Conclusion

This chapter proposed an architecture for disaster management intelligent decision support systems. The developed model main features can enhance the cooperation among agencies engaged in disaster relief operations, contributing to improve interoperability, information sharing, and shared situational awareness, hence conducting to a more effective and efficient decision-making in the context of complex disaster situations.

There is a perceived trend among some research agendas to develop ontologies for a number of domains, as a robust way to enhance understandability. The proposed system's infrastructure relies on an integrated hierarchy of ontologies, which formally conceptualizes the domain's terms and establishes relationships among those concepts. Ontologies are also viewed as a major contribution for applications' integration while underpinning the Linked Open Data Cloud, an infrastructure which allows the linking of data from different sources, related with disaster management.

The joint evolution of ontologies and linked data should be seen together with the use of the ISO/IEC 21838, an upper ontology and referential hat for mid-level ontologies, extended, on their turn, by domain ontologies such as disaster management, toward a semantic alignment of the DM ontological architecture.

A further research agenda on this subject shall develop and detail mid-level and domain ontology levels, promoting the FAIR principles, which within the realm of relief operations can not only increase effectiveness but also efficiency as well.

Acknowledgments The work was funded by the Portuguese Navy.

References

BFO. *Basic formal ontology*, http://basic-formal-ontology.org/. Last accessed 28 Feb 2022.

Bizer, C., Heath, T., & Berners-Lee, T. (2009). Linked data – The story so far. *The International Journal on Semantic Web and Information Systems, 5*, 1.

Bukar, U. A., Jabar, M. A., Sidi, F., Nor, R. N. H. B., Abdullah, S., & Othman, M. (2020). Crisis informatics in the context of social media crisis communication: Theoretical models, taxonomy, and open issues. In *IEEE access* (Vol. 8, pp. 185842–185869). IEEE. https://doi.org/10.1109/ACCESS.2020.3030184

Capterra. *Incident management software*, https://tinyurl.com/y6aq9qe9. Last accessed 28 Feb 2022.

Chen, H., Finin, T., & Joshi, A. (2005). The SOUPA ontology for pervasive computing. In V. Tamma, S. Cranefield, T. W. Finin, & S. Willmott (Eds.), *Ontologies for agents: Theory and experiences*. Whitestein Series in Software Agent Technologies.

Correia, A., Severino, I., Nunes, I. L., & Simões-Marques, M. (2018). Knowledge management in the development of an intelligent system to support emergency response. In I. L. Nunes (Ed.), *Advances in human factors and system interactions, AHFE 2017. Advances in intelligent systems and computing* (Vol. 592, pp. 109–120). Springer.

Cummings, J., & Stacey, D. (2017). The mid level data collection ontology (dco). In *Proceedings of KEOD*.

Cycorp. *OpenCyc Ontology*, https://old.datahub.io/dataset/opencyc. Last accessed 28 Feb 2022.

Di Maio, P. (2007). An open ontology for open source emergency response system. *Open Source Research Community, 43*, 1–12.

Dirgahayu, T., & Setiaji, H. (2020). Semantic web in disaster management: A systematic literature review. In *IOP Conference series: Materials science and engineering* (p. 12043). IOP Publishing.

Elmhadhbi, L., Karray, M.-H., & Archimède, B. (2018). An ontology-based emergency response system for interoperability in a crisis situation in smart cities. In *Enterprise interoperability: Smart services and business impact of enterprise interoperability*. John Wiley & Sons.

Galton, A., & Worboys, M. (2011). An ontology of information for emergency management. In *8th International conference on information systems for crisis response and management: From early-warning systems to preparedness and training, ISCRAM 2011*.

Gangemi, A., Guarino, N., Masolo, C., Oltramari, A., & Schneider, L. (2002). Sweetening ontologies with DOLCE. In *Lect. Notes Comput. Sci.* (*including Subser. Lect. Notes Artif. Intell. Lect. Notes Bioinformatics*).

GO. *The Gene Ontology resource*, Open Biological Ontologies Foundry, http://geneontology.org/. Last accessed 28 Feb 2022.

Grenon, P., & Smith, B. (2004). *SNAP and SPAN: Towards dynamic spatial ontology, spatial cognition and computation*. https://doi.org/10.1207/s15427633scc0401_5

Groen, P. *Open source resources for major disaster & emergency management situations*, https://tinyurl.com/y6p245su. Last accessed 28 Feb 2022.

Herre, H., & Heller, B. *General formal ontology*, https://www.onto-med.de/ontologies/gfo. Last accessed 28 Feb 2022.

ISO. *ISO/IEC-JTC1/SC32: ISO/IEC PRF 21838 Information technology – Top-level ontologies* (*TLO*), https://www.iso.org/standard/71954.html. Last accessed 28 Feb 2022.

Jain, P., Yeh, P. Z., Verma, K., Vasquez, R. G., Damova, M., Hitzler, P., & Sheth, A. P. (2011). Contextual ontology alignment of LOD with an upper ontology: A case study with proton. In G. Antoniou et al. (Eds.), *The semantic web: Research and applications. ESWC 2011* (Lecture notes in computer science) (Vol. 6643, pp. 80–92). Springer. https://doi.org/10.1007/978-3-642-21034-1_6

Kokar, M. M., Matheus, C. J., & Baclawski, K. (2009). Ontology-based situation awareness. *Information Fusion, 10*, 83.

Liberati, A., et al. (2009). The PRISMA statement for reporting systematic reviews and meta-analyses of studies that evaluate health care interventions: Explanation and elaboration. *PLoS Medicine*. https://doi.org/10.1371/journal.pmed.1000100

Lin, F. (2008). *Chapter 16 situation calculus – Handbook of knowledge representation*. Found. Artif. Intell.

Matheus, C. J., Kokar, M. M., Baclawski, K., Letkowski, J. A., Call, C., Hinman, M. L., Salerno, J. J., & Boulware, D. M. (2005). SAWA: An assistant for higher-level fusion and situation awareness. In: Proc. SPIE 5813, multisensor, multisource information fusion: Architectures, algorithms, and applications 2005, SPIE digital library, pp.75–85 (28 March 2005). https://doi.org/10.1117/12.604120

Mazimwe, A., Hammouda, I., & Gidudu, A. (2021). Implementation of FAIR principles for ontologies in the disaster domain: A systematic literature review. *ISPRS International Journal of Geo-Information. Multidisciplinary Digital Publishing Institute, 10*(5), 324.

Niles, I., & Pease, A. (2001). Towards a standard upper ontology. In: *Formal ontology in information systems: Collected papers from the second international conference*.

OASIS. *Emergency Data Exchange Language (EDXL) Distribution Element Version 2.0*, OASIS Emergency Management TC, https://tinyurl.com/y28jwa7m. Last accessed 28 Feb 2022.

Page, M. J., et al. (2021). PRISMA 2020 explanation and elaboration: Updated guidance and exemplars for reporting systematic reviews. *The BMJ. BMJ Publishing Group, 372*. https://doi.org/10.1136/BMJ.N160

Pease, A., Niles, I., & Li, J. (2002). The suggested upper merged ontology: A large ontology for the semantic web and its applications. *Imagine, 28*, 7–10.
PRISMA. *PRISMA – Transparent reporting of systematic reviews and meta-analyses*, Website. Available at: http://www.prisma-statement.org/. Last accessed 28 Feb 2022.
Sahil, N., & Sood, S. K. (2021). Bibliometric monitoring of research performance in ICT-based disaster management literature. *Quality & Quantity, 55*, 103–132.
Scherp, A., Franz, T., Saathoff, C., & Staab, S. (2012). A core ontology on events for representing occurrences in the real world. *Multimedia Tools and Applications, 58*, 293–331.
Segev, A. (2008). Adaptive ontology use for crisis knowledge representation. In *Proceedings of ISCRAM 2008 – 5th international conference on information systems for crisis response and management.*
Silva, T., Wuwongse, V., & Nidhi Sharma, H. (2011). Linked data in disaster mitigation and preparedness. In *Proceedings – 3rd IEEE international conference on intelligent networking and collaborative systems, INCoS 2011.*
Simões-Marques, M. (2017). Facing disasters – Trends in applications to support disaster management. In I. Nunes (Ed.), *Advances in human factors and systems interaction, AHFE 2016. AISC* (Vol. 497, pp. 203–215). Springer.
Smith, B., Ruttenberg, A., & Ceusters, W. *Information artifact ontology*, http://www.obofoundry.org/ontology/iao.html. Last accessed 28 Feb 2022.
Sowa, J. F.. *Sowa ontology*, http://www.jfsowa.com/ontology/. Last accessed 28 Feb 2022.
Turoff, M., Hiltz, S. R., White, C., Plotnick, L., Hendela, A., & Yoa, X. (2011). The past as the future of emergency preparedness and management. In M. E. Jennex (Ed.), *Crisis response and management and emerging information systems: Critical applications* (pp. 12–28). IGI Global.
UNDRR. *Terminology*, https://www.undrr.org/terminology. Last accessed 4 May 2022.
Wang, X. H., Zhang, D. Q., Gu, T., & Pung, H. K. (2004). Ontology based context modeling and reasoning using OWL. In: *Proceedings – Second IEEE annual conference on pervasive computing and communications, workshops*, PerCom.
Wilkinson, M. D., Dumontier, M., Aalbersberg, I. J., Appleton, G., Axton, M., Baak, A., et al. (2016). The FAIR guiding principles for scientific data management and stewardship. *Scientific Data, 3*(1), 1–9.
Yau, S. S., & Liu, J. (2006). Hierarchical situation modeling and reasoning for pervasive computing. In: *Proc. – The Fourth IEEE Workshop on Software Technol. for Future Embedded and Ubiquitous Syst., SEUS 2006 and the Second Int. Workshop on Collaborative Comput., Integr., and Assur., WCCIA 2006.*

Toward a Taxonomy for Classifying Crisis Information Management Systems

Marcos R. S. Borges, José H. Canós, Mª Carmen Penadés, Leire Labaka, Víctor A. Bañuls, and Josune Hernantes

Abstract In this chapter, we describe the process and the preliminary results of developing a taxonomy of Crisis Information Management Systems (CIMS). Building the taxonomy, we aim at orienting the understanding of the area (main topics, interrelations, challenges, gaps, etc.) and guide the search of the literature and systems focused on the topic of interest. Following the iterative method proposed by Nickerson et al. in 2013, we focused on the emergency response stage of the emergency management life cycle and defined a taxonomy organized along seven dimensions, namely, coordination, collaboration, information management, visualization, communication, intelligence, and global support; for each dimension, a number of characteristics understood as features of CIMS have been identified. The first version of the Tax-CIM taxonomy has been applied to the analysis of 15

The work was done while Marcos R. S. Borges was at TECNUN.

M. R. S. Borges (✉)
Department of Industrial Organization, TECNUN, Universidad de Navarra, Pamplona, Spain

Present Address:
PPGI-Universidade Federal do Rio de Janeiro, Brazil
e-mail: mborges@ppgi.ufrj.br

J. H. Canós · Mª. C. Penadés
Department of Computer Science (DSIC) and IUMTI, Universitat Politècnica de València, Valencia, Spain
e-mail: jhcanos@dsic.upv.es; mpenades@dsic.upv.es

L. Labaka · J. Hernantes
Department of Industrial Organization, TECNUN, Universidad de Navarra, Pamplona, Spain
e-mail: llabaka@tecnun.es; jhernantes@tecnun.es

V. A. Bañuls
Department of Business Management and Marketing, Universidad Pablo de Olavide, Seville, Spain
e-mail: vabansil@upo.es

H. J. Scholl et al. (eds.), *Disaster Management and Information Technology*, Public Administration and Information Technology 40,
https://doi.org/10.1007/978-3-031-20939-0_19

CIMS, showing that some changes had to be made and led to a second and more robust version.

Keywords Crisis Information Management Systems · Taxonomy · Emergency response

Introduction

Crisis management is a transversal discipline that integrates the results of many other areas. Therefore, it takes time and effort to understand its main topics, challenges, and open issues. Among these challenges, efficient information management emerged from the need for response teams to improve situational awareness and to deliver quality information to the different stakeholders. Consequently, advances in the design, development, and application of the so-called Crisis Information Management Systems (CIMS) have received much attention from both academics and practitioners, as well as from the software industry. Professional associations like ISCRAM[1] have fueled research, development, and innovation of tools covering completely or partially the crisis management life cycle.

A great amount of research in the area of Crisis Information Management can be verified by the contents of two important digital reference libraries: the Disaster Information Research Library (DIRL[2]), with 3933 references, and the ISCRAM Digital Library,[3] with 1827 references, both at the time of writing this proposal. In the specific subarea of Emergency Management Information Systems, a quick search in Google Scholar returns 1410 results (1210 of which correspond to work published in the last 20 years). Interest in the area has grown over the last 5 years, with the organization of several academic conferences and the publication of journals, meaning that we can expect a rapid growth in the years ahead. In the context of this great amount of research, it is difficult to navigate and find studies that are relevant to a particular research topic or project. The use of keyword search has low precision (many irrelevant instances) and low recall (many relevant instances not retrieved), yielding unsatisfactory answers. In addition, it is difficult to navigate through the literature without a guiding framework that describes the relationship between the various topics addressed.

The diversity in the field of crisis management has also propagated to the tools, and the number of CIMS available[4] makes it difficult to understand their features and choose the most appropriate system for an organization's specific needs. In this chapter, we describe the process and the preliminary results of developing a

[1] Information Systems for Crisis Response and Management, https://iscram.org

[2] http://faculty.washington.edu/jscholl/dirl/index.php, accessed on 2022/01/20.

[3] http://idl.iscram.org

[4] A search of the topic "Emergency Management Software" in the portal www.g2.com yields 61 tools that can be considered CIMS.

taxonomy of CIMS. Building the taxonomy, which we called *Tax-CIM*, our aim was to orient the understanding of the area (main topics, interrelations, challenges, gaps, etc.) and guide the search of the literature focused on the topic of interest.

Several taxonomies have been proposed in the field of emergency management. A topic search of the term "taxonomy" in the DIRL yields ten references, none of which has studied the domain from the perspective of software support for emergency response and recovery. Instead, they cover specific aspects of the emergency management life cycle. Consequently, a comprehensive view of the role of CIMS in response and recovery has yet to be published.

Tax-CIM aims to:

1. Be a guide for researchers, especially to help perform more focused literature searches and work descriptions.
2. Help end users (e.g., practitioners and civil defense authorities) to choose the right CIMS according to their particular context.
3. Discover gaps in the research on CIMS, opening new opportunities for innovative solutions covering those gaps.
4. Find inconsistencies in the use of terminology.

The multilevel classification developed in the taxonomy will help to structure knowledge about the role CIMS plays in the emergency management life cycle and particularly in the response phase. *Tax-CIM* has been developed following the method proposed by Nickerson et al. (2013). Specifically, we have performed an iterative process where empirical-to-conceptual and conceptual-to-empirical approaches have been applied. Building on our long-time research experience in emergency management systems, we were able to define a hierarchy of dimensions of emergency response (namely, coordination, collaboration, information management, visualization, communication, and intelligence), plus a set of characteristics for each dimension. The analysis of different CIMS based on the hierarchy led to refinements of these dimensions and characteristics, resulting in the taxonomy we present here. *Tax-CIM* is not a static taxonomy; we expect that further iterations of the process will result in refinements arising from new characteristics or the suppression of other characteristics for different reasons.

This chapter is organized as follows. We first provide some background on existing taxonomies in the emergency management domain and introduce the research method followed in our work. We then offer a detailed description of the development of *Tax-CIM*, which required two iterations of the method. The chapter concludes with a discussion of the results obtained and some conclusions.

Antecedents

Turoff (2002) establishes the origins of CIMS in the EMISARI system, developed in 1971 in the Office of Emergency Preparedness of the United States. According to Turoff, "past and future objectives [of CIMS] remain the same in crises, providing relevant communities collaborative knowledge systems to exchange information" (p. 29).

Some research has focused on the design of CIMS. Chen et al. (2005) present a framework to analyze the response to critical incidents. This framework conceptualizes four main elements for analysis: decision structure, information and resource structure, workflow structure, and responder structure. Other authors follow this path of proposing design principles for CIMS (Kyng et al., 2006; Jennex, 2007). Among these publications, we highlight the DERMIS model (Turoff et al., 2004), which proposes eight principles and five criteria (metaphor, human roles, notification, hypertext, and context visibility) for CIMS. These design principles are system directory, information source and timeliness, open multidirectional communication, content as address, up-to-date information and data, link relevant information and data, authority, responsibility, and accountability, and psychological and sociological factors.

Other papers have been oriented toward proposing ontologies for CIMS. Di Maio (2007) points out the need for an ontology for information exchange between CIMS. Xiang et al. (2008) build an ontology, dividing the tasks of emergency response systems in four major phases: response preparation, emergency response, emergency rescue, and aftermath handling. Liu et al. (2013) present 11 subject areas common to 6 ontologies useful in crisis management (resources, processes, people, organization, damage, disasters, infrastructure, geography, hydrology, meteorology, and topography).

Closer to our aim, some authors propose taxonomies in the crisis management field. Rauner et al. (2018) present a skills taxonomy to improve the interoperability and cross-border communication of emergency responders from different countries. However, rather than classifying CIMS, the aim of their taxonomy is to better cope with major disasters by identifying main national emergency responders needed for key emergency interventions. In this sense, Simpson (2012) proposes a taxonomy for crisis management functions including crisis communications and information management as one function. Additionally, we can find other taxonomies in fields close to CIMS, such as mobile emergency announcement systems (Addams-Moring et al., 2005), crisis management simulation tools (Barthe-Delanoë et al., 2015), community interaction in crises and disasters (Auferbauer et al., 2019), big data analytics, and IoT in disaster management (Shah et al., 2019).

These antecedents lead us to conclude that previous work on CIMS has been mainly oriented toward establishing design principles, rather than building a functional classification based on the CIMS characteristics.

Research Methodology

An important problem for understanding the domain of CIMS is the classification of systems into a framework that enables the identification of their purpose and usage. Emergency management has achieved a maturity level when many supporting systems are proposed and described but without allowing us to position them in the spectrum of existing systems and applications. Thus, an organized classification is very welcome. Making a general classification is not an easy task due to the variety of systems and application approaches. A set of common keywords is useful but not sufficient to understand the relationships among the systems and their purposes. A more systematic approach to the classification is required to reach this objective. Our proposal then is to develop a taxonomy that classifies the main aspects of CIMS based on a hierarchy of categories.

A taxonomy can be viewed as an evolution of a simple classification system, such as a set of keywords, and a previous step toward an ontology, which describes the relationship among objects as a graph instead of a hierarchy. Generating a good taxonomy, however, is not an easy task. The main characteristic of a good taxonomy is that it can differentiate between systems that have some variations at a relevant level of internal detail. In other words, they share the same roots of the hierarchy for coincident characteristics, but they belong to different branches for distinct characteristics. Due to its hierarchical nature, a taxonomy should be designed in such a way that the higher-level classes cover the more general categories, leaving the more specific ones to the lower levels. This requires a systematic development and, most importantly, an evaluation that demonstrates its suitability for the domain.

For the systematic development of the taxonomy, we adopted the method proposed in (Nickerson et al., 2013), aimed at guiding information system classification. To justify their proposal, the authors argue that "IS researchers have proposed a number of taxonomies over the years, but in many cases the development of these taxonomies has followed a largely ad hoc approach" (p. 337). The method they developed was based on the design science research paradigm, which aims to address new knowledge about artificial (i.e., man-made) objects that are designed to meet certain goals and provide utility to their users (Simon, 1969).

Figure 1 summarizes the iterative process defined by Nickerson et al. First, the scope of the taxonomy is defined in terms of the so-called meta-characteristic of the taxonomy; it is the most comprehensive characteristic in a domain, which will serve to derive the remaining characteristics of the taxonomy, so that each characteristic added to it must be a logical consequence of the meta-characteristic. The next step in the process is the definition of the *ending conditions* that will be used as criteria for finalizing the iterative process. Nickerson et al. (2013) distinguish two types of ending conditions. On the one hand, the objective conditions are those that help to ensure that the set of characteristics identified meets the requirements to be a taxonomy, that is, mutually exclusive dimensions and exhaustive characteristics in each dimension. On the other hand, subjective ending conditions need also to be examined to check that the following qualitative attributes are enforced; these conditions are as follows (quoting their own words):

- To be concise – "A taxonomy should contain a limited number of dimensions and a limited number of characteristics in each dimension, because an extensive classification scheme with many dimensions and many characteristics may

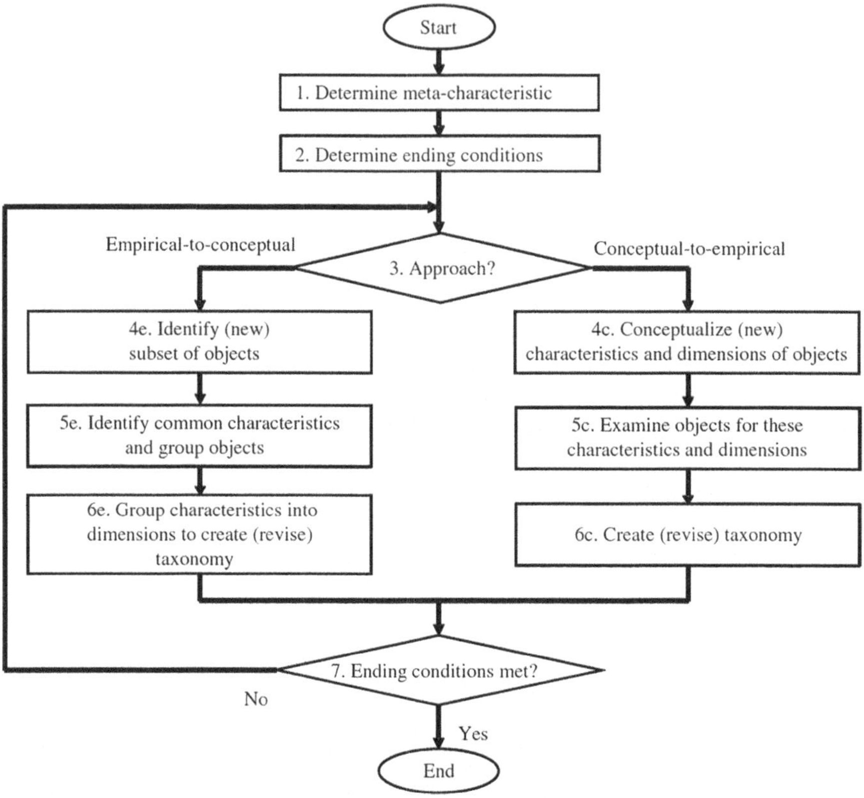

Fig. 1 Method for taxonomy development as proposed in (Nickerson et al., 2013)

exceed the cognitive load of the researcher and thus be difficult to comprehend and apply" (p. 341).

- To be robust – "A useful taxonomy should contain enough dimensions and characteristics to clearly differentiate the objects of interest. A taxonomy with few dimensions and characteristics may not be able to adequately differentiate among objects" (p. 341).
- To be comprehensive – "A useful taxonomy can classify all known objects within the domain under consideration" (p. 341).
- To be extendible – "A useful taxonomy should allow for inclusion of additional dimensions and new characteristics within a dimension when new types of objects appear. A taxonomy that is not extendible may soon become obsolete" (p. 341).
- To be explanatory – "A useful taxonomy contains dimensions and characteristics that do not describe every possible detail of the objects but, rather, provide useful explanations of the nature of the objects under study or of future objects to help us understand the objects" (p. 342).

Once the meta-characteristic and ending conditions are set, the iterative process can follow two alternative approaches, namely, conceptual-to-empirical (C2E) and empirical-to-conceptual (E2C). The choice of which approach to use depends on the availability of data on objects under study and knowledge of the domain. When little data are available, but the researcher has significant understanding of the domain, then starting with the conceptual-to-empirical approach would be advised, leading to the conceptualization of new characteristics, followed by the examination of the objects of interest for these characteristics, and revising the taxonomy. However, if the knowledge of the domain is not deep, but enough data about the objects in the domain are available, an empirical-to conceptual approach can be followed; in this case, identifying new sets or subsets of objects is followed by their examination to find relevant characteristics, which can be added to the taxonomy.

The development of a good taxonomy is a major challenge. It should be comprehensible to users and must cover the domain of interest in enough detail to be useful. The iterative refinement process must adhere to the following guidelines:

- If the complete categorization of an object does not fit entirely into the categories of the taxonomy, one or more new categories/subcategories must be created.
- If at the end of the categorization process a category has none or few objects, a targeted search is done using keywords that characterize the category. If a set of relevant articles cannot be added, grouping this category with another and putting all objects under the resulting category should be considered.
- If a category has too many objects, splitting the category into two or more categories/subcategories and moving the objects associated with this category to the new ones should be an option.

In the remainder of this chapter, we show how we adapted and applied Nickerson et al.'s method to the development of *Tax-CIM*.

Development of the *Tax-CIM* Taxonomy

In this section, we describe how we applied the method described in the previous section to develop *Tax-CIM*. The steps are numbered according to the process depicted in Fig. 1.

Beginning of the Process

Step 1. Definition of the meta-characteristic The meta-characteristic chosen for our taxonomy is *emergency response*. Consequently, we will define a set of relevant dimensions and conceptualize sets of characteristics within each dimension.

Step 2. Determination of the ending conditions Before starting the iterative development of the taxonomy, we must define the ending conditions of our process.

Regarding the objective ending conditions, the iterative process can be considered finished when we are able to group every object of study into the taxonomy categories, and no new splitting of categories is found. On the other hand, reaching subjective ending conditions should be particularly sought. A description of the taxonomy building loop follows.

Iteration 1 (I1)

Step 3.I1. Choice of the approach As stated above, the choice of the approach at each iteration depends on the current knowledge about the domain. After years of research on emergency management, we have become acquainted with many research prototypes and/or commercial systems supporting different stages of the emergency management life cycle and with the key aspects influencing the effectiveness of a response. Consequently, we assumed that our own knowledge of the objects in the domain was enough to enable an E2C approach.

Step 4e.I1. Identify (new) subset of objects The goal of this stage is to define a set of objects of study that must be analyzed in the following step. Instead of creating a closed set of CIMS, we relied on our previous research (Canós et al., 2004, 2005), where we studied the nature of emergency responses and identified six dimensions, namely, *coordination*, *information management and retrieval*, *presentation*, *communication*, *collaboration*, and *intelligence*, each one with their characteristics. We added a seventh dimension, *general support*, to include more general but relevant aspects not covered by the other dimensions. This was the input for the next step, where the grouping of objects began.

Step 5e.I1. Identify common characteristics and group objects From the set of all characteristics identified in the previous step, we started a process of selecting characteristics specifically related to the meta-characteristic, which were grouped by commonality relationships.

Step 6e.I1. Group characteristics into dimensions to create (revise) taxonomy Attending to the different nature of the characteristics found in the previous step, we defined seven dimensions, shown in the inner circle of Fig. 2. Each dimension corresponds to a relevant aspect of emergency response and groups several characteristics we considered relevant, which appear at the outer circle of Fig. 2. The number of dimensions and their characteristics were kept deliberately low to enforce the conciseness requirement of the ending conditions.

Step 7.I1. Ending conditions met The hierarchy of Fig. 2 was the first version of *Tax-CIM*. When evaluating the ending conditions mentioned earlier, it was clear that the taxonomy needed some refinement and, more importantly, some validation against the objects of interest. This made us to go for a second iteration, which is described below.

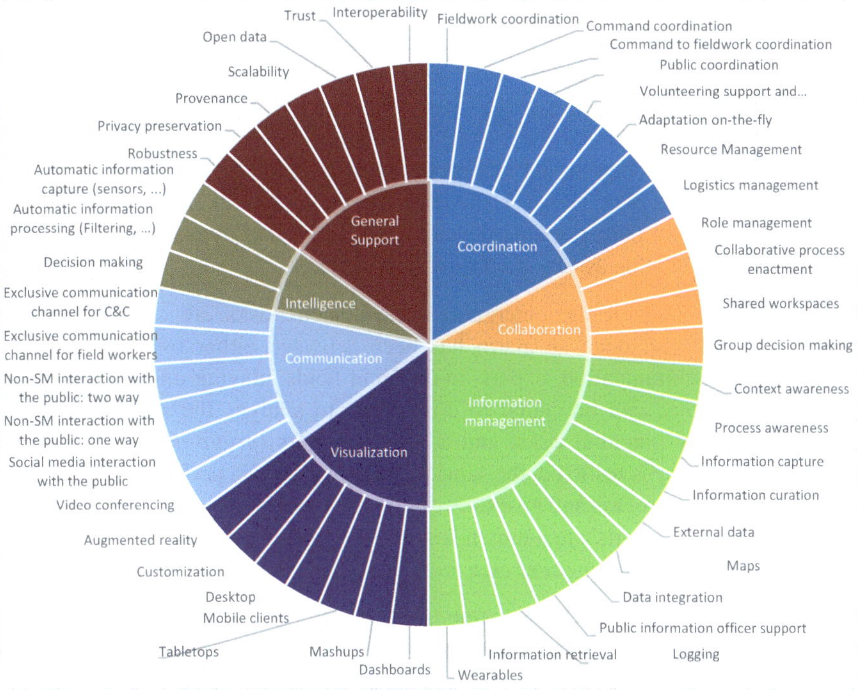

Fig. 2 Summary of Tax-CIM version 1

Iteration 2 (I2)

Step 3.I2. Choice of the approach In this iteration, our goal was twofold. To enforce explainability, we wanted to clearly define the meaning of each characteristic; to enforce robustness and comprehensiveness, we wanted to check whether or not the objects of interest fit well into the taxonomy. Consequently, we decided to follow a C2E approach.

Step 4c.I2. Conceptualize (new) characteristics and dimensions of CIMS The conceptualization of the first version of *Tax-CIM* was performed by adding a definition to each characteristic. The full definition appears in Appendix A, and a summary of the seven dimensions follows.

Coordination The response to an emergency is the result of the coordinated effort of actors working in a variety of settings so that coordination can be managed at different levels. Regarding the field operations, the different response teams must act according to well-established protocols that need to be enforced by team leaders (*fieldwork coordination*). Sometimes, action orders are sent to fieldworkers from the control room (*command-to-fieldwork coordination*). Some coordination is also needed inside the control room, where decision-making processes are developed in a hierarchical manner (*command coordination*). Finally, in cases where volunteering can help resolve a crisis, volunteers need guidance and protection from responders (*volunteering support and coordination*). Human resources coordination is complemented with coordinating access to resources (*resource management*) and *logistics management.*

Coordination is often based on protocols and procedures described in the emergency response plan; however, the unpredictable nature of crises makes it very difficult to cover all their possible development paths, and dynamic adaptation to the context is a valuable asset (*adaptation on the fly*).

Collaboration Many of the emergency management tasks are collaborative in nature. For instance, once an alarm has been activated either by sensors or by some human communication, experts in different fields, playing one or more roles (*role management*), can be called to e-meetings to analyze the situation, assess damages, identify potential risks, and advise managers (*group decision-making*). After the emergency is resolved, the same or other experts can perform collaborative assessments of the process and give safety managers insight for improving processes according to the experts' recommendations. In both cases, *shared workspaces* support the *collaborative process enactment.*

Information management Information is a key factor in the successful resolution of a crisis. As mentioned above, CIMS are complex systems that handle numerous pieces of information associated with the tasks to be performed by the different actors. Moreover, their relevance and/or validity may change according to the development of the emergency. Consequently, the information management problem in CIMS is challenging. CIMS should provide facilities for multimedia *information capture* from distinct sources, as well as *information curation* mechanisms to ensure the captured information is organized by means of descriptive metadata. Geotagged information (*maps*) and data coming from wearable devices of responders (*wearables)* are gaining relevance in the last years.

One of the key requirements we define for CIMS is dynamic delivery of information, that is, the information a user needs to perform a given task must be retrieved and delivered just at the usage time (*process awareness*). The information delivered must be context-sensitive (*context awareness*), eventually overriding information gathered previously. For instance, if a tunnel on a subway network has collapsed, the CIMS must not show a video playback of an open tunnel but rather a symbol of a blocked tunnel. Information resources can be owned by response organizations or be captured from some external sources, possibly heterogeneous and distributed (e.g., *open data* repositories). In these cases, *data integration* issues arise that need be managed using semantic interoperability techniques.

After being collected and organized, information must be usable. This means that appropriate *information retrieval* mechanisms such as (multimedia) content-based or keyword-based search must be provided. Using these mechanisms will not only enhance the situational awareness of responders but also public awareness via the role of the *public information officer*. Last but not the least, *logging* every decision made and every action taken during a response is crucial to enable later analysis of the response.

Visualization The emergency resolution process must be perceived in different ways by the different participating actors (*customization*). As stated above, the coordination mechanism must be able to "execute" all the actions comprising the process in the appropriate order; most of these actions are manual in the sense that they are to be performed by humans, where others can be done automatically. The set of tasks a given actor must perform are collected in a dynamic structure called the actor's worklist, in which the tasks are ordered according to the response process definition. Besides the default *desktop*-based interaction, other means such as *mobile clients*, *tabletops*, or even *augmented reality* sets can improve the user experience. For control rooms, *dashboards* and *mash-ups* can be valuable assets for decision-making.

Communication During an emergency, plenty of communications take place. All voice interactions between participants involved in emergency resolution need to be supported by reliable communication channels. *Videoconferencing* support must also be provided. Sometimes *exclusive communication channels for responders* and *for control room* can ensure that no interference between both nodes exist, thus avoiding possible confusion.

Informing the public is becoming more and more relevant. In the last decade, the use of social media (SM) to support crisis communication has been one of the most relevant research topics. *SM interaction with the public* has remarkably improved context awareness, although many challenges remain (Castillo, 2019). Besides SM interaction, other non-SM channels are still significant. Specifically, *one-way non-SM interaction with the public* is used to broadcast information of interest to the residents in an area affected by a disaster, and *two-way non-SM interaction with the public* enables dialogues to be established with the public as a way to gather context.

Intelligence By intelligence we mean two things. First, the ability of the system to generate valuable information from data coming from different sources. Sometimes these sources may be sensors or drones (*automatic information capture*), the data of which may be combined using information fusion techniques (*automatic information processing)* to provide CIMS users with meaningful interpretations, rather than raw data, thus saving time in crucial moments (e.g., fire detection systems). Secondly, advanced artificial intelligence techniques can support the *decision-making* processes.

General support This dimension aims at including characteristics that, while relevant for the analysis of CIMS, do not fit in the preceding dimensions. Many of them can be understood as nonfunctional requirements from a software engineering perspective, while others represent horizontal functionality affecting several dimensions. *Robustness* refers to how a CIMS deals with errors generated by unexpected data or actions during a response. *Privacy preservation* is key to ensure that sensitive information is kept safe and accessed only by authorized parties. *Provenance* relates to the existence of information traceability mechanisms that ensure the accuracy or authenticity of information sources. Related to provenance, *trust* focuses on the definition and implementation of means to ensure the reliability of external sources.

Table 1 CIMS analyzed during step I2.5c

CIMS	Type	Source
DisasterLAN	Commercial	https://www.buffalocomputergraphics.com/DLAN
D4H Readiness & Response	Commercial	https://d4htechnologies.com/incident-management/
Adashi C&C	Commercial	http://www.adashi.com/incident-command-software/
WhosOnLocation	Commercial	https://whosonlocation.com/visitor-management/
Veoci	Commercial	https://veoci.com/solution/emergency-management
Crisis control	Commercial	https://www.crises-control.com/solutions/public-alerting/
Safe reach	Commercial	https://safereach.com/en/emergency-notification-system/alert-app/
IBM Intelligent Operations Center for Emergency Management V1.6	Commercial	https://ibm.co/3rGrRJC
Cobra	Commercial	https://cobrasoftware.com/capabilities/
CEM platform	Commercial	https://www.everbridge.com/platform/technology/
Konexus	Commercial	https://www.konexus.com/
Crisis Track	Commercial	http://www.crisistrack.com/products/emergency-management/
Mission Track	Research	https://www.missiontrack.es
Tabletop system for situational awareness	Research	https://ieeexplore.ieee.org/document/5960190
Drones to the rescue: drone system for capturing situation awareness during response	Research	https://bit.ly/3HJwE2p

Scalability relates to the capacity of a CIMS to work not only at the local level but also at regional or nationwide levels if required. *Interoperability* is a technical capability allowing a CIMS to interact with other systems during the resolution of a crisis. From a semantic point of view, interoperability and trust are related to access and use *open data.*

A visual representation of the taxonomy with its dimensions and characteristics is presented in Fig. 2.

Step 5c.I2. Examine objects for these characteristics and dimensions The first version of *Tax-CIM* was used as a guide to examine a group of systems; to select them, we looked for "emergency management software" at the portal g2.com, a website specialized in reviews of software systems. We found 61 systems, from which we chose 12 for our study. We also selected 3 research systems to make a total of 15 objects of study (see Table 1).

Not all the systems in the portal were described in the same depth. In general, the information provided at g2.com was succinct, but a link to each CIMS's official vendor website was usually found. There, the technical level of the descriptions was not uniform: while some systems had a reasonable number of features listed, others were described in a purely commercial style, which made categorization difficult. What follows is a summary of the analysis performed and the changes introduced in each dimension to generate version 2 of *Tax-CIM*.

Coordination There was some difficulty in separating the *adaptation on the fly* done by the response teams and that was done automatically based on a predefined script. This dimension was thought to describe the support to human adaptation. If the support is in the form of recommendation or automatic decision, this should be part of the intelligence dimension and the *decision-making* characteristics. We changed the description of this characteristic and added the term "coordination" to the decision-making characteristic of the intelligence dimension. We do not foresee the need to separate the characteristics.

When dealing with volunteering, we found two subdimensions. The first one arises when the response team deals directly with the volunteers, having to coordinate their tasks, whereas the second one is shown when the response team deals with volunteer organizations, such as Red Cross, which coordinate their volunteers themselves. These require different types of coordination, and the taxonomy was adapted accordingly.

Collaboration There is a clear relationship between collaboration, coordination, and communication features, as teamwork requires all three to achieve its goals. These features overlap, and systems sometimes do not separate them clearly. However, they have different functions, and the taxonomy should reflect this by assigning the system to different subcategories even when systems do not separate the support. We did not make any changes to this dimension.

Information management Most systems analyzed in the first round provide and use some information management features. The characteristics in *Tax-CIM* covered all the systems. However, some of them were not found in the systems that we have analyzed so far; this is the case, for instance, of systems that make use of open data. We decided to keep all the characteristics unchanged, as we believe that some of them are quite new, appearing on academic proposals not yet implemented as a system. We foresee that future systems will include some of these features.

Visualization Visualization through mobile clients and desktops are the most common features provided by the systems. Mobile devices have been increasingly used for many purposes and the characteristics might overlap when analyzing the systems. Mobile clients such as smartphones have some limitations to support image visualization due to limited screen size. Tablets, on the other hand, are frequently mentioned as a better device for visualization. In the future, we may have to split the *mobile clients'* characteristic into three or four sub-characteristics to cover for different devices.

Communication The use of SM has been reported in many systems. The variety of solutions for SM with different characteristics might indicate the need for creating subcategories. In most cases, the SM channels have been used for one-way communication, i.e., not direct interaction. The two-way communication has been used mostly to support communication among responders in the field and in the command and control (C&C). Radio communication is still very popular among responders, but their operation is rarely supported by a system. This is why it was not included as a category. There are some alternatives to radio communication, but it seems it will take a while to replace the radio. Currently, we have found no reason to include them as a subcategory.

Intelligence Most of the intelligent systems provide recommendations; they do not provide autonomous decisions unless it is for simple decisions. In order to cover the recommendation feature, we changed the name of the characteristic to *recommendation and automatic decision-making*.

The characteristic *automatic information processing* was considered too broad. Although some systems combine them into one single feature, there are others that either separate them or provide part of them. There should be some separation between these characteristics. We decided to split this category into three: *automatic filtering*, *automatic categorization*, and *automatic inference*.

General support The categories listed under this dimension seemed to cover all systems that have been analyzed. Some, such as *open data* and *interoperability*, have not been present in any system yet. We kept all features assuming they will appear in the future systems.

Step 6c.I2. Create the taxonomy We generated version 2 of *Tax-CIM* according to the result of the analysis performed in step 5c.I2. Figure 3 shows the revised taxonomy. The three characteristics that replaced *automatic information processing* (*filtering*, *automatic categorization*, and *automatic inference*) at the intelligence dimension are highlighted. The small number of changes proved that version 1 was fairly comprehensive, but some refinements had to be made. A full definition of version 2 appears in Appendix B.

Limitations of the Work

We have developed a taxonomy of CIMS attending to their support to the response stage of the emergency management life cycle. We consider that given the high functional diversity of current systems and the growing interest in citizen and infrastructure protection of governments and organizations, a tool for helping users in the selection of the right system will be welcome. However, there is still work to do before reaching this goal, since the work described here has some limitations. Some relate to the application of the Nickerson et al. method, whereas others refer to the type and number of systems analyzed.

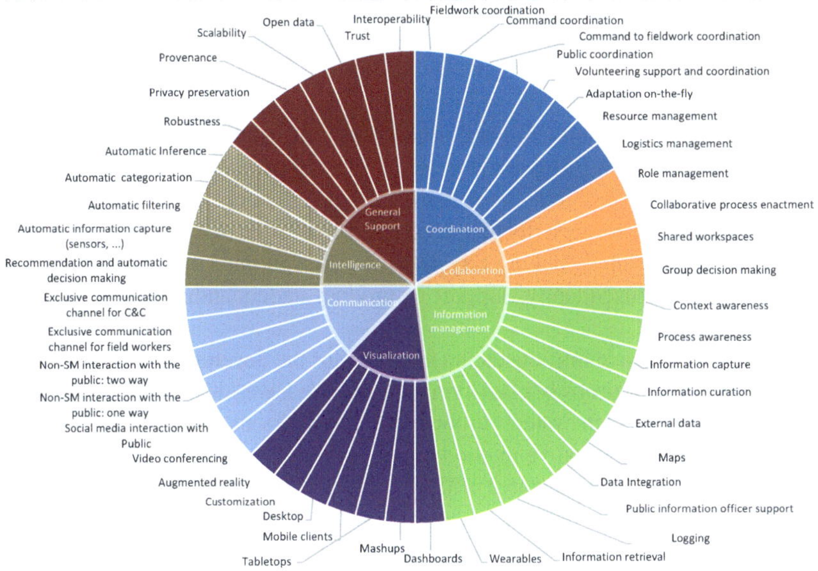

Fig. 3 Summary of Tax-CIM version 2

In the first iteration of the method, we decided to follow a E2C approach, which requires the identification and analysis of the objects of study from which the characteristics are drawn. In our case, instead of performing such an analysis, we based the identification of characteristics on our previous research experience in emergency management systems. From there we obtained a substantial number of characteristics that proved sufficiently comprehensive in further steps of the method.

In the second iteration, we studied 15 systems out of 62. This could be considered a low number, but we decided to use fewer systems since we were in an iterative process that will surely have more iterations. We expect to have many more systems analyzed in further refinements of the taxonomy. Another limitation comes from the bias toward commercial systems of our selection: 80% of the studied systems are commercial. We are aware that research systems can offer advanced features still not available in commercial systems, but, as a counterpart, information about the systems and their features may not be available in the form of a product description. It is our intention to incorporate more research systems in further iterations of the taxonomy development process.

Conclusions and Further Work

CIMS are at the core of emergency management digital transformation processes. In a world where more and more information is produced every second, tools for capturing, organizing, and disseminating information are required to perform safer and more efficient responses to crises. The need for such tools has been recognized worldwide, which explains the development of a great number of systems catalogued as emergency response software in the last decade. On the positive side, such diversity is good since potential users have a wide range of options to choose from. However, there is little guidance on how to select a particular system. A close look at the market of such systems shows much diversity in the way systems are described; often, the information found in the products' websites is sales oriented, lacking a systematic description of the systems' features and capabilities. Consequently, support to product understanding and selection is still missing.

In this work, we have introduced the first steps of the development of *Tax-CIM*, a taxonomy aimed at uniformly classifying CIMS. We have identified and organized the characteristics of such systems around seven dimensions relevant for emergency response following an iterative method combining conceptualizations with empirical study of the nature and features of CIMS. Using *Tax-CIM*, software vendors can produce systematic descriptions of their systems' features, while potential adapters of such systems can have an exhaustive description and comparison of the systems in the market, from which to select the one that best suits their requirements. Moreover, from an academic point of view, the taxonomy can serve as a keyword set for the description and retrieval of research literature.

The development of *Tax-CIM* is not finished; we estimate that at least one more iteration of the method should be made to include the classification of more CIMS. We expect that a new refinement of the characteristics set will produce a more comprehensive classification of existing systems. In the midterm, *Tax-CIM* is aimed at serving as a reference framework for the classification of CIMS. We expect the collaboration of system vendors or provide information to improve/extend the taxonomy. Along with these goals, we want to explore the use of a similar technique to develop taxonomies for other stages of the emergency management life cycle, such as preparedness or recovery, where there is a similar heterogeneity of systems.

Acknowledgments INCREMENTAL is a coordinated research project funded by Spain's *Ministerio de Ciencia e Innovación*. MRS Borges, J Hernantes, and L Labaka work under grant INCREMENT (PID2019-105414RA-C32), JH Canós and MC Penadés work under grant MIGRATE (PID2019-105414RB-C31), and V Bañuls works under grant RESISTE (PID2019-105414RB-C33). We also thank our anonymous reviewers, whose constructive comments helped to improve the quality of the chapter.

Appendix A Tax-CIM Version 1

Dimensions	Characteristics	Description
Coordination	Fieldwork coordination	Coordination between the response teams working in the operations field
	Command coordination	Coordination between the members of the control room
	Command to fieldwork coordination	Coordination of response teams from the control room
	Public coordination	Providing instructions for self-protection and/or to be first relief providers
	Volunteering support and coordination	Calling, accepting, and managing volunteerism (assignment of tasks, preparation assessment and improvement, coordination, etc.)
	Adaptation on the fly	Ability to change the action plan according to context changes or unexpected situations
	Resource management	Acquisition, maintenance, and allocation of material resources. Also, human resources management: allocation of duties, role assignment, etc.
	Logistics management	Definition of supply chains, fleet tracking, route optimization, etc.
Collaboration	Role management	Definition and assignment of roles to participants in the response
	Collaborative process enactment	Choreography of the response process, task lists, shared process awareness
	Shared workspaces	Role-based shared data spaces, collaborative planning
	Group decision-making	Support to the deliberation, voting and decision-making by formal or ad hoc groups
Information management	Context awareness	Users can access to fresh information coming from in-place sources that can overwrite the formal knowledge contained in the plan

(continued)

Dimensions	Characteristics	Description
	Process awareness	Every actor participating in the response knows what actions to perform at each moment
	Information capture	The system is able to catch information from different sources using video cameras, sensors of different types, UAVs, social media, etc.
	Information curation	The information is organized in the form of multimedia digital collections that are described using standard metadata schemas and eventually archived for further access or just preservation
	External data	External data sources are accessed to provide context to the different actors
	Maps	The information captures its geolocation and can be represented in spatial mash-ups
	Data integration	Data coming from heterogeneous sources can be merged into the CIMS schema by means of semantic integration techniques
	Public information officer (PIO) support	There are utilities for publication of information as well as for collecting requests and/or feedback from the public
	Logging	Every decision and action in the system is registered for further analysis
	Information retrieval	IR techniques allow the content-based retrieval of relevant information by means of text, picture, or audio-based queries
	Wearables	Different wearable devices can capture and send information about the responders' environment (including their health-relevant values)
Visualization	Dashboards	Functions for monitoring the situation awareness
	Mash-ups	Combining geolocated information with maps
	Tabletops	Use of interactive tabletops for both visualization and operation support
	Mobile clients	Responsive user interfaces adapt the dissemination to the screen dimensions
	Desktop	Default feature
	Customization	Role-based dissemination of information
	Augmented reality	Use augmented reality for visualizing the situation

(continued)

Dimensions	Characteristics	Description
Communication	Videoconferencing	Promote communication through videoconferencing, either for discussing or presenting information about a crisis
	SM interaction with the public	All types of interaction with the public through social media, either for receiving information or communicating information of common interest. It also includes requests to the public
	Non-SM interaction with the public: one way	Broadcasting information of interest to the public
	Non-SM interaction with the public: two way	Establishment of dialogues with members of the public
	Exclusive communication channel for fieldworkers	The same as C&C, but for fieldworkers, either to support the communication with the C&C and between the person operating in the field
	Exclusive communication channel for C&C	There is usually intense communication among members of the C&C teams, i.e., those who are not operating in the field (another category). Systems that support this interaction are in this category
Intelligence	Decision-making	All processes of automatic decision or recommendation after processing information available
	Automatic information processing (filtering, automatic categorization, and automatic inference)	After captured, the information has to be processed. This category embraces all processes that automatically filter, group, and generate conclusions from an information set
	Automatic information capture (sensors, drones . . .)	This category includes the dealing with all information coming from sources other than humans. It includes the selective and oriented capture of information without direct human intervention. Examples are sensors, autonomous drones, etc.

(continued)

Dimensions	Characteristics	Description
General support	Robustness	How to deal with errors generated by unexpected data or actions in the system. There are systems that address this issue because during a disaster response, the teams are under stress and can commit mistakes
	Privacy preservation	In many crises, the response teams deal with very sensitive information, such as the identification of people who are dead or injured. Functions in the system to preserve the authorized access to information are also part of this category
	Provenance	It refers to functions aimed to identify and preserve the provenance of information, not only for the purpose of trustworthiness but also to maintain the history of information transformation
	Scalability	It deals with how to evolve from a prototype or small number of users to a regional or national scale, particularly for crises involving teams from several regions/counties
	Open data	Some systems have their own data; others use data from open sources. There are some hybrid approaches, too. This category refers to systems that make use of open data
	Trustworthiness	This is an important aspect when dealing with information from external sources, particularly those that are not part of the network. Systems that deal with the trustworthiness of the information sources are member of this category
	Interoperability	There are two issues here: the first one relates to make systems used by different teams to share information and actions. The second one is to make systems for the same purpose but managed by different groups that can interoperate

Appendix B Tax-CIM Version 2

New characteristics are included *in italics typeface*.

Dimensions	Characteristics	Description
Coordination	Fieldwork coordination	Coordination between the response teams working in the operations field
	Command coordination	Coordination between the members of the control room
	Command to fieldwork coordination	Coordination of response teams from the control room
	Public coordination	Providing instructions for self-protection and/or to be first relief providers
	Coordinate with volunteer organizations	*Coordinate actions with volunteer organizations such as the Red Cross to avoid overlapping*
	Volunteering support and coordination	Calling, accepting, and managing volunteerism (assignment of tasks, preparation assessment and improvement, coordination, etc.)
	Adaptation on the fly dome by the response team	Ability to change the action plan according to context changes or unexpected situations
	Resource management	Acquisition, maintenance, and allocation of material resources. Also, human resources management: allocation of duties, role assignment, etc.
	Logistics management	Definition of supply chains, fleet tracking, route optimization, etc.
Collaboration	Role management	Definition and assignment of roles to participants in the response
	Collaborative process enactment	Choreography of the response process, task lists, shared process awareness
	Shared workspaces	Role-based shared data spaces, collaborative planning
	Group decision-making	Support to the deliberation, voting, and decision-making by formal or ad hoc groups

(continued)

Dimensions	Characteristics	Description
Information management	Context awareness	Users can access to fresh information coming from in-place sources that can overwrite the formal knowledge contained in the plan
	Process awareness	Every actor participating in the response knows what actions to perform at each moment and has the information he or she needs for acting
	Information capture	The system is able to catch information from different sources using video cameras, sensors of different types, UAVs, social media, etc.
	Information curation	The information is organized in the form of multimedia digital collections that are described using standard metadata schemas and eventually archived for further access or just preservation
	Open data	Open data sources are accessed to provide context to the different actors
	Maps	The information captured is geolocated and can be represented in spatial mash-ups
	Data integration	Data coming from heterogeneous sources can be merged into the CIMS schema by means of semantic integration techniques
	Public information officer support	There are utilities for publication of information as well as for collecting requests and/or feedback from the public
	Logging	Every decision and action in the system is registered for further analysis
	Information retrieval	IR techniques allow the content-based retrieval of relevant information by means of text, picture or audio-based queries
	Wearables	Different wearable devices can capture and send information about the responders' environment (including their health-relevant values)
Visualization	Dashboards	Functions for monitoring the situation awareness
	Mash-ups	Combining geolocated information with maps
	Tabletops	Use of interactive tabletops for both visualization and operation support
	Mobile clients	Responsive user interfaces adapt the dissemination to the screen dimensions

(continued)

Dimensions	Characteristics	Description
	Desktop	Default feature
	Customization	Role-based dissemination of information
	Augmented reality	Systems that use augmented reality for visualizing the situation
Communication	Videoconferencing	Promoting communication through videoconferencing either for discussing or to present information about a crisis
	SM interaction with the public	All types of interaction with the public through social media, either for receiving information or communicating information of common interest. It also includes requests to the public
	Non-SM interaction with the public: one way	Broadcasting information of interest to the public
	Non-SM interaction with the public: two way	Establishment of dialogues with members of the public
	Exclusive communication channel for fieldworkers	The same as C&C, but for fieldworkers, either to support the communication with the C&C and between the person operating in the field
	Exclusive communication channel for C&C	There is usually intense communication among members of the C&C teams, i.e., those who are not operating in the field (another category). Systems that support this interaction are in this category
Intelligence	*Recommendation and automatic decision-making*	All processes of automatic decision or recommendation after processing information available
	Automatic information capture (sensors, drones . . .)	This category includes the dealing with all information coming from sources other than humans. It includes the selective and oriented capture of information without direct human intervention. Examples are sensors, autonomous drones, etc.
	Automatic information filtering	*After captured, the information has to be processed. This category embrace all processes that automatically filter the data captured using some relevance criteria*
	Automatic information categorization	*This category embraces all processes that automatically classify the data according to the predicted usage*

(continued)

Dimensions	Characteristics	Description
	Automatic inference	*This category embraces all processes that automatically generate conclusions from an information set*
General support	Robustness	How to deal with errors generated by unexpected data or actions in the system. There are systems that address this issue because during a disaster response, the teams are under stress and can commit mistakes
	Privacy preservation	In many crises the response teams deal with very sensitive information, such as the identification of people who are dead or injured. Functions in the system to preserve the authorized access to information are also part of this category
	Provenance	It refers to functions aimed to identify and preserve the provenance of information, not only for the purpose of trustworthiness (another category) but also maintain the history of information transformation
	Scalability	It deals with how to evolve from a prototype or small number of users to a regional or national scale, particularly for crises involving teams from several regions/counties
	Open data	Some systems have their own data; others use data from open sources. There are some hybrid approaches, too. This category refers to systems that make use of open data
	Trustworthiness	Trust is an important aspect when dealing with information from external sources, particularly those that are not part of the network. Systems that deals with the trustworthiness of the information sources are member of this category
	Interoperability	There are two issues here: the first one relates to make systems used by different teams to share information and actions. The second one is to make systems for the same purpose but managed by different groups that can interoperate

References

Addams-Moring, R., Kekkonen, M., & Zhao, S. (2005). A simple taxonomy for mobile emergency announcement systems. In *Proceedings of ISCRAM 2005 – 2nd international conference on information systems for crisis response and management, Simpson, N*(April), pp. 309–316.

Auferbauer, D., Czech, G., Ruggenthaler, C., & Gojmerac, I. (2019). Taxonomy of community interaction in crises and disasters. In *Proceedings of the international ISCRAM conference, Simpson, N*(May), pp. 1031–1043.

Barthe-Delanoë, A. M., Truptil, S., & Bénaben, F. (2015). Towards a taxonomy of crisis management simulation tools. In *ISCRAM 2015 Conference proceedings – 12th international conference on information systems for crisis response and management, Simpson, N.*

Canós, J. H., Alonso, G., & Jaén, J. (2004). A multimedia approach to the efficient implementation and use of emergency plans. *IEEE Multimedia, 11*(3), 106–110. https://doi.org/10.1109/MMUL.2004.2

Canós, J. H., Borges, M., & Alonso, G. (2005). An IT view of emergency management. *IEEE Computer, 38*(12), 27.

Castillo, C. (2019). *Big crisis data: Social media in disaster and time critical situations*. Cambridge University Press.

Chen, R., Sharman, R., Rao, H. R., & Upadhyaya, S. J. (2005). Design principles for emergency response management systems. *Journal of Information Systems and E-Business Management Design, 15*(3), 81–98.

Di Maio, P. (2007). *An open ontology for open-source emergency response system*. http://ifipwg213.org/system/files/TOWARDS_AN_OPEN_ONTOLOGY_FOR_ER.pdf

Jennex, M. E. (2007). Modeling emergency response systems. In *Proceedings of the annual Hawaii international conference on system sciences* (pp. 1–8). https://doi.org/10.1109/HICSS.2007.386

Kyng, M., Nielsen, E. T., & Kristensen, M. (2006). Challenges in designing interactive systems for emergency response. In *Proceedings of the conference on designing interactive systems: Processes, practices, methods, and techniques* (pp. 301–310). DIS. https://doi.org/10.1145/1142405.1142450

Liu, S., Brewster, C., & Shaw, D. (2013). Ontologies for crisis management: A review of state of the art in ontology design and usability. In *ISCRAM 2013 conference proceedings – 10th international conference on information systems for crisis response and management, Simpson, N*(May), pp. 349–359.

Nickerson, R. C., Varshney, U., & Muntermann, J. (2013). A method for taxonomy development and its application in information systems. *European Journal of Information Systems, 22*(3), 336–359. https://doi.org/10.1057/ejis.2012.26

Rauner, M. S., Niessner, H., Odd, S., Pope, A., Neville, K., O'Riordan, S., Sasse, L., & Tomic, K. (2018). An advanced decision support system for European disaster management: The feature of the skills taxonomy. *Central European Journal of Operations Research, 26*(2), 485–530. https://doi.org/10.1007/s10100-018-0528-9

Shah, S. A., Seker, D. Z., Hameed, S., & Draheim, D. (2019). The rising role of big data analytics and IoT in disaster management: Recent advances, taxonomy and prospects. *IEEE Access*, 54595–54614. https://doi.org/10.1109/ACCESS.2019.2913340

Simon, H. A. (1969). *The sciences of the artificial*. Them MIT Press.

Simpson, N. C. (2012). On disaster response and emergent systems: A new taxonomy for operations management. *SSRN Electronic Journal*, 1–39. https://doi.org/10.2139/ssrn.2039466

Turoff, M. (2002). Past and future emergency response information systems. *Communications of the ACM, 45*(4), 29–32. https://doi.org/10.1145/505248.505265

Turoff, M., Chumer, M., Van de Walle, B., & Yao, X. (2004). The design of a dynamic emergency response management information system (DERMIS). *The Journal of Information Technology Theory and Application (JITTA), 5*(4), 1–35.

Xiang, L., Gang, L., Anhong, L., Jian, Z., Ning, A., Lian, L., & Yongzhong, S. (2008). Building a practical ontology for emergency response systems. In *Proceedings – International Conference on Computer Science and Software Engineering* (Vol. 4, pp. 222–225). CSSE. https://doi.org/10.1109/CSSE.2008.1044

Bibliography

Abbasi, A., & Kapucu, N. (2012). Structural dynamics of organizations during the evolution of interorganizational networks in disaster response. *Journal of Homeland Security and Emergency Management, 9*(1 (art. 23)), 1–19.

Abbassi, W., Harmel, A., Belkahla, W., & Rejeb, H. B. (2022). Maker movement contribution to fighting COVID-19 pandemic: Insights from Tunisian FabLabs. *R&D Management, 52*(2), 343–355.

Abdelghany, A., Abdelghany, K., Mahmassani, H., & Alhalabi, W. (2014). Modeling framework for optimal evacuation of large-scale crowded pedestrian facilities. *European Journal of Operational Research, 237*(3), 1105–1118.

Abrahamson, E. (2009). Necessary conditions for the study of fads and fashions in science. *Scandinavian Journal of Management, 25*(2), 235–239.

Addams-Moring, R., Kekkonen, M., & Zhao, S. (2005). A simple taxonomy for mobile emergency announcement systems. In B. A. van de Walle & B. Carle (Eds.), *2nd International Conference on Information Systems for Crisis Response and Management (ISCRAM 2005)*. Royal Flemish Academy of Belgium.

Adler, C., Krüsmann, M., Greiner-Mai, T., Donner, A., Chaves, J. M., & Estrem, À. V. (2011). *IT-supported management of mass casualty incidents: The e-Triage project*. Proceedings of the 8th International ISCRAM Conference (ISCRAM), Lisbon, Portugal, May.

Aftyka, A., Rybojad, B., & Rudnicka-Drozak, E. (2014). Are there any differences in medical emergency team interventions between rural and urban areas? A single-centre cohort study. *Australian Journal of Rural Health, 22*(5), 223–228.

Afzalan, N., Evans-Cowley, J., & Mirzazad-Barijough, M. (2015). From big to little data for natural disaster recovery: How online and on-the-ground activities are connected. *ISJLP, 11*, 153.

Agranoff, R. (2007). *Managing within networks: Adding value to public organizations*. Georgetown University Press.

Agranoff, R., & McGuire, M. (2003). *Collaborative public management: New strategies for local governments*. Georgetown University Press.

Aguirre, B. A., & Best, E. (2014). How not to learn: Resilience in the study of disaster. In *Learning and calamities* (pp. 236–252). Routledge.

Ahn, J., & Han, R. (2012). An indoor augmented-reality evacuation system for the Smartphone using personalized Pedometry. *Human-centric Computing and Information Sciences, 2*(1), 1–23.

Akerkar, R. (2013). *Big data computing*. CRC Press.

H. J. Scholl et al. (eds.), *Disaster Management and Information Technology*, Public Administration and Information Technology 40, https://doi.org/10.1007/978-3-031-20939-0

AlAwadhi, S., Aldama, A., Chourabi, H., Gil-Garcia, J. R., Leung, S., Mellouli, S., Nam, T., Pardo, T., Scholl, H. J., & Walker, S. (2012). Building understanding of smart city initiatives. In H. J. Scholl, M. Janssen, M. A. Wimmer, C. E. Moe, & L. S. Flak (Eds.), *Electronic government* (pp. 40–53). Springer Berlin Heidelberg.

Alberts, D. S., & Hayes, R. E. (2003). *Power to the edge: Command... control... in the information age*. Office of the Assistant Secretary of Defense, Command & Control Research Program (CCRP).

Alford, J., & O'flynn, J. (2012). *Rethinking public service delivery: Managing with external providers*. Bloomsbury Publishing.

Alipour, M., Dupuy-Chessa, S., & Céret, E. (2021). *An emotion-oriented problem space for ui adaptation: From a literature review to a conceptual framework*. 2021 9th International Conference on Affective Computing and Intelligent Interaction (ACII).

Alipour, M., Dupuy-Chessa, S., & Jongmans, E. (2020). *Disaster mitigation using interface adaptation to emotions: A targeted literature review*. 10th International Conference on the Internet of Things Companion.

Alsamhi, S. H., Almalki, F. A., AL-Dois, H., Shvetsov, A. V., Ansari, M. S., Hawbani, A., Gupta, S. K., & Lee, B. (2021). Multi-drone edge intelligence and SAR smart wearable devices for emergency communication. *Wireless Communications and Mobile Computing, 2021*, 1–12. https://doi.org/10.1155/2021/6710074

Ammenwerth, E., Iller, C., & Mahler, C. (2006). IT-adoption and the interaction of task, technology and individuals: A fit framework and a case study. *BMC Medical Informatics and Decision Making, 6*(1), 1–13. https://doi.org/10.1186/1472-6947-6-3

Anonymous. (2008). *National Incident Management System*. FEMA. https://www.fema.gov/pdf/emergency/nims/NIMS_core.pdf

Anonymous. (2010a, August). *Incident decision support software application note: System assessment and validation for emergency responders (SAVER)*. U.S. Department of Homeland Security. https://www.dhs.gov/sites/default/files/publications/IDSS_AppN_0810-508.pdf.

Anonymous. (2010b). *National Incident Management System Supporting Evaluation Program (NIMS STEP): Guide. Federal Emergency Management Agency*. U.S. Department of Homeland Security. https://www.hsdl.org/?view&did=693929

Anonymous. (2011a). Japan village that survived the tsunami. *Financial Express*, May 13, 2011, Story. Accessed May 15, 2011. http://www.financialexpress.com/news/japan-village-that-survived-the-tsunami/789960/1

Anonymous. (2011b). *Chief Executive/National Commander's Inquiry into Canterbury Earthquake 22 Feb 2011 – Final Report*. Director of Operational Efficiency (Wellington). http://www.fire.org.nz/Media/News/Documents/Christchurch%20inquiry%20report.pdf

Anonymous. (2011c). *Analytical baseline study for the Cascadia Earthquake and Tsunami*. Department of Homeland Security, National Infrastructure Simulation and Analysis Center, Homeland Infrastructure Threat and Risk Analysis Center, Office of Infrastructure Protection, National Protection and Programs Directorate.

Anonymous. (2012a). *About us*. [website]. Disaster Research Center. University of Delaware. Accessed November 20, 2012. http://www.udel.edu/DRC/aboutus/

Anonymous. (2012b). *Evergreen quake 2012 functional exercise: Regional after action report*. Edited by, Puget Sound (Seattle Metro area) city and county emergency management departments; Washington State Emergency Management Division; FEMA Region 10. Seattle: Puget Sound Regional Catastrophic Preparedness Grant Program (RCPGP). National Emergency Management Association (NEMA) Mutual Aid Grant. FEMA Regional Exercise Support Program (RESP).

Anonymous. (2012c). Strengthening activities on a global scale. *Risk Management Review*, August 29, 2012, 1–28. Accessed March 1, 2013. http://opim.wharton.upenn.edu/risk/review/WhartonRiskCenter-newsletter_2012.pdf

Anonymous. (2012d). Japan's 2011 earthquake and tsunami: remembrance, preparedness and rebuilding. *The Seattle Times*, March 9, 2012 at 3:42 pm, updated March 9, 2012 at 5:46 pm, 2012, 1.

Anonymous. (2013). National response framework. In *Homeland security*. FEMA.

Anonymous. (2015, February). *Common alerting protocol alert origination tools technology guide: System Assessment and Validation for Emergency Responders (SAVER)*. U.S. Department of Homelad Security—Science and Technology. https://www.dhs.gov/sites/default/files/publications/Alert-Protocol-TG_0215-508.pdf

Anonymous. (2016, September 6). *Cascadia rising 2016 exercise: Cascadia Subduction Zone (CSZ) catastrophic earthquake and tsunami*; Functional Exercise: June 7–10, 2016; Joint Multi-State After-Action Report. FEMA, Department of Homeland Security, Federal Emergency Management Agency.

Anonymous. (2017, January 5). *Washington State 2016 Cascadia rising exercise after action report catastrophic earthquake and tsunami scenario*. Washington State Emergency Management Division. https://www.google.com/search?client=safari&rls=en&q=Washington+State+2016+Cascadia+Rising+Exercise+After+Action+Report+Catastrophic+Earthquake+and+Tsunami+Scenario&ie=UTF-8&oe=UTF-8.

Anonymous. (2020, October 30). *Privacy impact assessment for the CBP Web Emergency Operations Center (WebEOC)—October 30*. U.S. Department of Homelad Security. https://www.dhs.gov/sites/default/files/publications/privacy-pia-cbp-065-webeoc-october2020.pdf

Ansell, C., Boin, A., & Keller, A. (2010). Managing transboundary crises: Identifying the building blocks of an effective response system. *Journal of Contingencies and Crisis Management, 18*(4), 195–207.

Antivachis, N. A., & Angelis, V. A. (2015). Network organizations: The question of governance. *Procedia-Social and Behavioral Sciences, 175*, 584–592. https://doi.org/10.1016/j.sbspro.2015.01.1241

Arbib, C., Dugdale, J., Arcelli, D., Moghaddam, M. T., & Muccini, H. (2019). Real-time emergency response through performant IoT architectures. In Z. Franco, J. J. González, & J. H. Canós (Eds.), *16th International Conference on Information Systems for Crisis Response and Management (ISCRAM 2019)*. Universitat Politécnica de Valéncia.

Arbib, C., Moghaddam, M. T., & Muccini, H. (2019). Iot flows: A network flow model application to building evacuation. In *A view of operations research applications in Italy, 2018* (pp. 115–131). Springer.

Arbib, C., Muccini, H., & Moghaddam, M. T. (2018). Applying a network flow model to quick and safe evacuation of people from a building: A real case. *RSFF, 18*, 50–61.

Argyris, C. (1971). *Management and organizational development; the path from XA to YB*. McGraw-Hill.

Argyris, C. (1990). *Overcoming organizational defenses: Facilitating organizational learning*. Allyn and Bacon.

Argyris, C., & Schon, D. A. (1996). *Organiational learning II*. Addison Wesley.

Arjun, P. (2019). *Machine learning and AI for healthcare: Big data for improved health outcomes*. Apress.

Aros, S. K., & Gibbons, D. E. (2018). *Developing an agent-based simulation model of the use of different communication technologies in inter-organizational disaster response coordination*. Proceedings of the 2018 Winter Simulation Conference (WSC), Gothenburg, Sweden, December 9–12.

Arslan, A., Golgeci, I., Khan, Z., Al-Tabbaa, O., & Hurmelinna-Laukkanen, P. (2020). Adaptive learning in cross-sector collaboration during global emergency: Conceptual insights in the context of COVID-19 pandemic. *Multinational Business Review, 29*(1), 21–42. https://doi.org/10.1108/MBR-07-2020-0153

Arthur, W. B. (1989). Competing technologies, increasing returns, and lock-in by historical events. *The Economic Journal, 99*(394), 116–131.

Atallah, D. G., Djalali, A., Fredricks, K., Arlington, L., Bussio, M., & Nelson, B. D. (2018). Developing equitable primary health care in Conflict-Affected settings: Expert perspectives from the Frontlines. *Qualitative Health Research, 28*(1), 98–111.

Atwater, B. F., Nelson, A. R., Clague, J. J., Carver, G. A., Yamaguchi, D. K., Bobrowsky, P. T., Bourgeois, J., Darienzo, M. E., Grant, W. C., & Hemphill-Haley, E. (1995). Summary of coastal geologic evidence for past great earthquakes at the Cascadia subduction zone. *Earthquake Spectra, 11*(1), 1–18.

Auferbauer, D., Ruggenthaler, C., Czech, G., & Gojmerac, I. (2019). Taxonomy of community interaction in crises and disasters. In Z. Franco, J. J. González, & J. H. Canós (Eds.), *16th International Conference on Information Systems for Crisis Response and Management (ISCRAM 2019)*. Universitat Politécnica de Valéncia.

Augustin, A., Yi, J., Clausen, T., & Townsley, W. M. (2016). A study of LoRa: Long range & low power networks for the internet of things. *Sensors, 16*(9), 1466 (1-18).

Babiak, K., & Thibault, L. (2009). Challenges in multiple cross-sector partnerships. *Nonprofit and Voluntary Sector Quarterly, 38*(1), 117–143. https://doi.org/10.1177/0899764008316054

Baghizadeh, Z., Cecez-Kecmanovic, D., & Schlagwein, D. (2020). Review and critique of the information systems development project failure literature: An argument for exploring information systems development project distress. *Journal of Information Technology, 35*(2), 123–142.

Bakos, L. (2020). *Knowledge management issues during organizational crisis: How human-machine communication helps*. 17th International Conference on Intellectual Capital, Knowledge Management & Organisational Learning ICICKM 2020, Toronto, Canada, October 15–16.

Bañuls, V. A., & Turoff, M. (2011). Scenario construction via Delphi and cross-impact analysis. *Technological Forecasting and Social Change, 78*(9), 1579–1602.

Bañuls, V. A., Turoff, M., & Hiltz, S. R. (2012). Collaborative scenario modeling in emergency management through cross-impact. *Technological Forecasting and Social Change, 80*(9), 1756–1774.

Barnett, D. J., Strauss-Riggs, K., Klimczak, V. L., Rosenblum, A. J., & Kirsch, T. D. (2021). An analysis of after action reports from Texas hurricanes in 2005 and 2017. *Journal of Public Health Management and Practice, 27*(2), E71–E78.

Barsky, L. E., Trainor, J. E., Torres, M. R., & Aguirre, B. E. (2007). Managing volunteers: FEMA's Urban Search and Rescue programme and interactions with unaffiliated responders in disaster response. *Disasters, 31*(4), 495–507. https://doi.org/10.1111/j.1467-7717.2007.01021.x

Barth, B., Friedemann, M., Mühlbauer, M., Vendrell, J., Riedlinger, T., De Cola, T., & Swaminathan, M. (2019). *Design of a multi-hazard collaborative system for scenario-based response planning*. INFORMATIK 2019: 50 Jahre Gesellschaft für Informatik–Informatik für Gesellschaft (Workshop-Beiträge), Bonn, Germany.

Barthe, A. M., Truptil, S., & Bénaben, F. (2015). Towards a taxonomy of crisis management simulation tools. In L. Palen, M. Büscher, T. Comes, & A. L. Hughes (Eds.), *12th International Conference on Information Systems for Crisis Response and Management (ISCRAM 2015)*. University of Agder (UiA).

Barton, M. A., & Sutcliffe, K. M. (2009). Overcoming dysfunctional momentum: Organizational safety as a social achievement. *Human Relations, 62*(9), 1327–1356.

Basu, M., Bandyopadhyay, S., & Ghosh, S. (2016). Post disaster situation awareness and decision support through interactive crowdsourcing. *Procedia Engineering, 159*, 167–173.

Baumgärtner, L., Gardner-Stephen, P., Graubner, P., Lakeman, J., Höchst, J., Lampe, P., Schmidt, N., Schulz, S., Sterz, A., & Freisleben, B. (2016). *An experimental evaluation of delay-tolerant networking with Serval*. 2016 IEEE Global Humanitarian Technology Conference (GHTC).

Beachwood, O. H., Weston, F. L., Coronado, C. A., Hollywood, F. L., & Calendar, M. C. M. E. (2013). Electronic siloing: An unintended consequence of the electronic health record. *Cleveland Clinic Journal of Medicine, 80*(7), 406–409. http://www.ccjm.org/topics/practice-management/single-article-page/electronic-siloing-an-unintended-consequence-of-the-electronic-health-record/a8187a47a625bb8c4d0ba2f1202afdf5.html

Becerra-Fernández, I., Madey, G., Prietula, M., Rodríguez, D., Valerdi, R., & Wright, T. (2008). Design and development of a virtual emergency operations center for disaster management research, training, and discovery. In *Proceedings of the 41st Hawaii International Conference on System Sciences*. IEEE.

Beck, E., Dugdale, J., Van Truong, H., Adam, C., & Colbeau-Justin, L. (2014). *Crisis mobility of pedestrians: From survey to modelling, lessons from Lebanon and Argentina*. International

Conference on Information Systems for Crisis Response and Management in Mediterranean Countries.

Beck, T. E., & Plowman, D. A. (2014). Temporary, emergent interorganizational collaboration in unexpected circumstances: A study of the Columbia space shuttle response effort. *Organization Science, 25*(4), 1234–1252.

Bélanger, F., Cefaratti, M., Carte, T., & Markham, S. E. (2014). Multilevel research in information systems: Concepts, strategies, problems, and pitfalls. *Journal of the Association for Information Systems, 15*(9), 1.

Benbasat, I., & Zmud, R. W. (2003). The identity crisis within the IS discipline: Defining and communicating the discipline's core properties1. *MIS Quarterly, 27*(2), 183–194. http://proquest.umi.com/pqdweb?did=352184641&Fmt=7&clientId=8991&RQT=309&VName=PQD

Berbakov, L., Pavkovic, B., & Vrane, S. (2015). *Smart indoor positioning system for situation awareness in emergency situations*. 2015 26th International Workshop on Database and Expert Systems Applications (DEXA).

Berbakov, L., Tripi, F. N., Abad, A. C., Gómez, J. V., & Pavković, B. (2017). *Android application for collaborative mapping in emergency situations*. 2017 25th Telecommunication Forum (TELFOR).

Berggren, P., & Johansson, B. J. E. (2010). Developing an instrument for measuring shared understanding. In S. French & B. Tomaszewski (Eds.), *7th International Conference on Information Systems for Crisis Response and Management (ISCRAM 2010)*. Information Systems for Crisis Response and Management.

Berlin, J. M., & Carlström, E. D. (2011). Why is collaboration minimised at the accident scene? A critical study of a hidden phenomenon. *Disaster Prevention and Management: An International Journal, 20*(2), 159–171. https://doi.org/10.1108/09653561111126094

Berlin, J. M., & Carlström, E. D. (2014). Collaboration exercises—The lack of collaborative benefits. *International Journal of Disaster Risk Science, 5*(3), 192–205.

Berman, J. J. (2013). *Principles of big data: Preparing, sharing, and analyzing complex information*. Morgan Kaufmann/Elsevir.

Berto, R., Napoletano, P., & Savi, M. (2021). A LoRa-based mesh network for peer-to-peer long-range communication. *Sensors, 21*(13), 4314 (1–12).

Betts, B. J., Mah, R. W., Papasin, R., Del Mundo, R., McIntosh, D. M., & Jorgensen, C. (2005). *Improving situational awareness for first responders via mobile computing*. STI Office, NASA.

Van Bezooijen, B., & Kramer, E.-H. (2015). Mission command in the information age: A normal accidents perspective on networked military operations. *Journal of Strategic Studies, 38*(4), 445–466.

Bharosa, N., Lee, J., & Janssen, M. (2010). Challenges and obstacles in sharing and coordinating information during multi-agency disaster response: Propositions from field exercises. *Information Systems Frontiers, 12*(1), 49–65.

Bharosa, N., Lee, J. K., Janssen, M., & Rao, H. R. (2009). A case study of information flows in multi-agency emergency response exercises. In *Proceedings of the 10th annual international conference on digital government research (dg.o 2009)*. Digital Government Society of North America.

Bhowmik, S. (2017). *Cloud computing*. Cambridge University Press.

Bigley, G. A., & Roberts, K. H. (2001). The incident command system: High-reliability organizing for complex and volatile task environments. *Academy of Management Journal, 44*(6), 1281–1299.

Birdsey, M., Islam, M. R., & Barmare, A. (2016). Sporting injuries, seasonal trend and impact on rural Australian hospitals: Implications and recommendations. *Australian Journal of Rural Health, 24*(6), 402–408.

Bizaki, H. K. (2016). *Towards 5G wireless networks: A physical layer perspective* (Vol. 232). BoD–Books on Demand.

Boersma, K., Büscher, M., & Fonio, C. (2022). Crisis management, surveillance, and digital ethics in the COVID-19 era. *Journal of Contingencies and Crisis Management, 30*(1), 2–9.

Boersma, K., Ferguson, J., Groenewegen, P., & Wolbers, J. (2021). The dynamics of power in disaster response networks. *Risk, Hazards & Crisis in Public Policy, 12*(4), 418–433.

Boersma, K., Wagenaar, P., & Wolbers, J. (2012). Negotiating the 'Trading Zone'. Creating a shared information infrastructure in the Dutch public safety sector. *Journal of Homeland Security and Emergency Management, 9*(2), 1–25. https://doi.org/10.1515/1547-7355.1965

Boersma, K., & Wolbers, J. (2021). *Foundations of responsive crisis management: Institutional design and information*. Oxford University Press.

Boersma, K., Wolbers, J., & Wagenaar, P. (2010). Organizing emergent safety organizations: The travelling of the concept 'netcentric work' in the Dutch safety sector. In S. French & B. Tomaszewski (Eds.), *7th International Conference on Information Systems for Crisis Response and Management (ISCRAM 2010)*. Information Systems for Crisis Response and Management.

Bogucki, S., & Schulz, K. J. (2015). Incident command system and National Incident Management System. In D. Cone, J. H. Brice, T. R. Delbridge, & J. Brent Myers (Eds.), *Emergency medical services: Clinical practice and systems oversight* (2nd ed., pp. 255–263). Wiley.

Boin, A., Ekengren, M., & Rhinard, M. (2020). Hiding in plain sight: Conceptualizing the creeping crisis. *Risk, Hazards & Crisis in Public Policy, 11*(2), 116–138.

Boin, A., Stern, E., & Sundelius, B. (2016). *The politics of crisis management: Public leadership under pressure*. Cambridge University Press.

Boin, A., & Paul t Hart. (2010). Organising for effective emergency management: Lessons from research1. *Australian Journal of Public Administration, 69*(4), 357–371.

Boloix, G., & Robillard, P. N. (1995). A software system evaluation framework. *Computer, 28*(12), 17–26.

Bolton, F. C. (2016). Use of the after-action review to improve learning. *Assessment Update, 28*(2), 3–15. https://doi.org/10.1002/au.30051

Bor, M., Vidler, J. E., & Roedig, U. (2016). *LoRa for the Internet of Things*. EWSN '16 Proceedings of the 2016 International Conference on Embedded Wireless Systems and Networks, February 15–17.

Borglund, E. A. M. (2017). The Role of Artefacts in Creating a common operational picture During Large Crises. In T. Comes & F. Bénaben (Eds.), *14th International Conference on Information Systems for Crisis Response and Management (ISCRAM 2017)*.

Borgman, C. L. (2007). *Scholarship in the digital age: Information, infrastructure, and the Internet*. MIT Press.

Bose, R. (2003). Knowledge management-enabled health care management systems: Capabilities, infrastructure, and decision-support. *Expert Systems with Applications, 24*(1), 59–71.

Bosman, J., & Renckstorf, K. (1996). Information needs: Problems, interests and consumption. In K. Renckstorf, D. McQuail, & N. W. Jankowski (Eds.), *Media use as social action: A European approach to audience studies* (pp. 43–52). John Libbey.

Botterell, A., & Addams-Moring, R. (2007). Public warning in the networked age: Open standards to the rescue? *Communications of the ACM, 50*(3), 59–60.

Bovaird, T. (2007). Beyond engagement and participation: User and community coproduction of public services. *Public Administration Review, 67*(5), 846–860.

Boynton, A. C., Zmud, R. W., & Jacobs, G. C. (1994). The influence of IT management practice on IT use in large organizations. *MIS Quarterly, 18*, 299–318.

Brinkerhoff, J. M. (2002). Government–nonprofit partnership: A defining framework. *Public Administration and Development: The International Journal of Management Research and Practice, 22*(1), 19–30. https://doi.org/10.1002/pad.203

Brown, J. T., Lindsay, B. R., & Petruzelli, J. (2017). *Congressional primer on responding to major disasters and emergencies*. Library of Congress. Congressional Research Service.

Bruneau, M., Chang, S. E., Eguchi, R. T., Lee, G. C., O'Rourke, T. D., Reinhorn, A. M., Shinozuka, M., Tierney, K., Wallace, W. A., & von Winterfeldt, D. (2003). A framework to quantitatively assess and enhance the seismic resilience of communities. *Earthquake Spectra, 19*(4), 733–752.

Bryson, J. M. (2004). What to do when stakeholders matter: Stakeholder identification and analysis techniques. *Public Management Review, 6*(1), 21–53. https://doi.org/10.1080/14719030410001675722

Buchetti, B., Parbonetti, A., & Pugliese, A. (2022). Covid-19, corporate survival and public policy: The role of accounting information and regulation in the wake of a systemic crisis. *Journal of Accounting and Public Policy, 41*(1), 106919 (1–21).

Buck, D. A., Trainor, J. E., & Aguirre, B. E. (2006). A critical evaluation of the incident command system and NIMS. *Journal of Homeland Security and Emergency Management, 3*(3), 1–27.

Buckland, M. K. (1991). Information as thing. *Journal of the American Society for Information Science, 42*(5), 351–380.

Bunker, D., Levine, L., & Woody, C. (2015). Repertoires of collaboration for common operating pictures of disasters and extreme events. *Information Systems Frontiers, 17*(1), 51–65.

Cak, S., Say, B., & Misirlisoy, M. (2020). Effects of working memory, attention, and expertise on pilots' situation awareness. *Cognition, Technology & Work, 22*(1), 85–94.

Callebaut, G., Leenders, G., Buyle, C., Crul, S., & Van der Perre, L. (2019). LoRa physical layer evaluation for point-to-point links and coverage measurements in diverse environments. *arXiv preprint* arXiv:1909.08300:1–2.

Canós, J. H., Alonso, G., & Jaén, J. (2004). A multimedia approach to the efficient implementation and use of emergency plans. *IEEE Multimedia, 11*(3), 106–110. https://doi.org/10.1109/MMUL.2004.2

Canós, J. H., Borges, M. R. S., & Alonso, G. (2004). An IT view of emergency management. *IEEE Computer, 38*(12), 27. https://doi.org/10.1109/MC.2005.410

Carlsson, L. (2000). Policy networks as collective action. *Policy Studies Journal, 28*(3), 502–520. https://doi.org/10.1111/j.1541-0072.2000.tb02045.x

Carr, N. G. (2003). IT doesn't matter. *Harvard Business Review, 81*(5), 41–49.

Carrier, M., & Nordmann, A. (2011). *Science in the context of application* (Vol. 274). Springer Science & Business Media.

Carter, J. (2017, July 6). *Department of Homeland Security Appropriations Bill*. TX John Carter. https://www.congress.gov/114/crpt/hrpt668/CRPT-114hrpt668.pdf

Carver, L., & Turoff, M. (2007). Human-computer interaction: The human and computer as a team in emergency management information systems. *Communications of the ACM, 50*(3), 33–38.

Case, D. O. (2007). *Looking for information: A survey of research on information seeking, needs, and behavior. Library and information science*. Elsevier/Academic Press.

Castillo, C. (2016). *Big crisis data: Social media in disasters and time-critical situations*. Cambridge University Press.

Cawley, K. S. (2020). *Assessing the impact of age and experience on the perceived ease of use of crisis information management software*.

Cecez-Kecmanovic, D., Kautz, K., & Abrahall, R. (2014). Reframing success and failure of information systems. *MIS Quarterly, 38*(2), 561–588.

Ceferino, L., Kiremidjian, A., & Deierlein, G. (2018). Probabilistic model for regional multiseverity casualty estimation due to building damage following an earthquake. *ASCE-ASME Journal of Risk and Uncertainty in Engineering Systems, Part A: Civil Engineering, 4*(3), 04018023.

Chambers, D., Cantrell, A. J., Johnson, M., Preston, L., Baxter, S. K., Booth, A., & Turner, J. (2019). Digital and online symptom checkers and health assessment/triage services for urgent health problems: Systematic review. *BMJ Open, 9*(8), e027743 (1–13). https://doi.org/10.1136/bmjopen-2018-027743

Chambers, R. (1994). The origins and practice of participatory rural appraisal. *World Development, 22*(7), 953–969.

Chang, H.-H. (2017). A literature review and analysis of the incident command system. *International Journal of Emergency Management, 13*(1), 50–67.

Chang, S. E. (2003). Evaluating disaster mitigations: Methodology for urban infrastructure systems. *Natural Hazards Review, 4*(4), 186–196.

Charmaz, K. (2006). *Constructing grounded theory: A practical guide through qualitative analysis*. Sage Publications.

Chatfield, A. T., & Reddick, C. G. (2018). All hands on deck to tweet# sandy: Networked governance of citizen coproduction in turbulent times. *Government Information Quarterly, 35*(2), 259–272. https://doi.org/10.1016/j.giq.2017.09.004

Chatfield, A. T., Scholl, H. J., & Brajawidagda, U. (2013). Tsunami early warnings via Twitter in government: Net-savvy citizens' co-provision of time-critical public information services. *Government Information Quarterly, 30*(4), 377–386.

Chatfield, A. T., Scholl, H. J., & Brajawidagda, U. (2014). #Sandy tweets: Citizens' co-production of time-critical information during an unfolding catastrophe. In R. Sprague (Ed.), *47th Hawaii International Conference on System Sciences (HICSS-47)*. IEEE.

Chatfield, A. T., Wamba, S. F., & Tatano, H. (2010). *E-Government Challenge in Disaster Evacuation Response: The Role of RFID Technology in Building Safe and Secure Local Communities*. 43rd Hawaii International Conference on System Sciences (HICSS-43), Koloa, Kauai, HI, January 5–8, 2010.

Chen, J., Arumaithurai, M., Jiao, L., Fu, X., & Ramakrishnan, K. K. (2011). *Copss: An efficient content oriented publish/subscribe system*. 2011 ACM/IEEE Seventh Symposium on Architectures for Networking and Communications Systems.

Chen, P.-H., & Feng, F. (2009). A fast flow control algorithm for real-time emergency evacuation in large indoor areas. *Fire Safety Journal, 44*(5), 732–740.

Chen, R., Raj Sharman, H., Rao, R., & Upadhyaya, S. (2007). Design principles for emergency response management systems. *Journal of Information Systems and e-Business Management, 5*(3), 81–98.

Chen, R., Raj Sharman, H., Rao, R., & Upadhyaya, S. J. (2008). Coordination in emergency response management. *Communications of the ACM, 51*(5), 66–73.

Chen, R., Sharman, R., Rao, H. R., Upadhyaya, S. J., & Cook-Cottone, C. P. (2014). Coordination of emergency response: An examination of the roles of people, process, and information technology. In B. Van De Walle, M. Turoff, & S. R. Hiltz (Eds.), *Information systems for emergency management* (Advances in Management Information Systems monograph series) (pp. 150–174). Routledge.

Choi, W., Hamacher, H. W., & Tufekci, S. (1988). Modeling of building evacuation problems by network flows with side constraints. *European Journal of Operational Research, 35*(1), 98–110.

Choo, C. W. (2002). *Information management for the intelligent organization: The art of scanning the environment* (ASIS monograph series) (3rd ed.). Information Today.

Choong, Y.-Y., Dawkins, S. T., Furman, S. M., Greene, K., Prettyman, S. S., & Theofanos, M. F. (July 2018). *Voices of first responders–identifying public safety communication problems: Findings from user-centered interviews, phase 1, Volume 1. U.S. Department of Commerce*. National Institute of Standards and Technology.

Chourabi, H., Nam, T., Walker, S., Gil-Garcia, J. R., Mellouli, S., Nahon, K., Pardo, T. A., & Scholl, H. J. (2012). *Understanding smart cities: An integrative framework*. System Science (HICSS), 2012 45th Hawaii International Conference on, January 4–7, 2012.

Chua, A. Y. K., Kaynak, S., & Foo, S. S. B. (2007). An analysis of the delayed response to Hurricane Katrina through the lens of knowledge management. *Journal of the American Society for Information Science and Technology, 58*(3), 391–403. https://doi.org/10.1002/asi.20521

Chung, K., & Park, R. C. (2016). P2P cloud network services for IoT based disaster situations information. *Peer-to-Peer Networking and Applications, 9*(3), 566–577.

Cimellaro, G. P., Malavisi, M., & Mahin, S. (2018). Factor analysis to evaluate hospital resilience. *ASCE-ASME Journal of Risk and Uncertainty in Engineering Systems, Part A: Civil Engineering, 4*(1), 04018002 (1–7).

Clarke, P. K., & Campbell, L. (2018). Coordination in theory, coordination in practice: The case of the clusters. *Disasters, 42*(4), 655–673. https://doi.org/10.1111/disa.12282. https://onlinelibrary.wiley.com/doi/abs/10.1111/disa.12282

Coben, J. H., Tiesman, H. M., Bossarte, R. M., & Furbee, P. M. (2009). Rural–urban differences in injury hospitalizations in the US, 2004. *American Journal of Preventive Medicine, 36*(1), 49–55.

Cole, D. (2000). *The incident command system: A 25-year evaluation by California practitioners*. National Fire Academy.

Comfort, L. K. (2002). Rethinking security: Organizational fragility in extreme events. *Public Administration Review, 62*, 98–107. https://doi.org/10.1111/1540-6210.62.s1.18

Comfort, L. K. (2007). Crisis management in hindsight: Cognition, communication, coordination, and control. *Public Administration Review, 67*(s1), 189–197.

Comfort, L. K., Boin, A., & Demchak, C. C. (2010). *Designing resilience: Preparing for extreme events*. University of Pittsburgh Press.

Comfort, L. K., Dunn, M., Johnson, D., Skertich, R., & Zagorecki, A. (2004). Coordination in complex systems: Increasing efficiency in disaster mitigation and response. *International Journal of Emergency Management, 2*(1–2), 62–80. https://doi.org/10.1504/ijem.2004.005314. internal-pdf://Comfortetal2004-CoordinationComplexSystems-2253890560/Comfortetal2004-CoordinationComplexSystems.pdf.

Comfort, L. K., & Kapucu, N. (2006). Inter-organizational coordination in extreme events: The World Trade Center attacks, September 11, 2001. *Natural Hazards, 39*(2), 309–327.

Comfort, L. K., Ko, K., & Zagorecki, A. (2004). Coordination in rapidly evolving disaster response systems: The role of information. *American Behavioral Scientist, 48*(3), 295–313.

Corbin, J. M., & Strauss, A. (1990). Grounded theory research: Procedures, canons, and evaluative criteria. *Qualitative Sociology, 13*(1), 3–21.

Correia, A., Severino, I., Nunes, I. L., & Simões-Marques, M. (2017). *Knowledge management in the development of an intelligent system to support emergency response*. International Conference on Applied Human Factors and Ergonomics, Los Angeles, CA, July, 25–29.

Cowper, T. J. (2000). The myth of the "military model" of leadership in law enforcement. *Police Quarterly, 3*(3), 228–246.

Coyle, D., & Meier, P. (2009). *New technologies in emergencies and conflicts: The role of information and social networks*. United Nations Foundation-Vodafone Foundation Partnership. http://www.unfoundation.org/assets/pdf/new-technologies-emergencies-conflicts.pdf

Creswell, J. W., & Miller, D. L. (2000). Determining validity in qualitative inquiry. *Theory Into Practice, 39*(3), 124–130.

Croteau, A.-M., & Bergeron, F. (2001). An information technology trilogy: Business strategy, technological deployment and organizational performance. *The Journal of Strategic Information Systems, 10*(2), 77–99.

Crowe, S., Vasilakis, C., Skeen, A., Storr, P., Grove, P., Gallivan, S., & Utley, M. (2014). Examining the feasibility of using a modelling tool to assess resilience across a health-care system and assist with decisions concerning service reconfiguration. *Journal of the Operational Research Society, 65*(10), 1522–1532.

Currion, P., de Silva, C., & Van de Walle, B. (2007). Open source software for disaster management. *Communications of the ACM, 50*(3), 61–65.

Daamen, W., & Hoogendoorn, S. P. (2012). Emergency door capacity: Influence of door width, population composition and stress level. *Fire Technology, 48*(1), 55–71.

Das, T. K., & Teng, B.-S. (1998). Between trust and control: Developing confidence in partner cooperation in alliances. *Academy of Management Review, 23*(3), 491–512.

Davis, G. L., & Robbin, A. (2015). Network disaster response effectiveness: The case of ICTs and Hurricane Katrina. *Journal of Homeland Security and Emergency Management, 12*(3), 437–467.

Davison, R. M., Martinsons, M. G., & Koch, N. (2004). Principles of canonical action research. *Information Systems Journal, 14*(1), 65–86.

Dawes, S. S., Birkland, T., Tayi, G. K., & Schneider, C. A. (2004). *Information, technology, and coordination: Lessons from the world trade center response*. Center for Technology in Government (CTG). http://www.ctg.albany.edu/publications/reports/wtc_lessons/wtc_lessons.pdf

Dawes, S. S., Cresswell, A. M., & Cahan, B. B. (2004). Learning from crisis lessons in human and information infrastructure from the world trade center response. *Social Science Computer Review, 22*(1), 52–66.

Dawkins, S., Choong, Y.-Y., Theofanos, M. F., Greene, K. K., Furman, S., Steves, M., & Prettyman, S. S. (2019). *Voices of first responders–examining public safety communication problems and requested functionality: Findings from user-centered interviews, Phase 1, Volume 2.1. U.S. Department of Commerce*. National Institute of Standards and Technology.

Nicola, D., Antonio, A. T., Vicoli, G., & Villani, M. L. (2012). An MDA-based approach to crisis and emergency management modeling. *International Journal on Advances in Intelligent Systems, 5*(1&2), 89–100. http://www.iariajournals.org/intelligent_systems/intsys_v5_n12_2012_paged.pdf

DeCapua, M. (2007). Letter to the editor regarding Incident Command System (ICS). *Journal of Homeland Security and Emergency Management, 4*(1), 1.

Deepak, G. C., Ladas, A., Sambo, Y. A., Pervaiz, H., Politis, C., & Imran, M. A. (2019). An overview of post-disaster emergency communication systems in the future networks. *IEEE Wireless Communications, 26*(6), 132–139.

Deffer, F. (2011, April 1). *Federal Emergency Management Agency faces challenges in modernizing information technology*. Office of Inspector General, Department of Homeland Security. https://www.oig.dhs.gov/assets/Mgmt/OIG_11-69_Apr11.pdf

Delaney, A., & Kitchin, R. (2020). Progress and prospects for data-driven coordinated management and emergency response: The case of Ireland. *Territory, Politics, Governance, 8*(6), 1–16. https://doi.org/10.1080/21622671.2020.1805355

Dempsey, R., & Chavous, J. M. (2013). Commander's intent and concept of operations. *Military Review*, November-December 2013, 58–66.

Department_Homeland_Security. (2008). *National Management Incident System*. United States Department of Homeland Security. http://www.fema.gov/pdf/emergency/nims/NIMS_core.pdf

DeSanctis, G., & Poole, M. S. (1994). Capturing the complexity in advanced technology use: Adaptive structuration theory. *Organization Science, 5*, 124–147.

Deutsch, E. S., Dong, Y., Halamek, L. P., Rosen, M. A., Taekman, J. M., & Rice, J. (2016). Leveraging health care simulation technology for human factors research: Closing the gap between lab and bedside. *Human Factors, 58*(7), 1082–1095.

Deverell, E., Alvinius, A., & Hede, S. (2019). Horizontal collaboration in crisis management: An experimental study of the duty officer function in three public agencies. *Risk, Hazards & Crisis in Public Policy, 10*(4), 484–508.

Dickes, L. A., David Lamie, R., & Whitacre, B. E. (2010). The struggle for broadband in rural America. *Choices, 25*(316-2016-7507), 1–8.

Dilo, A., & Zlatanova, S. (2011). A data model for operational and situational information in emergency response. *Applied Geomatics, 3*(4), 207–218.

Dirgahayu, T., & Setiaji, H. (2020). *Semantic web in disaster management: A systematic literature review*. IOP Conference Series: Materials Science and Engineering, Yogyakarta, Indonesia, November 15.

Dongare, S. S., Deokar, R. B., Patil, S. S., & Jadhav, P. L. (2017). Correlation of stature to arm span and biacromial shoulder width in young adults of Western Indian population. *International Journal of Education and Research in Health Sciences, 3*(2), 64–70.

Drabek, T. E. (1986). *Human system responses to disaster: An inventory of sociological findings* (Springer series on environmental management). Springer-Verlag.

Drabek, T. E. (2007). Sociology, disasters and emergency management: History, contributions, and future agenda. In D. A. McEntire (Ed.), *Disciplines, disasters, and emergency management: The convergence and divergence of concepts, issues and trends from the research literature* (pp. 61–74). Charles C Thomas.

Drabek, T. E., Hoetmer, G. J., & International City Management Association. (1991). *Emergency management: Principles and practice for local government*. Municipal management series, International City Management Association.

Drabek, T. E., & McEntire, D. A. (2002). Emergent phenomena and multiorganizational coordination in disasters: Lessons from the research literature. *International Journal of Mass Emergencies and Disasters, 20*(2), 197–224.

Drezner, J. A., Rao, A. L., Heistand, J., Bloomingdale, M. K., & Harmon, K. G. (2009). Effectiveness of emergency response planning for sudden cardiac arrest in United States high schools with automated external defibrillators. *Circulation, 120*(6), 518–525.

Dugdale, J. (2013). *Human behaviour modelling in complex socio-technical systems: An agent based approach*. Doctorate Habilitation, Informatique et mathématiques appliquées, Université Joseph-Fourier-Grenoble I.

Dugdale, J., Moghaddam, M. T., & Muccini, H. (2020). *Human behaviour centered design: Developing a software system for cultural heritage*. Proceedings of the ACM/IEEE 42nd International Conference on Software Engineering: Software Engineering in Society.

Dugdale, J., Moghaddam, M. T., & Muccini, H. (2021). Iot4emergency: Internet of things for emergency management. *ACM SIGSOFT Software Engineering Notes, 46*(1), 33–36.

Dugdale, J., Moghaddam, M. T., Muccini, H., & Narayanankutty, H. (2019). *A combined netflow-driven and agent-based social modeling approach for building evacuation*. International Conference on Principles and Practice of Multi-Agent Systems.

Dwivedi, Y. K., Wastell, D., Laumer, S., Henriksen, H. Z., Myers, M. D., Bunker, D., Elbanna, A., Ravishankar, M. N., & Srivastava, S. C. (2015). Research on information systems failures and successes: Status update and future directions. *Information Systems Frontiers, 17*(1), 143–157.

Dynes, R. R. (1970). *Organized behavior in disaster* (The disaster research center series). Heath Lexington Books.

Dynes, R. R., & Aguirre, B. E. (1979). Organizational adaptation to crises: Mechanisms of coordination and structural change. *Disasters, 3*(1), 71–74.

Dynes, R. R., & Tierney, K. J. (1994). *Disasters, collective behavior, and social organization*. University of Delaware Press/Associated University Presses.

Earl, M. J., Oxford Institute of Information Management, & PA Consulting Group. (1996). *Information management: The organizational dimension*. Oxford University Press.

Earle, C. R. (2018). C2 agility for emergency management: Examining the Katrina and Sandy responses. *Journal of Homeland Security and Emergency Management, 15*(4).

Echigo, H., Shibata, Y., & Takahata, K. (2007). Performance evaluation of a large scale distributed disaster information network system. *Journal of Interconnection Networks, 8*(4), 321–336.

Ehn, P. (2008). *Participation in design things*. Proceedings of the 10th Biennial Participatory Design Conference (PDC), Bloomington, Indiana, USA September 30 – October 4.

Eisenhardt, K. M. (1989). Building theories from case study research. *The Academy of Management Review, 14*(4), 532–550.

Eisenhardt, K. M., & Graebner, M. E. (2007). Theory-building from cases: Opportunities and challenges. *Academey of Management Journal, 50*(1), 25–32.

El Kafhali, S., Salah, K., & Alla, S. B. (2018). *Performance evaluation of IoT-fog-cloud deployment for healthcare services*. 2018 4th international conference on cloud computing technologies and applications (Cloudtech).

El-Jardali, F., Bou-Karroum, L., & Fadlallah, R. (2020). Amplifying the role of knowledge translation platforms in the COVID-19 pandemic response. *Health Research Policy and Systems, 18*(1), 1–7.

Elijah, O., Rahman, T. A., Orikumhi, I., Leow, C. Y., Nour, M. H. D., & Hindia. (2018). An overview of Internet of Things (IoT) and data analytics in agriculture: Benefits and challenges. *IEEE Internet of Things Journal, 5*(5), 3758–3773.

Elmasllari, E. (2018). Why IT systems for emergency response get rejected: Examining responders' attitude to IT. In K. Boersma, B. Tomaszewski, & Management (Eds.), *15th International Conference on Information Systems for Crisis Response and Management (ISCRAM 2018)*. Rochester Institute of Technology.

Elmasllari, E., & Reiners, R. (2017). Learning from non-acceptance: Design dimensions for user acceptance of E-triage systems. In T. Comes & F. Bénaben (Eds.), *14th International Conference on Information Systems for Crisis Response and Management (ISCRAM 2017)*.

Elmhadhbi, L., Karray, M.-H., & Archimède, B. (2018). An ontology-based emergency response system for interoperability in a crisis situation in Smart cities. In M. Zelm, F.-W. Jaekel, G. Doumeingts, & M. Wollschlaeger (Eds.), *Enterprise interoperability: Smart services and business impact of enterprise interoperability* (pp. 421–427). Wiley.

Endsley, M. R. (1995a). A taxonomy of situation awareness errors. *Human Factors in Aviation Operations, 3*(2), 287–292.

Endsley, M. R. (1995b). Toward a theory of situation awareness in dynamic systems. *Human Factors: The Journal of the Human Factors and Ergonomics Society, 37*(1), 32–64. https://doi.org/10.1518/001872095779049543

Endsley, M. R. (1995c). Measurement of situation awareness in dynamic systems. *Human Factors: The Journal of the Human Factors and Ergonomics Society, 37*(1), 65–84. https://doi.org/10.1518/001872095779049499

Endsley, M. R. (2001). *Designing for situation awareness in complex systems*. Second International Workshop on symbiosis of humans, artifacts and environment, Kyoto, Japan.

Endsley, M. R. (2015a). Situation awareness: Operationally necessary and scientifically grounded. *Cognition, Technology & Work, 17*(2), 163–167. https://doi.org/10.1007/s10111-015-0323-5

Endsley, M. R. (2015b). Situation awareness misconceptions and misunderstandings. *Journal of Cognitive Engineering and Decision Making, 9*(1), 4–32.

Endsley, M. R. (2017). Toward a theory of situation awareness in dynamic systems. In *Situational awareness* (pp. 9–42). Routledge.

Endsley, M. R., Bolté, B., & Jones, D. G. (2003). *Designing for situation awareness: An approach to user-centered design*. CRC Press.

Endsley, M. R., & Robertson, M. M. (2000). Situation awareness in aircraft maintenance teams. *International Journal of Industrial Ergonomics, 26*(2), 301–325.

Eysenbach, G. (2001). What is e-health? *Journal of Medical Internet Research, 3*(2), e833.

Fadok, D. S. (1995). *John Boyd and John Warden: Air power's quest for strategic paralysis*. Master Thesis, School of Advanced Airpower Studies, Air University (19950228 043). http://www.dtic.mil/cgi-bin/GetTRDoc?AD=ADA291621

Falegnami, A., Bilotta, F., Pugliese, F., Costantino, F., Di Gravio, G., Tronci, M., & Patriarca, R. (2018). A multicountry comparative survey about organizational resilience in anaesthesia. *Journal of Evaluation in Clinical Practice, 24*(6), 1347–1357.

Falkland, E. C., & Wiggins, M. W. (2019). Cross-task cue utilisation and situational awareness in simulated air traffic control. *Applied Ergonomics, 74*, 24–30. https://doi.org/10.1016/j.apergo.2018.07.015

Farazmand, A. (2009). Hurricane Katrina, the crisis of leadership, and chaos management: Time for trying the 'surprise management theory in action'. *Public Organization Review, 9*(4), 399–412.

Farmer, R. A. (2014, October 29). *FEMA's capability development after Katrina*. Federal Emergency Management Agency (FEMA), U.S. Department of Homeland Security. Institut de Seguretat Pública de Catalunya Barcelona. https://recercat.cat/handle/2072/249951?show=full

FEMA. (2015). *About Cascadia rising 2016*. [website]. FEMA. Accessed January 31. http://community.fema.govdelivery.com/connect.ti/cascadiarising2016/view?objectId=3233584

Ferber, J., & Weiss, G. (1999). *Multi-agent systems: An introduction to distributed artificial intelligence* (Vol. 1). Addison-Wesley.

Ferbrache, D. (2003). Network enabled capability: Concepts and delivery. *Journal of Defence Science, 8*(3), 104–107.

Fereday, J., & Muir-Cochrane, E. (2006). Demonstrating rigor using thematic analysis: A hybrid approach of inductive and deductive coding and theme development. *International Journal of Qualitative Methods, 5*(1), 80.

Ferris, E., & Petz, D. (2012, March). *The year that shook the rich: A review of natural disasters in 2011*. The Brookings Institution and London School of Economics (Project on Internal Displacement The Brookings Institution/London School of Economics). http://www.brookings.edu/~/media/research/files/reports/2012/3/natural%20disaster%20review%20ferris/03_natural_disaster_review_ferris.pdf

Fewell, M. P., & Hazen, M. G. (2003). *Network-centric warfare-its nature and modelling* (DSTO Systems Sciences Laboratory). Department of Defence Australian Government.

Fidel, R. (1984). The case study method: A case study. *Library an Information Science Research, 6*(3), 273–288.

Fischer, H. W. (2003). The sociology of disaster: Definitions, research questions, & measurements continuation of the discussion in a post-September 11 environment. *International Journal of Mass Emergencies and Disasters, 21*(1), 91–107.

Fischer-Pressler, D., Bonaretti, D., & Fischbach, K. (2020). *Effective use of mobile-enabled emergency warning systems*. Proceedings of the 28th European Conference on Information Systems (ECIS). Marrakech, Morocco, June 15–17. https://aisel.aisnet.org/ecis2020_rp/130

Fischer-Preßler, D., Bonaretti, D., & Fischbach, K. (2022). A protection-motivation perspective to explain intention to use and continue to use mobile warning systems. *Business & Information Systems Engineering, 64*(2), 167–182. https://doi.org/10.1007/s12599-021-00704-0

Fisher, K. E., Erdelez, S., & McKechnie, L. (2005). *Theories of information behavior* (ASIST monograph series). Published for the American Society for Information Science and Technology by Information Today.

Flachberger, C., & Gringinger, E. (2016). Decision support for networked crisis & disaster management – A comparison with the air traffic management domain. In A. H. Tapia, P. Antunes, V. A. Bañuls, K. A. Moore, & J. Porto (Eds.), *13th International Conference on Information Systems for Crisis Response and Management (ISCRAM 2016)*. Federal University of Rio de Janeiro.

Flanagan, J. C. (1954). The critical incident technique. *Psychological Bulletin, 51*(4), 327–358.

Flyvbjerg, B. (2006). Five misunderstandings about case-study research. *Qualitative Inquiry, 12*(2), 219–245.

Fotiou, N., Marias, G. F., & Polyzos, G. C. (2012). *Access control enforcement delegation for information-centric networking architectures*. Proceedings of the second edition of the ICN workshop on Information-centric networking.

Fowler, J. J., & Horan, P. (2007). Are information systems' success and failure factors related? An exploratory study. *Journal of Organizational and End User Computing (JOEUC), 19*(2), 1–22.

Franchi, F., Marotta, A., Rinaldi, C., Graziosi, F., & D'Errico, L. (2019). *IoT-based disaster management system on 5G uRLLC network*. 2019 International Conference on Information and Communication Technologies for Disaster Management (ICT-DM).

French, S., & Turoff, M. (2007). Decision support systems. *Communications of the ACM, 50*(3), 39–40.

Frøland, T. H., Heldal, I., Ersvær, E., & Sjøholt, G. (2020). *State-of-the-art and future directions for using augmented reality head mounted displays for first aid live training*. 2020 International Conference on e-Health and Bioengineering (EHB).

Fuchs, P. (2017). *Virtual reality headsets-a theoretical and pragmatic approach*. CRC Press.

Fuller, S. (2019). *Philosophy of science and its discontents*. Routledge.

Galindo, G., & Batta, R. (2013). Review of recent developments in OR/MS research in disaster operations management. *European Journal of Operational Research, 230*(2), 201–211.

Galton, A., & Worboys, M. (2011). An ontology of information for emergency management. In M. A. Santos & L. Sousa (Eds.), *8th International Conference on Information Systems for Crisis Response and Management (ISCRAM 2011)*. Information Systems for Crisis Response and Management.

Gangemi, A., Guarino, N., Masolo, C., Oltramari, A., & Schneider, L. (2002). *Sweetening ontologies with DOLCE*. Poceedings of the International conference on knowledge engineering and knowledge management, Siguenza, Spain.

Ganji, A., Savelli, S., Haselkorn, M., Wilson, T., & Dailey, D. (2019). *Cause and effect: A qualitative analysis of obstacles to information sharing during a regional disaster exercise*. 16th International Conference on Information Systems for Crisis Response and Management (ISCRAM 2019), Valencia, Spain, 19–22 May.

Ganz, A., Schafer, J., Xunyi, Y., Lord, G., Burstein, J., & Ciottone, G. R. (2013). Real-time scalable resource tracking framework (DIORAMA) for mass casualty incidents. *International Journal of E-Health and Medical Communications (IJEHMC), 4*(2), 34–49.

Gardner-Stephen, P. (2011). *The serval project: Practical wireless ad-hoc mobile telecommunications*. Flinders University, Adelaide, South Australia, Tech. Rep 230, pp. 1–29.

Gasco-Hernandez, M., Zheleva, M., Bogdanov, P., & Gil-Garcia, J. R. (2019). *Towards a socio-technical framework for bridging the digital divide in rural emergency preparedness and response: Integrating user adoption, heterogeneous wide-area networks, and advanced data science*. Proceedings of the 20th Annual International Conference on Digital Government Research.

Gazley, B., & Brudney, J. L. (2007). The purpose (and perils) of government-nonprofit partnership. *Nonprofit and Voluntary Sector Quarterly, 36*(3), 389–415. https://doi.org/10.1177/0899764006295997

Geisler, E. (2009). Tacit and explicit knowledge: Empirical investigation in an emergency regime. *International Journal of Technology Management, 47*(4), 273–273.

Giddens, A. (1984). *The constitution of society: Outline of the theory of structuration*. University of California Press.

Gil-Garcia, J. R., Dawes, S. S., & Pardo, T. A. (2018). Digital government and public management research: Finding the crossroads. *Public Management Review, 20*(5), 633–646. https://doi.org/10.1080/14719037.2017.1327181

Gillespie, D. F. (1991). Coordinating community resources. In T. E. Drabek, G. J. Hoetmer, & International City Management Association (Eds.), *Emergency management: Principles and practice for local government* (pp. 55–78). International City Management Association.

Gillespie, D. F. (2008). Disasters. In T. Mizrahl & L. E. Davis (Eds.), *Encyclopedia of social work* (pp. 1–13). Oxford University Press.

Gkeredakis, M., Lifshitz-Assaf, H., & Barrett, M. (2021). *Crisis as opportunity, disruption and exposure: Exploring emergent responses to crisis through digital technology* (Vol. 31, p. 100344). Elsevier.

Glaser, B. G. (1999). The future of grounded theory. *Qualitative Health Research, 9*(6), 836–845. https://doi.org/10.1177/104973299129122199. http://qhr.sagepub.com/content/9/6/836.abstract.

Glaser, B. G., & Strauss, A. L. (1967). *The discovery of grounded theory; strategies for qualitative research. Observations*. Aldine Pub..

Goldfinger, C., Kulm, L. V. D., Yeats, R. S., Appelgate, B., MacKay, M. E., & Moore, G. F. (1992). Transverse structural trends along the Oregon convergent margin: Implications for Cascadia earthquake potential and crustal rotations. *Geology, 20*(2), 141–144.

Goodman, E., Kuniavsky, M., & Moed, A. (2012). *Observing the user experience: A practitioner's guide to user research* (2nd ed.). Elsevier.

Granberg, T. A., Danielsson, N., Fredriksson, A., Nordstrom, J., Pilemalm, S., Tjernstrom, R., & Mojir, K. Y. (2016). *Using semi-professionals in emergency response*. Proceedings of the 13th ISCRAM Conference Rio de Janeiro, Brazil, May 22–25.

Granovetter, M. S. (1973). The strength of weak ties. *American Journal of Sociology, 78*(6), 1360–1380.

Granovetter, M. S. (1983). The strength of weak ties: A network theory revisited. *Sociological Theory, 1*(1), 201–233.

Graubner, P., Lampe, P., Höchst, J., Baumgärtner, L., Mezini, M., & Freisleben, B. (2018). *Opportunistic named functions in disruption-tolerant emergency networks*. Proceedings of the 15th ACM International Conference on Computing Frontiers, Ischia, Italy, May 8–10.

Greene, K. K., Dawkins, S., Prettyman, S. S., Konkol, P., Theofanos, M. F., Mangold, K., Furman, S., Choong, Y.-Y., & Michelle P. S. (2020, March). *Voices of first responders–Nationwide public safety communication survey methodology: Development, dissemination, and demographics*, Phase 2, Volume 1. U.S. Department of Commerce. National Institute of Standards and Technology.

Grenon, P., & Smith, B. (2004). SNAP and SPAN: Towards dynamic spatial ontology. *Spatial Cognition and Computation, 4*(1), 69–104. https://doi.org/10.1207/s15427633scc0401_5

Groenendaal, J., & Helsloot, I. (2021). Why technology not always adds value to crisis managers during crisis: The case of the Dutch nation-wide crisis management system LCMS. In A. Adrot, R. Grace, & K. Moore (Eds.), *ISCRAM 2021 Conference Proceedings–18th International Conference on Information Systems for Crisis Response and Management*.

Groenendaal, J., Helsloot, I., & Scholtens, A. (2013). A critical examination of the assumptions regarding centralized coordination in large-scale emergency situations. *Journal of Homeland Security and Emergency Management, 10*(1), 113–135.

Grogan, S., Pellerin, R., & Gamache, M. (2018). *The use of unmanned aerial vehicles and drones in search and rescue operations–a survey* (pp. 1–12). Proceedings of the PROLOG.

Grudinschi, D., Kaljunen, L., Hokkanen, T., Hallikas, J., Sintonen, S., & Puustinen, A. (2014). *Strategic management of value networks: How to create value in cross-sector collaboration and partnerships*. Doctorate Dissertation,. Lappeenranta University of Technology.

Gruening, G. (2001). Origin and theoretical basis of new public management. *International Public Management Journal, 4*(1), 1–25. https://doi.org/10.1016/S1096-7494(01)00041-1

Guah, M. W. (2004). *Today's health care demands knowledge management strategy*. 26th International Conference on Information Technology Interfaces, Cavtat, Croatia, June 07–10.

Guo, X., & Kapucu, N. (2015). Examining coordination in disaster response using simulation methods. *Journal of Homeland Security and Emergency Management, 12*(4), 891–914.

Hackos, J. A. T., & Redish, J. (1998). *User and task analysis for interface design* (Vol. 1). Wiley.

Haddow, G., Bullock, J., & Coppola, D. P. (2013). *Introduction to emergency management*. Butterworth-Heinemann.

Ham, B. (2018). *How often do Cascadia's megaquakes occur?* [website]. Annual Meeting, News. Seismological Society of America. Last Modified May 16. Accessed March 05. https://www.seismosoc.org/annual-meeting/how-often-do-cascadias-megaquakes-occur/

Hambridge, N. B., Howitt, A. M., & Giles, D. W. (2017). Coordination in crises: Implementation of the national incident management system by surface transportation agencies. *Homeland Security Affairs, 13*(2), 1–30. https://www.hsdl.org/?view&did=800160

Hamill, H. (2014). *Interview methodology. obo Sociology*. Oxford University Press.

Hang, H. M., Byass, P., & Svanström, L. (2004). Incidence and seasonal variation of injury in rural Vietnam: A community-based survey. *Safety Science, 42*(8), 691–701.

Hansen, R. R. (2007). Letter to the editor regarding incident command system (ICS). *Journal of Homeland Security and Emergency Management, 3*(4), 1–3.

Hanseth, O., Monteiro, E., & Hatling, M. (1996). Developing information infrastructure: The tension between standardization and flexibility. *Science, Technology, & Human Values, 21*(4), 407–426.

Hanson, P., & McDougall, C. (2018). *Enabling collaborative and resilient emergency management efforts: DFES and Western Australia's adoption of a common operating picture*. 1st International Conference on Information Systems for Crisis Response and Management Asia Pacific (ISCRAM Asia Pacific 2018), Wellington, New Zealand, 5–7 November.

Harrald, J. R. (2006). Agility and discipline: Critical success factors for disaster response. *The Annals of the American Academy of Political and Social Science, 604*(1), 256–272. https://doi.org/10.1177/0002716205285404

Harrald, J. R., & Jefferson, T. (2007). Shared situational awareness in emergency management mitigation and response. In *40th Annual Hawaii International Conference on System Sciences (HICSS-40)*. IEEE.

Hart, S. V. (2002, October). *Crisis information management software (CIMS) feature comparison report*. National Institute of Justice. Department of Justice. https://www.ncjrs.gov/pdffiles1/nij/197065.pdf

Hatamura, Y. (2011). Executive summary of the interim report, December 26, 2011. In *Investigation Committee on the Accidents at Fukushima Nuclear Power Stations of Tokyo Electric Power Company*. Secretariat of the Investigation Committee on the accidents at the Fukushima Nuclear Power Station.

Hatamura, Y. (2012). Executive summary of the final report, July 23, 2012. In *Investigation Committee on the Accidents at Fukushima Nuclear Power Stations of Tokyo Electric Power Company*. Secretariat of the Investigation Committee on the accidents at the Fukushima Nuclear Power Station.

Hayes, R. E. (2007). It's an endeavor, not a force. *The International C2 Journal, 1*(1), 145–176.

He, K., Zhang, X., Ren, S., & Sun, J. (2016). *Deep residual learning for image recognition*. Proceedings of the IEEE conference on computer vision and pattern recognition.

Heim, M. (1993). *The metaphysics of virtual reality*. Oxford University Press on Demand.

Helbing, D., & Molnar, P. (1995). Social force model for pedestrian dynamics. *Physical Review E, 51*(5), 4282 (1–18).

Henricksen, K., & Iannella, R. (2010). Towards standards-based resource management systems for emergency management. In B. Van De Walle, M. Turoff, & S. R. Hiltz (Eds.), *Information systems for emergency management* (pp. 327–343). Routledge.

Herranz, J. (2008). The multisectoral trilemma of network management. *Journal of Public Administration Research and Theory, 18*(1), 1–31.

Hickey, H. (2015). *Dating historic activity at Oso site shows recurring major landslides*. UWToday, December 22, 2015. Accessed December, 2015. http://www.washington.edu/news/2015/12/22/dating-historic-activity-at-oso-site-shows-recurring-major-landslides/

Hiltz, S. R., Van de Walle, B., & Turoff, M. (2014). The domain of emergency management information. In B. Van De Walle, M. Turoff, & S. R. Hiltz (Eds.), *Information systems for emergency management* (Advances in Management Information Systems monograph series) (pp. 15–32). Routledge.

Hodge, G. A., & Greve, C. (2005). *The challenge of public-private partnerships: Learning from international experience*. Edward Elgar Publishing.

Hoekstra, S., Kimberly Klockow, R., Riley, J. B., Brooks, H., & Erickson, S. (2011). A preliminary look at the social perspective of warn-on-forecast: Preferred tornado warning lead time and the general public's perceptions of weather risks. *Weather, Climate, and Society, 3*(2), 128–140. https://doi.org/10.1175/2011WCAS1076.1

Holdeman, E. E. (2020). *Use of WebEOC is insanity defined*. Emergency Management: Disaster Zone (blog), Government Technology. August 27. https://www.govtech.com/em/emergency-blogs/disaster-zone/use-of-webeoc-is-insanity-defined.html

Holland, J. H. (1996). *Hidden order: How adaptation builds complexity*. Addison Wesley Longman Publishing.

Hollnagel, E. (2013). *Resilience engineering in practice: A guidebook*. Ashgate Publishing, Ltd.

Holsapple, C. W., & Luo, W. (1996). A framework for studying computer support of organizational infrastructure. *Information & Management, 31*(1), 13–24.

Houghton, R. J., Baber, C., Cowton, M., Walker, G. H., & Stanton, N. A. (2008). WESTT (workload, error, situational awareness, time and teamwork): An analytical prototyping system for command and control. *Cognition, Technology & Work, 10*(3), 199–207.

Houghton, R. J., Baber, C., McMaster, R., Stanton, N. A., Salmon, P., Stewart, R., & Walker, G. (2006). Command and control in emergency services operations: A social network analysis. *Ergonomics, 49*(12–13), 1204–1225.

Howe, J. (2006). The rise of crowdsourcing. *Wired Magazine, 14*(6), 1–4.

Huang, J., Li, S., Chen, Y., & Chen, J. (2018). Performance modelling and analysis for IoT services. *International Journal of Web and Grid Services, 14*(2), 146–169.

Huey, C. W., & Terence, and Janice C Palaganas. (2020). What are the factors affecting resilience in health professionals? A synthesis of systematic reviews. *Medical Teacher, 42*(5), 550–560.

Huggins, T. J., & Prasanna, R. (2020). Information technologies supporting emergency management controllers in New Zealand. *Sustainability, 12*(9), 3716 (1–16).

Hundal, G. S., Thiyagarajan, S., Alduraibi, M., Laux, C. M., Furterer, S. L., Cudney, E. A., & Antony, J. (2021). Lean Six Sigma as an organizational resilience mechanism in health care during the era of COVID-19. *International Journal of Lean Six Sigma*, 1–23. https://doi.org/10.1108/IJLSS-11-2020-0204

Huxham, C., & Vangen, S. (2000). Ambiguity, complexity and dynamics in the membership of collaboration. *Human Relations, 53*(6), 771–806. https://doi.org/10.1177/0018726700536002

Inoguchi, M., Tamura, K., Horie, K., & Hayashi, H. (2014). *Implementation of web-based system for building damage assessment on online network: Case studies of Typhoon MAN-YI (1318) and Typhoon WIPHA (1326) in Japan*. Proceedings of the 2014 IEEE Asia Pacific Conference on Circuits and Systems (APCCAS), Ishigaki, Japan, 17–20 November.

Ion, M., Zhang, J., & Schooler, E. M. (2013). *Toward content-centric privacy in ICN: Attribute-based encryption and routing*. Proceedings of the 3rd ACM SIGCOMM workshop on Information-centric networking.

Ireson, N. (2009). *Local community situational awareness during an emergency*. 3rd IEEE International Conference onDigital Ecosystems and Technologies (DEST'09), Istanbul, Turkey, June 1–3.

Ismail, K. (2019). *JAMstack vs. LAMP Stack vs. MEAN vs .NET: Tech Stacks Compared*. CMS Wire, January 18, 2019, [1–7], Digital Experience. Accessed July 21, 2020. https://www.cmswire.com/digital-experience/jamstack-vs-lamp-stack-vs-mean-vs-net-tech-stacks-compared/

Iversen, L., Farmer, J. C., & Hannaford, P. C. (2002). Workload pressures in rural general practice: A qualitative investigation. *Scandinavian Journal of Primary Health Care, 20*(3), 139–144.

Iverson, R. M., George, D. L., Allstadt, K., Reid, M. E., Collins, B. D., Vallance, J. W., Schilling, S. P., Godt, J. W., Cannon, C. M., Magirl, C. S., Baum, R. L., Coe, J. A., Schulz, W. H., & Bower, J. B. (2015). Landslide mobility and hazards: Implications of the 2014 Oso disaster. *Earth and Planetary Science Letters, 412*(0), 197–208. https://doi.org/10.1016/j.epsl.2014.12.020. http://www.sciencedirect.com/science/article/pii/S0012821X1400781X; http://ac.els-cdn.com/S0012821X1400781X/1-s2.0-S0012821X1400781X-main.pdf?_tid=c2529568-a0e3-11e4-8994-00000aacb35f&acdnat=1421786260_1e2e0310a900bee958c91c6023fd86ad

Iyawa, G. E., Herselman, M., & Botha, A. (2016). Digital health innovation ecosystems: From systematic literature review to conceptual framework. *Procedia Computer Science, 100*, 244–252.

Jacobides, M. G., Cennamo, C., & Gawer, A. (2018). Towards a theory of ecosystems. *Strategic Management Journal, 39*(8), 2255–2276. https://doi.org/10.1002/smj.2904

Jacobson, D. D. (2016). How and why network governance evolves: Evidence from a public safety network. *Electronic Markets, 26*(1), 43–54.

Jaeger, P. T., Shneiderman, B., Fleischmann, K. R., Preece, J., Yan, Q., & Philip Fei, W. (2007). Community response grids: E-government, social networks, and effective emergency management. *Telecommunications Policy, 31*(10–11), 592–604. https://doi.org/10.1016/j.telpol.2007.07.008

Jain, P., Yeh, P. Z., Verma, K., Vasquez, R. G., Damova, M., Hitzler, P., & Sheth, A. P. (2011). *Contextual ontology alignment of lod with an upper ontology: A case study with proton*. Proceedings of the 8th Extended Semantic Web Conference, Heraklion, Greece, May 29–June 2.

Jalonen, H. (2013). The knowledge-innovation nexus in the welfare service ecosystem. *International Journal of Knowledge-Based Development, 4*(1), 34–49.

Janowski, T., Pardo, T. A., & Davies, J. (2012). *Government information networks-mapping electronic governance cases through public administration concepts* (Vol. 29, p. S1). Elsevier.

Janssen, M., & Estevez, E. (2013). Lean government and platform-based governance—Doing more with less. *Government Information Quarterly, 30*, S1–S8. https://doi.org/10.1016/j.giq.2012.11.003

Jennex, M. E. (2007). *Modeling emergency response systems*. Proceedings of the 40th Annual Hawaii International Conference on System Sciences (HICSS-40), Big Island, Hawaii, January 03–06.

Jennings, E. A., Arlikatti, S., Andrew, S. A., & Kim, K. W. (2017). Adoption of information and communication technologies (ICTs) by local emergency management agencies in the United States. *International Review of Public Administration, 22*(2), 193–210.

Jennings, P. A., Cameron, P., Walker, T., Bernard, S., & Smith, K. (2006). Out-of-hospital cardiac arrest in Victoria: Rural and urban outcomes. *Medical Journal of Australia, 185*(3), 135–139.

Jensen, J. (2011). The current NIMS implementation behavior of United States counties. *Journal of Homeland Security and Emergency Management, 8*(1, article 20), 1–25.

Jensen, J., Bundy, S. J., & Kirkpatrick. (2017). Local recovery coordinators and the national disaster recovery framework: Questions regarding the form, necessity, and potential of the role. *Journal of Homeland Security and Emergency Management, 14*(4), 1–13.

Jensen, J., & Thompson, S. (2016). The incident command system: A literature review. *Disasters, 40*(1), 158–182.

Jensen, J., & Waugh, W. L. (2014). The United States' experience with the incident command system: What we think we know and what we need to know more about. *Journal of Contingencies and Crisis Management, 22*(1), 5–17.

Jensen, J., & Youngs, G. (2015). Explaining implementation behaviour of the national incident management system (NIMS). *Disasters, 39*(2), 362–388.

Jo, D., & Kwon, Y. (2017). Development of rescue material transport UAV (unmanned aerial vehicle). *World Journal of Engineering and Technology, 5*(4), 720–729.

Johansson, B. J. E., Hellgren, C., Oskarsson, P.-A., & Svensson, J. (2013). Supporting situational awareness on the move – The role of technology for spatial orientation in the field. In T. Comes & F. Fiedrich (Eds.), *10th International Conference on Information Systems for Crisis Response and Management (ISCRAM 2013)*. Karlsruher Institut fur Technologie.

Johnson, A. (2011). Everything new is old again: What place should applied science have in the history of science? In M. Carrier & A. Nordmann (Eds.), *Science in the context of application* (pp. 455–466). Springer.

Johnston, L. M., & Finegood, D. T. (2015). Cross-sector partnerships and public health: Challenges and opportunities for addressing obesity and noncommunicable diseases through engagement with the private sector. *Annual Review of Public Health, 36*, 255–271. https://doi.org/10.1146/annurev-publhealth-031914-122802

Jones, C., Hesterly, W. S., & Borgatti, S. P. (1997). A general theory of network governance: Exchange conditions and social mechanisms. *Academy of Management Review, 22*(4), 911–945. https://doi.org/10.5465/amr.1997.9711022109

Jones, D., Lyle, D., Brunero, C., McAllister, L., Webb, T., & Riley, S. (2015). Improving health and education outcomes for children in remote communities: A cross-sector and developmental evaluation approach. *Gateways: International Journal of Community Research and Engagement, 8*(1), 1–22.

Jones, M. R., & Karsten, H. (2008). Giddens's structuration theory and information systems research. *MIS Quarterly, 32*(1), 127–157.

Jovanović, I. (2006). Software testing methods and techniques. *The IPSI BgD Transactions on Internet Research*, 30–41.

Jung, G., Joshi, K. R., Hiltunen, M. A., Schlichting, R. D., & Pu, C. (2008). *Generating adaptation policies for multi-tier applications in consolidated server environments*. 2008 International Conference on Autonomic Computing.

Jung, K. (2018). Mapping community diversity and e-participation in emergency management: Evidence from WebEOC in the city of San Francisco. *International Journal of Emergency Management, 14*(3), 275–290. https://doi.org/10.1504/IJEM.2018.094238. https://www.inderscienceonline.com/doi/abs/10.1504/IJEM.2018.094238

Jung, T., & Dieck, M. C. T. (Eds.). (2018). *Augmented reality and virtual reality*. Springer.

Jungk, R., & Müllert, N. (1987). *Future workshops: How to create desirable futures*. Institute for Social Inventions.

Kalkman, J. P., & Groenewegen, P. (2019). On frontline workers as bureau-political actors: The case of civil–military crisis management. *Administration & Society, 51*(7), 1148–1170.

Kaptelinin, V., & B NARDI, and Catriona Macaulay. (1999). The activity checklist: A tool for representing the Space of Context. *Interactions, 6*(4), 27–39.

Kapucu, N. (2005). Interorganizational coordination in dynamic context: Networks in emergency response management. *Connect, 26*(2), 33–48.

Kapucu, N. (2006). Interagency communication networks during emergencies. Boundary spanners in multiagency coordination. *American Review of Public Administration, 36*(2), 207.

Kapucu, N. (2008). Collaborative emergency management: Better community organising, better public preparedness and response. *Disasters, 32*(2), 239–262.

Kapucu, N. (2009). Interorganizational coordination in complex environments of disasters: The evolution of intergovernmental disaster response systems. *Journal of Homeland Security and Emergency Management, 6*(1).

Kapucu, N. (2011). The role of the military in disaster response in the US. *European Journal of Economic and Political Studies, 4*(2), 7–33.

Kapucu, N., Arslan, T., & Collins, M. L. (2010). Examining intergovernmental and interorganizational response to catastrophic disasters: Toward a network-centered approach. *Administration & Society, 42*(2), 222–247. https://doi.org/10.1177/0095399710362517. http://aas.sagepub.com/content/42/2/222

Kapucu, N., Arslan, T., & Demiroz, F. (2010). Collaborative emergency management and national emergency management network. *Disaster Prevention and Management: An International Journal, 19*(4), 452–468.

Kapucu, N., & Garayev, V. (2016). Structure and network performance horizontal and vertical networks in emergency management. *Administration & Society, 46*(8), 931–961. https://doi.org/10.1177/0095399714541270

Kapucu, N., & Qian, H. (2016). Understanding multiplexity of collaborative emergency management networks. *The American Review of Public Administration, 46*(4), 399–417. https://doi.org/10.1177/0275074014555645

Karagiannis, G. M., & Synolakis, C. (2017). Twenty challenges in incident planning. *Journal of Homeland Security and Emergency Management, 14*(2), 1–12.

Karagiannis, G. M., & Synolakis, C. E. (2016). *Collaborative incident planning and the common operational picture*. Proceedings of the International conference on dynamics of disasters, Kalamata, Greece, June 29–July 2.

Kaufhold, M.-A., Rupp, N., Reuter, C., & Amelunxen, C. (2018). *112. Social: Design and evaluation of a mobile crisis app for bidirectional communication between emergency services and citizens*. Proceedings of the 26th European Conference on Information Systems (ECIS2018), Portsmouth, UK, June 23–28.

Kayisire, D., & Wei, J. (2016). ICT adoption and usage in Africa: Towards an efficiency assessment. *Information Technology for Development, 22*(4), 630–653.

Kedia, T., Ratcliff, J., O'Connor, M., Oluic, S., Rose, M., Freeman, J., & Rainwater-Lovett, K. (2020). Technologies enabling situational awareness during disaster response: A systematic review. *Disaster Medicine and Public Health Preparedness, 1-19*, 341. https://doi.org/10.1017/dmp.2020.196

Kelly, J. V. (2014, July 1). *FEMA's initial response to the Colorado flood*. U.S. Department of Homeland Security, Office of Inspector General. https://www.hsdl.org/?view&did=755887

Kendra, J. M., & Wachtendorf, T. (2003a). Elements of resilience after the World Trade center disaster: Reconstituting New York city's emergency operations centre. *Disasters, 27*(1), 37–53.

Kendra, J. M., & Wachtendorf, T. (2003b). *Creativity in emergency response to the World Trade Center disaster* (pp. 121–146). Beyond September 11th: An account of post-disaster research.

Kenis, P., Schol, L. G. C., Kraaij-Dirkzwager, M. M., & Timen, A. (2019). Appropriate governance responses to infectious disease threats: Developing working hypotheses. *Risk, Hazards & Crisis in Public Policy, 10*(3), 275–293.

Kim, D. D. (2018). *Data+ disasters: Rethinking the role of metro Boston's data intermediaries in disaster management*. Master in City Planning, Urban Studies and Planning, Massachusetts Institute of Technology.

Kim, J.-E., & Hong, C.-H. (2019). A study on methodology of digital-SOP system for effective disaster response. In *Proceedings of the 2019 IEEE International Smart Cities Conference (ISC2)*. IEEE.

Kim, J. U., & Kishore, R. (2019). Do we fully understand information systems failure? An exploratory study of the cognitive schema of IS professionals. *Information Systems Frontiers, 21*(6), 1385–1419.

Kirillov, A., Girshick, R., He, K., & Dollár, P. (2019). *Panoptic feature pyramid networks*. Proceedings of the IEEE/CVF conference on computer vision and pattern recognition.

Klann, M. (2007). *Playing with fire: User-centered design of wearable computing for emergency response*. Mobile Response: Proceedings of the 1st International Workshop on Mobile Information Technology for Emergency Response, Sankt Augustin, Germany, February 22–23.

Klijn, E.-H., Edelenbos, J., & Steijn, B. (2010). Trust in governance networks: Its impacts on outcomes. *Administration & society, 42*(2), 193–221. https://doi.org/10.1177/0095399710362716

Klijn, E.-H., & Koppenjan, J. (2012). Governance network theory: Past, present and future. *Policy & Politics, 40*(4), 587–606.

Klijn, E.-H., & Koppenjan, J. (2014). Complexity in governance network theory. *Complexity, Governance & Networks, 1*(1), 61–70. https://doi.org/10.7564/14-CGN8

Klischewski, R., & Elmistikawy, Y. (2017). Designing information marketplaces for disaster management. In *16th International Conference on Electronic Government (EGOV 2017)*. Springer, Cham.

Koehler, G. A., Kress, G. G., & Miller, R. L. (2014). What disaster response management can learn from chaos theory. In A. Farazmand (Ed.), *Crisis and emergency management: Theory and practice* (pp. 111–130). CRC Press Taylor & Francis Group.

Kokar, M. M., Matheus, C. J., & Baclawski, K. (2009). Ontology-based situation awareness. *Information Fusion, 10*(1), 83–98. https://doi.org/10.1016/j.inffus.2007.01.004

Koubaa, A., & Shakshuki, E. (2016). Robots and sensor clouds. In J. Kacprzyk (Ed.), *Studies in systems, decision and control* (Vol. 36). Springer.

Krikelas, J. (1983). Information-seeking behavior: Patterns and concepts. *Drexel Library Quarterly, 19*(2), 5–20.

Kruke, B. I., & Olsen, O. E. (2012). Knowledge creation and reliable decision-making in complex emergencies. *Disasters, 36*(2), 212–232. http://onlinelibrary.wiley.com/store/10.1111/j.1467-7717.2011.01255.x/asset/j.1467-7717.2011.01255.x.pdf?v=1&t=id0ss8c5&s=2216e52667134f8aa22900f3677ed5e811969205

Kunnath, A. T., Pradeep, P., & Ramesh, M. V. (2012). *Locating and monitoring emergency responder using a wearable device*. Proceedings of the International Conference on Advances in Computing, Communications and Informatics.

Kyng, M., Nielsen, E. T., & Kristensen, M. (2006). *Challenges in designing interactive systems for emergency response*. Proceedings of the 6th Conference on Designing Interactive Systems (DIS'06), University Park PA, June 26–28.

Laakso, K., & Palomäki, J. (2013). The importance of a common understanding in emergency management. *Technological Forecasting and Social Change, 80*(9), 1703–1713. https://doi.org/10.1016/j.techfore.2012.12.012

Lamb, K., Boosman, M., & Davies, J. (2015). Introspect model: Competency assessment in the virtual world. In *Proceedings of the 2015 ISCRAM Conference*. ISCRAM.

Lamb, K. J., Davies, J., Bowley, R., & Williams, J.-P. (2014). Incident command training: The introspect model. *International Journal of Emergency Services, 3*(2), 131–143.

Landeg, O., Whitman, G., Walker-Springett, K., Butler, C., Bone, A., & Kovats, S. (2019). Coastal flooding and frontline health care services: Challenges for flood risk resilience in the English health care system. *Journal of Health Services Research & Policy, 24*(4), 219–228.

LaRose, R., Gregg, J. L., Strover, S., Straubhaar, J., & Carpenter, S. (2007). Closing the rural broadband gap: Promoting adoption of the Internet in rural America. *Telecommunications Policy, 31*(6–7), 359–373.

Lauria, M. J., Ghobrial, M. K., & Hicks, C. M. (2019). Force of habit: Developing situation awareness in critical care transport. *Air Medical Journal, 38*(1), 45–50. https://doi.org/10.1016/j.amj.2018.09.007

Lazreg, M. B., Chakraborty, N. R., Stieglitz, S., Potthoff, T., Ross, B., & Majchrzak, T. A. (2018). *Social media analysis in crisis situations: Can social media be a reliable information source for emergency management services?* 27th International Conference on Information Systems Development, Lund, Sweden, 22–24 August.

Le, N. P. (2021). The impacts of COVID-19 pandemic on Foreign Direct Investment: The case of Southeast Asian Nations. *Academia Letters*, 1–8.

Lefevre, A., Walter-Garcia, M., Hanson, K., & Smith-Easley, J. (2018). Not your typical "historian": Archiving successes and lessons learned during emergency response. *Disaster Prevention and Management: An International Journal, 27*(5), 523–533. https://doi.org/10.1108/DPM-05-2018-0136

Leknes, H., Aartun, E. S., Andersson, H., Christiansen, M., & Granberg, T. A. (2017). Strategic ambulance location for heterogeneous regions. *European Journal of Operational Research, 260*(1), 122–133. https://doi.org/10.1016/j.ejor.2016.12.020

Leong, C. M., Ling, S. L., Pan, P. R., & Kaewkitipong, L. (2015). ICT-enabled community empowerment in crisis response: Social media in Thailand flooding 2011. *Journal of the Association for Information Systems, 16*(3), 174–212. https://doi.org/10.17705/1jais.00390

Levius, S., Safa, M., & Weeks, K. (2017). Use of information and communication technology to support comprehensive disaster management in the Caribbean countries. *Journal of Information Technology Case and Application Research, 19*(2), 102–112.

Levy, J., & Prizzia, R. (2018a). Customizing web-EOC crisis management software to facilitate collaboration and increase situational awareness: Advances in Business Resource Center (BRC) Design for Business Continuity Management. In A. J. Masys (Ed.), *Security by design: Innovative perspectives on complex problems* (Advanced sciences and technologies for security applications) (pp. 291–316). Springer.

Levy, J., & Prizzia, R. (2018b). Building effective emergency management Public-Private Partnerships (PPP) for information sharing. In A. J. Masys (Ed.), *Security by design: Innovative perspectives on complex problems* (Advanced sciences and technologies for security applications) (pp. 375–401). Springer.

Li, N., Yang, Z., Ghahramani, A., Becerik-Gerber, B., & Soibelman, L. (2014). Situational awareness for supporting building fire emergency response: Information needs, information sources, and implementation requirements. *Fire Safety Journal, 63*(n/a), 17–28. https://doi.org/10.1016/j.firesaf.2013.11.010

Li, T., Xie, N., Zeng, C., Zhou, W., Zheng, L., Jiang, Y., Yang, Y., Ha, H.-Y., Xue, W., & Huang, Y. (2017). Data-driven techniques in disaster information management. *ACM Computing Surveys (CSUR), 50*(1), 1–45.

Li, X., Liu, G., Ling, A., Zhan, J., An, N., Li, L., & Sha, Y. (2008). *Building a practical ontology for emergency response systems*. Proceedings of the International Conference on Computer Science and Software Engineering, Wuhan, China, December 12–14.

Liang, S., & Gao, Y. (2010). Real-time notification and improved situational awareness in fire emergencies using geospatial-based publish/subscribe. *International Journal of Applied Earth Observation and Geoinformation, 12*(6), 431–438. https://doi.org/10.1016/j.jag.2010.04.001

Liapis, A., Kostaridis, A., Ramfos, A., Hall, I., DeGaetano, A., Koutras, N., Dobrinkova, N., Leventakis, G., Olunczek, A., & Seynaeve, G. (2015). *A position paper on improving preparedness and response of health services in major crises*. International Conference on Information Systems for Crisis Response and Management in Mediterranean Countries.

Liberati, A., Altman, D. G., Tetzlaff, J., Mulrow, C., Gøtzsche, P. C., Ioannidis, J. P. A., Clarke, M., Devereaux, P. J., Kleijnen, J., & Moher, D. (2009). The PRISMA statement for reporting systematic reviews and meta-analyses of studies that evaluate health care interventions: Explanation and elaboration. *Journal of Clinical Epidemiology, 62*(10), e1–e34. https://doi.org/10.1016/j.jclinepi.2009.06.006

Liebowitz, J. (1999). A look at why information systems fail. *Kybernetes, 28*(1), 61–67. https://doi.org/10.1108/03684929910253243

Lincoln, Y. S., & Guba, E. G. (1985). *Naturalistic inquiry* (Vol. 9, p. 438). Sage Publications.

Linkov, I., Eisenberg, D. A., Plourde, K., Seager, T. P., Allen, J., & Kott, A. (2013). Resilience metrics for cyber systems. *Environment Systems and Decisions, 33*(4), 471–476.

Liu, S., Brewster, C., & Shaw, D. (2013). Ontologies for crisis management: A review of state of the art in ontology design and usability. In T. Comes & F. Fiedrich (Eds.), *10th International Conference on Information Systems for Crisis Response and Management (ISCRAM 2013)*. Karlsruher Institut fur Technologie.

Liu, Y., Bild, D. R., Adrian, D., Singh, G., Dick, R. P., Wallach, D. S., & Mao, Z. M. (2015). *Performance and energy consumption analysis of a delay-tolerant network for censorship-resistant communication*. Proceedings of the 16th ACM International Symposium on Mobile Ad Hoc Networking and Computing.

Sardo, L., Ruggiero, D., Thurner, S., Sorger, J., Duftschmid, G., Endel, G., & Klimek, P. (2019). Quantification of the resilience of primary care networks by stress testing the health care system. *Proceedings of the National Academy of Sciences, 116*(48), 23930–23935.

Loia, V., D'Aniello, G., Gaeta, A., & Orciuoli, F. (2016). Enforcing situation awareness with granular computing: A systematic overview and new perspectives. *Granular Computing, 1*(2), 127–143.

Lombardo, K., Boggs, J. A., Boudreau, J., Chiles, P., Erickson, J., Gerstel, W., Montgomery, D., Shipman, L., Radcliff-Sinclair, R., Strachan, S., Sugimura, D., & Trimm, B. (2014). *SR 530 landslide commission final report. Edited by SR 530 landslide commission*. SR 530 Landslide Commission.

Long, B. (2018, May 29). *Web emergency operations center (WebEOC) interconnectivity: Fiscal year 2017 report to congress*. Federal Emergency Management Agency. https://www.dhs.gov/sites/default/files/publications/FEMA%20-%20Web%20Emergency %20Operations%20Center%20%28WebEOC%29%20Interconnectivity.pdf

Longstaff, P. H. (2005). *Security, resilience, and communication in unpredictable environments such as terrorism, natural disasters, and complex technology*. Center for Information Policy Research, Harvard University.

Loukis, E., Janssen, M., Dawes, S., & Zheng, L. (2016). Evolving ICT and governance in organizational networks-conceptual and theoretical foundations. *Electronic Markets, 26*(1), 7–14. https://doi.org/10.1007/s12525-015-0210-1

Low, S. P., Gao, S., & Wong, G. Q. E. (2017). Resilience of hospital facilities in Singapore's healthcare industry: A pilot study. *International Journal of Disaster Resilience in the Built Environment, 8*(5), 537–554.

Lucas, H. C. (1975). *Why information systems fail*. Columbia University Press.

Luna, S., & Pennock, M. J. (2018). Social media applications and emergency management: A literature review and research agenda. *International Journal of Disaster Risk Reduction, 28*, 565–577.

Luokkala, P., Nikander, J., Korpi, J., Virrantaus, K., & Torkki, P. (2017). Developing a concept of a context-aware common operational picture. *Safety Science, 93*, 277–295. https://doi.org/10.1016/j.ssci.2016.11.005

Luokkala, P., & Virrantaus, K. (2014). Developing information systems to support situational awareness and interaction in time-pressuring crisis situations. *Safety Science, 63*, 191–203.

Lutz, L. D., & Lindell, M. K. (2008). Incident command system as a response model within emergency operation centers during Hurricane Rita. *Journal of Contingencies and Crisis Management, 16*(3), 122–134.

MacFarlane, R., & Leigh, M. (2014). Information management and shared situational awareness: Ideas, tools and good practice in multi-agency crisis and emergency management. In *Emergency planning college occasional papers new series*. Emergency Planning College.

Magrin, D., Centenaro, M., & Vangelista, L. (2017). *Performance evaluation of LoRa networks in a smart city scenario*. 2017 IEEE International Conference on communications (ICC), Paris, France, May 21–25.

Manoj, B. S., & Baker, A. H. (2007). Communication challenges in emergency response. *Communications of the ACM, 50*(3), 51–53.

Mansab, F., Bhatti, S., & Goyal, D. (2021). Performance of national COVID-19 'symptom checkers': A comparative case simulation study. *BMJ Health & Care Informatics, 28*(1), 1–7.

Mansour, M., James, V., & Edgley, A. (2012). Investigating the safety of medication administration in adult critical care settings. *Nursing in Critical Care, 17*(4), 189–197.

Marincioni, F. (2007). Information technologies and the sharing of disaster knowledge: The critical role of professional culture. *Disasters, 31*(4), 459–476. https://doi.org/10.1111/j.0361-3666.2007.01019.x

Maritsa, E., & Kalemis, K. (2020). *Leadership readiness in crisis context: Health preservation through shared knowledge*. 17th International Conference on Intellectual Capital, Knowledge Management & Organisational Learning ICICKM 2020, Toronto, Canada, 15–16 October.

Markenson, D., & Howe, L. (2014). American Red Cross Digital Operations Center (DigiDOC): An essential emergency management tool for the digital age. *Disaster Medicine and Public Health Preparedness, 8*(5), 445–451. https://doi.org/10.1017/dmp.2014.102

Matheus, C. J., Kokar, M. M., Baclawski, K., Letkowski, J. A., Call, C., Hinman, M. L., Salerno, J. J., & Boulware, D. M. (2005). *SAWA: An assistant for higher-level fusion and situation awareness*. Proceedings of Multisensor, Multisource Information Fusion: Architectures, Algorithms, and Applications, Orlando, FL, March 28–April 1.

Matinrad, N., Granberg, T., Vogel, N. E., & Angelakis, V. (2019). *Optimal dispatch of volunteers to out-of-hospital cardiac arrest patients*. Proceedings of the 52nd Hawaii International Conference on System Sciences (HICSS-52), Wailiea, HI, January 8–11.

Matthews, D. (2015). *Special event production: The resources*. Routledge.

Mazimwe, A., Hammouda, I., & Gidudu, A. (2021). Implementation of FAIR principles for ontologies in the disaster domain: A systematic literature review. *ISPRS International Journal of Geo-Information, 10*(5), 324 (1-29). https://doi.org/10.3390/ijgi10050324

McCauley, S. F. (2015, November 20). *FEMA faces challenges in managing information technology*. Office of Inspector General, Department of Homeland Security. https://www.oig.dhs.gov/assets/Mgmt/2016/OIG-16-10-Nov15.pdf

McClendon, S., & Robinson, A. C. (2013). Leveraging geospatially-oriented social media communications in disaster response. *International Journal of Information Systems for Crisis Response and Management (IJISCRAM), 5*(1), 22–40.

McLean, I., Oughton, D., Ellis, S., Wakelin, B., & Rubin, C. B. (2012). Review of the civil defence emergency management response to the 22 February Christchurch earthquake. In *Civil Defence Emergency Management (CDEM)*. Civil Defence Emergency Management.

McMenemy, K., & Ferguson, R. S. (2007). *A hitchhiker's guide to virtual reality*. AK Peters.

Meijer, A. J. (2011). Networked coproduction of public services in virtual communities: From a government-centric to a community approach to public service support. *Public Administration Review, 71*(4), 598–607.

Mekiker, B., Wittie, M. P., Jones, J., & Monaghan, M. (2021). *Beartooth relay protocol: Supporting real-time application streams with dynamically allocated data reservations over LoRa*. 2021 International Conference on Computer Communications and Networks (ICCCN).

Melin, U., & Wihlborg, E. (2018). Balanced and integrated e-government implementation–exploring the crossroad of public policy-making and information systems project management processes. *Transforming Government: People, Process and Policy, 12*(2), 191–208. https://doi.org/10.1108/TG-12-2017-0080

Mendonça, D., Beroggi, G. E. G., & Wallace, W. A. (2001). Decision support for improvisation during emergency response operations. *International Journal of Emergency Management, 1*(1), 30–38.

Mendonça, D., Jefferson, T., & Harrald, J. (2007). Collaborative adhocracies and mix-and-match technologies in emergency management. *Communications of the ACM, 50*(3), 44–49.

Meng, Q., Zhang, N., Zhao, X., Li, F., & Guan, X. (2016). The governance strategies for public emergencies on social media and their effects: A case study based on the microblog data. *Electronic Markets, 26*(1), 15–29. https://doi.org/10.1007/s12525-015-0202-1

Mensah, P., Merkuryev, Y., & Longo, F. (2015). Using ICT in developing a resilient supply chain strategy. *Procedia Computer Science, 43*, 101–108.

Meso, P., & Smith, R. (2000). A resource-based view of organizational knowledge management systems. *Journal of Knowledge Management, 4*(3), 224–234.

Meyerson, D., Weick, K. E., & Kramer, R. M. (1996). Swift trust and temporary groups. In R. M. Kramer & T. R. Tyler (Eds.), *Trust in organizations: Frontiers of theory and research* (pp. 166–195). Sage Publications.

Mikhaylov, S. J., Esteve, M., & Campion, A. (2018). Artificial intelligence for the public sector: Opportunities and challenges of cross-sector collaboration. *Philosophical Transactions of the Royal Society A: Mathematical, Physical and Engineering Sciences, 376*(2128), 20170357 (1-20). https://doi.org/10.1098/rsta.2017.0357

Militello, L., Patterson, E. S., Bowman, L., & Wears, R. (2007). Information flow during crisis management: Challenges to coordination in the emergency operations center. *Cognition, Technology & Work, 9*(1), 25–25.

Milward, H. B. (1994). Nonprofit contracting and the hollow state. *Public Administration Review, 54*(1), 73–77.

Min, H.-S. J., Beyeler, W., Brown, T., Son, Y. J., & Jones, A. T. (2007). Toward modeling and simulation of critical national infrastructure interdependencies. *IIE Transactions, 39*(1), 57–71.

Misra, S., Roberts, P., & Rhodes, M. (2020). The ecology of emergency management work in the digital age. *Perspectives on Public Management and Governance, 3*(4), 305–322. https://doi.org/10.1093/ppmgov/gvaa007

Moghaddam, M. T., & Muccini, H. (2019). *Fault-tolerant iot*. International Workshop on Software Engineering for Resilient Systems.

Moghaddam, M. T., Muccini, H., Dugdale, J., & Kjægaard, M. B. (2022). *Designing internet of behaviors systems*. 2022 IEEE 19th International Conference on Software Architecture (ICSA).

Moghaddam, M. T., Rutten, E., & Giraud, G. (2021). *Hierarchical control for self-adaptive iot systems a constraint programming-based adaptation approach*. Proceedings of the 55th Hawaii International Conference on System Science (HICSS-55), Virtual.

Moghaddam, M. T., Rutten, E., Lalanda, P., & Giraud, G. (2020). *Ias: An iot architectural self-adaptation framework*. Conference on Software Architecture.

Mojir, K. Y., & Pilemalm, S. (2014). Emerging communities of collaboration: Co-location in emergency response systems in the 'Safety house' in Sweden. In S. R. Hiltz & M. S. Pfaff (Eds.), *11th International Conference on Information Systems for Crisis Response and Management (ISCRAM 2014)*. The Pennsylvania State University.

Mojir, K. Y., & Pilemalm, S. (2016). Actor-centred emergency response systems: A framework for needs analysis and information systems development. *International Journal of Emergency Management, 12*(4), 403–434. https://doi.org/10.1504/IJEM.2016.10000709

Mojir, K. Y., Pilemalm, S., & Granberg, T. A. (2018). Semi-professionals: Emergency response as an additional task in current occupations. *International Journal of Emergency Services, 8*(2), 86–107. https://doi.org/10.1108/IJES-11-2017-0059

Morris, J. C., Morris, E. D., & Jones, D. M. (2007). Reaching for the philosopher's stone: Contingent coordination and the military's response to Hurricane Katrina. *Public Administration Review, 67*, 94–106.

Moynihan, D. P. (2008). Combining structural forms in the search for policy tools: Incident command systems in US crisis management. *Governance, 21*(2), 205–229.

Moynihan, D. P. (2009). The network governance of crisis response: Case studies of incident command systems. *Journal of Public Administration Research and Theory, mun033*.

Muccini, H., Arbib, C., Davidsson, P., & Moghaddam, M. T. (2019). *An iot software architecture for an evacuable building architecture*. Proceedings of the 52nd Hawaii international conference on system sciences (HICSS-52), Wailea, Maui, HI, January 8–11.

Muccini, H., & Moghaddam, M. T. (2018). *Iot architectural styles*. European Conference on Software Architecture.

Muccini, H., Spalazzese, R., Moghaddam, M. T., & Sharaf, M. (2018). *Self-adaptive IoT architectures: An emergency handling case study*. Proceedings of the 12th European Conference on Software Architecture: Companion Proceedings.

Munkvold, B. E., Radianti, J., Rød, J. K., Opach, T., Snaprud, M., Pilemalm, S., & Bunker, D. (2019). Sharing incident and threat information for common situational understanding. In Z. Franco, J. J. González, & J. H. Canós (Eds.), *16th International Conference on Information Systems for Crisis Response and Management (ISCRAM 2019)*. Universitat Politécnica de Valéncia.

Neal, D. M., & Phillips, B. D. (1995). Effective emergency management: Reconsidering the bureaucratic approach. *Disasters, 19*(4), 327–337.

Netten, N., & van Someren, M. (2011). Improving communication in crisis management by evaluating the relevance of messages. *Journal of Contingencies and Crisis Management, 19*(2), 75.

Ngak, C. (2012). Social media a news source and tool during Superstorm Sandy. *CBSNews*, October 30, 2012. http://www.cbsnews.com/8301-205_162-57542474/social-media-a-news-source-and-tool-during-superstorm-sandy/

Nickerson, R. C., Varshney, U., & Muntermann, J. (2013). A method for taxonomy development and its application in information systems. *European Journal of Information Systems, 22*(3), 336–359. https://doi.org/10.1057/ejis.2012.26

Nielsen, J. (1994). *Usability engineering*. Morgan Kaufmann.

Nikolai, C., Becerra-Fernandez, I., Johnson, T., & Madey, G. (2010). *Leveraging WebEOC in support of the Haitian relief effort: Insights and lessons learned*. Proceedings of the 7th International Conference on Information Systems for Crisis Response and Management (ISCRAM 2010), May 2–5.

Niles, I., & Pease, A. (2001). *Towards a standard upper ontology*. Proceedings of the international conference on Formal Ontology in Information Systems-Volume (FOIS '01), Ogunquit, Maine October 17–19.

Norman, D. A., & Draper, S. W. (1986). *User centered system design: New perspectives on human-computer interaction.*

Norri-Sederholm, T., Joensuu, M., & Huhtinen, A.-M. (2017). *Ensuring information flow and the situation picture in public safety organisations' situation centres*. Proceedings of the 16th European Conference on Cyber Warfare and Security, Dublin, Ireland, June 29–30.

Norris, F., Stevens, S., Pfefferbaum, B., Wyche, K., & Pfefferbaum, R. (2008). Community resilience as a metaphor, theory, set of capacities, and strategy for disaster readiness. *American Journal of Community Psychology, 41*(1), 127–150. https://doi.org/10.1007/s10464-007-9156-6

O'Leary, R., & Bingham, L. B. (2009). *The collaborative public manager: New ideas for the twenty-first century*. Georgetown University Press.

O'Meara, P., Burley, M., & Kelly, H. (2002). Rural urgent care models: What are they made of? *Australian Journal of Rural Health, 10*(1), 45–50.

Obermeier, S. F. (1995). Preliminary estimates of the strength of prehistoric shaking in the Columbia River Valley and the southern half of coastal Washington, with emphasis for a Cascadia subduction zone earthquake about 300 years ago. *US Geological Survey Open-File Report, 94*, 589.

Oborn, E., Pilosof, N. P., Hinings, B., & Zimlichman, E. (2021). Institutional logics and innovation in times of crisis: Telemedicine as digital 'PPE'. *Information and Organization, 31*(1), 100340.

Oh, N. (2012). Strategic uses of lessons for building collaborative emergency management system: Comparative analysis of hurricane Katrina and hurricane Gustav response systems. *Journal of Homeland Security and Emergency Management, 9*(1, article 10), 1–20.

Oliver, W. M., & Meier, C. (2004). Stress in small town and rural law enforcement: Testing the assumptions. *American Journal of Criminal Justice, 29*(1), 37–56.

Oloruntoba, R., Sridharan, R., & Davison, G. (2018). A proposed framework of key activities and processes in the preparedness and recovery phases of disaster management. *Disasters, 42*(3), 541–570.

Olteanu, A.-C., Oprina, G.-D., Tapus, N., & Zeisberg, S. (2013). *Enabling mobile devices for home automation using ZigBee*. 2013 19th International Conference on Control Systems and Computer Science.

Onishi, N., & Glanz, J. (2011). Japanese rules for nuclear plants relied on old science. *The New York Times*, March 27, 2011, A1, Asia Pacific. http://www.nytimes.com/2011/03/27/world/asia/27nuke.html?_r=1&ref=asia&pagewanted=print

Opach, T., Rød, J. K., Munkvold, B. E., Radianti, J., Steen-Tveit, K., & Grottenberg, L. O. (2020). Map-based interfaces for common operational picture. In A. Hughes, F. McNeill, & C. W. Zobel (Eds.), *17th International Conference on Information Systems for Crisis Response and Management (ISCRAM 2020)*. Virginia Tech.

Orlikowski, W. J. (1992). The duality of technology: Rethinking the concept of technology in organizations. *Organization Science, 3*(3), 398–427.

Orlikowski, W. J., & Baroudi, J. J. (1991). Studying information technology in organizations: Research approaches and assumptions. *Information Systems Research, 2*(1), 1–28. https://doi.org/10.1287/isre.2.1.1

Orlikowski, W. J., Suzanne, C., & Iacono. (2001). Research commentary: Desperately seeking the "IT" in IT research—A call to theorizing the IT artifact. *Information Systems Research, 12*(2), 121–134. https://doi.org/10.1287/isre.12.2.121.9700

Orlikowski, W. J., & Robey, D. (1991). Information technology and the structuring of organizations. *Information Systems Research, 2*(2), 143–169.

Orlikowski, W. J., & Scott, S. V. (2021). Liminal innovation in practice: Understanding the reconfiguration of digital work in crisis. *Information and Organization, 31*(1), 100336 (1–6).

Osborne, D. (1993). Reinventing government. *Public Productivity & Management Review, 16*(4), 349–356.

Osborne, D., & Gaebler, T. (1992). *Reinventing government: How the entrepreneurial spirit is transforming the public sector*. Addison-Wesley Pub. Co.

Otto, K., Shekar, M., Herbst, C. H., & Mohammed, R. (2015, January). *Information and communication technologies for health systems strengthening: Opportunities, criteria for success, and innovation for Africa and beyond*. The International Bank for Reconstruction and Development/The World Bank.

Paci-Green, R., Boles, N., Black, T., Smith, K., & Munkh-Erdene, E. (2015, January). *Cascadia rising: Cascadia subduction zone (CSZ) catastrophic earthquake and tsunami* (Exercise Scenario Document).

Padli, J., Habibullah, M. S., & Baharom, A. H. (2010). Economic impact of natural disasters' fatalities. *International Journal of Social Economics, 37*(6), 429–441. https://doi.org/10.1108/03068291011042319

Page, M. J., Moher, D., Bossuyt, P. M., Boutron, I., Hoffmann, T. C., Mulrow, C. D., Shamseer, L., Tetzlaff, J. M., Akl, E. A., & Brennan, S. E. (2021). PRISMA 2020 explanation and elaboration: Updated guidance and exemplars for reporting systematic reviews. *BMJ, 372*(160), 1–36. https://doi.org/10.1136/bmj.n160

Palen, L., Hiltz, S. R., & Liu, S. B. (2007). Online forums supporting grassroots participation in emergency preparedness and response. *Communications of the ACM, 50*(3), 54–58.

Palen, L., Vieweg, S., & Anderson, K. M. (2011). Supporting "everyday analysts" in safety- and time-critical situations. *The Information Society, 27*(1), 52–62. https://doi.org/10.1080/01972243.2011.534370

Palen, L., Vieweg, S., Sutton, J., Liu, S. B., & Hughes, A. (2007a). *Crisis informatics: Studying crisis in a networked world*. Proceedings of the Third International Conference on E-Social Science.

Palen, L., Vieweg, S., Sutton, J., Liu, S. B., & Hughes, A. (2007b). *Crisis informatics: Studying crisis in a networked world*. 3rd International Conference on e-Social Science, Ann Arbor, MI, October 7–9.

Palm, J., & Törnqvist, E. (2008). Governing the sea rescue service in Sweden: Communicating in networks. *Journal of Risk Research, 11*(1–2), 269–280. https://doi.org/10.1080/13669870801939449

Pardo, T. A., & Scholl, H. J. (2002). *Walking atop the cliffs: Avoiding failure and reducing risk in large-scale e-government projects*. 35th Hawaii International Conference on System Sciences (HICSS35), Waikoloa, Big Island, HI.

Patrucco, A. S., Trabucchi, D., Frattini, F., & Lynch, J. (2022). The impact of Covid-19 on innovation policies promoting Open Innovation. *R&D Management, 52*(2), 273–293.

Patton, A. (2007). Collaborative emergency management. In K. J. Tierney (Ed.), *Emergency management: Principles and practice for local government* (pp. 71–85). ICMA Press.

Patton, M. Q. (2002). *Qualitative research and evaluation methods* (3rd ed.). Sage Publications.

Pease, A., Niles, I., & Li, J. (2002). *The suggested upper merged ontology: A large ontology for the semantic web and its applications*. Working notes of the AAAI-2002 workshop on ontologies and the semantic web.

Pechta, L. E., Brandenburg, D. C., & Seeger, M. W. (2010). Understanding the dynamics of emergency communication: Propositions for a four-channel model. *Journal of Homeland Security and Emergency Management, 7*(1, article 55), 1–18.

Pederson, P., Dudenhoeffer, D., Hartley, S., & Permann, M. (2006). *Critical infrastructure interdependency modeling: A survey of US and international research* (pp. 1–20). Idaho National Laboratory.

Pedrycz, W., & Chen, S.-M. (2014). *Information granularity, big data, and computational intelligence* (Vol. 8). Springer.

Peek, L. A., & Mileti, D. S. (2002). The history and future of disaster research. In R. B. Bechtel & A. Ts'erts'man (Eds.), *Handbook of environmental psychology* (pp. 511–524). Wiley.

Penning, A., Baumgärtner, L., Höchst, J., Sterz, A., Mezini, M., & Freisleben, B. (2019). *Dtn7: An open-source disruption-tolerant networking implementation of bundle protocol 7*. International Conference on Ad-Hoc Networks and Wireless.

Perla, P. P., Markowitz, M., Nofi, A. A., Weuve, C., & Loughran, J. (2000). *Gaming and shared situation awareness*. Center For Naval Analyses.

Perry, R. W. (2006). What is a disaster? In H. Rodriquez, R. R. Dynes, & E. L. Quarantelli (Eds.), *Handbooks of disaster research*. Springer.

Perry, R. W., & Quarantelli, E. L. (2005). *What is a disaster?: New answers to old questions*. Xlibris.

Pestoff, V. A., Brandsen, T., & Verschuere, B. (2012). *New public governance, the third sector and co-production* (Vol. 7). Routledge.

Peters, B. G. (1994). Managing the hollow state. *International Journal of Public Administration, 17*(3–4), 739–756.

Peters, D. T. J. M., Klijn, E. H., Stronks, K., & Harting, J. (2017). Policy coordination and integration, trust, management and performance in public health-related policy networks: A survey. *International Review of Administrative Sciences, 83*(1), 200–222. https://doi.org/10.1177/2F0020852315585061

Pfaff, M. S., Klein, G. L., Drury, J. L., Moon, S. P., Liu, Y., & Entezari, S. O. (2013). Supporting complex decision making through option awareness. *Journal of Cognitive Engineering and Decision Making, 7*(2), 155–178.

Pilemalm, S. (2018). Participatory design in emerging civic engagement initiatives in the new public sector: Applying PD concepts in resource-scarce organizations. *ACM Transactions on Computer-Human Interaction (TOCHI), 25*(1), 1–26. https://doi.org/10.1145/3152420

Pilemalm, S. (2020). Volunteer co-production in emergency management in excluded areas: Using civil citizens and semi-professionals as first responders. *eJournal of eDemocracy & Open Government, 12*(1), 61–86.

Pilemalm, S., Lindgren, I., & Ramsell, E. (2016). Emerging forms of inter-organizational and cross-sector collaborations in e-government initiatives: Implications for participative development of information systems. *Transforming Government: People, Process and Policy, 10*(5), 603–636.

Pilemalm, S., & Mojir, K. Y. (2020). Cross-sector collaboration in emergency response as network governance. *International Journal of Emergency Management, 16*(3), 249–280. https://doi.org/10.1504/IJEM.2020.113936

Pilemalm, S., Stenberg, R., & Granberg, T. A. (2013). Emergency response in rural areas. *International Journal of Information Systems for Crisis Response and Management (IJISCRAM), 5*(2), 19–31. https://doi.org/10.4018/jiscrm.2013040102

Pogrebnyakov, N., & Maldonado, E. (2018). Didn't roger that: Social media message complexity and situational awareness of emergency responders. *International Journal of Information Management, 40*, 166–174.

Pötsch, T., Schmitt, P., Chen, J., & Raghavan, B. (2016). *Helping the lone operator in the vast frontier*. HotNets '16: Proceedings of the 15th ACM Workshop on Hot Topics in Networks, November 9–10.

Pottebaum, J., Schäfer, C., Kuhnert, M., Behnke, D., Wietfeld, C., Büscher, M., & Petersen, K. (2016). *Common information space for collaborative emergency management*. 2016 IEEE Symposium on Technologies for Homeland Security (HST).

Prasad, R. (2014). *5G: 2020 and beyond*. River Publishers.

Prasanna, R., & Huggins, T. J. (2016). Factors affecting the acceptance of information systems supporting emergency operations centres. *Computers in Human Behavior, 57*(April), 168–181. https://doi.org/10.1016/j.chb.2015.12.013

Prince, S. H. (1920). *Catastrophe and social change, based upon a sociological study of the Halifax disaster*. Vol. XCIV. Vol. 1, Columbia studies in the social sciences, vol. XCIV, no. 1 whole no. 212. Columbia University.

Qiu, F., & Xiaolin, H. (2010). Modeling group structures in pedestrian crowd simulation. *Simulation Modelling Practice and Theory, 18*(2), 190–205.

Quarantelli, E. L. (1988). Disaster crisis management - a summary of research findings. *Journal of Management Studies, 25*(4), 373–385. https://doi.org/10.1111/j.1467-6486.1988.tb00043.x. <Go to ISI>://WOS:A1988P687000007.

Quarantelli, E. L. (1997a). Problematical aspects of the information/communication revolution for disaster planning and research: Ten non-technical issues and questions. *Disaster Prevention and Management: An International Journal, 6*(2), 94–106.

Quarantelli, E. L. (1997b). Ten criteria for evaluating the management of community disasters. *Disasters, 21*(1), 39–56. https://doi.org/10.1111/1467-7717.00043. <Go to ISI>://WOS:A1997WP03000004.

Quarantelli, E. L. (1997c). Problematical aspects of the information/communication revolution for disaster planning and research: Ten non-technical issues and questions. *Disaster Prevention and Management, 6*(2), 94–106.

Quarantelli, E. L. (Ed.). (1998). *What is a disaster: Perspectives on the question*. Routledge.

Quarantelli, E. L. (2000). *Emergencies, disasters and catastrophes are different phenomena*. University of Delaware, Disaster Research Center.

Quarantelli, E. L. (2005). A social science research agenda for the disasters of the 21st century: Theoretical, methodological and empirical issues and their professional implementation. In R. W. Perry & E. L. Quarantelli (Eds.), *What is a disaster?: New answers to old questions* (pp. 325–396). Xlibris.

Quarantelli, E. L. (2006). *Catastrophes are different from disasters: Some implications for crisis planning and managing drawn from Katrina*. Understanding Katrina: Perspectives from the social sciences, pp. 1–9. https://unitedsikhs.org/katrina/catastrophes_are_different_from_disasters.pdf

Quarantelli, E. L., & Dynes, R. R. (1977). Response to social crisis and disaster. *Annual Review of Sociology, 3*, 23–49. https://doi.org/10.1146/annurev.so.03.080177.000323. <Go to ISI>://WOS:A1977DS45900002.

Quek, T. Q. S., Peng, M., Simeone, O., & Wei, Y. (2017). *Cloud radio access networks: Principles, technologies, and applications*. Cambridge University Press.

Quinn, R. W., & Worline, M. C. (2008). Enabling courageous collective action: Conversations from United Airlines flight 93. *Organization Science, 19*(4), 497–516.

Raj, P., & Raman, A. C. (2017). *The Internet of Things: Enabling technologies, platforms, and use cases*. Auerbach Publications.

Rake, E. L., & Njå, O. (2009). Perceptions and performances of experienced incident commanders. *Journal of Risk Research, 12*(5), 665–685.

Ramsell, E., Granberg, T. A., & Pilemalm, S. (2019). *Identifying functions for smartphone basedapplications in volunteer emergency response*. 16th International Conference on Information Systems for Crisis Response and Management, Valencia (Spain), May 19–22, 2019.

Ramsell, E., Pilemalm, S., & Granberg, T. A. (2017). *Using volunteers for emergency response in rural areas: Network collaboration factors and IT support in the case of enhanced neighbors*. The 14th International Conference on Information Systems for Crisis Response and Management, May 21–24, Albi, Occitanie Pyrénées-Méditerranée, France.

Rao, A. S., & Georgeff, M. P. (1995). *BDI agents: From theory to practice*. ICMAS.

Rasmussen, J. (1983). Skills, rules, and knowledge; signals, signs, and symbols, and other distinctions in human performance models. *IEEE Transactions on Systems, Man, and Cybernetics, 3*, 257–266.
Rasmussen, J., Pejtersen, A. M., & Goodstein, L. P. (1994). *Cognitive systems engineering.*
Rauner, M. S., Niessner, H., Odd, S., Pope, A., Neville, K., O'Riordan, S., Sasse, L., & Tomic, K. (2018). An advanced decision support system for European disaster management: The feature of the skills taxonomy. *Central European Journal of Operations Research, 26*(2), 485–530. https://doi.org/10.1007/s10100-018-0528-9
Raymond, L., Paré, G., & Maillet, É. (2017). IT-based clinical knowledge management in primary health care: A conceptual framework. *Knowledge and Process Management, 24*(4), 247–256.
Reddy, M. C., Paul, S. A., Abraham, J., McNeese, M., DeFlitch, C., & Yen, J. (2009). Challenges to effective crisis management: Using information and communication technologies to coordinate emergency medical services and emergency department teams. *International Journal of Medical Informatics, 78*(4), 259–269.
Ren, S., He, K., Girshick, R., & Sun, J. (2015). Faster r-cnn: Towards real-time object detection with region proposal networks. *Advances in Neural Information Processing Systems, 28*, 1–9.
Resch, B., Schmidt, D., & Blaschke, T. (2007). *Enabling geographic situational awareness in emergency management.* 2nd Geospatial Integration for Public Safety Conference (GIPSC 2007), New Orleans, Louisiana, April 15.
Reuter, C., Kaufhold, M.-A., Leopold, I., & Knipp, H. (2017). *Katwarn, NInA, or FEMA? Multimethod study on distribution, use, and public views on crisis apps.* Proceesinds of the 25th European Conference on Information Systems (ECIS), Guimarães, Portugal.
Reuter, C., & Kaufhold, M.-A. (2018). Fifteen years of social media in emergencies: A retrospective review and future directions for crisis informatics. *Journal of Contingencies and Crisis Management, 26*(1), 41–57.
Ricci, M. A., Caputo, M., Amour, J., Rogers, F. B., Sartorelli, K., Callas, P. W., & Malone, P. T. (2003). Telemedicine reduces discrepancies in rural trauma care. *Telemedicine Journal and E-Health, 9*(1), 3–11.
Ristvej, A., & Zagorecki, J. (2011). Information systems for crisis management–current applications and future directions. *Communications, 2*, 59–61.
Ritchie, J., Lewis, J., & Gillian, E. (2003). Designing and selecting samples. In J. Ritchie & J. Lewis (Eds.), *Qualitative research practice: A guide for social science students and researchers* (pp. 77–108). Thousand Oaks/Sage Publications.
Rittel, H. W. J., & Webber, M. M. (1973). Dilemmas in a general theory of planning. *Policy Sciences, 4*(2), 155–169. http://offcampus.lib.washington.edu/login?url=http://search.ebscohost.com/login.aspx?direct=true&db=bth&AN=16620094&site=ehost-live
Ritter, F. E., Baxter, G. D., & Churchill, E. F. (2014). *Foundations for designing user-centered systems* (pp. 33–54). Springer.
Roberts, A., Nimegeer, A., Farmer, J., & Heaney, D. J. (2014). The experience of community first responders in co-producing rural health care: In the liminal gap between citizen and professional. *BMC Health Services Research, 14*(1), 1–10.
Roberts, N., Galluch, P. S., Dinger, M., & Grover, V. (2012). Absorptive capacity and information systems research: Review, synthesis, and directions for future research. *MIS Quarterly, 36*(2), 625–648.
Robertson, T., & Simonsen, J. (2012). Challenges and opportunities in contemporary participatory design. *Design Issues, 28*(3), 3–9. https://doi.org/10.1162/DESI_a_00157
Robinson, J. J., Maddock, J., & Starbird, K. (2015). *Examining the role of human and technical infrastructure during emergency response.* 12th International Conference on Information Systems for Crisis Response and Management (ISCRAM 2015), May 24–27.
Rodríguez, H., Quarantelli, E. L., & Dynes, R. R. (2006). Editors' introduction. In H. Rodríguez, E. L. Quarantelli, & R. R. Dynes (Eds.), *Handbook of disaster research* (Handbooks of sociology and social research) (pp. xiii–xx). Springer.
Rodriguez, J. (Ed.). (2015). *Fundamentals of 5G mobile networks.* Wiley.

Rogers, A. M., Walsh, T. J., Kockelman, W. J., & Priest, G. R. (1991). *Earthquake hazards in the Pacific Northwest: An overview*. US Geological Survey. https://pubs.usgs.gov/of/1991/0441o/report.pdf

Rogers, G. C. (1988). An assessment of the megathrust earthquake potential of the Cascadia subduction zone. *Canadian Journal of Earth Sciences, 25*(6), 844–852.

Rosenthal, U., Hart, P.'t., & Kouzmin, A. (1991). The bureau-politics of crisis management. *Public Administration, 69*(2), 211–233.

Rubin, J., & Chisnell, D. (2008). *Handbook of usability testing: How to plan, design and conduct effective tests*. Wiley.

Sahil, & Sood, S. K. (2021). Bibliometric monitoring of research performance in ICT-based disaster management literature. *Quality & Quantity, 55*(1), 103–132. https://doi.org/10.1007/s11135-020-00991-x

Saini, K., Kalra, S., & Sood, S. K. (2022). Disaster emergency response framework for smart buildings. *Future Generation Computer Systems, 131*, 106–120.

Sakurai, M., Watson, R. T., Abraham, C., & Kokuryo, J. (2014). Sustaining life during the early stages of disaster relief with a frugal information system: Learning from the great east Japan earthquake. *IEEE Communications Magazine, 52*(1), 176–185.

Salerno, J., Hinman, M., Boulware, D., & Bello, P. (2003). *Information fusion for situational awareness*. 6th International Conference on International Fusion (FUSION 2003), Cairns, Queensland, Australia, July 8–11.

Salmon, P. M. (2016). *Distributed situation awareness: Theory, measurement and application to teamwork. Human factors in defence*. Routledge.

Salmon, P. M., Stanton, N. A., & Jenkins, D. P. (2017). What is really going on? Situation awareness literature review. In P. M. Salmon, N. A. Stanton, & D. P. Jenkins (Eds.), *Distributed situation awareness: Theory, measurement and application to teamwork* (pp. 7–34). CRC Press.

Sánchez, C. E., & Sánchez, L. D. (2020). Case study: Emergency department response to the Boston Marathon bombing. In D. W. Callaway & J. L. Burstein (Eds.), *Operational and medical management of explosive and blast incidents* (pp. 363–367). Springer.

Sandvik, K. B., Jacobsen, K. L., & McDonald, S. M. (2017). Do no harm: A taxonomy of the challenges of humanitarian experimentation. *International Review of the Red Cross, 99*(904), 319–344.

Sarmady, S., Haron, F., & Talib, A. Z. H. (2009). *Modeling groups of pedestrians in least effort crowd movements using cellular automata*. 2009 Third Asia International Conference on Modelling & Simulation.

Satake, K., Wang, K., & Atwater, B. F. (2003). Fault slip and seismic moment of the 1700 Cascadia earthquake inferred from Japanese tsunami descriptions. *Journal of Geophysical Research: Solid Earth, 108*(B11).

Schakel, J. K., & Wolbers, J. (2021). To the edge and beyond: How fast-response organizations adapt in rapidly changing crisis situations. *Human Relations, 74*(3), 405–436.

Schein, E. (1969). *Process consultation: Its role in organizational development*. Addison-Wesley.

Schein, E. H. (1983). *Organizational culture: A dynamic model*. Alfred P. Sloan School of Management Massachusetts Institute of Technology.

Scherp, A., Franz, T., Saathoff, C., & Staab, S. (2012). A core ontology on events for representing occurrences in the real world. *Multimedia Tools and Applications, 58*(2), 293–331. https://doi.org/10.1007/s11042-010-0667-z

Schloter, M., & Skutella, M. (2017). *Fast and memory-efficient algorithms for evacuation problems*. Proceedings of the Twenty-Eighth Annual ACM-SIAM Symposium on Discrete Algorithms.

Schmidt, A., Wolbers, J., Ferguson, J., & Boersma, K. (2018). Are you Ready2Help? Conceptualizing the management of online and onsite volunteer convergence. *Journal of Contingencies and Crisis Management, 26*(3), 338–349.

Schmitt, T., National Research Council, Rao, R. R., & Eisenberg, J. (2007). *Improving disaster management: The role of IT in mitigation, preparedness, response, and recovery*. National Academies Press.

Scholl, H. J. (1999). Knowledge management and the vital organization. In R. Berndt (Ed.), *Management Strategien 2000* (Herausforderungen and das management (challenges for management)) (pp. 133–158). Springer.

Scholl, H. J. (2004). Involving salient stakeholders: Beyond the technocratic view on change. *Action Research, 2*(3), 281–308.

Scholl, H. J. (2005a). *Interoperability in e-Government: More than just smart middleware*. 38th Hawaii International Conference on System Sciences (HICSS38), Waikoloa, Big Island, HI, January, 5–8.

Scholl, H. J. (2005b). *Employing the mobility paradigm: The next big leap in Digital Government?* dg.o2005, The International Conference on Digital Government Research, Atlanta, GA, May 15–18.

Scholl, H. J. (2006). Electronic government: Information management capacity, organizational capabilities, and the sourcing mix. *Government Information Quarterly, 23*(1), 73–96.

Scholl, H. J. (2019). Overwhelmed by brute force of nature: First response management in the wake of a catastrophic incident. In I. Lindgren, M. Janssen, H. Lee, M. P. R. Bolívar, E. Tambouris, & H. J. Scholl (Eds.), *Electronic Government: Proceedings of the 18th IFIP WG 8.5 International Conference, EGOV 2019*. Springer.

Scholl, H. J., Ballard, S., Carnes, S., Herman, A., & Parker, N. (2017). *Informational challenges in early disaster response: The massive Oso/SR530 landslide 2014 as case in point*. 50th Hawaii International Conference on System Sciences (HICSS-50), Waikoloa, Hawaii, January 4–7. http://hdl.handle.net/10125/41458.

Scholl, H. J., & Carlson, T. S. (2006). Sourcing decisions in electronic Government and the knowledge transfer problem. In R. Traunmüller (Ed.), *Knowledge transfer for eGovernment: Seeking better eGovernment solutions* (Schriftenreihe Informatik (Informatics series)) (pp. 69–81). Trauner Verlag.

Scholl, H. J., & Carnes, S. L. (2017). *Managerial challenges in early disaster response: The case of the 2014 Oso/SR530 landslide disaster*. Proceedings of the 14th ISCRAM conference, Albi, France, May 15–19.

Scholl, H. J., & Chatfield, A. T. (2014). The role of resilient information infrastructures: The case of radio Fukushima during and after the 2011 Eastern Japan Catastrophe. *International Journal of Public Administration in the Digital Age (IJPADA), 1*(2), 1–24.

Scholl, H. J., & Dwivedi, Y. K. (2014). Forums for electronic government scholars: Insights from a 2012/2013 study. *Government Information Quarterly, 31*(2), 229–242. https://doi.org/10.1016/j.giq.2013.10.008

Scholl, H. J., Fidel, R., Liu, S., Paulsmeyer, M., & Unsworth, K. (2007). *E-government field force automation: Promises, challenges, and stakeholders*. 6th International Conference, EGOV 2007, Regensburg, Germany.

Scholl, H. J., Hubbel, K., & Leonard, J. (2018). *Communications and technology challenges to situational awareness: Insights from the CR16 exercise*. Proceedings of the 1st ISCRAM Asia-Pacific Conference, Wellington, NZ, November 5–7.

Scholl, H. J., Hubbell, K., & Leonard, J. G. (2019). Information sharing and situational awareness: Insights from the Cascadia rising exercise of June 2016. In *Proceedings of the 52nd Hawaii International Conference on System Sciences (HICSS-52)*. Maui, HI.

Scholl, H. J., Jurisch, M., Scholl, M. C., & Krcmar, H. (2014). Building sound foundations for smart city government: The case of Munich, Germany. *International Journal of E-Planning Research, 3*(4), 1–22. https://doi.org/10.4018/IJEPR

Scholl, H. J., & Klischewski, R. (2007). E-government integration and interoperability: Framing the research agenda. *International Journal of Public Administration, 30*(8), 889–920.

Scholl, H. J., Menten-Weil, W., & Carlson, T. S. (2017). Information artifact evaluation with TEDSrate. In *16th International Conference on Electronic Government (EGOV 2017)*. Springer.

Scholl, H. J, & Patin, B. J. (2012). *Resilient information infrastructures: Mobilizing adaptive capacities under extreme events*. 18th Americas Conference on Information Systems, Seattle, WA, August 9–12.

Scholl, H. J., & Patin, B. J. (2014). Resilient information infrastructures: Criticality and role in responding to catastrophic incidents. *Transforming Government: People, Process and Policy, 8*(1), 28–48.

Scholl, H. J, Patin, B. J, & Chatfield, A. T. (2012). *ICT-enabled city government field operations: Resiliency during extreme events*. 45th Hawaii International Conference on System Sciences (HICSS-45), Maui, HI, January, 4–7.

Schön, D. A. (1983). *The reflective practitioner: How professionals think in action*. Basic Books.

Schooley, B., Horan, T., & Marich, M. (2010). Managing IT collaboration in multi-organizational time-critical services. *MIS Quarterly The Executive, 9*(3).

Schroeder, J. M., Manz, D. O., Amaya, J. P., McMakin, A. H., & Bays, R. M. (2018). *Understanding past, current and future communication and situational awareness technologies for first responders*. Proceedings of the Fifth Cybersecurity Symposium, Coeur d' Alene, Idaho, April 9–11.

Schuler, D., & Namioka, A. (1993). *Participatory design: Principles and practices*. CRC Press.

Schulz, K. (2015). The really big one. *The New Yorker, 7*(20), 1–17.

Schwandt, T. A. (2001). *Dictionary of qualitative inquiry* (2nd ed.). Sage Publications.

Sciullo, L., Fossemo, F., Trotta, A., & Di Felice, M. (2018). *Locate: A lora-based mobile emergency management system*. 2018 IEEE Global Communications Conference (GLOBECOM).

Sciullo, L., Trotta, A., & Di Felice, M. (2020). Design and performance evaluation of a LoRa-based mobile emergency management system (LOCATE). *Ad Hoc Networks, 96*, 101993 (1–17). https://doi.org/10.1016/j.adhoc.2019.101993

Sebillo, M., Vitiello, G., Paolino, L., & Ginige, A. (2016). Training emergency responders through augmented reality mobile interfaces. *Multimedia Tools and Applications, 75*(16), 9609–9622.

Seedorf, J., Arumaithurai, M., Tagami, A., Ramakrishnan, K., & Blefari-Melazzi, N. (2020). *Research directions for using information-centric networking (ICN) in disaster scenarios*. Internet Research Task Force (IRTF). https://www.rfc-editor.org/info/rfc8884

Segev, A. (2008). Adaptive ontology use for crisis knowledge representation. In F. Fiedrich & B. A. van de Walle (Eds.), *5th International Conference on Information Systems for Crisis Response and Management (Proceedings of ISCRAM 2008)*. Information Systems for Crisis Response and Management, ISCRAM. Original edition, Segev, A. (2008). Adaptive ontology use for crisis knowledge representation. 5th International Conference on Information Systems for Crisis Response and Management (Proceedings of ISCRAM 2008). F. Fiedrich and B. Van de Walle, Information Systems for Crisis Response and Management, ISCRAM: 285–293.

Senge, P. M. (1990). *The fifth discipline: The art and practice of the learning organization* (1st ed.). Doubleday/Currency.

Senge, P. M., Kleiner, A., Roberts, C., Ross, R., Roth, G., Smith, B., & Guman, E. C. (1999). The dance of change: The challenges to sustaining momentum in learning organizations. *Performance Improvement, 38*(5), 55–58.

Seppänen, H., Mäkelä, J., Luokkala, P., & Virrantaus, K. (2013). Developing shared situational awareness for emergency management. *Safety Science, 55*, 1–9.

Seppänen, H., & Virrantaus, K. (2015). Shared situational awareness and information quality in disaster management. *Safety Science, 77*, 112–122.

Shah, S. A., Seker, D. Z., Hameed, S., & Draheim, D. (2019). The rising role of big data analytics and IoT in disaster management: Recent advances, taxonomy and prospects. *IEEE Access, 7*, 54595–54614. https://doi.org/10.1109/ACCESS.2019.2913340

Shapiro, D. (2005). *Participatory design: The will to succeed*. Proceedings of the 4th decennial conference on Critical computing: between sense and sensibility.

Sharma, S., Stigall, J., & Bodempudi, S. T. (2020). *Situational awareness-based Augmented Reality Instructional (ARI) module for building evacuation*. 2020 IEEE Conference on Virtual Reality and 3D User Interfaces Abstracts and Workshops (VRW).

She, M., Li, Z., & Ma, L. (2019). User-defined information sharing for team situation awareness and teamwork. *Ergonomics, 62*(8), 1098–1112. https://doi.org/10.1080/00140139.2019.1607910

Silva, T., Wuwongse, V., & Sharma, H. N. (2011). *Linked data in disaster mitigation and preparedness*. Proceedings of the 3rd International Conference on Intelligent Networking and Collaborative Systems (INCOS), Fukuoka, Japan, November 30–December 2.

Simo, G., & Bies, A. L. (2007). The role of nonprofits in disaster response: An expanded model of cross-sector collaboration. *Public Administration Review, 67*(s1), 125–142. https://doi.org/10.1111/j.1540-6210.2007.00821.x

Simões-Marques, M. J. (2017). Facing disasters—Trends in applications to support disaster management. In I. L. Nunes (Ed.), *Advances in human factors and system interactions* (pp. 203–215). Springer.

Simon, H. A. (1991). The architecture of complexity. In *Facets of systems science* (pp. 457–476). Springer.

Simpson, N. C. (2012). *On disaster response and emergent systems: A new taxonomy for operations management*. Available at SSRN 2039466. https://doi.org/10.2139/ssrn.2039466.

Slavin, K. (2016). Design as participation. *Journal of Design and Science*, 1–21.

Smart, P. R., Shadbolt, N. R., Carr, L. A., & Schraefel, M. C. (2005). *Knowledge-based information fusion for improved situational awareness*. 8th International Conference on Information Fusion (Fusion 2005), July 25–28.

Smith, K., & Hancock, P. A. (1995). Situation awareness is adaptive, externally directed consciousness. *Human Factors, 37*(1), 137–148.

Son, C., Sasangohar, F., Timothy Neville, S., Peres, C., & Moon, J. (2020). Investigating resilience in emergency management: An integrative review of literature. *Applied Ergonomics, 87*(n/a), 1–16.

Son, J., Aziz, Z., & Pena-Mora, F. (2008). Supporting disaster response and recovery through improved situation awareness. *Structural Survey, 26*(5), 411–425.

Sorensen, L. J., & Stanton, N. A. (2016). Keeping it together: The role of transactional situation awareness in team performance. *International Journal of Industrial Ergonomics, 53*(May), 267–273. https://doi.org/10.1016/j.ergon.2016.02.007

Spicer, S., Lowe, A. M., Cho, G., & Walton, M. (2019, September 19). *Disaster response: FEMA and the American red cross need to ensure key mass care organizations are included in coordination and planning*. United States Government Accountability Office. https://www.gao.gov/assets/710/701499.pdf

Stake, R. E. (1995). *The art of case study research*. Sage.

Stake, R. E. (2011). Qualitative case studies. In N. K. Denzin & Y. S. Lincoln (Eds.), *The Sage handbook of qualitative research* (pp. 443–466). Sage.

Stallings, R. A., & Quarantelli, E. L. (1985). Emergent citizen groups and emergency management. *Public Administration Review, 45*(1), 93–100. https://doi.org/10.2307/3135003. <Go to ISI>://WOS:A1985AAR3600014.

Stambler, K. S., & Barbera, J. A. (2011). Engineering the incident command and multiagency coordination systems. *Journal of Homeland Security and Emergency Management, 8*(1, article 43), 1–27.

Stambler, K. S., & Barbera, J. A. (2015). The evolution of shortcomings in Incident Command System: Revisions have allowed critical management functions to atrophy. *Journal of Emergency Management (Weston, MA), 13*(6), 509–518.

Stanton, N. A., Chambers, P. R. G., & Piggott, J. (2001). Situational awareness and safety. *Safety Science, 39*(3), 189–204.

Stanton, N. A., Salmon, P. M., & Walker, G. H. (2015). Let the reader decide: A paradigm shift for situation awareness in sociotechnical systems. *Journal of Cognitive Engineering and Decision Making, 9*(1), 44–50.

Stanton, N. A., Stewart, R., Harris, D., Houghton, R. J., Baber, C., McMaster, R., Salmon, P., Hoyle, G., Walker, G., & Young, M. S. (2006). Distributed situation awareness in dynamic systems: Theoretical development and application of an ergonomics methodology. *Ergonomics, 49*(12–13), 1288–1311.

Star, S. L., & Ruhleder, K. (1996). Steps toward an ecology of infrastructure: Design and access for large information spaces. *Information Systems Research, 7*(1), 111–134.

Starbird, K., & Palen, L. (2010). *Pass it on?: Retweeting in mass emergency*. 7th International Conference on Information Systems for Crisis Response and Management (ISCRAM 2010), Seattle, WA, May 2–5. http://www.cs.colorado.edu/~palen/starbirdpaleniscramretweet.pdf

Steen-Tveit, K., & Munkvold, B. E. (2021). From common operational picture to common situational understanding: An analysis based on practitioner perspectives. *Safety Science, 142*, 105381 (1–12). https://doi.org/10.1016/j.ssci.2021.105381

Stott, P. (2016). How climate change affects extreme weather events. *Science, 352*(6293), 1517–1518. https://doi.org/10.1126/science.aaf7271

Strauss, A. L., & Corbin, J. M. (1998). *Basics of qualitative research: Techniques and procedures for developing grounded theory* (2nd ed.). Sage Publications.

Sun, Y., Kuang, X., & Sun, D. (2016). The geographic concentration of China's e-business enterprises: Where they gather and why. *Electronic Markets, 26*(1), 31–42.

Surana, S., Patra, R. K., Nedevschi, S., Ramos, M., Subramanian, L., Ben-David, Y., & Brewer, E. A. (2008). *Beyond pilots: Keeping rural wireless networks alive*. NSDI.

Sutton, J., Hansard, B., & Hewett, P. (2011). *Changing channels: Communicating tsunami warning information in Hawaii.* Proceedings of the 3rd International joint topical meeting on emergency preparedness and response, robotics, and remote systems, Knoxville, Tennessee, USA, 7 – 10 August, pp 287–300.

Sutton, J., Palen, L., & Shklovski, I. (2008). *Backchannels on the front lines: Emergent uses of social media in the 2007 Southern California wildfires*. 5th International ISCRAM Conference.

Tan, M. L., Prasanna, R., Stock, K., Hudson-Doyle, E., Leonard, G., & Johnston, D. (2017). Mobile applications in crisis informatics literature: A systematic review. *International Journal of Disaster Risk Reduction, 24*, 297–311. https://doi.org/10.1016/j.ijdrr.2017.06.009

Tariverdi, M., Fotouhi, H., Moryadee, S., & Miller-Hooks, E. (2019). Health care system disaster-resilience optimization given its reliance on interdependent critical lifelines. *Journal of Infrastructure Systems, 25*(1), 04018044 (1–16).

Tashakkori, H., Rajabifard, A., Kalantari, M., & Aleksandrov, M. (2015). *Indoor incident situation awareness using a 3D indoor/outdoor spatial city model*. 2015 2nd International Conference on Information and Communication Technologies for Disaster Management (ICT-DM).

Taylor, J. E., Chang, S. E., Elwood, K. J., Seville, E., & Brunsdon, D. (2012). *Learning from christchurch: Technical decisions and societal consequences in post-earthquake recovery: Preliminary research findings August 2012*. Resilient Organisations Programme, University of Canterbury and University of Auckland. http://www.resorgs.org.nz/images/stories/pdfs/critical_decisions_in_the_recovery_of_christchurch.pdf

Thessin, J. (2003). Department of homeland security. *Harvard Journal on Legislation, 40*(2), 513–536.

Thomas, J. A., Pierce, L. G., Dixon, M. W., & Fong, G. (2007). *Interpreting commander's intent: Do we really know what we know and what we don't know*. U.S. Army Research Laboratory, Human Research and Engineering Directorate, Aberdeen Proving Ground, MD, 21005.

Thomas, K. (2004). *Office for Domestic Preparedness (ODP)*. US Department of Homeland Security.

Thomson, S., García-Ramírez, J. A., Akkazieva, B., Habicht, T., Cylus, J., & Evetovits, T. (2022). How resilient is health financing policy in Europe to economic shocks? Evidence from the first year of the COVID-19 pandemic and the 2008 global financial crisis. *Health Policy, 126*(1), 7–15.

Tierney, K. J. (2009). Recent developments in US homeland security policies and their implications for the management of extreme events. In H. Rodriguez, E. L. Quarantelli, & R. Dynes (Eds.), *Handbook of disaster research* (pp. 405–412). Springer.

Tiesman, H., Zwerling, C., Peek-Asa, C., Sprince, N., & Cavanaugh, J. E. (2007). Non-fatal injuries among urban and rural residents: The National Health Interview Survey, 1997–2001. *Injury Prevention, 13*(2), 115–119.

Tobias (Ed.). (2011). Using Twitter and other social media platforms to provide situational awareness during an incident. *Journal of Business Continuity & Emergency Planning, 5*(3), 208–223.

Tolea, M. I., Costa, P. T., Terracciano, A., Griswold, M., Simonsick, E. M., Najjar, S. S., Scuteri, A., Deiana, B., Orrù, M., & Masala, M. (2010). Sex-specific correlates of walking speed in a wide age-ranged population. *Journals of Gerontology Series B: Psychological Sciences and Social Sciences, 65*(2), 174–184.

Tomaszewski, B., Judex, M., Szarzynski, J., Radestock, C., & Wirkus, L. (2015). Geographic information systems for disaster response: A review. *Journal of Homeland Security and Emergency Management, 12*(3), 571–602.

Tranfield, D., Denyer, D., & Smart, P. (2003). Towards a methodology for developing evidence-informed management knowledge by means of systematic review. *British Journal of Management, 14*(3), 207–222.

Trentham, G., & Scholl, H. J. (2008). *Current practices in field force automation: Decision support and information management for the field force*. 41st Hawaii International Conference on System Sciences, Waikoloa, HI, January 7–10.

Treurniet, W., Boersma, K., & Groenewegen, P. (2019). Configuring emergency response networks. *International Journal of Emergency Management, 15*(4), 316–333.

Treurniet, W., van Buul-Besseling, K., & Wolbers, J. (2012). *Collaboration awareness–a necessity in crisis response coordination*. Proceedings of the 9th International Information Systems For Crisis Response and Management Conference (ISCRAM), Vancouver, BC, Canada.

Treurniet, W., & Wolbers, J. (2021). Codifying a crisis: Progressing from information sharing to distributed decision-making. *Journal of Contingencies and Crisis Management, 29*(1), 23–35.

Truptil, S., Bénaben, F., Couget, P., Lauras, M., Chapurlat, V., & Pingaud, H. (2008). Interoperability of information systems in crisis management: Crisis modeling and metamodeling. In K. Mertins, R. Ruggaber, K. Popplewell, & X. Xiaofei (Eds.), *Enterprise interoperability III: New challenges and industrial approaches* (pp. 583–594). Springer.

Tsai, J.-S., & Chi, C. S. F. (2012). Cultural influence on the implementation of incident command system for emergency management of natural disasters. *Journal of Homeland Security and Emergency Management, 9*(1, article 29), 1–22.

Turner, B. A. (1976). The organizational and interorganizational development of disasters. *Administrative Science Quarterly, 21*(3), 378–397.

Turoff, M. (2002). Past and future emergency response information systems. *Communications of the ACM, 45*(4), 29–32. https://doi.org/10.1145/505248.505265

Turoff, M. (2007). Emergency response information systems: Emerging trends and technologies. *Communications of the ACM, 50*(3), 29–31.

Turoff, M., Bañuls, V. A., Plotnick, L., Hiltz, S. R., Ramírez, M., & de la Huerga. (2016). A collaborative dynamic scenario model for the interaction of critical infrastructures. *Futures, 84*, 23–42.

Turoff, M., Chumer, M., Hiltz, S. R., & Klashner, R. (2004). Assuring homeland security: Continuous monitoring, control & assurance of emergency preparedness. *JITTA: Journal of Information Technology Theory and Application, 6*(3), 1–24.

Turoff, M., Chumer, M., van de Walle, B. A., & Yao, X. (2004). The design of a dynamic emergency response management information system (DERMIS). *JITTA: Journal of Information Technology Theory and Application, 5*(4), 1–35.

Turoff, M., Hiltz, S. R., White, C., Plotnick, L., Hendela, A., & Yoa, X. (2009). The past as the future of emergency preparedness and management. *International Journal of Information Systems for Crisis Response and Management (IJISCRAM), 1*(1), 12–28. https://doi.org/10.4018/jiscrm.200901010

Uhlarik, J., & Comerford, D. A. (2002). *A review of situation awareness literature relevant to pilot surveillance functions*. U.S. Department of Transportation, Federal Aviation Administration, Office of Aerospace Medicine.

United_Nations. (2012). *As quakes wreak havoc for second year, UN urges seismic threats be taken seriously*. United Nations, UN International Strategy for Disaster Reduction (UNISDR) and the Centre for Research on the Epidemiology of Disasters (CRED). Last Modified January 18. Accessed March 1, 2013. http://www.un.org/apps/news/story.asp?NewsID=40965

Urquhart, C., Lehmann, H., & Myers, M. D. (2010). Putting the 'theory' back into grounded theory: Guidelines for grounded theory studies in information systems. *Information Systems, 20*(4), 357–381. https://doi.org/10.1111/j.1365-2575.2009.00328.x

USGS. (2013). *Largest earthquakes in the World since 1900*. US Geological Survey. Accessed March 1. http://earthquake.usgs.gov/earthquakes/world/10_largest_world.php

Valenzuela, T. D., Roe, D. J., Nichol, G., Clark, L. L., Spaite, D. W., & Hardman, R. G. (2000). Outcomes of rapid defibrillation by security officers after cardiac arrest in casinos. *New England Journal of Medicine, 343*(17), 1206–1209. https://doi.org/10.1056/NEJM200010263431701

de Walle, V., Bartel, B. B., & Comes, T. (2016). Improving situation awareness in crisis response teams: An experimental analysis of enriched information and centralized coordination. *International Journal of Human-Computer Studies, 95*, 66–79.

Van de Walle, B., & Comes, T. (2014). *Risk accelerators in disasters: insights from the Typhoon Haiyan response on humanitarian information management and decision support*. Proceedings of the International Conference on Advanced Information Systems Engineering (CAiSE 2014), Thessaloniki, Greece, June 16–20.

de Walle, V., & Bartel, and Tina Comes. (2015). On the nature of information management in complex and natural disasters. *Procedia Engineering, 107*, 403–411.

De Walle, V., & Bartel, and Murray Turoff. (2007). Emergency response information systems: Emerging trends and technologies. *Communications of the ACM, 50*(3), 29–31.

De Walle, V., Bartel, M. T., & Hiltz, S. R. (2010). Information systems for emergency management. In V. Zwass (Ed.), *Advances in management information systems* (Vol. 16). Routledge.

De Walle, V., Bartel, M. T., & Hiltz, S. R. (2014). Coordination of emergency response: An examination of the roles of people, process, and information technology. In *Information systems for emergency management* (pp. 162–186). Routledge.

van den Homberg, M., Monné, R., & Spruit, M. (2018). Bridging the information gap of disaster responders by optimizing data selection using cost and quality. *Computers & Geosciences, 120*, 60–72. https://doi.org/10.1016/j.cageo.2018.06.002

Harmelen, V., Frank, V. L., & Porter, B. (2008). *Handbook of knowledge representation*. Elsevier.

Vecchi, V., Cusumano, N., & Boyer, E. J. (2020). Medical supply acquisition in Italy and the United States in the era of COVID-19: The case for strategic procurement and public–private partnerships. *The American Review of Public Administration, 50*(6–7), 642–649.

Venema, A. M., Groothoff, J. W., & Bierens, J. J. L. M. (2010). The role of bystanders during rescue and resuscitation of drowning victims. *Resuscitation, 81*(4), 434–439. https://doi.org/10.1016/j.resuscitation.2010.01.005

Venkatesh, V., & Davis, F. D. (2000). A theoretical extension of the technology acceptance model: Four longitudinal field studies. *Management Science, 46*(2), 186–204.

Vergne, J.-P., & Durand, R. (2010). The missing link between the theory and empirics of path dependence: Conceptual clarification, testability issue, and methodological implications. *Journal of Management Studies, 47*(4), 736–759.

Verma, S., Vieweg, S., Corvey, W. J., Palen, L., Martin, J. H., Palmer, M., Schram, A., & Anderson, K. M. (2011). *Natural language processing to the rescue? Extracting situational awareness' tweets during mass emergency*. Fifth International AAAI Conference on Weblogs and Social Media (ICWSM-11), Barcelona, Spain, July 17–21.

Vieweg, S., Hughes, A. L., Starbird, K., & Palen, L. (2010). *Microblogging during two natural hazards events: What twitter may contribute to situational awareness*. CHI10 conference, Atlanta, GA, April 10 to 15.

Vigoda-Gadot, E., & Vigoda-Gadot, E. M. (2003). *Managing collaboration in public administration: The promise of alliance among governance, citizens, and businesses*. Greenwood Publishing Group.

Wachtendorf, T. (2004). *Improvising 9/11: Organizational improvisation following the world trade center disaster*.

Wagnild, J., & Wall-Scheffler, C. M. (2013). Energetic consequences of human sociality: Walking speed choices among friendly dyads. *PLoS One, 8*(10), e76576 (1–6).

Waldrop, M. M. (1993). *Complexity: The emerging science at the edge of order and chaos*. Simon and Schuster.

Wang, W.-T., & Su-Ying, W. (2021). Knowledge management based on information technology in response to COVID-19 crisis. *Knowledge Management Research & Practice, 19*(4), 468–474.

Wang, X. H., Zhang, D. Q., Gu, T., & Pung, H. K. (2004). *Ontology based context modeling and reasoning using OWL*." Proceedings of the 2nd IEEE annual conference on pervasive computing and communications workshops, Orlando, FL, March 14–17.

Waring, S., Alison, L., Carter, G., Barrett-Pink, C., Humann, M., Swan, L., & Zilinsky, T. (2018). Information sharing in interteam responses to disaster. *Journal of Occupational and Organizational Psychology., 91*, 591.

Watson, H., & Rodrigues, R. (2018). Bringing privacy into the fold: Considerations for the use of social media in crisis management. *Journal of Contingencies and Crisis Management, 26*(1), 89–98.

Waugh, W. L. (2009). Mechanisms for collaboration in emergency management: ICS, NIMS, and the problem with command and control. In R. O'Leary & L. B. Bingham (Eds.), *The collaborative public manager: New ideas for the twenty-first century* (pp. 157–175). Georgetown University Press.

Waugh, W. L., & Streib, G. (2006). Collaboration and leadership for effective emergency management. *Public Administration Review, 66*(s1), 131–140.

Weber, E. P., & Khademian, A. M. (2008). Wicked problems, knowledge challenges, and collaborative capacity builders in network settings. *Public Administration Review, 68*(2), 334–349. https://doi.org/10.1111/j.1540-6210.2007.00866.x

Weichelt, B., Heimonen, T., Pilz, M., Yoder, A., & Bendixsen, C. (2019). An argument against cross-platform development: Lessons from an augmented reality app prototype for rural emergency responders. *JMIR mHealth and uHealth, 7*(3), e12207 (1–8). https://doi.org/10.2196/12207

Weichselgartner, J., & Pigeon, P. (2015). The role of knowledge in disaster risk reduction. *International Journal of Disaster Risk Science, 6*(2), 107–116.

Weick, K. E. (1988). Enacted sensemaking in crisis situations [1]. *Journal of Management Studies, 25*(4), 305–317.

Weick, K. E. (1993). The collapse of sensemaking in organizations: The Mann Gulch disaster. *Administrative Science Quarterly, 38*, 628–652.

Weick, K. E., & Sutcliffe, K. M. (2011). *Managing the unexpected: Resilient performance in an age of uncertainty* (Vol. 8). Wiley.

Weinholt, Å., & Granberg, T. A. (2015). New collaborations in daily emergency response: Applying cost-benefit analysis to new first response initiatives in the Swedish fire and rescue service. *International Journal of Emergency Services, 4*(2), 177–193. https://doi.org/10.1111/j.1540-6210.2006.00673.x

Weisfeldt, M. L., Sitlani, C. M., Ornato, J. P., Rea, T., Aufderheide, T. P., Davis, D., Dreyer, J., Hess, E. P., Jui, J., & Maloney, J. (2010). Survival after application of automatic external defibrillators before arrival of the emergency medical system: Evaluation in the resuscitation outcomes consortium population of 21 million. *Journal of the American College of Cardiology, 55*(16), 1713–1720. https://doi.org/10.1016/j.jacc.2009.11.077

Wenger, D., Quarantelli, E. L., & Dynes, R. R. (1990). Is the incident command system a plan for all seasons and emergency situations? *Hazard Monthly, 10*(3), 8–12.

West, D. O., & McCrumb, D. R. (1988). Coastline uplift in Oregon and Washington and the nature of Cascadia subduction-zone tectonics. *Geology, 16*(2), 169–172.

Whelan, C., & Molnar, A. (2018a). Organising across boundaries: Communication, coordination and conflict. In C. Whelan & A. Molnar (Eds.), *Securing mega-events: Networks, strategies and tensions* (pp. 91–122). Palgrave Macmillan, UK.

Whelan, C., & Molnar, A. (2018b). *Securing mega-events: Networks, strategies and tensions*. Palgrave Macmillan, UK.

Whitacre, B. E. (2008). Factors influencing the temporal diffusion of broadband adoption: Evidence from Oklahoma. *The Annals of Regional Science, 42*(3), 661–679.

Whitaker, G. P. (1980). Coproduction: Citizen participation in service delivery. *Public Administration Review, 40*, 240–246.

Wickens, C. D. (2008). Situation awareness: Review of Mica Endsley's 1995 articles on situation awareness theory and measurement. *Human Factors: The Journal of the Human Factors and Ergonomics Society, 50*(3), 397–403.

Wickler, G., & Potter, S. (2010). Standard operating procedures: Collaborative development and distributed use. In S. French & B. Tomaszewski (Eds.), *7th International Conference on Information Systems for Crisis Response and Management (ISCRAM 2010)*. Information Systems for Crisis Response and Management, ISCRAM.

Wilkinson, M. D., Dumontier, M., Aalbersberg, I. J. J., Appleton, G., Axton, M., Baak, A., Blomberg, N., Boiten, J.-W., da Silva Santos, L. B., & Bourne, P. E. (2016). The FAIR Guiding Principles for scientific data management and stewardship. *Scientific Data, 3*(1), 1–9. https://doi.org/10.1038/sdata.2016.18

Wolbers, J. (2016). Enhancing network centric operations doctrine to support civil military cooperation in disaster management. In *NL ARMS Netherlands annual review of military studies 2016* (pp. 115–131). Springer.

Wolbers, J. (2021). Understanding distributed sensemaking in crisis management: The case of the Utrecht terrorist attack. *Journal of Contingencies and Crisis Management*: (in print). https://doi.org/10.1111/1468-5973.12382

Wolbers, J., & Boersma, K. (2013). The common operational picture as collective sensemaking. *Journal of Contingencies and Crisis management, 21*(4), 186–199. https://doi.org/10.1111/1468-5973.12027

Wolbers, J., Boersma, K., & Groenewegen, P. (2018). Introducing a fragmentation perspective on coordination in crisis management. *Organization Studies, 39*(11), 1521–1546.

Wu, P. F. (2009). User acceptance of emergency alert technology: A case study. In J. Landgren & S. Jul (Eds.), *6th International Conference on Information Systems for Crisis Response and Management (ISCRAM 2009)*. Information Systems for Crisis Response and Management.

Wukich, C. (2020). More monitoring, less coordination: Twitter and Facebook use between emergency management agencies. *Journal of Homeland Security and Emergency Management, 17*(3), 1–29.

Yang, L., Guofeng, S., & Yuan, H. (2012). Design principles of integrated information platform for emergency responses: The case of 2008 Beijing Olympic Games. *Information Systems Research, 23*(3-part-1), 761–786.

Yang, Y. (2009). The 9/21 earthquake in Taiwan: A local government disaster rescue system. *Disasters, 34*(1), 112–136. https://doi.org/10.1111/j.0361-3666.2009.01117.x

Yankelevich, A., Shapiro, M., & Dutton, W. H. (2017). Reaching beyond the wire: Challenges facing wireless for the last mile. *Digital Policy, Regulation and Governance, 19*(3), 210–224. https://doi.org/10.1108/DPRG-01-2017-0002

Yap, N. T. (2011). *Disaster management, developing country communities and climate change: The role of ICTs*. Centre for Development Informatics, Institute for Development Policy and Management, SED. http://www.niccd.org/YapDisasterManagementDevelopmentICTs.pdf

Yau, S. S., & Liu, J. (2006). *Hierarchical situation modeling and reasoning for pervasive computing*. Proceedings of the 4th IEEE Workshop on Software Technologies for Future Embedded and Ubiquitous Systems, and the Second International Workshop on Collaborative Computing, Integration, and Assurance (SEUS-WCCIA'06), Gyeongju, South Korea, April 27–28.

Ye, J., Chen, X., Yang, C., & Jiaorong, W. (2008). Walking behavior and pedestrian flow characteristics for different types of walking facilities. *Transportation Research Record, 2048*(1), 43–51.

Yeo, J., & Comfort, L. K. (2017). An expected event, but unprecedented damage: Structure and gaps of large-scale response coordination of the 2011 Thailand floods. *Disaster Prevention and Management: An International Journal, 26*(4), 458–470.

Yin, R. K. (1981). The case study crisis: Some answers. *Administrative Science Quarterly, 26*(1), 58–65.

Yin, R. K. (1989). *Case study research: design and methods*. Rev. ed. Applied social research methods series; (Vol. 5). Sage Publications.

Young, D. R. (2000). Alternative models of government-nonprofit sector relations: Theoretical and international perspectives. *Nonprofit and Voluntary Sector Quarterly, 29*(1), 149–172. https://doi.org/10.1177/F0899764000291009

Zakour, M. J., Gillespie, D. F., Sherraden, M. W., & Streeter, C. L. (1991). Volunteer organizations in disasters. *Journal of Volunteer Administration, 9*(2), 18–28.

Zavattaro, S. M. (2013). Social media in public administration's future a response to Farazmand. *Administration & Society, 45*(2), 242–255.

Zhao, X., Miers, I., Green, M., & Mitrani-Reiser, J. (2019). Modeling the cybersecurity of hospitals in natural and man-made hazards. *Sustainable and Resilient Infrastructure, 4*(1), 36–49.

Zhou, L., Xianhua, W., Zeshui, X., & Fujita, H. (2018). Emergency decision making for natural disasters: An overview. *International Journal of Disaster Risk Reduction, 27*, 567–576. https://doi.org/10.1016/j.ijdrr.2017.09.037

Zhu, Y., & Li, N. (2021). Virtual and augmented reality technologies for emergency management in the built environments: A state-of-the-art review. *Journal of Safety Science and Resilience, 2*(1), 1–10.

Index

H. J. Scholl et al. (eds.), *Disaster Management and Information Technology*, Public Administration and Information Technology 40,
https://doi.org/10.1007/978-3-031-20939-0

T

U

The manufacturer's authorised representative in the EU is Springer Nature Customer Service Centre GmbH, Europaplatz 3, 69115 Heidelberg, Germany. If you have any concerns regarding our products, please contact ProductSafety@springernature.com

Printed and bound by CPI Group (UK) Ltd, Croydon, CR0 4YY
01/10/2026
02225892-0018